WALTER WANGERIN

THE BOOK OF GOD

THE BIBLE AS A NOVEL

Copyright © 1996 Walter Wangerin

The author asserts the moral right
to be identified as the author of this work

A Lion Book
an imprint of
Lion Hudson plc
Wilkinson House, Jordan Hill Road,
Oxford OX2 8DR, England
www.lionhudson.com
ISBN 978 0 7459 5539 1 (print)
ISBN 978 0 7459 5982 5 (epub)
ISBN 978 0 7459 5981 8 (Kindle)
ISBN 978 0 7459 5983 2 (pdf)

First hardback edition 1996
First paperback edition 1998
This edition 2011
10 9 8 7 6 5 4 3 2 1 0

Acknowledgments
Cover image © Lars Hesselmark/Nordicphotos/Corbis

A catalogue record for this book is available
from the British Library

Printed and bound in Great Britain by
MPG Books.

Walter Wangerin's website address is:
www.walterwangerinjr.org

To my family:
Thanne, Joseph, Matthew, Mary, Talitha

Now comes Ezra the priest down from the old palace mount, carrying the scrolls in his arms. He enters the square before the Water Gate and passes through a great congregation of people all sitting on the ground.

At the far end they have constructed a wooden platform. They've built a pulpit for this reading.

Ezra ascends the platform, steps to the front, and unrolls the scrolls.

Spontaneously the people rise up.

Ezra blesses the Lord. All the people raise their hands and answer, "Amen!" "Amen!"

And then, when they've sat down again, Ezra the priest begins to read.

"In the beginning God created the heavens and the earth.

"The earth was without form and void, and darkness was upon the face of the deep; and the Spirit of God was moving over the face of the waters.

"And God said, 'Let there be light.'

"And there was light."

CONTENTS

PART ONE

The
Ancestors

1

ABRAHAM

i

An old man entered his tent, dropping the door flap behind him. In the darkness he knelt slowly before a clay firepot, very tired. He blew on a coal until it glowed, then he bore the spark to the wick of a saucer lamp. It made a soft nodding flame. The man's face was lean and wounded and streaked with the dust of recent travel. He began to unroll a straw mat for sleeping but paused halfway, lost in thought.

Altogether the tent was rectangular, sewn of goatskins and everywhere patched with fresher skins of the goat. Across the middle a reed screen hung from three poles, dividing the space into two compartments, one for the man, one for his wife. These two were all that dwelt in the tent. There were neither children nor grandchildren. There never had been.

A vagrant wind slapped the side of the tent so that it billowed inward, but the man didn't move. He was gazing into the finger-flame of the lamp.

Old man. Perhaps eighty years old. Nevertheless, this present weariness did not come from age. In fact, the man had a small wiry body as light and as tough as leather. Nor was his eye diminished. It watched with a steadfast grey light, awaiting interpretation. It was not an old eye, but a patient one.

Not age, then. Rather, the man was made weary by this day's travel and yesterday's war.

His only relative in the entire land of Canaan — even from the Euphrates River in the east to the Nile in Egypt — was a nephew who had chosen the easier life. Though the old man himself lived in tents, Lot, his nephew, dwelt in the cities of the Jordan valley, the watered places, fertile places, desirable, sweet and green. But lately four kings of the north had attacked and defeated five cities of the valley. One of these was Sodom, the city Lot had chosen. Among the prisoners whom the northern kings carried away, then, was Lot.

As soon as the old man heard that his kinsman had been taken captive, he armed three hundred and eighteen of his own men, mounted donkeys, and pursued the enemy with a light and secret speed. In the night he divided his forces. He surprised the northern kings by striking from two sides at

once. He routed them. He drove them home. And all their plunder, all their
prisoners he brought back to the cities that had been defeated: Sodom,
Gomorrah, Admah, Zeboiim, Zoar. Lot was free again, and again he chose
Sodom for his dwelling — though the men of the place had a reputation for
extreme wickedness.

That was yesterday.

Today the king of Sodom had offered the old man all the plunder he'd
returned, but the old man refused.

Today the Priest-King Melchizedek had come forth with bread and wine to
honor the old man, and he honored him saying:

> Blessed are you!
> Blessed, too, be the God most high
> who delivers your foe into your hand!

And today the old man had come back to his tents, again, near the oaks of
Mamre, tired.

Today, in the evening, his wife had baked him a barley cake, though he ate
scarcely anything and she herself ate nothing at all.

"Is the young man safe, then?" she had asked.

"Yes," he told her.

"And his children?" she said, looking dead level at her husband. "How are
the children of the man who lives within the walls of houses?"

"Safe," said the man.

"They are home, then?" she said. "Lot sits contented among his children,
then? Lot looks upon the consolation of his old age, then, because he has an
uncle who saves him when his own choices get him into trouble?"

The old man said nothing.

"Because he has a good uncle?" she continued. "A generous uncle? An
uncle whose wife never did put the first bite of barley cake into the mouth of
her own child?"

It was then that the old man arose and left his food unfinished. He
trudged through the dusk to his own side of the tent and entered and
pulled the flap down behind himself and lit the lamp and fell to staring at
the single flame, the straw mat only half unrolled in front of him. He was
very tired. He was kneeling, sitting back on his heels. He maintained that
same posture, unwinking, unsleeping, through the entire first watch of the
night. All sound had long since ceased outside. The encampment slept. His
wife, finally, had fallen asleep on the other side of the reed screen. She was
sleeping alone.

Then, in the middle of that night, God spoke.

Fear not, Abram, God said, calling the old man by name. *I am your shield.
Your reward shall be very great.*

Abram did not move. He did not so much as shift his eye from the orange lamp-flame. But his jaw tightened.

God said, *Abram, northward of this place, southward and eastward and westward — all the land as far as you can see I will give to you and to your descendants forever.*

Still motionless and so softly that the wind outside concealed the sound of it even from his own ears, Abram breathed these words: "So you have said. So you have said. But what, O Lord God, can you give us as long as we continue childless?"

A wind took hold of the tent-flap and lifted it like a linen. The lamp-flame guttered and went out.

God said, *Come. Abram, come outside.*

On his hands and knees the old man obeyed.

God said, *Raise your eyes to heaven. Look to the stars, Abram. Count them. Can you count them?*

The old man said, "No. I cannot count them. They are too many."

Even so many, said the Lord God, *shall be your descendants upon the earth.*

With the same gaze as he had earlier turned upon the lamp-flame Abram gazed toward heaven. Now there was no wind at all. The air was absolutely still. Nothing moved in the land, except that the man could hear the sighing of his old wife inside her compartment.

He said, "Is it required then that a slave born within my household must be my heir?"

God said, *Your own son shall be your heir.*

Abram said, "How shall I know that? How can I know, when you have given us no offspring?"

Then the word of the Lord came to the old man.

Abram? said God. *Have you seen how a king will by a covenant establish his promise with his servant? Tomorrow, Abram. Tomorrow prepare the beasts. I am the Lord who brought you here to give you this land. Tomorrow I will make my covenant with you — and thereby shall you surely know my promises to you!*

∎

On the following morning the old man rose early. Without an explanation to any in the household, neither to his wife nor to his servants, he took from his herds a heifer, a she-goat, and a ram, all three years old, a turtledove, and a young pigeon.

These beasts he led to high ground, to a bare and lonely place where he tethered them.

Abram bound his robe to his waist and the sleeves to his elbows so that nothing hung loosely. He took a long copper knife and with quick cuts to either side of their necks he slaughtered the animals. They sank down and died without protesting. Then the old man drove the knife into the heifer at the top of her breastbone. Mightily he yanked the blade downward, cracking bone, slicing flesh, and cutting the carcass into two separate parts. He did the same for the goat and for the ram, though he did not cut the birds in two.

The halves of each animal Abram laid on the ground opposite each other, creating, as it were, a pathway up through the center of their bodies.

By late afternoon blood and the raw meat had drawn birds of prey to the sky above this lonely place. They circled lower and lower on watchful wings. Finally, in their hunger they dropped and tried to land. But Abram ran at them, shouting and waving his arms. The old man exhausted himself that day, driving the great raptor birds back from the carrion, protecting the animals of the covenant of God.

But then as the sun was going down it was more than mere weariness that came upon him. A deep sleep seized Abram. Dread and a marvelous darkness swept over him, and he sank to the ground, helpless.

When the sun was altogether gone and the whole world had descended into perfect night, there came a smoking firepot sailing through the dark — a furnace of smoke and a flaming torch. As they passed between the halves of the animals, the Lord God made a covenant with Abram, saying, *To your descendants I give this land, from the river of Egypt to the great river, the river Euphrates, the land of the Kenites, the Kenizzites, the Kadmonites, the Hittites, the Perizzites, the Rephaim, the Amorites, the Canaanites, the Girgashites and the Jebusites.*

∎

When Abram returned to his tents the following day, he bathed himself carefully and buried his clothes.

But he told no one where he had gone or what he had done or why he'd come back caked with dried blood.

ii

Sarai, for her part, was even more anxious than her husband regarding the promises of God. Abram had already entered his eighty-fifth year, and she herself was seventy-five.

And lo, O Lord: we are as childless as the day you first gave hope to my husband and me!

That hope had been planted a full ten years ago. Sarai was intensely aware of time. She had suffered the passage of every barren month since the coming of the promises of God. For the Lord had said to Abram, *I will make of you a great nation*. But a nation begins with the birth of one child.

Where is this child? Often the old woman placed her hands upon her sunken belly and thought, *Where is my child?*

❚❚

Sarai admitted that she had been unrestrained in laughter and dancing when the Lord God interrupted their quiet lives. It became the gossip of their city — "Old Sarai thinks she will bear a baby yet!" — and it might have been an embarrassment to Abram, if he had not already planned to leave.

They were living in Haran at the time, far to the north of this dry place, on the river Balik. Not in tents, in houses. Family and friends surrounded them, and though they were childless, by the time Abram was in his seventies they seemed content. Long ago Sarai had ceased to speak of children. She sincerely believed that she had accepted her sad fate.

But one night Abram came and woke her, his face ashen, his eyes smoky and enormous, his voice ghostly.

"Sarai, Sarai," he whispered, "prepare to leave."

"Leave? Where? Is your father sick again?"

Terah was failing in those years, often calling his son to his side.

Abram did not acknowledge the question. He looked like a blackened candle wick, rigid and breakable. "The Lord God has commanded me to go to a land which he will show me. Sarai," the man said, his voice issuing from his throat like wind from a cave, "he has made marvelous promises. He says he will make of me a great nation, and bless me, and make my name great so that I will be a blessing. *I will bless those who bless you, he said. And him who curses you I will curse. By you all the families of the earth shall bless themselves.* Sarai, get ready. We've got to go — "

And then when Abram had departed into the night, Sarai began to pant. She bowed her head and covered her face with both hands and burst into tears. *A great nation starts with a single child!*

Sarai, Abram's wife, was going to have a baby.

She could scarcely stand the sweetness low in her womb. A baby! Let people gossip about her strange behavior, her impossible expectations. Nothing bothered Sarai now.

Indeed, she traveled from Haran without complaint — she and Abram and his nephew Lot, their servants and their cattle. No matter that no one knew where they were going. The God of her husband was leading them. And a glad anticipation made the old woman young again. Blood flowed brightly in Sarai's face. No matter that they now became wanderers living in tents. No matter that, when Abram and his nephew had to divide their flocks and families, Lot chose houses in the cities of the Jordan valley, while her husband continued to roam in tents. None of this mattered — because she had received the promise of God: she who had been barren was about to bear a baby.

But that was ten years ago.

And the bloom had long since faded in Sarai's face.

Moreover, womanhood was as dead as leather within her, and the miracle itself seemed a withered thing now.

Yet God had aroused the desire inside of Sarai, and it would not lie down and die again. Every night it plucked at her heart: *Where is it? Where is the child of my own womb?* No, Sarai could never again be content with her fate — not after laughter and dancing and trust and all the changes the promise had caused in her life.

Therefore, she took matters into her own hands.

Sarai remembered a custom of Haran, a certain way by which to solve the problem of a woman's barrenness. Perhaps Abram had left most of *his* past in that land, but the promises of his God must not be left behind, so neither would Sarai leave behind this final chance for a child of her own.

"Abram?" she said. "I have an idea."

They were sitting outside and eating supper several days after he had returned all bloody from some private ceremony. He had not explained the blood and she hadn't asked. They were in the latter part of the meal. Sarai had cut a melon into parts for him, and he was eating them slowly.

"What is your idea?" he said.

She cast her eyes to the side, now cutting melon for herself. "I would not object," she said, "if you liked my idea and acted upon it. Another woman might object. I would not. In fact, I would be grateful."

Abram put a sticky finger to his tongue. "What is your idea?" he said.

"You know my maidservant, of course," she said, carefully cutting the rind from her fruit.

"Yes."

"Hagar. The sturdy woman whom we brought north from Egypt. That one. Young, she is. A good servant."

"Yes," said Abram. "I know her. What is your idea?"

"Now, then, are you finished with the melon? Have you had enough?"

Abram simply sat and gazed at his wife.

Finally she laid the pieces of her own fruit aside and wiped her hands and folded them in her lap and lifted her eyes to her husband.

"When certain wives are unable to bear children," she said, "they bring their maidservants to their husbands. They invite their husbands to go in to their maidservants in order that they, the barren wives, might in this manner get children of their own. For if the maid bears a baby upon the knees of her mistress, the baby becomes the child of the mistress. Abram, if you wished to do such a thing with Hagar my maidservant... I would not object."

For a long time the old man continued to gaze at the old woman. She lowered her eyes.

"It was just an idea," she said.

Abram said, "Bring her to me," and he rose and retired to his room in the tent.

∎

Hagar the Egyptian was not pretty. But Sarai always declared her handsome. She'd chosen this one in the first place because she had large hands and large feet, strength, bones like tent stakes. Only recently had Sarai also noted the generous width of Hagar's hips. Room. Wide black eyes, a broad forehead, not much learning, of course — but room.

On the morning after Hagar slept in Abram's compartment, Sarai saw for the first time that Hagar's hair was long and glossy and raven-black. One might call it beautiful. That same morning she commanded her maidservant to cut her hair short. "It has always interfered with your work," she said.

And then she saw that Hagar her maidservant had conceived. The Egyptian's complexion glowed so dark and fiercely that her eyes and teeth were a shock of whiteness. And when she began to show her teeth more and more in smiling, Sarai knew of a certainty that Hagar, too, knew a baby lay in her womb.

Soon another sign proved both Hagar's pregnancy and her awareness: she swaggered. Distinctly, she began to throw her hips left and right when she walked; and she began to look her mistress dead-level in the eyes; and she simply did not do the things Sarai commanded her to do. She never did get around to cutting her hair.

Sarai said, "Hagar, you go and draw the water this morning." But Hagar sighed and said she was tired, turned on her heel, went to Abram's side of the tent, sat down and ate figs.

And grew huge.

One day Sarai and a midwife were demonstrating how a maid might bear the babe on the knees of her mistress. The older woman made a roll of her sleeping mat and reclined against it, her legs thrust straight before her; Hagar sat on Sarai's thighs, leaning back on the old woman's breast, drawing her own legs up as high as she could; the midwife crouched over Sarai's ankles and faced Hagar, reaching down between Hagar's thighs.

"You see?" said Sarai. "The child will come out on my knees. I'll wrap my arms around you, Hagar, and press down on your belly like this — "

Hagar cried out and slapped Sarai's hands. "That hurts," she said. She stood up and swaggered out of the tent. Sarai sat stunned. The midwife lowered her face and said nothing.

On the following day, Sarai found Hagar sitting in the shade of Abram's tent with a bowl of figs.

Sarai stood above her. "You struck me," she said.

Hagar said, "Yes, and I told the master, your husband, that I was sorry. So I am sorry. And I told him, too, that you didn't mean to hurt me. It's just that I am soft and you are bony. I think he understands the difference, don't you? I said that maybe I am tender now because I am in the way of women, and that maybe you are rough because you are not."

Sarai opened her mouth to answer but groaned instead — a humiliating sound. So then she shouted her words: "It's your turn to... get water — "

Hagar said, "I'm sorry. Your husband commanded me to rest. I am obeying Abram."

The next time that Sarai sought to practice the bearing of this infant upon her knees, Hagar said, "Perhaps that won't be necessary anymore."

Straightway Sarai gathered her robe and, like a storm arising from the sea, she went in search of Abram.

This was a country of high grassy hills from which one could see many miles around. Sarai climbed a bald knoll and shaded her eyes and looked for the flocks of her husband, and then for the colors of his garments. He would be among shepherds today, choosing a lamb with which to trade for a particular luxury in the cities: a baby cradle.

There he was. There was Abram.

Even before she had reached the valley of his flocks, Sarai yelled, "Old man! Old man! May the wrong done to me be upon your head, old man!"

Her flesh was mottled brown by age and the harsh weather. Her hair had grown limp and thin and colorless. Nevertheless, when her body went taut with anger and her eye blazed, Sarai was young again, a warrior.

"The woman whom you embraced," she shouted, "the woman who now has conceived in her Egyptian womb, your maid and my servant — she looks upon me now with contempt," cried Sarai. "I will not abide it, Abram. I will not, and the Lord will have to judge between me and you, therefore!"

Abram stood facing her as she approached. When she paused to draw a breath he said, "She is in your power, Sarai. Do as you please. I won't interfere." Then he returned to his work.

Sarai was left to her own devices. She accepted that as power and freedom, and she became relentless.

From that day forward if Hagar refused to draw water, Sarai commanded two menservants to carry her by the armpits down to the spring and then to carry her back again while she bore the full waterskins however she might. Soon the maid found the strength to go for water on her own.

There were no figs for Hagar now. Nor naps during the day. And Sarai herself cut the Egyptian's hair so close to the skull that the tender skin burned in the sun.

When, finally, Sarai brought the raven-black tresses back to Hagar, together with a stiff linen cap, and required the maid to make of her own long hair a wig; when Sarai announced that she herself would wear the wig on special occasions in company with her husband Abram, Hagar the Egyptian disappeared.

In spite of her condition she ran far away from the tents of Abram — almost to the border of her homeland, Egypt. It was several months before she returned, exhausted, gaunt, but pregnant still.

She told Abram that the angel of the Lord had appeared to her by a spring of water on the way to Shur. The angel had promised her a son: *Name him Ishmael*, the angel said, *for the Lord has heard your affliction. He shall become a wild ass of a man, yet from him shall come so many descendants that they cannot be numbered for multitude.*

So Hagar bore Abram a son. And he named the baby Ishmael.

But it was not born on Sarai's knees.

Sarai was forced to watch all these things from a distance.

Yet even at a distance she saw the look on her husband's face as he laid the babe in the crook of his arm: tenderness! The old man's eyes were dewy.

iii

Then the Lord appeared to Abram and said, *I am El Shaddai. I am God Almighty. Walk before me. Serve me perfectly.*

Immediately, Abram fell on his face.

God said to him, *Behold, my covenant is with you. No longer shall your name be Abram. You are Abraham, for I have made you the father of a multitude of nations, and I will likewise establish my covenant with your descendants after you — an everlasting covenant!*

I give you and your descendants all the land of Canaan — an everlasting possession!

You, Abraham, and every male among you shall be circumcised in the flesh of your foreskins. It shall be a sign of the covenant between me and you.

As for your wife, Sarai: her name shall be Sarah. I will bless her. I will give you a son by her, and kings and peoples shall come from Sarah.

Abraham said, "Shall Sarah bear a child? Oh, that Ishmael might live in your sight, O Lord!"

God said, *No! Sarah your wife shall bear you a son and I will establish my covenant with him as an everlasting covenant!*

When he had finished saying these things, God went up from Abraham.

Then Abraham took Ishmael his son and all his slaves, every male in his household, and circumcised the flesh of their foreskins that very day, as God had said to him.

iv

Although Mamre, where Abraham often encamped, was on ground high enough to grow cool in the evening, during a summer's day the heat of the sun could be intolerable. It was Abraham's habit, then, to raise three sides of his tent on poles in order to cast a shade all round his room and to allow the dry wind to blow through it. Here he would rest in the afternoon, leaning against a straw mat that had been rolled up for his back.

By now the man was ninety-nine years old. He spent the hottest hours of the day dozing. Sometimes his old eye would roll open and he'd watch the oak trees floating in the heat waves; sometimes his eye would close and he would dream; sometimes he'd reach for a waterskin sweating and cooling in the wind.

And so it happened one afternoon that, opening a lazy eye, Abraham saw not trees but people standing by the tent, three men staring down at him. Strangers!

The old man jumped up and bowed down to the ground and said, "Stay a while. Rest a while."

Strangers must also be guests. Therefore, Abraham said, "Sirs, let a little water be brought to wash your feet while I fetch some food for you."

The men said, "Thank you. Do as you have said."

So Abraham went round to Sarah's side of the tent and asked her to make flat cakes of barley meal. He himself ran down to the herds and selected a tender calf for cooking. He roused his household from their afternoon naps and caused a general commotion throughout the encampment.

Finally he returned to his guests and spread goatskins underneath an oak tree and laid out cakes and meat and curds and milk, a generous meal.

He stood to the side and watched while they ate.

When they had finished they said, "Where is your wife? Where is Sarah?"

How could strangers know her name? Her new name! "In the tent," he said.

One of the men dipped his fingers in water to wash them, then leaned against the oak and said, "When I return this way in the spring, your wife Sarah shall be suckling a son."

Abraham felt the hairs on his neck begin to tingle. Suddenly this was not mere dinner conversation. It felt intimate and dangerous.

He was about to respond, when the stranger turned toward the tent and called out, "Sarah! Sarah, why did you laugh?"

A tiny voice in the dark interior said, "I didn't laugh."

The stranger said, "Yes, you did. When I said you would bear a son you laughed in your heart and mumbled, *Shall old age have pleasure anymore?* Woman," said the stranger, "is anything too hard for the Lord?"

Abraham gaped. His heart had begun to race wildly. His mind could scarcely keep pace with events. *The Lord!* This fellow had said, *Is anything too hard for the Lord?*

Once more, louder now but hidden still behind the reed screen of the tent, Sarah said, "I did not laugh!"

The three men were rising up, preparing to travel on. "You did, you know," the more glorious one said. "You laughed."

And then they left. They set out on the long road that descended to the city of Sodom.

For more reasons than he could contemplate, Abraham followed. It was the hospitable thing, surely, to accompany one's guest on his way. But Abraham had recognized in one figure something grander than a guest. By the cold in his bones he suspected that holiness was here. Therefore, Abraham followed, speechless, yet incapable of turning around and going home again.

As dusk darkened the earth, two of the strangers continued down the road alone. The exalted one paused and Abraham, too, stopped.

Then this one spoke in tones transcendent and powerful. It was indeed the Lord who said to Abraham, "The outcry against Sodom and Gomorrah is great. Their sin is very grave. I want to judge whether the accusation is accurate. That is why I am passing this way. That is why I am here."

Abraham glanced south-southwest to the cities in the valley far below. Citizens were lighting the night fires. A hundred tiny fires — they looked like a rash on the earth. Lot lived there.

Abraham closed his eyes and set his jaw. He thought that he should consider carefully his next action, but he could not. He couldn't think at all. He acted.

He said, "Will you destroy the righteous with the wicked?"

The holy figure did not respond.

Abraham wiped his mouth and spoke again. "Suppose there are fifty righteous in the city. Will you spare it for fifty? Surely the judge of all the earth would not slay righteous people because of the wickedness of others."

The Lord said, "If I find fifty righteous in Sodom, I will for their sake spare the city. Yes."

Old Abraham bowed his head and shut his eyes and took a deep breath and spoke. "I know I am but dust and ashes," he said. "But I started to speak and I must finish." He raised his face. "What if there are five less than fifty righteous? Would you destroy the city for lack of five?"

The Lord said, "For forty-five I will spare all."

Abraham said, "Ah, Lord, suppose there are only forty?"

"For forty I will not destroy the city.

"Thirty?"

"If I find thirty righteous I will withhold the punishment."

"What if there are only twenty?"

"And for twenty," said the Lord, "I will spare Sodom."

Abraham discovered that he was breathless, trembling and sweating. But he was not yet finished. "Oh, let not the Lord be angry with me," he said. "I will speak but this once more. Suppose, O Lord, that there are found only ten righteous within the city? What then?"

The Lord said, "For the sake of ten I will not destroy it."

Then the Lord went his way. But Abraham held ground where the dreadful conversation had taken place. He stared down toward Sodom, watching over his nephew Lot. Watching.

▌

Late that same evening two travelers arrived in Sodom. Lot, who was as hospitable as his uncle Abraham, invited them in and fed them and gave them pallets upon which to sleep.

But soon the men of the city surrounded his house, bellowing: "Bring out your visitors that we may lie with them!"

Lot himself stepped out and shut the door. "I beg you, brothers," he said, "don't act so wickedly. These men are my guests. But I have two daughters who are still virgins — "

The men of Sodom only roared the louder, "Get out of the way, Hebrew!" They rushed forward to break down the door.

But immediately the guests, angels of the Lord, snatched Lot in, shut the door, and by a mystery struck blind the entire company of men outside.

The angels said, "The sin of this city is so grievous that the Lord has sent us to destroy it. If there are any people here that you love," they said, "go now and warn them."

In fact, Lot's daughters were betrothed to men whom he respected. He ran to tell them of the Lord's decision. But they laughed outright at his news and scorned any suggestions he made about escaping. Lot was grieved by the prospect of their destruction.

By dawn, then, the angels actually had to drag him, his wife, and his daughters from their house. They drove them through the city gate, saying, "Run for your lives! Don't look back, don't stop in the valley, run to the hills or you will be consumed! Run!"

❚

In the morning Abraham stood on a high hill and watched as fire and pitch and a smoking brimstone rained down upon the cities of Sodom and Gomorrah. Abraham saw heaven lick the valley black, consuming every breathing thing and every green thing that had ever lived there.

When finally smoke went up from Sodom like the smoke of a furnace, the old man sat down and covered his face and wept. "Not even ten!" he said. "O Lot, God could not find as few as ten righteous people in the city you chose for yourself. Where are you now? Where are your daughters? Where is your wife?"

Lot and his daughters were safe in caves. But while they were fleeing the fire, his wife had stopped for a last glance at the city and in that instant had turned into a standing pillar of salt.

V

Soon after the destruction of Sodom, Abraham struck camp and traveled south into the Negev. Near Gerar he found new pasture for his flocks, so he stayed a while.

In the fall he and his men sheared the sheep, causing a daylong bawling from the terrified creatures while the women washed the fleeces clean of dirt and oils. They combed the wool out and packed it in bales. During the winter Abraham's household transported it to the city of Gerar and bartered for articles of copper and bronze, tools, utensils, weapons, pottery — and perhaps something pretty for one's wife if she were about to have a baby.

In the spring the sheep dropped new lambs.

And then the Lord kept his promise to Sarah.

In the small cool hours of a morning, Sarah bore Abraham a boy. The midwife brought the infant outside — a wiry, watchful child — and Abraham could not speak. The old man took the baby and gazed upon skin as fresh as petals — but he could not utter a word.

Eight days later, Abraham circumcised his son with a sharp flint knife. Then he made a great feast, gathering together his whole household to eat and drink and celebrate with him.

And before the day was over, Sarah's joy grew too great to be contained. The old woman laughed. She covered her face and laughed soundlessly, so that the entire company fell silent thinking she was crying. But then she rose up and clapped her hands and sang: "God has made laughter for me! Oh, laugh with me! Let everyone who hears my story laugh! Sisters, sisters, where was your faith? Who guessed yesterday that Sarah would suckle a child today? Yet I have borne my husband an heir in his old age."

Abraham stood to the side watching his wife. Now he went to her and took one of her hands in his own and held it until she stood still and returned his gaze. They were a small, wiry pair beneath the blue firmament.

Then Abraham looked down at Sarah's hand, this cluster of tendons and bone. One by one he touched the brown spots on the back of it. "Old woman, old woman, more precious than rubies," he murmured, "we will name the child for laughter. We will call him Isaac."

She was ninety years old. He was one hundred.

vi

At the birth of Ishmael years ago, Abraham had given Hagar her own tent in which to train and raise the boy. Hagar's tent never had pride of place. It was always pitched some distance from Abraham and Sarah's. And through the years Hagar, too, chose to keep distance between herself and the mistress of the household.

Abraham observed the choice and understood.

But privately he watched Ishmael grow into a youth of a nearly animal independence and dark intensities. Though he never spoke the thought aloud, it pleased Abraham to see the lad's spirit emerge both free and eager. On the other hand, it troubled him that the same spirit was wearing Hagar down. Large hands, large feet, her body was rawboned still; but her heart was tired and her mind uncertain.

■

It was just after Isaac had been weaned and Sarah's breasts were again flat and forever dry, that she came to Abraham among the flocks.

"Cast out," Sarah cried as she approached him, "cast out that slave and her son!"

Abraham turned to face his wife.

She didn't wait for response, but kept talking and coming at once. "I saw that Egyptian's wild whelp playing with little Isaac. There was absolutely no reverence there. None! I saw the future, Abraham, and I won't have it! The son of that slave woman shall not be heir with my son Isaac!"

Abraham said, "He is my son, too."

Sarah stood dead still, staring at Abraham. A little wind tugged at her colorless hair. Her voice, when she spoke, took on a husky quality. She uttered her words with individual softness and care. "Which of these sons," she said, "did the Lord God promise? And which did the Lord God give?"

So Abraham rose early the following morning and carried bread and a skin of water down to Hagar's tent. He spoke a word to her, then put his few provisions on her shoulder and sent her away with the child.

So Hagar and Ishmael went wandering in the wilderness.

■

But Isaac grew into a comely youth, a son of genuine respect and obedience, the blessing upon his father's old age. Abraham gave his heart completely to the boy.

There were days when the man would take Isaac with him to a high promontory and show him not only the tents, the servants, the flocks and herds of his household, but also the land as far as the lad could see, north and south, east and west.

"I, when I die," Abraham would say, "will give you the tents, my son. But God will give you the land."

The old man loved his son so deeply that he was like life inside his bones.

But then God said, *Abraham.*

The man said, "Here I am."

And God said, *Take your son Isaac to a mount in Moriah and offer him there as a burnt offering to me.*

In the evening Abraham carried his straw mat to a private place and unrolled it on a hill. All night he lay gazing up at the stars.

Early in the morning he returned to the tents and cut wood. He saddled a donkey. He asked two servants to accompany him on a journey he was about to make, then he entered Sarah's side of the tent and touched his son to waken him.

"Come," he whispered. "Don't disturb your mother. Come."

So they left the encampment together.

They traveled for three days in a northerly direction.

On the third day the old man lifted his eyes and saw the place of sacrifice afar off.

He said to the servants, "Wait here. The boy and I will go ahead and worship the Lord and then come back to you."

Abraham took the wood and laid it on the back of his son. In his left hand the man bore fire. In his right, the knife. So they walked together toward Moriah.

Isaac said, "Father?"

Abraham said, "Here I am, my son."

Isaac said, "We have the fire and the wood for our sacrifice, but where is the lamb?"

"Ah, the lamb," said Abraham. And then he said, "God will provide." So they continued forward, climbing the side of Moriah together.

When they came to the place, Abraham bent and built an altar. Wiry and silent, the old man laid wood on the altar. Then he bound Isaac his son and lifted him up and laid him on the altar, too, upon the wood.

So then Abraham bound his robe to his waist that nothing hung loosely, and with his left hand he touched the boy at the breastbone, and with his right hand he picked up a long copper knife and raised it very high in order to kill the boy with a single thrust.

Abraham! Abraham! It was the Lord God calling. *Abraham!*

"Here I am," the old man cried.

God said, *Enough. Do not hurt the boy. I know now that you fear God since you did not withhold your only son from me.*

Abraham lifted his eyes and saw a ram caught in a thicket by his horns. So he went and took the ram and offered it up as a burnt offering instead of his son. And he called the name of that place The Lord Shall Provide.

And the Lord said, *I will indeed bless you. I will multiply your descendants as the stars of heaven, and by them shall all the nations of the earth be blessed — for you have obeyed my voice.*

▌

After these things Sarah lived to be a hundred and twenty-seven years old. Abraham was again abiding near the oaks of Mamre. It was there that his old wife died.

Before he spoke the word to anyone else, Abraham sat by her bed for a night and a morning, weeping. He held her hand until it grew cold, and then he laid it by her tiny frame.

At noon he arose and went forth to find a place to bury his dead.

There was a field in Machpelah east of Mamre, owned by a man named Ephron, in which there was a cave. Abraham bartered with Ephron until he agreed to sell his field at a price of four hundred shekels of silver. In the presence of many witnesses the payment was weighed out and the sale made.

So the field belonged to Abraham.

He carried his wife Sarah to his small property and brought her into the cave and buried her there.

2

REBEKAH

i

Outside the city where Abraham's brother, Nahor, had lived and died, there was a well of fresh spring water. Abundant and dependable, the well served both the town and the travelers who passed by, caravans bearing rich goods east and west.

In order to draw water from this particular well, a woman had to descend steps of uneven stone, kneel down and dip her jar in the flowing water, then heave the full container back up to her shoulder and climb the steps again. Beasts of burden, of course, could not go down in the grotto themselves, so their water was brought up by the jarful and poured into stone troughs built at ground level.

Rebekah was familiar with the well and the routine. Daily at dusk she went with a group of friends to draw water for their families — bright young women, jars on their shoulders and laughter rising like flocks of birds. Rebekah herself moved more quietly than the others. She was tall. She took a longer, more graceful stride. She had a forehead of intelligence and a manner of immediate conviction. Even surrounded by crowds this woman seemed to stand alone.

And so it happened one evening that as the women were coming up from the well with full jars, an old man stepped forward and spoke to Rebekah as if she were the only one around.

"Please," he said, "may I have a drink from your jar?"

Clearly he was a traveler, dusty from the road, tired and very old — old enough to be her grandfather. Rebekah saw ten camels kneeling here and there around the well, their heads on high.

Her friends watched a moment, then left. It was growing dark, and Rebekah could take care of herself.

"Yes," she said, lowering the jar to her hand. "Yes, please do drink."

He took just a sip, never removing his eyes from her face. It caused her to blush.

She said, "I'll draw water for your camels, too, sir."

And she did. Down and up the stone steps she went, pouring water into the drinking troughs. While the old man still gazed at her, she gave a proper thump to one beast, which then rose and ambled forward to drink. The others followed. And Rebekah kept filling the troughs until all ten camels were satisfied.

It was dark when she was done.

And when the old man again approached her, he held in his hand objects so smooth and beautiful that they shined. A golden ring and two gold bracelets.

"Whose daughter are you?" he said.

Rebekah answered, "I am the daughter of Bethuel who is the son of Nahor."

"Nahor," the stranger murmured, "I know Nahor." He said the name with such emotion that he seemed about to burst into tears. He reached for Rebekah's hand and gently slipped the ring onto her finger. "Does Bethuel's house have room for me and my people to lodge a while?"

She said, "We have straw and provender, yes. And room. Yes."

Now, the old man went down on his knees and raised his arms and chanted softly: "Blessed be the Lord, the God of my master Abraham! He has led me to the house of his kinsman."

Without rising again, he clasped the bracelets around Rebekah's arms and said, "Please go. Please beg space for me for the night."

▎▎

Rebekah's father was old and infirm by then. It was her brother Laban who made most of the family's decisions. Laban didn't take an immediate interest in this story about a traveler from the west. He kept eating his supper. But then Rebekah removed her robe; he saw the gold and straightway left the house.

While he was gone, Rebekah and her mother prepared more food.

In time they heard Laban's voice outside. He was himself unbridling the man's camels. He was commanding his servants to bring water for the man's feet. And then he was saying, "Come in, O blessed of the Lord. Come and eat."

But when they were in the house and food was placed before him, the old man refused to eat.

"Not till I have told my errand," he said.

Laban said, "Speak on, friend!"

So he said, "I am Abraham's servant. The Lord has greatly blessed my master with flocks and herds, with silver and gold, menservants, maidservants, camels, and asses.

"But Abraham has only one son. Isaac. And he made me swear in the land of Canaan to return to this land and to the house of his kindred, here to find a wife for Isaac.

"This very day I arrived at the well outside your city and prayed that God would prosper me in my task. I said, *O Lord, when I ask a young woman to give me a drink, if she says, 'Drink, and I will draw for your camels, too,' let her be the woman you've chosen for my master's son.*

"And behold, even before I was done praying, your sister came. Rebekah came. This beautiful woman came and did all that I had asked of the Lord.

"Now, then," said the old man to Laban and Bethuel, "if you will deal loyally and honestly with my master, say so. And if not, say that, too. I must know whether to turn to the right hand or the left."

Laban said, "Clearly the thing comes from the Lord. Take my sister and go. Let her be the wife of your master's son, as the Lord has spoken."

All this Rebekah heard in shadow and in silence, standing erect in the same room while the men sat low around the oil lamp, speaking to one another.

It was Abraham's servant who finally raised his eyes and acknowledged her. "Rebekah, daughter of Bethuel," he said. She took several steps into the light, and he said, "Receive these things." Then he handed her jewels of silver and gold, and raiment closely woven. He also gave her brother and her mother costly ornaments.

Finally he ate his supper.

In the morning he said to his hosts, "Please allow me to go back to my master now. He's old and cannot live much longer."

Laban said, "Oh, sir — no! Let the maiden take time to say good-bye. Be our guest in the meantime. At least ten days."

"Please," said the servant. "The journey is a long one. The season will turn to rain soon. Please."

Laban said, "We should let Rebekah decide."

Immediately Rebekah said, "I will go."

Thus did Rebekah, this woman of quick conviction and utter self-assurance, in a night and a day transform her life thereafter and forever.

▌

In the month that followed, Rebekah and the old servant traveled from her home in Paddan-aram on the same road Abraham himself had taken more than sixty-five years earlier, a long southward route. They crossed the Jordan River at Succoth and journeyed yet farther south than the Salt Sea into the Negev.

On the evening of the thirtieth day, while the camels were moving with weary languor, Rebekah lifted her eyes and saw a man strolling alone across the fields, his head bent down in meditation.

"Who is that?" she said.

She alighted from her camel and went to the old servant of Abraham. "Do you see that man in the distance?" she asked. "Who is he?"

"Ah, that's the son of my master. That is Isaac."

So Rebekah covered her face with a veil and waited to be seen by the man who would be her husband.

In the Negev, then, Isaac took Rebekah to his tent, and she became his wife, and he loved her completely. He never loved another as long as he lived.

He said, "As soon as I saw the woman standing tall by the side of a white field, I fell in love with her."

He was forty years old.

ii

At the age of a hundred and seventy-five, Abraham breathed his last and died, an old man full of years.

His two sons came to bury him in the cave of Machpelah, in the field which he had purchased as a burial place for his wife.

So they were gathered together in the end, Abraham and Sarah.

But the brothers Isaac and Ishmael went their separate ways, never to meet again.

The children of Ishmael lived in the wilderness of Paran. They became a wild, fighting tribe, their young men expert with the bow, their hands against all other tribes.

But after the death of Abraham, God blessed Isaac.

For the next twenty years he wandered throughout the Negev wilderness, sojourning with his flocks and herds in the lands of other people, living in tents as Abraham had done before him.

And like Sarah before her, Rebekah was barren.

iii

"Isaac, why does the king want to see us?"

"Who knows why kings do anything?"

"No, but you know something. There's something you're not telling me."

"Well, yesterday when we were lying in the barley field Abimelech saw us."

"So what? Why should a king care about someone else's loving?" It wasn't so much a question as a meditation. Rebekah was beginning to wonder whether Isaac ought to strike camp and move away from this place — even before the harvest, if necessary.

She was riding a handsome donkey. A light breeze tugged at her veil. Her husband had insisted that she veil herself for this particular interview.

Isaac himself was washed and well dressed, leading the donkey up a long road toward the whitewashed walls of the Philistine city called Gerar.

They had been dwelling in this region for several seasons now, maintaining a fairly peaceful accord with the king and his people. In the beginning Isaac had even spent time in the city gates, gossiping with the citizens.

But lately his flocks and fields had been prospering more than those of Gerar. And when his servants discovered a fresh water in an old well, the men of Gerar came and demanded it for themselves. Isaac shrugged and gave it over and ordered his servants to dig another well. But when that well also brought forth a sweet water, the same men came to claim it, this time armed and angry, ready to fight. Isaac didn't want a fight. Though he himself was a good hunter he was not a fighting man. He relinquished this well, too.

So Rebekah was thinking that it was time for them to rise up and travel elsewhere.

Suddenly she snapped out of her meditations. "Isaac," she said sharply, "I think I want you to answer that question."

"What question?"

"Why Abimelech should be concerned about our lying together. If a wife wants children, what is that to a king?"

"A wife," Isaac mumbled low. "A wife, yes. Not a sister."

"What? What did you say?"

"I said, 'Not a sister.' "

"Isaac, turn and look at me! What do you mean, *not a sister?*"

Isaac turned but did not look at his wife. He said, "When we first came here the men of Gerar saw how beautiful you are, and they asked about you. I was afraid they might kill the husband to get at his wife — but for a sister they would let the brother alone. I told them you were my sister."

Rebekah gazed at Isaac a while, sitting as straight as a rod of iron upon her mount. Then she removed her veil and gathered her robes tightly around her body, snatched the bridle from her husband's hand, turned the donkey and rode alone back to the tents. Let Isaac keep his interview with the king. Let Isaac explain his own folly. Let Isaac grant her respectability again and with a confession make her his wife for the second time.

But now she was convinced. The time had come to move on.

A s her husband approached the sixtieth year of his life, Rebekah and Isaac encamped again at Beer-lahai-roi, near the same field where they first set eyes on one another.

She was younger than he, but they had been married for twenty years without children, and Rebekah longed for children.

One night she wept loudly and angrily on account of her longing.

The following morning Isaac came into her compartment, took her hand, and led her to a high, rocky hill where he lifted his hands in prayer on his wife's behalf. Then they went back down to their tent. They spent the rest of the day together, and soon Rebekah had no need to cry for want of a child. She had conceived. She was smiling and radiant again, and pregnant.

Ah, dark Rebekah! When she smiled her eye was the secret moon in a black galena sky. Her passage was so slow and so graceful as to bind men's hearts to the vision forever.

■

At three months to term Rebekah began to experience crushing pains in her womb. She would suddenly cry out, then clap her hand across her mouth in order to cover the sound.

If it has to be this way, she thought, *why should I go on living?*

This time she went alone to the sacred hill where Isaac had prayed before. She raised her hands and said, "What is it, Lord? O Lord, what is happening to me?"

And the Lord God said:

> *Two nations are wrestling*
> *within your womb;*
> *two peoples born of your body,*
> *Rebekah,*
> *shall suffer a lasting division.*
>
> *One shall be stronger than the other;*
> *the elder shall serve his younger brother.*

And so it was that when the time came for Rebekah to be delivered, she gave birth to twin boys. The first one came out wrinkled and red and so hairy he seemed to be wearing a coat. And the second came immediately behind, clutching his brother's heel.

So they named the first infant Esau. And the next they named Jacob, because already within the womb he was seizing his brother's heel.

V

As he grew into adulthood, Esau became a plainsman. Like his father he would go away by himself for months at a time, living off the land. Hunting. He had an accurate eye and an instinctive knowledge of his quarry: gazelle, oryx, ibex and all wild goats, mountain sheep — beasts of a gamier taste than fattened, domestic animals. A broad-chested, red-haired man, Esau lived by the strength of his arm. Even when he sat among the tents, he was not given to much talk.

Jacob, on the other hand, stayed continually in range of the household, the flocks, and fields and tents. He dearly loved a cunning conversation. Jacob's face, like his mother's, was smooth and mobile with intelligence. And he was a verbal fellow, more confident of his wit than of his arm.

Their father Isaac loved the game Esau brought home and cooked for him.

Their mother loved Jacob.

∎

One wintry dawn Esau returned from a long and unsuccessful hunt. He hadn't eaten for several days, and he had just traveled an entire night afoot. He was starving.

As he approached the tents of his father he smelled a morning stew on the air. It tightened his stomach and made him mad for food. He followed the scent directly to the tent of his brother.

There sat Jacob, stirring a bubbling red pottage.

Esau could scarcely form the words. "Please," he groaned, pointing toward the clay pot. "Please, Jacob, I am dying — "

Jacob said nothing for a moment. Then he looked up and smiled. "I think we can make a bargain," he said.

Esau wiped a big hand across his mouth. "A bargain?"

Jacob grinned and uttered his next words with such swift articulation that Esau felt at first confused, then angry and then just hungry, careless of anything else.

"Can a dead man inherit his father's wealth," Jacob said, "even if that man happens to be the elder of two brothers only? No, of course not. Dead men inherit nothing at all. If you die, brother, you've got nothing here and can get nothing hereafter. But if I give you food, I give you life now. In return for your life, then, you must give me that which, without your life, can mean nothing at all to you. Your birthright. So then here is the bargain, Esau: I give you life, you give me your birthright, and we are even."

Jacob always talked like this, too fast for common folk to follow. Esau could only think of food. "Yes," he said, reaching for the pot.

But Jacob pulled it back and with eyes suddenly steadfast said, "Swear it to me, Esau."

Esau yelled, "I swear," snatched the pot by main strength and carried it away in order to eat without the noise of his brother's voice to annoy him.

∎

In the days of their youth, most children give more thought to present desires than to the future necessities. Though it may mean nothing to a young man then when his blood is high and his arm is strong and his father is healthy, a birthright is a terrible thing to lose. It is double the inheritance any other sibling will receive.

Rebekah knew that.

More than that, Rebekah knew of the peculiar blessing which had been handed from Abraham to his son, her husband.

For the Lord God had also appeared to Isaac in the night, saying, *Fear nothing, Isaac. I am with you. I will bless you and multiply your descendants for the sake of Abraham my servant.*

The very next day Isaac built an altar in that place, and worshiped the God of his father. Rebekah had watched the mystery of her husband's behavior, and she had learned thereby both the faith and the prosperity of the family into which she had married.

vi

When Isaac had grown old and blind, he called Esau into his compartment and said, "I do not know the day of my death, except that it shall be soon. Now, then, Esau, take your bow and hunt game for me and prepare the savory food I love, that I may eat and bless you before I die."

As soon as Esau left the tents for the fields, Rebekah called Jacob into her compartment and whispered, "Don't talk, just listen. Just now your father sent Esau out to kill and cook meat for a very important meal. He plans to bless your brother before the Lord." Rebekah took Jacob's face between her hands and gazed sharply into his eyes. "There is no other blessing like the one he is about to bestow upon your brother," she said. "It is the blessing his father gave to him, the blessing of God which promises children and land to him who is blessed with it!

"Therefore, go down to the goat herd and slaughter two kids. I will cook one the way your father likes it, savory, and you will carry the meat to him so that he blesses you first."

Jacob whispered, "But Esau is hairy and I'm smooth. My father will feel the difference."

"What's hairier than a goat?" Rebekah said. "That's why you will kill two kids, one for its pelt. We'll cover your neck and arms with a good thick fur."

"But what if my father discovers me? What if I get a curse instead of a blessing?"

"Keep your voice down," said his mother. Then she hugged him briefly and said, "Upon me shall be the curse, my son. As for you, obey my word!"

So Jacob ran out and slaughtered two small goats with his own hand. Rebekah began to cook the one while Jacob skinned the other and scraped fat from the inside of the hide with the long edge of a knife. This fresh fur they tied to the backs of his hands, to his neck and shoulders — and over that they pulled one of the robes Esau used when hunting.

Rebekah placed a savory broiled meat into Jacob's hand and whispered, "Go."

So he entered his father's compartment bearing food.

"My father," said Jacob.

Isaac, sitting low upon his pallet, said, "Here I am. Who are you, son?"

Jacob said, "I am Esau. Your firstborn. I have done what you asked. Please sit up and eat that you might bless me — "

Isaac turned his blind face to the side. "Already?" he said. "How did you find game so quickly?"

"God gave me the speed."

Isaac said, "Come here, son. Let me touch you."

So Jacob drew near unto him, and Isaac stroked the goat hair. "The skin is Esau's," he murmured, "but the voice is Jacob's. Are you truly Esau?"

Jacob said, "Yes. I am."

Isaac said, "Let me kiss you."

Jacob bent down and held very still while his father kissed his neck at the hem of the hunting robe.

Finally Isaac said, "Yes. It smells like Esau, yes. So let me eat of your game, my son, and I will bless you."

When he had eaten, the old man spread his hands over the young man and, rocking to the rhythm of his language, chanted:

> *I smell the soil,*
> *I smell the field the Lord has blessed!*
> *May Heaven likewise*
> *grant you fatness, grains and grapes,*
> *both bread and wine abundantly.*

> *May peoples serve you,*
> *your mother's sons bow down before you!*
> *If any curse you*
> *he will be cursed,*
> *and blessed be all who bless you, son,*
> *forevermore.*

And so it was done. Old Isaac subsided into weariness, and Jacob left the tent.

Almost immediately Esau returned from the hunt with a fine catch. He dressed and cooked the meat and brought it into Isaac's compartment.

"Father," he said, "arise, eat the meat you love so much, then bless me as you said."

"Eat?" said Isaac, raising his head, blinking rapidly. "Eat? And what do you mean, 'Bless you'? Who is this? Who are you?"

"I am your son," said Esau. "I am your firstborn son — "

"Esau?" Isaac widened his blind eyes.

"Yes, Esau. And I have obeyed your word — "

"Then who was here before you?" Isaac cried. "Whose food have I eaten — "

"What?" Esau whispered.

"— and who did I bless — "

"Father! What are you saying?"

"—yes, and he shall be blessed — "

"You blessed someone instead of me? O Father!"

Esau lifted his voice in a wild, bitter cry: "Father, Father, Father," he wailed, "bless me also, O my father!"

Isaac said miserably, "Your brother has taken away your blessing, Esau."

"Jacob!" cried Esau. "Oh, they were right to name you Jacob! Twice have you tripped me from my rightful place."

"And I," whispered Isaac, "I have given him lordship over you."

Esau fell down to his knees and wept, "O Father, is there nothing left for me? Not one blessing left?"

The old man grew quiet. Finally he raised his hands above his elder son and spoke softly:

> *Far from fatness shall you live,*
> *far from grain and grapes and wine;*
> *and by the sword you must survive,*
> *serving Jacob for a time.*

> *But when you break the yoke of your brother,*
> *it shall be broken, my son, forever!*

So the second blessing, lesser than the first, was given.

And so Esau went forth from the tent of Isaac breathing threats against his younger brother: "I'll wait until our father dies," he said. "But then I will kill Jacob."

∎

In the early dark hours of the following morning, Rebekah slipped into Jacob's tent and woke him. "Get up," she whispered, stroking his cheek and chin. "Jacob, get up. Your brother has taken an oath to murder you. Flee to my family in the old country, Haran. Run to your uncle Laban. When Esau's anger has cooled, I will call you home again. But for now, go. Why should I lose two sons in a single day?"

So then Rebekah stood on a high rocky hill and watched the shadow of her dear one go. Softly he stole away as dawn began to touch the eastern sky.

∎

Rebekah never sent the message that Jacob could come home again. She died before she believed in his safety. She died without seeing her son again, and she was gathered to her husband's people, to Abraham and Sarah in the cave of Machpelah.

3

JACOB

i

Jacob ran a ridge road north by northeast. He kept to the spine of the hills which rose toward the oaks at Mamre, where his grandfather had so often sojourned. A stony road, it tore his sandals and cut his feet, but it didn't hit high bluffs or drop into impassable gorges. He felt the breath of his brother's threats upon his back. Jacob was outrunning his own death.

At noon he rested beneath an acacia tree — but grew too anxious to be still and then ran the rest of the afternoon without another pause. By evening the sun was low on his left, casting into darkness the treacherous descent toward the Salt Sea on his right.

Even into the night Jacob kept running, now tasting blood in his mouth, breathing hoarsely.

Then — in a barren place, suddenly — his legs failed him. He pitched face forward to the ground and lay still. He smelled the soil and the rock beneath his cheek. Above him the multitude of stars, the hosts of heaven, filled blackness with such tiny lights that the man felt diminished and solitary. His throat was raw. His muscles had seized like iron bands within him. The ground was cold. But he did not move. His head lay on a smooth rock. So then: that smooth rock would be his pillow. Jacob fell asleep.

And while he slept, he dreamed.

In his dream the night sky was completely empty, black, bereft of stars; but yet there was a falling and rising brightness near him. He looked and saw a broad staircase set with its foot on the earth and its head as high as the doors of heaven, and the angels of God were ascending and descending the staircase, coming and going, performing the myriad purposes of God.

He looked again, and there — standing above all, above the endless flight of stairs and the angels and the earth — he saw the Lord God himself.

And the Lord spoke to Jacob.

He said, *I am the Lord, the God of Abraham and the God of Isaac. The land whereon you lie I will give to you and to your descendants. And your*

descendants shall be like the dust for multitude. And in you shall all the
nations of the earth be blessed.

Behold, said the Lord, I am with you. I will keep you wherever you wander.
And I will bring you back to this land. I will never leave you, never, until I
have kept my promises —

Suddenly Jacob awoke from his dream, shaking with fear.

The night was visible again. The tiny stars had returned to their places,
cold and distant. But nothing was the same. An acrid scent of the sacred
lingered near the earth.

"Surely," Jacob whispered, "the Lord is in this place, and I did not know
it!" He rose to his knees. "Why, this is none other than the house of God!
And this," he said, gazing upward, "is the gate of heaven."

Even as the sunrise began to enflame the eastern sky, Jacob took hold of
his pillow-rock and heaved it from the ground. He set it on end as a pillar
and poured oil over it to mark the holiness of the place.

"O Lord," he cried, "if you will keep me and if you will bring me again to
my father's house in peace, then you shall be my God — and this standing
stone shall be your house."

So he named the place Beth-El, The House of God. And he went on his
journey less lonely after that.

ii

When Abraham had traveled this route a hundred years ago, he
came with flocks and herds and a sizable household. The days of
his journey were at least three times the days of Jacob's. Even
Abraham's servant, when he rode ten camels back to Haran to find a wife for
Isaac, took longer than Isaac's son did.

Jacob was light on his feet, young and healthy and swift after all.

After twenty days he came into a wide, flat plain where one could see
great distances unobstructed. There were sheep there. Jacob saw three
flocks of sheep, all lying down at noonday — not grazing abroad, as he
himself would have chosen if they had been his flocks.

Then he saw the shepherds. They, too, were lying down, their hands
behind their heads. Beside them, unremoved, was a heavy stone upon the
mouth of a cistern of water. So, then: not only were the flocks not grazing;
neither were they drinking, though the water was there for them.

"My brothers!" Jacob called as he approached the shepherds. They turned
their eyes toward him, but no one rose to greet him.

"Where am I?" he asked. "Where do you come from?"

A lean man said, "Haran."

"Haran? Truly?" Jacob grinned. He could scarcely believe his good fortune. "Where? Which way to Haran?"

The same man pointed north. Jacob looked and saw a fourth flock coming slowly through the sunlight.

"Is it possible that you know Laban?" he asked. "Does anyone know Laban, the son of Bethuel?"

Another man nodded. "We know him."

"Then I'm here!" cried Jacob. "This is exactly where I'm supposed to be." Several shepherds cast wry glances at the young man. Jacob said, "How is Laban? Is it well with him?"

The same lean shepherd said, "Yes, of course. Why not? That one has sons and daughters enough to care for his stock. Look there. That's one of his daughters coming now. Rachel."

"Rachel," Jacob said softly, glancing at the figure coming in her blowing robes.

Then with more vigor he said, "Why is everyone lying around? It's noon. Why don't you water your flocks and lead them off to pasture?"

Now, the lean shepherd squinted at Jacob as if to take his first true look at this foreigner, then turned over on his stomach. "It's the rule," he said. "No one waters his flock from this cistern till all the flocks are here. Besides, it takes more than three men to move the stone."

Rachel. As she came closer ahead of her flock, Jacob couldn't help but stare at her. Rachel: her eyes were wide and shy, as moist as the eye of a ewe lamb, and as kind. She had a beautiful fall of dark hair. She was herself small, her bones delicate, but she moved with such an economy that she seemed strong withal.

Moreover, she didn't have to utter a word. All she did was glance in Jacob's direction, and immediately the young man leaped to serve her. By himself he hooked his hands beneath the cistern stone, lifted it, and rolled it aside. He rushed to her, took the jar she was carrying, and began with speed and splashing to descend and ascend the steps of the cistern, pouring water down troughs for the sake of her flock alone.

The shepherds who had so little energy before now came running with their own flocks and jars and cursings. Who did this fellow think he was, breaking the rules?

But this fellow had lost all interest in brother shepherds. His eyes were filled with this sister shepherd who stood quietly by and waited till her sheep were satisfied. Then she smiled and, in tones as musical as the turtledove's, said, "Thank you, sir."

The very sound of her voice released such a rush of lonely emotion that Jacob walked toward her with tears in his eyes.

"Rachel, daughter of Laban," he whispered, "I am Jacob. I am the son of your father's sister, Rebekah."

"Jacob?" she said. "My father's kinsman, Jacob?"

He nodded and smiled and kissed her. "Jacob."

So Rachel ran north to Haran. And soon Laban himself came running back across the plain, a short, round, balding man, breathless from the run but full of compliments and attentions for his nephew. He threw his arms around Jacob and kissed him and led him by the elbow all the way back to his house.

"My bone and my flesh!" he announced. "You must stay with me at least a month."

∎

During that month Jacob worked for his uncle Laban with eagerness and a tireless efficiency. *I will be no lazy shepherd*, he thought. *I'll make myself indispensable.*

Therefore, he learned the lay of the land around Haran, the places of best pasturage, the caves where he might, if necessary, protect sheep from wild beasts or bad weather, the springs and wells and cisterns scattered in the wilderness. No matter where the shepherd led his flock, it must always be within a day's reach of water.

Laban's family lived in round stone houses with roofs of flat stone laid on wooden beams which radiated from a central pillar. The roofs were plastered and did not leak. Until this month Jacob had always dwelt in tents.

Moreover, Laban had created an elaborate system of sheepfolds by means of many low, stone walls. All his flocks could therefore return in the same night and still be kept separate.

In the evenings Jacob watched as hundreds of sheep and goats came home. He had a quick eye for the slightest limp and an easy hand with the crook to single out the sick kid. Better yet, he knew how to bind a wound and heal an infection.

At the end of a month Laban came to Jacob rubbing his jaw and shaking his head.

"Son of my sister," he said, slapping the young man's back, "I don't think I can do without you anymore. I have sons of my own, of course. And daughters, as you know very well: Leah, the older, and Rachel, the younger. Excellent children, all of them. Good workers, too. But you! You — " He started to laugh. Jacob, too, laughed. They laughed together.

"Will you stay?" said Laban. "Will you work for me? I'll pay you, nephew. You name your wage and we have a deal."

Jacob knew exactly the wage that he wanted.

"Rachel," he said.

Laban's smile stuck. "What? Who?"

Jacob said, "Sir, I'll serve you seven years for your younger daughter, Rachel."

His grin, when he pronounced the name, was dazzling; but his eye had a naked quality and a flash of panic: "That she might be my wife," he said.

Laban said, "Better I give the girl to you than to any other man. We have a deal."

∎

For seven years Jacob went forth every morning singing.

Everyone in Laban's house knew when Jacob was putting on his leather sandals and his cloak of leather. He sang about them. He sang about the girdle he wore. He named each bit of food in his scrip: bread, cheese, dates, raisins. To him his water bag contained a wine of criminal sweetness. And curdled goat's milk was the meat of kings and queens.

So he strode forth ahead of his flocks carrying three weapons: a sling, a stout studded club, and a voice of such garrulous confidence that any wild beast who heard him coming fled.

"Such long black lashes on these ewe lambs!" he sighed. "Eyes like Rachel's eyes."

He would lie on the ground in the midst of the flock, murmuring, "I'm surrounded by a host of Rachels!"

And the time passed as easily as a river at high water. Jacob the son of Isaac was very happy.

∎

At the end of seven years, Jacob washed himself, perfumed his hair, put on fresh clothes and new sandals, and went to the house of his uncle Laban.

"Sir," he said, "it's time. The years of my service are complete, and I wish now to marry your daughter."

Laban said, "Yes, it is surely time that you marry a daughter of mine!"

So the father of the bride sent out invitations to all the people of that region.

On the wedding day women gathered with Laban's wife and daughters in their private rooms to prepare the bride. By afternoon men had crowded into Laban's courtyards where they ate and enjoyed a variety of entertainments. Jacob sat in a seat of high dignity, beaming, speechless.

Finally at midnight Laban escorted his daughter, veiled face and foot in the most expensive raiment, to Jacob the bridegroom; then he led the couple through a pathway of grinning guests to a newly-built house, the doorway of which was graced by a carved stone lintel.

To the groom he said, "Here is your wife for the rest of your life. Take pleasure in her, my son."

The bride he admonished with these words: "My daughter, hold your tongue. Obey your husband ever in a humble silence."

Then he cried, "Tonight, no lights! Pleasure only, my dear children!" And he shut the door upon them.

In time the wedding guests departed, both the men and the women. Servants cleared away all signs of celebration.

■

In the morning there rose from Jacob's new house such a roaring that half of Haran woke.

Jacob burst out and crossed the courtyard to Laban's door. He didn't knock. He went straight inside and pointed at the man on his pallet, shouting, "What have you done to me?"

Jacob struck his forehead with a fist. "I served you for Rachel," he cried. "It is Rachel I love. All night long I thought I was with Rachel. Rachel! But this morning I look, and what do I see? I see Leah! Leah of the weak eyes! Leah! Why have you deceived me, old man?"

Laban sat up with a wounded look on his face. "How can you say such things to me?" he said. "One would think you were an enemy, not a nephew."

"*Enemy?* " shrieked Jacob. "Fraud! You are a fraud and not a father!"

"Please, Jacob. Please, let's not argue so," said Laban, smooth as honey. "Harsh words hurt me. This is all a mere misunderstanding."

He stood and reached up to pat Jacob's shoulder. "We have a custom here. I thought you knew. In this country we let the firstborn marry first, and the second-born second. It's the natural sequence. But," said Laban, throwing open his arms to embrace his son-in-law, "if you will serve me another seven years, you may marry the second-born, too. Within the week, in fact! Within the week you may lead the lovely Rachel, too, to your new stone house." The short man stood back and smiled. "What do you say? Do we have a bargain?"

Jacob's face was black as thunder. But his voice was small muttering, and he said, "Yes."

"What? What did you say, nephew?"

"Yes," said Jacob. "We have a bargain."

iii

LEAH SPEAKS

When my husband discovered that I was not my sister, I did not blame him for his anger. I had expected anger. I only hoped he would not hit me, and he didn't. He scarcely looked at me. At *me*, I mean. He did not see Leah. He saw not-Rachel.

Mine was the more elaborate wedding, of course, being first. Louder. More food, more guests.

It was when he led my sister into the same room where one week earlier he had led me; it was when he asked me to leave my new house and return to my mother's house a while; it was when he went into my sister fully knowing who she was and able, therefore, to call her by name; it was *then* that I surprised myself with sorrow.

I had said I would not love him. But I failed.

Thereafter I cooked well, and he praised my food. But he lingered over Rachel's.

At shearing time he weighed our portions of wool evenly. Each bundle was the balance of the other. But Rachel's wool, when it was washed, showed not a fiber that was not white.

I tried to hide my sorrow. It had not been planned that I should love Jacob. Nor was it his fault that I did. So he did not see my heart. But the Lord saw.

The Lord soon opened my womb and I conceived and I carried the baby nine months and I bore for my husband his firstborn son. I named him Reuben, because the Lord had looked upon my affliction, and I thought: *Surely now my husband, too, will notice me.*

Not long after that I conceived again and bore another son, and I thought, Because the Lord has heard that I am hated, he has given me this son also. So I named him Simeon.

Again I conceived and bore a son and I called him Levi. I thought that surely now my husband would be joined to me, seeing that I had borne him three sons.

Well, but I who was rich in one thing was poor in the other. Jacob loved his children, yes. And since that first night he nevermore looked with anger at me. Simply, he did not look at me with anything at all, neither a thought nor a word nor a feeling. When he looked at me he did not see Leah. He saw not-Rachel.

While I was bearing children all those years, my sister was barren. She was unhappy. So Jacob was unhappy, too.

I heard them whispering at midnight.

She said, "Jacob, either you give me children like Leah, or I shall die!"

He said, "Ah, Rachel, do you think I am in the place of God? I'm not the one who closed your womb."

When, therefore, I conceived and bore another son, I no longer sought the love of my husband by means of my children. I said out loud, "This time I will praise the Lord!" And I named the baby Judah.

But this fourth child tormented my sister. She stopped talking to me. She ignored my four sons. And if ever she was saying something to Jacob when I drew near, she broke it off and glared at me.

I saw that Jacob's shoulders began to droop and his eyes grew tired.

Then I saw that Rachel's maid, Bilhah, was with child, and I understood. Bilhah bore the baby upon my sister's knees, so it was considered to be Rachel's; and as soon as she saw that it was a boy she cried, "God has judged me and has heard my voice and has given me a son!" She named him Dan to commemorate this judgment of God.

Within a year Rachel's maid bore another son. I was not in the room at the time, yet the whole family heard Rachel's voice ring out when the boy was born. She said: "With mighty wrestlings have I wrestled with my sister, and I have prevailed." The word she used for "wrestle" is *niphtal*. So she named the baby Naphtali.

Shall I be blamed for offering my husband my maid then, too? By Zilpah I had two more sons. I named the first one Gad because he was for me good fortune; and the second I named Asher: Happy. And why should I not be happy, seeing that I was now the mother of six?

Still, my sister was not happy.

One morning during the wheat harvest my oldest son found mandrake roots. Roots shaped like a little man. They help women to bear boys. Rachel must have noticed. That afternoon she came to the threshing floor where I was working, picked up a flail, and began to beat the wheat beside me. Then she astonished me by speaking.

"Give me some of Reuben's mandrake," she said.

Those are the first words my sister had spoken to me in more than ten years. God forgive me, mine were no kinder than hers.

"Why should I?" I said. "Does the woman who stole my husband's love now want my son's roots, too?"

"Jacob visits you," she said.

"Not for years, Rachel," I said. "With Zilpah, yes. Not with me."

"Not for a single night?"

"Well, you tell me which night he has not been with you, and that will be the night he spent with me."

"Not one?"

"None."

Rachel fell silent, swinging her double stick, thumping the hard dirt, beating the wheat-sheaves into kernel and chaff — while I said nothing.

I had covered my face with my skirt. I did not want my sister to see that I was crying.

But then she stopped threshing and I felt her hand on the back of my neck.

"Leah," she said, "let's make a trade. I'll give you nights with Jacob, this night now and others hereafter, and we will not be enemies anymore, but sisters. And will my sister then give me some of her son's mandrake roots?"

This is the moment in my story which I most want to tell: that I embraced my sister. We burst into tears and held one another, and I found how deeply I loved her. No, I had never ceased to love the beautiful Rachel.

The mandrake did not help her. But she helped me. I bore two more sons and a daughter after that, and for each birth my sister was my midwife. We named the first of these three Issachar, and the second Zebulun, and the little girl Dinah. That was the end of my childbearing. I gave birth to no more children.

But my sister did.

Finally God hearkened to our ceaseless prayer on her behalf and opened her womb and the entire family rejoiced when Rachel conceived and bore a son.

On that day Jacob remembered how to smile again. Ah, his face was a flood of sunlight. He was happy. I was happy.

And Rachel gave beautiful voice to her own happiness. She said, "The Lord God has taken my reproach away!"

She named her first son Joseph.

iv

When Laban was happy he would grin so hard, that he produced beads of sweat on the top of his bald head. Lately the short man was sweating all the time, always dandling some new grandchild on his knee.

Jacob, the son of his sister Rebekah, had been for him an incalculable treasure. Ever since the young man's arrival nineteen years ago, Laban's flocks had continued to redouble themselves. Moreover, because his nephew held the rank of a servant in the household, the laws of the land gave Laban authority over Jacob's wives — his daughters — and over all their children.

Laban couldn't say that he'd actually planned such a rich old age; but neither would he deny that he deserved it. It was his cunning that had caused it, after all; a lesser man would not now be sitting so easy, dandling grandsons.

But there came a morning when Laban stepped outside to find Jacob standing by the door, hunched, haggard, and brooding.

"My son, what's the matter?" Laban boomed, full of good will.

Jacob said, "I have to leave Haran."

"What did you say?"

Jacob looked directly at Laban. "Sir, I beg you to let me go."

"Go? So you're speaking of going somewhere. Where?"

"Home."

"Ah," said Laban. "Of course. A visit."

"No, sir. No," said Jacob. He wore a full beard now, grizzled grey with his working. He was broad-shouldered; no day went by when he did not bend his back to some heavy labor. But he had in these latter years descended into silence. Who knew why talkative young men gave up that grander part of themselves? Laban, on the other hand, had kept his tongue oiled and was proud of his ready speech.

"Say on, my son," he said.

Jacob drew a deep breath. "You yourself know how your herds have increased all the years I've served you," he said. "And you know how honest I've been. Please, sir: release your daughters to me. Let me take my children and return to the land of my fathers. I want to be wandering again. This sitting in one place — " Jacob shook his head. "This working all in one place for so long... I... Laban, I haven't even been able to lay anything by for my family!"

"Right!" cried Laban. He seized Jacob's arm. "Exactly right! You must provide for your family before you do anything else! Before you even think of leaving, we must negotiate some better wage for you and the children. Tell me what you want, and it is yours."

Jacob gazed at his uncle a moment. He turned and looked toward the sheepfolds, then back at his uncle again. "Nothing," he said. "I don't want you to give me anything — "

"Jacob!" Laban shouted. "Nephew! Don't be hasty. I've a mind to be generous today. Just tell me what I should give you."

Softly Jacob said, "Give me nothing. But let me keep for myself those few lambs and kids born spotted or mottled or speckled or striped. Every white sheep shall be yours. Every goat born completely black or brown — yours."

Small sweat popped out on Laban's head, but he restrained his twitching grin. He frowned, murmuring, "Multicolored cattle to you, the rest to me. Hmm." But lambs are nearly always white, and kids all brown or black. Laban, subdued by the stress of this decision, said, "I agree. Keep them that drop speckled from their dams." Then he clapped his hands and cried, "So you'll stay, right? Building your herds? Working for me?"

"Yes."

"Good. It's a beautiful day. Let's go to work."

As soon as Jacob was out of sight, Laban called his sons and commanded them to separate every sheep with the slightest color, every goat with the tiniest white, and drive them away, a full three days' journey away.

That night when he returned from the fields, Jacob met cattle all one color. Not one goat had a star on its forehead, not one ewe showed one hair brown.

∎

One year later — in spring, when Laban, his sons, and all his shepherds were busy shearing their sheep — Jacob's servant found Leah and Rachel among the women, washing the wool.

The servant spoke secretly with them. "Veil your faces," he said, "and follow me. I'll show you where Jacob is."

This was curious. Both wives had assumed that their husband was with the rest of the family. Instead, they were led by a hard route westward, traveling all day till suddenly a valley opened below them, and there they saw huge flocks and herds, and strange people guarding them — and tents! Here were men and women and children, living in tents!

Jacob, bearded and light in a loincloth, strode up the slope of the valley and met them. He put his hands first on Rachel's shoulders and next on Leah's, gazing into their eyes so intently that they felt distressed and wondered what it meant.

He dismissed the servant, then led the women to a massive stone nearby. He himself did not sit.

"Jacob," Leah said, "I've never seen these cattle before, have I?"

"No," he said.

"Are they yours?"

"Yes."

"Does my father know about them?"

Her husband's eyes widened with an agitation Leah hadn't seen before. "No," Jacob said softly, "Laban doesn't know."

Leah turned to Rachel. "Not one animal has a solid color," she said. "See that? They're all speckled or spotted. But they look strong. Jacob, they look very large and strong."

Jacob said, "I have something to say to you. Listen first, then tell me what you think."

The man spoke quietly. There was such appeal in his voice — such concern for their present response — that the women felt a certain strength come into them, and a certain dread.

Jacob said, "Lately I've heard the sons of Laban complain about my presence here. They say I've taken their father's wealth. I think they fear for their own inheritance. On the other hand, I know for a fact that your father has no regard for me anymore. As far east of Haran as we are west of it, there are herds and flocks mottled exactly like these, except that they are weaker than mine. They belong to your father. On the day he promised to give me the multicolored cattle, he removed them all — every goat and sheep — and drove them east.

"You know that I have served him these twenty years with all my strength. Yet he has cheated me. He has changed my wages ten times. What am I to do in such a difficult position?

"I think I have to leave.

"Hush! Rachel, hush a minute. Let me finish."

Jacob knelt down and pulled a shepherd's scrip from under the stone. He opened it and offered each woman a bit of bread. Rachel nibbled at hers. Leah merely held it. Actually, her mouth was dry; but she didn't ask for a drink.

Jacob said, "But God has been with me. I dreamed a thing, and then I did it.

"I took fresh rods of poplar and almond and planed and peeled the bark so the white showed through. Whenever the stronger animals were breeding, I put before their eyes rods white with stripes and speckles and spots. But when the feeble animals bred, I hid the rods. So the mottled kids and the spotted lambs were strong — and they became mine, as you see before you now.

"In that same dream the angel of God said to me, 'Jacob.' I said, 'Here I am.' He said, 'I am the God of Bethel, where you anointed a pillar and made a vow to me. Now arise, go forth from this land and return to the land of your birth.'

"That is what God said, Rachel," Jacob whispered, gazing again with steadfast entreaty into her eyes. "Leah, the Lord God said, *Go*. What do you think?"

Rachel said, "Let Leah speak. She's older."

Leah said, "I'm thirsty."

Immediately Jacob drew a leather flask from his scrip. She put it to her lips and drank, grateful to find it was wine. Then she handed the flask to Rachel.

"I will tell you the truth," said Leah. "We are treated like foreigners in our father's house. Since we married you, there's been no guarantee that any property will fall to us or to our children hereafter. Now, then, whatever God has said to you, do."

This once, each in the presence of his other wife, Jacob kissed them. Yes: they felt both strength and dread in their souls. They did not feel young any more.

Jacob said, "Prepare the children. Tomorrow your father and brothers are going to shear the sheep they keep three days east of Haran. While they are there, we will steal away to the west."

■

So Jacob arose and set his family on camels and drove all his cattle westward — all that he had acquired in the land of Paddan-aram.

As his grandfather Abraham had before him, he crossed the Euphrates on inflated goatskins, then turned his face south to the land of Canaan and his father Isaac.

When Laban returned to Haran and saw his great loss, he called his kinsmen together and set out after Jacob. But God came to Laban in a dream by night and said: *Take heed that you speak no evil word to Jacob!*

Moreover, when he drew near to his nephew, Jacob rode at him in a towering anger. Jacob leveled at Laban a verbal attack so fiery that the older man began to shake.

He said, "These are my daughters. Their children are my children, and the flocks are my flocks. But what can I do this day to these my daughters or to their children? They are in your hand now. Come, let us make a covenant, you and I."

So Jacob took a stone and set it up as a pillar.

They called the pillar Mizpah because it was a watchpost between them. And each man said, "The Lord watch between you and me when we are absent one from the other. And I shall never pass over to you, nor you to me, to do the other harm."

V

South went the long household of Jacob, slowly. In the spring of the year there was good pasturage; but valleys thundered with the flooding rainfall and every small brook swelled into a river.

South, skirting the city of Damascus; south over the high plateau of Bashan, then descending a chalky, limestone land into Gilead; south through that beautiful country where Jacob grew contemplative and withdrew into himself. Here were sights he had not seen in half his lifetime: the western slopes of these hills were rich with olive orchards and vineyards and fields of a young, green grain; the hills themselves were covered in thick forest. Jacob was remembering, overwhelmed with the goodness of Canaan east of the Jordan.

But then they came to the Jabbok River, roaring through its gorges toward the Jordan, and another mood seized Jacob's heart, silencing him altogether.

He had sent messengers to his brother Esau, saying that though he was returning, there was no need for the brothers to meet or intrude on one another's private lives. But the messengers had ridden back at high speeds, crying: "He's coming! Esau is not staying away. He's crossing the Jordan at Jericho and riding north to meet you with four hundred men!"

His brother was coming to kill him. Jacob was afraid.

He led his household down a treacherous path into the Jabbok valley, to the narrow strip of land that ran along the northern bank of the river. There he began to divide his livestock and to send it all ahead of himself in great, successive waves. One wave alone consisted of two hundred and twenty goats, two hundred and twenty sheep, thirty camels, fifty cows and thirty asses — all in the care of several servants whom Jacob commanded to find Esau and say, "This drove of animals belongs to your brother Jacob. He gives them as a present to his lord Esau — and he himself follows behind."

But behind the first wave came a second, the same size, with the same message: "A gift, and your brother follows behind."

In this way Jacob sent a third wave and a fourth, an absolute deluge of wealth, a trick to soften his brother's heart or else to scare him with waves of power.

When his cattle and his drivers had all passed on before him, he saw to it that his wives and their maids and his eleven children likewise went safely over the Jabbok with his most trusted servants.

So then Jacob stood alone on the northern bank of the river: before him the roaring waters; behind him a wall of Nubian sandstone, perpendicular from its foot to the tangled black forest on its brow; right of him there was nothing except a stony, wet plateau; and left of him, nothing.

Night was descending. The gorge grew gloomier, leaving only a path of sky above him, where stars filled the blackness with such tiny lights that he felt small and solitary.

It had been Jacob's intent to make a private crossing of the Jabbok. But maybe he trusted the swimming stroke of his strong arm better in daylight than in the dark; and maybe the night fell faster within the walls of the gorge than he had expected. Whatever the reason, he did not dive into the waters. He did not move. He stood transfixed, surrounded by sound and soon by an absolute darkness — for even the tiny stars were suddenly swallowed as if by a beast of horrible size.

Jacob felt wind, then a chill.

Someone came flying down the riverbank. Jacob felt what he could not see. Then someone attacked him, struck him to the stony ground, and began to wrestle with him. They wrestled by the river. They whirled and heaved each other against the sheer rock wall. In a breathless silence they wrestled all night until a high grey dawn began to streak the sky.

Jacob's adversary touched him in the hollow of his thigh and put his thigh out of joint.

Jacob threw his arm around a huge waist and held on.

The massive foe said, "Let me go, for the day is breaking."

But Jacob shouted, "I will not let you go, unless you bless me."

"What is your name?"

"Jacob."

The contender said, "Your name shall no more be called Jacob, but Israel, for you have striven with God and with men, and have prevailed."

"Who are you?" Jacob cried. "Tell me your name."

But he said, "Why is it that you ask my name?" Then he blessed him and vanished, and he was there no more.

Immediately it was morning.

Jacob tried to rise from the terrible exertions of the night — then suddenly realized whom he had been struggling with all night, even all his life long. He began to tremble.

"I have seen God face-to-face," Jacob whispered, "yet my life is preserved."

He called the name of that place Peniel: The Face of God.

And the sun rose upon him as he left Peniel, limping because of his thigh.

vi

On the morning after God had changed his name to Israel, Jacob looked up and saw Esau approaching with four hundred men. He did not pause or turn away. He continued walking toward his brother. He limped. Moreover, he kept bowing to the ground in genuine humility.

And when Esau spied Jacob in the distance, he leaped from his donkey and ran as fast as he could to meet him, then fell on his neck and embraced him and kissed him.

Jacob wept because of his brother's kindness.

Both men were bearded. Both beards were shot with white. But Esau's was full and reddish while Jacob's was thin and black. Esau had the stocky body of his uncle Laban. Jacob had the native grace of Rebekah.

Jacob put his hands on Esau's shoulders and smiled. "To see your face is like seeing the face of God because you are receiving me with such favor."

Esau stroked the muscle and the bruises in Jacob's forearm. "You're stronger now," he said. "But, baby brother, your quarrels must be horrible."

Jacob laughed. He begged Esau to keep the presents he had sent him yesterday. And so the brothers were well-met after all. They spent the day together, and then they parted in peace, forever.

Esau returned to Seir, southeast of Canaan, where his family would dwell for centuries thereafter.

Jacob crossed the Jordan River at Succoth and traveled to Shechem. There he made public the name that the Lord God had given him. He purchased a small piece of land and built an altar on it. He called the altar El-Elohe-Israel: God! The God of Israel!

4

JOSEPH

i

Joseph, the only child of his mother Rachel, was a clever fellow, a boy with a mind of genuine complexity.

"Subtle," his father Jacob would say, tapping his temple. "Levi, why couldn't you learn to count so early?"

Even before he was weaned, Joseph learned that he could cause small explosions in any of his brothers, simply by raising his eyebrows and popping his eyes at the lad. "Stop that!" his brother would yell. "Stop it, you slithering — "

Of course, he only did that trick when their father was present — and then great Jacob would roar the name of the offended brother, "Judah! Judah!" laughing till the tears ran down his nose, utterly stunned by the wit of the infant. "Oh, Judah, the boy drives you like a donkey, doesn't he? Mark my words: he will be someone some day."

No one had the proof, but the brothers believed it was Joseph who told their father about Reuben's sin. Who needed proof? It was always Joseph. He was always sneaking off to tattle.

So one morning Joseph disappeared from the fields where the brothers had led their flocks, and just as they expected, Jacob came out that same afternoon.

"Oh, no," Reuben groaned.

The brothers lifted their eyes, and saw their father striding across the fields like the whirlwind of God, white with wrath. He passed through the flocks as if they were foam, bore down on Reuben, grabbed the young man's staff and began to beat him with it. Back-hand, back-hand, the big man cracked his son across the buttocks till the rod broke, and Reuben ran for the hills.

When their father departed again, never having uttered the first word, the brothers gaped at each other. What had Reuben done?

Well, Simeon knew. Simeon and Reuben shared the same room in their mother's tent. Three nights ago, with awe and pride and genuine dread, Reuben had described for Simeon his first experience with sex.

"Reuben had sex?" the brothers said.

"Yes," said Simeon.

"That's why father beat him so badly?"

"Well, yes and no. It gets worse."

"What could be worse than that?"

Simeon lowered his voice and said, "Reuben had sex with Bilhah, father's concubine, Rachel's maid — your flesh-mother, Dan, and yours, Naphtali."

All the brothers shivered at this last bit of news. And little lord Joseph! — so *he's* the one who told it to their father? Yes, and because of *him* every member of this family now is suffering. It probably never occurred to him what effect his tattling would have on Dan and Naphtali!

What, therefore, should be done about Joseph? What should the brothers do about him?

Reuben got a drubbing — and Joseph got a coat. A dress-coat! A garment so extravagantly long that one could not wear it while working. But then, the little lord never did physical labor anyway.

There was no proof that the coat was a reward for Joseph's witness against Reuben, but everyone assumed it because their father had chosen for his favorite son a coat with the sort of sleeve that only the royalty wore!

Right away the fellow began to dream.

Nor was he private about his dreams. Joseph would don that royal coat and regale the entire family with his dreams, raising his arms for emphasis.

"I dreamed that my brothers and I were binding sheaves in the field," he said. "And lo!" — here he threw up his arms and waved his sleeves — "lo, my sheaf stood upright while my brothers' sheaves bowed down before it."

Did he say *bowed*? Whoever heard of sheaves *bowing* like people? Besides, when did the little king actually cut a sheaf in his life?

"I dreamed of the sun and the moon and eleven stars," said Joseph. "And they were all bowing down before me."

Jacob cleared his throat. "This dream is different, isn't it?" he said, frowning. "By sun and moon, can you mean your mother and me?"

One would have wished that Jacob had probed the boy's insolence a little farther. He didn't. And seeing that their father did not, the brothers wondered more and more loudly among themselves: *What's to be done with this dreamer?*

ii

When Joseph was seventeen years old, his mother Rachel became pregnant for the second time in her life. It should have been a year of glad anticipation. But Rachel had ever had a delicate frame; and the same small bones that once had caused such love in Jacob now were frail and uncertain. Her large, lovely eyes were larger now and darker than ever.

Pregnancy made an invalid of Rachel.

Instead of gaining a cushion to soften the child inside of her, there came a month when she actually began to lose weight. Then the baby caused such pain in her pelvis that she had to lie down. Rachel spent the last three months of her term lying on her back. It broke Joseph's heart to see her so.

Whenever he crept into her tent, she smiled and reached to touch his cheek.

"Be good," she said. Often she said, "Joseph, are you befriending your brothers? Do you obey your father's word?"

"Yes," he would say. "Yes."

But then the baby would turn, and she would gasp, and Joseph hurt to see her hurt. Worse, he felt guilty that on his account she should struggle to cover the pain. His presence, then, increased her trouble.

"Be good," she said.

He said, "Yes," and left her alone in the darkness.

Then one night, while Jacob's household was traveling to Ephrath, Joseph was awakened by a long, crimson scream. This was not a lamentation. It was plain animal pain.

Joseph ran outside in time to see his aunt Leah duck into his mother's tent.

He went through the darkness to the back of her tent. He sat down and drew up his legs and wrapped his arms around them. He bit his lip. He bowed his head and rocked because he could hear the sounds his mother was making — woofing sounds, snarling, like the grunting of wild beasts when they tear their prey apart.

Joseph started to cry, but without sobbing. Tears ran down, soaking his robe at the chest.

Toward morning he heard Leah speak in a clear voice. "Don't be afraid, Rachel," she said. "You are bearing another son."

For just an instant Joseph felt almost giddy. Soon it would all be over.

But then he heard the whispering voice of his mother, a ghostly exhalation: *Benoni*, she breathed. This was her name for the infant. *Benoni.*

And then she breathed no more.

Joseph tried by the force of his will to make his mother breathe again. He held his own breath. Then someone touched his neck, and he jumped, and it was Leah. She said, "Joseph, go back to bed for a while. I need to speak to your father."

▮

Jacob buried Rachel on the way to Ephrath. He set up a pillar upon her grave.

It is the pillar of Rachel's tomb, which is there to this day, near the village of Bethlehem.

Exactly eight days after he had buried his wife, Jacob circumcised his son.
That night he crept into the darkness of Rachel's tent and crouched by her
pallet.

He heaved an enormous sigh. Then, suddenly, he smelled her.

He hadn't expected anything like the presence of Rachel to meet him
here; but her scent was on the air, something sweet and nourishing, like
milk. It was as if the spirit of Rachel herself were passing through the room.

Then it spoke: "But mother named the boy *Benoni*."

Ah, no, this was not Rachel. It had the lilt and the accent of her voice, but
it belonged to Joseph.

Joseph had been here ahead of Jacob, lying in shadows on his own pallet.
Perhaps he'd been sleeping here for eight days now.

Jacob turned toward his son and said, "What? What did you say?"

With some emotion Joseph said, "Mother named the boy *Benoni*. I heard
her. But today you circumcised him with another name: *Benjamin*."

"Yes, yes, I did."

"Why would you change my mother's wishes?"

"How long do you think a people should live with grief, Joseph?"

"I don't know."

"Always? Do you think Rachel would want us forever to grieve?"

"No."

"And your brother, how long should he be sorrowful? He will never be able
to remember his mother or his birth. Do you think his mother would want
him to go in gloom through the rest of his life?"

"No."

"No, surely she wouldn't. But Benoni means The Son of My Sorrow. And
Benjamin means The Son of My Right Hand. Joseph, your mother was sad for
a little while, and now she is sad no more. She named the birth. She named
the pain. She named the moment and the coming of her son, and we will
remember the name, you and I. This will be a covenant between us, together
to remember the name *Benoni* and all that it stood for. She named the birth;
let us name the boy. Why shouldn't your brother bear the brightness of his
mother's more lasting character? Why shouldn't he carry her confidence
into his life and into the world? Her right hand. My right hand. Our..."

"Oh, Joseph, hush," Jacob said. "My dear son, all is well now. The Lord is
with us. Hush, hush."

For Joseph had taken his father's hand and had laid the palm against his
face, and now the older man could feel the wetness on his boy's chin. Joseph
was crying.

So then they held each other, smelling Rachel's scent. And Jacob talked
long into the night telling his son of the past, his love for Rachel, his

wrestlings with God, his trust in the Lord God, the behavior that the Lord loves — and the covenant that had kept them safe through all these years.

∎

One morning while Jacob and his household were sojourning in the valley of Hebron, he called Joseph to himself and said, "My son, even your baby brother is smiling today. It's time to put your sorrow aside. Be busy. Talk to others. Listen to them. Share interests.

"Come, now," he said with cheer. "Your brothers are pasturing the flocks at Shechem, several days away. Go there, Joseph, to see whether it is well with them and with the flocks, then bring me word again."

In fact, it was the season for pleasant weather, after the rains but before the summer sun grew hot. And old Jacob knew from his own experience how pleasant a lazy trip north could be.

He sincerely wished to lift the spirits of his son; and he felt he was succeeding when Joseph came to say goodbye, wearing his gorgeous coat. It filled Jacob's heart with gratitude to see his son dressed thus. Yes, the coat had been an extravagance; but as long as it made the lad happy, it was worth the cost.

"Go safely," Jacob said, kissing Joseph and noticing that they stood on a level now. The child had grown as tall as his father.

"I will," said Joseph. Then he called out, "Where's my big brother Benjamin?"

Leah brought Benjamin out, and Jacob watched with tenderness while Joseph rained kisses on the baby, causing him to bark a husky laughter. Then the whole company was laughing, Jacob and Joseph and Benjamin and Leah.

Yes, yes, grief was coming to its conclusion.

"Goodbye, Joseph. God be with you, my son. Goodbye."

"And with you, Father. Goodbye."

∎

Seven days later, when the ten grown sons of Jacob returned from Shechem, Joseph was not among them. No, they hadn't seen him. They swore they hadn't seen Joseph anywhere since they had left Hebron more than a month ago.

On the other hand, they'd found a coat. A coat with long sleeves, very similar to Joseph's. Stiff with dried blood. It had been torn violently in three places.

"Father, can it be Joseph's coat?"

The old man took one look at the riven cloth and began to howl. "My son! My son!" he wailed. He tried to smooth the garment with the flat of his hand, then gathered it up and buried his face in it. "My son has been devoured by lions," he cried. "Surely Joseph is torn to pieces!"

Jacob rent his robe and put sackcloth upon his loins and mourned many days.

Reuben and Simeon and Levi and Dinah — all his children, one by one — came to his tent and tried to comfort him. But Jacob refused to be comforted. He said, "No, no — I will go to my grave lamenting Joseph, lamenting my dear son Joseph."

iii

B ut in the same days when the old man began to mourn the death of his son, Joseph was walking among the camels. He went in the midst of a caravan which followed an ancient trade route southwest along the coast of the Great Sea past Gaza, then west across the northern portion of Sinai to Goshen and into Egypt.

He went manacled neck and ankle. He was chained in line with twenty other men of several languages and various countries. His feet were bleeding.

His captors were not wicked. Nor were they merciful. They were merchants. Together with other goods — gum and balm and myrrh — they meant to sell the sleek young man at a profit. They had purchased him for twenty shekels, a reasonable price for a healthy male; but Egyptian coin would increase the investment, as long as he was healthy still when they got to that country. Therefore, they did not begrudge him bread. All their slaves improved in the passage. It was a matter of pride.

∎

Joseph had actually felt happy to see his brothers and their flocks spread out in a valley below him. They had been a surprising vision as he came over a grassy rise — and the lightness of his spirit at the sight had likewise surprised him. Yes, he had been lonely too long, too long mourning his mother.

"Brothers!" he called, grinning and waving. "Brothers, I am here!"

As he descended the slope in a little trot, he saw that they were gathering together and looking his way.

But they were not smiling.

Naphtali said, "The dreamer."

At this distance Joseph couldn't be sure, but it seemed that Naphtali had spat the word. His mouth looked twisted. Then Dan shouted with bloody savagery, "Let's see what becomes of his dreams," and Joseph slowed his step.

Two of the brothers, then three, then five broke from the group, running as fast as they could in Joseph's direction. All of the brothers were shouting now, all ten of them. Joseph's throat tightened. It felt as if he were in a dream. He absolutely could not move, trying and trying to make some sense of the moment.

Then his brothers were on him, whirling him around and ripping the long coat from his body. Someone hit him a solid blow to the side of his head. Joseph observed the impact and the pain with astonishment. There was meaning in that blow. Someone struck him in the small of his back and he crumpled. Then they were dragging him by his legs over dirt and rock, and then the earth opened up beneath him and he was falling. He hit bottom in an echoing place. He made an odd croaking sound. The wind was knocked out of him. He couldn't breathe. He glanced up and saw a small hole, the heads of his brothers blocking sunlight, then sank into unconsciousness. He was in a cistern. The thought accompanied him into the utter darkness: *I'm in a cistern. But I am not dead. I am in a cistern. O Lord, be with me now.*

∎

Joseph had not died. Instead, he was sold to slave traders; and two months later he found himself standing on a whitewashed platform, listening to the foreign tongues around him. The platform was surrounded by men with neat beards, trimmed to an oiled tuft at the chin. Some had side-whiskers from ear to jaw, but no one wore the sort of cheek-bushes he was used to. Men must pluck their hairs. And everyone, it seemed, bathed. Joseph couldn't smell sweat. People wore white linen in this country, a fabric as supple and smooth as human flesh. A marvel, nothing at all as rough as the wool he knew.

Clearly he was in a marketplace.

And those that stood on the platform were for sale.

To the left of the platform Joseph saw a small operation which caused him to become excited. Egyptians sat on chairs: here was a man sitting up on a chair behind a flat surface of wood. A table. And on that table was unrolled another sort of fabric altogether, stronger than linen. The man was making marks on that fabric with astonishing speed. For every slave sold, he would dip an instrument in black water, then form a series of swift, exquisite shapes on the fabric. Joseph peered more closely: the instrument was made from a rush that had been cut on a slant and frayed at the end, a brush for black ink! Joseph had heard of writing before. His father had explained to him the anonymous marks in clay and old stone. But this was a miracle of speed and simplicity, and it delighted him.

Before the bidding began for him particularly, Joseph realized one other wonderful fact about the man who wrote with rushes: that he was himself a slave.

Therefore, when the auctioneer asked him what skills he could perform, Joseph answered by pointing at the scribe on his left. "That," he said. "I can do that." In his soul he said, *Or if I cannot do it, I can learn.*

And if anyone had questioned him further, wondering how he knew the scribe was a slave or where he got the gall to say he knew the crafts of a nimble mind, Joseph would without hesitation have answered: "The Lord is with me."

∎

It happened that the man who purchased Joseph was a figure of importance in the land of Egypt. His name was Potiphar, "the one whom Re has given": Re, the sun-god of the Egyptians.

Potiphar held the rank of captain, commanding Pharaoh's personal guard. He carried — perhaps as a mere honorific, perhaps as a fact — the title "Eunuch," though he was married to a woman who was, said the royal gossip, both young and vital. Potiphar himself, despite his power, was not a physically imposing presence. On the other hand, his tiny eyes were shrewd and sure, as accurate as darts and as dangerous. He rode through the city, well-oiled, sweet-smelling, bejeweled, and revered wherever he went. He returned to a house built high above the river, a proud palatial edifice of marble-white walls, interior courtyards, many rooms, fountains outside, baths within, latticed windows to shape the light, and floors inlaid with bold mosaic. But the beauty above hid an official cruelty below. The captain of Pharaoh's guard was also the lord of his prisons, and Pharaoh's prisons were the basement chambers of the captain's house.

At Potiphar's insistence, every slave and servant wore linen as rich as his own. He wanted his household to reflect well upon his position and his evident generosity. Joseph, therefore, regularly washed his entire body with warm water and dressed himself in two pieces of clothing: the first an undergarment worn at all times, a long soft shirt tied about the hips; the second an elegant, close-fitting cape for wearing in public places.

In fact, Joseph seldom needed the cape. Potiphar kept him close to home because he genuinely liked the Hebrew.

This slave smiled. There was nothing cringing or fawning about him, but with good health and a glad disposition he would look his master straight in the eye and smile. What other slave was so peaceful in his position as to befriend the lofty Potiphar? None. And besides all that, it was a handsome, manly smile.

Joseph learned to write Egyptian as well as he spoke it, because he learned both skills at once. And swiftly — before the end of his first year in this master's service — the Hebrew had proven to be more than competent. Many accountants were competent; few were also trustworthy.

On impulse, once, Potiphar asked Joseph to inventory the goods of the household. When he was done, nothing was missing, not so much as a finger's breadth of wheat from the bins; but measures that had been falsified on previous lists now came to light. The Hebrew slave revealed these thefts without criticism or self-righteousness. He managed to make it a proper, impersonal report.

Therefore, Potiphar appointed Joseph to be overseer of his entire household. And then he was delighted to discover that his properties, his harvests and investments and even the transactions of the household, prospered.

"How is it you succeed so well?" he asked the slave. "And how can you take such pleasure in *my* prosperity."

The Hebrew replied with a smile, "God is with me."

■

God was with him. And this, to him, was the proof: that even as a stranger in a foreign land, Joseph had come to enjoy the daily routine of his life.

Early in the morning he entered the room from which he conducted his master's business. There, looking out an eastern window, he did as he had seen his father do — he gave thanks to God. Then he removed his cape, sat down in an Egyptian chair before an Egyptian table, mixed the inks and cut the rushes for his writing.

Within the hour Potiphar would arrive to discuss the day's projects, to receive reports, to give advice and to ask for it. After their conference, the master left for Pharaoh's court, while the slave stayed home and worked. So went his days. So passed the seasons, wet and dry.

Soon Potiphar's wife also began to bring various small tasks of her own into Joseph's room. He always rose to greet her. She always gave him a dead-level gaze and a thin smile. Though Potiphar was short, his wife was exactly Joseph's height. She would let him hold the tips of her fingers a moment, then she said, "Come, come, no need to be so formal."

But Joseph was never anything less than formal. It was more than his natural manner; it was a conscious choice. Often he went out to make purchases for the household. "Here is my seal," Potiphar had said to him. "If you think we need it, buy it. I trust your judgment." And since he acted in his master's name, it seemed right to act in self-effacing formality.

In a self-effacing formality, then, Joseph always waited until his master's wife was seated before he sat again to write.

She was, however, a perplexing woman. Clearly, her eye was lit with an interior intelligence. She could comport herself with a majestic dignity. Yet sometimes she would, exactly like a child, jump up the moment Joseph sat down, forcing him to rise again with embarrassment. It seemed to him she was testing the truth of his courtesy. He could be patient for whims of his mistress, of course; but it interrupted his work.

One day while she was sitting some distance away from his table, the woman began to murmur words so softly he scarcely heard them. He thought she was singing to herself. But suddenly he caught the words, *Hebrew, lie with me*, and his ears burst into flame. Joseph did not look up. Maybe he had imagined the phrase, for as soon as he heard it, she fell into a perfect silence. And after a moment she rose and left the room.

Joseph released a long, trembling sigh.

Three days later they happened again to be in the room alone.

Potiphar's wife said, "Joseph?"

He looked up.

She was gazing at him from dead-level eyes, the lids made green with malachite. "Joseph," she said. "Lie with me."

He gaped. Her neck was extraordinarily long, her throat naked.

Softly she said, "Did you hear me? Do you understand?"

Without a word he stood up, pulled on his cape, walked out of the room and through the courtyard and out of the house altogether.

When she entered the room on the following day, precisely at her usual time, Joseph rose as always to greet her, but he kept his eyes cast down and he did not take her hand. Neither did she reach for his. Nor did she sit. There was a servant standing at the door. She dismissed him.

So then they stood alone, his eyes lowered, hers burning the flesh of his forehead.

"Joseph," she said, "do you know what I want?"

"Yes," he said.

"Then why did you walk away from me yesterday?"

Now he looked at her. He wished he weren't panting like a child, but he had to speak: "My master," he said, then paused to breathe. "My master trusts me with everything he has — everything, my lady, except yourself, because you are his wife. How, then, can I do this great wickedness and sin against God?"

Potiphar's wife said nothing. Her lips drew thin and tight across her teeth. Her silences could be terrible. Perhaps she would leave now. Instead, abruptly, she sat. Joseph sat down, too. He tried to write. But every time he flicked up his eyes, he saw that she was staring at him in a cold silence.

Then she was gone. For ten days Joseph worked in his room alone.

But on the afternoon of the eleventh day, the woman appeared in the doorway, her hair loose, her eye unpainted, bright and wild. "Slaves," she hissed, "know nothing of gods and sin! Don't you ever pretend to be better than me!" She strode into the room. Joseph started to stand. She rushed at him and grabbed his undergarment at the shoulders. "Lie with me," she cried. "Hebrew, lie with me!"

Joseph rose up and pushed her backward. She fell against a cabinet filled with scrolls. But she was clinging to his garment. It ripped at the seam and came off. Joseph stood for an instant completely naked, then he leaped from the room and ran out into the courtyard blinded by his shame.

"Get off me! Get off me!" The woman was screaming inside the house. "Help! Help! The slave is trying to rape me! *Help!*"

Joseph whirled around. He saw Potiphar's wife stepping calmly through the doorway, though her mouth was open and she was making a powerful screaming sound. In her hand was his undergarment, in her eyes a cold, emotionless ice.

All at once there bounded from the door behind her four large Egyptian men, very angry. Joseph didn't try to run. Where would he go, naked? Nor did he fight back. He was beaten to the ground. He was struck on the back of his skull with the flat of someone's sword. Gratefully, then, he passed out.

▊

Joseph awoke in Potiphar's basement — the prisons of the captain of Pharaoh's guard.

The walls were thick. The rooms were narrow and dark and mostly bare. There were many such rooms, a labyrinth of rooms inhabited by men of every rank. Joseph discovered a hidden community of unfortunate men, none of whom knew when he might be released since there were no fixed sentences. There was only the whim of the powerful people upstairs.

But even the nether world was arranged like the world in light: prisoners who came down from high positions were served by prisoners who came from no position at all.

When two officers of Pharaoh's court were cast into these chambers — each for some offense which their lord must soon have forgotten — Joseph was charged to serve them. One was Pharaoh's butler. The other had been his baker. But Joseph was a Hebrew; therefore, they took his ministrations for granted and ignored him.

Time passed and neither courtier heard word from on high regarding his release. Each man sank into despair. They experienced horrible bouts of anxiety. And because slaves are nonentities, they confided their feelings to the Hebrew.

"What can we do to survive in here?" they asked. "Tell us," they begged, "how you endure this misery."

But the slave only said, "The Lord is with me."

■

One morning, as Joseph approached the cell of his masters with water and cloths to wash them, he heard an odd, choked moaning. When he entered, he found both Egyptians crouched in corners, shivering, holding their elbows as if cold to the bone. They were staring at the floor with gaunt eyes.

Joseph said, "What is the matter with you?"

The butler leaped to his feet and pressed his hands to his temples. "Hebrew, Hebrew, what do you know about us?" he cried. He turned to the wall. "We dreamed last night. Both of us. But there's no one in this pit to interpret the dreams. You have no idea, the agony. But it's not your fault. You've never lived as we have. Wash me and go away."

The delicate man sat down, tilted his head upward and closed his eyes.

Joseph wet his cloth and began to wash the butler's ears. "I have dreamed," he said softly. "And my dreams had meanings. Very good meanings, so I thought at the time. But no one had to interpret my dreams to me."

"What do you mean?" The butler opened one eye.

"I knew the meanings the moment I awoke."

The butler opened both eyes. "How? Are you a magician?"

"Don't all interpretations belong to God?" said Joseph. "And where is God *not*? God is everywhere."

The baker, much smaller than the butler, more private by profession, crept up to Joseph and touched his shoulder. "Here?" the baker whispered. "God is... here?"

"Everywhere," said Joseph.

"Do you think," the baker whispered with dreadful hesitation, "that God would perhaps be willing to interpret our dreams?"

Suddenly the butler seized both of Joseph's wrists. "Listen! Listen to this," he hissed and then launched into a breathless monologue: "I saw a grapevine with three branches, budding. Its blossoms burst open, and immediately there were clusters of ripe grapes, and I was pressing the grapes into Pharaoh's cup which was in my hand, and then I was taking the wine to him. What does your God think it means?"

Joseph plucked the butler's fingers from around his wrists, moistened the cloths and turned to the baker.

"The three branches are three days," Joseph said, beginning to wash the baker's face. "In three days Pharaoh will raise your head from here to himself above. He will restore you to your former office as his butler." Joseph turned to look at the butler. "This is the true meaning. When it takes place, remember me. When you are in Pharaoh's presence once again, please tell him of my situation. I beg you to ask for clemency."

Now, even the soft-spoken baker could not sit still. He wriggled beneath Joseph's hand, so Joseph touched the man's brow with the cloth and said,

"What was your dream?"

The baker closed his eyes. "I dreamed that there were three baskets on my head. The topmost basket carried cakes for Pharaoh, but the birds were pecking them. That is all."

The man fell silent. Joseph likewise said nothing for a long time. He washed the baker all down his arms, and when he came to the hands, he lingered.

"The three baskets are three days," he said. "In three days Pharaoh will raise your head from — " Joseph folded the man's hands within his own. " — will raise your head from your shoulders," he said. "He will hang you on a tree. The birds will eat the flesh from you."

∎

In three days the Pharaoh chose to celebrate his birthday by means of a feast for all his servants. On that occasion he remembered the butler and the baker, officers he had consigned to prison. The butler he brought back into his palace and his good graces. The baker he hanged.

But the butler forgot how he came to know the fortune that befell him.

So Joseph was in prison. In the dark pit of prison Joseph lay down on rotten bull-rushes, while the days passed into months and the months into years.

iv

Pharaoh slept on a couch. During the day it was a divan for sitting; at night it became his bed.

In the company of several wakeful servants, Pharaoh slept on a couch which was crafted of cedar and gold and silver. It was covered with thicknesses of linen; it was set on a raised pavement, itself a splendid mosaic of porphyry, marble, mother-of-pearl and other precious stones.

And the king of Egypt slept in light.

Oil lamps burned while Pharaoh was sleeping. Water flowed near his private chamber, murmuring softly, ready to slake or wash or cool the body of the king.

Curtains of a dark and curious weave stilled any wind that wandered the palace; rugs softened any step; and music could, if necessary, immediately comfort any nightmare; a harp and a lute waited to be brushed by the fingers of young girls. Likewise, a priest was never far away. Pharaoh was blood-kin to the gods. He slept attended. He slept in the company of many ministers. And yet this sacred personage slept on his beautiful couch in a loneliness deeper than any.

This was not so much his will as it was his station.

It could not be changed.

∎

One night Pharaoh lunged awake with a cry, staring about himself as if blind. His bedclothes fell aside.

Straightway two servants rushed in with moist towels. Young girls touched their instruments, causing shy chords to catch the air. A woman moved through the room brightening every lamp. Another brought new linen covers for the king's body.

Soon Pharaoh lay back and fell again into a fitful sleep.

But he mumbled and sweated and threw his arms about so that the servants who crept too close to fan him got cuffed.

Again the king lunged awake, panting and staring into the air.

"Where is the priest?" he cried. "Bring me the priest!"

The priest was already beside him, with a flask of wine and a silver cup.

Pharaoh gripped his arm. The cup splashed wine down the skirts of the priest.

Pharaoh said, "I dreamed. I dreamed a dreadful dream. I dreamed two dreams, very similar, very significant, very — "

Without releasing the priest's arm, Pharaoh told his dreams in sacred awe and in precise detail.

"What do they mean?" he said.

The poor priest had turned white during the recitation. Yes, the dreams were clearly heavy with meaning. So much the worse for the priest, who hadn't the first idea what they meant.

"Then bring me the magi!" the king commanded. "I want those who have made a profession of the sciences! Let them study this and interpret it!"

Pharaoh then recounted his dreams to a series of grave, thoughtful men, students of the universe. Courtly men pretended interpretations — and enraged the king. "You take me for a fool?" he cried. Men of honor bowed their heads and admitted failure. Men frightened even to approach the foot of Pharaoh stood gaping and mute.

"Is that it? Have I met every wise head in the kingdom? Is there no one to interpret my dreams to me?"

Then it was that the chief butler received his memory again. "O Pharaoh," he said, "There was a Hebrew slave in prison who interpreted my dream for me. He told me that my dream spoke of you, sir — that you would elevate me to your service again. And he was right."

"What is this Hebrew's name?"

"I never knew. Sir, I never knew his name."

∎

It was the captain of the king's own guard, Potiphar, who ushered into Pharaoh's presence a Hebrew man thirty years old, newly shaven, pale from the prisons, but confident in his carriage and level in his looking.

Pharaoh regarded the slave, who nodded and smiled.

"Hebrew, do you interpret dreams?"

"No," said the slave without embarrassment. "It isn't in me to interpret dreams. But God does. God can give an answer to Pharaoh concerning his dreams."

"Hebrew," Pharaoh said, slowly measuring the man from his foot to his face, "what is your name?"

"Joseph. I am the son of Jacob, who is called Israel."

"Joseph, then," Pharaoh said, "these are my dreams."

"I was standing by the Nile when seven cows, sleek and fat, climbed out of the water and began to graze on the reed grass. Immediately seven other cows came out. These were sickly cattle, very thin. They swallowed down the fat cows, and yet they stayed as thin as before. I woke from that dream, then slept and dreamed again.

"I saw seven ears of grain, plump and good, all growing on a single stalk. But then there sprouted seven more ears, thin and blighted by the east wind. Exactly as in my first dream, the thin ears ate the full ears.

"Joseph, son of Jacob, what does it mean?"

The Hebrew's expression had grown solemn. His voice now came soft with humility and perfect certitude. "God has shown Pharaoh what he is about to do through many lands," he said. "The seven good cows and the seven good ears are seven years. Your dreams are one. There will be seven years of great plenty in Egypt. But then the lean cows and the blighted ears stand for seven years of famine to follow the abundant years. Famine shall consume the kingdom so grievously that the time of plenty will be forgotten altogether. And the doubling of Pharaoh's dream means that the thing is fixed by God. It will surely be."

For a moment the halls of the Pharaoh were still. No one spoke, neither priest nor butler, wise man, or eunuch or slave. The king and the Hebrew looked at one another.

It was Joseph who broke silence.

"If Pharaoh wishes," he said, "I have a suggestion."

"Speak."

"Let Pharaoh appoint someone discreet, impartial, and wise to administer a gathering of grain during the seven years of plenty. Let granaries be built in which to store food against the seven years of famine that are to follow."

Two sentences. The Hebrew had uttered in two sentences such a clear common sense that Pharaoh stood up, stepped down from his dais, and confronted the man on an equal level, eye to eye.

"What would you say, Joseph? Shouldn't my administrator also exhibit the spirit of God? Shouldn't he be both bold and honorable?"

The Hebrew said, "Yes."

"Yes," said Pharaoh. "Yes, and since God is with you, interpreting dreams and offering prompt, impeccable counsel, I choose you."

The king of Egypt turned to a messenger and framed a decree to go forth through the entire kingdom:

"Watch, Philopater," he said. "Do you see how I put my signet ring on this man's hand?"

The messenger nodded.

"Yes, you have seen it," said the king. "Joseph, the son of Jacob, now has power to issue orders in the king's name and the ring to seal the same. He is no slave. He is no prisoner. He is under the authority of none but me, and all are under his authority. Mark it: he is my governor.

"Watch, Philopater. Do you see how I array the man in royal robes the like of my own? Do you see how I hang a golden chain around his neck? Yes, and when he rides through the kingdom, it shall be in a chariot whose glory rivals mine. And you, Philopater, shall command runners to go before him, crying, "*Abrek! Abrek!* Kneel before the governor's passing!'"

And so it was.

Pharaoh gave his new governor a new name: Zaphenath-paneah. By this name his fame went forth throughout Egypt and yet farther to the kingdoms north and east. Zaphenath-paneah, the Man who Lives when the Deity Speaks.

▌▌

So God was with Joseph.

He married Asenath, the daughter of the priest of On, and was comforted with human companionship.

Moreover, by the wisdom which God had invested in him, he accomplished the tasks he himself had recommended to the king. Joseph oversaw the building of spacious granaries. Then, during the plenteous years, he gathered so much food that finally it could no longer be measured.

During those years, too, his wife bore him two sons.

Joseph called the first Manasseh. It meant Making To Forget. For he said, "God has caused me to forget my hardship."

The second child he called Ephraim, To Be Fruitful. For in the evenings Joseph would ascend to a high window in his house and gaze down at the river valley, the fields, the crops of his adopted country: his life. And what was all this land, by the hand of God, if not fruitful?

But soon, exactly as the Lord God had communicated unto Pharaoh, the earth withered and hardened and cracked. Its plenty came to an end. Even the mighty Nile shrank and could not serve the soil. Famine began.

Months of drought became years of drought, so that the people despaired of rain and harvests. They ground dust between their teeth. It was a famine indeed.

As governor, Joseph opened the granaries slowly, sparingly. He knew he had to dole out their stores through seven years. The Egyptians, therefore, did not eat much. But they ate. And they did not die.

V

Old Jacob stood on a hill near Hebron, squinting across a stony gorge to the ridge road that traveled north and south in that region.

"See that?" he said. He raised his hand and pointed toward a file of travelers toiling along the ridge. They were silhouettes in a slow dance northward. Jacob's eyes watered in the dying sunlight.

"You see that lot?" he said. "They are tired, but their sacks are full. They are poorer, but they will eat for three months."

Jacob leaned heavily on a staff. He was speaking to his fourth son, Judah, who stood stout and strong beside him. This one was as quiet as his mother Leah. Once Jacob had mistrusted the child of his who did not talk. Now he believed that Judah's silences came of conviction and not of deceit.

"I think it is time we did the same," he said. "How many goats still give milk? There is neither milk nor cheese left. The rams live and the ewes die and even the lambs that are born die when their dams do. Judah?"

"Here I am, father."

"When did the last merchant caravan pass this way?"

"More than three years ago."

"Who travels through these dead lands?"

"Thieves. Gangs. The famished."

"Yes, and city-delegations to Egypt to buy grain. Those travelers there are proof that the rumors are true. Egypt has food, and it is time we went as well." The old man turned to face his son directly. "Take your brothers for protection. Leave your wives and children with me. Go down to Egypt and barter the best you can. Buy grain and come home again with full sacks."

Judah continued to gaze toward the sunset. His face took a bronze tinge. He had a broad forehead and a large nose. Jacob admired the nose on his son, but he wished the expression were more mobile. Judah's features chiefly showed restraint and rectitude.

"Father."

"Yes?"

"All my brothers?"

"No!" Jacob shouted. His stomach contracted. He gripped the staff for stability. Then, with more control, he said, "No, not Benjamin. All but Benjamin. Benjamin stays with me."

Soon Judah and his brothers, their donkeys, provisions, weapons and wealth, crossed to the ridge road themselves, where they turned south and slowly rode away, while Jacob and his youngest child stood watching the departure.

The old man put his arm around the boy. Benjamin was fourteen years old. He had a tangle of beautiful hair. He was a mere baby.

∎

The rainy season passed without rain. Only a few light showers fell to taunt the starving tribes.

Jacob went out every day to watch for the return of his sons. Every day was clear and hot. His old eyes could see very far across the land.

And then one afternoon he recognized their dark forms in the distance, so he hurried back to the tents to prepare a meal for their arrival.

They ate a solemn feast. The eating preceded any talking. Jacob kept jumping up and looking south. Ten of his sons had gone into Egypt. Only nine returned. Simeon had not come back. Judah grimly avoided his father's glances — and Jacob could scarcely stand the silence.

Finally he broke the ceremony of their feasting and cried, "Where's Simeon? What happened to Simeon? Why hasn't my second son come back?"

All the brothers ceased eating and sat in grave silence.

Judah said, "The grand vizier of Egypt, the most powerful officer, second only to Pharaoh, the governor in charge of foodstores — Zaphenath-paneah himself — required that Simeon stay behind in prison."

Jacob held onto his staff with both hands, or else he would surely have collapsed. He was the only one standing. His sons sat with their heads hung down, grizzled hair and sorrow covering their faces.

"Why? Judah, why? Why would the governor want Simeon? What crime did he commit?"

"The grand vizier," said Judah, "charged us all with a crime. All of us. He said we were spies."

"*What?* Spies? What did you do?"

"We don't know." Stout Judah now raised his face and looked helplessly at his father. "We were surprised that the man wanted to see us at all.

"Father," Judah said, "there are many people in Egypt to buy food, and there are officers to handle the traffic. But the governor himself came out to look at us. He asked where we came from. We said *Canaan*. He asked who our father was. We said, *Jacob, called Israel*. Then he said, *Yes, well, you are spies*. He accused us of spying. We said, *No, we are brothers, plain shepherds*. We told him there was no one else in Canaan except our father and one other brother.

What is your brother's name? he asked.

Benjamin, we said.

"The governor grew very angry then. We don't know the cause of his anger. Father, we could not understand this Egyptian. *Benjamin?* he said. We said, *Yes, Benjamin*.

"Then he said, *Bring Benjamin here, and I will know that you are not spies*."

At these words, Jacob slumped to the ground. Reuben rushed to catch him. Reuben and Levi together cradled the man while Benjamin ran for a flask of water. Judah watched unmoving. There was the tightness of genuine anguish in his face.

"What else?" Jacob whispered, lying in the lap of his sons.

Judah spoke softly. "We told him we could not bring Benjamin. We said it would kill you. We said you had already lost one son and could not lose another. The grand vizier only seemed to grow more furious as we talked. His face was white. His voice was a whisper. He spoke Egyptian, but the translator said, Then you shall stay in prison till one of you goes to Canaan and brings Benjamin here.

"So we sat in prison for three days. Then the governor came and said, *I've changed my mind*. He pointed at Simeon. *That one stays. The rest of you, go and come back with Benjamin. Your food is already in sacks on the backs of your beasts*, he said. *Go*.

"And so we have come."

In order to show that their journey had done some good, the brothers brought forth their sacks of grain and opened them.

But there arose into the night sky a howl of extremest sorrow. For old Jacob saw in each sack of his sons the money he had sent for payment. "What are you doing to me?" he cried. "You have stolen from the governor of Egypt! No, no, no, no, no, you will not take the son of my right hand into such danger. I am sorry for Simeon — but you will not bring my grey head down in sorrow to the grave."

∎

In the year that followed, no green thing grew for forage. Judah watched as the flocks and herds of his father sickened and died. People did not have the strength to drag the carcasses away.

Judah thought often of his brother languishing in an Egyptian prison. Simeon. Perhaps he was eating, but he was not here. Nevertheless, sins lay heavy on Judah's soul. And the pain of his father shut his mouth. He would not speak.

But when their previous stores of grain were gone, when his children and Jacob's grandchildren grew gaunt, and when their bellies distended with hunger, his father came into his tent and said, "Judah, go again. Try to buy a little food again from Egypt."

Judah said, "Father, sit down and listen to me."

He held his peace till Jacob sighed and sat. Perhaps the old man knew what was coming.

Then Judah said, "The grand vizier in Egypt solemnly warned us, saying: *You will not see my face unless your brother is with you*. Now, then, if you send Benjamin along, we will go. But if you won't, we cannot go to Egypt."

Jacob said, "How could you do this wickedness against me, telling the man I had another son?"

Judah said, "He questioned us closely. We only answered his questions."

Judah waited a moment in silence. Then he said, "Father, you know that we all will die if we don't do something now. Everyone will die. You and all your children and all our little ones. But send Benjamin with me and I will be surety for him. If I do not bring him back, let me bear the blame forever."

Long, long Jacob sat in silence.

Finally he said, "A little balm. A little wild honey." He pulled himself up by grabbing his staff. He limped to the door of the tent and turned. "Take gum to the governor and myrrh and pistachio nuts and almonds. Take double the money to pay for both loads of food." The old man turned away. He stood in the doorway staring out at the dusk, an ancient shadow, an enormous sorrow. "And," he whispered, "take your brother Benjamin."

▮

The chief steward of the grand vizier brought his master news at noon of a bright blue day: that the same men who had come from Canaan last year now had returned again.

"You wished to be informed," he said.

"Yes," said Joseph. He was in his working room in Pharaoh's palace. "How many are there?"

"Ten, my lord. I think ten."

Joseph felt his heart beat faster. "Wait for them in the marketplace," he said to the steward. "When they arrive, take them straight to my house. Slaughter an animal. Prepare a feast. I will share my evening meal with them."

By a stern self-discipline Joseph spent the day attending to his regular affairs.

Nevertheless, he placed himself near a latticed window from which he could watch the sons of Jacob. He saw his steward step forward to meet them. He watched the exchange of greetings — and then their faces fell, troubled by his invitation. Twice the steward tried to lead them to the governor's house, high on a hill; twice he had to turn back and beg them to follow. But all at once the men opened their pitiful sacks, pulled out a great deal of money, spread it on the ground and gesticulated, loudly explaining something. The good steward only put the money back again, grabbed their sacks himself, and in this way persuaded them to follow.

Next Joseph ordered Simeon's release. He, too, was led to the vizier's private quarters.

Then, late in the day, Joseph himself walked home.

As he approached his courtyard he heard a babble of Hebrew voices: "Simeon! Simeon, is it you? How are you? Oh, Simeon, how did they treat you?"

And Simeon's voice: "How is father? Oh, no! Reuben, you brought Benjamin — "

Joseph felt such a constriction in his throat that he feared he could not speak. *Benjamin is here!*

He strode into the courtyard and with a hard tone said, "How is your father? Is he alive?"

The brothers immediately fell on their faces before him. His interpreter repeated the question in Hebrew, but the brothers didn't move.

Joseph barked, "Stand up!" The interpreter didn't have to repeat it. The men rose slowly, gazing at Joseph with genuine fear. Wordlessly they pushed pots and jars toward him, balm and honey and gum and almonds.

Joseph said, "The old man of whom you told me, Jacob, Israel — is he well?"

In Hebrew the brothers murmured, "Your servant our father is alive. Yes, and he is well."

The breath was squeezed in Joseph's chest. Suddenly he saw the fourteen-year-old Benjamin, the image of their mother Rachel, a remarkable fall of dark hair — and then Joseph couldn't breathe at all. His face flamed with emotion. His nostrils flared. He pinched his lips and frowned like thunder. The brothers shrank backward from him. Joseph whispered, "This is your youngest brother?"

Judah stared at the governor. "Yes," he said. "Benjamin."

Joseph said, "Benjamin — "

But the name on his lips undid him. He covered his face and rushed from the courtyard into an inner room, where he burst into tears and wept: *Benjamin.*

During the meal that followed, Joseph watched how furtively his brothers ate. Eleven brothers: their hunger must be violent within them, but their fear must be greater. They nibbled. He sent them enormous portions. He sent Benjamin five times what he sent the others. Still, everyone only nibbled.

To his chief steward he whispered, "Go out and fill the sacks of the Hebrews with food and with their own money again. All of it." He pointed at Benjamin. "And in the sack of the lad place my silver cup. Go."

Speaking through the interpreter, Joseph required the shepherds to spend the night in his own quarters, then he left them.

He did not sleep at all that night.

Immediately at sunrise the following morning he heard the commotion of men preparing to leave. He ascended to the high window of his house and watched them go with haste and fear and elation. Eleven of them. Without turning around, he spoke to the steward waiting behind them. "Follow them," he said. "Block their progress. Ask why they would repay the vizier evil for good. Ask for my silver cup. Make them open their sacks. Call him who has the cup a thief, and bring him here."

Joseph watched his servant ride forth in a magnificent chariot, approach his brothers, command them to halt, command them to open their sacks. He watched the terror thicken in his brothers' faces as money fell out before the grain. And then, when the silver cup rolled out of Benjamin's sack, he saw how the ten older brothers all took hold of their robes and tore them. They made a terrible wailing. He could hear it even here, on his hill, in his house, behind the lattice of his window. He watched them slowly retrace their steps, returning to the house again.

He was sitting on a dais in his royal chair when they were ushered into his presence.

"What have you done to me this time?" he asked in Egyptian.

Judah spoke, broken by his anguish. "What can we say to my lord?" he said. "God has found out the guilt of your servants, and we shall be your slaves. All of us."

"No," said Joseph. "Not all of you. Only him whose sack had my silver cup. Him. The rest can go home to your father."

Judah's face twisted with grief. Joseph set his jaw. Judah crept toward him then bowed to the floor. "O my lord," he said, "let not your anger burn against your servant for speaking."

Joseph stiffened. He was fighting tears.

But Judah flinched in fear. He gathered strength and spoke nonetheless. "The first time we came, you asked about our father. We told you the truth: he is old. He has already lost one son. He will die if he must lose another. Especially his youngest son, Benjamin. But that is the one you demanded to see."

Joseph raised his face and shut his eyes tight.

Judah said, "Our father begged us not to bring the lad here to you. He said that any harm to Benjamin would bring his grey head down to death, because Benjamin's mother had two sons and one is gone. But you demanded it, my lord, so I argued hard for Benjamin's coming. I vowed to bear the blame of any trouble. I took an oath. Therefore, I beg you, let me stay in my brother's stead. Take me, not him. How can I go back to my father if his son is not with me? What could I say? I cannot. I cannot."

Joseph could not control himself any more.

In Egyptian he whispered, "Get out! Everyone but the Hebrews, leave the room."

When they were alone, he looked at his brothers and burst into tears. He knelt down in front of Judah and embraced him. In Hebrew he said, "Brother, didn't you know?"

He stood up and went to Benjamin and kissed him. "I am Joseph," he said.

"Reuben," he sobbed. "Reuben, look at me. Simeon, I am your brother. Levi, look, I am not dead. I did not die. I'm alive. It's me. Dan! Asher! Gad! Naphtali — it's me, Joseph!"

One after the other, he fell on the necks of his brothers and held them close until all the men were weeping.

"I have been in the hands of God from the time you took me from my father. Oh, my father! Please! Go to my father! Tell him who I am. Tell him Egypt is prepared to receive him in a royal glory. Issachar! Zebulun, run to our father and bring him here, to live the rest of his days in peace, with me, with us, with his whole family surrounding his tent all the days of his life."

vi

And so it happened that Jacob and his children and their children and all their goods moved south and west into the land of Goshen, where Joseph came in a splendid chariot to meet his father.

Joseph leaped from the chariot.

Jacob limped toward him, an old man with a thin white beard. Each man fell on the neck of the other.

Old Jacob said, "Now let me die, since I have seen your face and know that you are alive."

But he lived yet twelve more years. And before he died, he blessed his children, as well as the two sons of Joseph, Ephraim and Manasseh.

Then he drew his feet up into his bed and breathed his last.

But ages later, when God had fulfilled his promises and had made the family of Abraham and Isaac and Jacob multitudinous and strong; centuries later, when the Lord had led the children of Israel out of Egypt and back to the land he had covenanted to give them, they remembered their father with a creed repeated at every harvest, and thus did they give thanks unto their faithful God.

They said:

> *A wandering Aramaean was my father;*
> *he went down to Egypt and sojourned there,*
> *few in number,*
> *but there he became a nation,*
> *great and mighty and many.*
> *And the Egyptians treated us harshly...*

PART TWO

The
Covenant

PART
TWO

5
MOSES

i

The king of Egypt was far away from his homeland — northeast of the Nile, north of Canaan, more northerly still than Tyre and Sidon — fording the river Orontes. He was marching to meet the Hittites, whose king he called "the vile Fallen One of Hatti," and his army was so massive that it took several days to accomplish the river crossing.

The army was organized in four divisions, each named for one of the gods whom the Egyptians worshiped: Amun, Re, Ptah and Sutekh. And why wouldn't Pharaoh's forces be named after gods? Wasn't he himself their son? Didn't he ride and fight and rule in their power, daily renewing his strength with the sun?

Now, it happened that the division named Amun, which was under the king's direct command, had shortly completed the crossing when word came to Pharaoh that two nomads were requesting an audience with him. Re, the second division, was in the midst of its crossing, while Ptah waited in quarters on the far side till the ford was free. The fourth division, Sutekh, was yet several days to the rear.

"Nomads?" said Pharaoh.

"*Shasu,*" said the messenger, using an Egyptian term which meant To Wander Around. These were a landless people who lived at the edges of more sedentary civilizations, a nomadic folk who wandered the wilderness in tents. They were a class infinitely lower than the social refinement of Egyptians.

"What do they want?"

"To escape the power of the Hittite by serving Egypt."

"Ah," said the king. He paused a moment, then said, "Set my chair in an open space. Tell these two that I will listen with a smile and a stick, one for truth and one for lies, then bring them to me."

Pharaoh standing or Pharaoh sitting — he was ever a glorious figure. There flexed a visible strength beneath the bracelets of his arms. His eye was direct and steady. Unlike others, his loincloth was pleated and bound by a broad belt and a metal buckle engraved with his name; from the back hung a bull's tail, from the front an apron. Now, in preparation for the audience with these *Shasu*, he donned a blue helmet decorated with the sacred asp at the brow and two streamers hanging behind.

He sat down in his golden chair.

His lion came and lay beside him, tethered at the foot and peering into the blue distance.

Then the nomads were brought forward, fierce-eyed men of goatsmell and grizzled beards and robes of a woven wool. Uncut hair. He recognized the class. Even Egypt had become infested with them.

They bowed low before him.

He said, "What do you have to say?"

They rose up and in fawning voices said that their families were caught in the clutches of the Hittite king — but that king himself, the Fallen One of Hatti, was hiding in Aleppo, terrified of the Egyptian armies coming to engage him.

"*Shasu*," said Pharaoh, gazing at them with eyes like javelins. "You are *Shasu*."

"So we are called."

Pharaoh touched a short stick which lay across his knees and said, "Why should I believe you?"

They fell on their faces before him and whined, "For the sake of our children!"

Such abject selfishness is characteristic of this rank of human. Pharaoh, therefore, believed them.

He commanded the Amun Division to set up camp in the safety of this place and wait until the other three divisions should ford the river and join them. Even Re, the second division, was a long day's march downriver, busy about its crossing.

So the soldiers erected a square wall of shields upon the plain. The king's tent was set in the center. Oxen carts filled with provisions were gathered in; huts were built for the officers; stoves and stools and mats and basins lent a little comfort to these huts; and the soldiers themselves marked their personal areas with private bundles and weapons.

On the following day, while donkeys kicked their heels and rolled in the dust, while charioteers lay sound asleep in their chariots, a man came riding top speed from the south. His horse cleared the wall of shields in a single bound and thundered toward Pharaoh's tent.

"Re!" cried the man, flinging himself from his mount and stumbling forward: "The soldiers of Re are dead!"

Even as Pharaoh strode toward this messenger, he felt the ground trembling beneath his foot. "Speak clearly," he commanded.

The messenger wept, "The accursed Fallen One of Hatti had surrounded the second division in the night. He attacked us with the sunrise, and he comes behind me. King, he is upon you! Run!"

The *Shasu* had lied! They were spies after all.

But Pharaoh did not run.

Though the armies of the Hittites were thundering now into view, though his own soldiers exploded in panic, disordered and unready, the king swiftly grabbed his accouterments, donned his breastplate and helmet, slung a quiver over his shoulder and leaped into his chariot. He drove straight toward the Hittites, throwing up a cloud of yellow dust and drawing the best of his men behind, his personal bodyguard.

Riding at full gallop, Pharaoh tied the chariot reins to his belt, then began to release a hail of arrows upon the Fallen One of Hatti. The sheath at the side of his chariot was filled with javelins. These flew like raptor birds among the Hittites, killing two and three in a fall. Pharaoh was in his might! Pharaoh, unafraid, spread death around his hurtling chariot, opening a path through which his bodyguard followed, redoubling slaughter on every side.

The Hittites retreated before such courage. Like crocodiles they rushed belly-low back to the river. The Egyptian king charged them five times more, shining like his father Amon-Re. He set fire to the countryside.

▊

The word went home before Pharaoh did. *Triumph! This glorious, lionhearted warrior — he has bound the land and broken the back of Hatti.*

When, therefore, the king himself crossed the Egyptian frontier with prisoners of high rank and riches inestimable, priests met him with a profusion of flowers — and the sweet celebrations of victory and of grateful piety straightway began.

In a public place before Egyptian multitudes, the most important prisoners were commanded to make signs of submission. They turned the palms of their hands toward Pharaoh. He gazed impassively upon their defeat, nodded, and then, by the lifting of a small scepter, ordered their executions.

Next the various treasures of the Hittites were carried to a temple and spread out before the gods in order to be consecrated: cups and amphorae, rhytons and goblets of gold and silver, set with precious stones.

When Pharaoh himself appeared through a private doorway of the temple, he was frightening in magnificence. Upon his head he wore two crowns, one for the northern and one for the southern kingdoms of his realm. His chin was adorned by a ceremonial beard, dramatic in its length and plaiting. He wore a heavy necklace of gold from which hung chains and small silver flowers. Three pairs of bracelets flashed when he strode toward his seat, one on his upper arms, one at his wrists, and one upon his ankles. And down his back he wore a robe so light as to be transparent.

He was followed into the temple by more prisoners, their hands bound, ropes around their necks. These, too, in speechless dread acknowledged their defeat. But Pharaoh did not order their execution. Instead, he faced the images of his gods and raised his voice in a singsong hymn:

"I offer you homage, gods and goddesses, masters of heaven and earth and ocean, great of step in the boat of millions of years.

"Amon-Re! You unto whom I bring gold and silver, lapis lazuli and turquoise! I am your son, whom your two arms have brought forth. You have established me as sovereign over every land. For me you have made perfection on earth. I perform my duty in peace."

Thus Pharaoh declared that all victory was but a gift from his god, and that these treasures were but a return upon what he had first been given.

When the ceremony ended, when Pharaoh in blinding splendor stepped through the temple door ahead of his priests and the whole procession, he was suddenly met by two men who fixed him with fierce eyes. Their faces were sunbaked and creased. One was dressed in the Egyptian loincloth, but the other's robe was woolen, his beard full, his hair unruly, and his smell goatish.

A *Shasu.*

Pharaoh hesitated just an instant.

But swiftly into that instant the smaller man spoke.

"Thus says the Lord, the God of Israel." He spoke in the nasal squawk of an up-country slave. Why, the man was nothing but a Hebrew slave! "The Lord says, *Let my people go, that they may hold a feast to me in the wilderness.*"

ii

Something in that first encounter had seized Pharaoh's interest. An odd refinement in the Shasu which made his unruly appearance seem just that: an appearance. When, therefore, the same two men begged an audience with him the next day, Pharaoh granted it.

"Who is this little 'Lord' of yours?" he asked.

The grizzled *Shasu* spoke. With amazing rapidity he said: "The God of the Hebrews has met me face-to-face, and by his authority I beg you to let us go but a three days' journey to our ancestors' paths in the wilderness and sacrifice to the Lord our God — or else he will fall upon us with pestilence or with the sword."

This wanderer's eyes flashed a mordant fire. He grew more and more interesting as he spoke. Pharaoh leaned forward. It was the accent. The grammar and the vocabulary. Out of the mouth of a common *Shasu* was coming the most articulate Egyptian that Pharaoh had heard in years.

Therefore, he asked a second question of the *Shasu*: "What is your name?"

But the slave answered. "His name is Moses. Mine is Aaron. We are brothers."

"I wasn't speaking to you," said the king.

"Nevertheless, he wants me to talk for him."

To the *Shasu* the king said: "Who are your kin? Where are you from?"

Again, the other one said, "He is of Israel. His kin live here in the land of Goshen. The men are making bricks for your majesty's buildings — "

"Shut up, slave!"

The man named Moses was gazing with a smoky passion directly into Pharaoh's eye, working his mouth as if chewing, but saying nothing. An astonishing insolence, actually. A dangerous sort of audacity, because it could capture the fancy of more than one slave.

Abruptly, therefore, Pharaoh ended the interview.

"Lazy," he declared. "You, slave, are lazy. Your people are lazy. And now you wish to justify laziness by a long trip to a little god. Absolutely not. Go on, get back to work."

That same day the king called his vizier into his chambers and issued an order to those who supervised slave labor:

"Three points. One: no longer shall you give the people straw for making brick. Let them gather field stubble. Two: tell the Hebrew foremen that production quotas shall remain the same. Three: and if the people don't meet quota, beat the foremen."

To the vizier alone, Pharaoh said, "This people has caused trouble before. As long as eighty years ago my predecessors were trying by various bloody means to keep them in their place. Well, I will do it with work. I'll make them too weary to listen to any leader. Except myself, of course."

Every Egyptian city was surrounded by a wall of brick fifty feet wide and sixty feet high. Only the gate-pillars were stone. Likewise, all the city buildings were constructed more of brick than of stone. And in those days the king had begun to build grandly in the Nile delta, cities of beauty, cities of protection against the desert people in the west and the sea people of the north.

The quantities of brick required were astronomical.

And because the Hebrew slaves made and baked them, they, too, were necessary for the plans of Pharaoh.

I will weary them.

In great tubs the slaves mixed Nile mud with sand and straw, striving for the right consistency. They trod the mud. They stirred it with mattocks.

Then they poured it into brick molds, scraped it smooth, and snatched the mold away, leaving the single brick to dry in the sun a full eight days: brick by brick they worked.

I will weary them.

Without piles of chopped straw ready at their sides the whole operation slowed down. Slaves had to run the fields and yank roots from dried ground.

No, they could not continue to match the killing quotas for Pharaoh's cities, even though the foremen also began to work with them.

And so the foremen, their kinsmen, were beaten in sight of everyone. The dull crack of an Egyptian stick on Hebrew bone became a regular, horrible music. Every man, therefore, drove himself harder and harder, and in the houses of the slaves there was no laughter at night.

Finally the foremen went to the king himself. How could their lot grow worse than this?

Pharaoh was seated on his golden throne, wearing a diadem and plumes, so august a presence that the Hebrews kissed the earth and averted their eyes.

They said, "Perhaps the king does not know that his supervisors have stopped giving straw to us, his servants, but that they still demand the same number of bricks, and they beat us for failing the quota, but it is their fault — "

"Their fault?" Pharaoh raised a smooth and powerful arm. Pharaoh, who could turn the armies of the Hittites by personal force alone, whispered, "*Their* fault?" and the foremen began to tremble.

"Your fault, slaves," he said. "And I'll tell you the fault: you are lazy! You are a lazy breed! Lazy and cowardly besides, sending me a *Shasu* stranger to ask whether you can go into the wilderness to worship some minor deity of whom I have never heard — and I, the son of gods, know them all! Get out of my sight. Go and make brick."

The poor foremen stumbled backward, dismissed, silenced.

But when they stood outside the palace they saw Aaron and Moses, those who had stirred the trouble in the first place, and then they were not frightened. They were furious.

"Who do you think you are," they cried, "that you should speak for us? You've made us an offense to the king, and now his servants carry swords to kill us. Go away. Leave us alone!"

The man named Moses listened. He did not flinch. But neither did he answer, and his silence only enraged the men the more. Three men had to hold back one who offered to break the neck of this intruder.

They left him standing on the hard Egyptian dirt.

They did not see the sadness with which he watched them go.

■

When he awoke the following morning, the king of Egypt first sat on his bed-couch and read through his most recent correspondence. Then, attended by murmurous servants, he bathed and dressed and put on the insignia of royalty. Still within his palace and under the weight of divine authority, he was joined by the high priest of Amun, before whom he offered a sacrifice to that god and from whom he heard several prayers and exhortations.

This was customary, his daily ritual.

Somewhat unusual, however, was his decision to descend in the company of priests and magi to the banks of the river. Pharaoh decided to pay homage to Hapi, the Nile god shaped like a man so fat that his breasts hung down and his belly folded over his belt.

This trip was a whim of the morning. Pharaoh had not planned it. No one could have known that it was to take place. Nevertheless, as he approached the river's brink he saw that fierce-eyed fellow, Moses, standing directly in front of him, waiting, holding in his right hand a rod as tall as he was.

But Pharaoh stops for no man, certainly not for a nomad. Surrounded by his entourage, he strode toward the water, assuming that the *Shasu* would be swept aside by the king's cold countenance and royalty.

But the man stood ground, staring at Pharaoh — then all at once he began to roar in that articulate Egyptian tongue, causing others, if not the king, to hesitate.

"The Lord, the God of the Hebrews," he shouted, "sent me to you saying, *Let my people go, that they may serve me in the wilderness — and behold, you have not obeyed.*"

Now Pharaoh stopped. "I have not *what?*" he said.

But the wild man did not answer. He issued decrees of his own: "Therefore, by this you shall know that my God is the Lord: I will strike the water of the Nile with my rod, and it shall be turned to blood, and the fish shall die, and the river shall become foul, and everyone will be loathe to drink it."

Immediately, he turned toward the water, raised his long rod, and brought it down with a whistle and a slap on the face of the Nile.

Those who had watched the man's behavior with curiosity now stared at the water in astonishment. Where he struck it, the river began to bleed like a living thing. A bright red blood ran in ribbons downstream. It spread wider and wider. It began to creep upstream, too, against the current.

Pharaoh was furious.

"A trick!" he thundered.

He whirled around to one of the magi and threw his scepter at the man, commanding, "Do the same! Do it now! Make the river bleed!"

The magus obeyed. He scrambled down the bank and stirred Pharaoh's scepter in clean water and that water, too, boiled up bloody — so Pharaoh closed his mouth, glanced once at the man named Moses, then withdrew and returned to his palace. He would reverence Hapi another day, when the river's wounds had healed and there were fewer pests about.

iii

That night in the houses of Israel there was another sort of silence, not weariness: wonder.

They had seen the river run red with blood.

"Aaron," they said softly. "Aaron, who is this man?"

"He is my brother. Moses."

"He's one of us?"

"Yes."

"But he speaks like an Egyptian."

"Well, but he is of the tribe of Levi, just like me and Miriam, our sister."

"He has a foreign wife. A Midianite."

"My brother has been gone for forty years. There were no women of Israel where he was living. But he grew up in Egypt. He was forty years old when he left."

"Why did he leave in the first place?"

"He was running for his life. He had murdered an Egyptian."

"Aaron! Your brother is a rash man!"

"In fact, that's why he did it," Aaron said. "He happened to see the Egyptian beating one of our people. He saw no one was nearby, so he jumped the Egyptian and snapped his neck and buried the body in the sand.

"The next day he saw two of our people fighting together, a big Israelite beating a smaller one. Moses could never help himself. He grabbed the big man, threw him to the ground, and said, 'How can you hit your own brother?' But that man only laughed and yelled, 'So what? Are you going to kill me like you did the Egyptian yesterday?' So he knew that his crime was no longer a secret. He didn't even say good-bye to me or Miriam or our mother. He ran. That was forty years ago."

"That's when he went to live with the Midianites?"

"Yes," Aaron said. "And that's why he married a Midianite."

"Yet even after forty years he is still one of us?"

"Why do you keep saying that?" said Aaron. "Yes, he's one of us. He's circumcised. His son is circumcised — and that is especially due to his Midianite wife! For when Moses delayed too long, the Lord met him in the night and sought to kill him. But his wife took a flint and cut off the foreskin of their baby boy, then touched it to Moses' feet and said, 'Surely, you are a bridegroom of blood to me!' So the Lord did not kill him. He is one of us!"

"But why, after forty years, does he suddenly choose to come back?"

Aaron uttered the following words so softly that the people had to lean forward and cease their breathing a while.

"He says," said Aaron, "that God has heard our groaning. He says that God is remembering his covenant with our fathers, Abraham and Isaac and Jacob. Moses says that God has begun to deliver us from bondage, to redeem us with an outstretched arm and with great acts of judgment. He says that God has sent him here as a servant to accomplish these things."

■

On the seventh day after the Nile had been struck bloody, just as the king was ascending his golden throne to make himself available to the common people, the man named Moses appeared in the doorway. This time he didn't ask an audience. He entered boldly, perplexing the guards on either side, and began to speak in his headlong Egyptian:

"Thus says the Lord," he said, "*Let my people go, that they may serve me. But if you refuse to let them go, I will plague all your country with frogs. The Nile shall swarm with frogs, nor will it contain them. The whole country will crawl with frogs. Aaron will stretch forth his rod over the waters, and the waters will churn with an endless issue of frogs!*"

Pharaoh shook his head and said nothing. He lifted his left hand, a minor sign, and the guards stepped forward to remove the man. But the fierce-eyed Moses turned before they could touch him. He strode out of chambers, his robe billowing at the sleeves — out of the palace, down a long street and onto the king's own wharf. There he was met by the slave named Aaron. Together they walked along the edge of the wharf while Aaron trolled the end of his rod in the river. The small waves that the rod made were, in fact, frogs, a trail of frogs, individual, swimming, golden-eyed frogs. And the frogs tumbled up the banks of the river. Frogs went forth, swarming over the whole land, into the houses, into kneading bowls and ovens and bedrooms and beds.

Pharaoh commanded the magi to do the same, and they did, but that only doubled the populations of green, croaking creatures, filling the king's palace with frogs of his own making.

Pharaoh's roof dropped frogs like rain. His apartments were carpeted with moist bodies. He could not walk but that he squashed them. And when he entered his lavatory, when he sat on the limestone seat with a hole beneath, and when a frog fired itself upward from the sand below, *that* was one frog too many.

The king commanded that Moses be brought to him.

Moses came.

The king said, "End it."

Moses said, "Why don't you ask your magi to end it?"

The king said, "They can't. You must. Entreat your Lord to remove the frogs, and I will let the people go and sacrifice to him."

Moses said, "Then, sir, in order that you may know that there is no one like the Lord our God, you choose: tell me the precise time at which you wish the frogs to be destroyed."

"Tomorrow," said the king. "At sunrise."

Precisely at sunrise the following day all of the frogs, wherever they sat in their masses, died. The houses, the courtyards, and the fields were covered with dead frogs. The people raked them together into mountains, and the whole land stank.

But as soon as he recognized the respite, Pharaoh hardened his heart and canceled any promises he had made under the strain of an earlier moment.

◼

Now, in the houses of Israel — deep in the night and in privacy — people were whispering one to another.

"What is it? What's happening?" they said. "Some huge and holy thing is taking place."

"Moses knows," they said.

"He says it's the God of our fathers troubling creation. He says that God has heard our groaning and wants to take us for his people. His own people!"

"Moses. Is the man one of us after all?"

"And if he is," they said, "why don't we remember him?"

"But he was here," said Miriam, Aaron's sister. "He lived in Egypt, but not with us. Surely you remember the time when our afflictions began?" she said.

"Yes," said the people.

"You remember the king who first enslaved us because he was afraid of our great numbers?"

"Yes," said the people. "How could we forget?"

"He set taskmasters over us to wear us down. They made our lives horrible with labor in mortar and brick. But the more they oppressed us, the more we multiplied."

The people near Miriam smiled, recalling their toughness and the Egyptian's frustration.

"So the king conceived a plan," she said. "He told the midwives who served Hebrew women to kill our baby boys. But the midwives feared God. They let all our children live, male and female. They said, 'O King, Hebrew women are so strong, they drop their babies before we can get there.' "

"Ha ha ha!" The people barked a bitter laughter for the idiot Egyptian, tricked by the women.

Miriam paused a moment. Then in a softer, more serious voice she
continued: "So the king abandoned cunning and went straight to slaughter.
He sent his soldiers through our houses with orders to search out all the
baby boys, and to drown them in the Nile.

"It was then," said Miriam, "that my mother bore a beautiful baby boy.
For three months she hid him in the house, and the soldiers did not find
him. But then he grew too large and too loud, so my mother took a basket
and daubed it with pitch and laid her son inside and slipped it into the river
among the reeds. She told me to watch from a distance. That very day I
saw the king's daughter come down with her maidens to bathe. I saw them
stop at the little cove where my brother was floating. I watched the princess
undress and wade into the water. She disappeared among the reeds.
Suddenly she cried, 'Look what I found!' She came out of the reeds, pushing
the basket toward shore. All her maidens rushed to look. The princess
turned my mother's blankets aside — and there was my brother, his little
fists shaking. He was crying. I couldn't stand it. I started to run down the
bank toward her. She was saying, 'It's one of the Hebrew children,' and she
was holding the baby with such tenderness — such tenderness! I saw that
tenderness. I said, 'Do you want me to get a Hebrew nurse for the child?'
She looked up at me and said, 'Yes.' So I ran and got our mother, and by the
time we returned together, the princess had named him. Mosheh. She called
him Moses, because, she said, 'I drew him out of the water.' The daughter of
the king of Egypt adopted my baby brother. He grew up in Pharaoh's court.
That's why you can't remember him. But he suckled Hebrew milk. He drank
of the milk of our mother; he heard her prayers and learned our ways and
therefore has been one of us from the beginning. Believe it! Heart and soul
and might, Moses will always be one of us."

▌▌

On the following day, Moses and Aaron went out and stood alone in a
desert place.

At a word from Moses, Aaron whirled his rod like a threshing flail and
struck the dust of the earth, and the dust turned into gnats. The air in
Egypt grew thick with a rising dust, but the dust was gnats, and the gnats
landed on people and beasts.

The king in his palace, seeing the cloud of a new plague coming,
commanded his magi to do the same. But they could not. They could
neither do nor undo the thing.

They said to Pharaoh, "This is the finger of God."

Pharaoh curled his lip and dismissed his magi as useless fools.

iv

Pharaoh was not an old man. He was young and mighty. He had by the force of his glory and the smooth beauty of his arm turned back the accursed Fallen One of Hatti.

But physical strength counted for nothing now.

After the gnats, the man named Moses had appeared again on the bank of the river, promising flies — and the flies had come in swarms, making an infernal, universal *buzzing*, crawling on the faces and in the eyes of every Egyptian.

At the same time it was reported that the houses of the Hebrews were absolutely free of flies.

Something was favoring Israel.

▌

All his life Pharaoh had been a pious man, honoring his ancestors and building magnificent temples to the gods. He reverenced Re, Atum, Thoth and Ounnefer, and the Divine Ennead. He had, in every year of his reign, kept the great festival of Opet.

But where were the holy ones of Egypt now?

And who was this interfering, desert deity which the fierce-eyed Moses called "The Lord"? How could an unknown god make such violent distinction between Egypt and a pack of powerless slaves?

For when the flies had vanished (again, by an act of the God of Moses) there fell upon the cattle of Egypt a killing plague. Egyptian flocks perished. But the Hebrew flocks remained healthy! Egyptian donkeys and goats and camels perished. Yet not a beast of the Hebrews was touched.

The king of Egypt began to pace his chambers in the night, beseeching divine assistance. He was himself a child of the gods; it was his right to call and their duty to answer; but all the gods were as silent as stone — all save one. In his darkest moment it suddenly seemed to the king that the sun-god, Re, said: "I will rise in the morning." He took comfort in that promise.

And in the morning the sun did rise.

But soon it was shining on a new, more hideous plague. Several magi appeared uninvited before the king. "Majesty," they said, but they could scarcely speak: their faces were thick with red boils, their eyes puffed shut, their necks and shoulders wet with a yellow pus. "Majesty," they said, "the man named Moses took handfuls of ash from a brick kiln and threw them up, and the wind caught the ash and blew it abroad, and where it touched us... this happened. Everyone is breaking out in sores — "

"The Hebrews? The Hebrews, too?"

"No, sir. Not the Hebrews."

∥

When the world was not falling apart, Pharaoh took an extravagant pleasure in receiving the envoys of foreign lands. He blinded them with his splendor, building open pavilions in public and giving gifts of fabulous wealth.

But for this particular envoy, whom he himself had summoned, Pharaoh did not consider splendor. He didn't so much as change his clothes. He did nothing but wait, slouched on the golden throne, his knuckle in his mouth.

At midday, the man named Moses strode into his presence wearing woolen robes and carrying a long rod, his hair like a white wild smoke, his eye afire. *Shasu.* Pharaoh sighed to see this ragged ambassador: how does one negotiate with the wind and the sand and the furious stars?

Nevertheless, he muttered, "Go. Moses, go and sacrifice to your God. But do it within the land of Egypt."

The *Shasu* said, "No," then closed his mouth.

There was a silence.

Pharaoh said, "No? Suddenly you don't wish to sacrifice?"

"Oh, yes, we will sacrifice to the Lord our God. But we must go three days' journey into the wilderness, because he commands it."

"Into the wilderness?"

Moses kept his gaze on the Pharaoh, saying nothing.

So Pharaoh sighed again and said, "The wilderness, then. The wilderness. I will allow it. You may go three days' journey into the wilderness. But choose who is to go."

Moses said, "There is no choosing. We will all go."

Pharaoh said, "No, that's impossible."

Moses said, "All of us and all our cattle. Our young and our old, our sons and our daughters — "

Pharaoh raised his voice: "I said No! Take only the men among you — "

" — our herds and our flocks," said Moses, "because we must eat a feast to the Lord our — "

"Don't you hear me, man?" roared Pharaoh. "God help you, if ever I let you take your young away. *Shasu! Shasu*, you have some evil scheme in mind."

Now, Moses lifted his own voice and delivered a speech of elemental power, because the spirit of God was upon him:

"Thus says the Lord, the God of the Hebrews, *How long will you refuse to humble yourself before me? For by now I could have put forth my hand and struck you and your people with such pestilence that you would have been cut off from the earth. But for this purpose have I let you live: to show you my power, so that my name may be declared throughout the earth. Yet still you continue to exalt yourself against my people. Now, then: tomorrow in the middle of the day I will cause a heavy hail to fall, such as has never fallen* upon Egypt before. *If you believe this word, send your cattle to shelter. If not, cattle and people shall die together."*

Moses departed.

For a moment the king was speechless.

Then he issued a terse, private command, and soon a priest was standing before him, holding a lotus and a golden globe, signs of the sun-god, Re.

Pharaoh said, "Sing the song you sang at Neferhotep's funeral. I liked that song. Sing it again for me."

The priest didn't hesitate. In a eunuch's voice he sang: "As long as Re shall rise in the morning and Atum shall set in the west, men shall beget and women conceive and breath shall be in men's nostrils..."

By evening, then, though some of his counselors had ordered their servants and their cattle to take cover from the storm to come, Pharaoh did not.

∎

On the following day the sun rose and ruled the morning.

But directly at noon the light began to fail: a black cloud gathered over Egypt, and the wind blew. Lightning flashed. Thunder followed, and out of the cloud came hail, very heavy hail, hail such as Egypt had never seen before. It struck down everything and everyone in the fields; it tore limbs from the trees; both cattle and servants were killed; only those who stayed under cover survived.

But then the night came, and in the morning the sun rose up as strong as ever. It turned the hail to water. Re had arisen and ruled. The king, therefore, called for an excellent supper. In the night he thanked his god with many pious expressions and slept.

And the sun rose up the next day, too.

But so did a wind. An ominous wind. An east wind blew across the land with steady intensity. Everywhere Egyptians held their breath against some new calamity. Then they began to whimper, for from the northern kingdom to the south they saw the wind was drawing a vast cloud like a blanket over the land.

Pharaoh thought it was a dust storm, but the cloud came over the city and he could hear the sound of it: dry, chewing sounds and the rattle of a million wings. He looked, and the cloud had a million hungry mouths.

Locusts! It was an endless swarm of locusts so loud that a man could not call to his neighbor, nor could he see his orchards. Locusts were eating every sweet thing, every green and living thing.

Pharaoh's counselors burst into his chambers. "How long will you let this Moses be a snare to us?" they shouted. "Egypt is ruined. Call him! Give him what he wants. Let him go and let us live!"

Pharaoh set his jaw and nodded his head. Immediately a counselor ran out and returned with Moses and Aaron.

Pharaoh said, "This time I have sinned. The Lord your God is in the right; I and my people are in the wrong. Entreat your God only to remove this death from me!"

Without a word, the Hebrews turned and left. All at once the wind outside went into convulsions, and a strong west wind was sweeping the land, tearing the locusts from their million grips and driving them into the Red Sea.

Finally all the winds relaxed. In the night there was but a mild breeze.

But the king of Egypt could not sleep. He was seething with the humiliations now heaped upon him by his own people, his servants, his counselors. Therefore, his single prayer that night was a prayer of vengeance:

"By my life," he cried, "by Re, by my father Re who loves me, by the sun-god's bright imperial power upon this earth, I swear: my majesty shall rise in the morning to terrify all!"

And the morning came. But the sun did not arise.

If there was a day, none in Egypt could see it. For now there was darkness over the land, a darkness so thick it could be felt. No one could see his neighbor, no, nor his family either. The Egyptians did not stir from their houses.

Only the people of Israel had light where they dwelt.

So there passed one day and another day in sunless darkness. Three days. But who could count them without the heavenly lamp? Pharaoh paced in a rabid impotence, neither eating nor sleeping, growing more and more frenzied as the long night continued.

Finally he called Moses to himself. "Go!" he cried. "Go! Serve the Lord. Yes, and take your children with you. Take all your people. Only leave your flocks and herds behind."

The man named Moses showed neither triumph nor thanks at this grand capitulation. His expression was the same as when Pharaoh first met him on the banks of the Nile long, long ago.

And with damnable insolence he repeated precisely what he'd said before: "We will all go. All of us and all our cattle."

The king of Egypt leaped from his seat screaming, "Get out! Get out!" He had drawn a knife. His whole body trembled to use it. "Never look on my face again," he cried. "In the day you see my face, you shall die!"

Moses said, "So be it. Neither one of us shall see the other again."

V

Only the people of Israel had light where they dwelt.

And there it was that Moses, his hair like smoke on a mountain, took a stand before the whole congregation and spoke:

"Listen to me and believe what I say," he said. "I have seen the holiness of God."

In all Israel, no one uttered a word. Too much had happened since this man had arrived.

Moses said: "He called to me from a flame of fire in the midst of a bush. I saw the bush burning on the side of a mountain, yet it was not consumed; so I went to look, and as I did the voice of God said, *Moses! Moses!*

"I said, 'Here I am.'

"God said, *Remove your shoes, for the place where you stand is holy ground, and I am the God of your fathers, Abraham, Isaac, Jacob.*

"I hid my face, afraid to look at the living God.

"But God said, *I have seen the affliction of my people, and I am coming to bring them from bondage into a land flowing with milk and honey — the land I promised your fathers long ago.*

"Then God commanded me to carry his word to Pharaoh and to you. He said that I should lead you out of Egypt.

"But I said, 'Who am I to do such a thing?'

"God said, *I will be with you, and you shall know my name and use it.*

"In the midst of the flame of fire, then, the voice of God proclaimed: *I AM WHO I AM! Say to Israel that I AM — YAHWEH, the Lord, the God of your fathers — has sent me to you.*

"I dropped to my knees, shaking with fear. 'Lord,' I said, 'I cannot talk.'

"God said, *Who has made the mouth? Is it not I, the Lord? Then I will be your mouth.*"

Suddenly Moses lifted his voice and roared before the whole assembly of the people: "It is therefore not I but *YAHWEH*, the Lord, the God of our fathers, who has confronted the king of Egypt and by many signs has humbled him down in darkness.

"And even now, this very night, it is not I but the Lord our God who commands you to prepare for one more sign, the final, most terrible sign he shall perform.

"Prepare, O Israel!" cried Moses. "Accomplish the commands I now shall give you. By your obedience prove trust in the Lord. For tomorrow at midnight he shall with a mighty hand and an outstretched arm deliver you from bondage into the freedom of his beaming countenance!"

∎

And so it was that the people Israel spent the next day in speechless excitement fulfilling the commands of the Lord their God exactly as Moses directed them.

Every household took a lamb, a male one year old without spot or blemish, and killed it. They caught its blood in bowls, and with bunches of hyssop smeared the blood on the doorposts and the lintels of their houses. The flesh of the lamb they roasted.

In the evening, then, inside their houses, they ate the lamb with unleavened bread and bitter herbs. They ate all of it, as the Lord commanded, leaving none for the morning. And they ate in clothes ready for a journey, their loins girded, sandals on their feet, staves in their hands. They ate in great haste.

∎

At midnight the Destroyer went forth. The angel of the Lord passed through all the land of Egypt. When he came to a house that had the blood of a lamb smeared on its doorposts, he passed over that house. But every other house was open before him, and he entered, and when he left, a first-born child lay dead.

The Lord smote all the firstborn in Egypt, from the firstborn of Pharaoh who sat on his golden throne to the firstborn of the prisoner in his prison. All.

So there went up over the whole land a great and grievous weeping, for there was not a house where one was not dead.

And Pharaoh cried unto Moses and Aaron: "Rise! Go forth from my people! Go, you and your children, and serve the Lord with all your flocks and all your herds. Be gone. Be gone — and bless me, too."

∎

And so the people of Israel went out that night. They journeyed on foot from Rameses to Succoth, some six hundred thousand men and women and children.

They had lived in Egypt four hundred and thirty years; and now, as they left the long slavery of that place, the Lord God said to Moses: *Forever you must keep this feast as you kept it on the night I saved you — the lamb, the unleavened bread, the bitter herbs. Hereafter, this month shall be the first month of the year for you. And the feast shall begin on its tenth day. Make that day a memorial day throughout your generations forever. This is the ordinance of my Passover.*

So Moses told the people.

And the people, when they heard it, bowed their heads and worshiped.

6

SINAI

i

Why hat the children most remembered — the little children, the young ones stumbling behind their elders — was the strange silence of the night of their running. No one spoke.

Mothers and fathers walked swiftly with strained faces and many backward glances. They walked in the midst of an endless multitude of people; and though there were the sounds of a thousand sandals grinding sand and the stretch of leather, the huff of large cattle, the bleating of tired sheep, yet there was not a human voice to comfort them.

So the children went forward, big-eyed and frightened.

Even when dawn began to streak the eastern sky, people continued grimly hurrying, hurrying. They did not stop.

But sunlight and the warmth of the morning seemed to change things. Here and there the children heard soft talking. A little early whispering. Then giggling. The young women were giggling. Suddenly a man let out a bark of laughter and immediately shut up. But then another man started to laugh and could not stop. He covered his mouth, but the laughter came out of his nose. His shoulders were shaking. The people who saw him began to grin. Then they chuckled; then they, too, broke into outright laughter. They roared with laughter. They laughed till the tears ran down their cheeks. They covered their stomachs and gasped for air and howled as if they were hurting.

Like flocks of wild birds the laughter rose up and flew from family to family, from tribe to tribe throughout the entire congregation of Israel — and this, finally, is what caused the people to stop running: laughter.

They made the round desert ring with the sound of their joy.

And all the little children laughed along, though they didn't know why. They gathered kisses from mothers made beautiful by the mystery of this happiness, and from their fathers they received winks and pokes and mighty hugs.

So they remembered that the long night of silence had been followed by a day of laughter, loud, united, sweet, and free — and ever thereafter the children wished that such a day would come again. As they grew older they longed for one more day of a pure and infant innocence. It never came again.

ii

I srael traveled southeast to Succoth. They moved at the edge of the desert and encamped near Etham, a border fort where only a few troops were stationed. These poor soldiers stood on brick walls and stared in astonishment at a people who darkened the land for miles around: a plague of people!

Nor did the Egyptian soldiers sleep that night. They watched. And they saw a second wonder: a fire suddenly ignited itself in the midst of Israel, a fire which rose toward heaven then stood on one leg like a pillar. It did not go out. Rather, it began to move away at the pace of an old woman's walking.

Before morning the fire was gone. So were the people. They had followed the fire in darkness.

Now, finally, the soldiers shook off their trance and leaped to their horses and rode back to tell someone what they had seen.

∎

The pillar of fire that went before Israel in darkness — it was the Lord, leading them and giving them light. During the day it led them as a pillar of cloud. It was never again absent from them.

And Moses was the prophet of God, speaking his will in words the people could understand.

For forty years Moses had lived as a *Shasu*, a nomad. He knew the wilderness very well; and the Lord knew him: in a holy, terrible privacy, they spoke together.

When, therefore, Moses led Israel by a winding way along the eastern frontier of Egypt, it was not because he was confused. It was God's command.

By the will of the Lord, Israel finally stopped and camped between the sea on their east and another border fort, Migdol, some distance to the west.

∎

While Israel was encamped near the sea, a young woman happened to notice a tiny puff of dust near the distant fort called Migdol. *Soldiers*, she thought. She squinted, and what she saw comforted her: *They're riding away. Good.*

Just before these months of upheaval, she had married a man named Carmi, a good man of the tribe of Judah. But then the river had turned to blood and the heavens went to war and the poor woman was never able to savor her marriage — not till now. Now they were free, and the wife of Carmi often went out alone to gather firewood. Then she would wander farther and farther from camp, heedless and completely happy, because she was huge, soon to bear their first child.

One afternoon, then, just as she knelt to pull dry roots, a flash of light caught her eye. She stood and peered westward. There was another tiny flash, and she thought, *The Egyptians are riding away.*

But then she saw that the entire horizon from north to south was seething with an angry yellow dust. Another flash! Another! Metal reflecting sunlight. Now, it seemed to the woman that the earth itself was trembling, and the wind blew odors of leather and sweat — and that metal! It was weapons! The sun was striking helmets and spearheads and the bright sides of chariots!

She dropped her few sticks and turned and ran back to camp as fast as her big body could go. "Egypt!" she cried. "Egypt! The soldiers are coming to get us!"

Just like that, their freedom was gone. A lie! An illusion.

By the time she reached her people, the woman was wild with sobbing. Her terror was like an arrow in the heart of the Israelites, who lifted their voices in wailing. The people looked and saw the armies of Egypt. They saw yellow dust stretch like a curtain across the west. But the east was blocked by water. They were caught between swords and the sea — and though Egypt was still distant, their skin already tingled for the whips and arrows to come.

They found Moses and screamed at him: "Why did you bring us here? To kill us? Weren't there graves enough in Egypt to bury us?"

Moses turned his back on the accusers, climbed a solitary rock, then raised his arms and shouted: "Silence! Israel, be silent! Be still! Don't try to fight! Do nothing at all, but watch and see how the Lord will defend you today."

"Do nothing?" Israel thundered. "*Nothing?*"

"You need only be still," Moses cried, "because the Lord will fight for you."

"The Lord! Where is the Lord? For all his signs and all his wonders, here comes Egypt again — "

"LOOK!" cried Moses. "LOOK!"

He was pointing at the pillar of cloud. It was moving. It had risen above the people and now was sailing westward through blue air. At the same time it was spreading wider and wider, a thick grey curtain — higher and lower at once, like a wall between heaven and earth. The children of Israel were struck dumb by the sight.

For the cloud of God had divided Egypt and Israel one from the other.

At the same time, Moses took his rod and strode to the shore of the sea. There he turned and cried to Israel, "Break camp! Prepare to travel." Then he stretched out his rod to the sea, and a strong east wind arose. It blew all night long. It blew mightily upon the sea until its waters were driven backward left and right.

Israel, surrounded by the elements of the Lord their God — by cloud and wind and water whirling — said nothing. They broke camp and stumbled eastward where the sea had been. In a stunned wonder and on dry ground they crossed all the way to the other side while the east wind beat their backs and pushed them forward. Moses was the last to go.

In the morning the pillar of fire and of cloud soared up from the ground, and the Egyptians saw where Israel had gone. They mounted their chariots. They whipped their horses and rode in wild ranks after their escaped slaves, plunging down into the bottom of the sea and racing between the walls of water.

But Moses, climbing the far side of the sea, stretched out his rod again, and the wind ceased and the waters were released. They collapsed upon the Egyptians who were whirled about in foam, who sank beneath a jubilation of waves. Wood only floated to the surface. Here and there a horse beat water, screaming. But armor held the soldiers under. So the horsemen and the hosts of Pharaoh perished.

The Lord saved Israel that day from the hands of the Egyptians.

Then Miriam, older than her brothers Moses and Aaron, took a timbrel and began to sing. For a while she sang alone, an old woman giving sweet expression to her faith and the praise of the Lord.

But then another old woman — the mother of the wife of Carmi — stepped forward and began to dance to the timbrel with gestures smooth and unspeakably lovely. "Because my daughter gave birth to a son," she said, "in the midst of the sea she bore a child, and they did not die."

Other women, both old and young, wept in the knowledge of deliverance. They could not contain themselves. They clapped. They joined the mother of the wife of Carmi, dancing. Soon all the women of Israel were following Miriam with timbrels and motion, and she sang to them these words:

Oh, sing to the Lord,
for he has triumphed gloriously:
the horse and rider he has thrown into the sea!

The Lord is my strength,
my God and my father's God the same!
And he who is salvation now has given me his name:

his name is the Lord!
I will exalt him day and night!
Forever will I praise my God, my song, and all my might.

iii

The children of Israel followed Moses from the sea through the wilderness of Shur for three days. They found no water.

Carmi kept watch over his wife, who was nursing their baby. He saw that she was growing pale and fearful.

"Elisheba," he whispered, "Are you sick?"

"It's the baby," she said. "My milk is drying up."

"What can I do for you?"

"I need something to drink," she said.

"Moses told us that we're coming to a pool tomorrow. Be patient, Elisheba. Wait till tomorrow."

But when Israel arrived at a spare desert oasis, they found the water brackish and bitter.

Carmi was desperate. He ran from family to family looking for water, but he only found others distressed and wondering what they were to drink.

Then Moses came through the congregation, dragging an odd, wiry tree he had cut in the desert — Moses, intent upon the bitter pool.

He raised his voice. "If you listen to the Lord your God and do what is right in his eyes — " He heaved the tree into the water. "—then the Lord shall be your healer. Drink!"

Carmi was the first to kneel and drink. "Elisheba!" he cried. "Elisheba, come! The water is sweet."

▌▌

Next Israel encamped in a large oasis where there were twelve springs of water and seventy palms. They were glad for the abundance and begged Moses to stay here. But inexorably he led the people toward the wilderness of Sin.

It was now a month and a half since they'd left Egypt and entered the desert. They scarcely knew how to survive apart from civilization. They had never foraged in a dry land. They hadn't learned to hunt, to live in skins, to patch old tents, to walk the day long carrying all their possessions and all the provisions wherever they went.

Abraham and Isaac and Jacob had been nomads. So had the twelve fathers of the twelve tribes of Israel. But this vast and mighty company, their descendants, knew a better life, houses and gardens and ready food.

"Moses!" they said. "Where are you taking us?"

Fierce-eyed Moses didn't answer. He kept walking forward through the blistering desert, swinging his long rod, his wild hair like a thundercloud.

"Moses!" they yelled. "We wish we had died in Egypt, where we sat by the fleshpots and ate bread till we were full. But here you will kill us with hunger!"

And Carmi, who knew how to make brick but who could not make one morsel with which to feed his hungry son, named the child Achar. He did it in a fit of despair. The name means Man of Trouble.

But his wife hid the harder meaning from her baby by calling him Achan instead.

Finally Moses stopped and spoke to the people. "Who am I that you should blame me?" he said. "Your complaining is not against me but against the Lord!"

The Lord. Even the anxious Carmi cast his eyes down to the ground.

Moses said: "But the Lord has heard you. And to show you that it is he who brought you out of Egypt, at twilight he will give you flesh, and in the morning you will be filled with bread."

Even while he was speaking, the people saw across the wilderness the glory of the Lord: a great black cloud was rushing toward them. When it had approached the camp they saw that the cloud was quails, a huge migration of quails flying low for sheer weariness.

Carmi took a club and beat several quails out of the air, then he ran to Elisheba with arms full of meat.

In the morning another wonder appeared, a gentle thing, a snow from heaven.

There had fallen on the face of the wilderness a fine, white, flake-like substance, sweet as coriander, something that tasted like wafers made from honey.

The children of Israel went out and gazed at a wilderness of white, whispering, "What — ? What — ?" which in their tongue sounded like the single word, *Man? Man?*

"What is it?" they said. "*Manna?*" they said.

And Moses said, "It is the bread which the Lord has given you to eat. He will send it as long as we need it — even until we are done with our wanderings. Gather it, every man among you; gather one omer for each member of your family, no more, no less; then eat it all that same day. Trust the Lord. He will send you more in the morning."

So there was a great and sudden harvest. The people called their new food *manna*, and most of them obeyed Moses' instructions.

Carmi, however, was a man of extremes. He was worried for his baby and brought home six omers. During the day they ate three. That night he congratulated himself on having provided for the next day, but by dawn his store was stinking and crawling with worms. So Carmi had to go out and gather again with the rest of the children of Israel.

iv

By stages the people crossed the wilderness of Sin. Moses walked in the vanguard, following the glorious pillar of cloud whose head was in the heavens.

But one morning the children of Israel saw that the cloud was gone and Moses was leading them alone.

When someone asked whether God had abandoned them, Moses pointed. "Don't you see where we are going?" he said.

Far, far ahead of them, almost invisible for distance, the children of Israel saw something like smoke rising from a stony hill.

"What is it?" they said.

"It is our cloud upon the mountain of God," Moses said.

Day by day as they moved forward, it seemed to Israel that the stony hill was growing on the horizon. It became a crag. A grey, bleak eminence. The wrinkled face of an ancient effigy.

The Mountain of God.

In a week the rock had filled the entire southern sky. It filled their hearts, too, with a gaping trepidation. All talking had died among the children of Israel; their bodies had shrunk; they could not tear their eyes from something so huge on a flat plain — this grisly, rough, and frowning mountain whose summit was covered in cloud. It was not green. It was a heap of obdurate rock.

But the cloud was alive. Lightning troubled its interior. Thunder muttered.

In the third month since their escape from Egypt, Israel entered the wilderness of Sinai, which was dominated by a mountain of the same name: *Sinai, the Mountain of God.*

"There!" cried Moses over the thunder: "There is the ascent where I saw the bush which would not burn up. It is there I first met God. And now it is there, O Israel, that the Lord your God is coming to you in thick cloud and thunder-blasts and fire and smoke.

"For he says: *You have seen what I did to the Egyptians, how I bore you forth on eagle's wings and brought you to myself. If, then, you will obey my voice and keep my covenant, you shall be my own possession among all peoples; for all the earth is mine. You shall be to me a kingdom of priests and a holy nation.*

"Therefore," Moses said, "prepare for the Lord. In three days he is coming down upon the mountain in your sight. Wash your garments. Do not go near one another for sexual contact. Build a fence around the base of the mountain so that every living thing stays back. For if anyone touches the mountain when it is holy, he shall die."

█

The morning of the third day broke with violent lightning and thunder. The ground itself began to quake. Smoke like the smoke of a kiln went up from the mountain, for the Lord was descended upon it in fire. And a sound like the blast of a trumpet began, growing louder and louder until the people ran backward for fear.

"Moses!" they cried. "Speak to us and we will hear. Let not the Lord God speak to us, or we will die."

Moses shouted, "Don't be afraid. God has come to test you, so that your awe for him may keep you from sinning."

But the people ran farther and farther away.

So Moses himself crossed the bordering fence and by a steep, stony ascent went into the darkness where God was. He climbed the mountain alone.

And when he stood in the rolling blackness of cloud, the Lord God spoke to him, and Moses remembered the glorious words which he heard. Ten words. These words:

I am the Lord your God, who brought you out of the land of Egypt, out of the house of bondage. You shall have no other gods besides me.

You shall make for yourself no graven image nor the likeness of any created thing, to bow down and worship it. For I the Lord your God am a jealous God, visiting the iniquity of the fathers upon the children to the third and fourth generation of them that hate me — but showing mercy unto thousands who love me and keep my commandments.

You shall not take the name of the Lord your God in vain.

Remember the Sabbath day. Keep it holy. Six days you shall do all your work, but the seventh is a sabbath to the Lord. On that day none of you shall work — for in six days I created the heavens and the earth and everything in them, but on the seventh I rested, and I made that day holy.

Honor your father, honor your mother, that your days may be long in the land that I shall give you.

You shall not kill.

You shall not commit adultery.

You shall not steal.

You shall not bear false witness against your neighbor.

You shall not covet your neighbor's house or suffer a secret desire for his wife — not for his wife, nor his servants, nor his cattle, nor for anything that is his.

When the Lord had uttered these ten words, Moses climbed down the mountain and took a stand before the whole congregation of Israel and told them what God had said.

The people said, "All that the Lord has spoken we will do. We will be obedient."

So Moses built an altar for God at the foot of the holy mountain. He also raised twelve pillars there, one for each of the sons of Jacob, the father of the tribes of Israel.

Then he sacrificed burnt offerings and peace offerings. The blood of an ox he caught in bowls. While it was yet warm he threw half the blood against the altar of the Lord, and half upon the people themselves, to consecrate their promise.

He cried, "Behold the blood of the covenant which the Lord has made with you!"

The bloody sacrifice was a sign that God and all the children of Israel were now bound by a covenant together. He was their God. They were his people. And the covenant would last as long as they kept their promise and obeyed the word of the Lord their God, his commandments and statutes and ordinances.

For the people had said, "All the words which the Lord has spoken we will do."

❚❚

Again, God called to Moses, saying, *Come up and I will give you tablets of stone upon which I myself have written the law for the people's instruction.*

So Moses went again into the boiling cloud which was the glory of the Lord upon the mountain.

For six days the Lord was silent, and Moses waited.

Then on the seventh day God began to speak to Moses out of the cloud. He spoke a very long time. Through forty days and forty nights God gave to Moses his ordinances and his statutes.

He outlined a social code, civil and criminal laws, distinguishing the crimes that deserved death from those that warranted lesser punishments. *If any harm is caused, then you shall give life for life, eye for eye, tooth for tooth, hand for hand, foot for foot, burn for burn, wound for wound, stripe for stripe. . . .*

Property rights were detailed and secured.

Moral and religious codes were given equal weight with all other laws of the covenant.

Justice was defined. The very spirit of justice was required of those who held authority in Israel.

The great ritual festivals of the people, by which they would keep their calendars thereafter, were named.

The Lord God touched upon the core of the covenant: *If you do all I say, then I will be an enemy to your enemies and an adversary to your adversaries. I will bless your bread and your water. I will take sickness away from you. I will drive your enemies out of your land until its borders reach from the Red Sea to the sea of the Philistines, from the wilderness to the Euphrates.*

And in order that I may be with you wherever you go, said the Lord, *let the people build a sanctuary where I may dwell. Build it as a Tabernacle thus:*

So then Moses learned the exact size and the right materials for a holy tent — together with all its appointments and furnishings. There would be an Ark in which the stone tablets of the law should be kept and upon which would rest the golden Mercy Seat of God. The Ark would sit in the innermost chamber of the tent. God would meet the people in darkness there, and his presence would make this the holiest place in Israel.

The Tabernacle would have two rooms. The outer must be divided from the holy of holies by heavy veils and should contain three pieces: a table for the sacred bread, a lampstand, and an altar for incense.

Outside the tent altogether, yet within a courtyard, should stand a brass altar for burnt sacrifice.

Moreover, the Lord described all the duties and the garments of a priesthood devoted unto him. And he appointed Aaron, Moses' older brother, to be his first priest.

When he had made an end of all this speaking, God gave Moses two tablets of stone upon which he had inscribed the testimony with his own finger.

V

To Aaron the glory of the Lord was like thick smoke and a red fire raging in the high gorges of Sinai. It frightened him.

He had watched his brother walk away from Israel toward the mountain. He had seen Moses, so small among the boulders, take a deep breath and begin to wind his way upward — a toilsome journey, a tiny man enfolded by heaves of brown rock, disappearing and appearing again on the wild escarpment.

Finally Moses disappeared altogether.

During the first week of his brother's absence, Aaron walked among the tents of the children of Israel, marveling at how quickly they could return to the daily business of satisfying their own wants. While Moses confronted the Lord on their behalf, the people were boiling quail and baking a hard cake on clay, gossiping, napping in the midday shade. Husbands and wives were quarreling over trivial matters. Old people crouched beneath tent-flaps, missing the very air of Egypt. The children wandered the alleys between tents, grumbling about how bored they were.

Aaron heard the smallest children ask for water, and then for the first time he heard his brother's name mentioned. Mothers said, "We have to save our water. Wait till Moses comes back."

"But I'm thirsty now."

"Be patient."

"When is he coming back, Mama?"

"Soon, Raffi. Soon."

So it went for a week. Aaron shook his head over a people who could stand so casually upon such convulsions of the universe.

In the following week Moses' name was used more often. "Where is he?" the people said. Now they were growing anxious. They cast glances at the mountain and its unquenchable fire. "What happened to him?"

"We have almost no water left."

"Where do we go from here?"

During the third week the people became angry. They started to shout at the mountain. "Moses! What are you doing up there? Here is where your responsibility is! You brought us here! Come and help us now!"

The persistent muttering of the thunder only infuriated them the more. "Don't you care about us?"

Aaron couldn't tell whether they were speaking to Moses or the Lord.

"Have you forgotten us?"

The fourth week of their abandonment produced a genuine panic.

"He's dead," the people said. "We're alone out here."

Now there were tears in the camps of Israel. Little children watched with wide eyes as their parents groaned and wept out loud.

"Where is our God? Where is his pillar to lead us? Where is his right arm now?"

Some of the old people rolled over and covered their faces, hoping that they might swiftly die.

No one was cooking. No one was eating now. No one was sleeping or washing or grooming himself. The universe had gone through convulsions. Heaven and earth had collided, leaving Israel lonely under the thunder of this solitary mountain, and now they knew not what to do.

Aaron felt their agitation as a storm that was about to break. He could scarcely breathe. All the laws were gone. Bloody passions soon would destroy this people right where they sat, at the foot of the mountain.

When, therefore, the children of Israel came to him at the end of the fifth week and begged for gods that they could see — humbler gods, gods who would comfort them by a gentler, visible presence — Aaron agreed.

This is the way Aaron consoled the heart of Israel: he asked for all their golden jewelry; they obeyed immediately, heaping the gold before him; he melted it and molded it and graved it into the shape of a bright, golden calf. Then he lifted the figure up in the sight of all the people.

"Here it is!" they said, truly relieved. "Here is the god that brought us out of Egypt."

Aaron himself was moved by the depth of their gratitude and by the sudden healing of this whole congregation. In that same spirit, then, he built an altar before the shining calf and proclaimed, "Let tomorrow be a feast to the Lord!"

And so their contentment turned to joy.

In the morning they woke early and offered burnt sacrifices on the altar before the calf. Then they sat down to eat a rich feast. They drank wine, and then they rose up to play.

On that day in the sixth week of their loneliness, the children of Israel were lonely no longer. They were laughing again. They sang songs with lusty jubilation. And they danced. They danced in wild abandon, clapping, whirling in circles, crying out, streaming a salty sweat down their foreheads. They had forgotten the mountain —

—till suddenly thunder tore heaven in two. The air itself exploded, and there stood Moses on a crag above them. He was holding a flat tablet of white stone. Another lay in blinding white pieces down the skirts of the mountain. *That* had been the thunder which destroyed the joy of the people, for now he lifted the whole stone in his hand and threw it down to the foot of the mountain, and a second mighty quaking shook the earth.

Aaron stood at a great distance from his brother, yet he could feel the heat of his fury.

Moses now came striding into the midst of the camp. People stepped backward, mute, making a path for him. He took a great hammer and beat the golden calf and burnt it and ground it to powder. This he mixed with water, which water he forced down the throats of Israel.

Moses cried out to Aaron and said, "What did the people do to you, that you should bring such a sin upon their hearts?"

"Yes, it was the people!" Aaron said. He shook before the wrath of the prophet of God. "An evil people! They told me to make them a god."

But Moses had already turned away from him, and the poor man fell down and covered his face in both hands. He stayed that way the rest of the day, hiding in shame from the sight of Moses and the sight of the Lord God upon his mountain. He did not see what followed. But he heard it.

Aaron heard Moses cry out: "Who is on the Lord's side? Come to me!"

He felt the ground shudder under the feet of many men, and Moses said, "Sons of Levi, thus says the Lord: *Put on your swords, every man of you, and go to and fro throughout the camp and kill them that turned away from me —* "

So then Aaron pulled his knees up to his chest. He made a sad ball of himself — for he heard the sounds of a slaughter in the wilderness of Sinai. Men chopped and bleeding and dying.

The night passed in an unnatural silence.

Aaron did not move. Nor did he sleep.

In the morning Moses spoke again. It was a softer voice, but it, too, could be heard everywhere in the camps of Israel:

"I'm going back up the mountain," he said. "You have sinned a great sin. Yet perhaps I can make atonement for you with the Lord."

Shortly thereafter Aaron felt the touch of a hand on his neck. Very near his ear, Moses whispered, "Stand up, brother. Wash your face. If I return, I will have good news for you."

∎

Once more the man named Moses stood before the Lord upon the mountain, wrapped in darkness, praying:

"Alas, the people have sinned exceedingly. Graven images, gods of gold, petty deities that they think they can control. They have sinned grievously.

"But now I beg you, Lord: forgive their sin. Blot it out."

No, spoke the Lord God from the mountain: *Those that sinned I will blot out. I have seen this people. It is a stiff-necked people. Let me alone, that my wrath may consume them!*

Slowly Moses lifted his blind face. "O Lord, if you will not forgive them, then I pray you to blot me, too, out of the book which you have written."

Not you, Moses! No, it is of you that I now intend to make a mighty nation.

Moses began to wring his hands. "What will the Egyptians say of you if you slay your people here? They'll say that your powerful arm is evil after all. That you save a people to kill them! Oh, turn from your wrath! Remember the promises which you swore unto our fathers, to make of their descendants a great nation and to give them Canaan as an inheritance forever."

There was silence in the universe. Then the sound of the mountain was somewhat softened. *They may go. Tell that stiff-necked people they may go to the land I promised. But they go alone. For if I went with them, my wrath would consume them.*

"So," said Moses, "you want me to lead this people alone to the land of promise? How can I do this thing alone? I thought I had found favor in your sight."

Moses, you have found favor in my sight. I know you and I call you by name.

"What favor is it if you depart from me? How can I know your favor if Israel must travel alone? Isn't it precisely in your presence, O Lord, that we are made distinct from all other peoples upon the earth?"

Moses, Moses. All thunders ceased. The darkness lightened. And the Lord said, *Moses, this very thing which you have spoken — I will do it. For you have found favor in my sight.*

Now, Moses closed his mouth and lowered his hands and turned his face aside. His hair was like smoke. His brow concealed a difficult thought.

Finally he whispered, "I pray you, O Lord, show me your glory."

Straightway the wind died. The yellow air stood still. The mountain hushed, as between the heaves of storm.

And all at once the Lord God lifted his prophet bodily and set him down in the cleft of a rock. He covered Moses with his hand — that he might not, by the direct sight of the holy God, die. Then the glory of the Lord began to pass that crack in the mountain, crying: *The Lord! The Lord!*

Only when he was going away did God remove his hand, and Moses saw the back of him.

But while it went, his glory proclaimed: *The Lord, merciful, gracious, slow to anger — a God abounding in love. Forgiving iniquity, blotting out sin, but by no means clearing the guilty —*

And Moses, as soon as he saw such majesty, bowed his head and worshiped.

∎

This time when Moses came down the mountain carrying two new tablets of the law, the skin of his face shined with a terrible splendor. So bright was his countenance that Aaron and all the people fell backward in fear.

"Cover your face!" they cried, "or we cannot come near you!"

So Moses covered his face with a veil.

And for the rest of that year, the first year of their deliverance, Israel continued obedient unto the Lord. As Moses recounted the plans which God had given him for a Tabernacle, they built it.

And when it was built, the cloud of the presence of the Lord came down and rested upon it, and the glory of the Lord filled its rooms, and not even Moses could enter it then.

vi

In the first month of the second year since the children of Israel had gone forth from the land of Egypt, they gathered into families and kept the Passover festival exactly as the Lord their God had commanded them. A lamb without blemish. Seven days of unleavened bread. Bitter herbs.

Miriam sang two songs, a sad song for remembrance and a sweet song for their freedom.

All was well.

Come, then, said the Lord unto Israel, his firstborn child. *Come, let us go home together.*

7

THE CHILDREN
OF ISRAEL

i

On the twentieth day of the second month of their second year of freedom, the cloud was taken up from the Tabernacle, and the children of Israel set out by stages from the wilderness of Sinai. This vast company followed the cloud toward the wilderness of Paran.

The standard of the camp of Judah set out first, and the host of Judah went in companies.

Next went the host of the tribe of Issachar, then the host of the tribe of Zebulun.

When the Tabernacle had been taken down, some of the men of Levi bore forward its poles and its covering only. Then in slow succession there followed the tribe of Reuben and the tribe of Simeon and the tribe of Gad.

In the center of the train, priests carried the Ark of the Covenant on long staves. By the time it arrived at the next encampment the Tabernacle would be ready to receive it.

As six tribes went in front of the Ark, so six tribes came behind: Ephraim, Manasseh, and Benjamin; Dan, Asher, and Naphtali.

This was the order of march for the hosts of Israel as long as they traveled the wilderness.

Whenever the Ark set out thereafter, Moses cried: "Arise, O Lord. Let your enemies be scattered!"

And whenever it came to rest, he said, "Return, O Lord, to the ten thousand thousands of Israel."

ii

Little Achan was one year old when his mother gave him new sandals and his father finally took down their tent. Then they were walking together. Away from the mountain. They were almost the first to go — they and their family, the Zerahites, and their tribe, which was Judah.

Achan knew the names of his blood-kin. They were the names of his identity. Achan, the son of Carmi, the son of Zabdi, the son of Zerah, of the tribe of Judah — Achan was not one. He was many. The children of Israel, *they* were one, and little Achan was a part of that.

His mother had taught him these things.

For a little while he walked by her side. Soon she picked him up and wrapped him in the folds of her robe and carried him on her back. He became drowsy. Each time she took a step he could hear a huff of wind in her lungs. He loved that sound.

His father said, "Elisheba, you have big feet."

His mother's voice hummed through her back to the ear of her son. "So I will have an easier time walking."

"Well, why don't you put sandals on?"

"My toes grip. And my soles can stand the rock. They have grown hard."

"Fine, fine," said his father, "but have you thought about me?"

"What about you?"

"What do you think? My wife's feet are big and hard. It is an embarrassment to me."

Achan's mother stopped talking then. Her son heard only the huff of her trudging, that comforting sound. He fell asleep.

∎

Every morning manna covered the face of the ground. Israel never wanted for something to eat. They could grind the manna in mills or beat it in mortars; they could boil it or make cakes of it; and though it tasted good enough, like cakes baked in oil, it always tasted the same.

One evening, then, when Elisheba set manna before Carmi, he jumped up and began to fling his arms around.

"I have been talking with Nahshon and Zuar," he shouted. "Do you want to hear what they say?"

Elisheba didn't answer, but neither did her husband wait for an answer. "They say their strength is being dried up, that's what they say," he shouted. Achan sat chewing and watching his father with big eyes.

"And they are not alone," Carmi shouted. "Eliab and his father Helon say the same thing. And Elizur — I talked to him. And Shelumiel. We need meat to eat! Meat! Savory meat! We remember the fish of Egypt, cucumbers and melons and leeks and onions and garlic. Oh, the garlic! Just a little garlic! But there's nothing to look at here but... *manna!*"

Little Achan also looked down at his little bits of manna. He pushed it away. Immediately he felt a burning like a bee-sting at the tip of his ear. But this was no bee. It was a clip from his mother's fingernail. He took back the manna and ate it.

∎

Moses led the twelve tribes and all their hosts north by northeast from the wilderness of Sinai, through the wide wilderness of Paran, and into the wilderness of Zin.

Now, it happened on the way that he heard crying in the camps of Israel. At night the people were weeping over their miserable lot.

Moses was dismayed. He turned to the Lord and said, "Did I conceive this people? Did I bear them that you, O Lord, should command me to suckle them like a wet nurse? Where am I going to get meat for these, these — *children!* Six hundred thousand mouths and gullets and stomachs of craving!"

Then the anger of the Lord burned hot against Israel. *Tell them*, he said to Moses, *that they shall eat meat tomorrow. And the next day. And the next! Tell them they shall eat meat for an entire month! Meat till it comes from their nostrils. Meat till it looks loathsome to them. Meat — because they are rejecting the Lord their God!*

So there came from the Lord a violent wind. It crossed the sea and brought quantities of quails, flocks of fat quails that fell all round the camp, covering the wilderness two cubits deep in meat, even to the distance of a day's journey in every direction.

The people began to gather it. They kept on gathering meat till no one had less than the load ten donkeys could carry. But as soon as the meat was between their teeth, the fury of God shot forth and smote the people with a plague, and many perished there.

That place was called Kibroth-hattaavah: The Graves of Craving.

iii

At the southern edge of the Negev, near Kadesh, the cloud of the presence of the Lord came down and the northward journey of Israel was over.

"Canaan is across that desert," Moses said to them. "The land the Lord God swore to our fathers, to give to their descendants forever — it is just across that desert."

So the children of Israel pitched camp in that place, according to the instructions of the Lord. The Tabernacle was assembled in the center of two huge circles of tents. Aaron and his people constituted the eastern side of the circle closest to the Tabernacle — the side to which its door opened. The rest of the inner circle belonged to the families of Levi, so that the priests and the servants of the Lord were ever near to serve him.

The great outer ring was composed of the other tribes, so the Lord was in the midst of them all. From his central seat, God called to Moses, and Moses bore his word to all the people:

You have seen the signs I wrought for you in Egypt. In the same manner shall I go with you into this land, that you might take it for yourself. Now, then, O my people, do these two things: send men to spy out the land of Canaan; and when they return, go in yourselves and by my might make it your own, for it is yours!

Moses chose twelve men, one from each of the tribes of Israel, and all of the people came out to watch them go. A mere handful of kinsmen went north, walking until they were too distant to be seen.

Then the people returned to their tents. Land! *Rehoboth!* They tingled with anticipation.

■

Carmi lay outside his tent in the cool of the evening. He was talking out loud.

Elisheba, who was inside washing their son with the leftover drinking water, thought that a visitor had come by. She was hurrying so she could go out and enjoy the conversation before night forced them to sleep.

"Yes, yes, yes," Carmi was saying. "It will be two fields. At least two fields. One for planting and one for grazing. I myself will tend the flocks. There will be very large flocks. Many sheep, I assure you. No more bricks for me — I am going to be a rich man. And I'll let the woman take care of my crops. She can plow and plant. She walks well. She has big feet. Yes, yes, yes, I will have my own land. Three fields. Why not three? Of course, three! And I will order my servants to build big bins for the harvest."

Just as Elisheba laid young Achan down on his mat, the boy opened his eyes wide and said with slow wonder: "Bins, Mama. Bi-i-ins."

"Hush, don't worry about bins," she said. "You go to sleep, Achan."

Then she stepped outside, smiling. Elisheba didn't talk much. It wasn't in her nature. But she loved to listen. Therefore she was sorry to find Carmi lying on the ground alone, his hands locked behind his head.

"Where is he?" she said softly.

"Where is who?" The tone of her husband's voice implied that she had asked a ridiculous question. But he answered her question with a question, so she was bound to speak again.

"Him," she said as softly as she could. "Our visitor. Him."

"Well, I haven't seen anyone around here. You must have better eyesight than me, woman."

Elisheba put her head down and said nothing.

From inside the tent there came a tiny voice: "Mama? Mama? What's bins? Can I have one, too?"

∎

A cry went up: "They're coming!"

All Israel rushed out of their tents. They ran to the north side of the encampment, breathless with anticipation and glee, squinting to see where the spies were.

There they were!

Yes, there they were — but they, too, were running. They were not in a group. They were stretched across the Negev, every man for himself, the young ones racing top speed, the old ones nearly dead with exhaustion. Their clothing was torn! They were disheveled and frightened.

Shaphat's mother began to scream. Of all the spies, Shaphat was the youngest. The wives of the others covered their mouths with fear.

Shaphat, the first to arrive, fell down gasping. He couldn't speak. He could only shake his head. Others came in with bloody feet. Water was brought. The people surrounded them. And then they began to speak.

"We can't," they said. "No, we cannot do this thing!"

Their faces reflected such horror that the rest of the people felt it, too. Here on the edge of a strange land, Israel trembled and waited to hear the name of the horror in Canaan.

"The cities there are large and fortified. And the people!" The spies rolled their eyes remembering. "We saw there the descendants of Anak! No, this is a land that devours its inhabitants. The people are of enormous stature. Giants! Yes, we saw the Nephilim! And we seemed no bigger than grasshoppers next to them!"

Moses had come through the multitude in time to hear the last part of the spies' recitation: *Nephilim. Grasshoppers.*

"What?" he said, astonished. "Is there no good news?"

Just then the last two of the spies arrived, Caleb and Joshua. They were not bleeding. They were not disheveled. They had not been running, but walking — and they were the last to come because they were carrying a single cluster of grapes so huge that it hung from a pole between them.

"Yes," they said, grinning, "there's wonderful good news. This is a land flowing with milk and honey. See the sort of fruit it produces? And there are figs and pomegranates just like this! The Lord has made it an exceedingly good land for us."

Caleb raised his right arm and said, "Let's go now, at once, and occupy it."

But the other spies yelled at him. "What's the matter with you? Didn't you see what we saw? Our wives and our children will be food for those giants!"

At that the whole congregation began to whine and wail.

Caleb and Joshua were stunned. They had expected everyone to share their triumph. "The Lord delights in us," they said. "Don't fear the people of this land. God will make them bread for us. The Lord is with us. He has taken their protection away — "

But all the children of Israel wept aloud: "Oh, why didn't we die in the wilderness! Why did the Lord bring us to this land, to fall by the sword? Let's choose our own captain! Let's command our captain to take us back to Egypt."

Then Caleb the son of Jephunneh and Joshua the son of Nun tore their clothes in shame. "Israel!" they cried, "Do not rebel against the Lord our God!"

Moses said nothing at all. He had seen enough to know what the Lord thought of this people now. He turned and walked back through the camp to its center, to the Tabernacle; and there the Lord met him, and the Lord spoke:

How long will this people despise me? And how long will they not believe in me, despite the signs which I have wrought among them? I will disinherit them.

Moses lay down on his face. He spoke in tones so quiet that none but God could hear him: "But I have heard the word in your own mouth, O Lord. You declared yourself to be slow in anger and abounding in love. You said you forgive iniquity. I beg you, then, to pardon the iniquity of this people according to the greatness of your own steadfast love. I beg you, O Lord."

In the dark interior of the Tabernacle, above the mercy seat in the holy of holies, the Lord God said: *Even so, I pardon them. Even so. But none of those who saw my glory against Egypt shall live to enter the land. Only my servants Caleb and Joshua, because they have followed me truly — they and the children whom Israel thought would be food for the giants — shall enter and dwell there.*

Moses, tell this people that they must wander the wilderness yet forty more years. I, the Lord, have spoken.

So Moses rose up and went out and told the people this unhappy word.

There was no laughing in the camps of Israel that day. No, nor was there much laughter for years to come; but the children longed to hear it again. They remembered the day when the whole congregation had laughed aloud. The little children longed to laugh like that again.

iv

While yet the twelve tribes of Israel were encamped near Kadesh, Miriam, the sister of Moses and Aaron, and the oldest of the three, died.

She who had watched over the infant Moses with tenderness and wit; she who had sung at the redemption of Israel and who had taught the women to dance — she was buried in that place.

∎

So Israel became *Shasu*, a nomad wandering from place to place without plan or direction, waiting. Waiting until this time of dying was over.

When they lacked water, the people complained to Moses and Moses prayed on their behalf.

Once, when God had commanded Moses and Aaron to speak to a rock that it might pour forth water for the people, the brothers chose rather to strike it with Aaron's rod.

The striking worked. Water indeed came out, and the people drank.

But unto Moses and Aaron the Lord said, *Because you did not believe in me, neither of you shall bring this assembly into the land which I have promised.*

∎

One night Achan was awakened by a strange sound in the tent — a strangled, choking sound, as if someone couldn't breathe.

Achan was seventeen years old by now; he slept in a compartment of his own; the sound was coming through the wall of his father's room.

He almost got up to see what the trouble was, but then he heard his mother's voice. She, too, had heard the sound and had crept into Carmi's room.

"What's the matter?" she whispered in her low, gentle voice.

"Nothing!" Achan's father was gasping for air. "Go away."

His mother whispered, "But why are you crying, Carmi?"

"Because," the man sobbed, "because I think I will never have a plot of land for myself."

"Hush, hush." His mother's voice was so familiar, so consoling. "Don't worry about land," she said. "Go to sleep now, Carmi."

∎

When the congregation of Israel was encamped near Mount Hor, the Lord said to Moses, *Take Aaron up the mountain. Tell him to don his priestly garments, then lead him together with his son Eleazar up Mount Hor, for he shall be gathered to his people now.*

Moses did as the Lord commanded.

Early in the morning he and his brother and his nephew, climbed the mountain together. They sat and looked out over the tents of the people. After a little while, Moses stripped Aaron of his garments. He put them on Eleazar.

Aaron lay down, then, and died there on the top of the mountain.

Moses and Eleazar came down alone.

And when the house of Israel saw that Aaron was dead, they wept for him thirty days.

Moses was silent all those days. He did not weep. He did not speak a word.

∎

From Mount Hor the people of Israel set out by the way of the Red Sea, moving south-southeast toward Ezion-geber, where they camped.

Then they encamped at Elath.

They set out by the way of the plain northward from Elath and encamped in Punon.

Again, they set out from Punon and encamped at Oboth.

They set out from Oboth and began to climb to higher ground. They encamped at Iye-abarim.

From there they set out and encamped in the valley of Zered.

∎

On the way the people became irritable and impatient. They murmured against God and against Moses.

Despite the rigid order of their lives, despite the many commands of God, their movement lacked a plan or point or purpose! It was ridiculous. Wandering, wandering nowhere — but doing it all with stiff rules and wonderful precision!

A general mood of bitterness infected Israel, until it seemed to some that everyone must feel the same, though few had the courage to *say* it. So those few became bold on behalf of the rest. With the added swagger of self-righteousness, they complained loudly, in public places.

Carmi was among the loudest.

Sixty years old, thin and stooped, gaunt in his cheeks, balding and blotched on the top of his head, Carmi chose to speak of the food. He stood in front of his tent and shouted, "There is neither food nor water!"

His son, now thirty years old, watched with a scornful indifference. He wasn't embarrassed or ashamed. In fact, he no longer felt anything at all for this disappointed old man.

Carmi's wife, on the other hand, was terrified of his rash behavior. She begged him to come in and be quiet. She said, "Carmi, you know better. There is water when we need it, and there has been manna every morning — "

But the man bellowed the louder: "When I think what my life could have been! When I think what I might have made of myself! A little land! A few fig trees, a few sheep — no, Elisheba, this is not food. Moses!" he roared, waving his hands. "Moses, do you hear me? I am the voice of ten thousand now. I am pointing at a jar of manna! I am remembering manna, day after day for thirty years, manna! And I gag! I say for ten thousand: we loathe this worthless food!"

That same night, Carmi the son of Zabdi died.

He was bitten by a snake. And though the bite produced a fiery inflammation all over his flesh, the man chose silence at the end. He did not cry out. He did not speak. His wife took him in her arms and stroked his sweating forehead and rocked him. Once he opened his eyes and looked up at her. His swelling countenance seemed to say, *I expected nothing else.* And then he breathed his last.

But from other tents in Israel there went up many an agonized cry that night.

The entire camp had been overrun by serpents. They came in silence, surprising the people by the sudden fire of their bite.

And in the morning light the serpents were visible everywhere, dropping from loose clothing, lying in the folds of the tents, sliding through the dry grass — and killing the children of Israel.

So they went to Moses with wounded bodies and broken hearts. They found him at the Tabernacle in the midst of all. And they said, "We have sinned. We've spoken against the Lord and against you. Moses, we repent the iniquity! Please pray to the Lord, that he take away the serpents from us!"

Moses listened, his fierce old eyes probing the faces of those who surrounded him, then he turned and entered the Tabernacle, and there he stayed for the space of an hour.

During that same day, Elisheba also was bitten by a snake.

Achan heard the tiny sigh his mother made for the pain she had sustained. He went into her room and saw the dry eye of the serpent. Immediately he crushed its head and gathered his mother into his arms and ran outside. He raced westward through the wide encampment from the tents of Judah to the center of all the circles — the Tabernacle.

As he arrived, he saw several of the men of Levi lifting a dull yellow snake to the top of a pole. It had been molded of bronze.

Moses was calling to all the people: "The Lord has commanded me to raise this serpent before you. In mercy he says, *If those who have been bitten look upon the serpent, they shall live.*"

Achan laid his mother down before the pole. Already her breath was labored and foul. Her face was swollen and red.

Slowly she opened her eyes. She looked upward. She gazed upon the bronze effigy for a brief moment. Then she closed her eyes and relaxed and fell into a deep sleep.

When she woke, she was well.

■‖

From the valley of Zered the children of Israel set out and encamped on the far side of the Arnon.

From there they continued to Beer. This is the well at which the Lord said to Moses, *Gather the people together, and I will give them water.*

And this is the place where Israel sang:

> *Spring up, O Well! (Come, sing to the water.)*
> *Run sweet for the lips of our sons and our daughters!*
> *You are the source our nobles once dug*
> *with scepters and staves and faith and love.*
> *Spring up, O Well, for the good of our daughters:*
> *forever our princes! Forever your waters!*

From that wilderness they went on to Mattanah, and from Mattanah to Nahaliel, and from Nahaliel to Bamoth, and from Bamoth to the valley lying in the region of Moab by the top of Pisgah which looks down upon the desert.

■‖

While they were here, at the edge of the desert of Kedemoth, Moses sent messengers to Sihon, the king of the Amorites, asking permission to pass through his territory. The Amorites dwelt east of the Jordan River, from the Jabbok on their northern border to the Arnon, which flowed into the Dead Sea on the south.

"We will go by the king's highway," Moses said. "We will neither turn into your fields nor drink the water of a single well."

But Sihon refused the request.

Moreover, when he had sent spies to estimate the strength of the people of Israel, he began to fear them. They were too many and too near. Quickly, then, he mounted an army and rode toward this threat in the desert.

Israel, likewise, gathered together an army of fighting men and went westward toward Sihon.

The armies met near Jahaz. In sunlight they fought a dusty, bloody battle, and by nightfall the hosts of Israel had slain Sihon with the edge of the sword.

Thus, the children of Israel took possession of all the lands of the Amorites. And Moses settled some of the people as governors in Heshbon, the city from which King Sihon had ruled.

■|

Next Israel turned north and went up the road to Bashan.

When Og, the king of Bashan, heard of their coming, he gathered forces from everywhere within the kingdom of Bashan. He armed them and marched south to meet the people of Israel.

Now, Og ruled all the land north of the Jabbok as far as Mount Hermon, sixty cities fortified with high walls, gates, and bars. He was a mighty enemy.

It became clear to Moses that he would have to meet the armies of Og on the fields near Edrei, north of Ramoth Gilead.

During the night before the battle — when the men of Israel sat silently, hearing the enemy eating and singing and shouting taunts across the way — the Lord said to Moses, *Do not fear them. I have given Og into your hand, him and all his people, all his cities, all his land. You shall do to him as you did to Sihon the king of the Amorites, who dwelt in Heshbon.*

And so it was:

By noon of the following day, Israel had beaten Og so completely that no survivor was left, none to carry the sad news back to the cities, no messenger at all — until the children of Israel themselves arrived to take possession of that city.

So Israel also controlled the entire tableland of Gilead and Bashan, all the territory east of the Jordan.

■|

Finally, then, forty years after they had set out from Egypt as a people redeemed by the Lord their God, the children of Israel encamped in the plains of Moab between Beth Jeshimoth and Abel Shittim, on the eastern side of the Jordan, across the river from Jericho.

V

Moses had been eighty years old when he led the hosts of Israel out of Egypt. He was a hundred and twenty when finally the Lord allowed Israel to stand again at the borders of Canaan — here on the shores of the Jordan. And though his strength had not abated in all those years, it had come time now for Moses to die.

He would not enter the land with his people.

∎

On the first day of the eleventh month of the fortieth year since Israel left Egypt, Moses called the entire congregation together, and when they stood in a vast circle around the Tabernacle he lifted up his voice and spoke to them:

"The Lord your God is determined now to keep his promise and to lead you into the land of Canaan, even as he led your parents with signs and wonders out of Egypt."

The fierce eye of this old man shot left and right among the people. He was looking for someone. His hair was as white as the snows on Mount Hermon, his cheeks creased like the cataracts that ran down Hermon toward the Jordan. Suddenly, he pointed.

"Joshua, son of Nun!" he cried. A small, studious man glanced up, then glanced around himself as if embarrassed to be singled out.

"Joshua, you were faithful," Moses cried. "You and Caleb the son of Jephunneh — you two alone trusted the Lord to lead us into Canaan when the rest of Israel whimpered. The Lord therefore has chosen you to lead this people over Jordan into the land.

"As for you!" Moses swept his eyes across the entire assembly, a magnificent nation, young and strong and bright-eyed, not a slavish soul among them, not a face over fifty. "As for you, never forget the lessons of the wilderness. When you beget children and grandchildren; when you have grown old in the land, remember still to seek the Lord your God. If you search with all your heart, you will find him.

"For ask now of time past, since God created people to walk on earth, ask from one end of heaven to the other whether such a thing as this has ever happened. Did any people ever hear the voice of God speaking out of fire, as you have heard, and live? Or has any god ever attempted to take a nation for himself from the midst of another nation, by trials, by signs, by wonders and by war, by a mighty hand and an outstretched arm, by terrors, great terrors, according to all that the Lord your God accomplished for you in Egypt? To you it was shown. To you, that you might know that the Lord is God! There is no other besides him. Because he loved your ancestors and chose their descendants, he brought you out of Egypt with his own presence.

"And he made a covenant with you at his holy mountain! Not just with your parents, but with you, all of you alive and here today. He said, *I am the Lord your God, who brought you out of the land of Egypt, out of the house of bondage: you shall have no other gods besides me —*

"Hear, O Israel: the Lord your God is one Lord! And you shall love the Lord your God with all your heart and with all your soul and with all your might. And all the words which I have taught you of the commandments of God, his statutes and his ordinances, shall be upon your heart. You shall teach them diligently to your children and shall talk of them when you sit in your house and when you walk by the way and when you lie down and when you rise up."

Moses fell silent. No one moved. His eyes wandered away from the people toward some region none of them could see. He seemed to depart from them a while; yet no one grew restless, and no one moved.

This old man had been alive as long as anyone could remember: leading them, angry, aloof, willful, right — always *right*, yet ever faithful — and sometimes kind. When one caught him gazing upon the people in the evening, there appeared in his eyes a dreaming gentleness. A kindness.

Softly, now, Moses said: "For you are a people holy to the Lord your God. For the Lord chose you out of all the peoples on earth to be his own possession."

His eye sharpened: "It was not because you were many or mighty or righteous that he chose you. You have been a monumentally stubborn people. But it is because the Lord loves you. He is keeping the oath which he swore to your parents.

"Tomorrow, Israel, you will pass over the Jordan to dispossess nations greater and mightier than yourselves. But the Lord your God goes before you like a devouring fire. He will fight on your side. He will subdue these nations for you.

"And now, what does the Lord require of you but to fear him, to walk in his ways, to love him, to serve him with all your heart? Circumcise the foreskin of your heart. Be no longer stubborn. For the Lord your God is God of gods and Lord of lords, the great, mighty, terrible God, who executes justice and loves the sojourner and feeds the hungry and covers the naked.

"Love the sojourner likewise," said Moses, and he paused, gazing at the people.

"Cleave to the Lord," he said.

"He is your praise.

"He is your God."

Moses was almost whispering. Most of Israel could no longer hear him. But they knew what he was saying. He had said it often before. They loved the words. Already they recited them to their children: *Your ancestors went*

down to Egypt seventy persons; and now the Lord has made you as the stars
of heaven for multitude. . .

As the stars of heaven for multitude.

As the stars of heaven.

∎

That afternoon Moses walked alone to Mount Nebo, some distance east of
the encampment. His stride was cautious and short. He leaned heavily on
his rod. But by evening he had climbed the mountain and was standing on a
high ridge, gazing westward into a vermilion sun.

The Lord said, *Moses, look. Look: this is the land I swore to Abraham and
Isaac and Jacob, to give it to their descendants. Look, Moses. Can you see?*

The old man squinted against the bloody sunlight. Yes, he could see. In a
mystery, he saw the entire territory from Dan in the north even unto Zoar in
the south.

Yes. Yes, he could see.

∎

So Moses, one hundred and twenty years old — though his eye was not dim
nor his natural force abated — died on Mount Nebo.

The Lord gathered up the body of his servant, and God himself buried
him, and no one knows the place where he was buried, even to this day.

There has never since arisen in Israel a prophet like Moses, whom the
Lord knew face-to-face.

PART THREE

The Wars of
the Lord

PART
THREE

8

JOSHUA

i

The kings in Canaan ruled small cities set on hills, five to ten acres crowded with buildings and surrounded by a wider skirt of farmland and fields outside the wall. They ruled a population that lived in the second stories of well-built houses, a people that drove its livestock inside the wall every night, into the ground level of their own houses.

Twice annually the Canaanite kings petitioned their gods for rich crops. It was the necessary ceremony of a sedentary race: if one could not go forth to find goodness, goodness must be coaxed home. Of Ba'al, the god of the thunderclouds, the kings prayed rain; of Astarte, his consort, they pleaded fertility and a fruitful harvest.

But in the spring of a particularly wonderful abundance — precisely at the harvest when northern rains and the melting snows had swelled the river Jordan to an impassable flood — the king of Jericho was praying a different prayer. One of desperation.

"O thou who mountest the clouds," he cried. "O great Storm-god, Ba'al!"

He had been watching a new people massed on the eastern shores of the Jordan, a desert-hardened lot who, like locusts, seemed capable of eating the countryside. Already they had devoured the kings of the Amorites and the Moabites.

The king of Jericho had considered his city protected by the river. There simply were no fords in the Jordan at full flood. But this morning his outposts brought word that this people had crossed anyway. Suddenly they were at Gilgal on the west side, building altars. Men and women and children. All of them!

"O great Storm-god, Ba'al, stride the skyways, shake your spear of thunderbolt — and fight for us! Save us from this wild, dry, and swarming plague of the desert!"

ii

Joshua the son of Nun was picking his way through the darkness toward the city of Jericho. Step, step, he went by slow steps. He was a nearsighted man. He peered intently at things in order to choose where to set his foot.

But the night was dark by design. Joshua had chosen a moonless night because he planned to steal right up to the city walls and touch them.

Jericho had to be defeated first if Israel would enter Canaan to dwell there. In fact, Joshua was not going there for information. He had already dispatched two spies into the city. Their report had been remarkably accurate because a prostitute named Rahab had given them room and protection. *A canny choice,* they had laughed at their return. *A whore's not likely to ask questions, right? — but no one's able to answer them better than her.*

No, he needn't spy. Joshua was making his solitary way to Jericho in order to touch its spirit and assess its strength before the children of Israel began to take the land their God had promised to their ancestors.

It was in this land that the Lord God had required of Abraham that he circumcise the males of his household, in this land that God attached promises to that sign of the covenant. And now Israel was about to receive more than words and more than signs; Israel was about to receive the soil itself!

Therefore, as soon as Israel had crossed the Jordan, Joshua, too, had required every male born in the wilderness to be circumcised in accordance with the covenant. They used flint knives, the same as Abraham had in the beginning.

Next he ordered the people to keep the Passover, and so they did on the fourteenth day of the month. On the fifteenth, Israel ate of the produce of the land, unleavened cakes and parched grain — and on that day manna ceased falling forever.

There! Close before him Joshua saw the huge black shadow of Jericho, its wall a high, wide absence of stars. Joshua the son of Nun paused. *O Israel, how will you breach such stone?*

But Israel had crossed the Red Sea dry-shod.

And Israel had again, in these latter days, crossed also the Jordan River on a dry bed because the Lord had blocked its waters in the north and all the water south had drained away.

Why should not Israel cross this hard wall, too?

Then step, step: Joshua resumed his slow progress toward the wall, staring straight ahead, straining his poor eyes, raising his hands, preparing to touch the stones of the powers of Canaan.

Suddenly Joshua saw with terrible clarity a man standing with a drawn sword before him.

Joshua dropped his arms and gaped a moment. Then he whispered, "Are you for us — or for our adversaries?"

The man with the sword said, "No, but as commander of the armies of the Lord have I come."

Immediately Joshua fell facedown on the earth and worshiped.

He said, "What does my lord bid his servant?"

The commander of the Lord's armies said, "Put off your shoes from your feet, for the place where you stand is holy."

Joshua did so.

And then it was that Joshua the son of Nun, the leader of the forces of Israel after Moses, learned how the stones of the walls of Jericho might be breached.

iii

The king of Jericho had shut the gates of his city and barred them with timber. Citizens, farmers, soldiers, all were inside. Sheep and goats and cattle; mattocks, rakes, and weapons — everything the city owned had been gathered in. The spring that watered Jericho, the best such spring in all of Canaan, ran bright and unabated. Moreover, the greatest part of an excellent barley harvest had already been stored. Not only were the new stone granaries full, but food had overflowed as well into the ancient underground silos of the first farmers of Jericho.

Jericho was ready for the longest siege. Jericho would endure.

In the middle of the night the king of Jericho climbed his wall in order to inspect its readiness for a direct attack.

There were jars of oil arranged at intervals along the top. And sluices cut through the stone. The king put his finger in these. There were smoking smudge-pots ready to ignite the oil for a rain of fire. And short arrows, the sharp bronze bolts of Jericho, bristled in the narrow stone cavities. Spears stood at the corners for men whose arms were mighty, whose eyes were accurate. And loose stones were piled here and there for the older men and the angry women to push upon the heads of Israelites who came too near with ladders.

The king inspected everything personally. Yes: whether for siege or for assault, Jericho was ready.

And the wall he stood upon was doubled. Two walls, one inside the other, connected by intermediate stone and a strong lattice of timber. Previous regencies had permitted the building of rooms between the walls. The poorest people lived there. Outcasts and whores. And stores were kept in the spaces. And though the stones had only been hammer-trimmed and laid in clay mortar, this king had himself commanded the outside wall to be coated with a thick yellow plaster up to fifteen feet high. That was his own contribution. It would require ladders to climb the wall these days. Yes: Jericho was ready.

But the king paced his wall the whole night through and prayed:

Asherah, consort of El, mother of seventy gods and of Ba'al —

He was restless. He had heard rumors regarding the might and the fury of this desert breed, this flinty nation come from Egypt. They worshiped a mountain God.

— O Asherah, beg the bloodiest of your children to protect us from the deity that can dry the sea for the feet of its people!

There was a moment that night when the king thought he heard the gentlest of murmurings outside the wall, almost womanly in solicitude. But it was a quick word as quickly gone, and he was left with a deeper sense of loneliness — as though Asherah had stolen away to love another better than he.

▌

At dawn, as the sky began to gather a grey light, the king could see the forms of his watchmen standing at the corners and in the towers by the gate. People stirred in the city. Smells of old sleep arose. A few sticks crackled into flames.

Families began muffled conversations.

The king had just decided to descend and wash himself, when a distant sound arrested him. It came from the northeast, almost inaudible, a soft rhythmic beating. But the guards were not reacting. Perhaps there was no sound after all. Yet he seemed to feel a vast pulsing in the earth and in his bones.

There!

"Guards!" cried the king of Jericho. "Captains!" he roared down to the city. "Rouse your warriors! Archers, get up! Get up! Get ready!"

There was motion at the northeast horizon. A dusty motion, like a cloud billowing up from the distant earth.

Now Jericho broke into a hectic activity. The wall sprouted warriors, rushing to their posts and their weapons.

The eastern sky streaked red. An angry boil burst at the horizon, and that northeastern cloud caught fire of the sun.

It was the armies of Israel! The entire force of the nation was marching hither in perfect order. No one hurried. All came in a wide file, a very long line.

Jericho watched. Jericho fell into a waiting silence. Jericho crouched on the wall and watched.

Now the king would learn what strategy he'd have to contend with. He glanced swiftly at his archers and the spearmen. They knew exactly their killing distances. They would not release an arrow till the enemy was within reach.

But Israel never came that close.

While the line of Israelites was still at a safe range, horns began to blare and the vanguard soldiers turned. They turned parallel to the city wall. They kept marching in a measured step, gazing straight ahead. They would not even look at Jericho! The entire file of Israel's army circled the city. The trumpets snarled and tore the air and did not cease.

Archers on Jericho's wall shivered, so strong was their desire to shoot. But their captains, glancing at the king, commanded patience. And the king kept twitching his eyes left and right along the strange procession that now surrounded his city.

Where would the attack come from? From everywhere at once?

The faces of Israel revealed nothing. They were grim, controlled, fixed, and unforthcoming. Every warrior stared straight ahead.

There: in the very middle of the march. The king saw seven men in priest's robes of stunning luxury, gold and blue and purple and scarlet, fine twined linen. Each man held a hollow ram's horn to his lips, and all were blowing together brutal harmonies, causing the flesh on Jericho's neck to shiver. There: that's where the orders were coming from, from that sound!

And immediately behind these seven men came four more carrying a box of beaten gold by means of two long staves, two men before and two men after it.

So the file of the hosts of Israel passed round the city all that day. Not one arrow was released between the enemies. Not a word was exchanged. No, not so much as a glance from the eyes of one to the eyes of the other. And when one slow circumference had been accomplished, Israel turned back to Gilgal. The rams' horns ceased their sounding. And in silence the host departed again.

The men of Jericho were exhausted, drenched in an acid sweat. But the king could not console them. He sent them down from the wall, commanding them to eat and to sleep and to prepare for the attack tomorrow.

Yet even now he did not know what strategy the desert swarm had chosen against him. If this were siege there was no sense to it. Or perhaps it was some ritual by which to bind the city's strength and soul. If so, then the assault would come tomorrow at daylight.

Therefore, the king was on his wall the following dawn.

All his warriors accompanied him.

And Israel came out of Gilgal as before. But — precisely as before — Israel marched once around the city, blowing seven horns, displaying its mysterious golden box, and returning to camp by the setting of the sun.

So it was the third day. And the fourth: Israel encircled the city once and departed.

On the fifth day the king of Jericho began to shout from the top of his wall. All morning long he shouted taunts and execrations. It heartened his people a while. He gave his words the bite of bitter poetry. He pronounced vile maledictions on the heads of Israel. But Israel's eyes remained forever forward. Israel's horns did not cease to blow.

By afternoon the king despaired of cursings and of his gods as well. A suffocation was overcoming his city. People trembled. They could neither eat nor sleep. Children had long since ceased to cry.

On the sixth day the king cracked a door in the city wall and, flanked by four bodyguards, boldly approached the head of Israel's marching column in order to attempt negotiations. There he saw a small man whose eyes were bent ever to the ground, a shuffling fellow given to much thought. A reasonable man, perhaps. The king tried to engage him in conversation, but the studious man didn't answer. He looked up at the king. He squinted fiercely and finally produced an otherworldly stare as if the king were but a phantom. The horns blew and blew, while all Israel passed this personage with no acknowledgement. He might have been a beggar.

So the king of Jericho returned to his city, to his wall, to his ignorance and his futile observation.

The seventh day was different.

On this day, Israel circled Jericho not once, but seven times, from dawn to late afternoon. Suddenly, in the midst of their seventh passage, the sound of the ram's horns changed. It rose to the shrieks of eagles. And all the voices, all the throats of Israel opened. Ten thousand warriors turned inward, roaring, and charged the city. The city walls themselves began to shudder. The king felt a terrible agitation in the stones beneath his feet. His archers leaped up. Spearmen reached for spears. Women brought smudge-pots to ignite the oil in sheets of fire. But just as Israel entered the range of Jericho's arrows, the city walls rose three feet into the air, bellowed like a living thing, cracked at every join and mortar, then collapsed — a great crush of stones on all the people below.

The king of Jericho tumbled down into his dying city. The burning oil spilled inward. Fire and timber and rock fell with him. And the final vision vouchsafed unto the king was of a piece of wall which neither crumbled nor burned, a slim finger of stone with one window two stories up, from which hung a scarlet cord.

In his last instant of life all the world seemed to the king a bitter joke — for why should that one live at last and not another? The window belonged to an outcast! A whore named Rahab.

iv

Joshua watched the flames. He had heard the thunderclap, the voice of the Lord that cracked the walls of Jericho and dropped them into a heap, and now he let the watery curtain of red flame play upon his poor eyes. Dark figures rushed here and there, the hosts of Israel reducing the city to dust.

Except for certain metals which God had reserved for the treasury of the Tabernacle, absolutely everything of Jericho had been placed under a sacred ban. It was devoted to the Lord for destruction. *Herem*: the Lord God commanded that neither the people nor the possessions of this city should ever again serve a human purpose.

Joshua was watching the utter obliteration of a city, all the cattle, all its citizens young and old, all the wealth it had gained throughout its generations, the riches that would have enriched another army — all.

And when Jericho was but an acrid smoke arising from ashes, Joshua bowed his head and in a quiet, frightened voice said, "Cursed be the one who shall ever rise up to rebuild this city."

Those near him heard what he said. But what he said next was so terrible that the words were imprinted on their memory forever:

> *At the cost of his firstborn*
> *shall he lay foundations;*
> *for the price of his youngest*
> *shall he buy new gates.*

So the fame and the fear of Joshua went throughout the land of Canaan, for the Lord was with him.

v

We will cut Canaan at its middle, then take each half individually." Joshua was squatting on a dusty plot, drawing lines with his finger. "I've studied this," he said. He fussed with the accuracy of his picture. "Here is the Jordan River; at its south is the Salt Sea; at its northern reach, the Sea of Kinnereth. We are here, northwest of the Salt Sea. Jericho."

Joshua peered at the ground. The officers of Israel made a circle around him, taller, younger, more robust than he. They kept changing position, trying to see; but the little man hovered so blindly over his map that he blocked their view.

"Here is Ai," he said softly, "and Bethel, west of it. These cities sit on the ridge route running north and south from Beersheba, here, to Shechem, here. This road is the spine. Break it and we break Canaan in two."

Joshua squinted up at the officers. "And we will break Canaan in two," he said quietly. There was neither triumph nor urgency in his voice. It was a matter of fact. "For when he chose me, the Lord said, *No man shall be able to stand before you. I will be with you; I will not fail or forsake you — for you shall cause this people to inherit the land which I swore to their fathers to give them.*"

Joshua returned to his map, marking and naming cities first in the south and then in the north. This was the sequence he intended for the campaign to come: secure the land west of the Salt Sea, a hilly, less populated country, and *then* reach for the richer regions of the north.

But start with Ai.

"Othniel," Joshua said, trying to find that man among the faces, "what did you say of that city?"

A young man of large, grinning cheeks said, "It sits on a ridge, but the people have made little of that defense — and they are so few you needn't send more than two thousand men." He grinned broadly. "I'll shake my spear and that army will scatter, so scared are they of us!"

Joshua nodded.

▌

In the morning Joshua sent three thousand warriors westward to Ai, to defeat that city with a single strong assault.

At the same time he met with a group of impoverished travelers who were requesting to live among Israel. They said they had come from a far country because of the wonders the Lord had performed in Egypt.

They said, "We will be your servants. Come, make a covenant with us..."

But before this conversation or any covenant could be concluded, Joshua heard shouting at the western tents of Israel. It sounded like an outcry of grief.

Joshua began to walk in that direction, and soon the young man of grinning assurances came dashing through the camp.

When he saw Joshua, he fell before him and gasped, "We are beaten!" His body stank of a sweaty fear.

"Beaten, Othniel?" Joshua said. "*Beaten?*"

"They came out of the gate like bees and killed ten men before we could speak," Othniel panted. "We fled. We ran down the ridge — but they followed as far as some stone quarries, killing, I don't know, thirty, forty men. Yes, beaten."

Joshua was astonished. "What's forty among three thousand! Why didn't you stand and fight?"

"Our courage died in us."

"Why?"

"Sir, I don't know. But the spirit was snatched out of the whole army of Israel!"

Then Joshua went to the Tabernacle and tore his clothes and bowed down in front of the Ark and whispered, "Alas, Lord God, it has only just begun! Yet already Israel has turned tail to the enemy! Why are we defeated now? Why should we be stopped at the start of our campaign?"

The Lord said to Joshua, *Israel has sinned. They have stolen treasures of Jericho, the very things I placed beneath a sacred ban. Israel cannot stand before their enemies, because the whole people has become like that which was stolen. They are a thing devoted to destruction.*

Joshua said softly, "What, then, can we do?"

The Lord said, *Find and destroy the devoted things that were stolen.*

"How shall I seek them?" said Joshua.

Divide the people. Let the tribes pass by until I choose one tribe. Of that tribe, let the clans pass until I choose one; and of the clans, households; and of the households, men.

And so it was.

On the following morning, after a sacrifice to sanctify the people for this solemn trial, Joshua commanded representatives of the twelve tribes of Israel to come before him at the Tabernacle.

One by one they passed by while lots of judgment were cast. And the tribe of Judah was taken.

Then representatives of the clans of Judah passed by Joshua. Lots were cast, and the clan of Zerah was taken.

Among the households of Zerah, Zabdi was taken.

And of the sons of Zabdi, Carmi. But Carmi had perished in the wilderness with everyone else of his generation. Therefore, the final lot fell upon Achan, the son of Carmi, the son of Zabdi, son of Zerah, of the tribe of Judah.

Achan had stolen the treasures of Jericho.

Joshua squinted against the sunlight, identifying Achan. Forty years old. He had been the firstborn of the new generation, for his mother delivered him even as Israel was passing through the sea from Egypt into freedom. Achan. The son of his mother Elisheba, a faithful soul who died at their second crossing, from the wilderness, over Jordan, into this land of promise.

"Achan," said Joshua so softly his breath was but wind on sand, "Achan, my son, render praise to the Lord God of Israel and tell me now what you have done. Do not hide it from me."

"My father wanted two fields and got none," said Achan. "I want only one. But even my one is uncertain. The land is filled with enemies. Many of us are going to die."

"Achan," Joshua said, "what did you do?"

The man sighed and lowered his head. "When I saw among the spoils of Jericho a beautiful mantle from Shinar, close-woven and dyed with a deep purple dye, I took it. I took silver weighing two hundred shekels, a gold bar of fifty shekels. I buried these in the earth inside my tent. I planned to buy the field my father never had."

And now it was Joshua who sighed. He got up and walked away, his head bowed down as always, his poor eyes peering at the ground before his feet.

As he went, he gave orders softly, and the orders were accomplished, and all Israel was sober and thoughtful that day.

They dug in Achan's tent and brought out the things that had been devoted to destruction. These they carried with Achan into a separate valley, and there they burned all that Achan was: his oxen, his asses, his sheep, his tent, his possessions, his sons, his daughters, his wife, and himself. They burned him with fire, and they stoned him with stones, and he was no more, and Carmi's heritage passed from the earth.

Thereafter the name of the place was the Vale of Achor, Valley of Trouble.

▌

After that Israel defeated Ai easily.

Joshua, in the strength of two victories, established covenants with four cities south of Ai: Gibeon, Chephirah, Beeroth, Kiriath-jearim. So the back of the land of Canaan had been broken indeed.

▌

Without hesitation, then, the small, studious man led his forces southward according to lines once drawn on the dusty ground.

The kings of five southern cities strengthened themselves by forming a coalition and moving north as a single army: Jerusalem and Hebron and Jarmuth and Lachish and Eglon. But Joshua heard of their union and drove Israel all night long in a forced march uphill from Gilgal to the pass of Beth-horon where at sunrise he astonished the enemy by his mere and massive presence. He attacked them, routed them, and pursued them southward into the foothills, striking again and again, at Azekah, at Makkedah. The Lord went with him, once hurling great hailstones down from heaven, once holding the day itself, the sun and the moon, dead still while Joshua finished battles that needed more time than a single morning and an evening.

Marching southward he attacked the main fortresses of the foothills, Libnah, Eglon, and Lachish. Then he turned east and mounted straight into the heart of the southern highlands, taking Hebron and Debir.

∎

As he did in the south, so he did in the north.

Again, kings in fear for their cities joined forces against this common enemy.

Again, the soft-spoken Joshua directed the hosts of Israel in assaults so accurate, so balanced, and so well-timed that the natural weakness of any coalition, the lines along its join, cracked. Joshua divided his enemy and conquered them one by one by one.

The number of kings whom Joshua defeated on the west side of the Jordan, from the valleys of Lebanon in the north to Mount Halak in the south, was thirty-one kings.

vi

When Joshua the son of Nun was very old, he summoned to himself the elders and heads and officers of Israel.

When he began to speak, he scarcely lifted his head. It seemed too large for his thin neck. And his body was small, bent round like a shepherd's crook. Those who listened had to press in close and tip their heads sideways.

Moreover, the man's voice was but a hollow whisper. He seemed to speak from the caves of the ancients. None remembered Egypt but him. He alone had seen the griefs of Egypt.

"Behold," he breathed, "we have divided the land as best we can among the tribes of Israel. Every tribe has a territory, every tribe an inheritance, fields and houses and land. So it is, and so it shall be. The Lord has kept his promise to Abraham and Sarah, Isaac and Rebekah, Jacob and Rachel and Leah. My children, look about you. We are home."

It was a day of radiant sunshine, though Joshua still had not raised his head. He kept silence a while, and it occurred to the heads of Israel that he really meant it: they should look around at the land, the soil, the magnificent oak by which they had gathered, the earth.

But Joshua could not look. His eyes were blinded by the sunlight.

"Your work is not altogether done," he said. "Many foreign nations remain among us. In time the Lord will push them back before you.

"But until that time you must not mix with these nations, or mention the names of their gods, or swear by them, or serve them, or bow down to them. You must cleave to the Lord your God as you have done to this day. Israel, love the Lord your God!"

As he spoke, more and more people gathered. The small group grew. Mothers holding babies came, and the young men and young women together, farmers and shepherds, priests and weavers and potters.

Joshua was at Shechem, between the mountains of Ebal and Gerizim, a holy place before the Lord — and perhaps that was why so many soon began to hear a man who spoke so softly. They were listening as much with their spirits as with their ears.

"I am about to go the way of all the earth," said Joshua. "Before I go, I must hear your faithfulness.

"Our most ancient ancestor — Terah, the father of Abraham — served other gods beyond the Euphrates. But the Lord took Abraham and led him here and gave him Isaac; to Isaac he gave Jacob; and to Jacob, twelve sons and a daughter. Then Jacob and his children went down to Egypt. The Lord! The same Lord who delivered your parents from the bondage of Egypt is he who has led you here. God has kept his promise. Israel, you are like the stars of heaven for multitude! You are the descendants God swore to give to our father, the fruit of our mother's barren womb! You are the nation that was to come from them — and you are home!

"Now, therefore," said tiny Joshua, "fear the Lord. Serve him in sincerity. Keep his statutes now as he has kept his promises to you. Be his people, for he has chosen you, and he is your God. Love him."

Suddenly Joshua lifted his face. He opened his eyes, eyes moist and unfocused in the sunlight, and he raised his thin voice like an eagle's claw upon the air.

"But if you are not willing to serve him, then choose this day whom you *will* serve, whether the gods your most ancient ancestors served beyond the river, or the gods of the Canaanites in whose land you dwell. As for me and my house, we will serve the Lord!"

Silence returned. It was the same waiting silence with which Joshua had begun his valediction — but then he desired their looking. Now he required their speaking. His raised face sought some word of the people.

Almost as one, then, the children of Israel said, "Far be it from us that we should forsake the Lord to serve other gods! It is the Lord our God who did great signs in our sight! He preserved us all through the wilderness. Therefore, we will serve him. Yes! He is our God!"

Joshua said, "You cannot serve him and another, too. You cannot serve him with words only, or with emotion. Israel, he is a holy God. He is a jealous God. If you forsake the Lord to serve foreign gods, he will turn and consume you after having done you good — "

"No!" cried the people. This was thunderous. It was the united voice of men and women together. In a sacred manner the entire nation had gathered at Shechem, and the whole nation cried, "No, we will serve the Lord."

Joshua said, "You are witnesses against yourselves that you have chosen the Lord."

They said, "We are witnesses."

"Then incline your whole heart to the Lord, the God of Israel."

They said again, "The Lord our God — him will we serve, and his voice will we obey."

So Joshua made a covenant with the people that day. He ordered a great stone to be set up under the oak tree in the sanctuary at Shechem, and he said, "Behold, this stone shall stand witness to all that has been said here, both for your generation and for the generations to come."

█

After these things Joshua the son of Nun, the servant of the Lord, died. He was a hundred and ten years old. They buried him in his own land, on his own inheritance at Timnath-serah, which was in the highlands of Ephraim, north of the mountain of Gaash.

Likewise, the bones of Joseph, which the people had carried with them out of Egypt, were buried at Shechem. Joseph, finally, was gathered to his people in that same portion of ground which his father Jacob had purchased from the sons of Hamor for a hundred pieces of money.

Thus he, too, after many centuries, had land and a home, and lay in it.

9

EHUD

Now, these are the nations which were left in Canaan when Israel took possession of it: the five lords of the Philistines, who controlled the southwest seacoast and the plain from Gaza to Ekron and as far inland as the foothills of Judah; the Canaanites in pockets and cities everywhere among Israel; the Sidonians on the northwest and the seacoast there; the Hivites, who dwelt on Mount Lebanon from Mount Ba'al-hermon as far as the entrance of Hamath; some Hittites; Amorites, Perizzites, and Jebusites.

As time went by, the memories of Moses and Joshua began to fade among the people. They forgot the mighty signs which God had done for them in the wilderness and even at their entering into this land. By degrees Israel slipped into sinning. They took as wives the daughters of these nations. They also gave them their daughters in marriage, and in the homes where such crossings occurred, the people began to serve foreign gods.

They served Ba'al and his consort, Asherah.

When they planted crops; when they sought the early and the late rains upon their seed; when they wished their fields to be fruitful, they went to the god who mounted the clouds, Ba'al, whose figure was a bull and whose province was fertility.

This is how the people of Canaan propitiated Ba'al: they lay with the prostitutes who represented his consort, the receptacle of seed and rain, the soil. They did for Ba'al as they desired the storm-god to do for them. It was a ritual of like to like.

The children of Israel copied this ritual and the anger of the Lord was kindled against them. God allowed enemies to arise against his own people.

∎

In those days, Eglon the king of Moab began to subdue his neighboring lands. He established an alliance with the Ammonites; he swelled his armies with warriors from the Amalekites; then he invaded the territories of Israel. He crossed the Jordan and seized territory as far west as the city of palms near old Jericho.

For eighteen years King Eglon oppressed Israel, requiring them to bring him an annual tribute of their produce. And during the last six of those years King Eglon grew fat. Each time Israelites returned from paying tribute, the description of his corpulence grew. It was said that he seldom stirred outside the courtyards of his own house.

Israel said, "He drinks our sweat. He eats the meat of our bones and swells while we are starving here! O Lord God, save us from the hand of Eglon!"

Their tears and their prayers were a repentance before the Lord. Therefore he raised up a deliverer for his people, Ehud, the son of Gera the Benjaminite.

In the eighteenth year of the rule of Moab, the people elected to send Ehud with tribute to King Eglon. And the spirit of the Lord came upon Ehud so that he fashioned for himself a sword with two edges as long as his forearm. He sewed, too, a scabbard of tough cloth and girded it under his clothing on his right thigh, because he was a left-handed man.

Then Ehud led seventy men eastward, all of them with donkeys bearing wool and wine and figs and fresh grapes and sacks of barley. They were a caravan of value. They forded the Jordan at low water and continued southwest without a guard. No one would attack them, because all the land belonged to Eglon.

The king received his tribute at a low, stone house, sitting on a bench, wide and deep. He did not rise. He scarcely acknowledged the Israelites before him. Instead he commanded his servants to relieve the donkeys of their burdens and then, without ceremony, sent the delegation away, donkeys and all.

Indeed, this was a very fat man. He wore flesh like an apron hanging down between his spread knees.

Just as the Israelites began to re-cross the Jordan, Ehud turned back toward Moab on his own.

He came again to King Eglon's house and said, "I have returned in secret to tell the king something regarding the loyalty of Israel."

A traitor is always welcome to tyrants. Therefore one of the guards checked the left side of Ehud's robe for weapons, then led him by a stone staircase to the roof of the king's house, where a cool room had been built. Within the shade of this room, Eglon sat on a wooden board through which was a hole under which was a chamber pot. Evidently the king spent much time in this place. It was surrounded by courtiers, advisors, servants, and a cook.

"Well?" said the king.

Ehud said, "The message is a secret, O King."

Eglon cried, "Silence!" to the crowd around him and invited Ehud into his small room alone.

So Ehud entered and closed the door.

"It is a matter of life and death," he said, reaching to his right side where couriers kept diplomatic correspondence.

King Eglon raised his right hand to receive a written message.

Ehud said, "I have a message from God for you" — and with his left hand he drew the double-edged sword and thrust it into the king's belly, and the hilt went in after the blade, and the fat closed over both blade and hilt so that Ehud could not withdraw the sword again. The dirt came out of Eglon and a tremendous odor filled the air.

Ehud stepped out of the small room and shut the door behind himself.

"The king is very busy," he said to the attendants, and he left.

Eglon's attendants sniffed the air and recognized what sort of business it was. Politely they waited for the king to finish. They waited until the evening. They waited until they became alarmed — and then, despite the shame, they opened the door of his chamber, and there lay their lord dead on the floor.

In the time of their delaying, Ehud had run as fast as he could to the Jordan and over the ford to Seirah. Then up and down the hills of Ephraim he went, sounding the ram's horn of war, declaring the death of King Eglon. Ehud gathered the forces of Israel to attack the leaderless armies of the oppressor.

"Follow me!" he cried, filled with the spirit of the Lord. "God has given your enemies the Moabites into your hand!"

So the men of Israel went down with him and seized the fords of the Jordan, cutting off the escape of the occupying Moabites. Then they turned and destroyed altogether the armies that had ruled among them.

So Moab was subdued that day under the hand of Israel.

And the land had rest for eighty years.

10

DEBORAH

In time the people of Israel began again to do what was evil in the sight of the Lord, and the anger of the Lord was kindled against them.

Jabin, a Canaanite king who reigned in Hazor, grew strong and subdued the northern tribes of Israel. He empowered Sisera of Harosheth-ha-goiim to command his armies — a force of nine hundred iron chariots, stupefying to the foot soldier of Israel who carried but a bronze sword — and together these two oppressed Israel for twenty years.

Jabin and Sisera controlled the Esdraelon plain, the rich valley of Jezreel which was watered by the Kishon River and which swept eastward from the sea as far as Mount Tabor, cutting the tribes of Israel nearly in two.

For fear of Jabin and Sisera, caravans avoided the Israelite highways. Trade ceased, and Israel was impoverished.

Travelers took the crooked paths, the back roads, in order to guard against attack and plunder.

Even the farmers disappeared. They were targets in the daylight. There were no crops in this rich plain. The land looked bleak and abandoned.

■

As they had before, the people of Israel repented. They cried for help unto the Lord.

So the Lord raised up for them a deliverer: Deborah, the wife of Lapidoth, a woman whose language issued from her mouth like liquid fire.

The spirit of the Lord came upon her, and she grew wise in the laws of the covenant. Beneath a palm near the cities of Ramah and Bethel, Deborah sat and resolved private disputes for the people. As a mother in Israel she judged them. Her name was spoken everywhere among the tribes. She won their admiration.

And then by the spirit of God she also began to prophesy.

Deborah sent word everywhere in Israel, south to Benjamin, near to Ephraim, north to Issachar, Zebulun, and Naphtali, saying:

> *Arise! Arise!*
> *Even peasants must take the field!*
> *For the Lord is emerging from Sinai!*
>
> *Look how the heavens*
> *crack and tremble at his coming!*
> *The earth shakes! Mountains roar before the Lord!*
>
> *Barak, arise!*
> *Man of lightning, come and take captives!*
> *For the people of God will rule the mighty, come!*

Thus Deborah summoned Barak to herself, the son of Abinoam from Kedesh in Naphtali.

When he stood before her she removed the hood of her robe and faced him bareheaded. Her hair was very long, iron-grey, and uncut — the sign of one who has made a vow before the Lord and who will not cut her hair again until the vow is fulfilled.

There was an absolute conviction in this woman. Mother in Israel, her eyes were steadfast on Barak.

She said, "The Lord commands you to gather ten thousand men on the wooded slopes of Mount Tabor. He himself will draw Sisera into the valley along the river Kishon, where you must attack the chariots. God will give the Canaanite armies into your hand. Go."

When this word had been spoken, Deborah turned away and sat again beneath her palm. She lifted the hood to cover her head, glanced up, and saw Barak still standing in the same place, staring at her.

"Well?" she said.

Barak pinched his lips and dropped his eyes.

"Sisera's chariots number nine hundred."

"Yes."

"They're made of iron. They are pulled by one and two horses each."

"Yes."

"We are on foot. We have scarcely a shield or a spear anywhere in Israel."

"I know that."

"Well," said Barak, gazing at the tips of his fingers, "if you, Deborah, will go with me, I will go. But if you will not go with me, I will not go."

Deborah let fall the hood behind her. She gathered her long hair and began to wind it into a thick rope, which she coiled around her head. All the while she looked directly at Barak.

"I will go this road with you," she said. "But it will not lead to your glory, Barak, nor to the glory of any man."

And she prophesied, saying:

> *Praise Jael.*
> *Of women, praise Jael.*
> *Of tent-living women, praise Jael*
>
> *whose left hand grips one stake of her tent,*
> *whose right hand holds a workman's hammer,*
> *whose eyes are bright on the vein in the temple*
> *of him who commands an army of chariots —*
>
> *he drives nine hundred chariots*
> *all armored in iron*
> *and heavy.*

∎

So Barak and Deborah went north to Kadesh, where they gathered farmers and fathers, shepherds, vine dressers and boys — the armies of Israel. They made no secret of their recruitment. They blew the ram's horn of war. And then they conducted a noisy march ten miles south to Mount Tabor.

All this was observed by Sisera's spies, who told him that Barak the son of Abinoam had positioned ten thousand fighting men in the forests on the southern slopes of Mount Tabor. The woods might hide them a while, but they were poorly armed and vulnerable.

Sisera wasted no time. He called out his chariots and his armies from Harosheth-ha-goiim near the sea and drove them in a swift, massive march along the river Kishon, over the Esdraelon plain toward Tabor.

Deborah sat on a high mountain crag. Through eyes as stony as the hills she watched the dust of Sisera's advance. "Wait," she murmured to Barak. "Wait. Wait. Wait — "

Suddenly there rose a cold, urgent wind. It snapped her robe and tore down the mountain, westward. At the same time a black cloud began to overshadow the river, the valley, the dust, the armies, the entire mountain.

"There," said Deborah, pointing to heaven. "There: that is the Lord." And she cried suddenly, at the top of her lungs, "Up, now! Barak, attack! The Lord goes forth before you: Go!"

So Barak led ten thousand men out of seclusion, down to the plains. They charged directly into the onrushing chariots.

And at the same time, the Lord God struck with convulsions of nature:

From heaven the stars threw spears to the earth;
from their courses they fought the chariots —
for the black cloud broke
and lightning dropped
and rain like arrows
ripped the soil —

and the river rose!

It rose like an ox
to gore the warriors,
trampled their chariots,
and drove them back to Megiddo!

Through the blinding rain and the mud that mired every chariot, Barak and his men pursued the Canaanites westward, past Megiddo, as far as Sisera's city, Harosheth, toward the sea.

But Sisera himself was not among the slaughtered.

He had leaped from his chariot and run straight north toward Hazor, the city of Jabin. But as he ran through the black rain and the furious wind he became more and more exhausted. So when he saw tents and recognized the camp of Heber, a Kenite who had made peace with Jabin, Sisera turned aside to seek some kind of asylum.

He found only women in the camp. He was comforted by that.

Moreover, when the wife of Heber heard his story, that the forces of Israel had routed his army and soon would come looking for him, she invited him into her own tent.

"Don't be afraid," she said. Her whole manner was kind and consoling.

"What if Barak comes looking for me?" Sisera said.

The woman thought a moment. She glanced around the interior of her tent, then said, "Lie on the ground. I'll cover you with a rug, and tell him that I am alone."

Sisera began to relax. "May I have a drink of water?" he asked.

The woman smiled and shook her head. "Oh, sir, better than water, I have milk to replenish your strength."

So she opened a skin of milk, and he drank until he was full. Then he lay down and she covered him completely in a new rug. The scent of the thing was homely and familiar. Very soon he fell asleep.

■|

And Deborah sang this song:

> *Most blessed of women is Jael*
> *the wife of a Kenite!*
> *Of tent-dwelling women give praise*
> *to this one, Jael:*
>
> *when the enemy begged for cover*
> *she offered a rug;*
> *when Sisera asked for water*
> *she gave him milk;*
>
> *she brought him the sweet curd*
> *in a king's bowl,*
> *and laid him down in safety*
> *and he slept.*
>
> *Jael: she kneels beside him,*
> *a stake at his temple.*
> *Jael: she raises a mallet,*
> *and her rug blooms*
> *a bright round flower of blood.*
>
> *Now through her window a woman is looking;*
> *the mother of Sisera calls through her lattice:*
> *"Why does he tarry? Where is his chariot?*
>
> *"Perhaps they're dividing the spoils of Israel.*
> *Shirts dyed purple, shirts embroidered:*
> *perhaps there's a shirt for the neck of my son...."*

So Jabin and Sisera were subdued that day. Their yoke was lifted from the people of Israel.

And Deborah returned to her palm tree between Ramah and Bethel in the hill country of Ephraim. She covered her head and began again to judge the people.

And the land had rest for forty years.

11

GIDEON

The people of Israel did what was evil in the sight of the Lord.

A farmer named Joash, of the tribe of Manasseh, built an altar to Ba'al. He lived not more than twenty miles southwest of Mount Tabor. Beside the altar he erected a tall wooden pole upon which was carved the image of Asherah, swelling goddess of fertility. Joash still called on the name of the Lord; yet, at seedtime he also made judicious appeals to Ba'al and Asherah. So did most of his clan, the Abiezerites. So did many in Israel.

But just as the fields that had been planted under a pagan ritual grew ripe to the harvest, a wild desert people came riding from regions east of the Salt Sea. Midianites! They terrified Israel. Riding monsters as swift as the wind, they appeared at dawn, seized the fresh grain, trampled the standing crops, burned the fields, killed peasants from the backs of their impossible beasts, and disappeared again before the dusk.

Camels — they rode *camels*! They reached *down* to club the skulls of Israel. They covered more than sixty miles in a day. And they were able to bear enormous quantities of produce away, two hundred miles away. The distance once protected Israel. But Midian had learned to ride camels.

They returned the following year, again at the harvest. This time they slaughtered the livestock, too, leaving not a sheep nor an ox behind.

Next the Midianites came with their tents. Like locusts they swarmed over the Jordan, too many to count, feeding off the green land and driving many Israelites into the mountains to hide in caves and strongholds.

So it went for seven years.

And the people of Israel cried for help to the Lord.

One night, under cover of darkness, someone came and pulled down the altar which Joash the Abiezerite had built for Ba'al. In the morning people found the old stones scattered; but new stones had been laid to form another altar — upon which one of Joash's bulls had already been sacrificed. And the wood that burned the sacrifice was the pole of the image of Asherah. Her face had turned to ashes.

The people said to one another, "Who did this thing?"

∎

Now, one of the sons of Joash, Gideon, was threshing wheat in a square stone pit as deep as his chest.

This was his father's wine vat. In better times he would be singing here, roaring happy songs with other men as they trod the grapes, and as the sweet juice flowed down channels to lower, cooler vats. In better times he would be threshing grain on a high, open ground with the help of his ox and his children. For the ox would pull the threshing sledge while his children gave it weight and laughed while he led them round and round on piles of stalks, separating the hard, good kernel from the chaff.

But these were bad times. Midian might sweep down at any moment. Gideon was hiding. He was beating the stalks with a stick and a flail, threshing in the old way, crouching lower than the walls of his pit, hoping no one noticed.

Suddenly, he heard a voice and he dropped to the ground.

The voice was melodious, like strong music. It came from an oak near the winepress. It said: "The Lord is with you, you mighty man of valor."

Mighty man of valor. Gideon hoped it meant someone else. But he feared it meant himself. Slowly he rose to his knees and peered over the edge of the vat. Chaff stuck to his sweaty chest.

Yes, it meant him.

For there beneath the oak sat a man of regal appearance. Gazing straight back at Gideon. Smiling, seeming well contented.

Gideon, hiding all but his eyes below the stone, said, "What are you talking about?"

"Go," intoned the marvelous figure, speaking to Gideon; there was no one else in sight. "Go in this might of yours, and deliver Israel from the hand of Midian "

Gideon considered the man and the madness of his utterance.

All at once he jumped up and shouted, "Did someone tell you it was me? Well, it wasn't! I'm not the sort that dishonors his father. Besides, I'm nothing. I'm no one. Look at me: Gideon, the least of the little clan in the weakest of tribes — "

"Isn't it I who send you?" said the smiling figure. His voice had the force of mountain water. "I will be with you."

"I hated that altar," Gideon pleaded. "The face of Asherah frightens me."

"I will be with you," the voice rolled on: "And you shall smite the Midianites as one man."

Gideon swallowed and fell silent.

The two men looked at each other a while.

Then Gideon said, "I am going to bring you something to eat. Please don't leave while I am gone."

The man said, "I will stay till you return."

So Gideon went into his house and prepared a young kid and unleavened cakes. He put the meat in a basket and the broth in a pot, and brought it all to the man who sat beneath the oak.

The man said, "Lay the meat and the cakes directly on this rock."

Gideon did so.

The man said, "Now, pour the broth over them."

Gideon did.

Then the man reached with the tip of his staff and touched the food. Immediately fire shot from the rock and consumed the meat and the cakes together, and the man vanished.

"Alas!" cried Gideon. "Alas, O Lord God! I have seen the angel of the Lord face-to-face — "

But the voice of the Lord, the voice of many cataracts said, *Be at peace, Gideon. You will not die. But go. For haven't the Midianites and the Amalekites and the people of the East all come together and crossed the Jordan? Yes, and even now they are encamping in the valley of Jezreel.*

That night Gideon did not return to his house. A solitary man, he sat on the wall of his father's wine vat, staring at a pile of new fleeces which lay on the stone floor exactly where he had been threshing wheat that day.

"If you will deliver Israel by my hand," Gideon prayed, "then give me a sign. Let the fleece be wet in the morning, but all the floor around it dry."

And so it was. At sunrise Gideon wrung enough dew from the fleece to fill a bowl. But he stared at that bowl all morning long, and by the afternoon, when the wool was still moist, he was thinking that wool would naturally hold water longer than stone.

So that night he put the fleece back in the same spot.

"Don't be angry with me," Gideon prayed. "Let me make just one more trial. This time, O Lord, let the fleece be dry and all the ground around it wet with dew."

Gideon sat vigil over the pile a second night through, and in the morning the fleece was dry. All the ground around was wet with dew.

∎|

The spirit of the Lord came upon Gideon the son of Joash. It filled him as a body fills a garment — and Gideon sounded the horn of war, and the clan of Abiezer rose up ready to fight.

Likewise, Gideon sent messengers throughout Manasseh and Asher and Zebulun and Naphtali. Men came from all four tribes with tents and weapons to follow him.

This army Gideon led to the spring of Harod, somewhat south of the hill where Midian lay encamped in a valley.

That same day the Lord spoke to Gideon.

The people with you are too many, lest Israel should boast in victory, said the Lord. Therefore, tell those who are afraid that they may go home.

Gideon did as the Lord said, and twenty-two thousand men went home. Ten thousand remained.

Again the Lord said, *They are still too many. They will think it was their hand that delivered them. Therefore, march your armies to the water and command them to drink.*

Gideon did so, and while the men were drinking the Lord said, *Those that put their hands in the water and lap as dogs do, count them and keep them. Those that kneel, send them home.*

Nine thousand seven hundred men had kneeled down to drink! That left only three hundred! Gideon felt as if he were back in his wine vat, helpless and small and frightened.

But the Lord said, *With three hundred will I give the Midianites into your hand. Tell the others to leave their jars and their trumpets behind and to depart before the darkness.*

That night Gideon led his small band to the ridge overlooking the valley where Midian lay encamped. Their red fires filled the dark as stars fill the heavens. They made a constant noise, like crawling insects in the night, like bees in their hive.

The Lord said, *Arise, O mighty man of valor, and go against the camp.*

Gideon said, "It is the night, Lord! No one fights in darkness."

The Lord said, *I have given the enemy into your hand.*

"O Lord! O Lord God, you have reduced us to nothing before this horde, and I am not a mighty man. I have always been afraid."

Look, then, little man, said the Lord, and in a vision Gideon became aware of a small barley cake tumbling down the hillside into the camp of Midian. It rolled toward a tent and bumped it — and the tent was knocked so hard that it turned upside down and fell flat to the ground.

You, Gideon, are that barley cake, said the Lord. *Obey me now, and go.*

In darkness, then, Gideon issued each of his men a ram's horn, a hollow jar, and a torch. While they were yet close before him he whispered their orders: "Whatever I do, do likewise," he said. "When I blow my horn, blow yours exactly where you stand. Shatter your jars and light your torches and shout, *A sword for the Lord and Gideon.*"

Gideon divided the three hundred men into three companies, and sent them north and west and south of the valley, until they became a thin invisible loop in the hills surrounding Midian.

In the tents of the Midianites, one hundred and thirty-five thousand warriors slept in the assurance of their great numbers. Watch fires burned at intervals throughout the wide installation, ten thousand of those. Camels were gathered in great herds, the easier to feed — five thousand corrals, a hundred thousand head. And men stood watch around the entire perimeter, gazing out into the darkness, expecting nothing.

Then, just as guards went forth to start the middle watch, a single horn wailed in the hills west of the camp, a snarling irascible sound, as if it were a wild beast upon its prey.

The watchmen of Midian turned. *Who prowls the darkness blowing a ram's horn?*

But other horns joined their voices to the first. As if the sound were a fire, it raced left and right around the hills, violent, loud, predatory. *Who fights in the night?* Naked Midianites started to step out of their tents. *Who hazards a perfect darkness? What madness is this?*

Suddenly, from all the hills around the camp, great crashings and shatterings came down. *What? What?* cried Midian, seizing swords and spears. *What army is charging down the slopes at us?*

Now torches were exposed on high, a ring of flame encircling Midian, and human throats were bellowing: "A sword for the Lord and Gideon," and all the warriors of the Midianites were awake, now, crying: *They've cut us off! Even their rear guard is swarming down the hills! Fight! Fight! Fight!*

But those whom Midian slaughtered were their brothers. Terrified by the night attack, sightless, fearing infiltration, they slew whomever came near. They killed each other. Gideon bellowed on the hillside and then watched Midian destroy itself, until there were no more than fifteen thousand left.

These fifteen thousand he pursued.

In the next days, Gideon followed them as far as Karkor, which was their own city. They considered themselves safe. The miserable army collapsed and began to rest — when suddenly Gideon appeared above them, even here, throwing them again into such a whining panic that he beat them with the edge of his own sword.

There Gideon captured two kings of the Midianites, Zebah and Zalmunna. He bound them and carried them home and set them up before himself in the square stone wine vat.

"If you had not slain my kin," Gideon said to them, "I would not slay you now. But in the day you chose death for Israel, you chose death for yourselves. Jether!" Gideon called. "Jether, come here."

A slim, beautiful youth stepped forward, both solemn and scared.

Gideon said to Zebah and Zalmunna, "This is my firstborn." And then to the lad Gideon said, "And these men are your task. Kill them."

Young Jether walked slowly toward the Midianite kings. He took the hilt of his sword in his right hand and drew it. His arm was lean. It shook uncontrollably. His face remained solemn, but his huge eyes developed tears. He raised the wobbly sword over his head — and there he stopped.

"Sir!" cried Zebah, and it became evident that he, too, was in anguish. "Sir, we are kings. You have already debased us by placing us in a wine vat. But to execute us by the hand of a beardless boy — "

Poor Jether lifted his eyes to his father in piteous agreement.

Zebah said, "Rise yourself and fall upon us — for as a man is, so is his strength."

With a horrible bellow, Gideon leaped into the pit and slew Zebah and Zalmunna in two strokes, and there was an end to it.

But in remembrance of the time of his might, Gideon kept among his own possessions the crescents that once had hung on the necks of the camels of the kings of Midian.

■

The men of Israel said to Gideon, "Rule over us, you and your son and your grandson, too. You have delivered us from the hand of Midian. Why not continue the peace for the generations that will come after us?"

Gideon said to them, "I will not rule over you. And my son will not rule over you. The Lord alone rules over you."

So Midian was subdued. Neither their kings nor their people returned to cause harm in Israel anymore. And through all the days of Gideon thereafter, the land had rest: forty years, a generation.

12

JEPHTHAH

i

After Gideon there arose to deliver Israel Tola, the son of Puah, a man of the tribe of Issachar. He lived at Shamir in the hill country of Ephraim. He judged Israel twenty-three years, and when he died he was buried where he had lived, at Shamir.

After Tola arose Jair the Gileadite, who judged Israel twenty-two years. He is remembered as a man of wealth, for he had thirty sons who rode on thirty asses and who governed thirty cities in the land of Gilead. Jair died and was buried in Kamon.

Again the people of Israel did what was evil in the sight of the Lord. The pattern of their behavior became like a wheel rolling. Over and over again, when the generation that had known and obeyed the Lord passed away, the next one would forget him and seek the peculiar power of some other god.

Then, inevitably, the wheel turned and Israel would suffer at the hand of a new enemy, who gathered strength against them, troubled them, subdued them, and taught them how weak was their hold on the land after all.

So Israel would remember the Lord their God, and would cry unto him for deliverance. That was the third turn of the wheel. Marvelous in mercy was the Lord! He always turned the wheel its fourth time, completing a full revolution and bringing his people back to peace and rest again. For the Lord God grew indignant over the misery of Israel. Again and again, upon their prayer, he sent his spirit into someone and raised up a deliverer for his people Israel.

ii

So after Jair had died, and after the land had rest for more than a generation, the people of Israel again did what was evil in the sight of the Lord.

Then the Ammonites, perceiving a weakness, sought opportunity to regain territory they had lost long ago when their great King Og had been defeated by Moses of the Israelites. They raised a large army and marched into Gilead, east of Jordan, where they encamped and prepared to attack Israel.

The elders of Israel in Gilead came together at Mizpah, but there was no one among them capable of dramatic military leadership.

"What man can fight the Ammonites?" they said. "Let him lead us now, and we will give him headship over all the inhabitants of Gilead hereafter!"

Now, Jephthah was a mighty warrior. He dwelt in the southeastern regions of Gilead with a band of wild fellows. His father had been a man of wealth and reputation, but his mother was a whore. Therefore, he had been driven out by the legitimate children of his father and had made his own reputation as a free man, a rider, a raider, a soldier of fortune.

Unto Jephthah the elders of Gilead turned, "Come and be our leader," they said. "Fight the Ammonites for us."

As it was, Jephthah liked his life. He had a house in Tob, east of Ramoth-gilead. He had one child, a daughter, who loved him and for whom he had built the house in the first place.

But the elders were offering him the lifetime leadership of all the clans of Gilead.

In the evening he went into his daughter's room and sat down beside her. "Those that hated me are humbling themselves before me," he said. "Those that drove me out as a bastard are now begging me to be their judge. How can I say no?"

Father and daughter sat in dim light a while. She was a lovely maiden with slender fingers.

"You can't say no," she said.

Jephtha said, "But I will be gone a long time."

His daughter kissed his forehead and said, "Go."

In the morning he and his men rode to Mizpah with a roaring, fierce delight. Jephthah had no doubt that the Lord, the God of all the tribes of Israel, had reached down and lifted him from his low degree to this exalted position.

Indeed, the spirit of the Lord came upon Jephthah, and he gathered armies from Gilead and Manasseh and Israel, and just before he marched them into war against the Ammonites, he made a vow to the Lord.

"O Lord, my best for your best," he said. "If you give me this victory, then I will give you the first good thing that meets me when I return! I will burn it as an offering to you."

The adventurer laughed a laugh of such spectacular anticipation that not a warrior in Israel was fainthearted thereafter. Jephthah raised a thunderous shout and led them into battle.

He crossed over to the Ammonites, attacked them, and the Lord gave them into his hand. He smote them from Aroer to the neighborhood of Minnith, twenty cities, and as far as Abel-keramim with a very great slaughter.

Then Jephthah the Gileadite returned to his house. And behold, his daughter came out to meet him with timbrels and with dancing. She was his only child.

iii

THE MAIDEN SPEAKS

Her Seventh Day

My flow began today. The way of women is upon me. In these last weeks I had forgotten that it would come. But the times have not changed my body. Of course it would come.

Milcah, do you think the times have changed the law for me? Will I have to sacrifice two turtledoves in eight days in order to purge myself again?

But for me there shall not be an eighth day.

∎

Her Sixth Day

They carve in stone the laws that govern the nations!

They raise marble obelisks upon which to write the histories of great and bloody battles! Kings who triumph want their triumphs remembered.

Covenants are baked into an everlasting clay.

Even the transactions of wealthy men are etched in tablets and preserved.

O eternal God, let this also be inscribed in stone, for it is as monumental as any battle that any man has ever fought to the death: that Jephthah's daughter wept because of a word her father spoke. His speaking stopped her womb forever.

Jephthah's daughter howls in the mountains because no child shall ever call her Mother.

Write this in stone and save it: that at the end of all battles, Jephthah's daughter dies a virgin.

∎

Her Fifth Day

But how can a daughter blame her father?

This is true: a man need not make a vow. Nothing compels him.

But if he chooses nonetheless, and if he makes his vow before the living Lord, then he must keep it. After the oath has been established, there is no longer a choice. There is only obedience and the deed. Or what is a covenant for?

But the world is always larger than the man, always larger than his knowing or his ability to know. And his vow binds him to the universe. It causes wheels to grind that he can no longer stop.

The man who forgets this largeness — he shall suffer when his oath returns to him with a strange face and a fateful consequence.

How, then, can a daughter blame her father? He is as sad as she is now.

Ah, he was ignorant. He did not know.

∎

Her Fourth Day

He loves me! He loves me! He has always loved me!

He built a beautiful house for me.

He set it on a stone foundation exactly where I paced the sides for it, and I asked that my house look like all the houses of Israel, and it does!

He said, "Where shall I build it?"

And I said, "On a hill!"

So he built its walls of a baked mud brick laid in perfect rows. He plastered the outside and whitewashed it. My house is radiant! It catches a golden evening light.

When you enter the doorway you stand in a lovely little court. There is not much room for flowers, but the sunlight comes down from above, and I have my oven there, my own *tabun*, where I prepare food for the two of us.

On the right side of the court are four strong posts and an open room. On the left is the door to my room. In the back is the door to his.

I chose to dress in his room.

On the day when they said he was come home again, I went into his room and put on clean white linen — his room because I wanted to smell his scent. I was filled with such joy for him!

I planned to follow custom, to go out dancing as Miriam danced when the Egyptians were defeated at the Sea. Hadn't my father defeated the Ammonites?

So when I heard his mount coming up the long road to our little house, I laughed. I laughed aloud and grabbed my timbrel and ran outside to meet him, dancing.

▌

Her Third Day

My father's mother was a concubine and an outcast. Yet she had a child, and her child loved her and took care of her until she died.

I am not a concubine. I am not an outcast.

But I shall die with no children at all.

▌

Her Second Day

Sisters, sisters, come and sit by this stream a while. We will be home soon.

The Lord has watched our going and now our coming. No one has harmed us, though there was no other guard to protect us. Seven women, walking the mountain roads two months long in safety. My father has brought peace to the land. The highways are free of raiders now. Yes. Peace.

I'm thirsty.

Thank you, Milcah.

Oh, don't cry! We have cried. We've cried through seven Sabbaths, and when you cry I begin to cry all over again, too.

Here. Drink water from my cup.

It is surely a grief we grieve, isn't it? — though no one has died.

You say: *But you shall die.*

Yes, but I say, *But I do not cry for that.*

Sisters, I cry no differently than any woman whose child was taken from her by war or by famine, by sickness or by the bloody sins of men. We cry for absent children. They cry for the one that is no more; I cry for the one that shall never be.

Ah, sisters, I lament for us all! I lament the bearing itself! The travail that promises such joys and delivers such sorrows. I lament this, that we can and do and must bear — but may never hold one good thing still and here in the crook of our arm forever.

I cry that every birth is the beginning of death.

No, no, no, no, my father hath gotten us no peace at all in the land, no peace whatsoever.

Come.

Let's walk before I find the words for cursing.

◼

Her Last Day

Milcah, wake up. It will be dawn in an hour. I want to ask two things of you before we have to separate.

Please remember me. This is the first thing.

Perhaps in the years to come you might lift your eyes to these mountains and remember that we wandered here and that we lamented together, yes? Milcah, my friend, I love you.

I must go and bathe while it is still dark and I am alone. You stay here. I must wash my clothes and anoint myself and so prepare to meet my father. He is there. He is in the little house, waiting.

And this is the second thing I have to ask you:

Will you take care of my father when I cannot? If you agree, you must swear to serve him not only for my sake, but also for his.

Because he loves me, Milcah. That was never in doubt. From the beginning my father has loved me completely, and he will only love me the more tomorrow.

Therefore, you must be there when the sun arises and he looks out to see what has changed in the world.

iv

As Jephthah the Gileadite, after having destroyed the Ammonites, approached his home in high spirits and laughter, he heard a small, sweet laughter in the distance, mixing with his. It quickened his heart.

Then, to his even greater joy, he saw his daughter emerge from the house in long white linen, laughing, striking a timbrel, and dancing.

Almost he kicked his mount into a gallop.

But the Lord said, *She is the one. As I have given you a victory, so shall you give this child to me as the burnt offering of your vow.*

"Alas!" cried Jephthah. Laughter and dancing died together. "Oh, my daughter, you have brought me very low!"

The child stood transfixed by the horror in her father's voice. He dismounted and walked to her on foot. As he went, he told her his vow in every sad particular: *the first good thing that meets me.*

Softly she set down her timbrel. "Father, let this thing be done for me," she said. "But let me alone two months that I may wander on the mountains, I and my companions, and bewail my virginity."

He said, "Go."

And she departed, to return at the end of her appointed time.

▌

Jephthah the Gileadite judged Israel six years. Then he died and was buried in a city in Gilead.

After Jephthah, Ibzan of Bethlehem judged Israel. He had thirty sons and thirty daughters. He gave his daughters in marriage outside of his own clan and brought thirty women in from the outside for his sons. He judged Israel seven years, then he died.

After him, Elon the Zebulunite judged Israel. He judged Israel ten years, then died and was buried at Aijalon in the land of Zebulun.

After him, Abdon the son of Hillel the Pirathonite judged Israel. He had forty sons and thirty grandsons who rode on seventy asses, a wealthy man. He judged Israel eight years.

13

S<small>AMSON</small>

In those days Israelites north and south began to tell stories of a mighty man who came from the village of Zorah, of the tribe of Dan. It was said that he had never cut his hair in his life, for that was his vow before the Lord. In return, God had bestowed upon him more strength than the lion or the ox.

What flowing hair the man must have! Like a black robe blowing, when he lets it down.

His name was Samson. Named for the sun. And he was as cunning as he was strong, for single-handedly this hero could distress the Philistines, enemies of Israel.

Oh, it stirred their blood to hear of his adventures. It made them proud and it caused them laughter, both at once.

█I

Once upon a time Samson was in the Philistine town of Timnah. There he spied a maid so lovely that his heart grew sick on account of her.

He rushed home to Zorah and said to his parents, "Get her as a wife for me."

His parents said, "Samson, don't take a wife from the uncircumcised Philistines. Look among your own people."

But Samson's heart ached and he could not forget the maiden. So he went by himself to Timnah to speak with her father about a marriage.

On the way a young lion roared against him, and the spirit of the Lord stirred mightily within him, and he tore the lion as one tears a kid, breaking its joints apart. He left it dead and continued on.

The second time he saw the maiden, she pleased him even more than the first. With passion and eloquence, then, Samson persuaded her father to grant him his daughter in marriage.

*Remembering his parents' objections, Samson said, "Let it be a sadiga," —
a marriage in which the wife remains home with her family and the husband
visits from time to time.*

*Now, while he was traveling from Zorah to Timnah for the wedding feast,
he noticed the carcass of the lion he had killed, that bees were swarming
around it. He looked closely and found a hive in the lion's bones, and honey
in the hive. Samson scraped honey into his hands and continued to Timnah,
eating as he went.*

*The wedding feast lasted seven days, at the end of which the formal acts of
marriage would be accomplished. In the meantime there was dance and food
and merriment. Thirty Philistine men came to celebrate with Samson.*

*On the first day, Samson proposed a game. "Let me put a riddle to you,"
he said. "If you can guess it before the end of the seventh day, I will give you
thirty linen garments and thirty festal garments, too. But if you can't, you
must give me the thirty and thirty."*

There was wine, and there was gladness.

The Philistine men said, "Put your riddle to us."

Samson grinned and said:

> *"Out of the eater, something to eat;*
> *out of the strong one, something sweet."*

*The thirty companions laughed and returned to their wine. In private they
discussed the riddle, but none could guess its meaning. Not the first day, nor
the second, nor the third.*

*On the fourth day they took the bride aside and said, "Either you find the
meaning of Samson's riddle, or we will burn your father's house with fire."*

*On the fifth day the maiden came to Samson and burst into tears. "You don't
love me," she said. "How could you keep secrets from me if you loved me?"*

"What secrets?" Samson said.

"The riddle you put to my countrymen. That one."

"But that's a riddle, not a secret," he said.

But she only wept the louder.

*On the sixth day the maiden refused to speak to Samson. This caused his
heart such sorrow that he told her the meaning of the riddle.*

*On the seventh day, exactly at sundown, when the husband and the wife
were preparing to enter a private chamber to consummate their marriage,
thirty companions cried out together, "Israelite! We know the meaning of
your riddle!"*

"What is it?" said Samson.

And the Philistine men said:

"What is sweeter than the bee?
Or the lion, stronger than he?"

Samson glanced at the woman beside him, hidden in veils; then in a low,
cold voice he spoke to the Philistines: "If you had not plowed with my heifer,
you would never have discovered my riddle! But I will keep my promise to
you in my own way!"

Samson bolted from the wedding house. The spirit of the Lord came upon
him and he went to Ashkelon, where he killed thirty men and took their spoil.
That same night he returned to Timneh with thirty festal garments, and then
he went home to Zorah in a rage.

∎

There were five lords of the Philistine people, each controlling a strong
walled city: Gaza, Ashkelon, and Ashdod on the coast of the Great Sea west
of Dan; Gath, in the foothills of Judah, and Ekron, six miles inland.

Hundreds of years ago when the children of Israel were still wandering
in the wilderness, the Philistines had been a marauding, seagoing people,
bold enough to invade Egypt. Egyptian armies had repelled them; but then,
even as Moses was marching against Sihon and Og east of the Jordan, the
Philistines began to seize cities north of the Negev and to destroy the people
who inhabited them. Therefore, Israel and Philistia had entered Canaan at
the same time, one from the wilderness, one from the sea.

The children of Israel chose to work the soil, to herd flocks, and to live in
a loose federation of tribes.

The Philistines, on the other hand, gathered in whitewashed cities where
they developed military aristocracies, hierarchies of power. Altogether they
became a society formed for war, training their sons already in childhood
to fight.

Israel plowed as farmers had plowed for ages, behind the slow ox with a
wooden plowshare sheathed in bronze.

Philistia was learning a new thing: how to work iron. And the lords of the
Philistines were beginning to make weapons of iron.

∎

It was just at the start of the wheat harvest when Samson's heart again grew
sick for his Philistine wife, with whom he had never yet lain.

So he took a kid for a meal of reconciliation and traveled to Timnah, to
her house.

Samson was about to enter, when her father met him at the door and
prevented him.

"She is not here," he said.

"Then I will wait for her," Samson said.

The old man hung his head. "No, she is never coming back."

"Then where can I find her?"

"What could I do?" the old man said. "I really thought you hated her."

"I do not hate my wife. Where is she, that I might lie with her now?"

"Son, it would have disgraced us if there had been no marriage at the end of the feast."

Samson began to frown. The cords in his neck stood out. "What did you do?" he said.

"Please, son, her younger sister is fairer than she. Take her sister instead."

"What, old man? What did you do?"

"I gave your wife to the best man and she married him."

Slowly, Samson gathered his hair into seven locks and tied them back from his face. "This time," he said, "I shall be blameless in regard to the Philistines."

Then he went and took torches and caught three hundred foxes. He tied them tail to tail with a torch between each pair. And that night he set the torches afire and released the foxes, and they ran throughout the standing grain of the Philistines, burning the fields, exploding the shocks that had already been tied, and leaping even to the olive orchards.

Seeing the flames, the Philistines cried, "Who has done this to us?"

And they said, "Samson! The son-in-law of the Timnite, because he took his wife and gave her to another!"

Therefore they seized both her and her father and began to burn them with fire.

But Samson, who was returning with another kid, heard the screams of the woman he had married, and in a rage he smote the Philistines hip and thigh, a very great slaughter.

Then he ran from their land to a cleft of rock in Etam, which was in the territory of Judah. There he hid himself while an army of several thousand Philistines went looking for him.

▌

There were no kings in Israel in those days, only the judges whom the Lord sometimes appointed as leaders of his people in times of crisis.

In contrast, each of the five cities of the Philistines was ruled by a tyrant who held complete authority. Moreover, these five lords were capable of joining into a single force for war. And in these latter days that expediency looked more and more likely, for they had a complex system of trade routes to protect, and their populations were growing larger and hungrier every year.

Israel had rich valleys, vineyards, orchards, herds, and fields. But Israel had no standing army. Her warriors were her farmers. Philistia had weapons of iron. And her citizens were an army. The lords of the Philistines, considering it infinitely more efficient to take than trade, now began to arm themselves.

In the night-time, therefore, in the privacy of their houses, the Israelites increased their confidence and courage by telling stories of their national hero.

■

Once upon a time an army of a thousand Philistines entered the territory of Judah, breathing threats of war.

The men of Judah were terrified.

"Why have you come up against us?" they said.

The Philistines said, "We have come to bind Samson the Danite, to take him back and to do to him what he did to us."

So the men of Judah asked among themselves and discovered that Samson was hiding in Etam.

They went to him, saying, "What is the matter with you? Why have you put us in such danger? You know we can't win a war against the Philistines."

Samson said, "I have never done more to them than they did to me."

The men of Judah said, "That is nothing to us. We have come to bind you and to give you into their hands."

Samson said, "Kinsmen, do one thing for me."

"What thing?"

"Swear that whatever happens, you will not fall on me yourselves."

"We swear, we will not kill you," they said.

So he came forward and allowed them to bind him with two new ropes, and they led him up from the rock to the Philistines.

Then, just as the army of the Philistines closed in around their prisoner with shouting and triumph, the spirit of the Lord came upon Samson, and his ropes became like flax in flames: they snapped. He saw on the ground the jawbone of an ass and seized it, and with that weapon Samson slew a thousand men, the entire army.

Then he mounted a hill and cried out:

> *"With the jawbone of an ass I made an army red!*
> *With the jawbone of an ass a thousand men are dead!"*

So the place was called Ramath-lehi: The Hill of the Jaw-bone.

■

But for some of the Israelites, tales of a single hero were no comfort at all. These people hated the waste. They considered such stories to be a dangerous diversion, because they provided only a false hope while covering up the actual danger which the Philistines were becoming to Israel.

These Israelites asked the realistic questions: "When their armies attack, who will fight for us?"

"The Lord," was the answer. "The Lord has always raised up leaders for us."

"Yes, and until then we remain twelve tribes who sometimes talk and who sometimes don't. How often has a leader been able to bind all twelve tribes into a single fighting army? Never! There are always some who refuse to fight."

"But the few who fought, haven't they always won the victory?"

"This is a new enemy. He fights with iron. He comes under captains who were born to slaughter Israelites."

"The Lord God himself is our captain."

"Yes, the Lord! And didn't the Lord also say that he made us a nation? Look around, children. We are no nation! Nothing unifies us — nothing and no one. We need a king."

"No! Gideon said it long ago: the Lord must rule as king among us."

"We need a king, to train men in fighting, to give us continual leadership and a center like other nations — or else we will die on the point of an iron sword!"

∎

Once upon a time Samson fell in love with a Philistine woman named Delilah, and he went in and lay with her.

When the lords of the Philistines learned that Samson regularly slept with Delilah, they came to her and said, "If you can tell us where his strength abides, so that we can bind him and subdue him, we will each give you eleven hundred pieces of silver."

Late one night Delilah said to Samson, "Please tell me where your great strength lies."

Samson smiled and said, "Bind me with seven fresh bowstrings, new and never dried, and then I shall be as weak as any other man."

He stretched himself out on her couch and fell asleep.

Immediately, Delilah told Philistine soldiers what he had said. They brought her seven bowstrings which had not been dried, and she bound Samson with them, wrist and ankle, and then she cried out, "Samson! The Philistines are upon you!"

But when he woke he snapped the bowstrings as a thread snaps in fire, and he struck the soldiers unconscious. So the secret of his strength was not known.

On the following night Delilah said, "Bowstrings don't weaken you, do they, Samson? Bowstrings have nothing to do with it, do they?"

"No," he said.

"What binds you then?" Delilah asked.

And Samson said, "Ropes, Delilah. New ropes, never used, shall make me weak like any other man."

So when he had fallen asleep, she took new ropes and bound him arms and legs, neck and thigh. She invited soldiers into her inner chamber, and she cried out, "Samson! The Philistines are upon you!"

But he snapped the ropes like thread and dispatched these soldiers as he had their brothers.

The next night Delilah fell to sobbing. She wept piteously and said, "Until now you have mocked me and told me lies. Tell me, Samson, how you might be bound."

Samson said to her, "If you weave the seven locks of my head with the web of a loom and make it tight with the pin, then I shall become weak, like any other man."

So while he slept Delilah took the seven locks of his head and wove them into the web. She made them tight with the pin and then cried out, "Samson! Samson, the Philistines are upon you!"

But he awoke from his sleep and pulled away the pin, the loom, the beam, and the web.

So then Delilah slapped the man in the face and grew angry. "How can you say you love me," she cried, "when your heart is not with me? You have mocked me three times. Three times you have lied about your strength. When will you ever tell me the truth?"

And when she pressed him hard day after day, and urged him, his soul was vexed to death, and he told her all his mind.

"A razor has never come upon my head, not since I left my mother's womb. If I am shaved, then my strength will leave me, and I shall become weak, like any other man."

When Delilah saw that he had told her all his mind, she sent for the lords of the Philistines, saying, "Come at once."

Then the lords came to her and brought the money in their hands.

In the night she caused Samson to sleep on her knees, and she called a man to shave off the seven locks of his head.

Then she began to torment Samson, and his strength left him.

She whispered in his ear, "The Philistines, Samson. The Philistines are upon you."

He tried as before to break free, but he could not.

So the Philistines seized him and gouged out his eyes and brought him down to the city of Gaza and bound him with bronze fetters and set him to turning the millstone in the prison, like any ox.

As the years passed the hair of his head began to grow again.

Then came the day when the lords of the Philistines gathered to offer a great *sacrifice to their god, Dagon.*

And when their hearts were merry they said, "Call Samson! Let him make sport for us!"

So Samson was brought from prison into the magnificent house of Dagon. They commanded him to stand between the pillars of the temple, where everyone could see him, those on the ground, those in balconies, and those who lay on the roof — about three thousand people.

Samson, raising his blind eyes, heard the roar of three thousand throats and felt their heavy breath upon him. He put out his hands until he found two pillars, and he asked the lad who led him, "Are these the pillars that the whole house rests on?"

The lad said, "Yes."

So Samson prayed, "Lord God, remember me and strengthen me only this once, that I may be avenged upon the Philistines for one of my two eyes."

Then he grasped the pillars and leaned his weight against them, his right hand on the one, his left hand on the other. And crying out, "Let me die with the Philistines," Samson bowed with all his might, and the temple fell upon the lords and upon all the people that were in it.

So the dead whom he slew at his death were more than all those whom he had slain during his life.

These are the stories of Samson, hero of the Israelites.

14

THE LEVITE'S CONCUBINE

In those days there was no king in Israel. People did what was right in their own eyes, and tribes were not always friendly one to another.

Now, the concubine of a certain Levite became angry with him and ran away to her father's house in Bethlehem of Judah. She was young. She stayed there four months without returning.

Though she was no more than a concubine, purchased from an impoverished family, the Levite had developed an affection for the girl. So he arose and went after her, planning to speak kindly to her and to bring her home again.

For two days he traveled south through foreign territory with one servant and two donkeys.

When the girl's father saw him coming, he ran out with joy and invited the Levite to stay a while. So the man ate and drank and lodged there. By the end of three days he had persuaded his concubine to come home of her own will. Therefore they decided to leave early on the fourth day.

But that morning the father said to his son-in-law, "Strengthen your heart with a morsel of bread, and after that you may go."

So the two men ate and drank together, and the time passed, and soon it was the middle of the afternoon. When the Levite and his concubine rose to go, her father said, "The day has sunk into the evening. Stay one more night. Let your heart be merry and tomorrow you may rise early for the journey."

But the man had made up his mind. He saddled his donkeys and left Bethlehem, his concubine, his servant, and himself, traveling north.

As they were passing Jerusalem, the servant said, "Let's turn aside and spend the night in this city."

But the Levite said, "This city belongs to Jebusites. We cannot stay in a city of foreigners."

So they continued until they came into territory of Israel, land held by the tribe of Benjamin — and just at dusk they arrived at the city of Gibeah. They entered there and sat down in the open square, but no one offered them lodging for the night.

Finally an old man came in from his work in the field. He was an Ephraimite sojourning among the Benjaminites. When he saw the Levite and the girl, he said, "Where are you going?"

The Levite said, "Into the hill country of Ephraim, where my home is. But no one here will take us into his house. We have bread and wine enough for everyone. There is no lack of anything."

The old man said, "Peace be to you. I will care for all your wants. Come, stay with me."

So he brought them to his house and gave the asses provender; and they washed their feet and ate and drank.

But in the darkness the young men of Gibeah, wicked fellows, surrounded the house and beat on the door.

"Old man!" they cried. "Send out your visitor so that we can lie with him!"

The Ephraimite went out and begged them to stop. "The man is my guest," he said. "How can you even ask such a vile thing?"

But the crowd became louder and more brutal. They struck the old man aside, broke his lock, reached inside and seized the Levite by his robe. Knives flashed. With one hand the Levite braced himself against the door; with the other he grabbed his concubine and pushed her outside and slammed the door and leaned his body against it.

The young men of Gibeah, sons of Belial, raped the girl all night long. And as the dawn began to break, they let her go.

In the grey light the girl came and fell down at the door of the house where her master was.

And the Levite rose up in the morning. When he opened the door of the house and went out, there was his concubine lying at the door with her hands on the threshold.

He said to her, "Get up. Let us be going."

But there was no answer.

He kneeled down beside her and heard the breath go out of her body. She sighed and did not breathe again.

The Levite stood up and lifted the girl in his arms and laid her across the back of one donkey. He rode the other, leading her home the entire day without a rest or a pause; and when he entered his own house he found a knife, and laying hold of his concubine's corpse, he divided it limb from limb, into twelve pieces.

He sent the pieces throughout all the territory of Israel.

And all who saw them said, "Such a thing has never happened from the day the people of Israel came up out of the land of Egypt! Consider it! What shall we do?"

So the people of Israel gathered at Bethel, and the elders said, "Tell us how this wickedness came to pass."

The Levite said, "When the men of Gibeah came against me and attacked the house by night, I knew they meant to kill me! They raped my concubine and killed her. They have committed an abomination. People of Israel, all of you, what shall we do?"

They said, "Not one of us will return to our houses until we make Gibeah of Benjamin pay for the vile crime which they have committed in Israel."

So they sent messages to the tribe of Benjamin, saying, "Give up those wicked fellows in Gibeah, that we may put them to death and put this evil away from Israel."

But the Benjaminites would not listen to the voice of the other tribes. Instead they mustered an army from all their cities and came to join Gibeah in battle against the rest of Israel. Now, the men of Benjamin could shoot a bow with either hand; and they could sling a stone at a hair without missing.

The people of Israel inquired of God: "Which of us shall go up first to battle against Benjamin?"

And the Lord said, *Judah shall go up first.*

So the people of Israel rose in the morning and encamped against Gibeah. Their armies went forth into battle. Judah first. Judah took the field first, but Benjamin beat the men of Judah backward with terrible attacks, killing them as they ran. Moreover, Benjamin drove the rest of Israel from the field.

The people of Israel then wept before the Lord until evening, and they inquired of him, "Shall we again attack our brethren the Benjaminites?"

The Lord said, *Go up against them.*

Therefore the men of Israel took courage and again formed the battle line in the same place where they formed it the first day. And Benjamin came out of the city of Gibeah this second day, and again they defeated the men of Israel. So the armies withdrew to Bethel again and wept louder than before. They sat before the Lord and fasted and offered burnt offerings and peace offerings. Phinehas the son of Eleazar brought forth the Ark of the Covenant of God, and the people asked, "Shall we yet again go out to battle against our brethren the Benjaminites, or shall we cease?"

And the Lord said, *Go up; for tomorrow I will give them into your hand.*

On the third day Israel set an ambush behind the city of Gibeah — otherwise, they formed the same battle line as on the previous two days. And in the morning the entire army of Benjamin rushed forth from the city, attacking Israel. As before, Israel fought a little while, then turned and ran, and Benjamin followed, killing about thirty men of Israel.

But then the men hidden in ambush broke out and rushed to the city of Gibeah. They struck the whole city with the edge of their swords.

A signal had been arranged between the men of Israel and the men in ambush: *When smoke goes up from Gibeah, turn! Turn and fight.*

And so it was. A column of smoke rose from Gibeah; the armies of Israel saw it and turned to attack their brothers. Benjamin, too, saw the city going up in smoke, and were so dismayed that they retreated from Israel in violent disorder.

The men of Benjamin fell that day; the cities of Benjamin were burned; women and children perished with the cities, and the tribe was reduced to almost nothing. Six hundred men fled toward the rock of Rimmon and hid in the shadow of that rock four months.

Then all the rest of Israel came together again at Bethel and sat before God until the evening, weeping bitterly. For they said, "O Lord, why has this come to pass, that there should be today one tribe lacking in Israel?"

For the sake of their brothers, they went armed to the city of Jabesh in Gilead and seized four hundred young women, none of whom had ever lain with a man. With these they offered peace to the men at the rock of Rimmon. So the virgins of Jabesh-Gilead became wives and mothers in Benjamin, and the tribe did not die.

▌

In those days there was no king in Israel. Every man did what was right in his own eyes.

PART FOUR

Kings

PART
FOUR

15

SAUL

i

By the gates of Jabesh-Gilead there stood a stone fortress several stories higher than the rest of the city. One could stand in the northwest corner of this fortress and look down into the Jordan valley at some of the richest soil on the east side of the river. From its southwest corner one could see the magnificent hills of Gilead, their lower slopes terraced for olive orchards and vineyards, their highest reaches covered with forests as thick as those of Mount Carmel or Lebanon.

Into the wet dew of an early dawn three men crept through an outer door of that fortress and began to run west along a dry riverbed toward the Jordan River. No one else was in view. The houses of Jabesh were empty. All its citizens were huddled in the fortress itself. The children still were sleeping.

As the three men approached a low break of trees just beyond bowshot of the fortress, they slowed to a walk. They bowed their heads and lifted their arms, revealing empty scabbards. A small detachment of Ammonite soldiers stepped out of the break and surrounded them, holding spear-points to the backs of their necks.

"King Nahash has given us leave," said the tallest of the three, his head still bowed. "We have seven days. At the end of seven days you can kill us, but till then the king's order grants us safe passage."

One of the soldiers grabbed the hair and yanked backward. When his face was tilted to the morning light, it was evident that the man of Jabesh had but one eye. His right eyeball was gone. The lid fluttered, sucked into the skull like the cheek of a toothless grandfather. The Ammonite soldiers burst into a sneezing, scornful laughter. They pulled back the heads of the tall man's companions and their laughter redoubled. These two also were blinded in their right eyes. And because they were also afraid, their lids were open. The sockets writhed with white tendons. A foolish flow of tears fell from the empty eyes.

"Warriors!" sneered the Ammonites. "Warriors that can't aim an arrow or stab with the right hand! Pass by. Pass by. What harm can half a soldier do? Ha ha ha!"

Their heads bent in humiliation, the three men of Jabesh continued running down the riverbed. They stumbled often, for the lack of an eye. They clung to one another in order to ford the Jordan, its current swift here, but shallow. They cut through dense vegetation on the western side, willow and cane in a soft marsh, reeds as tall as a man. Wild beasts roamed these thickets. Lions, leopards, jackals. But even to a one-eyed man, animals were nothing next to the Ammonites that besieged his city.

King Nahash had heard of the weaknesses of Israel. He knew that Philistines had attacked and routed their armies at Ebenezer and pursued them as far east as Shiloh, where they destroyed the Tabernacle, that ancient sacred tent which Israel had brought from the desert two hundred years ago. Nahash knew that even the most holy shrine of Israel, the Ark of the Covenant, had been captured by the Philistines and carried back to their own cities. Only recently had it been returned.

Therefore, Nahash of Ammon had mustered his armies and attacked the tribes of Reuben and Gad, finally laying siege to Jabesh-Gilead. He intended to make a reputation for himself.

When the elders of Jabesh offered tribute in exchange for a treaty of peace, King Nahash clapped his hands in delight. "On this condition will I make a treaty with you," he said. "That I gouge out all your right eyes."

The elders took counsel together and replied, "Give us seven days respite, that we may beg Israel for help. If none comes, we will give ourselves to you."

"Yes, yes, beg Israel," Nahash said. "Let that mighty nation come to save you. The greater the number of eyeballs plucked, the greater the disgrace of my neighbor!"

Because Israel seemed everywhere to be in tatters, King Nahash felt confident of a final victory. Therefore he picked three men, gouged their eyes as a sign of his threat, and gave them safe passage over Jordan.

∎

It was late in the day. The men of Jabesh had climbed the western side of the Jordan valley, a dry, crumbling clay, that tore their knees and elbows, and were running south on the ridge route. They had passed Shechem an hour ago. Below them on the left and the right the hills were lost in an evening shadow. All three were exhausted, but they did not stop. They were going to Gibeah. The elders of Jabesh had sent them to find Saul the son of Kish who lived at Gibeah of Benjamin. If anyone could save them, it would be Saul.

The city of Gibeah was the place where Jabesh virgins had been taken several generations ago, by whom the men of Benjamin rebuilt their families after Israel had slaughtered their wives and children. There was kinship between Saul of Gibeah and the blind messengers of Jabesh.

Moreover, Saul himself had fought in Moab, south of the Ammonites.

He had raised his own force, had struck according to his own designs, proving himself beholden to no one! He himself had laid a foundation for a fortress at Gibeah and had acquired his own smith in spite of the Philistine monopoly. Saul fought, therefore, with weapons of iron, sharper, more durable, and more deadly than the bronze the rest of Israel had to use.

At noon on the second day of their journey, the messengers of Jabesh-Gilead arrived in Gibeah. Immediately, though they were tired and filthy, they stood in the gate of the city and reported the threats of Nahash. When the people of Gibeah saw the empty eyesockets of their cousins, and when they heard what horrors might befall the rest of the city, they began to weep aloud.

At that same time a man was coming in from the fields behind a team of oxen. He was tall and strong across the chest. His hair flowed down to his shoulders. His eyes were dark and his hearing quick. "What's wrong?" he called as he approached the gate. "Why are you crying?"

The one-eyed messengers stepped forward and said, "King Nahash has surrounded Jabesh-Gilead. What he's done to us he promises to do to all the city. So we've come looking for Saul the son of — "

Even before the request was finished, the handsome man's eyes crackled and blazed a black fire. His face grew dark. He seized an iron sword, whirled it over his head and slew his oxen where they stood, then he began to cut their carcasses into huge pieces of meat and bone.

The messengers from Jabesh-Gilead fell silent. They had found the man whom they were seeking. Saul the son of Kish handed twelve hunks of bloody meat to his servants, saying, "Take these to the tribes of Israel. Declare that whoever does not come to follow Saul in battle, even so shall it be done to his oxen! Tell the fighting men to meet me at Bezek! In four days! By dusk on the fourth day I shall be waiting with a sword and a helmet and a coat of mail. Go!"

To the three men from Jabesh he said, "No king shall gouge the right eyes of your brothers. Return and say to the elders of Jabesh-Gilead that in five days, by the time the sun is hot on that day, they shall have deliverance."

So the order and the cry went forth from Gibeah.

Saul the son of Kish was a fire in Israel. Several thousand warriors came to Bezek directly west of the Jordan from Jabesh-Gilead. So sudden was the muster of this army that no warning ever reached Nahash.

But three one-eyed messengers slipped back into the city with the pledge of Saul. So on the sixth day of their respite, the elders of Jabesh sent a written capitulation to King Nahash: *Tomorrow we will give ourselves up to you, and you may do to us whatever seems good to you.*

That night Saul drove his armies in a remarkable march through darkness east of Bezek, over roadless hills, down treacherous scrabble, the loose clay and gypsum of the western descent into the Jordan valley. They crossed the waters quietly, then climbed up the east side, through vineyards and orchards, creeping like cats, thousands of warriors from Israel and Judah.

At a checkpoint every man passed Saul, where with silent gestures he divided them into three companies and pointed each in its own direction, till the camps of the Ammonites were altogether surrounded.

Exactly at sunrise, Saul let out a yell of rage and ringing delight, releasing all his warriors into the midst of the camps of Nahash. Spearheads and arrows roused the Ammonite army and laid them quickly down again. Israel slaughtered Ammonites until the heat of the day, and those who survived were so scattered that no two of them were left together.

ii

The dramatic salvation of Jabesh-Gilead by Saul the son of Kish transformed the governance of Israel forever. It would no longer be a loose association of tribes — a single God, a common history, but each with its own inherited territory and every tribe independent of the others.

For more than forty years the people had been beseeching the Lord to anoint a king in Israel. But God, through his priest, Samuel, had denied them. Samuel said, "God is your king."

Now, the judgment of Samuel was powerful in the land. He spoke for God. Even from his birth he had been dedicated unto the Lord; as a child he had served in the Tabernacle at Shiloh — and he became a priest because the Lord God himself had called him.

The word of the Lord was rare in those days. There was no frequent vision. Therefore, this divine appointment was extraordinary. *Samuel!* the Lord called to a young lad in the dead of night: *Samuel!* And the boy had answered, "Here I am." And God said, *Behold, I am about to do a thing in Israel at which the two ears of every one that hears it will tingle.*

When Samuel was a young man, the lords of the Philistines invaded Israel with terrible devastations. They destroyed Shiloh. They burned the beautiful Tabernacle of the Lord. They captured the Ark of the Covenant and carried it into their own cities.

It was as if the hands and the feet of the people had been cut off. They despaired, and they said to Samuel, "We need a king."

As Samuel grew older, the Philistines had cut the land nearly in two, dividing the hill country of Manasseh and all tribes north from the hill country of Ephraim and all tribes south. They controlled the trade routes, choking off Israel's exchange of goods. They smelted the iron for tools and weapons, but there was not a smith in all Israel! This enemy was entrenched, unlike any Israel had encountered before.

When Samuel had grown old, the elders of the twelve tribes came to him in a formal body and stated their request as an absolute, unanimous demand. "Appoint a king to govern us like all the nations," they said.

But the very concept still troubled Samuel. "You have a king," he said. "You have had a king since Egypt! Who else but the Lord sent Moses to bring your fathers through the wilderness to this place? Yes, and it was the Lord who raised for you deliverers here, Barak and Deborah, Gideon and Jephthah. How can you say 'A king shall reign over us,' when the Lord your God is your king?"

But this time the elders were prepared for the priest's refusal. "Samuel, you are a good man and a righteous judge," they said. "Israel hasn't seen a priest like you for hundreds of years. But you are old, now — and your sons do not walk in your ways."

"My sons? Why do you mention my sons?"

"They judge the people in Beer-sheba."

"I know where my sons are."

"But you don't know what they do, Samuel! They have turned from God in order to seek gain. Your sons take bribes. They pervert justice. After you, who shall lead us with righteousness? Please, give us a king to govern us."

Samuel fixed the elders with his eyes. "Do you understand the ways of any king who would reign over you?" he said. "A king will take your sons and appoint them to be his horsemen and to run before his chariots. Your children are free now. How will they be then? A king will command some of them to plow *his* ground, some to reap *his* harvest, some to make *his* weapons. Listen to me! He will take your daughters to be perfumers and cooks and bakers. He will take the best of your fields and vineyards and orchards and give them to his *servants*. Have you considered this? Today you own your goods; you owe nothing to anyone except to the Lord your God. But tomorrow a king will take a tenth of your grain and your grapes, a tenth of all your produce. He will take your menservants and maidservants and the best of your cattle and put them all to *his* work. You shall be his slaves. In that day you will cry out because of the king whom you have chosen for yourselves — and why, then, should the Lord God answer you?"

But the elders and the people refused to listen. Again they said, "No! We will have a king like all the nations, a king to govern us and go out before us and fight our battles!"

In the end Samuel withdrew to a private place and repeated the words of the people in the ears of the Lord.

And the Lord said, *Grant it, Samuel. Anoint a king for them*!

It was just then that Saul the son of Kish led his dramatic attack against Nahash of the Ammonites. It was then that the spirit of the Lord exploded mightily in him for the sake of Jabesh-Gilead.

The people in a delirium of triumph began to cry, "This is the man! This is the one! Let Saul reign over us!"

Therefore the Lord said to Samuel, *Anoint this man of Benjamin to be prince over my people Israel and to save them from the hand of the Philistines.*

Obediently, Samuel called the tribes of Israel to Gilgal, there to renew the kingdom.

And joyfully representatives of all twelve tribes arrived.

Samuel stood up before them and said, "Here, then, is the man whom the Lord chooses to rule over you. Saul son of Kish, step forward!"

A storm of roaring greeted that name. The noise grew louder and louder as a handsome man strode forward, a dark, passionate man, a man of magnificent height. Saul stood a full head higher than anyone else in Israel. Yet he bowed his great frame down before Samuel, and upon Saul's head the priest of God poured the oil of his office: King of Israel.

iii

Immediately, Saul invited the stonemasons of Israel to come to Gibeah, there to build a fortress upon the foundation he had already prepared. The men who came were old, but they were filled with new hope and they loved the king who strode among them praising their labors, laughing, and clapping his hands in a bright and boyish delight. Soon they had built a citadel of massive, rough-hewn masonry with four short towers at the corners and a casement wall: two stories high. Unpretentious. There was neither ornament nor beauty in the thing, and very little furniture. All was functional and strong. But Saul embraced every dusty old man as if he had built an Egyptian palace.

At the same time Saul gathered in Gibeah several hundred young men of vigor and courage; with these he created a new thing in Israel, a standing army.

❚

Now, the Philistines had garrisons stationed in cities west, north, and northeast of Saul, some as close as three miles. They controlled the Beth Horon road westward to the coastal plain, and they could at any time strike across the north-south ridge route, cutting off communication north and south in Israel.

Saul, therefore, positioned tiny divisions of his new army in central and eastern Benjamin: Michmash, the hill country of Bethel, Gibeah. The soldiers stationed in Gibeah he placed under the command of his own son,

Jonathan, who, though he wasn't as tall as his father, was filled with the same swift daring.

Saul now planned to wait a while, building his forces and entrenching them quietly in regions beyond the Philistine reach. He wanted to increase his arsenal of iron weapons. There were no chariots in his army, but his soldiers needed more than slings and copper daggers and bronze swords. They needed small shields for quick attack and large shields for the battle line. Saul wanted to craft them properly, curing leather for the wooden frame — but Jonathan took matters into his own hand, and at once Israel was at war.

Very early one morning Jonathan led his little division three miles north-northeast and surprised the small Philistine garrison at Geba. He defeated them and sent them running to the garrison at Gibeon. Even while the young man enjoyed his triumph, a message was flying back to the five Philistine cities: *There is a king in Israel! He has seized Geba. He has weakened us in Benjamin and broken the eastern branch of the Beth Horon road!*

A king in Israel?

The armies of the Philistines reacted immediately. They mustered at Aphek, northwest of the new king's armies, then began by a more northerly route to march toward the hill country of Benjamin, avoiding the Beth Horon road altogether.

This army was both large and experienced. Horsemen restrained restless mounts; chariots were driven by two men, chariots of wickerwork with cases attached to the dashboards for spears and whips and battle-axes; drovers prodded pack animals; oxen pulled wagons heavy with iron armament and siege equipment: long Philistine divisions raised several miles of a dim red dust.

When Saul heard of their mighty approach, he blew the horn of war, calling forth fighting men from all twelve tribes in order to augment his standing army. There was a king in Israel! Shepherds responded, leaving their flocks. Farmers dropped their mattocks and picked up swords. Carpenters exchanged hammers for daggers. The common men of the kingdom of Israel ran from their houses to meet Saul at Gilgal, and the king's hundreds swelled to thousands.

The armies of the Philistines rolled through Bethel without obstruction and massed on the horizon north of Michmash. Saul's little garrison in that place broke camp and ran all the way to Gilgal, crying, "The Philistines have covered Michmash with troops as many as sand on the seashore!"

Indeed, having found high, open fields protected by a deep gorge on the south, the Philistines had begun to dig elaborate installations for their forces. At the same time they sent their raiders galloping through the countryside to seize provisions, food and wood and water. Wherever they

rode they burned farmers' houses, scorched the fields, and slaughtered the
sheep so that Saul would find nothing with which to supply his own soldiers.

The women and children of Israel were terrified. Those too old to fight
suffered horrors at the hands of the marauding Philistines. Having no
homes, they hid in caves and tombs and cisterns.

When Saul marched his armies toward Michmash, the soldiers saw no
green thing left. The earth was black and stinking, homesteads deserted.
Every citizen who ran to them for safety had a story to tell, and every story
contained a new violence in Israel. The militia, therefore, began to desert.
Fathers sneaked home to look for their families. Farmers threw away their
swords and escaped over Jordan to the lands of Gad and Gilead.

By the time Saul arrived at Geba to join his forces with Jonathan's, they
numbered no more than six hundred men between them.

Israel also encamped on high ground, southwest of Michmash. They, too,
used the gorge that ran east and west as protection, since it was a defile too
deep for crossing, its walls rocky and steep, its brow covered with thickets.
But the south side had a higher vantage than the north, and Israel was able
to look down into the Philistine camp.

Jonathan was fascinated by the view. Morning and evening he lay among
the thorns at the edge of the precipice, gazing at the enemy, calculating.
He saw that the main camp sat some distance back, but a small tough guard
had been positioned immediately at the crest of the canyon wall.

Early one morning Jonathan withdrew from the thicket grinning exactly
like his father: white teeth, flashing black eyes, and a fierce conviction. He
slipped through the sleeping army of Israel to his tent.

"Etam," he whispered as he entered.

A youth stirred inside and woke.

"Etam, I have a plan for the two of us, if you're willing."

Jonathan began to gather his weapons. The lad pulled on a tunic and
rushed to help.

"A plan?"

"Maybe the Lord will work with us. Why wouldn't the Lord save Israel?"

Etam whispered, "I am with you, sir."

Jonathan faced the lad and grinned. "Good for you, Etam, armor-bearer!
Quickly, now: dress me." He put out his arms. Etam heaved a coat of mail
over his shoulders and while he was tying the cords behind him, Jonathan
said, "You and I are going to descend the near side of the gorge. At the
bottom we will show ourselves to the Philistine guard on the other side. If
they say, 'Wait till we come down,' we'll stand still, right where we are. But
if they say, 'Come up to us,' that, Etam, is exactly what we're going to do!"

"Sir," Etam whispered, "no one can climb that chasm wall."

"Yes, yes, the Philistines will mock us with their words — but those very
words will be a sign that the Lord has given them into our hands."

Jonathan grabbed a length of braided rope, then led Etam through dawn to the thicket that hid the southern rim of the canyon.

He tied one end of the rope to a stout oak, bound a bag of heavy equipment to the other end, and lowered it into the gorge. It bumped stone and disappeared into morning mists. When the whole rope had been paid out, Jonathan took it in his two hands and without a word descended to a dry riverbed below, then tugged the rope three times and felt the weight of Etam's coming.

When they were together between the crags, Etam helped Jonathan don the rest of his battle gear. Then, when the mists had blown away, they moved to a clear space and Jonathan began to bellow like a madman: "Dogs! Dogs! Philistine dogs, look out! The armies of Israel are upon you!"

Faces came and peered over the edge of the high rock, first with frowns and then with wide gaps at the mouth. The Philistines burst into laughter. "You?" they howled. "You are the armies of Israel? Then let these two great armies fly up to us, and we will show you a thing or two!"

The guard retired, laughing heartily.

Jonathan whispered, "Did you hear what they said?" He embraced his armor-bearer and stood back, flashing a white grin in perfect delight. "God has given them into our hands. The name of this wall is Bozez: the Shining. Etam, I am going to climb the Shining, and you, like an eagle, will fly behind me!"

During the hottest portion of the day, King Saul was sleeping in the shade of a pomegranate tree.

Suddenly the ground beneath him trembled. He jumped to his feet, blinking, trying to gather his wits, when he heard his watchmen cry, "Look! The camps of the Philistines! Look!"

As if in a dream, Saul saw the entire army of the enemy surging back and forth — panicked! It seemed to him that they were hopelessly panicked.

"Who is gone?" Saul cried. "Which of my captains is missing?"

While the tumult among the Philistines increased, Israelites ran to their tents and discovered that Jonathan had left with his armor-bearer, his sword, and all his equipment.

King Saul of Israel uttered a bark of laughter, rose to his glorious height, and cried, "The battle has begun! Let's finish it!" He sent half of his forces around to attack from the west while he led the rest eastward to cross the gorge at an easy pass and then to strike the eastern flanks of the Philistines. As he galloped through the countryside he saw farmers and shepherds emerging from their hiding places. They had heard fright in the enemy and strength in Israel. Saul's militia was swelling again. He galloped with a sweeter fury, roaring laughter, a king to his people!

As he closed in upon the camps of the Philistines, he recognized a marvelous confusion: they were fighting each other! No hesitation, then! King Saul spurred his mount into the midst of the enemy, laying about with his iron sword, causing carnage. He thrust stomachs. He cut jaws to their joints and split skulls and opened bright fountains in human necks, thundering taunts and imprecations, terrifying Philistines and cutting a path for Israelites. Rivers of blood flowed into the battlefields of Michmash. When his horse therefore slipped and fell beneath him, Saul leaped to his own feet and fought hand to hand with dagger and sword. He stepped backward, backward — until he bumped another body. He whirled to dispatch it, but discovered his son, and roared in delight, "Jonathan, Jonathan! What a beautiful day this is!"

They turned back to back and fought four-legged, invincible.

"Jonathan!" Saul cried. "What did you do to the Philistines?"

And Jonathan, killing those who would kill the king, cried, "I climbed Bozez! I caught the guard by surprise. I slew twenty in two minutes. The rest ran to the camps, bleating that Israel had soared over the gorge. Then the earth quaked — and that was the Lord our God, and that was more than they could take."

Back to back, father and son terrified the entire army of the Philistines so that they fled from Michmash. They retreated westward, and the farther they ran, the more of Saul's old militia poured down from the hills where they had been hiding. Israel chased the Philistines all the way to Aijalon.

∎

Now, this is the family of Saul the son of Kish. When he was anointed king of Israel he had three sons: Jonathan, Ishbaal, and Malchishua. The names of his two daughters were Merab and Michal. Michal was the youngest, just an infant at the coronation of her father. She never knew a time when she was not the daughter of a king.

Saul's wife, the mother of these five, was Ahinoam, whose name means My Brother Is Joy. After her husband became king, Ahinoam had one more son, Abinadab.

Later Saul took for his concubine Rizpah, the daughter of Aiah. She bore him two sons, Armoni and Meribbaal. Her name means Glowing Coal. She was a woman of infinite love and desperate loyalty for her children. Rizpah was a stone that kept its red heat even after two of her children had perished.

Despite his victory at Michmash, there was hard fighting against the Philistines all the days of Saul. Whenever he saw a strong man or a valiant man, he invited him to join the standing army which he kept at his fortress in Gibeah. Saul's army, therefore, grew into a smooth, obedient, and ready force, a military power beholden to the king alone. And as its commander he appointed his cousin Abner.

iv

S amuel, the white-haired priest of God, now traveled down from Ramah to Saul in Gibeah. They met in the gate of the city. Samuel sat down to rest before he spoke. As long as the old man kept silence, so did the king. He stood, his dark hair brushed glossy for the sake of the priest, his tall frame like a column, waiting.

Finally, Samuel raised his eyes and said, "You remember that it was the Lord who sent me to anoint you king over Israel."

"Yes, I remember."

"Then listen to the words of the Lord who made you king: *Amalek is harassing the tribe of Judah. He has never changed his ways, nor have I forgotten how he opposed Israel when they came up out of Egypt. Now I will punish him. Saul son of Kish, go and smite Amalek. Utterly destroy all that he has. Spare no person and no thing, but kill both man and woman, infant and suckling, ox and sheep and camel and ass.*"

Hearing this, the king seemed to sag and grow tired. "The *herem*," he said.

"Yes," said Samuel, "the ban. Amalek is devoted to the Lord for destruction. Neither you nor your people shall touch anything that is of Amalek, lest you bring trouble upon Israel."

Saul said, "This thing has not been asked of Israel since Joshua entered Canaan and destroyed Jericho."

Samuel squinted up at the king. "Why do you say so, Saul? Is there something here you do not understand?"

"No," said the king, "no."

But the lines in his face were deeper than before. In the years of his reign until now there had been no peace for Saul. He had fought the Philistines admirably, but he had not been able to subdue them. At the same time, Israel's older enemies took advantage of that constant preoccupation, so that King Saul had to blow the horn of war against Moab, against Ammon, against Edom. By the sheer force of his personality, he had to raise the militia over and over again.

And now Samuel said, "Go. Utterly destroy Amalek."

So once again Saul ignited the black flame in his eyes and blew the ram's horn of war, this time summoning Israel to Talaim in Judah. And once again the charismatic king succeeded. Farmers turned into fighters. They took their weapons and prepared to enter the wilderness, to attack the tribes that once had attacked their ancestors.

In Talaim King Saul issued orders. "This shall be the *herem*! Nothing shall be left of Amalek when we are done. It is devoted to the Lord for destruction."

Then he mounted his horse and rode out before them all. His personal bodyguard went next, then Abner and his captains, and finally the body of Israel left on foot. Saul and Abner and Jonathan wore bronze helmets. The rest wore helmets of leather, rounded at the top with long flaps to cover their ears and cheeks.

In the valley near Amalek, Israel halted.

Saul sent Jonathan out by night to scout the camps of the nomads. With his son's information — still under cover of darkness — he dispatched Abner with seven regular soldiers to hamstring the camels and the asses while he himself led the armies of Israel in a great circle around the camp: a noose.

Exactly at sunrise, Saul cried a command. The captains picked it up. Like wildfire their voices encircled Amalek, and then Israel *was* the fire, rushing in from all sides and slaughtering the Amalekites in a holy conflagration. Many were destroyed. Most were destroyed — even those who did escape: they were pursued as far as Shur near Egypt and destroyed.

Yet, not everyone was destroyed. Saul spared Agag, the king of the Amalekites. And some of Saul's soldiers kept back the best of the sheep and the oxen, the fatlings and the lambs.

▮

Then the word of the Lord came to Samuel at Ramah.

The Lord said, *I repent that I made Saul king; for he has turned away from following me. He has not performed my commandments.*

Samuel was furious.

In the morning he rose up and went forth to find the king.

They told him that Saul had been victorious. They said that he had been making a triumphal procession northward, pausing at Carmel long enough to set up a monument to his accomplishment and then passing on to Gilgal, there to make sacrifices to the Lord. They told Samuel, too, that Saul had brought back proof and a personal trophy: the king of the Amalekites, Agag, alive.

So Samuel went to Saul at Gilgal, a day's journey for the old man.

Saul saw him coming and went to meet him.

"Blessed be you to the Lord," he called even as he strode to Samuel, grinning. "Sir, I have performed the commandment! Amalek is punished."

Samuel waited until the king came near, then said, "What then is this bleating in my ears?"

Saul paused, still grinning.

Samuel said, louder: "What is the lowing that I hear?"

"Oh, well," Saul said. "The people have brought some sheep and oxen back to sacrifice to the Lord your God — "

"Stop," said Samuel.

"—the rest," Saul continued, "the rest we have utterly destroyed — "

"Stop!" Samuel cried. "Do you want to hear what the Lord said to me this night?"

Saul began to blink rapidly, all his triumph suddenly gone. He drew a deep breath and said, "Say on."

Samuel said, "You are the head of the tribes of Israel. The Lord anointed you king. That same God sent you to destroy the Amalekites, to fight against them until they were consumed. Why didn't you obey the voice of the Lord?"

Saul said, "But I did. I did what the Lord sent me to do. I only brought back Agag, and the people brought the best cattle for a sacrifice here in Gilgal."

"Does the Lord delight in sacrifice as much as in obedience?" Samuel cried, his old eyes flashing. "Behold, to obey is better than sacrifice, and to hearken is sweeter than the fat of rams. But rebellion is as bad as sorcery, and stubbornness no less than idolatry. Because you rejected the word of the Lord, the Lord has rejected you from being king."

Now all the lines in Saul's face deepened. His shoulders sagged, and he said, "I have sinned. I transgressed the commandment of the Lord. Samuel, priest of God, I beg you, pardon my sin. Return with me, that I may worship the Lord."

But Samuel's anger was unyielding. "I will not return with you," he said. "The Lord has rejected you."

The old man turned to go.

"Wait!" cried Saul. He moved in front of Samuel, blocking his way. "Why can't I be forgiven like any other man?"

"Because you are changing, Saul. Because you are impatient and arrogant. Because you have usurped authority which does not belong to you. Because you offered burnt offerings unto the Lord without waiting for me, his priest!"

"Yes!" cried Saul in anguish. "Yes, I remember that offering. But I had to do it. Samuel, the armies of Israel needed the blessing of God, but you were delaying. I waited for you, but you didn't come!"

"Get out of my way!" the old man snapped. "Since you no longer wait upon the Lord, neither does he wait on you. He has rejected you from being king of Israel."

Samuel pushed Saul backward. The tall man stumbled as if struck by a club. Samuel began to walk away, but Saul reached out and grabbed his robe so forcefully that the fabric tore. He let go of the robe. He went down on his knees and folded his hands in supplication. But Samuel held the rip with two hands in front of Saul's face. "This is a sign," he said, all his old limbs trembling. "As you have torn my clothing, so the Lord has torn the kingdom of Israel from you this day and has given it to a neighbor worthier than you!"

"I have sinned, I have sinned," Saul wailed. His great shoulders shook with this weeping. "O priest, yet honor me before the elders of my people. Return with me that I may worship the Lord your God!"

Samuel was stooped and gaunt and exhausted, and now it seemed his anger died within him. Slowly he extended his hand and placed it on Saul's head. He began to stroke the beautiful hair. For a long time, while the king continued bowed before him, Samuel stroked his hair, and neither man said a word.

Once more the old priest relented and went a day's journey with the king, and Saul worshiped the Lord.

But after that Samuel returned to Ramah, and Saul traveled to his fortress in Gibeah, and that was the last time they saw one another until the day that Samuel died.

V

The Philistines never ceased to test the mettle of Israel's king and of his armies.

Regularly, annually, disciplined soldiers established battle lines by driving their wide rectangular shields side by side into the ground and sticking lances between them. From behind this fortification, they rained arrows upon poor Israelite villagers, who would then cry out and beg the king to come and save them.

So Saul would rekindle his personal fires and blow the trumpet and summon the militia to fight on behalf of Israelites in trouble. But the people of Israel grew less and less inclined to heed their king.

Sometimes, therefore, Saul drove the Philistines back by the desperate slashings of his own sword and the support of his standing army only. Sometimes the young men whom he loved the most, whom he himself had trained in the yards surrounding his fortress at Gibeah, died beside him. Then a new rage came upon the tall king and none could withstand him. He made wooden shields explode with blows from his war club. And sometimes he would fall asleep in full battle dress, bloody and unwashed — exhausted.

But with his new rages came a new trouble. Saul began to suffer nightmares, after which he woke up in a running sweat, filled with anxiety, grabbing his temples and desperately trying not to howl out loud.

Saul had never been a fearful man. He had no idea what to *do* with fear. But now it caused a tremendous noise in his brain which he thought might issue from his mouth. So he buried his face in blankets and tried to keep his condition a secret.

There were whole months when the man felt equal to the responsibilities of his office. Then he would grin again and clap the young men on their backs and eat with them. Then the wars of Israel seemed no greater than the wars of any nation.

But suddenly his terrors would return, and for three nights together he would dream and wake and dream again.

One night, when he rose up in horror from his pallet, he saw Rizpah sitting in his room, watching him — an apparition of perfect calm.

With a mighty effort he restrained himself, drawing his knees and his elbows to his stomach, breathing loudly in his nose.

Rizpah, his concubine, was a young and gentle woman, thin, of sad countenance. He was embarrassed so to be seen by her.

But she said, "This isn't the first time, is it?"

And he shook his head. The silent woman knew more than he had realized.

Rizpah stood up and came to him, and he saw that she was walking on bare feet. She sat down on the floor beside his pallet, drew her feet beneath her skirts, took his head between her cool hands, and laid it gently down upon her lap. She began to sing to him in a high, untutored voice. She sang a lullaby. She sang until his spirit grew calm and his eyes closed and he slept.

In this way, Saul learned that music could restore his soul.

And this is how it went for several months: Rizpah, recognizing when he had entered the black mood, would come in the night and comfort him with touching and with singing.

But it occurred to Saul that there would be no one to sing for him when war carried him away from home.

And then Rizpah became pregnant. Soon all of her nights would be devoted to another. So who would come and sing for the king of Israel then?

■

Between the hill country of Judah and the flat coastal plains of the Philistines lay a rumpled land, humped and wrinkled as if it were a blanket someone had tossed down. This was a north-south strip of foothills ten miles wide, twenty-seven miles long, divided by five rich valleys. The hills were encased in nari, a crusty rock covered by the merest skin of soil, making the hills themselves useless for planting. They were bearded with scrub forests. Sycamore trees grew there, producing a sweet, small, figlike fruit. But the valleys were fertile. Little limestone villages clung to the hillsides in order to leave the valleys free for farming.

This region was called the Shephelah, because an Israelite in the high hills of Judah would look down to see it nearly as far as the sea.

Now, the Philistines, probing eastward in the Shephelah, had suddenly seized Azekah, a town at the eastern passage of the valley of Elah. Their own city of Gath dominated the same valley at its western extreme; therefore they moved swiftly to strengthen this foothold in Judah. They marched a large army up the valley a mile past Azekah, took a hill on its south side, and dug in. They encamped on top of that hill, then established a battle line yet farther up the valley, a mile west of Socoh.

The people of Socoh woke to find a wall of shields across the floor of the valley of Elah, and Philistines behind that wall, and more Philistines farther back on the high hill behind them. Immediately they sent runners to the king of Israel, begging him to come and fight for them.

King Saul blew the trumpet for war.

Very few men came down from the northern tribes of Israel. Some came from Benjamin. Most came from Judah. With these men and his standing army, Saul marched south to Bethlehem, then west along the little brook of Elah into the valley as far as Socoh. He camped on a hill on its northern side, two miles from the Philistine hill.

In the morning he and Abner and all his warriors attacked the shields of Philistia. They charged across the flat valley floor, trampling the wheat fields and running directly at the thin line of uncircumcised soldiers. But then a hail of arrows hit them short of the battle line. Archers were in the hills on the right and the left: an ambush! Abner screamed a retreat. Israel lost twenty-seven men. And that night Saul woke in his tent, trembling again with his terrors.

The next days went no better.

And on the fourth day, Israel heard laughter in the camps of the Philistines.

It was the booming voice of a single colossal man. A giant, in fact, who could make himself heard from hill to hill across the valley, roaring scorn for Israel's militia.

This mockery went on for five weeks unabated, the most humiliating engagement Saul ever had endured.

He maintained a princely dignity in daylight. But his nights were intolerable. Within an hour of falling asleep he started up in fear and in blinding pain. He could neither think nor plan nor pray nor sleep. He could scarcely breathe. He struggled mightily not to cry out — and at dawn he fought to seem a king again.

Saul began to ask his soldiers whether they knew anyone who could sing well. He said he needed someone to stay with him in his tent and to sing soft songs at midnight.

One day a man named Shammah came and said, "I know a lad who plays the lyre and sings well."

"Who is he?" said the king.

"My youngest brother," said Shammah. "He has a wooden lyre of six strings, but he can play on three strings or twelve."

"And who are you?" said the king.

"Shammah, the third son of Jesse of Bethlehem in Judah. My brothers and I are following you into battle, O King. But David is the one who sings. He's just a lad still living at home, feeding the sheep of our father."

"Bring him, Shammah. Bring him to me as soon as you can."

So Shammah went up to Bethlehem and brought his brother back to the camps in the valley of Elah and presented him to the king.

Saul stepped out of his tent and saw a light-boned youth no taller than the king's own breastbone. But the lad moved with grace. He had delicate fingers and a tangle of red hair and eyes with long lashes, flecked with gold.

"David, son of Jesse?"

"Yes, sir."

"Have you brought a bed-mat and a lyre?"

"Yes, sir."

"And you have your father's permission to be here?"

"Yes, sir."

"Then we will try this arrangement for a night or two: sleep in my tent. If you see that I have awoken, don't ask questions. Don't talk to me. Don't even try to understand what I am doing. Just take your lyre and sing until I sleep again."

"Yes, sir."

So the lad unrolled his bedding in the tent of the king.

▌

Every evening and morning the giant came out of the camp of the Philistines, took his stand across the valley, and roared derision against Israel. "Choose a champion!" he bellowed. "I defy the ranks of Israel to send one man to fight me!"

Because of this single figure, Saul's armies had ceased to attack the battle line that transected the valley of Elah. If they were afraid of one Philistine, what could they do to one thousand?

But this one was terrible. He stood more than nine feet high at the brow. He wore a helmet of bronze and a coat of mail weighing more than two hundred pounds. He had greaves of bronze on his legs, a javelin of bronze slung down between his shoulders, and a spear in his hand whose shaft was the size of a weaver's beam. He came from Gath. His name was Goliath.

Morning and evening, day after day, he mounted his southern prominence and thundered, "Am I not a Philistine? Are you not the soldiers of Saul? Choose one man to fight me. If he kills me, we will be your servants. If he dies, then you will serve us!"

∎

In the fifth week of this mortifying war, Saul suddenly woke at midnight shouting aloud his anguish. It felt as if a vulture were piercing him through at the bosom. "David!" he choked. Spittle had soaked his beard. "David, David, son of Jesse!"

Then he realized that the lad was already singing.

Saul held his breath.

God is here, he heard. *God is here*: a full and tender voice, a tone as pure as burnished gold. Saul felt the eating beak soften and withdraw. His fierce staring relaxed. He lay back and drew a deep breath. His eyelids drooped and closed of their own accord.

David the son of Jesse was running his fingers over six soft strings and singing:

> *I am not lonely. God is here.*
> *Hand at my shoulder. Word in my ear.*
>
> *The Lord is the shepherd who leads me down*
> *to quiet pools and a soft green ground.*
> *He feeds, restores, beholds, relieves me,*
> *shows the right road, then precedes me:*
>
> *I am not lonely. God is here.*
> *Strength for my going. Song in my ear.*
>
> *Yea, though I cross the valley of dying,*
> *I do not fear. I am not crying.*
> *Thy rod for the beast, thy staff for my leaning,*
> *thou art my comfort and thou my redeeming.*
>
> *Thou art my present, beginning and ending,*
> *the oil that I feel on my forehead descending,*
> *the goodness that follows my every endeavor,*
> *the temple I'll dwell in forever and ever —*
>
> *O Lord, I am not lonely now,*
> *for thou art with me, my shepherd — thou!*

∎

On the fifth day of the sixth week of Goliath's thunderous ridicule, Shammah came to the king's tent and asked an audience. It was noon. The armies of Israel were lying about in positions of defeat and desolation. No one was eating.

The king stepped out and sat in the shade of the tent-flap. Standing beside Shammah was his youngest brother, David.

"Well?"

With every sign of discomfort, Shammah said, "David wants to fight the giant."

Saul uttered a short bark of laughter. But David was gazing straight into the king's eye, not at all intimidated.

"You're no more than a youth," Saul said. "A shepherd. And Goliath, besides every other advantage, has been a warrior from *his* youth."

Shammah cuffed his brother's shoulder. "I told you so," he said. "Let's go."

But David stepped past him to the king. "No one else will fight Goliath," he said, his eyes as steadfast as sunlight. "The heart of every warrior in Israel fails on account of this one man."

"Yes. Exactly. And if mature men won't fight him, why should I let a lad go?"

But in Saul's heart there flickered a small black flame. *A savvy lad.* He began to make a narrow assessment of the shrewdness and the ability here before him.

"Yes," said David, "and exactly as *you* have said, your servant keeps sheep. But that, O King, argues for my going."

"What?" Saul flashed a quick grin. "How?"

"When lions or bears snatch lambs from the flock, I go after them. I whack them with my rod and take the lambs out of their mouths. If they turn to attack me, I catch them by the beard and kill them. Sir, it is the Lord who delivers me from the tooth of the lion and the claw of the bear! The Lord will surely deliver me from the hand of an uncircumcised giant."

By the time David finished his speech, his eyes blazed a golden fire, and Saul could not stop grinning.

He's a dagger dipped in venom, thought the king, then aloud he said, "No one has ever spoken truer words, sir! It is the Lord who gives the victory. Wait here."

Saul went into his tent and came out carrying his own armor.

"Yes, and I, too, commend you to the Lord. Here." He hoisted the coat of mail over David's back. He placed his helmet on David's head, and the poor lad peered out like a turtle under so much metal. Saul wanted to laugh at the sight. But he also discovered tender fears for David. The armor was no good. The youth would have to go light on his foot, unprotected and vulnerable.

"But if you can't swing a sword," said Saul, lifting the armor from David's small frame, "how do you kill wild beasts?"

"With this." David raised his right hand. Tied to the middle finger was one end of a long leather sling. The hollow of the sling, the stone-pocket woven between two thin cords, was worn and well used.

"With that?"

"Yes, sir."

The king of Israel laid his hand upon the lad's wild red hair. "Go," he said earnestly, "and the Lord be with you."

So David departed, his sling wrapped like a sleeve around his forearm, his shepherd's pouch at the small of his back.

King Saul never took his eyes from the young adventurer. As David descended the north slope of the valley, Saul mounted a lookout in order to keep watch.

It was early evening, the second time today when Goliath would emerge to challenge Israel.

There was no avoiding the battle now: Saul saw the giant striding toward his stone platform on the south side of the valley, followed by a servant who, though he was a full-grown man, struggled under the weight of his master's armor.

Goliath climbed a dolmen, an enormous stone table, threw back his great head and boomed: "I defy the ranks of Israel to send me a man that we may fight together!"

Quickly Saul looked for David on the valley floor. There he was — and he wasn't even paying attention to the Philistine! The lad was down on one knee by the brook of Elah, reaching into the water. *He's choosing stones!* While Goliath of Gath made the hills quake with his bull's voice, David was hefting wet stones and dropping them into his pouch. *Four of them*, Saul counted. *Five.* Then the lad stood up again and jumped the stream and continued walking toward Goliath. *He walks on the balls of his feet, like dancing.*

All at once the giant noticed the Israelite approaching. "Finally!" he cried. He positioned his armor-bearer with a shield in front while he raised his own helmet, preparing to put it on — but then he leaned forward, scowling. "What?" he roared. He threw the helmet to the ground, knocked the armor-bearer aside, and launched into a lumbering run. "What! Am I a dog?"

Saul ran forward, the better to see. Goliath had ceased laughing. He was not scornful: he was enraged, his brow as black as a thunderhead.

"Am I a dog," he bellowed, "that you come at me with sticks?"

David didn't hesitate. He maintained an easy pace, his face set directly toward the shambling foe, his shoulders back, his neck an ivory column.

Goliath stopped. "Come, then!" he raged. He drew his sword and lifted his spear the size of a weaver's beam. "Come and I will give your flesh to the birds and the beasts!"

Neither faster nor slower, David kept trotting at his own easy pace. Saul saw him slip a stone from the pouch at his back and wrap it in the hollow of his sling. Then the gentle tenor voice rang out in the valley: "You come with iron weapons. I come in the name of the Lord, whom you have defied. This day the Lord will give you into my hand, and I will strike you down, and all the earth will know that there is a God in Israel."

A boy! Goliath was dumbfounded. His lips retracted. Saul heard an inarticulate growl of a warrior humiliated. And new fury propelled the giant forward. He began to charge downhill toward David. He leveled his spear at the lad's breast. He raised his sword in his right hand.

Saul stood transfixed, as speechless as the giant.

But David never varied his pace. He had begun to whirl the sling above his head, causing the leather to sing in the wind.

With a snap he released it. The stone streaked for Goliath's skull.

Suddenly that champion of the Philistine armies slowed to a walk, perplexed. He turned to the side, as if to ask a question, then toppled backward upon the ground, like a great cedar felled.

Even now David did not pause. He trotted uphill toward Goliath supine, slipped the huge sword from his hand, took a stance with his right foot at the giant's shoulder, his left foot at his ear, then heaved the iron weapon high and brought it down with all his might. The blade cut through flesh and bone to the earth below. Goliath's head rolled free, and Saul began to laugh. King Saul opened his mouth and laughed as he had in the early days of his reign. For David was walking back across the valley, holding the head of Goliath by the hair, and in the perfect center of the giant's forehead was a small round hole.

All Israel now raised a shout of triumphant joy — while Philistines wildly pulled their shields from the battle line and threw themselves into a messy retreat.

Immediately the men of Israel and Judah gave chase. They followed the enemy down the valley as far as Gath and even to the gates of Ekron, slaughtering cowards all along the way. Then they returned to plunder the empty camps, exchanging their dull bronze weaponry for bright new iron.

But Saul stood apart, contemplating another victory. And in the night he found David, the fire of his latter years and his delight in life again.

"Son of Jesse," he said, "hereafter you must be my armor-bearer. More than that, enter the battle with me. Fight beside me, David. And if you continue tomorrow as gallant as you were today, I will set you over a thousand troops. Oh, David, what glories God has won for us today!"

Suddenly the king knelt down and seized the slender shepherd in a mighty embrace.

It may be that another son of Saul would have felt jealous at such an open display of affection. These were princely promises after all.

But Jonathan stood back in the darkness smiling. He, too, was overwhelmed with gladness. Saul was strong again! Saul was robust and happy and whole again. The soul of his father had been restored.

So Jonathan gazed at the ruddy young man who had accomplished such goodness, and he loved him.

vi

"David, come here. My father has a new weapon. Look!"

Saul had built stone stables behind his fortress in Gibeah. He and his captains rode horses into battle; therefore, he had appointed servants to feed and groom his mounts even in peacetime. And — though Israel thought of horses as the playthings of rich pagans — he had begun to use them for his swifter journeys. Yes, even for his pleasure.

Moreover, he had permitted Jonathan to teach David how to ride. Jesse disapproved. But the young man was of the king's court now.

"Here. Come round this way."

Jonathan led David to a low building at the back of the stables. He unlatched the wooden door and began to swing it open. On his cheeks Jonathan felt the chilly morning air; in his heart he felt a keen excitement. It always delighted him to show David some new thing.

This lad from the country was so genuine in his appreciations that Jonathan himself was elevated. With David he was wise and skilled. A teacher. No competition here! Until now all of Jonathan's friends had turned everything into a contest; so had Jonathan; it was in his nature to run, if he ran, faster than others. But *this* friend seemed to feel no need to outrun anyone; rather, he would out-compliment everyone. And his intelligent eyes fairly crackled with glad thanksgivings when some particular friend — like Jonathan — took time to grant him gifts of knowledge and insight.

"What do you think?" said Jonathan, standing back so David could see the treasure inside.

It was a chariot.

Jonathan couldn't contain himself. He burst out laughing. David didn't. He gave his friend an amber smile; then, with intense curiosity he approached the device and began to touch its tongue, the pole that ran back under the box to the axle, the wicker weave of the box itself, the interior dashboard, the exterior cover of hard leather front and sides.

David did all this in silence. It fascinated Jonathan, how restrained this young man was. He himself would have been boisterous in the examination, every thought jumping out of his mouth. When Jonathan fought, he shouted. When he spoke with his father, they both shouted. When he made love, he laughed and he shouted together. That someone might feel many things, and feel them as deeply as David did, yet present to the world an exterior so controlled and courtly and kind — that amazed Jonathan, and confronted by David's silences he felt infinitely younger than his friend, immature, a noisy pupil with much to learn after all.

David stood back from the chariot and said, "There is no reason why Israel shouldn't use this weapon in war."

Jonathan said, "Let's go hunting."

"With this?"

"Yes!"

"Where? We're in the mountains here."

"Flatland in the valley of Aijalon!"

"Do you know how long it takes just to get to the city of Aijalon?"

"Come on! Come on! In the open country we'll fly faster than the hart! The roebuck! David, the *gazelle*!"

"And you know how to hitch this thing."

"Yes. I'll teach you. Two horses. Let's go!"

■

In those days Saul was told that the king of Zobah had begun to harass the tribes of Manasseh and Naphtali in the north. Again he blew the ram's horn of war. Again he raised a militia and placed himself at the head of it and by the force of his passions led it north and north to fight.

David rode beside him, skillful on a donkey, the captain of a thousand men. David rode in a busy silence, his red hair tugged by the wind, his copper-flecked eyes scanning the land ahead; for this captain had the ability to conceive battle strategies in his mind and to test them in imagination.

Saul marveled. It was like this: both he and his new warrior could read the words on a scroll. But he read aloud. The young man read silently. Saul had never heard of such a thing before.

David continued, too, to sleep in the king's tent. And though no one else in Israel may have known when the black mood tormented him, David knew. David woke and stroked his lyre and sang. He sang in a soothing tenor. He sang — so Saul began to realize —*for* him as well as to him. That is, he sang to God on behalf of Saul:

> *We call on thee, O Lord. Lord, hear our cry.*
> *Thou refuge both of shepherds and of kings,*
> *keep us as the apple of thine eye,*
> *and hide us in the shadow of thy wings.*

Always Saul was eased by the singing. Always he fell asleep before the music ceased. But sometimes he woke the following day disquieted. Some small thing nagged in the back of his mind. What was it?

Saul and Abner and Jonathan and David defeated the king of Zobah. He was an Aramaean, an ancient relative of Abraham and Israel. Saul ordered his execution, and he was executed, but there was little satisfaction in the victory. This petty kingdom would rise up again. Moab had. And Ammon and Edom and Amalek. And three of these were kin.

That night Saul woke himself by crying out the name of Samuel. His throat was thick with sobbing. His head was roaring like a waterfall, and he was crying, "Samuel, come back! Samuel, Samuel, I have sinned! Come back!"

David was already singing. A complex song, so it seemed. Saul fought the noise inside his skull in order to hear the song.

> *O Lord, rebuke me not in fury,*
> > *nor chasten me in wrath!*
> *Thine arrows have found me! Their heads are buried*
> > *in my heart, point and shaft!*
>
> *My wounds are foul and festering*
> > *because of foolishness;*
> *O God, I'm sorry for my sin!*
> > *My sin! Lord, I confess.*
>
> *Do not forsake me, O my Lord!*
> > *O God, deliver me!*
> *I wait upon thy kinder word;*
> > *O Lord, I wait for thee —*

In the morning Saul could repeat the entire song from memory. He went out of his tent whispering it. The song had become the cry of his heart. It gave expression to the furnace burning within him, and therefore it gave him comfort.

But suddenly — just as he was reaching for his horse's bridle — the king yelped and whirled around and glared back at the tent. A thought had just pierced him like an arrow, and he understood why David's nighttime presence was so troubling: the man knew too much! With David the king had no secrets! Neither, then, could he maintain a personal privacy with that one — no, nor authority either! David had dared to give expression to the sins of his king!

And how *ever* could he presume to talk about his, Saul's, sin?

■

After hunting, Jonathan hobbled the horses, and allowed them to graze in a green field. He took a long drink from his leather flask — a good, sweet wine — offered the flask to David, then threw himself down on the grass, lay back, and heaved a sigh of happiness. David came and lay beside him. They gazed into the blue sky.

They had been gone from Gibeah three days. Though they could beg cakes from the villages because Jonathan was recognized as the crown prince of Israel, they had mostly eaten the meat of their hunting. They felt proud and independent.

Jonathan said, "You know the old priest named Samuel, don't you?"

"Yes," David said. "Why?"

Jonathan shifted his shoulders and locked his hands behind his head.

"The people of Ramah say that he has taken to his bed. They say he's dying."

"He's very old."

"Old like a skeleton. Have you ever seen him?"

"Once."

"Well, until this sad news my father sent him regular invitations, but he never came. My father requested permission to go to Samuel himself. He never answered. Now the old priest is sick unto death, and my father has stopped asking altogether."

Jonathan lay quietly a moment, biting the inside of his lip. "I don't know why Samuel wouldn't come. It hurt my father. Now the wound is worse than before."

Jonathan turned his head and glanced at his friend. David had a scattering of freckles over his cheeks and the bridge of his nose.

"Once?" said Jonathan. "When did *you* see the priest?"

David sat up. "I've never told this to anyone else. Even my family doesn't know the whole of it," he said. "And I don't altogether understand it either. It makes me feel sad."

David reached down and took Jonathan's right hand in the gesture of a pledge. "You've got to promise to keep this between us," he said. "You cannot tell it to your father."

David's gaze was so penetrating and at the same time so full of pity that Jonathan responded as if in ceremony: "This is between us alone."

"Samuel came to Bethlehem several years ago just after your father had attacked the Amalekites. He said he came to sacrifice a heifer to the Lord with the elders of the city. 'Consecrate yourselves,' he said to them, 'and come with me to the sacrifice.'

"But to my father he said, 'I will myself consecrate you and your sons.'"

David lay back down and closed his eyes. Jonathan was watching him closely. His friend's voice had an undertone of urgency.

"I was in the fields that day, keeping the sheep," David said.

"The priest performed the ritual washing of my father. Then he washed my brothers one by one, Eliab, Abinadab, Shammah — all seven. My father says that when the last had been washed, the priest asked if those were all the sons that Jesse had. It was then that they sent for me.

"Jonathan, when I stood in front of that old man he grabbed my head with such strength in his hands that I thought he would crush me. He whispered a few words so softly no one could hear them except me: *The Lord sees not as people see,* he said. *People look on the outward appearance, but the Lord looks on the heart.*

"Then he drew from his robes the horn of a wild ox. He held it over my head and tipped it and I felt oil soaking my hair. As if it came from a great cut, oil ran like blood down my temples, down my forehead and my face. It dripped from my chin. Oh, Jonathan, there was so much oil and the ancient priest seemed so furious that I felt afraid. I smelled smoke, and I thought we were both going to die.

"All at once he was done. He put his things away, and he left. The priest never did sacrifice the heifer, though most of the village had consecrated themselves. They said, 'He is old and forgetful,' and they forgave him.

"Well," David said, standing up and staring toward the hills. "That is the time I saw Samuel."

Jonathan followed David with his eyes. "No," he said, "I will never tell anyone this story." He, too, stood up. "But I think you will know when the time has come to tell it aloud yourself, and then everyone will know its meaning." He looked at the back of his friend, the tangled red hair, flesh so white and vulnerable.

Suddenly Jonathan turned and ran to the chariot. He reached into the dashboard case and drew forth his sword and his best black lacquered bow. Then he returned to David, softly calling his name.

The two men faced each other.

Jonathan said, "You have just given me a thing of inexpressible value, a gift like nothing anyone has given me before. Now I want to give you something." Jonathan paused. He was more than ten years older than his companion, taller, darker, more rugged. Yet his manner grew bashful. "David," he said, "can these gifts make a covenant between us?"

David bowed his head.

Jonathan said, "I want us to make a covenant together, you and me. Friendship unshakable and everlasting. Because I love you, son of Jesse, as I love my own soul — "

Jonathan stopped speaking. Abruptly he stepped forward and held out his sword and his bow that David might take them.

But for a long while David didn't move. He stood with his head bowed so low that his face was hidden. Then he made a small sound, and Jonathan realized that his friend was crying.

Immediately he dropped his weapons and went to David and embraced him.

"Let's go home," he whispered. "It's time to go home."

■|

The Philistines attacked villages in the Guvrin valley of the Shephelah. Three villages, one right after the other.

Saul blew the trumpet of war. A militia was mustered.

West of Keilah, which would have been the next town attacked, Israelite warriors rushed out of the hills in a blunt, head-on counterattack. The valley was narrow at this point. Rock rose on both sides to create a bloody corridor.

Saul and Jonathan and Abner all charged the enemy on horses.

David rode a mule.

Saul argued that the horse was larger and faster than any other mount. He said it had military advantages, especially for the tall, long-legged man. But in those days, a rider controlled his horse by the bridle alone. It took a warrior of volatile temperament and genuine strength to make the horse work well in the midst of battle. For all its speed, the horse was a fractious, shivering, nervous beast.

Mules may have been stolid and lower-slung. But they were steadfast creatures, altogether dependable — and in the hills of Judah, surefooted.

On a mule, then, David brought his division down difficult rock into the valley, surprising the foe at its left flank. David's division struck the telling blow of the battle — and David, in the thick of things, slaughtered Philistines with such dazzling dexterity that the people of Keilah, huddled on the top of the rocks, broke into cheering.

David killed with a minimum of motion and of blood. His sword was shorter and sharper than most. So quickly did he slip his blade in a heart and out again, his victim seemed merely puzzled before he died. And he fought silently. David neither laughed nor cursed nor taunted his foe. His eyes were not angry, but alert. And because of the lack of tumult where he went, Philistines were unaware how near they were to dying.

But the people on the ridges saw. Israelites screamed their admiration. And when the enemy turned in retreat, they leaped up and began to shout a certain refrain in unison. Saul heard the rhythm of their voices, but at this distance he couldn't make out the words.

The next day, after Israel had broken camp and the militia had demobilized, Saul and his captains mounted their horses and began to ride back to Gibeah.

As they passed through cities on the way, women came out with timbrels to meet King Saul, singing songs of joy and dancing. But in every city one refrain dominated the music of the women — the same one Saul had heard from the rocks surrounding the battlefield. This time he heard the words, and his face fell:

> *Saul has killed his thousand again,*
> *and David his ten thousand men!*

That same night Saul woke in his chambers, filled with the black mood, grabbing things and breaking them, a table, a clay basin. He couldn't remember beginning; neither could he stop. His mind bright with hatred. And as always when Saul woke, David was sitting in the corner of his bedroom singing, strumming his instrument and singing some sweet song:

> — *A thousand foe may fall at thy right,*
> *ten thousand at thy left;*
> *yet the pestilence that stalks by night —*

The song was a damnable outrage! Saul grabbed a jar of water and smashed it to the floor. He seized a spear. He flung it at David, screaming: "I'll pin you to the wall!"

David ducked. The spear shattered against stone. And suddenly Saul was overwhelmed with remorse. He stood gaping at his hands and gasping as if he could not breathe. Then he rushed to David, crying, "I'm sorry! I'm sorry! I didn't mean to hurt you."

David opened his mouth to speak, but Saul clapped his hand over it. "No, no," he cried, "it's not your fault. It's my fault." Then he stumbled backward and turned and lifted his hands as high as he could and wailed, "Lord God, where are you? Why have you taken your spirit away from me?"

King Saul collapsed to the floor. He felt no hatred now, except as one hates himself. He drew his knees up to his chest and wrapped his great arms around them and rocked side to side.

"Why, why?" he sang. It sounded like a song. "Why has this evil spirit come upon me? O God, won't you tell me what I am to do?"

■

In those days Saul's youngest daughter came to him and asked for something.

"What is it?" he said.

As far as Michal's memory went, she had always been the daughter of a king, and her father loved her by giving gifts.

"David," she said, "the son of Jesse."

"What?" Saul stared at his daughter. "What are you asking?"

"I want you to make David my husband."

Saul caught his breath. For a moment he trembled to think of his flesh joined to David. But then he began to smile. He took Michal into his arms and said, "Yes. Yes, I will offer you to David. Of course. Yes."

She beamed and kissed her father and ran from the room.

But Saul was thinking: *Let Michal be the snare that turns the hand of the Philistines against David.*

That same day he sent servants to David, saying: "Behold, the king delights in you. All his servants love you. Even his youngest daughter,

Michal, loves you. Now, then, David son of Jesse, at the king's request, become his son-in-law."

Within the hour they returned and reported David's response: "He says he is a poor man and of no repute. He asks whether it seems a little thing to become the son-in-law of a king."

Saul said, "Tell him I desire no expensive marriage present, just the proof that a hundred Philistines have perished. Ask him whether he thinks he is valiant enough to enter the territories of the Philistines for a hundred foreskins."

The servants went again to David. Saul paced in his chambers and waited to hear the fate not so much of his daughter as of his captain.

In the evening the servants came and said, "David has accepted the offer. He has left with some men for the cities of the Philistines."

"Already?" the king said, frowning. This was good, of course. It was his plan for the killing of David, and the sooner, the better. Why, then, did Saul feel as if the affair had just outrun him?

Three days later he heard a shout go up outside the fortress, the voice of his warriors praising a hero for some wondrous accomplishment.

King Saul rushed outside, and there came David, leading an ass and a simple cart and ten sacks filled — so everyone in Gibeah knew — with Philistine foreskins.

Gibeah? Why, everyone in Israel knew. And everyone knew that David had done double the king's request. City to city, rumor flew and Israelite pride had burst in Israelite bosoms: *David invaded the strongholds of the Philistines and killed two hundred men and took two hundred foreskins and then escaped unscratched! David!*

In the merriment of the moment, some soldier presumed fellowship and slapped his king on the back. Saul, with a backward shot of his elbow, broke the man's jaw.

He kept his promise, of course. King Saul gave David his youngest daughter for a wife, and he granted them a room upstairs in his fortress. But the unrestrained affection with which the kingdom now greeted David — that caused in Saul a dynastic fear.

▌

In those days Samuel died, and the elders of Israel assembled to mourn him. Priests came from the north and the south. Soldiers gathered with their captains, men and women, young and old. But not the king.

Samuel was but a wisp at death, sunken eyes and bones like dry reeds. His face was fixed in an expression of sorrow.

They buried him where he had lived, in Ramah.

■

Whenever an army marched through Israel, it was the farmers who suffered most. Troops plucked their fruit, ate their grain, stole their cheeses and cream, butchered their cattle. The battles themselves were engaged in cultivated fields, destroying crops even before they could be harvested. Friendly armies commanded, enemies stole — but David the son of Jesse distinguished himself from either of these. He honored the common farmer. He asked for his food.

And when his fighting men had been fed, he blessed his benefactors, saying, "Blessed be the Lord, the God of Israel, and blessed be your kindness, and blessed be you who kept us this day from hunger and thirst."

Soon everyone in Israel knew David on sight. And more than the women sang his praises. Men, too, the young and the old, farmers and shepherds and shopkeepers: the common folk of Israel shouted:

> *Saul has killed his thousand again,*
> *but David his ten thousand men!*

Lately David was making slower and slower marches home. It was not just that he met with adulation; he also chose to stop at various homes along the way in order to share the spoils of his victory with those who had supported him.

Thus it happened that after a brief skirmish against the Philistines Saul went home, but David delayed.

On the third day the king asked why David had not yet returned and it was told him that the son of Jesse was visiting all the cities of Israel. "He eats with the people and then he blesses them. They rejoice in his presence."

The king said, "How do you know that?"

And it was told him: "Wherever David stays, there is dancing in that village."

That night King Saul sat inside the door of his room with a spear across his knees. He did not light the lamp. The only sound he made was a harsh catch of breath, struggling to control himself. His muscles all were taut. He was waiting for the door to open, waiting to see the silhouette of David returning.

■

Michal woke suddenly out of deep sleeping. Something had shocked her awake, but she recalled no sound.

Then she sensed motion. Then someone was standing over her. Then the man knelt down, and it was her husband David.

"Your father," he whispered, "just tried to kill me."

"What?"

"Hush, Michal. This isn't the first time. He threw his spear at me."

"*Kill* you, David? This isn't a dream or a misunderstanding?"

"He ordered soldiers to guard the doors. I bolted from his room, but he knows I haven't left the fortress."

Michal realized that her bedding was wet. The moisture was warm, and so she hadn't noticed before; but now the blanket was sticking to her stomach.

"David! You're bleeding!"

"My left side, under the arm."

"Oh, David! If you don't save your life tonight, you'll die tomorrow."

Michal got up and began to tear the linen bedding into strips. "Tie these together," she said. She tore more strips, these much wider. "Raise your arms." She washed the wound, a long horizontal slice, then bound his ribs, his back, and his breast with the linen bandages. She went to her window and opened the lattice wide.

"Send for me," she said.

David kissed her, then went out the window and down the side of Saul's fortress by a linen rope.

Send for me, she said, believing she would see her husband again in a few days.

Michal pulled the lattice closed and went to work. She laid a teraphim, a wooden image, on her bed. She stuffed a small bag with goats' hair, and placed it at the head of the teraphim, then covered both with clothes and blankets. Finally she went to the corner of the room and trimmed the wick of her lamp so that it shed but a dim light.

Almost immediately guardsmen burst into her room.

Michal cursed them. "Can't you see he's sick?" she said.

The guards retreated from her ferocity, but then Saul came into the room with torches.

"I will see him sick or well," he said. "And if the poor man has bled too much to move, then we'll take the whole bed downstairs!"

He snatched back the blankets. The head-bag bounced softly away, and the teraphim lay blank in bed.

Saul covered the top of his head with two hands and howled: "Michal! How could you deceive me? How could you give my enemy time to escape?"

"He told me to," she said. She cringed from her father as from a madman. "He said to me, 'Why should I kill you?' And he said, 'Let me go.' Father, Father, what else could I do?"

∎

"Tonight he planned the deed!" David was out of breath, crouched in the shadow in Jonathan's courtyard. "I opened the door to his chamber, and there he sat, framed and facing me, the spear drawn back, his eyes blazing. I leaped to my right but caught the spear in my left side."

Jonathan touched David's breast. Bandages.

David said, "Truly, as the Lord lives and as your soul lives, Jonathan, there's but a step between me and death."

"I believe you," Jonathan said. "What do you want me to do?"

"Tomorrow is the new moon. I will not be at the feast with your father. I will be hiding by the heap of stones in Ribai's field. When your father misses me, tell him I went to Bethlehem to celebrate the feast with my own family. I won't appear for three days. If your father accepts that, then the evil spirit has come and gone, and it will be safe for me to return. But if he continues angry, then this evil is of his own will. In that case, Jonathan, keep faith with me. Love me still. But if you find that I am guilty, slay me yourself. Don't let Saul do it."

"Oh, David!" cried Jonathan. "How could I ever hurt the hairs of my beloved?"

David said, "Who will tell me if your father answers you roughly three days through?"

Jonathan said, "I will."

"How? I won't be able to show myself. And you will be watched."

"I know the heap of stones," said Jonathan. "On the third day I'll go to Ribai's field with my bow. I'll bring a boy with me to gather the arrows I shoot, and I will call loudly to him. If I say, 'The arrows are near you,' you will know that all is well. My father is kind again. But if I say, 'The arrows are far beyond you,' stay hidden. Go in secret. For the Lord has sent you away."

When they had said these things, David went out and melted into the night.

Jonathan stood alone in the center of his courtyard. He thought he would go inside and sit. But he didn't. By sunrise he was still in the courtyard.

∎

In the evening of the day of the new moon, the king sat down to eat. As always, he sat on the seat by the wall. Jonathan sat opposite. Abner sat by Saul's side. David's place was empty.

They passed the meal in silence. King Saul said nothing at all regarding David.

But David's place was empty the next night, too.

Saul said, "Yesterday I thought David was unclean and couldn't eat the feast. That can't be a problem today. Why isn't he here this evening?"

Jonathan said, "David asked leave to go to Bethlehem. He said that his brother commanded him to be there for a sacrifice which his family holds at this time of year."

"Well, let me tell you what you are, Jonathan," Saul said, standing and facing his son. "You are a bastard! You're the issue of a perverse, rebellious, deceitful woman. You are no child of mine! Don't you understand? As long as the son of Jesse lives, you will never succeed me. Your kingdom will never be established! Jonathan, find that pretender! Fetch him to me, and I'll kill him myself!"

∎

Early the third day, Jonathan stood in a green field, facing a rough heap of rock and the brush that surrounded it. He saw no motion. But somewhere in that place his friend lay concealed.

Beside him was a boy.

Jonathan said to the boy, "Do you see these arrows?"

The child nodded.

"How many?"

"Three."

"I'm going to shoot all three arrows at a mark beside that heap of stones. Run and find them for me."

The child nodded again and stood still, waiting.

"Boy!" Jonathan barked, and the poor child jumped. "Run! Go! And don't come back until you have found all three arrows! One, two, three!"

The lad began to run toward the stones, and Jonathan notched the first arrow. With a fierce expression, he drew the shaft to his ear and shot. The arrow flew far past the stones. He shot the second arrow even farther. The third, when he had drawn it, trembled in the bow; his arms trembled; he didn't look fierce now; he looked sad. Jonathan knew he should simply let his brother vanish. It was not wise to see him. But how could he let him go and not see him?

The lad was just coming to the heap of stones. Jonathan shouted, "The arrows are beyond you! Beyond you!"

The child glanced back and ran on.

"Farther!" yelled Jonathan, then he drew the third arrow and shot it short. It struck by the stones. As if he hadn't the voice to call anymore, he said sadly, "I'll help you," and he walked toward the stones himself, peering narrowly at the thicket surrounding them.

He knelt among the bushes. "David?" he whispered.

Soon David was kneeling in front of him.

Jonathan gazed at the lean, freckled face a while. "So you know," he said.

"Yes, I know."

Suddenly Jonathan embraced David, and they clung to one another.

"I understand something now," Jonathan whispered into David's ear. "What Samuel did when he poured oil on your head: he was anointing you. He was preparing you to be the next king in Israel."

David pulled back, frowning. *"You're* the son of the king. You will succeed your father."

"No... no, I won't," Jonathan said softly. "You will. My father has helped me to see that. I think it is his final favor to you — that insight. I only pray that when you come into your kingdom, you'll show me the love of the Lord and will not kill me, David."

"Kill you? Jonathan, *kill* you? How can you think such a thing?"

"I live in a king's court."

"Oh, Jonathan, I'd rather my eyes were burned in their sockets!"

"Shhh, I believe you. And I bless you, David. May the Lord be with you even as once he was with my father."

The two men sank back on their heels and gazed at each other. Jonathan heard the distant crashing of the child still searching an arrow. Slowly he stripped himself of his robe and handed it to David. Flecks of amber in his friend's bright eyes! Shining eyes. How white was David's skin!

Jonathan said, "Take it as a token, and go in peace. Haven't we sworn in the name of the Lord, *The Lord be between me and thee, and between our descendants, forever*? Yes. David, go in peace."

He rose to his feet and shouted over the bushes, "Here it is. Here is the third arrow, boy!"

∎

In the months that followed, rumors reached Saul in Gibeah regarding David.

"David stayed in Nob with Ahimelech the priest, who gave him the holy bread to eat, the bread of the Presence. And when he left, he took the sword of Goliath the Philistine."

Again: "David was seen in Gath, the city of the Philistines. He was acting the part of a madman, scratching marks on the doors of the gate, drooling and gibbering! And Achish the king said, *Do I lack madmen, that you have brought this fellow here to haunt my house?* So they drove David away."

And again: "David has gone to the cave of Adullam! He's gathering a band of bloody adventurers. Soldiers of fortune! And those who follow him are men in distress, men in debt, men discontented with their lot."

Rumors filled the kingdom. David had captured the imagination of the people, and everyone knew some story about him.

"David and his men have fought against the Philistines at Keilah."

Again: "David lurks in the strongholds in the hills and the wilderness of Ziph."

And then again: "David and his men are in the wilderness of Maon!"

And Saul couldn't help it. A man obsessed, he responded to the rumors. With regard to Nob and the priest who gave food and a weapon to David:

Saul led an army there, killed Ahimelech, his family, and all eighty-five persons who served the holy place. He slaughtered Nob, men and women, children and sucklings, oxen, asses, and sheep — he put them all to the sword.

With regard to Keilah the king rode there as fast as he could, with his own swift army. But by the time he arrived, David had vanished.

When Saul heard that David was in Maon, he mounted a strong horse and rode all night, black fire in his eye. When he came to the mountain in that wilderness, he began to circle it — until a messenger came from the north, saying, "The Philistines are attacking us!" To the north, then, Saul rode in frustration.

But soon another rumor came:

"While you, King Saul, were marching round the west side of the mountain in Maon, David and his men were hiding on the east side of the same mountain."

∎

In those days the Philistines gathered their forces for war, intending to crush Israel once and for all.

Each of the five cities sent its armies northward by hundreds and by thousands. Chariots ground over the flat, dry earth; horses and mules and donkeys and soldiers caused the ground to shudder; the air felt heavy, as before a storm. This vast company assembled at Aphek, then marched north through the plains of Sharon and east into the Jezreel valley.

A small division of Israelites was encamped by the fountain in Jezreel. In fact, that division was the pretext and focus for this tremendous military display. The lords of the five cities declared that Israel threatened communications between them and their allies in Beth Shan.

So the Philistines established camps north of Jezreel, on the southern slopes of Mount Moreh at Shunem. They transformed the face of the mountain into a city, tents and pavilions and roads and watchtowers, all networked with trenches. There had not been so concentrated a preparation for war since they had gone to fight Israel at Michmash.

When King Saul heard of the mobilization of Philistine armies and their invasion of the Jezreel valley, he mounted his horse and rode north blowing the horn of war, desperately trying to inspire the men of Israel and to raise an army.

But the militia grew slowly, and then it moved sullenly. Israel was tired. These wars were unwinnable. This enemy had deep roots and magic branches. Cut one and two grew in its place. Besides, there were in those days some serious questions about the ways of kings in Israel. *He will take your sons —*

Saul's leadership had lost fire since Michmash. That man was more weary than any — his face heavy and seamed, his mind divided, his heart consumed by troubles the people could not name. Sometimes he emerged from his tent in the old style, furious and magnificent, blazing like Moses on the mountain. More often his eyes were dead, like ashes.

Thus the king led Israel to the Plain of Jezreel. He encamped on the north side of Mount Gilboa, more than ten miles away from the Philistine armies.

And then, in the night, Saul himself rode over the plain to Mount Moreh to see what sort of fight this would be.

He saw a mountain burning. He saw myriad Philistine fires. He saw ten thousand thousand troops gazing into flame and laughing. He saw a smoke go up that blackened the moon and swallowed the stars of heaven. Saul's knees buckled. He kneeled and cried out: "O Lord, what shall I do?" He repeated the prayer over and over again, "What shall I do?" But the Lord did not answer him.

Saul mounted his horse and rode back to his own camp. There he inquired of the Lord again, this time by means of the Urim. But the Lord did not answer him.

The king called prophets to himself. By the prophets he begged the Lord to tell him what he should do in the face of such Philistine mobilization. But the prophets could say nothing, and the Lord did not answer him.

Saul began to fast. He would not break his fast, and in that state, by dreams, he supplicated the Lord.

But the Lord God remained silent and did not answer him.

Then the king said to his servants, "Find me a medium. Find me a woman who can talk with the dead."

So haggard was his manner that no servant could refuse him or pretend not to know there was sorcery in the land.

They said, "There is a woman at Endor — "

But the king was already gone.

∎

Now, Saul covered himself in the rough leather of a goatherd. He dressed as if for cold weather, pulling a hood over his head, and rode north around Mount Moreh and the Philistine horde. He passed them in shadows by night. Outside Endor he hid his horse in a grove of trees, then he walked barefoot into the town. He came to a low stone cottage. He knocked on the door.

Someone lit an oil lamp inside.

The door opened a crack.

"What do you want?" A woman's voice.

Saul said, "Divine a spirit for me. Bring up the one I name for you."

"What, are you trying to kill me?" hissed the voice. "You know the king outlawed mediums and wizards. Is this a trap?"

"Ahhh!" cried Saul, a spasm of anguish. "Please! I know the king. I know him well, and I swear no punishment will fall on you if you do this for me."

"How can I? I'm not a medium."

"You are — or you wouldn't be so quick to smell a trap."

"Go away!"

"For God's sake, woman, help me! There is nowhere else I can go."

Slowly the door opened inward. Saul ducked down, pulled his hood close, and entered, murmuring, "Bless you, bless you, the Lord bless you — "

"Sit there," the woman said, pointing to a stool in the corner of the cottage. She placed the lamp in the center, then sat in the opposite corner. She was soft and round, a woman of maternal proportions. She spread her knees to sit. She bowed her head and pressed her fingers into her eyes.

"Whom shall I bring up for you?"

Saul swallowed. He leaned forward and looked intently into the woman's face. "Bring up Samuel the priest for me," he whispered.

The woman did not rock. She did not mutter a foreign language or else make pagan signs. In a soft voice, as a mother calls her child to a difficult task, she said, "Samuel, Samuel." There was a deep breathing silence in the cottage. Again, she said kindly, "Samuel." Again, the room held still. Saul was panting.

A third time the woman called, "Samuel! Samuel!" — and almost immediately another voice came out of her mouth, saying, *Saul, Saul, is that you?*

Suddenly the woman looked up and shrieked. It was genuine terror. "*You* are the king! Why did you deceive me? What are you doing?"

Saul could scarcely contain the emotion mounting within him. "Go on! Go on!" he cried throwing back his hood. "The king swears safety if you go on: what are you seeing?"

The woman had begun to tremble. Tremendous forces were colliding in her cottage. Slowly she bowed her head, and then she pressed her knuckles deep into her eyesockets.

"I see — "she said. She was sobbing. "—I see a god coming up out of the earth."

"Don't be afraid," Saul whispered. "What does he look like?"

"Like an old man. A bony old man rising from the ground. He's wrapped in a torn robe."

"Samuel," Saul hissed. "Samuel." He slipped from his stool and bowed down.

The strange voice said, *Why have you disturbed me?*

Saul said, "Oh, Samuel, I am lost. The Philistines will attack tomorrow, but God has turned away from me! The Lord will not answer me! Samuel, tell me what to do."

The voice said, *Why do you ask me? You know that the Lord has already given the kingdom to David.*

"Ahhh, let it be. Then let that be," Saul whispered. He rose up on his knees. He folded his hands before the woman who had driven her eyes back into her head. "I will not dispute what has been done. Only, tell me about tomorrow. What can I do to save Israel?"

Nothing.

"I am ready for anything. I'll make any sacrifice. Just tell me what to do."

It is already done.

"What is done?"

Tomorrow you and your sons shall be with me. That is done. And the Lord will give the army of Israel into the hand of the Philistines. That, too, is done. All is done.

Saul fell full length on the floor and lay on his back. There was no strength left in him.

The woman looked up, then rose and ran to him and knelt beside him.

"My lord," she said. "My lord! What is the matter?"

His great frame filled half her cottage. His hair had fallen like a shining grey splendor all around his head. He had been a handsome man.

"My lord?"

He didn't answer. His breathing was slow and even.

"My lord, what have we done, that you can't talk?"

The king's eyes were open, gazing into the middle distance. His eyebrows were raised, as if he were asking a sad question.

The woman began to stroke his shoulder. "Peace, peace," she said gently. And then she tipped her head and in the tones of a mother said, "When was the last time you had anything to eat? Can I get you something to eat?"

16

DAVID

i

D avid the son of Jesse sat in darkness on the brow of a cave near
En-gedi. His men lay sleeping inside the cave. He had taken the last
watch of the night — a solitary, moonless hour suited to his mood.
"I lie in the midst of lions," he murmured. He sighed. He turned his head
to the right a moment, to the ceiling of stars in the south, then softly he
began to sing:

> *Be merciful to me, O God:*
> *I lie in the midst of lions.*
> *Protect me by the sweep of thy wing*
> *from the ravening bite of the lions!*
>
> *Their teeth are spears and arrows clashing,*
> *their tongues the bloody sword.*

David fell silent. He sank into a brooding meditation. Vagrant breezes
blew up from the Salt Sea — massive, flat, black before him. High on his left
a waterfall tumbled several hundred feet down into a sweet oasis.

These were the Wildgoats' Rocks. The cave where his strong men slept
was an old sheepfold, girdled by low stone wall across the entrance. David
had considered this a good hiding place.

Apparently, not good enough.

For nearly a year the king of Israel had been pursuing him with horses and
warriors and a fixed will to kill the man. Several times David had only barely
escaped: at Keilah, by a mountain in the desert of Maon.

But yesterday, while he and his men crouched in the dark recesses of this
same cave, Saul's armies came marching past the entrance. They stopped.
David could hear the shouting and the laughter of troops cooling themselves
in the oasis pool.

Then someone darkened the entrance and came into the cave. Just inside, the man stripped off his robe, his tunic, and his loin cloth. He squatted between two stones and groaned.

By the size of this figure and by the heedless force of his gestures — he had flung the robe ten feet deeper into the cave — David knew who it was. King Saul himself.

No, En-gedi wasn't good enough. David would abandon the site tomorrow. In fact, he had to find another strategy altogether. He was a renegade, an outlaw whom people might either befriend or betray. Running and raiding, then, must finally end in exhaustion or else on the point of a royal spear.

"But my heart," David whispered, "my heart is steadfast, Lord." He glanced up and saw that the eastern sky was lightening to grey. The smooth horizon beyond the sea was a black line visible against the dim light.

Suddenly, David drew breath and began to sing aloud:

> My heart is steadfast, O my God!
> My heart stands fast in thee!
> I'll sing this morning's morning song,
> dawn-dappled melody:

He stood up. He took a stance on the limestone ledge above the cave and sang:

> Awake, my harp! Awake, my lyre!
> My soul, look to the skies!
> We'll brighten night with a song of fire
> and cause the dawn to rise!
>
> Be thou exalted, O Lord God,
> above the firmament!
> Come, let thy glory walk the world
> with steps benevolent.

He sang the last passage as a refrain over and over, seven times over, and when he finished, the east indeed was afire, the sea was lost in burning mist, and his young men were wandering out of the cave below, stretching and rubbing their faces.

David looked down and saw one man of bullish stature and wiry, close-cropped hair.

"Joab!" he called.

That one turned and looked up. A hard, weathered face. Smooth-shaven. As ageless as stone, though he was in fact no older than David.

"Let's go to the Philistines," David called down to him. "What do you think? We can offer our services to Achish of Gath."

The man named Joab regarded David a full minute, then shook his head and shrugged and walked down to the pool.

"What then, cousin?" David called. "Are you angry with me?"

The rest of the men were already splashing morning water on their faces, blowing plumes of spray, rolling their muscles below the waterfall at cliffside. Thirty men formed the core of those that followed David, independent fellows, men of shrewdness and courage and power. Heroes.

There sat Benaiah by a new fire molding barley cakes for baking against the rocks. Benaiah — who seldom spoke, whose obedience was as sure as sunrise — had shoulders like the beam of a house. David knew that this man had slain bare-handed a lion cornered in a pit in a snowstorm. He was fearless. With nothing but a staff Benaiah would await the attack of an armed soldier, then he'd tear the weapon from his enemy's hands and kill him with the edge of his own sword.

"Benaiah," David said, "when you've eaten, take several men to forage for grain and cheeses, dates and raisins. We're going to travel to Gath."

David came down from his perch above the cave and approached a lean man. "I'm going to talk with your brother a while," he said. "Pass the word to everyone that we will begin to travel at dusk." This was to Abishai, smooth as an eel, lantern-jawed, and so thin that, running, he seemed all neck, impossible to grab, cut, hit, stab, or kill. "Tell them we'll take a hard route through the valleys, dark and treacherous but safe."

As he passed among the men, David spoke all his words softly, as though every word were personal to the man addressed.

There was Abiathar, returning from the pool with washed clothing. David stopped him and said, "This morning and this evening, I want you to sacrifice peace offerings unto the Lord." Abiathar nodded and smiled. He had the gift of sweetness. In spite of grief he could smile a perfect radiance upon those he loved — especially David, who was all his family now.

"Prepare us for a change," David said. "Beg God to bless the change. I have decided to put an end to raiding."

Abiathar was the son of Ahimelech, the priest at Nob whom Saul had murdered for giving David bread to eat. Saul had slaughtered every member of Ahimelech's family *except* Abiathar, who fled to David with his father's ephod. So David had an oracle whereby he could seek the will of the Lord.

And then there was Joab, David's sister's son, a warrior and a tactician who could read the field in an instant — terrain, enemy, weather, the cold political consequence of any act. David found Joab among the cypress trees on the far side of the pool, standing in shade.

"So, what do you think?" David said.

216 | THE BOOK OF GOD

Joab was shorter than he was and stockier. His manner was gruff. David looked directly into his eyes, though he stared ever into the distance.

"King Achish of Gath," Joab said.

"Yes," said David.

"Why?"

"Saul must be persuaded to stop hunting us, or we will perish at his hand. He has never fought anything but a defensive war against the Philistines. He won't breach their borders by an offensive invasion. And Achish knows the enmity between us. I believe he will make space for us in Gath. What do you think?"

"Isn't it treachery to treat with the enemy?"

"Treachery? That never bothered you before. Besides, who is our enemy? The one who would kill us, right?"

"In the lion's den no one is the lion's foe. Everyone's his food."

"I think we can deceive both Saul and the Philistines by *seeming* to serve Achish while actually serving ourselves in Judah. Who knows the hill country and the Negev better than we do?"

"My cousin goes around the stream he could cross in a step."

"Joab, stop these aphorisms and speak plainly."

"*Nabal*," Joab barked. "Fool!"

"So you are angry with me."

Now Joab looked directly at David. "If you had killed the king yesterday, there'd be no need for deception today."

David's face felt suddenly hot. "How could I have killed the king?" he said.

"He was squatting in the cave as dumb as a lamb at the sacrifice. If you could creep close enough to cut off the hem of his robe, surely you could have cut his throat."

"That's not what I mean, Joab. How could I kill the Lord's anointed? How could I live with such a sin?"

"Is it a sin to kill a killer? Is it a sin to relieve Israel of a dangerous, maniacal *tyrant*?"

"Joab!" David's voice was a whipcrack. His cousin flinched, then frowned and looked out over the Salt Sea.

David said, "The chosen one of God is the will of God made visible among us. Saul is Saul, but the king is the Lord's, and I will not sin against the Lord."

Joab's hair was wiry, iron-grey. His eyes were a cold grey, his jaw strong, his cheeks soldier-seamed. He was deep-chested and bandy-legged and brusque. And now he was as mute as grey stone.

Actually, though David had just experienced his own anger, immediately he liked his cousin again. Silence in this iron countenance tickled David and made him feel light-hearted.

He laid his hand on Joab's shoulder and said, "While we are in Gath I want you to observe the organization of the Philistine army, the sizes and the purposes of its various units. Identify the ranks and authority of its officers. Memorize the weaponry. Learn its methods of supply and transport, its division of duties, its stratagems in different terrains, the most effective deployment of chariots. Everything. Steal every military thought they have. We will not waste our time in Gath, whatever happens. And I've made up my mind: when we are an army, Joab, you will be its commander-in-chief."

█

When David was joined by everyone for whom he was responsible, more than six hundred people encamped around him. The entire families of his fighting men depended upon him. They were the kin of outlaws: what city was safe for them now? David's sisters and brothers, likewise, were fugitives, their spouses and their children — and their parents, Jesse and Nahash.

But Jesse and Nahash were very old. Their bones were brittle and their eyes dim and they could not travel safely, however smooth the road or peaceful the countryside.

At noonday David sat in the shade of his father's tent.

His mother brought them cool water to drink. She was so bent by age that her face looked straight down to the ground when she walked.

David watched how slowly she sat down, then he said: "When we strike camp and leave tonight, we cannot take a high road. We'll climb the gorges, down one side and up the other. We are going over the mountains to Gath."

Jesse nodded. Nahash raised bright eyes and looked shrewdly at her son. "You mean to say that we cannot come," she said.

"Yes," said David, "I do. I'm sorry. I think it would kill you."

Nahash said, "Right now there is no place in Israel that will not kill us."

David felt sad. "I've brought trouble to your old age."

"King Saul has troubled our old age." Nahash said. Her tone was strong, her eye direct. Only her body was infirm.

"But then where can you go?" David said. "If all of Israel is deadly to my parents, where can they find refuge?"

Nahash said, "Send us to Moab."

"Moab, Mother? Moab is an enemy of Israel."

"No, an enemy of *Saul*. Moab is your lineage, my son."

"What?"

"There is Moabite blood in your veins."

"How — ?"

"Not every truce is won by fighting. Some are by discussion. And some by love. Send us to Moab."

Then, without moving her old bones, Nahash told David a tale of his heritage.

Long ago there was a famine so severe in Israel that Elimelech of Bethlehem took his wife and his two sons to Moab, to survive there until rain returned to Judah.

Soon after their journey Elimelech died, and his wife Naomi was left to raise her sons alone.

In time each man married a Moabite wife, one whose name was Orpah, one whose name was Ruth.

But then her sons died, too, and the woman was bereft altogether. In sorrow she decided to return to her own people.

Naomi said to her daughters-in-law, "Go back to your mothers' houses, and may the Lord deal as kindly with you as you have dealt with the dead and with me."

She kissed them, and they began to weep. "We will go with you to your people," they said.

Naomi said, "Do I have more sons in my womb? Daughters, I am too old to marry, but you should not refrain from marrying again."

So Orpah kissed Naomi and departed. But Ruth clung to her.

"Entreat me not to leave you or to return from following you," Ruth said. "For where you go I will go, and where you lodge I will lodge. Your people shall be my people, and your God my God. Where you die I will die, and there will I be buried."

Naomi saw that Ruth was determined. She said no more.

David watched his mother tell this story. Ancient, bent and wrinkled, she took such delight in the remembrance and in her words that her voice had a husky quality.

If David had an aptitude for language, he had received it with this mother's milk.

When the two women arrived in Bethlehem, the people said, "Is this Naomi?"

"No, no, don't call me Naomi," she said. "Call me Mara, bitter, because the Almighty has dealt bitterly with me."

Now, they had returned at the time of the barley harvest.

Naomi said to Ruth, "My husband's cousin owns fields outside the city. His name is Boaz. Go, daughter. Glean ears of grain and bring us enough to grind for cakes."

So Ruth went and gleaned after the reapers.

*Boaz himself came walking in the fields that day. When he saw Ruth, he
said to the supervisor, "Whose maiden is that, so lovely and so alone?"*

*The supervisor said, "She is the Moabite who came with Naomi. She has
worked since the dawn without a rest."*

Boaz went to her and said, "What is your name?"

She bowed and said, "Ruth."

*"Ruth," he said. "Ruth, do not go into anyone else's fields. Glean in mine
beside my servants. They will protect you. If you get thirsty, drink from our
vessels."*

Ruth whispered, "Why should you notice me, a foreigner?"

Boaz said, "Because of all you have done for your mother-in-law."

"You are most gracious to me, my lord."

*In the evening Ruth beat out what she had gleaned. It was about an ephah.
And Naomi said, "Blessed be Boaz by the Lord, whose kindness has not
forsaken the living or the dead."*

*Now, when the barley had been reaped, Naomi said to Ruth, "Shouldn't I
seek a home for you, that it may be well with you? Daughter, tonight Boaz will
be winnowing his barley at the threshing floor. Wash and anoint yourself. Put
on your finest clothes and go to the threshing floor, and when he lies down
to sleep, uncover his feet and take your place beside him. He is one of our
nearest kin. He will tell you what to do."*

So Ruth went to the threshing floor by night.

*When Boaz had eaten and drunk and his heart was merry, he lay down by
the heap of grain. Then she came softly and uncovered his feet and lay down.*

*At midnight the man was startled. He turned over and found a woman
lying at his feet.*

"Who are you?"

*"I am Ruth. Oh, sir, spread your protecting skirt over your maidservant,
for you are my next of kin."*

*"Ah, daughter, bless you," Boaz said. "You've made this last kindness
greater than the first, because you haven't gone after young men, rich or
poor. Yes, I will try to do for you all you ask. But you have a nearer kin than
I. If he chooses to marry you, I must let you go. But lie here until the morning,
and I will see what I can do."*

*So she lay wakeful at his feet until the morning and arose and departed
before anyone could recognize her face.*

*That day Boaz went to the nearer kin of Naomi. "I have a matter to discuss
with you," he said. "We need ten men to witness the decision you are about
to make."*

The kinsman thought that Boaz' proposal must be serious.

*When the ten men had been gathered, Boaz said, "Naomi is selling a parcel
of land. If you want it, buy it. If not, I will buy it because I am next in line."*

Quickly the kinsman said, "I want to buy it."

Just as quickly, Boaz said, "One more thing: he who buys the field also buys Ruth the Moabite, and he must have children with her in the place of her first husband, so that his lineage can continue."

"What?" cried the kinsman. "Then the land will go to her children?"

"Any son of Ruth's must be the son of her first husband."

"In that case," said the kinsman, "take the field."

"You give up all rights?" Boaz said in front of ten men. "Even your rights to Ruth the Moabite?"

"Yes, of course."

Boaz turned to the ten men and announced, "Then Ruth shall be my wife."

The elders said, "We are witnesses. May you prosper in Bethlehem."

So Boaz married the beautiful Ruth, and soon she bore a son.

The people of Bethlehem said to Naomi, "Blessed be the Lord! For your daughter-in-law, who is more to you than seven sons, has borne a nourisher for your old age."

Naomi took the child and smiled. "Call me by my rightful name again," she said. "Naomi. Call me 'Pleasant.' "

They named the baby Obed.

"David," Nahash said, "I remember Ruth. When I married Jesse she came and blessed us — as old to me then as I am to you now. She is your father's grandmother. Obed you know: your own grandfather. David?"

David found that he had slipped completely into the consolation of his mother's tale.

"David?" she said, and it was as if he woke up.

"What, Mother?"

"Send us to Moab. We will live out the rest of our days in Moab."

"And I am but a renegade," he whispered.

He went to his mother and lightly hugged her brittle bones. "To Moab, then," he said. He kissed her. With crooked fingers she brushed the hair back from his forehead.

It was the last time he ever laid eyes on his parents, Jesse and Nahash.

ii

A rider came riding at breakneck speed. He made no effort at stealth. He could be shot from the back of his mount, and for that very reason David allowed him to approach unharmed.

Asahel, the youngest brother of Joab and Abiathar, had seen dust in the distance and had called David to the tower by the gate. David had climbed an interior stair and looked north. The donkey was lathered by long travel, running numbly now. The man, too, was exhausted, leaning heavily left and right. His clothes were torn to ribbons. He was an Amalekite.

Asahel said, "I'll spear him at the gate!"

The young man's threat was understandable. Amalekites, camel-riding nomads of the south, had burned this same city when David and his army were absent: Ziklag, his base of operations for the last two years.

The Philistine King Achish had given Ziklag to David who had been conducting raids against the enemies of Judah and sharing his spoils with the elders of the tribe. In this way David bound their hearts to his own. He was consolidating personal power in the hill country of Judah and the Shephelah to the west and the Negev to the south. Achish knew nothing of the adventurer's successes. Lately, in fact, all five lords of the Philistines and all their armies had marched north to fight Saul near Jezreel.

"He's an Amalekite," Asahel hissed. "I'll run out and pin him to the ground!"

David said, "Wait. He's coming from the north, not the south."

The rider had already spied David at the tower window. He was waving both arms and crying, "My lord! My lord, a message!"

David touched the back of Asahel's hand. "We'll meet him together," he said, "without your spear."

So Asahel left his spear but kept his sword. They went down and stood within the gate, and immediately the Amalekite came clattering in, his poor mount stumbling sidewards. He jumped down and ran to David, bowing again and again. There was dirt in this messenger's hair. No — dust. The dust of mourning.

David said, "Where do you come from?"

The Amalekite said, "Only yesterday I escaped from the camp of Israel."

Israel! David grabbed the man's hair, forcing him to look up. "How has the fighting gone?" he said. "Tell me!"

The Amalekite managed a fawning smile. "May the Lord your God do to all your enemies what he did last evening on Mount Gilboa."

"My enemies? Who are my enemies? And what did the Lord do on Mount Gilboa?"

The messenger grinned. He had a hawk's head, a raptor beak, and thick brows. He said, "The people of Israel fled from battle. Many have fallen and are dead. King Saul is dead. And his son Jonathan — " the nomad paused, revealing tiny yellow teeth "—he, too, is dead."

David turned aside. His right knee began to tremble. He focused tremendous energy in that place to control the trembling.

He whispered, "How do you know that Saul and Jonathan are dead?"

Suddenly the Amalekite was garrulous. "By chance I was on the mountain," he said. "I saw the king leaning on his spear, and the chariots and the horsemen of the Philistines were closing in upon him. He looked back and he saw me and yelled, 'Who are you?' I told him, and he said, 'Stand beside me and slay me.' He said, 'Anguish is upon me!' Then he rolled up his eyes and he fell like stone to the ground. I saw the Philistines coming. I was sure he would not live when they got there, so I stabbed him and took the crown from his head and the bracelet from his arm, and, look: I've brought them here, to you, my lord, to you, my lord.''

The Amalekite began to bow again, up and down. But David stood immobile. His knee was not shaking now. Asahel, beside him, likewise remained perfectly still. Silence and stillness finally caused the Amalekite to cease his mindless obeisance. He murmured, "My lord?" and smiled.

Pronouncing his words with a terrible quietude, David said: "How is it... that you were not afraid to put forth your hand... to destroy the Lord's anointed?''

The Amalekite lowered his head, an excellent show of humility. He did not see David nod to Asahel and walk away. He did not see the sword flash from the sheath at Asahel's side. He did not see death descending to the back of his naked neck.

███

By nightfall David had wandered into the wilderness south of Ziklag, scarcely aware of his own motion. The air was cold. He stepped on white stones, radiant in moonlight, and then he paused at the edge of a gorge, a black slash in the earth.

There was no planting in this place, no seedtime here, no harvest.

David spoke aloud.

"Jonathan, where are you lying now?" he said. "Where is the hand that gave me its bow, black lacquered, as tough as the cords of your heart? At what stars do the dark eyes stare that looked into mine and loved me?''

Suddenly David cried out: "Israel!" He threw back his head and howled, "Israel, your glory is dead on the mountains!''

Where David's voice went, the wild goats bounded awake. Badgers and creatures of the night made an intense and nearly inaudible rustling, escaping.

David cried, "A shield lies on the rock, forgotten! On the grey face of Mount Gilboa a round shield lies cracked and dry, which once protected the breast of King Saul!

"Saul and Jonathan," David keened. He crouched and wound his fingers in his tangled hair. His voice rose several octaves and grew soft, and he sang:

> *Saul and Jonathan!*
> *Lovely and beloved!*
> *In life and in dying not divided:*

swifter than eagles!
Stronger than lions —
but tonight, O daughters of Israel,
weep for Saul
who dressed you in scarlet.
As for Jonathan...

David sank to the ground, his cheek against stone. He drew his knees up and wrapped his arms around them, making himself smaller and smaller. Very quietly he began to sob. "Jonathan, I am sick with sorrow. Here: I lie down here in the night that holds your right hand somewhere. And here I whisper how I loved you, brother. I loved you past the love of women."

Oh, how the mighty are fallen,
and these sweet weapons of the Lord's old warring,
dead.

∎

After a month had passed, David summoned his closest advisors to a hill outside Ziklag: Joab, the commander of his slick small army; Benaiah, as loyal as an ox, David's personal bodyguard; thin Abishai, the young, swift Asahel, both of them Joab's brothers; and Abiathar, whose countenance was ever suffused with sunlight.

Abiathar brought with him the ephod oracle so that David could inquire of God what they ought to do.

The men sat down in a circle.

"Joab," David said, "what do you have to say?"

The commander glanced once at David and then delivered a terse report. "Briefly: Abner still commands Saul's standing army. He has established Ishbaal as king of Israel in Mahanaim, east of Jordan. Ishbaal is the last living son of Saul. Abner knows of our activities in Judah. He wants to talk. He has asked to meet me at the pool near Gibeon."

David said, "Abishai, what *about* Judah? What are their elders saying?"

Abishai uncoiled his length and said, "They like you. Especially now that Saul is dead, they are looking to you for leadership."

David tilted his head. "What sort of leadership?"

Abishai shrugged. "You've given them goods and security. They respond with praise and loyalty. They say these things publicly, in the gates, in the fields."

David turned to Abiathar. In tones suddenly hushed he said, "Inquire something of the Lord for me."

Abiathar took up the ephod. David said, "Ask what I should do. Should I leave Ziklag and go up into the hills and into the cities of Judah?"

The Lord said, *Go up.*

David said, "Which city? To Hebron?"

And the Lord said, *Yes. Go up into Hebron.*

So David arose and spoke again to Abishai, "Tell the elders of Judah that I am about to move my army and all my people to Hebron. Tell them it is the will of the Lord."

And to Joab: "Send word to Abner that you will indeed meet him — but that the meeting take place after certain ceremonies in Hebron. Tell Abner that those ceremonies shall be a sign: 'When they are complete, come to the pool of Gibeon.' "

David turned and walked away — not toward Ziklag, but out into the wilderness again.

■

And so it was that David moved to the high hills of Hebron where there was abundant water, springs, wells, and natural defenses. Hebron sat astride the ridge route passing north and the history of David's ancestors: for Abraham had sojourned here; and here, by the oaks of Mamre, God had said that Sarah would bear a son, and Sarah had laughed but she bore that son and named him Isaac.

David loved the smell of these stories, one thousand years old. He walked in the ancient places. During the day he gazed down into the Jordan valley, trying to imagine where Sodom had been. At night he lifted his eyes and whispered the old, old words:

> *Look toward heaven and number the stars,*
> *if you are able to number them.*
> *So shall your descendants be.*
> *And Abraham believed the Lord,*
> *and he reckoned it to him as righteousness.*

Within a month of his arrival, the elders of Judah came to David. They brought oil in the hollow horn of an ox, prepared to accomplish the ceremonies that David had announced to Abner.

Solemnly the elders wrapped David's head in a turban. They encircled the turban with a simple ring of gold to signify this man's rule over them. Then they anointed him with the oil, ordaining David as chosen by God and empowered with the authority of the Lord.

Abiathar raised a ram's horn and began to blow long blasts.

Spontaneously the people shouted, "Long live King David!" Then all the people went out after David, playing on pipes and rejoicing so loudly the air was split by their joy.

▌

So Joab went out with twelve officers of David's army to the reservoir near Gibeon, representing a king. His men carried their weapons in a casual manner.

Abner arrived with twelve officers of his own, likewise at ease in the meeting. There was laughter and greeting in the sunlight by the pool. Strong men who had not seen one another in more than four years now met and began to exchange stories. Many of them once had fought the Philistines side by side; then they had chased one another for a while — but Saul died and David prospered.

"What shall we do?" they said.

And in rough goodwill of their reunion they said, "A tournament! While Abner and Joab talk, we'll test our strength with wooden swords and the butts of our spears."

With taunts and boasts the men of Israel and the men of Judah stripped off their tunics and lined up in two lines. Then, bellowing, they fell upon each other, wrestling, swinging the dull ends of spears with power, bruising and beating each other in this rugged warrior's sport.

Abner and Joab sat face-to-face. Joab held his peace, grey-eyed and taciturn. Abner was talking about the Philistines. He made countless references to Achish, the king of Gath, and he kept leaving small pauses in his speech where Joab might introduce a word or two as well regarding this king.

Abner was saying, "— only the stronger after Gilboa, of course, though King Achish has returned, as I'm sure you know, to Gath, confident of his control over Jezreel and the land between and the Shephelah of Judah, too. Wouldn't you say so... ? Confident, I mean, insofar as he may be confident of the friendship of David... ? Not to suggest that we don't appreciate David's choices in the old days — the difficult days when the king pursued David... ?"

Abner breathed deeply and allowed a long pause to pass.

Joab sat staring with the fixed, shining eye of a serpent, watchful, revealing nothing.

Abner said, "Sir, I will be plain with you. I seek a word. We know that David has not always loved the Philistines and that his raids these last years have not served Gath or its king. Therefore, I have come to discover to what extent David intends to honor that old association."

Joab said nothing. He did not ease the moment by so much as a blink of his eyes. Apparently, tension did not trouble him; nor did he care about protocol between the envoys of kings.

Abner said, "Is David a friend of the Philistines?"

Joab didn't answer.

Abner said, "More to the point, does David set his face against Ishbaal, the son of Saul, the king of Israel?"

Joab stared straight into Abner's eyes.

"If we must fight the lords of the five cities, will David take the field at all?"

All at once the noise of the mock battle changed. The sport had gone out of it. Warriors meant their taunts. They had turned their spears round to the blade-end with murderous intent. Someone must have taken fierce offense.

Both Abner and Joab leaped up and ran toward the bloody melee.

Abner seized a spear and swung it over his head like a club, cracking the backs of those who were tearing at each other. In fact, his men had suffered the worse beating. Six were dead, six alive but panicked.

Joab's men, filled with fury, were gathering for a unified assault.

Abner cried a retreat and led his men away, racing for their lives.

Joab and his brothers gave chase. Lean Abishai ran well, but Asahel, youngest, was also the swiftest. Like a gazelle he outran the others, his eye on Abner. He was flying toward his first battlefield kill.

Abner saw the pursuit and cut left. So did Asahel, closing distance. Abner gripped the spear in his right hand and ran flat out across two fields in fast succession. Asahel kept gaining on him.

Abner glanced back. "Is that you, Asahel?" he cried.

The young man shouted, "It is I."

Abner cried, "Turn away. Go for one of my warriors and take his spoil!"

Marvelously, Asahel increased speed and kept on coming.

Suddenly Abner turned and faced the young man. "Go back!" he yelled. "Why should I strike the blood of Joab?"

Asahel, drawing his sword, seemed to become airborne.

Abner turned his spear backward, intending a lesser wound — but the young man came upon him with such velocity that the butt of the spear pierced him through the belly and broke out the small of his back.

Abner released his spear. Asahel curled around it like a serpent stabbed. Before Joab or Abishai arrived at this spot, Abner dashed away.

But the sight of his brother impaled on the shaft of a spear transfixed Joab. As he approached Asahel, he slowed to a walk. Then he stopped altogether, drained of motion and all speech.

Asahel looked up and croaked, "I'm glad to see you, brother. Would you pull this tree-trunk out of me — " He attempted a grin. "—so that I could breathe again?"

But then the young man's eyes crossed, and he died.

Joab began to walk. He did not run. Neither did Abishai run. They walked in the direction that Abner had gone. At a steady, unbreakable pace, they followed Abner all the rest of that day.

In the evening Abner appeared on the top of a hill, surrounded by a band of Benjaminites.

"Shall the sword devour us forever?" he shouted. "Joab, don't you know that the end must be bitter? How long will it be before you bid your people to turn from pursuing their brethren?"

Joab and Abishai and the men of David looked for a moment at the figures on the hill, then silently they withdrew and walked back to Asahel. They took up his body and buried him in the tomb of his father at Bethlehem.

So war broke open between the house of Saul and the house of David. Civil war continued in Israel through the next five years. David's strength increased more and more, but the house of Saul grew weaker.

▌

Ishbaal of Israel was a youth, a pale fellow frightened even of his own officers. He did not have the nature of a king. His family consisted completely of women. Every man except Ishbaal had been murdered.

When Abner brought him issues demanding decisions, this king withdrew into a pout and stared out the window. He was puffy from inactivity and self-pity. No decisions were ever forthcoming.

So Abner gathered certain men who were loyal to him alone and sent them to David in Hebron with a message:

"To whom does the land belong?" he said. "Make a covenant with me, David, and my hand shall carry all Israel over to you."

David answered, "Good. I will make a covenant with you. But one thing I require, that when you come you bring Michal, Saul's daughter. Give me my wife, whom I haven't seen since I escaped her father with my life."

Abner agreed.

But years had passed since their separation, and Michal had married Paltiel the son of Laish. Nevertheless, Abner sent a band of soldiers to their house and by force brought Michal to himself.

As the expedition of twenty soldiers set out toward Hebron, Michal's husband followed on foot, weeping for his wife.

At Bahurim Abner rode back to the man and said, "Return to your house, Paltiel. There is no help for it. Michal is David's wife now."

Paltiel stood still and watched the whole procession ride away. Michal showed no emotion of her own, but her lips were white.

As they traveled south, Abner conferred with many of the elders in Israel and Benjamin. "Now is the time to make David king over us all," he said. "The Lord has promised that it would be David who will save us from the Philistines.

"I'm on my way to talk with David," Abner said. "Are you with me?"

When he came to Hebron, David welcomed him with an elaborate, formal feast.

Michal sat in a stony silence beside David, king of Judah. The flesh had thickened on her bones. There were lines at the corners of her mouth.

David, for his part, had lost his freckles — though his skin had fared poorly in constant sunlight. It was scarred on his face and arms from burning; but his breast was lily white and tender underneath his robe. His hair was as tangled as ever, but the red of it had deepened to a dark copper sheen.

There was a melancholy in his golden eyes.

When everyone had eaten, Abner rose to his feet and said, "The elders of Benjamin wish to make a covenant with you, David, that you reign over them. So do all the tribes between Mahanaim and this place. I have spoken with them. With your leave, therefore, I will travel north and gather all Israel to my lord the king."

David gazed at the commander of Israel as if interrogating him. Abner maintained his military bearing. Finally David said, "Go. You have my leave."

On the following morning, as Abner was departing through the gate of the city, he happened to pass Joab returning to Hebron with his men after a raid.

Abner in the clean clothes of diplomacy, Joab in the sweat and the grit of warfare: they paused, facing one another.

Joab said, "What are you doing here?"

Abner answered with grace: "To honor your lord David and seek his agreement to become my lord king."

Joab hunched his broad shoulders.

Suddenly he said, "Come here. I have something to say to you in private."

Joab led Abner into one of the small rooms at the side of the gate. Just as they entered, he turned and stabbed Abner in the belly with a knife so long that it came out his back and cut through the robe.

Joab left the room without a word and went to bathe himself.

When David heard of Abner's death he tore his clothes and put on sackcloth and mourned for him. The next day he walked behind Abner's bier all the way to the grave, lamenting in a loud voice:

> Should Abner die surprised like Nabal the fool?
>> Your hands were unbound!
>> Your feet were unfettered!
> You fell as they fall who die on the knives of the wicked.

Joab stood at the side of the road and heard the lament. He watched the funeral procession, unblinking and indifferent.

The people knew that it had not been David's will that Abner should die. But no one uttered blame against Joab.

■

Abner's death caused Ishbaal, king of Israel, to sink into despair. Even outside his house people could hear him pacing the rooms, bemoaning his fate.

One afternoon in the heat of the day, two captains of Saul's old army came to the young king's house. The doorkeeper was sleeping. They entered unhindered and found Ishbaal dozing face down on his bed. Without waking him, they cut off his head.

The names of these men were Rechab and Baanah. They were brothers, the sons of Rimmon the Beerothite.

All night long they traveled to Hebron, carrying the head of Ishbaal to David himself.

When they came before David, they said, "He sought your life. But the Lord has avenged you this day on Saul and on his offspring."

David walked to Rechab and Baanah where they stood. He put out his fingers and touched the solemn, puffy face of Ishbaal.

Quietly he said, "Yesterday afternoon and evening. Last night all night long. Dawn and daybreak and morning." David raised his eyes and looked from Rechab to Baanah. "During all your walking you did to get from Mahanaim to this place, for every step you took, did it never once occur to you that I might object to the murder of an innocent man in his own house on his own bed?"

David turned and said to his bodyguard Benaiah, "Execute them."

In the heat of that same day, Rechab and Baanah were hung up without their hands and feet beside the pool at Hebron, dead.

But the head of Ishbaal was buried in the tomb of Abner.

■

In those days the elders of the tribes of Israel came to David at Hebron and said, "Behold, we are your bone and your flesh. In times past, when Saul was king over us, it was you who led Israel in war. And the Lord has said to you, You shall be shepherd of my people Israel."

So David made a covenant before the Lord with the people of Israel: he who was king in Judah now was anointed king of all the tribes, uniting Israel under his sole rule.

David, when he began to reign, was thirty years old.

iii

Someone is singing in the streets of Hebron. Early in the morning before the small shops open, before the daily bread is baked or any merchant has begun to call out the name of his wares, someone is passing below the king's window, singing in a beggar's rough voice these words:

> *The Lord says to my lord:*
> *"Sit at my right hand,*
> *until I make your foe*
> *   your footstool."*

David wakes and hears that small snatch of song. Who is singing? A man or a woman? One of the prophets? One of those unkempt, alien beings, the whirling, wild-eyed dancers who used to attract Saul?

> *The Lord says to my lord:*
> *"Sit down in power!*
> *Send forth your scepter!"*

David rolls back the blanket and stands up in his room. Even so, the voice grows distant, swiftly receding:

> *For day by day*
> *like dew from the womb of the morning*
> *your youth shall wash you strong again—*

Gone.

By the time the king gets to the window and looks down, the dim streets of Hebron are empty.

Moreover, it's snowing. The air is visible and silent, all filled with falling. The low stone wall across the way has a woolen hood. Suddenly it occurs to David that snow would preserve the singer's foot-tracks.

He throws a robe around his shoulders, runs downstairs, crams sandals between his toes, and rushes out into the early cold of the morning.

But when he gets to the side of the house where his window looks, he finds only Rothem, an ancient domestic servant hunched over her broom of twigs, sweeping the snow from the street. She is destroying the steps of the singer. She is humming tunelessly in her great nose. She glances up and sees the king and twists her face into an expression of greeting.

"For your pretty foot, m'lord," she croaks. "Because the king's foot shouldn't be bitten by winter."

David returns to his chambers and lies down again. But he can't go back to sleep. He has been living in Hebron seven years now, and this is the thought that occupies his mind: his house is too small. He has seven wives, Michal among them, each woman with chambers and servants of her own. He has six sons; only Michal is barren, though she keeps nurses and tutors and toys as if she had a child. David's house has counting rooms and a feast room and a place to stand before the Lord — but it has no place for the treasures his raids bring home, nor halls required by a king: a waiting room, a throne room, a place to render judgment. Moreover, there is no place for the ministers who serve him in the maintenance of a kingdom. His house is too small.

Two years ago David spent time in the city of the Jebusites, called Jebus or Jerusalem, studying their methods of governance. Even before the tribes of Israel had anointed him king, he slipped into the city and spoke with the common scribes, those who labored in their king's employ but whose level was beneath their king's attention. From them he learned the administration of kingdoms.

Lately David has been applying this knowledge. He has been appointing officers and counselors with which to rule Israel. Today the king has a royal cabinet — but he has no room for it!

Seraiah, his secretary, knows seven languages and writes all of David's correspondence. Seraiah keeps an account of the acts of the king, but he has no room for the records.

Jehoshaphat is the king's herald. He handles most of the affairs of state; but he lives at a distance from David's house. He should be *in* the house.

Benaiah now commands an entire band of fierce, loyal troops: David's personal bodyguard. These men absolutely require space in the king's house.

And Joab's duties as commander-in-chief have increased enormously, for he has organized the military into several distinct divisions: regiments of a thousand, companies of one hundred, platoons of fifty, and squads of ten men each. He who fights Philistines actually admires their effective declension of authority. It produces a remarkable coherence on the battlefield, however chaotic the fighting becomes.

David knows what delights his passionless commander: that one word from his mouth can be multiplied by a thousand mouths to ten thousand troops, transforming a host of men into a singular, smooth, and murderous attack. Joab has the tactician's mind. He also has the tyrant's arrogance and the soldier's impatience.

But he has no *room* for his officers or for the keeping of his troops. Hebron is in the territory of Judah, whose elders want to exert control over Joab's army. And the citizens of Hebron resist the imperious attitude and the categorical command of generals.

Hebron loves the king.

Hebron only tolerates his grim commander.

But Hebron hates the army that sleeps in its houses and eats its food. Therefore David is contemplating change. Not just his house, but this whole city is too small for him — There! There it is again! The singing. Outside his window, cloaked in snowfall, David hears the rough voice singing:

> *The Lord is at your right hand!*
> *The Lord will shatter kings!*
> *He will crack the heads of the nations,*
> > *that you,*
> *when you pass that way, my pretty lord,*
> *may pause to drink from the small brooks*
> *peace.*

This time David doesn't disturb the warmth of his bedding.

He looks up at the oakwood beams and the grey clay troweled between them.

"Tomorrow my ceiling will be cedar. And my house — " David ponders the thought, his hands behind his head, gazing upward, gazing *through* the ceiling, and then he whispers: "My house will be in Jerusalem."

▮

The advance of David, king of Israel, against Jerusalem of the Jebusites was no secret.

His armies marched from Hebron in full view of every village and city on the ridge route north. His troops moved in such a disciplined silence that the Israelites who stood along the way also fell silent at their passage.

David had initiated no discussions of treaty, nor had he responded to the ambassadors of the Jebusites. He did not want tribute. He wanted the city. And he wanted to take it by a force so fatal that no one would doubt his possession thereafter. The city would belong to him and then to the sons who came after him. And because the world should know the glorious thing which was occurring, David rejected stealth. But Jerusalem was mightily fortified. Parts of its walls were more than five hundred years old. And in the three hundred years since Joshua had invaded Canaan, Israel had not been able to defeat this city.

The king of Jerusalem sent a messenger to David when he appeared in the hills south of the city. The messenger rode a horse. David rode a mule. As they approached each other in an open space, David called, "Does Jerusalem have something to say to David?"

The messenger said: "The king says, 'It is no use to attack our walls.' My lord the king says, 'With such walls even the blind and the lame could drive back David, the shepherd.' "

David sat astride his mount, smiling with a sunny praise upon the Jebusite messenger, as if the man had just sung a delightful song.

The messenger cleared his throat. "Sir," he said, "does Israel have a reply?"

"Thank you for asking," said David. "Yes. I do." He turned to Joab and in conversational tones said, "Tell the troops that whoever reaches the water shaft first and there smites Jebusites who are by nature lame and blind — he shall be my chief and my commander."

Joab nodded and repeated the order to an aide.

David turned to the messenger and said, "You'd best not hesitate." The poor fellow was gaping past David, where Joab's command was multiplying itself over and over, farther and farther away. "Someone is liable to get home ahead of you."

The man whirled about, whipped up his horse, and tore north over the hills to Jerusalem screaming: "The water shaft! Garrison the water shaft!"

David watched him go, his face now fixed in a pale mask. Softly he said to Joab, "Go."

Joab barked a more brutal command. The horn of war awoke all down the column of warriors, and the armies began to move.

David turned his mount aside and climbed a high bluff in order to watch the campaign.

Joab bent his body and galloped forward at breakneck speed, ten men riding immediately behind him. They outdistanced the foot soldiers, who ran in companies of a hundred.

Indeed, the commander-in-chief was the first to arrive at Gihon, a spring in the Kidron valley just below Jerusalem. Here was the water shaft that David had named. It had been cut upward through rock so that the city could come down for water during a siege. A Jebusite guard was stationed here, but Joab and his men attacked with such astounding savagery that they scattered.

Enemy soldiers appeared in the mouth of the water shaft.

Joab's men shot them with arrows.

Soldiers began to pour from the shaft.

Joab dismounted and threw himself bodily against these, killing them with two short daggers in close spaces. Then he began himself to ascend the narrow tunnel, meeting the Jebusites one by one and climbing their bloody corpses like steps.

The ten Israelites came immediately behind him. None of them spoke. Every man knew precisely the plan their commander had conceived.

Within the city itself, they burst from the shaft like a fountain of bright iron. Side by side they fought toward the great gates in the western wall. Two Israelites died, bitten by Jebusite arrows. Another stumbled with a spear in his side. A fourth man ran forward, drawing a hail of arrows from all the warriors of Jerusalem, emptying their bows so that Joab could safely lunge the last few feet to the gates. There, surrounded by six Israelites in leather armor, Joab heaved the bar from its metal braces and swung wide the gates to the city, and so a great stream of troops surged in, flooding the pavements, the streets, the houses of Jerusalem, slaughtering soldiers and driving the citizens back against their walls.

David entered the western gate on his mule, unhindered.

The king of the Jebusites was brought before him.

David said, "Is it better to live blind and lame or better to die entire? A shepherd wants to know."

The king gave David a wicked look, but he said nothing.

David sighed. "Well, then I will choose for you and grant you an honorable death. But know this first before you die: that the city has a new name now. I have named it the City of David."

‖

Late that same night, King David walked along the northern ridge of his new stronghold. He stopped at the ravine that had for centuries protected Jerusalem against assaults from the north. He stood in the cold night wind and gazed across at a hill yet higher than this one. But David wasn't thinking about fortifications just now. He was thinking about the history of these hills, and their future.

"Moriah," he said. He murmured the word slowly: "Mount Moriah," the ancient name of that higher hill before him, grizzled with brush and rock and age. It was there that Abraham had almost slain his son Isaac and sacrificed him to the God whose name he did not know. But God — even David's God, the Lord — had saved Isaac by providing a ram for the sacrifice. "And so you saved us too, by saving the seed of our grandfather." David was speaking aloud in the wintry night. His breath made ghostly puffs in the cold air. "Right there, on that hill, one thousand years ago, the flint knife of an old man did not cut his son's throat. O Lord God of Israel, now that you have given it to us again, it is on that same hill I want to build a house for you, on Moriah, the place of saving!"

‖

One month later, news came to David that the Philistines had mustered their armies in Gezer and were now marching into the valley of Rephaim.

David was not surprised. As long as he had stayed in Hebron, the Philistine lords saw him as a soldier of fortune raiding the useless hills of Judah. But now he was king of territories north and south with a city of his own between the two. Now a stronghold of ancient reputation bore his name and protected his person. There was in Israel a king greater than Saul!

David summoned his advisors to the western gate of the city. Abiathar brought the ephod so that the king could seek the will of the Lord.

David asked, "Shall I ride forth against the Philistines? Will you give them into my hand?"

The Lord said to David, *Ride forth. I will certainly give the Philistines into your hand.*

So David and Joab and all their mighty men gathered in the hills east of the valley of Rephaim. They spread through rocks and the rugged terrain and concealed themselves. When the Philistines appeared at the far end of the valley, David whispered to his armies, "Wait." The Philistines were looking for a place to establish the camps of a long campaign. They came closer and closer, but David whispered, "Wait."

Only when the greater body of their cavalcade had entered the eastern reaches of the valley of Rephaim did David cry: "Up, Israel!" All at once the Israelite warriors burst forth from the rocky heights of Rephaim like cataracts, like a thousand spouts of water. Israel astonished the Philistine forces who turned and ran in a panic, leaving their carts, their supplies, their gear, their food — and their gods! That night David made a mighty bonfire. He commanded the men to shout the names of the gods whose images they had captured. Benaiah in particular had a voice so huge that the enemy could hear him even in their camps on the distant hillside. "Dagon!" Benaiah roared. "*Dagon!*" thundered the hosts of Israel.

David heaved the image of Dagon into the fire, and then the remarkable Benaiah bellowed: "Lo! Dagon is in flames! How can a god whose image is ashes fight for his people?"

At midnight David inquired of the Lord whether he should go forth against the Philistines a second time.

The Lord said, *You shall not go forth. In darkness go around to their rear and come upon them opposite the poplar trees that cover the hillside. When you hear the sound of marching in the tops of the trees, bestir yourself.*

David did as the Lord commanded. All night he positioned his armies behind the lords of the Philistines.

In the morning the wind was still. Israel didn't move. Every soldier could hear the preparations of the enemy as he dressed in chain mail and tightened his bridles and made metal sing against its sheath.

Suddenly the million loose leaves of the poplar forests started to flutter, to rattle and chatter and run. The Philistines hesitated, thinking they heard armies in the sky. But the Israelites heard the hosts of the Lord, and instantly they rose from the forests, struck the unprotected rear, routed the Philistines, and drove them in terrified confusion out of their own camps. This is the foe whom Saul could never completely defeat. This is the nation that had grieved the mothers of Israel ever since Samson had perished between the pillars of their temple. On that day David chased them from the valley of Rephaim, all the way back to the gates of Gezer.

And this, then, is how David perceived that he had become a king among kings and that the Lord had exalted his kingdom Israel: Hiram, king of Tyre, sent a royal embassy to honor David after this dazzling victory over the Philistines. Moreover, Hiram offered him gifts so fine and generous that all the nations knew that Tyre was seeking diplomatic relations with Israel. "If you wish cedar trees," Hiram said, "I will send as many as you ask. If you wish carpenters and masons, I will send them, too."

And David in Jerusalem responded: "Friendship is ever better than war. Yes, I have a thing to build with your cedar trees, Hiram. A house — "

■

So David built a magnificent house high on the northern ridge of Jerusalem. His house was the crown of the city. Cedar panels covered the walls. Cedar beams upheld the roofs. Gardens were planted on those roofs, and when he strolled in his gardens the king could see down into every courtyard of every other house in his city.

A little lower than his own apartments, yet higher than the rest of the house, David built rooms for Michal, the wife of his youth.

Saul once had placed her on the second floor of his own rough fortress. Maybe, thought David, she would appreciate this more wonderful elevation. He wanted to make Michal glad again. She had scarcely spoken since he brought her to Hebron a year ago. He sat beside her at every festival, but she remained withdrawn. He gave her an onyx brooch, white engraved in black. But she never wore it. For his other wives, all of whom were bearing children, David built thirty chambers, three rows of ten each on the second story of an entire wing. Already he had taken new wives from Jerusalem, following the custom of the nations round about whereby a king proclaimed his personal force in the size of his harem and the numbers of his children.

It was a grand house, a royal house. He who had slept in stone caves now lived in a palace of his own conceiving, in which were the spaces of governance, a throne room, a waiting room, working rooms for his officers, space for archives, a treasury for the king's wealth, stalls for Benaiah and his personal bodyguard. Room! *Rehoboth!* David thought with joy. *Isaac in the wilderness, David in his city: the Lord has made room for us — and I too shall be fruitful in the land.*

It was precisely then, in this mood of gratitude, that another duty forced itself upon David. *The Ark of the Lord's Covenant has been neglected all these years in Kirjath-jearim.*

The Ark of God, which is called by the name of the Lord of hosts who sits enthroned on the cherubim!

■

In those days David, king of Israel, arose and went with his officers and with elders of the twelve tribes to the house of Abinadab, which was on the hill near Kirjath-jearim.

They brought with them a new cart.

At the command of the king, the sons of Abinadab, Uzzah and Ahio, carried the Ark from their father's house and placed it with sacred care upon the new cart. Then they drove the oxen, Ahio before the cart and Uzzah behind it.

David and the people of Israel who were with him began to sing. The king sang a verse and the people echoed it word for word. But then the king grew excited that the shrine of the Lord was moving to his city. He laughed and lifted his voice and sang with such a driving delight that the people also sang faster songs. They played lyres and harps and tambourines and castanets and cymbals — and they abandoned themselves to dancing. As they followed the Ark toward Jerusalem they moved their feet harder and swifter. Uzzah threw his arms to heaven and whirled about behind the cart. But just as they approached the threshing floor of Nacon, he slipped on some warm ox droppings and fell. Uzzah cracked his skull on the stones of the threshing floor and died instantly.

The word of his death flew backward like an arrow, striking every dancer with mortal terror. They stood still and whispered, "He must have touched the Ark! Uzzah defiled the Ark, and the wrath of God has killed him!"

No one moved. Who knew what God might do next?

The king had heard the word of the people, and he, too, grew fearful. "If the Lord has broken forth against Uzzah," he said, "how can the Ark come to me now?" David commanded that the cart, the oxen, and the Ark of the Covenant all be taken to the house of Obed-edom, a man from Gath, a Philistine who lived nearby among the Israelites.

The elders and all the people of Israel stole home abashed.

David returned to his city without the Ark of God.

But within three months young Abiathar came to King David and smiled. "A remarkable thing has happened, my lord," he said. "I have been to see the Ark, and I tell you, the Lord has blessed Obed-edom because of it."

David said, "The anger of the Lord is passed?"

Abiathar nodded. A light returned to the king's golden eyes, and he, too, began to smile. "Then let us bring the Ark of God into the citadel!"

This time the king wore a white linen apron under his royal robes.

This time priests bore the Ark by staves on their shoulders, as it had been carried in the wilderness. And this time, when they had gone just six paces from the house of Obed-edom without a rebuke from God, David slaughtered and sacrificed an ox and a fatling in glorious thanksgiving.

Then the procession wound up toward Jerusalem, and the king ran ahead of everyone, breaking into whoops of joy. The Lord was with him! David clapped his hands and laughed more loudly than he had before. He danced. Everyone danced with him. They sounded horns in thrilling harmonies. David erupted in a fire of praise and poetry. He stripped his clothes in order to move more freely. He took off everything except the linen apron at his waist, and he leaped white-legged as high as a gazelle.

As the Ark entered the city, the citizens leaned from their windows and clapped. They lined the streets and, affected by the dancing of the king, roared with delight. The thunder of their voices followed the Ark to the tent which David had prepared for it, and there he offered burnt offerings and peace offerings before the Lord. He blessed the people in the name of the Lord and distributed to every man and woman a loaf of bread, a portion of meat, and a cake of raisins.

Then everyone returned home.

David, too, went to his house to give his family his personal blessing. They gathered in a courtyard, his wives, his children, all his servants and laborers, maids, bakers, herdsmen — even Rothem the ancient domestic who swept the streets with her bramble broom. Only Michal was not there. This disturbed David.

When he had pronounced the blessing on everyone else, then he climbed the stairs to his first wife's chambers.

He found her sitting at the window, looking down on the city streets.

"Michal," he said, "are you ill?"

She sat profile to him, framed by the window. She did not move.

He said, "This is the day when the Lord has come into the City of David. Couldn't you have come down to stand beside me?"

Michal blinked. Water filled the creases below her eyes. More severely David said, "Why did you neglect the day? Why did you refuse my blessing just now?"

Slowly she turned to face him. Her lips were pinched and trembling. "For shame," she said, her throat thick with emotion.

"Shame?" said David. "Shame, Michal? What does shame have to do with the day that has made this city sacred?"

Michal glared at him, her eyes bright with tears. "Oh, how the king of Israel honored himself today," she wailed. "Like any vulgar fellow he flaunted his nakedness before the eyes of men and women together."

"Ah," said David, peering out of Michal's window. "My wife has turned her vantage into the seat of judgment." He looked at her. She returned the look, lowering her chin and glaring upward. Softly David said, "I danced before the Lord today. I made merry before him who chose me over your father as the prince of Israel. And I will make myself yet more contemptible than this, Michal. Surely, I will be abased in your eyes. But the men and women of whom you speak — by them I shall be held in honor."

David turned and left.

Michal continued to live in her lofty apartments.

But even to the day of her death, she had no child.

∎

King David stood in darkness on the higher hill, the ancient, rocky Moriah, and looked across the ravine at his own generous mansion.

Its windows shined like a hundred eyes in the night, warm on the inside, bright in the rooms of his dwelling place.

But this scrub hill was a thorny place, dark and unprotected.

David prayed that night. He paced the rock and said, "O Lord God, I dwell in a house of cedar, but your Ark dwells in a tent. Let me build you a house — here, on this mountain. Mine on Zion, yours on Moriah — "

But the Lord said, *Since the day I brought the people of Israel up from Egypt I have used a tent as my dwelling place.*

No, David, do not build me a house. Rather, I will make you a house! I took you from following the sheep and made you prince over Israel. I have been with you and I will be with you all your days — and when you lie down with your ancestors I will raise up your offspring and establish his kingdom. I will establish his throne forever. He shall build a house for my name, and I will be his father, and he shall be my son.

David stood rigid on the dark hill. "O Lord my God," he whispered, "is this a promise?"

The Lord said, *It is a promise.*

David whispered yet again, "Lord, but is it like your word to Abraham? Is it like your word to Moses on Sinai? Is it a covenant?"

The Lord answered, *It is my covenant with the house of David. It is an everlasting covenant, ordered in all things and secure.*

A wind blew up and tugged at David's tangled hair. It billowed his loose robe and bathed his body in the cold. But he was lost in the knowledge of the Lord. David's thin white frame stood erect, his face tipped up to heaven. "It is a decree of the Lord," he said. "Oh, I will sing the decree of my God!"

> *God said to me, "You are my son,*
> *today have I begotten you.*
>
> *I make the nations now your heritage,*
> *even as far as the ends of the earth."*

iv

In those days David the king of Israel defeated the Philistines in the west and subdued them altogether. He took Methegammah out of their hands.

He traveled to the king of the Ammonites in the east and offered friendship instead of war. Nahash, very old and very wise, accepted.

Moab rose up and fought with David. He defeated them. He measured them with a line, making them lie down on the ground. Two lines he measured to be put to death, and one full line he spared. The Moabites became his servants and brought tribute.

David won a name for himself by slaying eighteen thousand Edomites in the valley of Salt. He stationed garrisons throughout all the kingdom of Edom, and they became his servants, sending tribute.

In time he ceased to march with his armies. His commanders went forth in his name, and in his name his envoys levied an annual tribute which enriched the treasuries of this king.

Nahash the king of the Ammonites died in his old age, and Hanun his son reigned in his stead. David sent several emissaries into Ammon to console the young king and to congratulate him. But even before they arrived at the Ammonite capital of Rabbah, Hanun seized the Israelite ambassadors and accused them of spying in his land. He shaved half their beards and tore open their robes at the waist, exposing their genitals. "The cheek declares you women," Hanun said, "but the hip will prove that you are men. Go on home! Get out of here!"

When David learned of the humiliation of his servants, he dispatched Joab with a regiment to Rabbah, to teach the callow fool a lesson: Ammon would be bound to Israel one way or the other.

Joab crossed the Jordan by the ford at the north end of the Salt Sea. This took him through open country on the way to Rabbah.

As he approached the city, the armies of Ammon came out and began to draw up in battle lines. So did Joab, facing them.

But suddenly a shout went up at the back of his troops. Joab turned and saw that a huge army, thirty thousand foot soldiers and chariots, was bearing down on his rear. Syrians! Mercenaries! Hanun had purchased their help and put Israel in a nutcracker, and the open country gave chariots a place to play.

"Abishai!" Joab called to his brother. "Divide the troops! Now! If the Syrians get too close we'll have no room to maneuver. Take four companies and check Hanun while I fly in the face of this ambush. Go!"

Joab spent a moment looking south, judging distances and speeds and points most vulnerable in the advancing line. Then he barked orders, redistributed his own forces, and suddenly charged to attack the attackers.

Sling-stones and javelins and a rain of arrows, the marauding bravery of Joab's forces, and a rush on foot as swift as chariots — all at once things doubled in speed. The Syrians were astonished at this turn of events. They hesitated. Joab did not. They stopped. Joab charged the harder. Syria broke and scattered, escaping by any means possible.

And the young Hanun, when he saw his allies failing, retreated into the walls of his city. Joab gave David an accurate report of the events near Rabbah. "I was overconfident," he said. "Worse, because some Syrians were put to shame, many Syrian cities are preparing to fight us. Hadadezer of Zobah is bringing forces from Damascus and from as far as the Euphrates."

David said, "We will not be overconfident the second time. Raise the militia of all Israel. I myself will take command."

There were three fords over the Jordan. The second was near Jericho. The third, farthest north, was at Adamah, leading into the valley of Succoth.

David said, "We'll cross at Adamah. There will be no haste, Joab. When this is done, it will be done indeed, and it will not occur a third time." David spoke in pragmatic tones. There was neither censure in his voice nor anything like shame in Joab's countenance. "Therefore, arrange supply lines for our armies from Succoth and from Mahanaim. When we have entered the valley, we will not turn south toward Rabbah, but north to Helam and Damascus and Zobah. I must attend to Hadadezer first and Hanun of the Ammonites second."

In three weeks King David of Israel had crossed the Jordan to meet the armies of Hadadezer at Helam. Israel and Syria drew up battle lines with shields and spears and fought against each other. David slew seven hundred Syrian horsemen and forty-two thousand foot soldiers. David corralled and hamstrung all the chariot horses, keeping back one hundred chariots with which to equip his own army. When all the captains and commanders of Hadadezer saw that they had been defeated by David, they made peace with him and became his subjects. Now, David sent Joab and the armies of Israel south to lay siege to the fortified city of Rabbah.

"Patience," he said to Joab. "There never was haste to the thing. Let the young Hanun grow old inside his walls, and the Ammonites will never challenge Israel again."

King David himself returned home. With Benaiah and his bodyguard he carried thirty shields of gold taken from the officers of Hadadezer, as well as great quantities of bronze.

∎

On a summer's day at noon, when farmers were harvesting wheat and the olive trees had just begun to bloom, King David put his hands behind his back and went out to walk in the gardens on his rooftop. He strolled among the redbud, the pomegranates, roses, and oleanders. He wore a cool linen tunic and Egyptian sandals turned up at the toe. He was nearly forty, a lean man, light on his feet and vastly content.

The siege which Joab was conducting against Rabbah east of the Jordan had entered its second month. According to reports, Israel fought daily skirmishes at the city walls to keep Hanun's forces frightened and unbalanced; but Joab had not yet tried to breach the walls. There was time.

Apart from this war with the Ammonites, the kingdoms of Judah and Israel enjoyed peace with the rest of the world. Tribute was enriching the treasuries in Jerusalem, and David ruled solely. King David dominated all the territory from Egypt to the Euphrates: by governors he controlled the Aramaeans, the Syrians, Edom; he was himself chief of the Moabite tribes; he had established treaties with Tyre and Hamath; and when Rabbah fell, he would become king of the Ammonites, too.

He was almost restless in his successes.

David plucked dry ears of the ornamental wheat that grew in the beds of his garden. He wandered toward the southern parapet of the roof, rubbing the ears in his palms, placing fresh kernels between his front teeth and cracking them. He glanced down into the city. A sparkling caught his eye, a flash of sunlight in one of the courtyards below. It was water in the cistern of a wealthy house. David looked more closely and saw a woman bathing there, alone, secluded. She lay on her back in the bright water, her body ivory white, her black hair floating like a radiance round her head. She had kicked a delicate foot. That was the flash that caught the king's eye. And now he could not take his eyes from her.

In a little while she rolled over, stood, and stepped up onto the pavement, raining water. She covered herself in a blue robe and vanished into the house.

David woke. The wheat had turned glutinous on his tongue. He rushed into his own house and ran downstairs to the chambers of his secretary, Seraiah. He described the house with its open cistern. He named the street that bordered it, and he said, "Who lives there?"

Seraiah said, "Ah, that's Uriah's house."

"Uriah? The Hittite? The building belongs to my Uriah?"

"Ever since we were running from Saul, he has been your soldier. The same one."

"I appointed him an officer next to Joab," David said. "He is very loyal."

"And he's fighting even now at Rabbah."

"But there's a woman in his cistern, someone I've never seen before."

Seraiah smiled. "Old Uriah has married a young wife. She's the daughter of another good fighter of yours, Eliam — and her grandfather is Ahithophel."

"Yes, yes, friends of mine — but I've never seen her before," the king repeated thoughtfully.

His secretary nodded.

Suddenly David demanded: "What is her name?"

Seraiah said, "Bathsheba. Eliam called her his Daughter of Abundance."

"Bathsheba," David said.

That night he couldn't sleep. Nor could he think of anything but the woman bathing. The image caused him a greater restlessness than he had ever suffered before, and the more he considered it in solitude and in darkness, the more convinced was David that he could not survive this torment.

"Tobias!" cried the king. "Tobias!"

An aide appeared in the doorway.

David said, "Go to the house of Uriah the Hittite and tell his wife that the king of Israel has need of her immediately."

Tobias lit two oil lamps in David's room, then left.

David lay on his couch unmoving, willing himself not to think, waiting. He decided that he did not know what would happen. The night would grind on and he would see where it led him.

But when the woman whom he had seen swimming in sunlight actually entered his bedroom and stood between the lamp flames looking at him, he knew. He knew what he would do.

"Bathsheba," David whispered, his voice thickened, breathless: "come here."

She came toward him like a white cloud. He put his arms into the coolness and drew her down to himself, and then he was making love to her and there was no stopping now, no thinking, no talking — but David heard someone sobbing and he hoped it was himself. He hoped it wasn't Bathsheba. How dreadful, if he had caused Bathsheba to cry!

Shortly before dawn the woman left the king's palace and returned to her own home.

David didn't see her after that. The opportunity to meet seemed never to arise — and her courtyard, when he looked into it, was always vacant.

But two months later, on the first day of the week, Bathsheba sent a message by her maid to the king, saying, "I am with child."

On the third day of that same week, a brief command was received by Joab at Rabbah:

Uriah the Hittite, having served with distinction, deserves a rest. Cousin, send him home a while. Tell him his bed is soft and his wife is lonely.

King David had no better servant than Uriah. None was more honorable, none more loyal than he. It should have been anticipated, then, that the man would greet his king as soon as he returned to Jerusalem. Yet David seemed baffled by the Hittite's visitation, his helmet beneath his arm, his coat of mail still bound to his body.

David said, "You haven't bathed yet."

Uriah grinned, black grit wreathing his countenance. "I haven't been home yet, sir." He had a square face and generous eyelids. His hair was going grey. "I came first to venerate my lord."

"Ah," said David. It was the evening of the Sabbath. His own hair and beard were perfumed, a contrast that caused him some discomfort. He, too, smiled and said, "How is Joab?"

"The anvil? Oh, he laughs and jokes and loves us all."

David frowned. "I asked about Joab."

"I know." Uriah ducked his head. "I was poking fun at the commander."

"Oh. Of course. And how do the troops fare?"

"We do not rush matters," Uriah said more seriously. "Few of us have died. Joab is more patient than I've ever known him to be."

"Good, good," said David. Now he smiled like sunlight and put his hand on the officer's shoulder. "Thank you for the news," he said. "Go down to your house and your new wife, Uriah. Wash your feet. Take your ease. Have pleasure. Go."

Uriah bowed and went out the door.

King David took his own ease that night. He slept better than he had in a week.

But when he stepped outside in the morning to speak a word to Benaiah, he found Uriah the Hittite sleeping in the doorway with the rest of the king's bodyguard.

"Uriah!" David shouted, louder than he had intended.

The man woke and bounded to his feet.

"Why are you here? Why didn't you go down to your own house?"

The Hittite said, "All my brothers are camping in the open field. Shall I eat and drink and lie with my wife when they have no comfort at all?"

David frowned. He glanced at Benaiah. "You let a tired soldier sleep here, as if on duty?"

Poor Benaiah didn't know how to answer such a question.

David stared at Uriah a moment, then he said, "Stay with me the rest of the day. Eat with me. Drink with me." He smiled and said, "These are commands, Uriah. Obey me."

Uriah did. On the first day of the week David fed him royal food, and from noon until night he gave him a rich wine for drinking.

When it was dark outside, Uriah went to the king and threw his arms around him, a crushing embrace.

David laughed. "You're drunk, my friend," he said.

Uriah tipped his strong, grey face to the ceiling and roared with laughter.

David said, "Go home. Go home to the woman who is waiting to please her soldier. Go."

Uriah winked at the king. He waggled a forefinger of caution, then rolled out of David's chambers, down the stairs, out of the palace.

David was too taut to sleep again that night.

As soon as dawn broke in the east, he dressed and went downstairs. He opened the great doors of the palace, and his heart sank. There was Uriah, snoring among the king's bodyguard, still stinking and unwashed.

So the king returned to his room. In his own hand he wrote on a new clay tablet:

> *Set Uriah in the forefront of the hardest fighting, then draw back that he may be struck down and die.*

David closed the tablet, sealed it with his royal seal, carried it out to Uriah the Hittite and gave it to him, saying, "Return to Rabbah. When you get there, give this to Joab."

On the Sabbath of the second week a messenger came to the king in his palace, craving an audience. David met him in the midst of his bodyguard. Benaiah was present.

"They may all hear your news," said David.

So the messenger said, "Joab told me to ride as fast as I could, to tell you that he attempted a direct attack on the city. But archers shot at your servants from the wall. Four of the king's officers are dead. Uriah the Hittite is dead, too."

David nodded sadly. "Tell Joab not to let this matter trouble him, for the sword devours now one and now another."

But when Benaiah went and told Bathsheba that her husband and his friend Uriah had died, she lifted her voice in a loud wail of lamentation. She went into her courtyard and paced continually, weeping and wringing her hands.

David watched her from his lofty gardens. He watched for seven days, a proper period for mourning.

On the first day of the third week, King David sent Tobias and ten royal maidservants to Uriah's house with crimson garments, a gold necklace, and an onyx brooch carved white on black. They returned to the palace with the pale Bathsheba now robed in exquisite raiment, and she became his wife.

Late in the winter, during the latter rains when almond trees bloomed white in the streets of Jerusalem, Bathsheba gave birth to a son.

She never named the child.

David thought to name him, for the baby was alabaster, fragile, translucent, and his father's heart was moved by the pale beauty and the weakness of the tiny boy.

But David was interrupted.

A prophet named Nathan requested an audience, saying he could not wait till the child was circumcised. The matter wanted an immediate judgment.

"Sir," said Nathan, "two men have a dispute. The one is rich, with many flocks and herds. The other is so poor that he had but one little ewe lamb which he brought up with his children. She used to eat from his table, as dear as a daughter to him.

"Now, a traveler came to the rich man, but he was unwilling to give up any of his own sheep, so he seized the poor man's lamb and slaughtered her and cooked her for his visitor's food."

When David heard the nature of the dispute and the injustice done to someone so powerless, he was outraged. "As the Lord lives," he said, "anyone who can do such a thing deserves to die."

"Is that," said Nathan, "the king's judgment?"

David said, "Surely the rich man must restore to the poor man four times what he took."

Nathan said, "How does one restore a life?"

David looked at the prophet with exasperation. "Even a rich man can't make the dead to live again."

"Exactly," Nathan said. He took a stand immediately before the king and said, "David, you are that rich man. As for the poor man, thus says the Lord: *I delivered you from Saul. I gave you the houses of Judah and of Israel. I gave you wives — and if that were too little, I would add as much more. Why, then, have you despised the word of the Lord? Why have you slain Uriah the Hittite with the weapons of the Ammonites — and then taken his wife to be your wife?*"

David took hold of the throat of his garment and began to tear it slowly, from top to bottom. His face had gone haggard with grief.

"I have sinned," he whispered, staring at Nathan, his thin chest appearing where his royal robe had been. "I have sinned against the God of Israel."

"Yes, my lord."

"Nathan! I have sinned!"

"Yes."

In that same moment a nurse came to the king. When she saw his condition, she almost withdrew, but he said, "What!"

She bowed and trembled. "Sir, I'm sorry," she said in a faint voice. "Your son is sick."

"Which of my sons?" David cried. "Which one?"

"The infant."

King David ran down the corridors of his palace. He ran to the thirty rooms reserved for his wives and his children. He ran into the apartments of Bathsheba, and found them crowded with women.

"Get out!" he cried, and they departed in absolute silence.

David saw the baby, seven days old. There could be no circumcision tomorrow. Its tiny body was hot and dry, its breath but fleeting pants. All its skin seemed shrunken, but the baby wasn't crying. David's son was not complaining. It turned huge eyes toward its father, and its father could not tolerate the trust he thought he saw in them.

David rushed from the room. He fled upstairs to his own rooms and fell on his face and cried out, "Have mercy on me, O God! Wash me from my sin! I know my sin. I have seen my sin. It is against you that I have sinned, and you are right to punish me. Me, O Lord my God. Punish me — but let my poor son live — "

All day long King David prayed, loud enough that Tobias and all the servants heard him. He didn't eat. He fasted. And he prayed the next day, too, the eighth day of his young son's life.

"Wash me, and I shall be whiter than snow," he prayed. "O Lord, let me hear gladness again, that the bones which you have broken might rejoice — "

Tobias came into the king's room to read a message from Joab:

> *I have taken Rabbah's water supply. We are ready to take the city itself. Come, O King, and lead the defeat, lest it be called by my name.*

But David did not respond. He did not rise from the floor. He continued fasting and praying.

Two days later Tobias came and read a second message:

> *Are you the king, or am I? Which of us shall defeat the Ammonites for the Lord and for Israel?*

David remained where he was. Tobias had no evidence that he had even heard the words. Neither did Joab.

On the fourteenth day after the birth of the infant, Joab wrote:

> *Is the king of Israel dead, that he no longer answers his commander?*

And on the fifteenth day the nameless baby died.

Tobias was afraid to tell David that the child was dead. He spoke to servants outside the chambers, saying, "When the baby was still alive the king wouldn't listen. How can I say it's dead? King David may do himself harm."

But David heard the whispering, and he called out, "Is my son dead?"

Tobias couldn't find the words. He stood mute in the hallway.

But old Rothem, the ancient broom-woman, answered. "He is dead," she said.

David said nothing. Soon Tobias heard motion in the king's apartment, water poured from jar to basin, the rustle of raiment.

That evening the king appeared downstairs in the palace, his hair brushed clean, his red beard trimmed and anointed, his clothing clean. He went out to the tent where the Ark of God was, and he worshiped. Then he returned and called for food and ate.

Tobias gaped at his lord the king. He was a helpful servant, but he was not old. There was much he did not understand.

David saw his bewilderment and said, "As long as my son had life, I thought the Lord might be gracious and let him live. But now he is dead. No fasting can restore his life. I cannot make him live again. One day I shall go to him, but he will never return to me."

On the following day, King David rode out with Benaiah to Rabbah and joined Joab in fighting the Ammonites. Rabbah fell before their assault, and its citizens crept out like skeletons. Young King Hanun went down on his knees and begged for his life. David put the heel of his right foot on the back of Hanun's neck, a sign of absolute subjection. Then there was brought to him a crown weighing sixty-five pounds, set with a most rare jewel. David went to a public place in the city and placed this crown upon his own head, declaring himself to be the king of the Ammonites.

When all these wars had ceased, David remembered the day he had seen his small son sick, the tiny body tight inside its pitiful skin. He recalled the trust in the baby's eyes, and how he rushed from the room in anguish. Now, these many days later, it occurred to him that he and the infant had not been alone in the room. A woman had been sitting and weeping silently behind him. She had stayed when he escaped. Bathsheba, the baby's mother.

In the days of his kingdom's complete peace, then, David went and comforted his wife with soft words and with singing. Soon she conceived, and in midwinter, shortly after the barley fields had been sown, Bathsheba gave birth to a second son.

On the day of its circumcision, they named the baby Solomon.

Then Nathan the prophet came to David and Bathsheba to say that the Lord loved this infant with a particular love. So they added to his name a second name: Jedidiah, Beloved of the Lord.

V

David had many sons older than Solomon. By his fortieth year he had produced a handsome generation from which would come a king to rule Judah and Israel in his stead.

Hadn't the Lord God promised it?

For he has made with me an everlasting covenant, ordered in all things and secure.

Born to David in Hebron — now grown and strong and stalwart, each in his own right — were five men. Amnon, the oldest, was a man of hungers and passions not unlike David's own. Absalom, next oldest, was simply beautiful. He had that abundance of black hair which David had loved in Saul and Jonathan. The father's heart was moved even just to gaze upon Absalom. A straight, smooth brow; a cunning mind; a man of sweet words; a man most politic and courtly, yes: he had a royal bearing.

Adonijah, the third living son, displayed a tendency to pout. A bit withdrawing and woundable. But he was an excellent student! He needed no scribe to write his letters for him. David took pride in the learning of his third son.

But he scarcely noticed the fourth and the fifth, perhaps because their births occurred when he was consumed with the consolidation of his kingdom. Shephathiah and Ithream, then, remained close to one another all their lives. They were the last children born in Hebron, just before David's move to Jerusalem — and there the king's new house seemed to teem with sons, thirteen born in less than ten years. It was natural that these two should form a quiet alliance. Neither one had aspirations to power nor any desire to reap the rewards of their parentage. When they were thirteen and fourteen years old they watched, as did everyone in the palace, the dramatic birth of a pale child, the surviving son of Bathsheba, Solomon; they noted how carefully the boy was raised, how little real freedom he had, how seldom he was alone — and how sober it made him. They were glad to be plain and unnoticed. And then, through no fault of their own, they were witnesses of an assassination between brothers — their own brothers! — so cold-blooded that these two gathered their things together and moved away from the house of David forever.

▌▌

When he was twenty-two years old, Amnon — the son of David by his wife Ahinoam — fell violently in love with Tamar. It was a forbidden love, and he grew sick with it: for she was also a child of David, by his wife, Maacah, who was also the mother of Absalom. Tamar was Amnon's half-sister.

She was just entering womanhood, a virgin of slant eyes, deep red hair, and dark complexion. Her face was older than her soul. She had no idea what passions she aroused in men.

In Amnon. So tormented was he by his inability to have this woman that he took to his bed and soon the entire royal household began to worry about him.

David himself came to his oldest son and said, "Is there anything I can do for you?"

Amnon said, "Yes. Yes, let my sister Tamar come and make some cakes while I watch, that I might eat them from her hand."

The king granted his request. He sent Tamar to Amnon, saying, "Prepare food for your brother."

She did. Tamar came to Amnon's house and there took dough and kneaded it and made the cakes in his sight. She baked them and carried them to him that he might, exactly as he had requested, eat them from her own hand.

But he refused to eat.

He said to his personal aide, "Send the servants away, and you — wait out in the courtyard."

When they were alone, he said to his sister, "Bring the food into my chamber."

Tamar obeyed. She brought the cakes into Amnon's private room. She took one and knelt and reached it carefully toward his mouth.

Suddenly Amnon grabbed her wrist. He was panting, bathed in a sick sweat, his eyes moist with pleading. "Lie with me!" he said.

Tamar uttered a frightened cry. "No! You are my brother! No!" she said. "Where could I go in my shame? No — "

But Amnon, growling, did not release her. He tore her robe open and threw her backward on his bedding and raped her. As soon as he finished, he jumped away from her.

She was crying. Her face was blotched white and red. She still lay on his bed, bleeding into the blankets. She had drawn her knees up and seemed to contract into herself like a larva curling around the point of a knife. Amnon said, "Get out of here!"

She shook her head and kept crying. He began to pace in the small room. "Get up! Get off my bed!" he said.

She tightened into a hard ball. Her red hair now seemed obscene, sticking to her face. Amnon said, "Stop your whining. What's the matter with you? Don't you know when you're not wanted? Go on — get out of my rooms."

"No," she sobbed. "I will stay with you." Then the hatred with which Amon hated her was greater than any love that he had felt for her before.

"If you don't go," he roared, "I will throw you out!"

She said, "My brother, this wrong in sending me away is greater than the other which you did to me."

Amnon, seething with fury, called his aide in from the courtyard. "Pick this whore up, and carry her from my house!" Gingerly the young aide carried Tamar from the room while Amnon shouted, "Bolt the door behind her!" Tamar had come to Amnon wearing a long robe with sleeves, the dress of the daughters of kings who are yet virgins. Now she did not change the garment, despite its long rip and its soiling. Instead, she tore it almost to rags and covered her hair with ashes and went to the house of her brother, Absalom.

"What? Tamar, what happened?" Absalom asked. She fell into his arms, and he held her tightly until she could control her sobbing. Then she whispered into his ear, "Amnon, Amnon — "

Absalom grew very still. "Hold your peace, my sister," he said. "Stay here. Live here with me, and wait. Wait."

So she lived with Absalom as a desolate woman. And they waited. They heard that David knew of the crime. They heard, too, that their father the king was very angry with Amnon. But a whole year passed in which he did nothing to punish Amnon or else to right this wrong.

Absalom said bitterly, "Like father, like son. Maybe one sinner can't bring himself to condemn another sinner. Wait, Tamar. Be patient, and perhaps I will find a way to take matters into my own hands."

Another year passed.

Then, at the time of sheepshearing, Absalom announced that he would celebrate the season by giving an elaborate feast at Baal-hazor. He invited all of his brothers, the sons of the king, to come and eat with him. They did, in a high good humor.

Here, then, gathered the glory of David's kingdom, the next generation, eighteen men and lads all talking and laughing. They ate succulent food. They drank remarkable wines. And when the evening came and their hearts were merry, the servants of Absalom walked quickly through the banquet hall, holding knives beneath their robes. They surrounded Amnon, and just as that man felt an alien presence around him, Absalom cried a command, and his servants stabbed his oldest brother to death.

The rest of the king's sons rose up, horrified. They ran out of the hall, leaped to their mules, and rode hard to Jerusalem in order to separate themselves from the bloody scene and to prove their innocence.

Shephathiah and Ithream did not stop in Jerusalem. These two continued on into the hill country of Judah, where they settled at a distance from royalty and intrigue. They chose, rather, to follow the sheep as their grandfather had, and their father, before royalty had consumed him.

Absalom fled in the opposite direction, to Geshur, the kingdom northeast of Israel where his mother's father ruled as king. Immediately, King David issued a decree that the murderer of his son must remain in Geshur as an exile, forbidden to come home again. It was an appropriate punishment.

But David's heart yearned for his beautiful boy. Who else displayed such grace and bearing as Absalom? In which other son did David find his own deepest notions of royalty reflected? Amnon could never be recovered. And Absalom was as good as dead.

King David, the ruler of many nations, paced his rooftop gardens, sad and distracted. He built a booth on the roof of the palace, so that he might stay there even in the rains and in the noonday sun.

Joab cared nothing for appearances — except when they betrayed hidden truths. And in these latter months he could not help observing changes in the king's demeanor. David's red hair was shot with white. His quick eyes had lost their golden flecks; they were merely brown and tired. His body was growing sickly white and hollow. He wasn't eating well. He spent his time alone on the palace roof.

This was Joab's interpretation of internal truth: the king was pining for Absalom. It was an indulgence Joab did not share. He never pined. Nor did he have feelings for Absalom. In fact, he thought the fellow a bit affected — cutting his hair but once a year, then weighing the cut as though this were a ceremony of some significance. On the other hand, as long as the king languished in loneliness, the kingdom itself was compromised.

For purely pragmatic reasons, then, Joab devised a way to draw David out. He fetched from the town of Tekoa a wise woman. He dressed her in the clothes of one who is mourning, and he sent her to the king with a carefully constructed speech.

The woman said, "Help, O king!"

He said, "What is your trouble?"

She said, "Alas, I am a widow. I had two sons to carry his name — but they quarreled with one another, and one of my sons struck the other and killed him. Now the whole family is demanding that I hand over to them my last son, to destroy him. But he is the heir. They would quench my coal and leave my husband neither name nor remnant on the earth."

Quickly King David rendered a decision, "Go to your house," he said. "I will give orders to protect your son."

The woman pressed her case, "Pray, let the king invoke the Lord," she begged, "that the avenger of blood slay no more and my son be not destroyed."

David said, "As the Lord lives, not one hair of your son shall fall to the ground."

Immediately, then, the woman stood up straight and true. "Doesn't the king realize that he convicts himself in this decision?" she said.

David drew back, frowning.

The woman said, "My lord the king is like the angel of God, able to discern good and evil. You likewise had two sons. One killed the other, and you banished the living one. But what has been the result? Not only is a father deprived, but a whole kingdom is deprived of its heritage. Sir, Absalom is heir to your throne! Bring him home again. We all must die. We are like water spilt on the ground, which cannot be gathered up again. Amnon cannot come back. But Absalom can — "

King David gazed narrowly at the woman. "Is the hand of Joab in this?" he said.

She answered, "The king has wisdom like an angel of God. Yes, Joab bade me say these words exactly as I've said them."

David nodded and nodded, the flash of something like anger and something like glee in his eye. "The man needs no helmet. He has a skull of bronze."

So David reversed his earlier decree. He allowed Joab to bring Absalom back to Jerusalem. But he folded his arms and added: "Let him dwell apart in his own house. He is still banished from the king's presence!"

David was on the rooftop when Absalom entered Jerusalem through the western gate. From above, the father saw his beautiful boy, the flowing black hair and the bearing more martial and magnificent than any other son of his. He also saw Absalom glance up and then raise a hand in greeting — but he, the king, only looked and did not return the salute.

For two years David watched Absalom from a distance. For two years he felt it necessary to continue the difficult discipline. He hardened his expression whenever the young man rode by. But he watched, fascinated by Absalom's boldness. The son looked directly at his father, steadfastly into his eyes, unashamed, looking and looking as if searching for something. How long could David maintain the juridical pose? Sometimes to be king was almost more than he could bear.

And then one day Joab entered the king's chambers with a growl of irritation and a strong smell of smoke. His clothing was streaked with sweat and ash. A grass fire. "My lord," he said, "as far as I'm concerned you can do what you please with that son of yours. His word bears no force with me; I have no complicity in this. Nevertheless, he has persuaded me to bring you a message."

"Absalom," David said.

"Absalom, son of Maacah. Yes."

"Please," said David softly, "what message?"

"Lord Absalom says, 'Why have I come from Geshur? It would be better for me to be there still. Let me come into the presence of the king, and if there is guilt in me, let him kill me.' "

"That's what he said? He thinks I might kill him?"

Joab shrugged. "I don't pretend to interpret."

"Were his spirits crushed? Kill him! What else did he say?"

"I didn't wait to hear more." Joab turned to leave. He paused at the door of David's chambers and said, "My lord, the boy kept sending for me as if I were some sort of servant. I ignored him — until this morning when someone set my barley field afire, and I ran to put it out, and there he was, holding the torches, and that's what he said. No, his spirits were not crushed."

Joab went out in disgust.

David scarcely noticed. "That I might kill him!" he murmured. "He thinks the king's discipline could ever go so far as to *kill* him?"

So David broke his hard pose. He called Absalom to himself, and when the handsome man strode through the main door of his house, David ran to him and embraced him and kissed him. "Absalom!" he wept. "Oh, my son, how I have missed you!"

■

In those days Absalom got himself a chariot and horses and fifty men to run before him wherever he went, a personal bodyguard. He began to rise early in the morning and to stand all day in the city gate. When anyone came to Jerusalem seeking the king's judgment over some matter, Absalom would call to the man and say, "What city are you from? Which tribe? How are your children?"

After questions like these and close conversation with the supplicant, Absalom would earnestly declare: "See, your claims are good and right, but the king is busy and there's no one to hear you." He would shake his head in deep sympathy. "Oh, that I were judge in the land!" he would sigh. "Then everyone with a suit could come to me and I would give him justice!"

Often, now, people bowed down before Absalom. Wherever he went in Israel — and especially in Judah — people offered him a formal obeisance. But he always raised them up and took them by the shoulders and kissed them. So he left the people filled with wonder for the handsome prince in his rich chariot.

And then, in the fourth year after his return to David's graces, Absalom began to confer secretly with various leaders in Israel. He met his cousin Amasa outside Jerusalem at night. Amasa was a warrior with much combat experience. Moreover, he was a nephew of Joab; he had learned leadership from the commander-in-chief himself.

At the end of their meeting, the cousins embraced and separated. Amasa traveled north and began to move among all the tribes of Israel, talking to the local leaders of the militia.

Absalom rode south into the hill country of Judah. He went to the town of Giloh, about five miles from Hebron, to the house of Ahithophel, an old man, grave and white-headed, a man of national reverence.

Ahithophel had long been King David's wisest counselor. His word was received by everyone in Israel as if it were an oracle of God. Until eight years ago he had lived near the king in Jerusalem; but then he retired to his home in Giloh and served David only upon the king's particular request.

Absalom believed he knew why Ahithophel had left. He sat facing the man a long time before he spoke. The silence was meant to convey a personal respect as well as the weight of the matter which he brought for discussion.

Finally Absalom said, "Sir, I intend a vengeance on your behalf."

Ahithophel's eyebrows rose up. "On my behalf?" he said. "What vengeance do I seek?"

Absalom said, "Of David, my father. For his sin against your granddaughter Bathsheba."

Absalom paused. The old man gave the slightest squint of true remembering. Yes. Absalom's instinct had been accurate.

He drove forward, therefore, with conviction: "Not to mince words, David raped her. Worse, I suspect he ordered the death of Uriah." Ahithophel said nothing. But his pale eyes were clearly struggling with emotion.

Absalom said, "I am planning to take my rightful place upon the throne. This will require the overthrow of my father. He will go down, sir, for many sins, not least of which is his persisting offense against the woman of your house, Bathsheba. Ahithophel, say nothing to me now. Only consider whether you may be willing to serve with me as my highest, most trusted counselor."

The eyebrows had lowered. Absalom could not read the old man's mind.

So he brought his suit to its conclusion. "In several weeks I will be in Hebron, where the king once lived, where even now people remember and regret the loss of their prestige. To Hebron shall come the armies of Israel under the command of Amasa, my cousin. Sir: as soon as you hear the trumpet and the cry *Absalom is king at Hebron*, then, perhaps, you may choose to help me reestablish justice in the land."

∎

Now, David received a respectful message from his son Absalom. The prince craved a meeting with his king.

David laughed aloud at the formality of the thing.

"Tell him to come!" said David. "Tell him we will eat a meal together!"

So David had a calf slaughtered and prepared in the richest manner. He asked that the most excellent wine be brought to his rooftop, and that a table be set in the booth built among his gardens. In a good humor David intended to outdo the formality of his son. He dressed in purple. He perfumed his hair — hair silver-white but as soft as ever, falling in loose curls, though nothing like the grand black cataracts of Absalom's hair. On impulse he placed a royal ringlet around his brow.

Then he and his oldest son sat down to eat.

Absalom, handsome in the king's bower, said, "My lord, I beg leave to go — "

"Wait!" cried David. "Whatever you ask, I will give you. But let's wait with beggings and givings a while. My son," he said, sunshine flooding his heart, "how are you?"

"Well," Absalom blinked at the intensity of the question. "I am well."

"Ah, then the Lord has been good to both of us. I am well, too," said David. "Yes, yes — all is well," he said. And it was. There had been rest from war for many years now. The rains had been regular and abundant. The king had returned to his old joy in music, singing songs he had not sung before, songs filled with praise and not complaint.

Absalom was looking narrowly at his father.

He said, "You know no trouble in the kingdom then?"

"No," said David. He thought a moment. "Well: Rothem died," he said. "My ancient domestic. My dear broom-woman who was old when I was young, who swept the streets outside my house in Hebron. Faithful Rothem has died. I am sorry for that."

Absalom frowned. "A broom-woman. For a broom-woman the king is moved to notice trouble in the kingdom."

"Yes," said David. "Why? Are you aware of something I should know?"

Absalom applied his attention to the food a while. The sun had slanted downward. Evening approached.

David said, "There is no house for the Ark of God. That is a wrong which I couldn't right, but it must finally be righted. Absalom, the Lord — " David felt heat in his cheeks, but the word was begun and he couldn't contain it: " — the Lord told me my offspring would build a house for his name. When he is king my son will right that wrong." Such a sweet commotion danced in David's breast! It was as if he were speaking love to a young woman.

Absalom said, "Where would a house of the Lord be built?"

"There. Over there." David pointed to the higher hill north of them, where shadows struck strongly eastward. "On Moriah. Look: the next king should fill this ravine with stone and earth, and smooth a path from here to there, from hill to hill, so the Lord might dwell inside the City of David!" He grinned. He had just, for the first time since he had conceived it, spoken his dream out loud. "What do you think?" he said. Absalom stood up and walked to the northern side of the roof. He looked a while at the higher hill. Then he went to the western side and looked down into the streets of the city. "A king's view," he said.

David rose and joined him. "What did you say?"

"So this is what the king sees when he bends his gaze to the lives of his people below."

"Yes. It causes both pity and affection. It causes me to pray."

"Can the king also recognize loneliness from here? Can the king also pierce to the hearts of the children and discern when they suffer various kinds of isolations?"

Before David could answer, Absalom began to hum a low tune. Then he put words to it: "O God, the waters are up to my neck. Remember that?" he said. And he sang in a strong, melodious voice:

O God, the waters are up to my neck;
   I sink in mire; there is no foothold.
I am tired with crying, my throat is broken,
   my eyes are thick with waiting for my God —

"Remember that?" Absalom asked. "Do you remember singing that?"

Somewhat subdued, David answered, "Yes. I didn't know anyone heard me then."

"Heard you, sir, and memorized the smart lash of your language, too." Absalom continued to sing:

Those that hate me without cause
   are more than the hairs on my head;
they attack me with lies, saying I've stolen,
   saying I've stolen and must restore —

Absalom, looking down from the palace roof toward the western gate of the city, said, "Did it ever occur to the king that his sorrows might be suffered by others as well, even to the same degree of poetry?"

"Yes. Often." A piece of the sun had stuck on the western horizon. The city below was sinking in shadows. Both men peered into the shadows.

"Once I waved while you leaned down and looked from the rooftop. Do you remember that I waved to you?"

David stood beside his son and said nothing.

"My sister lives as a widow," Absalom said. "She has worn the widow's weeds for eleven years now."

David murmured, "Tamar."

"Yes, sir. Tamar, the only daughter of Maacah, my mother."

"And mine, Absalom. My daughter, too."

Abruptly Absalom straightened and squared his shoulders and said, "Sir, I beg leave to go to Hebron. I vowed a vow to the Lord when I was in Geshur, that if the Lord would bring me back to Jerusalem, I would worship him in Hebron too."

"Yes," David said, "Go."

Absalom turned to face his father. "It is my hope that I might take two hundred men with me as invited guests for the sacrifices I intend to offer."

David kept looking down into the dark city. Softly he said, "Go in peace."

Absalom put forth the finger of his right hand and touched the gold ring around his father's head. Then he bowed low with a formal decorum. He turned on his heel, strode to the stone stairs, and descended.

David did not move.

Early next morning the king watched as his son rode a rich chariot out of Jerusalem, preceded by fifty men and followed by two hundred.

∎

In the months that followed, rumors reached Jerusalem from many parts of the kingdom, but especially from Judah: "Absalom has been declared king in Hebron."

"Elders of the twelve tribes are blowing the horn of war and crying, *Absalom is king at Hebron!*"

"Ahithophel the Gilonite, King David's ancient counselor, has joined Absalom in Hebron."

"Rebellion! The people with Absalom are daily increasing."

Then this: "The hearts of the men of Israel have gone after Absalom!" Everywhere tribes were declaring their separation from David.

And finally: "O King, Amasa is leading the militia of Israel down from the north! Absalom is marching up from the south with Ahithophel!"

"Arise," said David. He tied his clothing close to his person and sent swift messengers through the city, to every officer and counselor: "Let's flee now, before our escape is cut off!"

So the king went out of Jerusalem with all his household and those who were loyal, with Joab, Abishai, Benaiah, and the six hundred men of his standing army. He left ten concubines behind to watch over the palace. Men and women wept as they passed through the gates of the city.

King David took a position by the brook Kidron to watch the procession of his people as they hastened toward the wilderness.

The last to come was Abiathar, David's priest since the days when Saul pursued them. Abiathar and the Levites came bearing the Ark of the Covenant of God.

David stopped them.

"Go back," he said. "Carry the Ark back into the city. If I find favor in the eyes of the Lord, he will bring me home and let me see it again. But if he says, *I have no pleasure in David*, let him do to me what seems good to him."

David drew the priest aside and said, "You, too, my friend. Stay here with your sons. When Absalom enters Jerusalem, listen to his plans, then send word to me at the fords of the Jordan." So Abiathar returned into Jerusalem with the Ark of God.

But David went up a high hill on the east side of the city, weeping as he went. He walked barefoot, his head covered. The name of this hill was the Mount of Olives.

When he reached the summit, a foreigner named Hushai ran to him, also with earth on his head, his coat torn for grief. "Oh, my friend," he said to David, "let me go with you."

David embraced him a moment, then said, "Hushai, you would do me more good in the city. Offer yourself as a counselor to Absalom. Call him king without embarrassment. Tell him you will serve him better than you served his father. Then perhaps you can defeat whatever counsel Ahithophel might give. And when you know my son's designs, pass the word to Abiathar the priest. He'll pass it on to me."

∎

Hushai the Archite arrived at Jerusalem just as Absalom in new purple robes was preparing to make a triumphal entrance. Of those who stood along the ridge road outside the city, Hushai alone was not weeping. He contrived delight.

"Long live the king!" he called. "Long live the king!"

Absalom recognized the man. "Hushai, you hardheaded counselor! Is this the loyalty you give your friends? Why didn't you go with David?"

Hushai said, "Oh, no! I belong with the one whom the Lord and the men of Israel have chosen. Who else can prevail? Sir, if I served your father well, I will serve you better."

So Absalom, inviting Hushai to follow, entered the city grandly. He rode through narrow streets to his father's palace with a ready retinue, with bright eyes and a hard young hunger.

Absalom mounted the throne of David, attended by his counselors, Ahithophel, Amasa, Hushai.

"Friends," he said, "You see the grief of David's citizens. Advise me: How shall I make this city mine?"

Ahithophel lowered the bushes of his eyebrows. His eyes could not be seen. Softly he said, "My lord, go in to your father's concubines. All Israel will hear that you have usurped absolutely the place of the king, and that you have made yourself odious to your father; then the hands of all who are with you will be strengthened."

"Excellent!" said Absalom. "And I know the place to do it."

While he stayed in Jerusalem, then, Absalom regularly ascended to the booth on the roof of the king's house, where everyone could see his comings and his goings. There, one by one, the vital young man walked King David's concubines through the gardens, then led them into the booth and lay with them.

But Ahithophel was daily urging another piece of advice upon Absalom, who seemed to desire the comforts of royalty more than the labors.

"You can't delay," he said. "Let me choose twelve thousand men and pursue David immediately. I'll catch him weary and discouraged, and throw him into a panic. His people will flee. But I will strike the king only. Everyone else I'll bring back to you as a bride comes home to her husband."

Absalom ascended the throne and mused over the advice.

Ahithophel's face was strained with anxiety.

But Absalom turned to Hushai the Archite and said, "What do you think?"

Hushai was shaking his head. "This counsel is weak, sir." He threw his hands behind his back, and rose to the balls of his feet. "You know that your father and his men are mighty. Worse than that, now they are as enraged as a she-bear robbed of her cubs. Do you think an old warrior like David would be lingering in the open? Even now he's gone to ground. He's concealed himself. Moreover, Israel knows how strong he is. At the first attack, no matter who wins, the people will say there's been a slaughter among the armies of Absalom. No, my lord, I advise you to wait: first gather all Israel to yourself, from Dan to Beersheba, as the sand by the sea for multitude, and *then* go into battle yourself. We shall descend on David and cover him as the dew covers the ground; and of him and all the men with him not one will be left. Then, O King, there shall be no doubt who is king in the land."

Ahithophel had bowed his head. He held his peace through Hushai's long speech, but his face was hidden, his deeper thinking concealed.

Absalom was wearing the slim golden ring his father sometimes wore. A smile spread across his countenance. "Hushai," he said, "you are right. I should fight. But I should first gather the force to win that fight."

So then Hushai bowed and went out of Absalom's presence to pass this news to Abiathar the priest.

Ahithophel also left Absalom's presence. But the old man saddled his donkey and left Jerusalem altogether. There seemed no urgency anymore. He rode slowly south to his own city. Once there, he set his house in order, and then he hanged himself.

▌

In the meantime, David arrived with his standing army in Mahanaim. He moved into the houses Abner and Ishbaal had occupied when poor Ishbaal was striving to be king in Israel. Then he began to develop strategies with which to meet his son, Absalom.

He knew the boy. However Absalom might judge him lacking in pity and insight, David knew his son as well as he knew his own soul. He knew that Absalom loved power more than he understood it. The crown would control him because he could not yet control himself. Absalom, the honey-tongued. His father would have given him so much more than the boy could, by his own hand, take.

King David reviewed his troops, then set over them commanders of thousands and commanders of hundreds. He divided the entire army into three large divisions, one under Joab, one under Abishai, and one under a soldier of fortune named Ittai, a Gittite.

When scouts came saying that Absalom and Amasa had crossed the
Jordan and were camping in Gilead, David gathered his commanders for a
final war counsel.

"I will march with you, as I have in the past," he said.

"No, sir," said Joab. "It isn't practical. They can wipe out half of us and we
would go on fighting. But if they killed you alone, the war would be over."

David gazed at his cousin, the cold self-confident mouth, hard grey eyes,
a man in whom there never had been tenderness nor any sign of remorse.
"Whatever seems best to you," David said.

The king took a stand at the gate of the city. He cried the command
that set his armies into motion, then saluted them as they marched out by
hundreds and by thousands.

"Deal gently!" he cried. "For my sake deal gently with the young man
Absalom!"

That day Joab acquitted himself as well as he ever had. Neither his
intellect nor his physical force had abated with age. It was Joab who chose
to engage the armies under Absalom and Amasa in the forest of Ephraim.
He knew silence and speed among the trees. He knew how to separate the
enemy into a thousand bands blinded by the woods, while communication
among his own experienced troops was as swift as the wind. He created
feints and dodges and ambushes of sudden savagery. Amasa had planned to
field the hundred chariots that David stabled in Jerusalem, but none could
drive through the forest of Ephraim.

So the armies of Absalom and Amasa were utterly defeated. Twenty
thousand perished, the forest devouring more than the sword.

Absalom likewise was fleeing for his life on the back of a mule. He was
riding at heedless speeds through the bush and the brambles, when his hair
caught fast in the branches of an oak. The mule galloped away, leaving the
man hanging between heaven and earth.

Absalom cried out. His sword had fallen to earth. He could not hack
himself free. He eased his scalp by winding his fingers in his long hair and
pulling himself up.

A young soldier stepped out of the bushes and gaped at him. "Quick!"
Absalom called. "Hand me the sword!"

But as soon as he heard Absalom's voice, the soldier dashed away like a
frightened hare.

The forest fell silent. Not so much as a breeze moved. The air was still and
hot. Absalom's arms ached. His fingers slipped and were cut on thin strands
of hair. He let go. His scalp was lifted from his skull.

Then he heard a swift tramping through the woods. And voices.

"But the king commanded us to save his life!"

"Ah!" A growl of disgust. "I will not waste time like this with you!"

Absalom recognized the latter voice.

Joab stepped into the clearing, glanced at Absalom, and kept walking forward, pulling three arrows from his quiver. The young man didn't move. He didn't kick. He saw nothing in Joab's face except a sober attention to duty.

Absalom felt the first arrow strike with such surprising force that his body swung backward. Joab, bare-handed, thrust the second one deep between his ribs. There was no sensation of pain, just a tough tugging. Absalom was grateful for that.

The third arrow was driven up under his ribcage and into his heart.

∎

Now, David was sitting within the gates of the city. A watchman was on the roof of the gate, by the wall. When he lifted his eyes, he saw a man running alone across the fields in this direction.

The watchman called out, "A soldier is coming!"

The king said, "If he is alone, he has news of the war."

But as that runner drew near, another man came out of the far woods, also running at a breakneck pace.

"See," called the watchman, "here comes a second man, also running alone!"

The king said, "Then he also has news."

The watchman called: "I think the man in front is Ahimaaz, the son of the priest! The man behind is a slave, an Ethiopian."

David said, "Ahimaaz is a good man. He comes with good news."

Then Ahimaaz cried out as he approached the gate, "All is well! All is well!"

David rose up to meet him, and the son of his old friend bowed his face to the earth.

"Blessed be the Lord your God," Ahimaaz puffed, flushed and happy, "for he defeated those who raised their hands against my king."

David said, "Is it well with the young man Absalom?"

Ahimaaz stood up. "When Joab sent me," he said, "I saw a great tumult, but I couldn't tell what it was."

The king said, "Turn aside, Ahimaaz. Stand here."

So he turned aside and stood still.

Then the Ethiopian came. Immediately he grinned at the king and clapped his hands. "Good tidings!" he cried. "For the Lord has delivered you this day from the power of all who rose up against you."

David said to the Ethiopian, "Is it well with the young man Absalom?"

The Ethiopian said, "May all the enemies of my lord the king be as that young man is now!" He clapped his hands again with glee. "Dead!" he cried.

David did not answer. He stumbled sideways, groaning, as if a great weight had been laid on his shoulders. Then he began step by step to climb the stairs to the chamber over the gate. As he went he wept and he said, "O my son Absalom, my son, my son, Absalom! Would God that I had died instead of you, O Absalom, my son, my son!"

vi

The king never was not tired after that.

One year he conducted a census throughout his realm in order to develop a system for national taxation. But the Lord God said, *What, will you now place confidence in your numbers and in your strength and cease trusting in me? Are you now a king like any other king among the nations?*

And the Lord sent an angel into the kingdom, killing by a pestilence. The angel advanced by terrible degrees toward Jerusalem, to destroy it — but just as death was ascending Mount Moriah north of the city, the Lord repented and said to the angel, *It is enough. Now stay your hand.*

David looked and saw the angel on the side of the hill, at the threshing floor of Araunah, a Jebusite. "O Lord," he cried, "I have sinned. I have done wickedly. But my sheep, my citizens, what have they done? Let thy hand, I pray thee, be against me and my father's house — "

It was precisely there that the pestilence ceased. Not another human perished.

So David went to Araunah and said, "Sell me your threshing floor, that I might build an altar to the Lord on it."

Araunah said, "Take whatever you wish and offer it up. Here are the oxen for a burnt offering; here are the threshing sledges and the yokes of the oxen for wood. O King, Araunah gives them as a gift to you."

But David said, "No, I will buy it for a price. I will not offer to my God offerings that cost me nothing."

King David bought Araunah's threshing floor and the oxen for fifty shekels of silver. He built there an altar and offered burnt offerings and peace offerings.

And he returned to his palace more weary than ever.

∎

David was an old man now. He could not keep muscle on his bones. The flesh of his chest folded down upon itself like leather flaps. "The grinders," he used to say to a young woman named Abishag, "the grinders cease because they are few." He would give her a self-deprecating smile, showing the loss of teeth. Then he would place the tips of her fingers upon his eyes and say: "Those that look through my windows are dimmed. The doors of my ears are closing, too, Abishag; so the sounds of the household are low — though I jump at the voice of a bird." David was fond of Abishag the Shunammite. Often he placed her hand on his silvery hair and said, "The almond tree, it blossoms white. The grasshopper drags his poor body along. And not even the caper-berry can rouse the cricket's song again. Poor Abishag. Not even the caper-berry."

King David spent most of his waking days on the roof of his palace. He seldom moved through the city. And he never traveled beyond its walls. His gardens were a comfort. His booth became his bedroom.

Nor did he grant audiences to many people.

Not to foreigners seeking alliances. Not to citizens with disputes.

Not even to Joab. Lately King David had simply stopped seeing the commander-in-chief. That hard, grey eye had become repugnant to him. For many years after Absalom's rebellion it had been necessary to allow the cold man still to lead the armies of Israel. Other rebellions had followed. At least once David's dominion and the unity of the twelve tribes were maintained by a military force — and none but Joab could drive that spike with accuracy and efficiency.

But the hand that killed for the sake of the kingdom had also killed Absalom.

In his old age David felt he no longer needed to suffer the presence of the man that had murdered Absalom.

Therefore, though Joab regularly requested an audience, the king refused.

Regality. Power. Decisions of state. The administration of a complex kingdom — these things occupied David's attentions less and less. He sat in his garden all covered with blankets, his dim eyes lidded, his old lips pursing around soundless words. From the streets below rose up the cries of the merchants. And fifty men ran clamoring in front of the chariots of Adonijah, the king's oldest son. Far away they seemed to be running. Adonijah, handsome man — he rode far, far away into mists and dreamings.

But here was Michal! — his eager, passionate princess. She was clapping her small hands and laughing. Her nostrils always flaring when she laughed. And her laugh was like the tiny bells of the priests. David loved Michal. David had loved Michal first of all. Thin child! Small-bosomed —

Ah, but Michal had died hardened and angry and fat and disappointed. David had not anticipated the depth of his sorrow when she left him. He missed Michal. There was a host of people whom he missed.

Jonathan? Jonathan, brother, I am here, in the corner! And even now Jonathan was grinning with his white teeth and walking toward David among the palms and the pomegranates, and immediately both of them were young men, hunting in a wicker chariot, laughing, throwing themselves lightly down on the green grass, and David was saying with great earnestness,

Where is your bow, Jonathan? He was reaching for his friend's hand in order to express the urgency of his question: *What have you done with your bow, Jonathan? I thought you gave it to me, but I can't find it anywhere.*

No! David should not have asked the question! Immediately Jonathan vanished. Jonathan wasn't here. *His beautiful face is under the earth, smiling behind the black soil. There is dirt where his tongue had been —*

David the king would sit for hours, sunken under his blankets by the booth on the rooftop, murmuring: "The silver cord is snapping, the golden bowl is breaking, the pitcher is breaking at the fountain, the wheel is cracking at the cistern. Abishag, come sit by me. Abishag, come lie with me and keep me warm."

And always Abishag obeyed. She would bring near to him her beautiful body and kindness. Abishag the Shunammite was the result of careful searchings through all the land of Israel. Abishag and David would go into his booth and lie down together under heaps of clothing. She would put her warm flesh next to his. For the king was cold. He was seventy years old. His servants had sought everywhere for a maiden to minister unto him in his old age. They had found no one more lovely than she. David lay next to the naked Abishag, but even so he could not get warm. The coldness creeping through his bones was the ice of mortality.

∎

Someone is singing in the king's room. The softest voice, the brush of a bird's wing:

> *Fairer thou art than the children of women;*
> *grace is poured into thy lips,*
> > *God hath blessed thee —*

Someone is combing the king's hair carefully and singing:

> *Gird thy sword upon thy thigh;*
> *O mighty one, O majesty,*
> > *ride forth in victory —*

Suddenly the door opens, bright sunlight cuts into the room, and two figures enter. One walks straight to the king's couch. The other, a black silhouette, remains by the door.

The king's eyes begin to water because of the light.

The near figure says, "Thank you, Abishag. That's enough for now." It is Bathsheba's voice. This is Bathsheba beside him.

David says, "Please. Would someone close the door?"

Bathsheba says, "Solomon, close the door."

The one by the sunlight turns and pushes the door closed.

David blinks his tears away. Bathsheba has iron-grey hair, strong brows, hoods of flesh above her eyes. She stands erect and very handsome. Abishag has withdrawn into a corner.

Solomon remains by the door.

"David, this is important," Bathsheba says. "It requires an immediate, official act. Please sit up."

Abishag steps forward. She slips her hands beneath the king's shoulders and helps him to sit.

"My lord," Bathsheba says, "you swore by the Lord your God that Solomon would reign after you. It is time to remember your oath. This very morning, though you do not know it, Adonijah is being declared king. He is sacrificing oxen and sheep by the Serpent's Stone outside Jerusalem. He has invited all your sons except Solomon. Israel is waiting, O King, for you to choose who shall sit on the throne after you. And if you do nothing now, you know that Solomon and I shall suffer hereafter — "

While Bathsheba is speaking, the door flies open, the light strikes David like a sword and a third figure enters.

Quickly Solomon closes the door.

This is Nathan the prophet. "Did you order the elevation of Adonijah?" Nathan asks. "He's eating a coronation feast this very hour. Abiathar the priest and Joab, commander of your armies, are raising cups of wine and crying 'Long live King Adonijah!' The whole city can hear it. O King, I was not invited. Neither was Benaiah or your bodyguard — or Solomon here. Solomon is your only offspring not invited. Did you decree the move?"

For just a moment David presses his fingers into his eyes. Before he removes them, he says, "Nathan, go and bring Benaiah here. Bring Zadok the priest." The door opens. The door closes. Then David frees his vision and finds Solomon. "Come here, my son," he says.

The slender man steps forward.

David reaches and takes his son's hand. "As I swore by the Lord that you would reign after me, so will I do this day — "

Bathsheba sinks to her knees. She bows her face to the ground. David prevents Solomon from making the same bow.

"Be strong," he says. "Listen to me, Solomon. Show yourself a man. Keep the charge of the Lord your God. Walk in his ways, keep his commandments, and you will prosper."

Solomon's eyes are large and dark. His hair falls in smooth waves, as black as a raven's. His cheek is sallow, his step soundless, his fingers as light as reeds. How stalwart is the young man's heart?

David says, "Kneel."

Solomon kneels.

David places his two hands behind the head of his son, as if cupping a lotus. He gazes into the young man's eyes, then softly begins to whisper:

> *The Spirit of the Lord blows through me,*
> *the Rock of Israel has said unto me:*
> *"The king that rules in the fear of God,*
> *   shall dawn like the morning light!*
> *   Like the sun in a cloudless sky!*
> *   Like the rain that kisses the tender grasses!"*
>
> *Doesn't my house stand so with God?*
> *My son, the Lord has established with me*
> *   an everlasting covenant,*
> *   ordered in all things and secure.*
>
> *Will he not, like a root in deep earth, bring all I desire*
> *   to bud and to flower?*

Now David lifts his son's chin on the crook of his finger and breathes a word that none but Solomon hears:

"When you are king, deal no differently with Joab than he has dealt with others. Let the end match the rest of this hard man's life."

The door opens. Three men enter. The sudden sunlight blinds King David, but he continues: "Here is Benaiah my bodyguard — deal loyally with him and he will be forever loyal to you.

"Rise, Solomon," the king says. "Bathsheba, rise."

Now David begins to issue a series of commands:

"Benaiah, put Solomon on my mule and lead him down to the spring and the water shaft where we first fought to take this city a lifetime ago.

"Zadok, thank you for your love. When Solomon is at the water shaft, take a horn of oil and anoint him king over Israel.

"Nathan, blow the trumpet and cry, 'Long live King Solomon!' Let there be multitudes of people shouting and dancing and playing music and rejoicing. Let them make such a noise that the earth is split by their joy. I want to hear it even up here, where I lie. Then bring Solomon into the king's palace, and seat him upon the king's throne, and let his mother sit beside him, queen for the rest of her life."

The enormous Benaiah, slower in his old age but as strong as ever, finds his tongue and rumbles, "Amen! May the Lord, the God of my lord the king, say so!"

"Go!" David whispers. "Go, go, before Adonijah believes his fevered visions."

One by one four people go out and are swallowed by sunlight. The fifth, Bathsheba, pauses in the doorway, a shadow black and erect, glancing back. Then she pulls the door closed, and the room falls into darkness.

David releases a long, shuddering sigh and slides down into the bedding on his couch. He is so cold. He is so mortally cold.

I will extol thee, my God and king. I will bless thy name forever —

This last labor laid him lower than a week of physical combat. His hands are feckless, trembling. He can't take hold of the hem of the cover. And the sunlight that cut to the back of his skull is aching in that place still.

The silver cord is snapping.

I named one son for the Lord, to say that God is our Lord: "Adonijah." I named the other "Shalom," for peace. What then? — are peace and lordship striving together?

David allows his eyes to close. The dark of the room and the dark of sightlessness are one with him. A serious fit of shivering seizes his entire body.

There was another son whose name —

Ah, I can't remember his name!

Bathsheba?

I have had many children by many wives, but this one —

Bathsheba, what was the name of our first child? The one who died because of my sin? — what did we name him?

David's feet are so cold that they ache, as if someone were beating the soles of them. The cold and the hard pain rise together through his bones. He cannot bend his legs at the knee, but all his limbs — and his jaw as well — are shaking violently.

Is it snowing? Did I walk in the snow with no shoes on? I have lost the feeling in my legs.

A great multitude is shouting something. Somewhere pipes and timbrels are making music. But they are so far away that the word of the people is muffled. It is something both rare and familiar. David has heard that word before, though not often.

Build the Temple on the threshing floor of Araunah! Do you hear me? I am calling as loud as I can. Someone, run and tell my son that he must build a house for the Ark, and it must be built on Mount Moriah!

All at once the shaking ceases. David's body relaxes. It melts. It runs down like water in the morning.

Darling, did you sweep the snow away?

Someone is combing the king's hair. The touch of her hand upon his forehead is so infinitely merciful that it draws warm tears into his eyes.

"Who are you?" he whispers.

A voice replies, "Your maidservant, sir." Then the same feathery voice is singing:

> *Your robes, my lord, are woven of fragrance,*
> *   myrrh and aloes, cassia;*
> *in rooms of ivory stringed instruments*
> *   play and make you glad.*
>
> *At your right hand stands your queen*
> *   clothed in the gold of Ophir —*

"Abishag?" David whispers.

In this instant the king is lucid. His eye is bright; all sound and sight are clear; nothing is remote; absolutely nothing resists his knowing it.

Kneeling beside him in the night and lamplight is a young woman so beautiful that he cannot stop weeping. Her breath in his nostrils is solemn and warm. Her skin is knit of white cloud. "Abishag, is that you? Are you the one who is singing to me?"

Abishag the Shunammite says, "Yes, my lord. I am singing to you."

"Yes. Yes, I knew it was you."

David smiles with a genuine gratitude and closes his eyes and dies.

❙❚

So David slept with his ancestors. He was buried in the city that bears his name. And the time that he reigned over Israel was forty years, seven years in Hebron and thirty-three years in Jerusalem.

So Solomon sat upon the throne of David his father; and his kingdom was firmly established.

> *I will extol thee, my God, my King,*
> *and bless thy name for ever and ever;*
> *great is the Lord! Greatly to be praised!*
> *His greatness is unsearchable.*
>
> *One generation shall praise thee to another*
> *ever declaring thy mighty acts.*
> *They shall pour forth the fame of thy goodness,*
> *and shall sing aloud thy righteousness.*

The Lord is gracious, full of compassion,
slow to anger, abounding in love;
the Lord is good; his tender mercies
are over all that he has created.

The Lord is faithful in all his words,
gracious in all his deeds;
he catches the falling —

17

SOLOMON

i

TAMAR

This morning I left my house near the gate of the city and joined the river of Israelites flowing through the streets of Jerusalem up to the bright new building of my brother. It sits high and beautiful, itself like a heaven under heaven — stone walls freshly hewn and white, windows like the eyes of God observing creation, two bronze pillars in front of the porch that gleam sunlight and seem strong enough to bear the weight of the firmament. We have been busy. The city, I mean. Stone dust still blows in the streets and whitens the ground and puts grit between our teeth. It has taken seven years to complete the temple. Seven years and thirty thousand of our own men, not to mention the craftsmen King Hiram sent from Tyre.

Jerusalem exploded. No one did not have something to do. Feeding them alone was itself a national task. I can shape a barley cake in the time it takes to draw two breaths. My hands have cracked, patting cake dough all day long, all year long.

But the king required it.

The labor and the building, I mean. I chose to serve by baking. Except for the start, except for the widowhood, I have always chosen my own lot. Except for the widowhood and the love that sometimes stirs in me.

Solomon built the temple on the northern hill which once was outside Jerusalem. But Solomon ordered all the earth removed from the temple site to be dumped into the ravine that used to divide the hill from the rest of the city. And when foreign stonemasons were dressing the great stone blocks for the temple wall, Israelite laborers carried their rubble to the same ravine. It doesn't exist any more. We call it the Millo now. Things are changing at a dizzy speed.

Already the king has begun constructing a new house for himself — a palace whose size I will not be able to believe until it is done. I saw the outlines laid down on the ground. I simply cannot imagine the finish. I will be baking barley cakes for a long time to come. So we walked past the house of my father, David, and I thought, *How modest it has become in a brief eleven years*.

Scarcely considering the newness of it, we crossed the Millo to the temple Mount. We walked through the ground-markings of my brother's magnificent palace yet to come. And because I arrived among the earliest groups, I was then able to enter the temple's inner court, surrounded by a fence of three courses of hewn stone and one of cedar beams.

O Solomon! Where do these visions come from? How wealthy you must be!

I was transfixed by the furniture outside the temple, the high altar directly in front of the porch, thirty feet by thirty and fifteen feet high; the molten sea that sits on the backs of twelve bronze bulls and holds, they say, ten thousand gallons of water! People filled the inner court.

At midday I could hear by the clamor that multitudes now filled Jerusalem. They stood all down the hills in order to be near, if not in hearing, when the Temple of the Lord was dedicated.

Then the sound died. Ten thousand people grew suddenly, enormously quiet. I heard another sort of walking. The tramping of soft feet in a marching rhythm, the pressing of bodies backward. A path was opening through the crowds — coming across the Millo and into the inner court of the temple. I turned and looked. I, too, stepped back. Then priests appeared, carrying on staves the Ark of the Covenant of God.

Behind them came an entire column of priests and Levites, some bearing the holy vessels that had been in the tent with the Ark, others leading so many sheep and oxen I could not count them.

Then came King Solomon.

My brother is so beautiful, he breaks my heart.

He walked behind all. He walked past me without glancing to the left or the right. His eye is brown, the color of the fawn's eye, with a perfect radiance of black lash. These are like darts. They wound.

While the priests who bore the Ark stood high on the temple porch, and while others began to slaughter animals under the morning sunlight, King Solomon himself mounted the platform of the high altar and presided over the sacrifices. Still the aweful hush of the peoples continued, and I could hear the crackling and the hissing of sacrificial meats. I could smell the strong delicious odors. There was a tumult of emotions in my breast. Oxen and sheep went up to God. Solomon stood in the midst of it all, not a big man, neither tall nor muscled, but of unutterable authority and royal calm, presiding.

All at once he turned to the temple and sang in a level chant:

> *The Lord has set his sun in the heavens,*
> *but said he would dwell in the thick of the darkness!*

Then the king faced us and called to all the people: "Blessed be the Lord, the God of Israel, who has fulfilled what he promised to David. For I have risen in my father's place and sit on the throne of Israel, and I have built this house for the name of the Lord God of Israel, and there have I provided a place for the Ark of the Covenant, which the Lord made with Israel when he brought our parents out of Egypt.

"There is a room in the temple, dark with a thick and holy darkness, the Debir: there shall the priests set down the Ark, beneath the outstretched wings of two cherubim."

I think I did not breathe all the while that Solomon spoke his blessing.

Then he raised his arms to heaven. His voice soared. He prayed, "O Lord, God of Israel, there is no God like thee in heaven above or on earth beneath, keeping covenant with thy servants!"

I said, *Yes.*

"Lord, confirm the word spoken to David my father, that there would never fail a son of his on the throne in Israel, so long as they kept thy commandments — "

I thought of my brother, of him who prayed the prayer, and in my heart I said, *Yes.*

"But will God indeed dwell on the earth? Behold," Solomon cried, "heaven and the highest heaven cannot contain thee! How much less this house which I have built. Yet have regard for the prayer of thy servant, O Lord my God, that thine eyes may be open night and day toward this house. Hearken to the supplications of thy people when they pray toward this place. Hear in heaven, thy dwelling place, and when thou hearest, forgive. For thou didst separate them from among all the peoples of the earth and made them thy heritage, O Lord, O Lord God!"

My brother then nodded toward the priests who bore the Ark of the Covenant, and slowly, with dreadful solemnity, they entered the temple. There was a space of time in which no sound was made nor any motion. A great weight lay upon us all. The king stood in a rigid attitude, watching. From his vantage he could see inside. We could not. I watched him. He wore a slim circle of gold around his locks. His cheeks had a sunken quality. His jaw flexed slightly, as if chewing. Then he squinted his dark eyes. Then a light smile touched his lips. A door shut within the temple, reverberating. Suddenly my brother stepped backward, averting his face. I looked and saw the priests running out the temple door, over the porch and down the steps. Behind them a black smoke was rolling. Cloud filled the house of the Lord, so that no priest could stand near it. I looked and saw that my brother was laughing. It was a soundless laughter, altogether contained. His lean body bent, his mouth remained closed and his eye open — but there was within him such a hilarity that, though no one else seemed to see it, I, too, began to laugh. But I laughed aloud, an embarrassing cackle.

I went down to my knees, laughing. The people beside me drew back. I knelt in a small circle of sunlight, frightening my neighbors, but I couldn't help it. I couldn't stop. I covered my face with my two hands and squealed and shook like a madwoman.

I said, *It's Solomon's laughter! I'm laughing for King Solomon!*

Several people tried to grab me. No matter, I kept laughing. I said: Because of my brother, the glory of the Lord has entered his temple like smoke! I was trying to explain my ecstasy.

But then that ox Benaiah came and picked me up and started to carry me away from the temple. I cried, *Solomon! Solomon!* I twisted around and saw the king on the high altar. He wasn't paying any attention to me.

Then I wondered whether Solomon himself hadn't signaled his commander to bear me away. So laughter vanished, and joy went out of the thing. I recall that I began to kick Benaiah. I bit him. But without conviction, really. What else should I expect after all these years? This old warrior doesn't hate me. He wasn't going to hurt me. Still, I bit his forearm and said, "Are you going to kill me, too, the way you killed Joab?"

Benaiah the son of Jehoiada, commander of all my brother's armies — he is an ox, mute and mountainous. Joab was clinging to the altar of the Lord, begging refuge; but because King Solomon had ordered it, Benaiah ignored the altar and murdered the man. He's loyal. He is not unkind. He won't hurt me. But I don't like him.

I don't think there is anyone in Jerusalem whom I like anymore.

I don't even like Solomon. He knows nothing of my long sorrow. Widowhood doesn't touch him. Poverty, the scorn of all Jerusalem, the stink of other men's sinning — what does the king know of these things? Did my father David ever tell his son Solomon that I was raped by my brother, David's first son, Amnon? Surely my father whispered the sins of Joab into Solomon's ear, or else Joab would not have been murdered. Did he whisper, too, that Tamar was raped? Did he care that Tamar was raped? Did he tell Solomon that the only person who befriended Tamar was himself murdered? That Absalom was murdered, leaving Tamar widowed and friendless — a madwoman?

I don't like Solomon.

I do not honor his wealth or his power.

But I love him. I love him. God help me, I can't stand the torture it causes me, but neither can I control it: I dream about my brother. I pant to see him passing in the city. I burn in the flesh of my face. I have fallen in love with Solomon.

ii

It took seven years to build the temple of the Lord. After that it took another thirteen years for the king to build the houses and halls of his own royal compound.

Through twenty years the queen mother watched the glorious constructions of her son in silent satisfaction. Not only did he create habitations of splendor for the Lord and the Lord's anointed, he also surrounded Jerusalem with a new wall, expanding both the city and its population.

Farther abroad, he fortified cities crucial to the defense of the kingdom. He built great stables of stone for the horses of his cavalry and of his charioteers. He built naval yards in order to control trade both by land and by sea, and from those yards he launched a fleet of new ships — also his own construction.

And in the midst of these national labors the king did not forget his mother. He designed apartments for Bathsheba in his personal palace. And she sat nearest him for any public feast. When the king went forth to welcome foreign dignitaries, it was his mother who walked beside him. There was no queen in Israel equal to Bathsheba.

This is not to say that there were no other queens in Israel. Solomon married often. Bathsheba could not choose wives for her royal son. But she made it a practice to attend every wedding, and then to indicate her supremacy by leading the new wife to rooms in the house where all the king's wives dwelt. This was a building huger than the temple, rich by reason of its many cedar pillars and called, therefore, the House of the Forest of Lebanon. It had forty-five rooms in the upper story alone and was connected to Solomon's palace by several public rooms, the waiting hall and the throne hall.

But on any given evening, Bathsheba herself did not have to pass through public places in order to see her son. She walked on floors of cypress down a hall whose walls were cedar, polished, inlaid with gold and ivory. She had but to whisper his name, and he was present to her, available and alert.

She loved her son. She was proud of his power and accomplishments, though she was not surprised by them — hadn't she groomed him for this glory? In everything Bathsheba praised Solomon.

But she also knew the mind of the man.

All the world was aware of his wisdom. People stood in awe of the king because his judgments were wise and just. He moved among the nations in a manner most sovereign and tranquil — but the mother knew the mind of her son. Therefore, she kept as close an association with him as love and motherhood allowed. It was not prestige that caused her to walk at his elbow. It was caution. Bathsheba in her sixtieth year was a realist. She knew there was in this splendid king a flaw that could cost him the kingdom.

∎

In the twentieth year of his reign, as he approached the fortieth year of his life, King Solomon sealed a covenant with Pharaoh Shishak, king of Egypt, by taking his daughter in marriage.

Through his highest ambassadors, Egypt said to Israel: "You are now my son-in-law."

And Israel replied: "Peace shall be our gateways and trading shall be the talk between us."

Perhaps to make a dramatic gesture of the opening of doorways — and, at the same time, to display the sort of power that now was allying itself with Israel — Pharaoh Shishak attacked a city that sat on the Egyptian highway north and south along the Great Sea: Gezer, due west of Jerusalem, but still controlled by Canaanites. He defeated it, burned the place to the ground, then gave it as a dowry to Solomon.

Clearly, this marriage was made for its political benefits.

What a great blasting of horns, therefore, accompanied the king's appearing in the portal of his palace! What a shiver of timbrels and bleating of flutes as he descended the stone roadway to the city gates where he would meet King Shishak's daughter. Solomon was sunlight in white linen. There went through the crowds that lined the road a trembling, as horse-flesh trembles, a physical reaction of awe.

The king went bareheaded. Behind him walked the queen mother with two crowns. And behind her the daughters of Jerusalem prepared to dance the king and his bride back up to his palace again.

But if the king caused shivers in the multitude, the bride caused explosions of delight and applause.

She came through the gates in a palanquin borne upon the shoulders of eight men. Its wide canopy covered her in shade, covered the child whose complexion was like milk, whose cheek was breakable alabaster, whose lip was a scarlet thread. The people thundered approval. She was all the art and the sweetness of Egypt, condensed into a single, perfect face.

The palanquin was a gift of Solomon to his bride. He had made its pillars of silver, its chair of gold, the seat deep, soft, and purple, its whole interior fitted with leather. But even so rich a sedan looked brutish next to its passenger. The palanquin was set down before the king. Then Shishak's daughter smiled and arose and stepped out on a foot as translucent as seashell.

From the moment Egypt put forth her fingers and touched his hand, the king of Israel ceased breathing.

And his mother noticed the difference.

Egypt had fixed an enormous gaze directly upon Solomon's dark eyes. It was a brazen act, really. She did not so much as blink. Even when the queen mother stepped directly in front of her to place the wedding crown upon the bride, Egypt peered through her as though she were air. And Solomon answered stare for stare. Neither did he acknowledge his mother's formal word when she spoke to him, or her kiss, or her placing of the wedding crown upon his head. He gaped like a shepherd.

Then Egyptian beauty and Israelite splendor turned and walked together toward the palace — and now the dancers followed with ceremonial whirling and laughter, and Jerusalem joined the procession. But Bathsheba had stepped away from the festivities. She stood to the side, watching her son ascend the streets with this new woman. As light as frost, she was. As dainty and thin and white. And, perhaps as cold.

Already the city had thrown itself into revelry, celebrating the mighty union made. But the queen mother was not hungry. She was alarmed.

iii

H ere is the sort of story that the citizens of Judah and of Israel told regarding the wisdom of their king:

Two harlots came to wise King Solomon. They had a dispute which no one could resolve.

One woman said, "My lord, this woman and I share one house and two rooms. In the same week we both gave birth to children. But then this woman's baby died in the night because she lay on it. At midnight she arose and while I slept she took my son and laid in my bosom her own dead son. When I woke in the morning to nurse my child, behold, he was dead. But I looked closely and saw that it wasn't mine at all. It was hers."

The other woman cried, "No! The living child is mine! The dead one is yours."

The first woman said, "No, the dead child is yours!"

Then the king said, "Since you cannot agree I will divide the matter evenly between you. Give me the baby."

They placed the living infant in his lap.

The king said, "Bring me a sword!"

So a sword was brought to the king.

And the king said, "Cut the living child in two equal halves. Then give half to the one woman and half to the other."

Immediately the first woman wailed, "Oh, my lord, don't kill the baby! Give him to her!"

But the other woman said, "Let it be neither mine nor yours. Divide it."

The king said, "Give the living child to the first woman, and do not slay it. She is his mother."

Tales like this were told far beyond the borders of Israel. The fame of wise King Solomon spread west through Egypt into Africa, and as far east as the Indus River. People declared that the largeness of his mind was like the sand on the seashore.

Likewise, the grandeur of his personal household was rumored as far south as Sheba in Arabia. It was reported to the queen of Sheba that Solomon — whose kingdom controlled the trade routes which her caravans traveled — kept forty thousand horses and twelve thousand riders. She heard that for one day alone his private provisions consisted of thirty measures of fine flour and sixty measures of meal, ten fat oxen, twenty pasture-fed cattle, and a hundred sheep, besides harts, gazelles, roebucks, and fatted fowl. That much food was required to feed the king's officers and counselors, his many wives and servants, his multitudinous family.

And his guests.

The queen of Sheba determined to be one of the guests of this resplendent king, to prove the tales concerning him and to test his wisdom with hard questions.

There was no secret to her going. The journey was a long time in the planning and then again as long in execution. News flew through the deserts of Arabia and the high plateaus of Africa. Ships on the Red Sea learned of it. Nomads knew. They moved toward the high roads in order to watch passage of the caravans of Sheba. It was a very great retinue with camels bearing spices and gold and precious stones. It stretched as far as the eye could see both north and south along the trade route. And in the center of it all, in her own golden carriage, came Queen Bilkis as if she were a burning onyx for brilliance.

Jerusalem was ready. Jerusalem had also heard the news.

South of the city the caravans of Sheba were met by the chariots of Israel, in the foremost of which stood three persons: a driver; a woman handsome, erect, and formidable; and a man of dark, remarkable beauty. This man wore a thin circle of gold around his hair. This was Solomon himself, who led Queen Bilkis into Jerusalem with fanfare and elegance.

The king of Israel had built a pavilion in the greater court of the temple of his God, where he and Sheba could sit as luminaries above the public. He had stretched purple canopies over the platform. And when the day came for them to take their places there, servants appeared on every side, waving fans of an Egyptian design.

Four figures met and sat on the high pavilion: Queen Bilkis of Sheba and her vizier, King Solomon of Israel and that woman of magnificent silence, the queen mother. She had been a wife of David. Solomon introduced her as Bathsheba.

Bilkis opened her formal inquisition. "Solomon, master builder, I put you a question," she said. "You have scattered fifty new forts across the Negev south of your kingdom. I saw them as I journeyed here. All around this city you have built a new wall. I admired it when I arrived. You have chariots and armies and shields and spears, vast protections against your enemies. But here am I within the forts, inside the wall, on the soft side of your every soldier. What if I, behind my smile, were that enemy? What good then, O King? What value are all the stones and metals you can measure?"

Solomon nodded. His black hair tumbled to his shoulders. His brown eyes were like an oiled wood, untroubled though filled with thinking. Queen Bilkis found that his looks alone consumed her attention and gave him an intellectual advantage.

"Queen, you are right." He gave her a radiant smile and said, "In themselves my walls and all my munitions are useless. But their strength is in a weak thing, and their power is in that which powerful men despise."

The queen of Sheba said, "What weak thing can save a nation?"

King Solomon answered: "There was a little city with few men to guard it. A great king came and besieged it. But there was found in it a poor wise man, and he by his wisdom delivered the city. The queen of Sheba has not yet passed the last defense of Israel. It sits beside her on this platform."

"You must mean yourself," said the queen. "And you suggest that you are a poor man. But the house behind us and the one in front of us belie you, Solomon. How can you call such a life poor?"

"But this is what wealth has revealed to me," said Solomon: "the poverty of *all* life." He raised his voice so that everyone gathered might hear him. "I've made a test of pleasure and found that it was vanity. Yes, I have accomplished many great works: I've built houses and planted vineyards and made gardens and dug pools from which to water a forest of growing trees. I own herds and flocks greater than any before me in Jerusalem. I have been entertained by the most excellent singers, both men and women. But when I considered what my hands had done and the toil I had spent in doing it, I saw that all was vanity. It was all a striving after wind, and nothing was gained under the sun. I tell you, there is no difference between the rich and the poor, except that one may deceive himself with dreaming and another may not. Wisdom is in this, to know that one *is* poor."

A preacher! This Israelite was a man of exhortations. Queen Bilkis smiled openly at the passion of his delivery. He was persuading her. Nevertheless, she leaned near Solomon and whispered, "My lord, the words of the wise heard in quiet are better than the shoutings of rulers to fools."

King Solomon grinned at her wit. "Yes!" he countered: "As one dead fly makes a vat of perfume stink, so one word of folly outweighs a lifetime of wisdom. Should I hold my peace now?"

Bilkis said, "He who digs a pit will fall into it."

Solomon answered, "If the serpent bites before she is charmed, what good is the charmer?"

Bright as an onyx, Sheba beamed at Israel. "Ah, the charmer has done well," she said, "very well indeed. There is no serpent here to bite him, nor an enemy to attack." Queen Bilkis rose and faced the people. "Happy are you, O Israel," she said, "for your king is the son of free people. He feasts at the proper times, for strength and not for drunkenness! The report which I heard in my land concerning his wisdom and prosperity are true. Blessed be the Lord your God, who has delighted in this son of David! It is because the Lord loves you, Israel, that he has made Solomon your king, to execute justice and righteousness throughout the land!"

In the days of her visitation, Solomon gave the queen of Sheba all that she desired. Likewise, she made him a gift of one hundred and twenty talents of gold, together with precious stones and a quantity of spices so great that never again came such an abundance of spices into Jerusalem. She stayed in Solomon's city for the length of a season. During that time she observed the building of a new house not far from the palace of the king, a small house by comparison, but one of unparalleled luxury. A jewel.

Shortly before her departure she happened to ask Solomon who was of such importance as to receive a house like that. The king colored and didn't answer. But the queen mother did. It was the only time Bilkis heard her speak — and though the woman seemed otherwise patient and generous, the comment sounded caustic. "Egypt requests a house of her own," the queen mother said, "and Israel obeys."

iv

The daughter of Pharaoh, the wife of Solomon, has made herself known in Jerusalem. She does not mix with the people. She remains aloof from the court of the king. But she is not ashamed to sing boldly from the high windows of her new house:

> *What is that coming from the wilderness*
> *   like a column of smoke,*
> *perfumed with myrrh and frankincense*
> *   the fragrance of merchants?*

> *Behold, it is the litter of Solomon,*
> *   surrounded by sixty,*
> *mighty men all girt with swords*
> *   against the alarms by night!*

Go forth, O daughters of Jerusalem!
Behold King Solomon,
crowned with the crown his mother gave
on the day of our wedding, go!

▮

Bathsheba is striding through the private apartments of the palace, looking for her son. There is something she has to tell him. It cannot wait any longer. She must confront him now.

But he is not in his chambers. He is not in any of the officers' rooms, nor in the room where he writes, nor in the places of prayer. Unless he has gone to the temple. It is evening. Perhaps he is in the temple.

Bathsheba walks through the dusk across the great court into the inner court.

▮

In her little cottage, Tamar holds up a mirror of polished bronze. It is one of the few luxuries preserved from her past, when she was a princess.

She has lit four oil lamps, all in a row on a rough wooden table. She is kneeling at the table and gazing at her face in the mirror.

She pulls an ivory comb through her hair. "It was red once," she whispers to the mirror. "Like my father's." But her hair is straw-colored now, dry and thin. The comb scarcely notices as it passes over her scalp. Tamar's face is long and tired. She has washed it, preparing for sleep. The eyes that stare back at her — who could love such doleful eyes?

"Dark, dark," she whispers, as if accusing the visage in polished bronze. "O daughters of Jerusalem, I am as black as goat's hair, black as the knotty weave of the tents of Kedar. I wish it were the curtains of Solomon."

Solomon! She said "Solomon," and the eyes in the mirror are immediately startled. They gape, and she cannot soften them again.

"Do not gaze at me," Tamar hisses between her teeth. She lays the mirror down. "I am swarthy! The sun has scorched me! My brothers were angry with me. They made me the keeper of their vineyards. But my own vineyard — " Tamar covers her face with her hands. "My own vineyard I have not kept!"

So then she snuffs the four lamps in her cottage. A little moonlight falls through a narrow slot in the wall. She rises and goes to the bed-mat already unrolled in the corner farthest from the door. She lies down and stares up into the darkness.

She doesn't think that she will sleep this night either.

∎

The daughter of the Pharaoh has a trilly, breathless voice, a baby voice, though the words are a woman's. Passionate.

Even when she sings within her house the sound flies out the windows. She is not ashamed to let Jerusalem hear her business. Such a woman doesn't give a fig for the opinions of the daughters of Jerusalem. Or perhaps she cares very much what they think.

She sings into the fresh dark of the evening. She emits little cries as she sings, overcome, perhaps, by the sentiment of her song:

> *The voice of my lover!*
> *Behold, he comes*
> *leaping on mountains,*
> *bounding the hills!*
>
> *My lover is*
> *a young gazelle!*
> *He dances like*
> *the large-eyed stag!*
>
> *Behold, he stands*
> *behind my wall*
> *looking through lattices,*
> *gazing in windows!*
>
> *"Arise!" he calls.*
> *"My fair one, come!*
> *The winter is past,*
> *the rains are gone.*
>
> *The flowers appear*
> *and singing bursts forth.*
> *Arise, my love,*
> *and come away!*
>
> *O my white dove,*
> *in clefts of rock*
> *let me see your face:*
> *your face is comely!*

Oh, catch us the foxes,
the little foxes,
that plunder the vineyards:
Our vines are in blossom — come!"

∎

The queen mother has found her son. He is sitting alone in the throne hall, upon his great throne of ivory.

"Do you hear it?" Tonight Bathsheba cannot control herself. Finally her patience is gone and the words shoot from her mouth like arrows. "Yes, you hear it! You are in here listening to it, and before you return to your chambers you will visit Egypt, and she will do some little thing for you and then you will promise some majestic thing in return. And this is the evil, Solomon: not that you go to her, nor even that you promise extravagantly, but that to this woman you keep your promises! *You hear her, don't you?"*

The king neither answers nor looks at his mother.

His throne rests on a dais which is mounted by six steps, each step guarded by carved lions. The throne itself is shaped like a high-backed chair with wide arm rests. On the back a bull's head is carved, power! On either side stand two terrible lions with wings extended backward, as if in flight. An ivory inlay adorns the whole, together with gold leaf hammered into intricate designs.

The king is both glorious and small in such a chair. Just now he offers no acknowledgement that his mother is even in the room. There is no expression on his delicate face. Nothing but a kind of vacuity in listening, as some people use music to rest from thinking.

Bathsheba tempers her anger. With the language of an intelligent advisor she says, "My son, I must in love and good reason speak. No one else will speak as forthrightly as I. It is good that the people fear you, but not if *all* the people fear you. I am the one who does not fear.

"And I would not be speaking now if you had never built a house for her. That gift teaches me your weakness, Solomon.

"Your weakness. It is not that you make love to many women, but that you let women instruct you, and you obey. God appointed you to decide for Israel. Not your wives, no matter how powerful their fathers are. But those whom you love are controlling you. Women are controlling Israel!"

King Solomon turns his head and says one thing: "Mother, *you* are a woman."

As if a bowstring snapped, Bathsheba begins to shout at her son. "A woman!" she cries. "Your mother is a woman. Is she also Egyptian? Does she look like a Moabite? An Ammonite? An Edomite? Is your mother an iron Hittite, Solomon? There are hundreds of those, all wives to you, and every one of them worships a god who is not our God, and what shall I say in the name of your father David when I see you prostrate yourself before the pagan goddess Ashtoreth? Ho, the king of Israel has gone after Milcom the abomination of the Ammonites — "

Solomon arises from his throne and begins to descend the steps.

Bathsheba cannot stop. She knows she's shrieking. She knows her face is twisted in fear — not *of* the king but *for* him. Yet she follows him to the door of the throne hall, crying, "The king has built a high place for Chemosh the abomination of Moab, and for Molech the abomination of the Ammonites, on the mountain east of Jerusalem — "

But then her son is no longer here. He has departed by the side door, into the night.

Bathsheba snaps her jaw shut. She bites her words off as a woman bites thread. She stands trembling for a long time. She is considering what sort of prayer to pray.

▌

Tamar is dreaming.

It seems to her that her beloved is knocking at the door.

He is calling, "Open to me, my sister, my love, my dove, my perfect one, open the door! My head is wet with dew." Tamar is smiling. Her cheeks ache with the smiling. "My locks drip with the drops of the night," calls her beloved.

But her garment has been laid aside, and she has bathed her feet for sleeping. She hesitates an instant.

She thinks she hears his hand to the latch. Her heart jumps within her. Yes! She will go!

She rises to open the door. Her lovely hands drip myrrh. Her fingers are moist with the myrrh. She puts them to the handle and opens — But her beloved is gone! Because of her hesitation he is gone.

Perhaps Tamar is no longer dreaming. She is a gaunt woman in bed clothes, running barefoot through Jerusalem, whose stones are cold. This cold is not a dream. She is running among the houses, seeking her beloved, calling to him. But he gives her no answer.

Far ahead she hears the quavering voice of a night bird, singing. As fast as she can, Tamar runs toward the voice.

My beloved is radiant and ruddy.

That is the song she hears. It descends from a high place, from on a hill and yet higher than the hill. Tamar runs through the dark night, listening:

His head is the finest gold;
his locks are waves,
black as the raven.

His eyes are like doves
by rivers of water,
bathed in milk
and fitly set —

Suddenly three men block Tamar's way.

Watchmen, whose duty it is to defend the king's palace, have heard a disturbance between the palace and the newly built house of the daughter of Pharaoh. They see a woman dancing there. She is dancing with her arms stretched out and her head thrown back, as if she were catching rain on her face.

When the watchmen touch her, the woman screams and dashes toward the palace door. So they hit her. But she keeps running, oblivious of pain. They chase her, beating her until she falls in the street and covers her head. They strip her even of her bed clothes.

Then the watchmen pick her up and carry her down to the gates of the city.

As she goes, the woman cries out at the top of her lungs, "I adjure you, O daughters of Jerusalem, if you find my beloved, tell him — tell him that I am sick with love."

And so they put her outside the city in darkness. They close the city gates.

Yet in the jewel-bright house of Egypt, all lit with candles and lamplight, a song is heard, a nasal voice in childlike confidence:

His cheeks are beds of spices
breathing sweetness;
his lips are lilies,
distilling a liquid myrrh.

His arms are rounded gold
set with beryl;
his body bright ivory
encrusted with sapphires.

His legs are alabaster columns
on bases of gold.
His countenance like the slopes of Lebanon,
forested of cedars.

> *His speech is a dear milk,*
> *and he is altogether lovely.*
> *This is my beloved. This is my friend,*
> *O daughters of Jerusalem.*

V

Now, the weight of the gold that came to Solomon in a single year was six hundred and sixty-six talents. This was tribute from the nations, and more besides that came from traders and merchants.

King Solomon made two hundred large shields of beaten gold, each shield worth six hundred shekels of gold. He also made three hundred smaller shields — all to be used in ceremonial display by his bodyguard. He kept these ritual weapons in the House of the Forest of Lebanon. All his drinking vessels were of gold; none was of silver; for the king had a fleet of ships at sea. Once every three years the fleet would come bringing gold, silver, ivory, apes, and peacocks. Solomon made silver as common as stone in Jerusalem. He made cedar as plentiful as the sycamore of the Shephelah.

And he gathered together chariots and horsemen. The king had fourteen hundred chariots and twelve thousand horsemen, whom he stationed in the fortress cities, as well as in Jerusalem. He imported his horses from Egypt. One mare cost a hundred and fifty shekels of silver, and a chariot six hundred. These he exported again to kings both north and east of Israel, the kings of the Hittites and of Syria.

It was a lucrative trade.

But it was supported upon the backs of Israelites, since the king maintained a labor tax not just among foreigners but among the men of Israel as well. The men of his own tribe, Judah, he did not burden with difficult tasks. The southern portion of Solomon's kingdom experienced his favor, while the north suffered.

Of those working in Jerusalem to build its strength and its sanctuaries, many were Amorites and Hittites and Perizzites and Hivites and Jebusites. But thirty thousand men were levied also from Israel, and taskmasters were placed over them as over any gang of workmen.

David had never done such a thing!

And Saul had lived in a rough fortress not much larger than any laborer's house.

One of the taskmasters heard the complaints of the Israelites and never forgot them. He saw their faces grimed with the king's sweat, lonely for their families, angry that their farms were lying fallow — and he read there an outrage that would not soon pass away. These men were Ephraimites. So was he — and it was only by the fortune of the king's appointment that he was himself an overseer and not doubled down like his brothers beneath the heavy stones of the houses of Egyptian princesses.

The taskmaster's name was Jeroboam, the son of Nebat. One day when Jeroboam was walking outside Jerusalem, the prophet Ahijah found him and led him out to open country.

Ahijah was wearing a new garment. When he was alone with Jeroboam, he took hold of the cloth and tore it into twelve separate parts. Then he said to Jeroboam, "Take for yourself ten pieces. For thus says the Lord, the God of Israel: *I am about to tear the kingdom from the hand of Solomon, and I will give you ten tribes. For the sake of my servant David and for the sake of Jerusalem, I shall leave yet one tribe to Solomon's offspring. He shall himself reign over Israel all the days of his life. But I will take the kingdom out of his son's hand and will give it to you, ten tribes.*"

That day Jeroboam fled to Egypt. He stayed in Egypt until the death of Solomon.

vi

The time that Solomon reigned over Israel and Judah was forty years. Then he who had been splendid in living became most plain in dying. In the same day that he died, King Solomon's body was carried on a wooden bier to a tomb outside the city. A door that had sealed a small cave was cracked along its stony seams, and the stones were set aside. Then two men bowed down and bore the king's body through the low entrance, one stepping backward and one forward.

So the king in white linen, wearing no adornment, was laid on rock inside the cave where the bones of his father David lay.

Immediately the stones were mortared in place again, the door closed, and the tomb was sealed. The shadows of the people grew longer and longer. The day-wind ceased. Briefly, the evening kindled cold fire in the western sky. But the east breathed grey over the whole earth. Then the night came and swallowed everything in darkness. The crowd turned and went back into the city.

But when the hard moon appeared and cast pale light on the hills outside Jerusalem, two figures became visible. Two women still stood near Solomon's tomb. One was so gaunt that the darkness pooled in her eyes and her cheeks, making a skull of her vigil. She was bowed down and abjectly poor. The other stood rich, erect, and proud — but aging.

Each woman gave signs of a solitary existence. They did not acknowledge one another. Perhaps neither knew that the other was there.

The night wind began to blow from the east to the sea. It was a cold wind. It caught the fresh scent of the mortar now drying in the door of Solomon's tomb. Both women drew their robes close about their bodies. They covered their faces. Only their eyes showed above the veils. Neither woman wept.

So Solomon slept with his fathers, and Rehoboam his son reigned in his stead.

PART
FIVE

Prophets

PART
FIVE

18

THE MAN OF GOD
FROM JUDAH

i

In the seventh year after the kingdoms of Judah and Israel had split in bitterness, a rawboned man walked the ridge road north, intense and frightened, but unswerving.

He was young and sunburnt. He walked with the long stride of a farmer, and he came from the hills of Judah. If he worked a plot there, it was small and stony; and if his crop was barley, then his journey was costing him a harvest since this was the eighth month of the year, when barley is cut in the hills.

The man's manner was rural, his aspect blunt. But his eyes had a hunted quality, staring straight ahead. He seemed fixed on some terrible task.

He was muttering aloud: "O altar, altar, men's bones shall be burned upon you — "

Bareheaded, barefooted, the man from Judah did not pause to eat or to drink or to rest.

It was noon when he passed Jerusalem going north.

A band of soldiers was patrolling the land between Judah and Israel.

"Turn back!" they cried.

The young man neither stopped nor answered.

One of the soldiers ran after him, calling, "Brother, there's no one in Israel to protect you. Now that they have their own king, Judah is their enemy!"

The soldier fell in step with the farmer. He looked into his face and, seeing there both dread and youth, pitied him.

"Why are you so fierce? Are you seeking some vengeance?"

"No."

"Are you angry?"

"No."

"Then turn back. Come back with me."

"No."

"Why not? Where are you going?"

"To Bethel."

"Oh, sir! Not Bethel! Not now!" The soldier grabbed the young man's garment, but the traveler had the mindless strength of a mule, and the soldier was nearly yanked from his feet.

"King Jeroboam is holding a feast in Bethel today," the soldier pleaded. "Jeroboam himself will be offering sacrifices to the golden calves that he has fashioned."

The farmer said, "I go to talk to the king." His voice trembled with dread. He was in anguish. But he never once broke stride. He said, "God has sent me to talk to King Jeroboam."

The soldier stopped in the middle of the road and watched the farmer toil north into the land of Israel.

"They'll kill him," he said.

ii

When Solomon died, his son Rehoboam was immediately anointed king of Judah. But just as David had been crowned twice, once over Judah and once over the northern tribes of Israel, so Rehoboam knew that he must travel north to receive the coronation of that kingdom, too.

Israel had loved David, because David loved them as much as he loved his own tribe, Judah.

But Solomon had distinguished between Israel and Judah, laying on Israel a greater burden, rigor, and taxation.

Therefore, when Rehoboam came seeking their allegiance, the northern tribes decided to exchange it for promises of equality. Before they would crown him, they began a negotiation with him, under the leadership of Jeroboam the son of Nebat.

With a formal dignity, Jeroboam said, "Welcome, Rehoboam, King of Judah."

Rehoboam said, "Is this the best that Israel can offer, a welcome from one who supervised workers in my father's kingdom?"

"It is," said Jeroboam, "the only welcome the king of Judah can expect."

"Didn't you spend these last years hiding in Egypt? Why do you suddenly appear when I come to receive the crown of Israel?"

The two men were seated among their advisors on a large platform. People of the northern tribes surrounded the platform listening intently, since their future would be defined by these discussions.

Jeroboam stood up and walked five paces away from the king of Judah, then turned and said, "King Solomon made our yoke heavy. He did not deal with Israel as gently as he did with Judah. He crushed us with labor as if we were a conquered race. If you, Rehoboam, will lighten the hard service of your father, we will serve you."

Rehoboam turned to his advisors.

In slow, uncertain tones, the old man counseled compromise, encouraging him to accept Israel's offer. But the young men were adamant: "The weak are eaten," they said, "but the strong are respected."

So Rehoboam rose up on the platform and delivered his answer: "My little finger is thicker than my father's waist. Did he chastise you with whips? Well, I, sir, will chastise you with scorpions. Do not expect me to weaken before you."

Jeroboam didn't hesitate. He lifted his voice to the multitude, crying, "Go home! Go home, Israel. We have nothing to do with the house of David anymore." Then he pointed a finger at Rehoboam and said, "But you, sir — *you had better look after your own house!*"

The northern tribes did not anoint Rehoboam their king.

He tried to command their obedience, but they murdered the officers he sent to them.

Israel anointed Jeroboam their king, so the northern tribes divided themselves from the southern tribes of Benjamin and Judah, and though they were rooted in the same history, there were two kingdoms, now, and these kingdoms were at war.

iii

The city of Bethel was crowded with pilgrims. They had gathered for the king's festival on the fifteenth day of the eighth month, and the king himself was there, luminous in the robes of a priest, robes of an Egyptian cut and glory.

The day was stately, its ceremonies majestic, for Jeroboam had learned the manner of absolute monarchs. In Dan he had built a holy shrine and a golden calf for worship; in Bethel, likewise, there was a shrine and an altar of awful proportions.

Even now King Jeroboam, having ascended the steps of this altar, was raising a bowl with incense above his royal head, preparing to pour it on burning coals. And the crowd, awaiting the white smoke of the deity, had caught its breath. Bethel was tense and still.

The bowl began to tip —

When suddenly a rough, untutored voice cried out at the foot of the altar: "O altar, altar! Thus says the Lord, *A son of the house of David shall sacrifice on you the priests who burn incense on you — "*

The crowd fell back from this outrage. It was a fellow in goatskin, a farmer! And like a madman, sweating and fierce, he was addressing the altar.

"Thus says the Lord, *Men's bones shall be burned on you!*"

King Jeroboam peered down at the solitary figure. "Who are you, sir? Your accent is from Judah?"

"And this," cried the young man, "is the sign that the Lord has spoken: *The altar shall be torn down, and the ashes upon it shall be poured out —* "

"Seize him," commanded the king. He stretched out his right hand toward the man from Judah and said, "Someone seize him and — "

But in that instant the king's hand dried up. It shrank and cracked like skeletal bones.

"Man of God!" he cried. The king could not pull his arm back to his body. The crowd drew farther and farther back. Even the young farmer gaped at what had happened. "Man of God, entreat the Lord your God for me, that he would restore my hand."

Never blinking, never moving, the young man muttered, "Lord, could you restore it as he said?"

While everyone watched, the blood crept into the king's right hand again, pinking the pale color and fattening the flesh until his fingers opened and closed and he put it under his robe and pressed it to himself.

The man of God from Judah released a huge sigh.

King Jeroboam gazed at him a moment, then he said, "Come home with me. Refresh yourself, and I will reward you."

The young farmer shook his head. From this moment on he was unable to lift his eyes up to the king's face again. He said, "No. The Lord commanded me neither to eat bread nor to drink water until I returned home. No."

With every sign of simple fear, he glanced around himself, then turned and began to walk through the crowd with great haste, evidently going home.

But at the same time five other men dashed to their father's house to tell him what they had seen. He was a prophet of some repute in Bethel. When he heard what another prophet had been able to accomplish in his own territory, he said, "Saddle my donkey! I want to meet this man of God!"

iv

In the seventh year after he had lost the northern kingdom to Jeroboam, King Rehoboam of Judah died. His son Abijam ascended to his throne and did what was evil in the sight of the Lord. He permitted male cult prostitutes to practice in Judah.

So both kingdoms turned from the Lord their God. For Jeroboam had established priests in all the pagan high places. His shrines at Dan, on his northernmost border, and at Bethel, on his southern border, ten miles from Jerusalem, were meant to prevent his people from worshiping at Solomon's temple. Of the golden calves in those places, he said, "Behold your gods, O Israel — the gods who brought you out of the land of Egypt."

So evil was the house of Jeroboam, that the Lord determined to wipe it out altogether. King Jeroboam died a natural death; but his son reigned less than two years and then was murdered by an officer of his army, Baasha. This man Baasha proclaimed himself ruler of Israel, and then he tried to ensure his royal authority by slaughtering every member of the house of Jeroboam.

But the evil done by Jeroboam was repeated by Baasha and by his son Elah. A pattern of evil had developed among the kings of the north, and the Lord — the God who had led Israel on eagle's wings out of Egypt — restlessly kept seeking a ruler who would remember his covenant and honor him.

The house of Baasha fell exactly as had Jeroboam's, and the commander-in-chief of the armies of Israel was elevated to the throne. This was Omri, who ruled with more foresight and a wiser administration than any king before him in the northern kingdom.

Omri built a new city for his capital. He named it Samaria, and he fortified it with strong walls and soldiers, as he did other cities near his borders. His reputation grew in the nations around him, and when he died, his son ruled in his place: one of the greatest kings of Israel, Ahab.

V

The young farmer from Judah was exhausted. As soon as his task had been completed and the terrible force of the Lord had released him, he found that his bones were quivering like reeds in the wind.

Two miles south of Bethel he turned from his path and collapsed beneath an oak tree. It seemed to him that he dozed, but the sun made a buzzing in his ears.

Then a voice called, "Ho! Are you the man who came from Judah to speak against the altar?"

The farmer opened his eyes. He saw an old man climbing from a donkey, white hair, a full white beard.

"I am," he said.

"Come," said the old man, crinkling his eyes, smiling. "Come home with me and eat my bread."

The poor farmer shook his head. "I can't," he said. "The Lord commanded me neither to eat bread nor to drink water until I am home again."

"Yes," said the old man. "I heard about that command. But I am a prophet as you are, and an angel spoke to me by the word of the Lord, saying, *Bring him back with you to your house, that he may eat and drink.*"

The young man still shook his head.

But the old man put out a hand and touched his shoulder. "You have had a difficult task, and you have accomplished it well, and now you are weary. Don't I know the sacred weariness that comes over prophets?"

The farmer felt his chin trembling. He was very close to tears.

"And," said the white-haired man, "the deed is done, isn't it? Of course it is. Come. Come home with me."

He slipped his hand beneath the farmer's elbow.

With tears the young man rose up. The old prophet persuaded him to ride the donkey, and together they returned to Bethel and to the prophet's house. They ate. They drank. In the dark, they lay down to sleep.

In the morning the man from Judah, rose up refreshed and prepared to travel the ridge route home again. His host saddled a donkey and gave it to him as a gift.

But the young farmer never arrived at home. He never harvested his barley.

vi

Abijam the king of Judah did what was evil in the sight of the Lord. He reigned only three years.

When he died, his brother Asa was anointed king — and this man did what was right. Asa burned the pagan images Abijam had allowed. Moreover, he removed the idols of his grandfather Solomon, reversing that great king's policies in order to make the worship of the Lord God exclusive in Judah.

Asa ruled in Judah forty years.

When he died, his son Jehoshaphat ruled in his stead. He, too, was a just and faithful king. He ruled during the years when Ahab was king in the north; nevertheless, though Ahab's foreign wife Jezebel brought priests of Ba'al into Israel, no such priest ever entered Judah so long as Jehoshaphat ruled in the south.

He initiated judicial reform in Judah by installing objective judges in key cities throughout his realm. At the same time he set up in Jerusalem a court of appeals, in order to root out injustice wherever it might occur. He ruled twenty-four years.

But when he died, his son Jehoram did what was evil immediately. He ordered the assassination of all his brothers, together with their captains and their followers, so that no one would dispute his rulership. Bloody footprints were left in the halls of Solomon's glorious palace. Soon pagan practices leaked down from the north. Priests of Ba'al found place in Judah, and leaders in Judah neglected the Lord their God.

∎

But God never forgot his people. God never forgot the ten tribes of Israel in the north, or Benjamin and Judah in the south. Passionately the Lord kept calling them to repentance and to faithfulness again. For their own sake he pleaded with them to remember his covenant and to obey his statutes, because they could not survive apart from him. They would lose the land! They would be scattered among the nations, and they would die.

So said the Lord who had met them at Sinai. So said the mighty God who had chosen to dwell among his people.

Year after year God uttered his love to them by means of fierce and sacred figures, solitary souls of terrifying eloquence: the prophets.

vii

The same day in which he had sent the young man back to Judah, news was brought to the old prophet in Bethel. His donkey was seen standing on one side of the ridge route. On the other side stood a lion. Between them lay a corpse with its throat torn open — a bite of the lion, no doubt.

The old prophet rode out to see this sight.

Indeed, the donkey was his.

And the dead man was the young farmer from Judah.

The white-haired prophet said, "Indeed, this was a man of God. Everything he spoke was the word of the Lord. When he disobeyed and ate bread, he was punished."

The old prophet walked past the jaws of the lion and gathered the young man's body up in his arms.

"Alas, my brother," he said. He laid the dead man on the back of the donkey that stood waiting, then he mounted his own beast and rode back to Bethel, mourning: "Alas, my brother!"

At evening he buried the man from Judah in his own tomb, and he said to his sons, "When I die, bury my bones by the bones of this prophet. For the saying which he cried against the altar in Bethel and against all the pagan places in the cities of Israel — that saying shall surely come to pass."

19

ELIJAH

i

There was a grand wedding in the city of Samaria. King Ahab was taking a new wife — a woman of Tyre, the daughter of King Ethbaal: for the two great kingdoms of Israel and Tyre were sealing an alliance. Hereafter they would exchange goods and join military force against common foes in Damascus and Mesopotamia. Tyre would draw food from Israelite farmland for colonial expansion all along the northern coast of Africa. Rich landholders in Israel would gobble tiny farms and grow yet richer. Ahab, having thus strengthened his hand, would have the means to make a similar alliance with Judah to the south — and new blood would enter the family of Omri and Ahab.

The king's wife was Jezebel. She was strong and handsome, a woman to the purple born. Ahab's father had not always been king. Ahab, therefore, continued to feel the constraints of common law. He would grow morose and gloomy when some law denied him his desire. But sunny Jezebel simply broke the laws. They did not exist for royalty. Ahab delighted in the license of his magnificent queen.

There was a wedding in Samaria.

The Tyrian bride set her eyes in antimony, drawing black lines at the edges of her eyelids to make of her merest glance a flash of brilliance. She adorned her head in sinuous oriental fashion. She clothed herself in shimmering purple with a gold weave beneath the bosom. She rode through the city on a plush divan, causing the faces of her people to blush and to bow. Behind her walked forty priests of Ba'al Melqart, the god whom she had worshiped in her land, the god she would surely worship in this land, too. Ahead of her waited a powerful husband and a bed, an ebony masterpiece inlaid with ivory. Wealth went with the woman. Wealth preceded her. She would not have married Israel if it had not been said that Ahab had a house of ivory and rooms of precious stone.

There was a wedding in Samaria.

There was celebration in this city of new stone and modern fortification; city whose massive walls of salients and recesses were a better defense than any Solomon had built; Samaria, whose wide avenues and fresh houses exploded with the population of Israel. People cheered the progress of their new queen. The king had said: *Behold the future!* And merchants and soldiers and landholders, vintners, masons, carpenters, smiths, and children all went wild at the declaration. A dull roaring deafened the city, a glad hilarity because of this future.

But just as her caravan reached the porch of the palace, where Ahab himself stood smiling his welcome, Jezebel noticed one man in the multitude who did not bow before her antimony glance. He looked like a desert creature, desiccated. He wore a mantle of camel's hair. He was unshorn, head and face. His body was hardened as for war. He stood straight up, looking back at her. His eye was altogether too bold, direct; it seemed contemptuous! Immediately, the queen was disgusted by this man.

■|

After the marriage of Ahab and Jezebel, Samaria experienced a period of renewed construction. The wide avenues were narrowed to make room for the houses of the priests of Ba'al Melqart, whom Jezebel worshiped. Not forty houses for forty priests, but four hundred, and then again another fifty. Jezebel's father was not only the king of Tyre but also a priest of Ba'al Melqart. So Ahab commanded a temple to be built to the god of his wife and her father. In an elevated space within the city walls the land was excavated, pillars were raised, a house of lovely proportion was hewn of stone and cypress and cedar. Now thousands of people could worship the god whom the Tyrians believed to control the skies and bless the earth with rain and rich fertility: Sky-strider! Cloud-rider, Ba'al Melqart.

But fertility needs a female. The gods must be male and female together in order to produce fruit. Therefore, Asherah, the goddess consort of Ba'al, also entered Israel and Samaria. And she required priests, and they required houses. So the streets grew narrower: four hundred more houses for four hundred more priests. And all these servants of Ba'al, together with their families and their servants — a very great company — ate at the queen's table. Eight hundred and fifty Tyrian priests were supported by the state.

For Jezebel intended to do more than worship the gods of her homeland. She wanted as well to enlighten the rude people of this backward nation, that they would worship her gods too. Thus the great number of priests: she had come with a zeal. The Lord of Israel was law-hard and austere. He was the God of a stony code, a mountain deity of wind and earthquake and frightening fires. Such holiness lacked all sweetness. Let Israel compare green fields with the forbidding mountain and make a choice.

The temple which Ahab built for Ba'al Melqart and Asherah was as luxurious as their religion. Within its pillars there was neither darkness nor dread nor severity — but lightness, luminance, soft fountains of a gentle water, and kindness to every sense of the body. But on the day that this pleasant edifice was dedicated to her gods, a man stood up in the streets of the city and cried, "Ahab! Ahab!"

He had an irritating, nasal voice: "King Ahab, hear what the Lord God says to you!"

Ahab had already entered the temple. Jezebel, ten steps behind him, made the mistake of turning. She turned and recognized a face she had seen before.

The hair of this man, as thin as tow, was uncut and wild. His shoulders were draped with a mantle of camel's hair. His arms had the stringy strength of a nomad.

He kept yelling, "Ahab! Ahab!" until the king himself appeared in the doorway of the temple — and then he said, "As the Lord the God of Israel lives, before whom I stand, there shall be neither dew nor rain these years — "

Queen Jezebel experienced an intense hatred for this ranter who spoke of the things her Ba'al controlled.

He cried: "There shall be neither dew nor rain these years — except by my word!" And then he vanished.

Jezebel hissed, "I despise that fellow."

Ahab said, "So do I. But even the opinions of kings have never mattered to him."

"What is his name?"

"Elijah. He is from Tishbe in Gilead. Elijah the Tishbite."

"He doesn't wash."

Ahab shrugged. "There are laws for those who make special vows to the Lord: they don't drink strong drink or cut their hair till the vow is done. But they wash. He washes."

"Except by *his* word!" Jezebel trembled at the blasphemy and the arrogance of this desert thing. "Ba'al is god of the rains, but he said it wouldn't rain except by his word. I hate Elijah the Tishbite."

But the word of the blasphemer came true.

ii

In the months that followed the dedication of the temple of Ba'al Melqart and his consort Asherah, no rain fell in Israel — neither the early rains nor the late rains a whole year through. There were no harvests.

Seedlings perished in dry ground. The crops looked like hair on leprous flesh, a standing deadness.

King Ahab said, "Where is Elijah?" He said it privately, then he demanded it publicly: "Has anyone seen Elijah the Tishbite?"

The people couldn't answer him. They said, "He travels on the winds of the Lord. He is here, and then he is not here. How can anyone know where Elijah is?"

A second year passed without a rainfall. So widespread did the drought become that it included Tyre and Sidon in the north. The king repeated his question as a royal command. It carried with it anger and the burden of punishment: "Tell me where Elijah the Tishbite is!"

A boy said, "I saw him."

That boy was brought into the king's presence.

"Where?" said the king. "Where did you see Elijah?"

The boy said, "The prophet is living in a cave by the brook Cherith, east of the Jordan." He lowered his voice and opened his eyes very wide: "Ravens," he whispered: "Every evening ravens bring the prophet bread and meat. That's how he lives."

Ahab sent soldiers to the Cherith. They searched up and down the dry streambed. They found the signs of dead fires, but Elijah they did not find.

"Where is he?" Ahab cried. A third year began without rain. The bins and the storehouses in Israel were empty. Even the rich were going hungry.

Moreover, the mules of Ahab's armies and all his chariot horses were starving for lack of grass. He commanded soldiers to look everywhere in Israel for green grass and grazing.

At the same time Jezebel sent her own troops as far abroad as Tyre and Sidon, looking for Elijah. She told the soldiers to threaten the people and to swear a solemn oath if they said they had not seen him.

In the tiny town of Zarapheth north of Tyre, the soldiers discovered a widow who said that she had seen Elijah the Tishbite. In fact, she had fed him and let him live in her house.

But when they asked where Elijah had gone, she said that even if they killed her she wouldn't speak a word to harm Elijah.

The widow told Jezebel's soldiers that she and her son had been preparing to eat their final meal and to die, when this man Elijah came and asked for food. She had only a handful of meal left and a little oil in a cruse. But Elijah said, "Fear not, for the Lord the God of Israel says, *The jar of meal shall not be spent, and the cruse of oil shall not fail until the day that the Lord sends rain upon the earth.*"

"He must be a prophet," the woman said, "because his word came true. We always had enough food for one more meal."

But then the widow's son became sick and stopped breathing. Elijah stretched his body over the boy's body three times, asking the Lord to give him breath again and he did. "The boy lives," the soldiers reported to Jezebel in Samaria. "We saw him. And the widow will only say that Elijah is a man of God in whose mouth the word of the Lord is truth."

In the day that Jezebel heard this story, she ordered her troops to cease looking for Elijah. Rather, they were to ride through the whole land of Israel and cut off all the prophets of the Lord wherever they were to be found. Kill them. The prophets of God went into hiding. They inhabited caves. Certain Israelites protected them, feeding them scraps of bread; but the queen's armies were beginning to learn the territory, and soon no cave would be safe.

Then suddenly Elijah appeared outside Samaria. King Ahab was walking in a dry field by himself; he looked up and saw the wild aspect of the prophet, as rough as mountain rock.

"Is that you?" he said. "Is it you, you troubler of Israel?"

Elijah said, "I have not troubled Israel. You have. You and your father have split this nation into two by forsaking the commandments of the Lord and following Ba'al."

Ahab said, "How can you say I have forsaken the Lord? I name my children with his name. I fear his glory in the firmament. I know his strength to shut up the rain."

"So the king who fears the Lord has married a woman who hates the Lord and murders his prophets! Not both, King Ahab! No one can worship both the Lord and another. Yet you force Israel to hop from leg to leg between two cliffs! If the Lord is God, follow him! But if Ba'al, then follow him!"

King Ahab turned his back on the prophet.

"I," cried Elijah, "even I only am left a prophet of the Lord!" Now he sang out in his nasal voice so that the people of Samaria heard him. People on the road outside the city stopped to watch, and the king was caught in discourse with the prophet of God. "I am one alone," yelled Elijah, "but Ba'al's prophets are four hundred and fifty men. Now listen to me, O King, and hear the end of famine and the return of the rains. I am going to Mount Carmel above the sea. Bring two bulls to that place and all the priests of Jezebel's god, and we shall each pray to our own god, and everyone shall see which is God indeed. The God that can send both fire *and* rain, is he not God?"

iii

Mount Carmel juts northwest from Israel into the sea. On its southern side there was a strip of land more fertile than any other in the kingdom; therefore it was called the *carmel*, the Garden Land. Just below the summit of the mountain — also on the southern edge,

but sixteen hundred feet above the seashore — was a natural platform, a flat
stretch of thin soil and limestone.

It was there that the prophet Elijah was found again.

To that place came all the priests of Ba'al Melqart and of his consort,
Asherah.

Moreover, since most of Israel had heard of the challenge of Elijah, they
climbed the mountain, too, covering it with a vast congregation, curious
and hungry and hopeful.

The queen had not deigned to leave her palace at the behest of a Tishbite.
King Ahab, likewise, was absent.

But bulls were there for sacrifice. And here in the middle of the mountain
platform were scattered the old stones of an altar that Jezebel had torn down.

Among these stones stood Elijah, wrapped against the mountain winds
in his mantle of camel's hair. "Choose for yourselves one bull," he cried to
the priests of Ba'al Melqart. His wild hair whirled in the wind. "Cut the bull
in pieces," he cried. "Lay it on wood, but put no fire to it. Then call on the
name of your god, your sky-strider, lord of the clouds, to see whether he will
send the fire to burn his own sacrifice."

They did. They slaughtered the bull and butchered it. They arranged
the bloody meat on dry wood, and then they began to pray. "Ba'al! Ba'al
Melqart, answer us!"

All morning long, Elijah rolled the stones of the Lord's old altar together
again, and the pagan priests called upon their god. Nothing happened.
Nearly a thousand priests, they shouted louder and louder. By noon they
began to limp around the sacrifice, begging the deity to manifest himself —
but there was no voice. No one answered.

Elijah, lifting now one stone upon the other, paused and yelled, "Louder!
Louder! Maybe Ba'al is sleeping. Maybe he's gone on a trip."

The priests drew swords and cut themselves till the blood streamed down
their faces and their limbs. As midday passed they spun in circles, raving
and shrieking. But there was no voice. No one answered.

Suddenly Elijah cried out to the people of Israel, "Come near to me!"
They drew near and saw that the twelve stones had been built again into an
altar of the Lord. All around the altar Elijah had dug a trench. The wood was
on the stones, and the sacrifice had been laid on the wood.

Elijah said, "Fill four jars with water and pour it on the offering and on
the wood."

They did.

He said, "Do it a second time," and they did.

"Again," he said. So then the water soaked the whole altar and filled
the trench. Elijah the Tishbite lifted his hands and said, "O Lord, God of
Abraham, Isaac, and Israel, let it be known this day that you are God in
Israel and that I am your servant. Answer me, O Lord. Answer my water

with your greater rains. Answer me, that this people may know that you are God."

Then in the middle of a cloudless afternoon, the fire of the Lord forked out of heaven. It struck the earth, consumed the offering, the wood, the stones, the dust, and swallowed the water in the trench.

The people of Israel dropped to the ground, roaring, "The Lord, he is God! The Lord, he is God!"

But Elijah, full of a holy fury, wanted action. "Seize the priests of Ba'al!" he commanded. "Grab them where they stand! Let none escape!"

At the sound of his voice, Israel became a host of warriors. "Bind the pagans in strips of their clothing," he cried, "and follow me!"

Already wounded and amazed, the priests of Ba'al Melqart and Asherah were overcome by the congregation of Israel and driven down the mountain into the valley of Kishon below. "Kill them," said Elijah, and Israel slaughtered the personal priests of Jezebel. In a universal delirium, they killed every one of them.

Almost immediately, when the voice of Ba'al had been drowned in blood and a hollow silence stunned the evening air, the people were horrified by what they had done. They stared at the carnage around them, trembling.

"What will the queen do to us now?" they wailed. Then they saw Elijah on a low crag, and they cried out: "What will Ahab require of us now?"

Elijah swept the people with eyes drained of passion. He shrugged and whispered, "Go home."

As if a great sickle had cut among them, the congregation of Israel vanished. They scattered, and in a short time no one living soul was left near Carmel except the prophet and a lad whose arm he had caught and held.

"Come with me, boy," Elijah said, and they climbed the mountain again.

On the high plateau, the prophet wrapped his mantle around his upper body and walked west along the ridge that reached out over the sea. He sat down and drew his legs up and lowered his face between his knees.

"Boy," he said, "go up and look over the sea to the horizon. What do you see?"

The boy went up and looked and came back again. "I don't see anything," he said.

Elijah said, "Go again. Go seven times again."

Seven times the lad walked to the edge of the mountain and peered westward. After the seventh time he came and said, "I see a little cloud like a man's hand rising out of the sea."

"Then run to King Ahab," the prophet said, "and tell him that the word which is soon to break from heaven is of the Lord and of no other god. Run."

In a little while the heavens were rolling with black clouds. The wind woke up and blew from the west. The prophet kept his head bowed down.

He drew his mantle over his shoulders — and then there fell a great rain. The mountain was beaten with a blowing water all down its slopes; sheets of rain swept over the valleys and the borders of Israel, out into the desert. The prophet sat on Carmel, and the roofs of Samaria dripped.

iv

T hree days later an Israelite crept to Elijah where he was hiding in a ravine near Tishbe and told him that Queen Jezebel was seeking to kill him.

The messenger said, "She sent me herself, saying, 'So may the gods do to me and more also, if I do not make Elijah's life as the life of my priests by this time tomorrow.' "

Then Elijah was afraid. He left Tishbe, traveling south as fast as he could past Jericho and Jerusalem and Hebron. He ran through the night, by dawn coming through southern Judah near Beer-sheba. Still, the prophet did not stop. He traveled in sunlight through the wilderness all day long.

At dusk he collapsed beneath a broom tree and cried out, "It is enough! O Lord, take my life away. I am no better than my fathers."

When the night descended, the air grew cold. Elijah covered himself in his mantle and fell asleep under the broom tree.

Suddenly there appeared beside him a column of white light, and an angel touched him and said, "Arise and eat."

Elijah saw at his head a cake baked on hot stones and a jar of water. He ate and drank, and then lay down again.

But the angel came a second time and touched him and said, "Arise and eat, or else the journey will be too great for you."

So Elijah arose and ate and drank — then he went in the strength of that food forty days and forty nights, all the way to Sinai, the mountain of God.

He found a cave in the base of the mountain and entered into the darkness there. But the word of the Lord came to him and said, *Elijah, what are you doing here?*

Elijah wound his fingers into the wild hair on his head. "I have been zealous for the Lord," he said. "The people of Israel have forsaken your covenant, O God of hosts! They have thrown down your altars and killed your prophets. I, even I only, am left; and now they seek my life, too, to kill me."

The Lord said, *Go forth, Elijah, and stand on my mountain.*

So the man crawled out of the cave and climbed Sinai, the mighty crag in an endless wilderness. He labored upward as Moses had five hundred years before, then he stepped out on a rocky promontory.

At once a screaming wind swept over the summit and ripped down the mountainside, spraying pebbles, dislodging boulders, and driving the prophet back beneath the brow of a rust-red rock. But the Lord was not in the wind.

After the wind died, the entire mountain began to tremble, riding an earthquake. Rifts opened in its ruined face, pinnacles toppled, and enormous stones careened down in dust to the dead plains below. But the Lord was not in the earthquake.

After the earthquake, fire spouted from the holes that had opened in Sinai. Red flame shot from its hollows, a black smoke boiled upward, ash went up as high as heaven, and the prophet cried out in terror. But the Lord was not in the fire.

Then after the fire came the very sound of stillness, a calm so vast and quiet that Elijah could hear it. When he heard the voice of the daughter of silences, he bowed and hid his face in his mantle, weeping.

For the voice said, *Elijah, what are you doing here?*

Elijah whispered, "I told you, Lord. I have been zealous for you — "

But the Lord said to him, *Elijah, I will always keep a remnant in Israel, seven thousand people who have not bent their knees to Ba'al and seven thousand mouths who will not kiss him.*

Elijah, desiccated, tired, filled from his skull to his loins with pain and trouble, sobbed like an infant.

And the Lord said, *Go to Damascus and anoint Hazael king over Syria. Then anoint Jehu king over Israel in Ahab's place. Then find Elisha and anoint him prophet in your place. Those who escape the sword of Hazael shall Jehu slay, and those who escape the sword of Jehu shall Elisha slay.*

And it seemed to Elijah that a promise arose from the daughter of the voice of God, a gentle benediction to wipe his tears away:

And when all is done, come home. Come home.

▮

Six months after the drought had ended in Israel, a young man named Elisha went out to plow the fields of his father. His was a wealthy family with large landholdings in the region of Abel-meholah, near Tishbe in Gilead.

On this particular day Elisha was supervising twelve teams of oxen, all moving in a long indented row, each team touching the furrows of those in front. Elisha was driving the twelfth team, watching the plowmen ahead of him.

Then he became aware of a man walking beside him, an older man of rocky features, wild hair, and stern gestures.

The man removed the mantle that was draped over his shoulder, shook it open, and cast it over Elisha.

Immediately Elisha knew who the man was: Elijah from Tishbe, the prophet of the Lord, mighty against every ba'al, and death to Ba'al Melqart whom the queen had brought from Tyre.

And Elisha knew yet more: that the camel hair mantle bore prophetic power; that it fell on his person with promise — and though Elijah had said nothing at all, Elisha heard a holy command: *Follow me.*

Right away the young man left his team of oxen and went after the older man.

"My lord," he said, "my lord, can I kiss my father and my mother good-bye?"

The old man said, "Go. Nothing I have done prevents you. Go."

In high delight, Elisha rushed back to the team of oxen. He led them home, slaughtered them, butchered them, boiled them with fire from the wooden yokes they had been wearing, then served them to his mother and his father and to his entire household. When he had completed his farewell, Elisha rose up and went after the prophet Elijah and ministered to him.

V

In the days when Ahab was the king of Israel and Jehoshaphat the king of Judah, these two kingdoms ended their long wars and concluded a treaty together.

Ahab and Jezebel gave their daughter Athaliah in marriage to Jehoshaphat's son Jehoram. Blood bound them now. And Ahab soon took advantage of this alliance. He invited Jehoshaphat to join him in a campaign against the king of Damascus.

"If we can control the king's highway east of the Jordan," he argued, "we will control all the trade that goes north from Sheba and Arabia to the seaports in the cities of my father-in-law, Tyre and Sidon. But the key to the king's highway is Ramoth Gilead."

The king of Damascus held Ramoth Gilead as his own.

Ahab proposed to attack the Syrian king there. Jehoshaphat, who was strengthening the economy of Judah, agreed.

So the armies of Israel and Judah marched over Jordan under direct command of their kings. They advanced through a narrow valley that cut between the towns of Tishbe and Abel-meholah, and then in glittering military display they encamped in the fields west of Ramoth Gilead.

The king of Damascus himself arrived with thirty-two Syrian captains and established opposing battle lines.

But Ahab's nerve began to fail. A certain prophet had prophesied, "I saw Israel scattered on the mountains like sheep without a shepherd, and the

Lord said, *These have no master.*" The king had ordered the prophet thrown into prison; but before the dawn of the battle day, he came to Jehoshaphat's pavilion and asked him to wear the insignia of the king of Israel, while he, Ahab, wore the plain armor of a charioteer.

At sunrise, then, it was Jehoshaphat who commanded Israel and Judah to charge, and Jehoshaphat who rode in the midst of the brave assailing foot soldiers, their soul and their center.

But the king of Damascus had prepared his captains for a more cunning war than frontal slaughter. "Fight neither the small nor the great," he said, "but seek the king only."

The engagement of the battle lines created an odd confusion among the warriors. Damascus seemed to retreat, but only feigned withdrawal, doubled back, and ran in another direction — always looking for the colors of the king.

Frustration made the hosts of Israel and Judah tingle in their sinews. They lost concentration and grew merely angry.

But then a Syrian archer drew his bow and shot blindly into the thick of his enemy and happened to hit King Ahab. The arrow struck between the chain mail and his breastplate, piercing through his abdomen.

The king fell forward on the dashboard of his chariot. "Turn around," he growled to the driver. "Carry me from the field. I'm wounded."

Jehoshaphat rode with dexterity through the mêlée crying encouragement, never staying in one place, always dashing for another. Damascus could never come near him. The battle continued into the afternoon, and Ahab watched from the western hills, propped up in his chariot.

By nightfall, when a servant came to speak to him, it was discovered that he was dead. The blood from his wound had filled the bottom of the chariot.

So the cry went up: "Every man to his city! Every man to his country! The king is dead!"

Israel and Judah retreated.

King Ahab's body was brought back to Samaria, where he was buried. Soldiers washed his chariot out by the pool of Samaria, and in the night the dogs came and licked up his blood.

vi

All through a winter's night at the height of the rainy season, young Elisha heard his master stirring in the cottage where they slept. Old Elijah shuffled back and forth in the darkness, back and forth slowly, painfully, like a fox crippled and caged.

Dawn came cold and indistinct. It lay on Elisha like a grey weight. Suddenly he realized that Elijah's shuffling had ceased: it was the silence that felt so heavy.

Elisha jumped up and dashed outside. Little Gilgal still was sleeping.

The young man ran to the gates and out of town, and there he saw his master, nearly a mile away, toiling south over the hills of Ephraim. Elisha hurried to catch up.

Elijah's hair, as defiant as ever, had become a smoke of white, his beard a briar of white. He was angular at every joint. His face, rough, impenetrable, was a little Sinai. He did not glance at Elisha when the young man came beside him, but he said, "Go back to Gilgal. The Lord has sent me on to Bethel."

Elisha said, "It's too cold to travel."

"I have my mantle."

"You are too old."

"I have always been old."

Elisha said, "It's going to rain."

But Elijah didn't answer, so they walked in silence for the next three hours.

When they were passing through Bethel, a small band of prophets took Elisha aside while the old man walked on. Elisha was anxious to follow.

But the band of prophets said, "Don't you know that the Lord will take your master away from you today?"

"Yes, I know," Elisha said, and he ran after Elijah.

"Stay here," Elijah said. "The Lord has sent me to Jericho."

Elisha said, "I will not leave you."

So they walked in silence on a downward grade to Jericho. The prophets from Bethel followed at a distance. It began to rain.

More prophets met them in Jericho. They whispered to Elisha, "Don't you know . . . ?"

But Elisha would not leave the side of his master, and these prophets joined the others, like a flock of timorous creatures creeping behind.

Old Elijah's hair shook raindrops. His face streamed water, but he did not cover his head with the camel hair mantle. He said, "Elisha, stay in Jericho!"

Elisha said, "No!"

They descended in silence to the Jordan.

Now a cold evening wind was blowing, driving the rain like ice against the land. The river churned and raced through its channels, a treacherous thing, an impossible crossing.

But Elijah rolled his mantle into a stout rope, and struck the waters with it, and the Jordan parted to one side and to the other, and the master and his student walked over on the riverbed, but the river roared back into its course behind them, and the prophets who followed them were blocked and helpless.

As he toiled up out of the valley of the Jordan, Elijah called through the violent weather: "Ask what I shall do for you before I am taken from you!"

Elisha cried back: "Sir, let me inherit a double portion of your spirit!"

For a moment Elijah paused and turned to the young man. They were dark figures in a darker storm. The old prophet put his hand on Elisha's shoulder. "You talk like my firstborn," he said. "My son, if you can see the hosts of heaven, it shall be done for you."

Elijah walked away. Elisha did not move. He watched his master go, the old man's body flashing in the sudden white of lightning, his mantle whipped by the wind. Thunder rolled all down the Jordan.

And then it was not lightning at all, but vermilion flames in heaven, a blazing mass descending. Elisha looked and saw a chariot of fire and horses of fire. They rushed the earth. They separated him from Elijah. They gathered the old man up, and Elisha saw him ascended by a whirlwind, living, into heaven.

"My father! My father!" he cried. "The chariots of Israel and the horsemen!"

The fires vanished. The howling night was black again. Elisha seized his robe and began to tear it in two — when he saw the mantle of his master sailing down from heaven to earth. He caught it and buried his face in the rough camel hair.

When he came again to the east side of the Jordan, Elisha rolled the mantle and struck the waters exactly as he had seen Elijah do it; but the river roared on, unabated.

Elisha cried out at the top of his lungs: "Where now is the Lord, the God of Elijah?" and he struck the water again.

This time the Jordan parted, and the young prophet walked over on the solid riverbed.

20

AMOS, HOSEA

i

After her husband died, Queen Jezebel took control of the kingdom of Israel.

Her eldest son perished within a year of his own coronation. Her second son Joram was a man given to luxury and pleasant pursuits. When he ascended the throne, then, he was grateful for his mother's counsel — and she was glad for the power.

She maintained the rich connection with her father's city, Tyre, importing the best of the world's trade. While Judah preserved the old ways, living a poorer, more isolated existence, Israel enjoyed commerce with all the nations and changed. It was in these days that Jezebel's sister Dido became the queen of Carthage on the coast of northern Africa. Likewise, her daughter Athaliah was queen mother in Judah. They formed a family of powerful women. Jezebel liked her life. She felt equal to the contests of kingdoms.

▋

"Joram," Queen Jezebel said, "I think you should do as David did when he ruled from Egypt to the Euphrates."

"More than a hundred years ago," said her son. "What did David do?"

They were sitting in the queen's apartments in the palace of Samaria. Damascus had a new king who was marching to regain possession of Ramoth Gilead, the city that had taken Ahab's life.

The new king of Damascus was Hazael. He had been an officer in the old king's bodyguard — until he suffocated the king in his sleep and by a savvy manipulation rose to the throne himself.

Go to Damascus and anoint Hazael king over Syria.

Jezebel said, "He let another man fight his wars, and he lived to a very old age. Joram, I think you should appoint a commander-in-chief over all your armies, someone strong and dogged, but without imagination. Stand back in safety until victory is assured, then as king ride to triumph in the final engagement."

Joram said, "There is an officer who came up through the ranks, a soldier since he was fourteen, completely fearless."

"Can he take command?"

"He's the sort that the hardened troops will follow."

"But will he obey you, Joram? Can this leader also follow?"

"He fights the way other men plow fields, dutifully, routinely. I doubt he's ever suffered an original thought."

"Do I know him?" Jezebel asked.

Joram said, "Do you know Jehu of the house of Nimshi?"

Jezebel knew everyone of any rank in Israel. She said, "A true Israelite. A grim and sober man, isn't he? Small-minded. Unlettered."

Joram smiled. "Exactly," he said.

So Jehu the son of Nimshi was appointed commander-in-chief of the armies of Israel, and Jezebel sent him to fight the Syrians at Ramoth Gilead.

Those who escape the sword of Hazael shall Jehu slay.

■

Again, Jezebel and Joram were in the queen's apartments, eating delicate roasts of African monkey and drinking the famous wines of Syria, skins from Helbon and from Uzal, both.

In the midst of this meal, a watchman asked to speak with King Joram.

He was admitted to the room.

"My lord," he said, but his eyes kept straying toward the presence of a genuine force, Jezebel. "While I was watching from the tower by the gate, I saw a company of soldiers riding at great speed from the east. They are armed. They are not messengers."

Joram said, "Send a horseman out to meet them. Ask if they come in peace."

The watchman bowed and left. But within the hour he returned, anxious and perplexed.

"I sent the horseman as you commanded, sir," he said. "But when he reached them, and when they had spoken together, he joined them! He drew his sword and is riding this way *with* them!"

Jezebel said, "Send a second man. Send a captain and an equal company of horsemen. Arm them."

"I will," the watchman said. He hurried from the room.

Neither the queen nor the king ate now. Jezebel had risen to her feet and was striding about the room. "From the east," she said. "There is no close enemy in the east. Except — "

The watchman burst in without asking leave.

"Madam! Sir! The captain and his company have joined the warriors, too! They're coming with a hard determination. They are walking their mounts!"

Jezebel said, "Can you identify these people? Do you know their tribe or race?"

The watchman lowered his eyes. "Yes," he said.

"Then who are they?" Jezebel's eyes flashed. Her beauty was a deadly thing.

"Israelites," said the watchman.

"What? Our own forces?" The queen snapped erect. "Answer me, watchman: could you tell who leads them?"

The watchman whispered, "Jehu the son of Nimshi, commander of your armies."

Jezebel spoke in a low, honeyed voice: "Joram, go out yourself. He is your subordinate."

The king was not dressed for combat. But he went, and Jezebel went out of the palace after him. When Joram rode out of the city gates, she mounted the wall and watched him go, he and a bodyguard of three.

When the coming company saw King Joram approach from the city, the men halted in a semicircle, Jehu in front of all.

Joram cried, "Jehu! Jehu son of Nimshi, is it peace?"

The grim commander said, "What peace, when the whores of Jezebel fill the land?"

He had not yelled the words, but Jezebel heard them. It was the very language of that wilderness lizard, Elijah.

The scene in the distance took on a dream-like quality. Everything moved slowly, now, detached from Jezebel's immediate attention — though she felt she knew exactly what was going to happen.

Jehu the Israelite drew an arrow from his quiver. Joram her son wheeled his mount around and whipped it toward Samaria, crying, "Treachery! Treachery!"

Jehu took a thousand years to draw the arrow taut in his bow, and the arrow sailed in a beautiful arc, like a rainbow. It sank into her son's back between the shoulder blades. He spread his arms and soared from his horse, higher and higher. Jezebel closed her eyes, and the whole scene vanished.

She returned to her palace and ascended to her apartments above the central entrance.

In a private room Jezebel sat down at a table where ointments and powders were arranged, and she began to groom herself. She anointed her flesh with oil. She coiled her long hair on her head in oriental fashion. She drew black lines of antimony along the edges of her eyelids, so that the whites became a blaze of beauty. She covered herself in purple raiment and gold embroidery at the bosom, and then she walked to the window and threw open the lattice and stood there, while Jehu, the commander of the armies of her son, rode into Samaria.

Jezebel stood like a cedar tree, majestic and immovable.

She said, "Is it peace?"

Jehu leaped to the ground, looking around for the source of the question. It had fallen upon him from on high.

"Is it peace?" Jezebel repeated, and Jehu saw her. So she made her voice a thick run of honey: "Do you come to my city in peace, you murderer of your master?"

Jehu did not answer her. He was a lout, unmannered, unlettered, undistinguished in anything except killing. Royalty confounds rude boors. In the presence of a noble soul, they are reduced to brutality.

Jehu opened his mouth and bellowed, "Who is on my side?"

Jezebel felt the presence of four servants in her chambers, eunuchs. She smelled them. They wore a delicate calamus. "Who is on my side?" Jehu bellowed, and the eunuchs stepped up behind the queen of Israel, two on her left, two on her right.

"Throw the woman down to the dogs!" the man commanded. She felt the soft hands of her servants. They lifted her bodily, tilted her from the window, and dropped her. She fell without a sound, turning once in the air and striking her skull on the pavement below, where she died.

ii

As soon as power was in his hands, Jehu destroyed the entire house of Ahab.

He commanded the people of Samaria to slaughter Ahab's children. They obeyed and brought their commander a prize of seventy heads in seventy baskets — all the sons of Ahab. Next Jehu annihilated the dead king's servants, his counselors, his administrators, his policies, his structures of government, his leadership.

When Jehu the son of Nimshi was anointed king in Israel, the kingdom itself was nearly dead from retribution.

Hazael of Damascus took advantage of the weakness. He attacked Israel east of the Jordan, seizing Ramoth Gilead, the king's highway, and all the territory as far south as Moab. Likewise, he attacked west of the Jordan, across the plain of Esdraelon and down the coast of the Great Sea, enclosing Israel in a Syrian grip.

By the time King Jehu died, his son's armies were reduced to ten chariots, fifty horsemen, and an internal force of ten thousand foot soldiers.

Israel suffered a poverty worse than ever since kings ruled the land.

But during the next generation, the whole world began to shift and the fortunes of Israel and Damascus were reversed. A new, more massive enemy emerged from the east, fighting with a cruelty so unspeakable that cities capitulated even before they were attacked. Assyria, from the Tigris River east of the Euphrates, was consolidating an empire. Assyrians cut open the wombs of pregnant women as a matter of course. They tossed living infants into the air and caught them on the points of their spears.

Assyria laid siege to Damascus, now ruled by the son of Hazael, Ben-hadad II.

In the open field these armies fought from enormous four-cornered chariots with wheels of eight spokes, wheels as high as a man. Their soldiers rode horses. This was Assyria's peculiar reach and speed, that they were the first to field great cavalries of mounted lancers and archers who shot while riding.

Their leaders plaited the hair on their heads and the beards on their faces, taking upon themselves the image of a thundercloud bearing down. They were bulls. Assyria trampled the fields like a bull enraged, goring and shaking its victims to tatters.

And they had also perfected methods of siege.

In the hills north and east of Damascus they felled great trees and constructed three huge engines of war. One was a platform on eight wheels, as high as the city walls. From this elevation they shot dead ahead at the enemy.

The second weapon, built on six wheels, was a tower in whose belly swung a battering ram and on whose shoulders crouched the archers of Assyria behind shields.

Slowly they rolled their siege machines down newly graded causeways toward Damascus. At the same time their soldiers were digging tunnels to weaken the walls from beneath.

When, after three months, the city was judged ready to fall, soldiers on the platform sent a furious hail of arrows into Damascus while the tower was trundled directly to the city gates. And then the third machine was swung into place. The Assyrians called it *nimgalli*, the hurler of "large flies": a catapult.

At a cry from their commanders, every weapon groaned to life. Boulders beat the city walls. The great timber in the belly of the tower battered the city gates again and again. Armed troops rushed forward under shields, carrying light ladders. They swarmed up the walls on all sides, and by night Damascus had fallen to Assyria.

The king of Assyria required tribute from Damascus thereafter.

Tyre and Sidon and Edom and Israel also paid an annual tribute, but they had not been plundered or defeated.

Israel, therefore, strengthened the military, rebuilt fortresses, reclaimed territories as far north as Hamath and all down the east side of the Jordan: Ramoth Gilead, the king's highway. The economy improved.

Thirty years after Jehu had died, a new king reigned in Israel: Jeroboam II, cunning, educated, alert to the great and delicate balance of powers throughout the world. Copper came into his kingdom and tin from lands east of Assyria; spices and perfumes arrived by caravan, purple linens, combs and brooches, precious stones, luxuries.

The walls of Jeroboam's palace were paneled; his furniture was inlaid with ivory; he slept on a bed of ivory.

Such good fortune persuaded the people that God approved of them again. The priests of the shrine in Bethel taught Israel that wealth was a sign of divine favor — and they themselves grew rich in the practice.

A grateful people brought constant gifts of sacrifice. The golden calf placed here by the first Jeroboam more than a hundred and fifty years ago now proved its power in the sunny reign of the second Jeroboam.

The population of Israel increased. The number of pilgrims journeying to Bethel also swelled. These were a confident people. Their sacrifices were born of a glad self-satisfaction. The altar in Bethel produced a delicious smoke daily — a sweet scent, surely, in the nostrils of God. Loud and beautiful was the music in the court of the calf, lutes and harps and strings and pipes, loud clashing cymbals.

Amaziah, the priest of that place, stood at the altar in royal colors, presiding with a dramatic flair and courtesy. He was beloved by this people. He was also beloved by his king. All was well!

Amaziah the priest reached to turn the meat broiling on the altar. He spilled its juices to the hot coals, creating a great spitting billow of white cloud. He threw his arms up, preparing to chant a blessing upon the heads of his people —

— when a sharp voice like an ax blade split the air, screaming:

I hate, I despise your feasts! I take no delight in your solemn assemblies! Even though you offer me burnt offerings, I will not accept them!

iii

In the region of Tekoa, six miles south of Bethlehem and ten miles south of Jerusalem, there lived a shepherd who had also been observing the elemental shifts of power in the world. But his interpretation did not favor Israel. He saw punishment on the horizon.

Amos was a plain man. In the higher Judean hills he pastured a flock of sheep. In lower valleys he maintained a grove of sycamore trees, the fruit of paupers. When it was small and green, each fruit had to be pinched. Amos broke the husk, opening it to sunlight so that the insects inside would die and the fruit would ripen to an edible softness. Even so, it never achieved sweetness. But it fed the belly and it nourished the peasant and it was very cheap.

Amos knew poverty firsthand, though his own shape tended to corpulence no matter how little he ate. He was fat. He puffed hard and turned red when he labored.

Amos dressed in a leather jerkin older than his father. His hut was stone and grass. His friends were indentured to the wealthy, working all their lives for someone else's benefit and watching their children enter the same unseemly life. Amos, too, was poor. But a poor man need not lack intelligence. And a poor man's God need not be poor.

In the eyes of Amos, Assyria moved within the designs of a mighty God — and Assyria, therefore, was not the salvation of Israel. Unless attitudes changed and faithfulness returned, Assyria would become the natural consequence of sinning!

It distressed him that the people of God could be so ignorant of God.

But he would have suffered his distress alone and in private, if the Lord had not driven him into public places, speaking.

Amos never wanted to be a prophet. He had contempt for prophets: so many wanted fees for their oracles.

But in the spring of the year, twenty years after Jeroboam II had been anointed king of Israel, Amos looked down into the soil and saw locusts hatching. This was when the tender shoots were just appearing. He saw newborn locusts, rosy-white like worms. He saw them split their early skins and begin to hop about.

Then the Lord God caused this brood to rush into maturity. Five times the locusts molted while Amos watched, swelling ten times over and sprouting wings. They swarmed upward. Their wings made a dead-dry whirring. They went forth to consume the green grass, all the grass of the land, and Amos understood the prophecy, but he could not tolerate the horror of its meaning.

"O Lord God," he cried, "forgive Israel! How can Israel stand if you do not forgive?"

The Lord repented of the thing he had revealed, and he said, *It shall not be.*

But in the summer of that same year the sun grew hot on Amos' shoulders. So fiercely did the heat beat down on him, that he heard the Lord God calling, and he saw a flaming fire, and the fire was devouring the ancient deeps of creation, the source of all waters in heaven and on earth, and he saw that the fire had begun to eat the land, too, and he cried, "Cease, O Lord God! I beg you, cease! How can Israel stand if you do not cease?"

And again the Lord repented, saying, *This also shall not be.*

But yet a third time, while he was gazing at a wall which the builders were building, Amos saw a plumb line hanging for the straightness of the corner.

And the voice of the Lord said, *Amos, what do you see?*
Amos said, "A plumb line."
Then the Lord caused him to see that it was God who held the plumb line in his hand, and the Lord said,

> *Behold, I have set a plumb line*
> *in the midst of my people Israel:*
> *I will never pass by them again.*

This time Amos could not answer the Lord. He could no longer beg for mercy. He could not pray for Israel.

And the Lord said: *Their high places shall whistle with desolation. Their sanctuaries shall fall into a stony waste. I shall with the sword cut off their kings.*

Amos could not stay home after having had these visions. They drove into his bones a holy restlessness. He knew. He knew what the Lord required of him, and he hated it. But he could not refuse it.

Therefore, he pulled his leather jerkin down over his round body, and left his flocks and his sycamore grove, and traveled north to Bethel.

The city astonished him. On the one hand, its luxury was a killing thing, like rot in summer fruit; but on the other hand, these people were grinning and congratulating themselves for many successes.

The Lord said, *The songs in the palace shall be wailings, and the bodies in the silent streets shall lie, fly-blown, in heaps*, and Amos looked around to see whether anyone else had heard the horrible declaration. No one had.

Amos, puffing for all his exertion, walked through the city to the altar raised upon its highest hill of Bethel. He pressed through the crowds until he saw a priest above all. But Amos was a short man. He climbed the base of a pillar, grabbed the pillar in his left arm and swung outward, just as the priest caused a white plume of smoke to explode before him.

Then the Lord God was crying out in Bethel: *I hate, I despise your feasts! I take no delight in your solemn assemblies!*

But the words issued from Amos' own mouth. His heart hammered so hard against his ribs, that he thought he would die.

The Lord said, *Even though you offer me burnt offerings, I will not accept them! Take away from me the noise of your songs!*

The priest had seen Amos.

"Sir!" he called. An affable voice. "Sir, why don't you and I go apart and talk together?"

But the Lord cried out: *Let justice roll down like waters and righteousness like an ever-flowing stream! You shall take up your abominable thing, your gods and your images which you made for yourselves, or I will take you into exile beyond Damascus, says the Lord, whose name is the God of hosts!*

The priest turned pale. "Guard!" he called. The Israelites, gathered before this altar and the calf, were becoming skittish, covering their ears to block out the words uttered against them.

Amos felt a genuine pity. He understood very well the affliction which was being prophesied. He was sweating; his heart hurt as if from spasms; he wanted to go home, but the Lord had not yet ceased his outcry:

For three transgressions of Israel and for four I will not revoke the punishment — because you sell the righteous man for silver, and you buy the needy woman for a pair of shoes! You trample the heads of the poor in the dust, and you turn away from the afflicted —

Suddenly Amos was seized from below. Soldiers tore him from the pillar and dragged him after the priest into a small private room. There the door was shut upon them, Amos and the priest alone.

The priest fixed the shepherd with furious eyes. "My name is Amaziah," he said, "priest of God in Bethel." He began to remove the sacred articles of his clothing. "You may believe that your ranting is of God. I don't. We keep absolutely every ritual God commanded Moses to keep: sacrifices, offerings, feasts, memorials, festivals. Shame on you! Shame on you, Judean, for playing the false prophet before me — "

"Amaziah, priest in Bethel," Amos interrupted, "swallow the spit of your accusations and let it burn within you. I did not want to come. It was the Lord who took me from the flock and drove me here! And you, keeper of every ritual — what you do *not* keep before the Lord is his covenant!"

Amos was sweating and puffing and miserable and despising the fact that he had no stature in his struggle on the Lord's behalf. He was short and fat, and his voice sounded like a whine.

Amaziah said, "The firstfruits of everything go to God. There is a continual offering of thanks for the goodness he has showered upon — "

"What do all the right words matter," Amos shouted, "when people are wrong with their neighbors? It isn't how you sacrifice, but how you *behave* that proves you righteous."

"This land is bathed in the goodness of God! Look about you. How can you suggest that God does not love and reward us?"

"Oh, God has loved you. But you do not love in return, neither the Lord nor his people. These blessings have turned to rot in you. They divide the nation, and those who keep riches unto themselves hurt the others! Amaziah, priest in Bethel, your rich lords loan money to the farmer in order to foreclose! I have seen it. They use false weights when they pay. They sell a poor man for a pair of sandals, and then they build for themselves summer houses of hewn stone. They sleep on ivory beds — and they thank God for their reward!"

While Amos poured forth his words, Amaziah had grown very calm. He sat down at a small table, took tablets from a shelf, and now was writing on them.

Amos said, "Therefore Israel shall be the first of those to go into exile. The revelry of those who stretch themselves on couches shall pass away — "

Amaziah snapped the tablets shut, rose, opened the door, and handed it to the guard who stood outside.

"Take this to the king," he said. "Come back immediately with his answer."

When the door was closed he faced Amos and spoke in unctuous, mannered tones:

"You'd better flee, you seer, to the land of Judah. Eat bread in Judah. Prophesy in Judah. But never again return to prophesy in Bethel. It is the king's sanctuary, the temple of the kingdom. Fat little man, for your own sake I counsel flight. For this is the message I just sent the king: 'There is a man here conspiring against you. He says that Israel must go into exile and that Jeroboam shall die by the sword.' "

Amaziah never realized the enormous relief he had granted the shepherd from Tekoa. For the Lord fell silent in that very moment, and Amos was indeed free to go home again.

iv

What shall I do with you, O Israel?
I desire steadfast love, not sacrifice!
Yet your love is like a morning cloud,
like the dew that goes early away —

Once more the Lord tried by love to draw his people back again.

There was in Israel a prophet named Hosea who married a woman named Gomer. In the early years of their marriage she bore her husband three children.

The first was a son whom they named Jezreel.

When the second child, a daughter, was born, the Lord said, *Call her name Lo-ruhamah, Not Pitied, because I will no longer have pity on the house of Israel to forgive them.*

When Lo-ruhamah was weaned, Gomer conceived again and bore a son.

And the Lord said, *Call his name Lo-ammi, Not My People, because Israel is no longer my people.*

She raised her children quietly for several years. But after they had grown into stout youths, Gomer suddenly gathered her things and ran away from her house, her husband, and her family.

She took a lover. She descended into harlotry. Soon she was possessed by another man as a slave is possessed by a master.

∎

Then the Lord said to Israel:

*When you were a child, I loved you. And I called you, my child, out of Egypt.
But the more I called you, the more you went away from me. You burned
sacrifices to Ba'al. You burned incense to idols.*

*Yet it was I who taught you how to walk. When you grew tired, I
carried you in my arms. I healed your weariness. I led you with cords of
compassion. With bands of love I drew you through the wilderness to myself.
Where you chafed with your burdens, I eased you. When you were hungry, I
bent down to feed you.*

*What shall I do now, O my people — now that you refuse to turn back to me?
I will send you back to Egypt!
I will let Assyria rule over you!
I will send a sword to break the bars of your gates and to rage in your cities!
I will ignite war inside your fortresses, and war will devour you!
Oh, Israel!
Oh, my child!
How can I give you up? How can I hand you over to destruction? My heart
recoils within me. My compassion grows warm and tender.*

*No, I will not execute my fierce anger. I will not destroy Israel, for I am God
and not a mortal. I am the Holy One in your midst. I will not come to destroy.*

∎

And to Hosea himself, the Lord God said:

*Go again and love the woman who has become an adulterer with another
man. Love her, Hosea, even as I the Lord love the people of Israel, though
they have turned to other gods.*

So Hosea bought his wife back again for fifteen shekels of silver and a
measure of barley.

And he said to her, "You must live faithfully to me. You cannot belong to
another man anymore. And I will be faithful to you."

So he took her back again and loved her.

And the Lord changed the names of their children. *Don't call your
daughter Not Pitied*, said the Lord. *Call her She Has Obtained Pity. And call
your son My People.*

∎

Again, the Lord spoke with the faithful few who lived in Israel, saying:

Plead with your mother. Plead that she put harlotry away from her face, and adultery away from between her breasts!

She has said, "I will go after lovers who give me bread."

She does not know that it is I who give her grain and wine, who lavish silver upon her.

But now I will allure her. I will lead her again into the wilderness as at the beginning and speak tenderly to her. And even in the desert will I give her vineyards. No other lover can do this thing. Ba'al cannot do this. So she shall answer me again as in the days of her youth.

She shall call me her husband.

O Israel! I will betroth you to me in righteousness and justice, in steadfast love and in mercy.

For I have pity on Not Pitied!

And I say to Not My People, no! You are my people!

Please answer me now. Please say unto me, "You are our God."

V

Israel never returned unto the Lord.

Jeroboam II never changed his heart. He died believing that his kingdom was a bowl of healthy fruit. But as soon as he died, the rot in the center rose to the surface, and the sweet skin burst its putrefaction.

The time that passed between the day of Jeroboam's death and the fall of his kingdom was a mere twenty-five years. Six kings reigned in swift succession, not one of whom trusted in the Lord more than he trusted in his sword and the easy promises of nations.

Jeroboam's son Zechariah was assassinated by a man named Shallum, who reigned one month in Samaria before he himself was murdered by Menahem the son of Gadi.

Menahem ruled for seven years by killing his citizens and by extorting money from them — fifty shekels of silver a year from every family in Israel — in order to buy peace from Assyria.

When Menahem died, his son took the crown, but was immediately murdered by one of his own officers, Pekah the son of Remaliah.

Pekah sought to throw off the Assyrian yoke. With the king of Damascus, he revolted against the eastern empire.

The king of Assyria marched west to Israel, destroying nations in the way and deporting populations to the far reaches of his realm, where they were swallowed by other cultures. This was the Assyrian method of weakening rebellious peoples, to remove them from their homeland and to settle others in their places.

While Judah watched from its isolation in the southern hills, while Jerusalem begged God to protect them from such universal disasters, the king of Assyria turned his forces against the coalition of Israel and Damascus and found it to be no stronger than dry tinder. He crushed it utterly.

King Pekah was murdered by one of his own people, Hoshea, the son of Elah, who surrendered to Assyria, who paid tribute and was allowed to live on a small patch of land around the city of Samaria: thirty miles by forty in size.

For six years Hoshea paid tribute, but when the king of Assyria died, he thought he might, with the help of the armies of Egypt, make a successful revolt.

But when the new king of Assyria marched west to destroy Israel completely, Egypt did not appear.

Hoshea shut himself within his capital. Assyria laid siege to the city, built mighty engines of war, rolled them up to the city gates, dug tunnels beneath the walls to weaken them, and on a summer's day stormed into Samaria, killing its last king, its final king forever.

Twenty-seven thousand two hundred and ninety persons were deported from Samaria. The leaders, the last best minds of the land, were carried away to Assyria and scattered from Halah to Gozan on the river Habor. Some went to the cities of the Medes.

But none were heard from again.

∎

In Jerusalem a prophet watched the long departure of the tribes of the north, suffering both pity and fear. He pitied Israel. But he feared for his own tribe, Judah.

"And will my king listen to this word of the Lord?" he said.

The prophet was Isaiah the son of Amoz. His king was Ahaz, who had erected an Assyrian altar in the courts of the Lord, of whom it was rumored, "He offered his son as a sacrifice."

Isaiah said, "The Lord of hosts has a day against all that is proud and lofty. Look how those people have cast their idols to the moles and the bats, and have covered themselves in rocks and caverns from the terror of the Lord!

"But the Lord says, *Come, let us reason together: though your sins are like scarlet, they shall be white as snow; though they are red like crimson, they shall become like wool. If you are willing and obedient, you shall eat the good of the land. But if you refuse and rebel —* "

21

ISAIAH

i

A young man of wealthy dress and a noble bearing walks in solemn procession with seven priests across the courtyard of the temple. He has clear eyes and a soft, well-cut beard. They are moving from the altar of burnt offering toward the eastern gate. It is dawn, just before sunrise. And it is autumn. The early air is sweet and cold. People have crowded the courtyard. Worshipers. Citizens of Jerusalem and Judah. A few come down from scorched Israel. Now, as the priests pass through the crowd eastward from the temple porch to the gate, the people begin to sing. Theirs is the multitudinous voice of the untrained, but they have often sung this song before. They know it well, and they love it. "The earth is the Lord's," they sing, "and the fullness thereof, for he has founded it upon the seas — "

At the eastern gate the procession stops. One priest steps forward and takes hold of the knot of the rope that has kept this gate closed the whole year through. The knot is sheathed in a hard clay seal. The priest raises it to the level of his eyes. The young nobleman also steps forward, draws a hammer from the folds of his robe, and with one blow smashes the clay seal.

The rope is pulled from its track.

Six priests lean against the doors, three for either one, and the gates of the temple courtyard swing open, revealing the Mount of Olives just outside of the city. There! Right there over the Mount of Olives, the sun will appear in a few minutes. Already the sky is crimson. This is *Rosh Hashanah*, the first day of the new year.

Quickly, now, the procession returns across the courtyard. The great doors of the temple are already standing open, flanked on either side by Jachin and Boaz, the two brazen pillars built by Solomon. One strong voice from the people cries, "Who shall ascend the hill of the Lord? Who shall stand in his holy place?" And the people boom their answer: "They that have clean hands and a pure heart, they will receive the blessing of the Lord!"

At the great altar the procession separates, priests to the right, priests to the left, followed by the young man who carries the hammer. This man sees everything. He glances backward through the gate to the mount and the rosy sky beyond. He peers forward, deep into the temple. Before they mount the steps, his sight is on a level with the interior floor. His nostrils are flaring. His eyes are wide with anticipation. The priests have paused between the altar and the porch.

Suddenly, sunlight!

A ram's horn whoops. A trumpet cracks the sky with a long, loud blast.

The people sing a thunderous song: "Lift up your heads, O gates! Be lifted up, you everlasting doors, and the King of Glory shall come in!"

The sun has broken over the mount. It is sending a single shaft of light through the eastern gate, over the altar, into the temple, down the long nave thick with smoke from the altar of incense, and even to the holiest place, the deep room, the dark recess where the Lord God sits! There! The holy of holies! There!

That spear of sunlight in smoke is a burning thing. It grows brighter and wider, and one voice sings, "Who is the King of Glory?"

And the people answer, "The Lord, strong and mighty — "

Though the seven priests remain unmoving in front of the porch, the young nobleman continues forward as if drawn by bands invisible. Up the porch steps, one by one, gazing into the temple, pierced by sunlight. Then, just between the massive doorposts, he sinks to his knees.

A voice behind him cries, "Who is the King of Glory?"

The people reply, "The Lord of hosts! He is the King of Glory."

And the sound is so loud, the song and the blowing of trumpets, the shaking of timbrels, the ululation of women's tongues, that the doorposts tremble in their sockets and the young man murmurs, "Woe is me! I am lost." He is transfixed where he kneels. His eyes are bright with fear, and his words are uttered in anguish. "I am a man of unclean lips," he whispers, "but my eyes have seen the King, the Lord of hosts!"

■

In his words, the vision of Isaiah the son of Amoz:

In the year that King Uzziah died I saw the Lord sitting upon a throne, high and lifted up.

The train of his royal robes swirled in the temple.

And around him stood the seraphim, the burning ones that wait on him. Each had six wings. With two they covered their faces, with two they covered their feet, and with two they flew.

And one was crying to another: "Holy! Holy! Holy is the Lord of hosts! The whole earth is full of his glory!"

At the voice of him who called, the great doors shook in their sockets, and the house of God was filled with smoke.

I said, "Woe is me! I am lost, for I am a man of unclean lips, and I dwell in the midst of a people of unclean lips! But my eyes have seen the King, the Lord of hosts!"

Then one of the seraphim flew toward me, holding in his hand a burning coal which he had taken with tongs from the altar.

"Behold," he said, "this has touched your lips. Your guilt is taken away, and your sin is forgiven."

And then I heard the voice of the Lord in the counsels of heaven saying, "Whom shall I send? Who will go for us?"

Immediately I cried out, "Here am I! Send me!"

And he said, "Go. Speak to this people, even if they will not understand. Show them again and again, though fat hearts and heavy ears and blind eyes are unable to perceive."

I said, "For how long, O Lord?"

He said:

> *"Until the cities lie abandoned,*
> *and houses lack inhabitants,*
> *and the fields and hills are desolate,*
> *and the Lord has removed the people far away!*
> *"Though a tenth remain in it,*
> *it will be burned again and again,*
> *like an oak whose stump is standing*
> *after the tree is felled."*

ii

During the two hundred years of Israel's existence, the southern kingdom of Judah had been ruled by eleven kings. Every one of them was of the house and lineage of David. His line had not been broken in all these years.

Yet not every king remained faithful to the covenant of God. The present king Ahaz believed that he, not the Lord, had saved Judah from the destruction suffered by the northern ten tribes. For when Assyria came like the bull, goring nations to death, Ahaz took treasures from the temple and from his own house, and sent them as gifts to Assyria, begging protection and offering vassalage.

The prophet Isaiah had urged him to trust the Lord. He told Ahaz to ask a sign of God. "Let it be as deep as Sheol or as high as heaven! Ask anything, that he might prove his strength to you."

Ahaz had said, "I will not put the Lord to the test."

Isaiah answered, "Then the Lord will give you a sign without your asking: *A maiden will conceive and bear a son, and will call his name Immanuel — and even before the child can choose between good and evil the land whose kings now frighten you will be deserted!*"

But Ahaz sent his splendid gift to the Assyrian king, and his nation was not destroyed when Israel was.

In fact, for two centuries, Judah had enjoyed peculiar protections. He had always been poorer than the northern kingdom, his living more austere; but that which impoverished him also preserved him. Judah's hills were hard to negotiate. No trade routes crossed his soil. Nor did he have goods that others wanted. Therefore, Judah remained relatively isolated from the rest of the world. Luxurious pagan influences were weaker where pagans did not travel.

Judah's economy was rural. The land was spare. The population was generally pastoral, unwilling to change and fierce in its independence.

And as a capital, Jerusalem was scarcely international: intensely national, rather, hard to get to, culturally separated, devoted unto God, holy. For Judah had a temple where the Lord of heaven and earth had chosen to dwell. Judah had an elaborate ritual of worship. And Judah had a king, a son of David, with whom the Lord had established his covenant forever.

But the word of the Lord came to Isaiah the son of Amoz, saying:

Sons have I reared. Daughters have I raised, but they forget me. The ox knows its own, the ass its master's crib, but my children do not know and my people do not understand.

▌

The wife of the king of Judah bore a son, and called his name Hezekiah: The Lord Is My Strength.

The boy was sober even from his mother's womb. He grew up conscious of the elemental changes in the nations around him and in the earth — as though mountains were cracking and crumbling into the sea. Nothing was stable. Judah in particular seemed small among the kingdoms. Edom attacked her from the south. The ancient Philistine cities found strength and weapons and attacked from the west. Even Egypt, as old as deserts and rivers, had shattered into helpless divisions; dynasties were passing away. Hezekiah questioned the advisors of his father, seeking explanations. He sat with the priests in the temple.

And then Assyria marched against the northern kingdom.

Hezekiah was eighteen years old when the Assyrians laid siege to Samaria. He listened intently to the reports that poured down from the north. He heard of the horrors. He went out himself and watched the melancholy deportations, thousands and thousands of those that had been kin to him, the old and the young now trudging away in ropes, their herds and cattle driven eastward, carts filled with goods now bound for the storehouses of Assyria.

When Hezekiah was twenty-five his father Ahaz died, and he was himself anointed king of Judah. There was little joy in the coronation.

The sober king was asking in his heart: *How shall I rule? What course is left for a king in Judah?*

In the seven years since Israel died, wild animals had begun to prowl the hills of Ephraim. The land was deserted of its old activity and its sunny populations — and the few who lived there now were an alien breed, people of impenetrable behavior and curious dress whom Assyria had imported from other defeated, dispirited cities: Babylon, Cuthah, Hamath, Avva.

If the kingdom of Israel could suffer such defeat, Hezekiah wondered, *is the God of Israel diminished? Is the Lord less than Asshur, god of the Assyrians?*

How could he ask such questions aloud in the streets of Jerusalem? How could he — a son of David in whose very person rested the covenant God made with David — ask whether the hand of the Lord was weakened? Judah hid in these ancient promises the way the hunted hides in rocks and caves.

But which god was god of the other? Asshur or the Lord?

The Assyrians made pictures of their gods. The people of Judah did not. These pictures were fashioned of wood, plated in gold, given staring white eyes of precious stone. And what did the face of the god of the Assyrians look like? Why, like the face of the king of Assyria! Here was their leader in heaven and on earth, here visible before them: the one who had destroyed Israel and made Judah bow down with splendid gifts and tribute.

But the God of Judah was invisible. Was he also unreachable? He had an unspeakable name. He was a deity wrapped in thick darkness, a God present in word but not in image, a smoky thing, a thing of the wind. Was he also a thing who, if he did not answer, was not there?

So which was the god of the other god?

In the privacy of his palace, King Hezekiah bent down by the sash of a window and whispered his question. He did not mean it as a prayer. He was too frightened to pray such a thing. He meant it merely as an expression of a mystery which, if it could not be solved, he could not reign.

The king whispered, "What shall we now say of the Lord, the God of Israel?"

Immediately a voice came in the window, saying:

That even from the beginning he has been the God of all creation!

iii

Isaiah had ceased to prophesy when King Ahaz refused to obey the commands of God. He wrote in a scroll all the prophecies he had uttered as a young man, then he retired from public places and was not seen again for seventeen years.

By the wealth and heritage of his family, Isaiah had access to the royal courts. His was noble blood. No one questioned his presence where rich men gathered or his participation in the counsel given to kings. At the invitation of the high priest, he joined the most sacred processions of the temple.

Though his prophecy condemned injustice in the kingdom, yet Isaiah himself was not a brooding fellow. He was educated, polished, articulate, and generally pleasant in the company of others.

People did not, then, understand his sudden withdrawal. Was there some offense they were unaware of?

But Ahaz died, and suddenly the Lord roused Isaiah with a tingling sense of hope. The Lord sent the prophet forth again in deliberate joy.

He was fifty. His hair had not turned grey. His body was healthy, his mind was stout — and one morning, under pressure of the deity, Isaiah rose early, trimmed his beard, washed and oiled himself, dressed in his finest raiment, and went out into the streets of Jerusalem to fulfill a command of God.

In his left hand he carried a ram's horn, in his right a timbrel. Swiftly he ascended the temple hill, then took a stand at the southern gate between the courtyard of the Lord and the private quarters of the king, Solomon's palace.

"Hezekiah!" he cried. "Hezekiah, come out! Let's make your coronation more joyful than it was, so that your reign may become more blessed than it is!"

The prophet raised the ram's horn to his lips and blew on it. He sent a thrilling blast through Jerusalem. He blew till the people began to fill the entire area between the temple and the palace.

And when the young king leaned out of an upper window, Isaiah began to sing. He beat the timbrel and raised his left hand and danced as if he were at a wedding:

> *The people who walked in darkness*
> *have seen a great light!*
> *Those who dwelt in the land of deep darkness,*
> *upon them the light has shined!*

> *For unto us a child is born,*
> *unto us a son is given;*
> *and the government shall be upon his shoulder,*
> *and his name shall be called:*

Wonderful Counselor,
Mighty God,
Everlasting Father,
Prince of Peace.

Of the increase of his kingdom and of peace,
of justice and of righteousness,
there shall be no end;
the zeal of the Lord of hosts will do this!

Now Hezekiah the king come down out of his palace and walked across the pavement to Isaiah. Prophet and king stood face-to-face a while, neither breaking the gaze. The older man was smiling at the younger, but the younger had the solemnity of a serious question. Hezekiah, taller than Isaiah but bent by his meditations, had developed deep lines between his brows, so that he seemed always frowning. Finally he said, "But the Lord of hosts was defeated by Asshur of the Assyrians. How can he accomplish the things you say he promises?"

Isaiah, shorter than the king but as straight as a tree stump, laughed. "No! No!" he cried. "O my son, the Lord was not defeated," he said. "Rather, the people of the Lord were defeated because they would not trust in him. Hezekiah, so young and so somber, listen to me: even Assyria is the servant of our God! Hasn't he called that nation *The rod of my anger, the staff of my fury?* It was the Lord who sent Assyria to plunder Israel.

"And now the Lord declares that he will punish the king of Assyria for his arrogant soul and his pride:

The light of Israel will become a fire
and his Holy One a flame,
and it will burn and devour
the thorns and briars of Assyria
all in a single day!

"In that day," Isaiah said, "the remnant of Israel and the survivors of the house of Jacob will lean on the Lord, the Holy One of Israel!"

Isaiah stepped forward and laid his hands on the bony shoulders of the king. "Trust the Lord," he said softly, "though your father did not. Serve him, serve him faithfully, and no enemy will be able to trouble you."

Then the prophet jumped backward and cried, "But this is a coronation! Judah, you have a new king!" As erect as a pillar, he blew seven quick blasts on the ram's horn, and then it was the Lord who spoke in Jerusalem, saying:

O my people, do not fear the Assyrians when they smite with the rod. Soon my anger will turn to their destruction. I will lift my rod as I did in Egypt! In that day Assyria's yoke will be broken from your neck!

> And there shall come forth from Jesse
>   a shoot;
> a green branch shall sprout
>   from his root —
>
> And the spirit of the Lord shall rest upon him:
>   He shall not judge by what his eyes see
>   but with righteousness shall he judge the poor,
>   and with equity choose for the meek of the earth.
>
> The wolf shall dwell with the lamb,
>   and the leopard lie down with the kid,
> The lion, the calf, and the fatling together —
>   and a little child shall lead them.
>
> They shall not hurt nor destroy
>   in all my holy mountain;
> For the earth shall be full of the knowledge of God
>   as the waters cover the sea.

Who could remember the last time a prophet had laughed and danced for gladness? Oh, it had been long since the Lord had spoken so kindly unto his people.

But there was a king in Judah who obeyed the Lord. There was reason for celebration.

iv

For the rest of that day King Hezekiah sat in a dark corner of the temple, contemplating what the prophet had said. It required a whole new view of the God of Israel. But, oh! — what a glorious sight was spread before him now! As if he stood on a mountain, and the world lay down before him.

The Lord was not lesser, but greater than the king had conceived! And if a people perished, it was not because God had forgotten them, but because they had forgotten God.

"He is our strength," Hezekiah murmured, weaving the meaning of his name into the word.

And how did Israel forget the Lord? Their rituals were more elaborate than Judah could afford. Their ceremonies were rich and noisy, splendid displays. But they did not remember the covenant. They had lost humility and obedience. Doing good.

"God is my refuge and strength," the king said. His voice echoed in the empty temple. A little daylight drifted through dust in the upper reaches of the room — a cruel light, really, because the sacred place was cluttered with junk, wooden images, the sins of his fathers. Idols. Abominations.

The king stood up and spoke in a full voice:

"God is our refuge and strength! Therefore we will not fear though the nations change, though the mountains shake in the heart of the sea, though the waters roar and foam!"

He walked to the lampstands that Solomon had fashioned two hundred years ago. They were gathered all along one side, dead out.

"This," he said, "should be the habitation of the Most High God" — then he walked out into sunlight and stood on the porch of Solomon's temple. He saw a priest in the courtyard and called him over.

"God," said the long, lugubrious king, "is in the midst of us. We shall not be moved."

"No, sir," said the priest. "We shall not be moved."

The king frowned, deepening the lines between his brows. He pondered the priest a moment, then he said, "Do you believe that?"

"I believe that the Lord of hosts is with us. Yes, my lord: I believe it."

The king said, "And I'll tell you another thing: it is the Lord who causes desolations in the earth! Likewise, the Lord can stop war altogether."

"He shatters the spear and burns the chariots with fire."

"Extraordinary!" the king murmured, gazing grey-eyed at the man before him. "Priest, what is your name?"

The priest said, "Azariah."

The king said, "Azariah, work with me. I appoint you the chief officer of the house of God. Gather the priests and Levites. Command them to sanctify themselves. It is now time to purge the temple and again to sanctify it!"

In those days a great reform took place in Jerusalem and in all Judah.

All the desecrations that had accumulated in the temple were carried outside the city and thrown into the brook Kidron, where they were burned. The temple doors were repaired and opened. The altars were purified, the utensils, the lampstands, and the room which in darkness contained the Ark of the Covenant, the Holy of Holies.

Hezekiah then led Judah in a sacrifice of thanksgiving. Six hundred bulls were slaughtered and offered on the great altar — and three thousand sheep.

Then the king sent out an edict to all Judah and even to the remnant of Israel who still lived in the desolated lands north: *Come! Keep the Passover to the Lord in Jerusalem.*

Ever since Moses had commanded it, the Passover had been kept by families in their own tents and their own houses. This was a new thing, that all the people should gather in one place for the festival! Then all the households and all the tribes of Israel constituted a single family before God.

Hezekiah tore down the high places. He broke pagan images in the land. He shattered pillars erected to other gods. He kept the commandments which the Lord had commanded Moses.

And he had rest.

For the Lord was his fortress.

V

But the years passed, the wheels of power ground forward, and the world began to change again.

There arose a new Pharaoh and a new dynasty in Egypt. He unified that ancient nation and strengthened its armies and then began to seek diplomatic relationships with all the smaller kingdoms to its east. It was this Pharaoh's strategy to make these kingdoms stones in a great wall between himself and Assyria.

Ambassadors of Egypt began to arrive in Jerusalem, begging private consultations with the king of Judah.

Hezekiah admitted them into his throne hall once, twice.

And the prophet Isaiah grew wary. His counsel was not sought during these visitations, nor was his presence invited.

Everyone knew that the old Assyrian king had died and that rebellion was breaking out everywhere in the empire. King Midas of Phrygia, Carchemish in Syria, the powerful Babylon, the king of Elam — all were testing the strength and the resources of the New Assyria. The nations were raging again and — as Isaiah saw it — little kingdoms who leaped into the maelstrom seeking power or advantage would more likely drown.

Hezekiah ceased appearing in public. Isaiah could not find him to speak to him.

But evidence of the king's thinking began to appear everywhere in the kingdom.

A new wall was built around Jerusalem, protecting buildings that once were outside the old wall. New stables and storehouses were constructed. A tunnel was carved through solid rock, starting from both ends at once. It went seven hundred feet from a spring of water in the Kidron Valley up into the city and assured Jerusalem a continuous water supply — even during a siege!

Troops and chariots were sent forth to garrison strategic cities, and watchtowers appeared like a necklace around the throat of Judah, a border of fortresses!

In the sixty-sixth year of his life, Isaiah was again roused by God and driven into the streets of Jerusalem to prophesy.

The next time the Egyptian ambassadors arrived at the city gates, an angry man ran at them, crying, "An oracle!" He was wearing sackcloth. He grabbed the bridles; the horses reared and whinnied, and the Lord spoke:

> I am riding on the swift clouds to Egypt
> > to confound your plans!
> Your Nile will be parched and dry,
> > your fishermen will mourn,
> because your princes are deluded
> > and your wise men fools.
> The leaders of Egypt have led her astray!
> She's like a drunk who staggers in his vomit —

But the Egyptian charioteers whipped their horses until the great beasts broke into a bewildered gallop and Isaiah was knocked to the side.

His head hit a stone baluster, so that he lay stunned in the street a while.

When he came to his senses, Isaiah pulled himself up, took a few unsteady steps, then set his face toward the king's palace and began to walk.

The longer he walked, the more erect he became. His expression was fixed and bleak. He made the sackcloth seem a noble robe by his bearing alone.

So aristocratic did his manner become, that the guards outside the throne hall shuffled backward, and the old man entered without hindrance.

King Hezekiah was sitting six steps high on his ivory chair, his long countenance lined and melancholy. The Egyptian envoy was evidently in the midst of formal greetings. Everyone looked up at the sound of Isaiah's intrusion, but no one spoke.

Isaiah walked directly to the throne, ignoring the Egyptians.

"When did you cease to listen to the Lord?" he said.

Hezekiah only looked at Isaiah, pursing his lips. He said nothing.

Isaiah, then, took hold of the hem of his sackcloth and pulled it off over his head. There were startled grunts in the room. Courtiers were offended. But the prophet continued. He kicked his sandals off. He stripped his old flesh of all its covering except the loincloth.

Then, standing in the throne hall with his buttocks visible, thin, and shining white, Isaiah said, "This is a portent against Egypt, King Hezekiah. This is all that nation has to offer you. Thus says the Lord your God!"

Leaving his clothes behind as his counsel, the old man went out from the presence of the king. Nor did he wear anything but the loincloth from that day forward — until Hezekiah began to trust the word of God again.

For three years Isaiah walked naked and barefoot through Jerusalem. His skin burned in the summer sun. It cracked and withered in winter. At all times people hid their faces from him because nakedness was such a shameful thing.

But Hezekiah was establishing alliances with the kingdoms of the world. Nearby, Moab and Edom and Ashdod and cities of the Philistines joined him, each one a stone in the wall against Assyria. From greater distances, Hezekiah received an embassy from Merodach-Baladan, the king of Babylon. International promises, international intrigue, and the maneuverings of power.

At home the king was manufacturing weapons for his soldiers and chariots for their horses — and in huge clay jars he was sending grain to the fortresses where they were garrisoned.

The citizens of Judah began to delight in the prospect of independence again. Hezekiah's father had brought upon them the crushing yoke of Assyria. He had initiated an annual tribute that had burdened them ever since. But now the good and shrewd king Hezekiah, having magnified himself by associations with other embittered kingdoms, decided to withhold the tribute from the iron empire. Jerusalem, a little breathless at the dare, grinned and grew proud of their amazing boldness: Jerusalem was free!

But the Lord God said:

As my servant Isaiah is walking naked and barefoot, so shall Assyria lead away the Egyptians naked. And those who hope in Egypt shall be dismayed and confounded! In that day you will say, "And we? — how will we escape?"

vi

King Hezekiah fell sick with a deadly sickness. He went into his private chambers and lay down, intending to suffer through to health again. But he didn't get well.

Hezekiah had always been a monarch of internal meditation, thoughtful and quiet. This, now, was the measure of his physical pain: he groaned so loudly that his voice could be heard throughout the palace.

Day by day his servants came to wash him. He was covered with an eruption of boils so fiery and violent, he could scarcely move. His servants wiped the discharge away. They lay wet cloths on his flesh to cool a raging fever. They changed his bedding, scrubbed the floor and the walls, poured

ointment, spread spices — but the odor in his room only grew more foul
and his pain increased.

Then one morning the prophet Isaiah was standing in the king's room.
Despite the fire all around his body, Hezekiah felt the presence. He looked
through the haze of his sickness and saw Isaiah at his feet. "Have you come
to comfort me?" he whispered.

The prophet, his beard as trim as ever but snow white, spoke with an
impersonal exactitude.

"Thus says the Lord: *Set your house in order, for you shall die. You shall
not recover.*"

Isaiah left.

The king gazed where the prophet had stood, tears rising in his eyes.
All his life a melancholy man, yet he had never until this moment wept.
Hezekiah turned. Through a slow cycle of suffering, Hezekiah turned to the
wall and prayed a silent prayer, moving his lips and releasing a corrupted
breath, but making no sound:

"O Lord, remember now how I have walked before you in faithfulness and
with a whole heart. Remember the good I have done in your sight."

The king wept bitterly.

Suddenly he was hearing the voice of the prophet:

"Even before I had left your courtyard, the Lord stopped me and sent me
back to you."

King Hezekiah lifted his head. Indeed, Isaiah stood at his foot again.

And the Lord said, *Hezekiah, I have seen your tears. I will heal you. On
the third day you shall go up to the temple, and I will add fifteen years to
your life. I will deliver you and this city out of the hand of the armies of
Assyria. I will defend this city for my own sake and for my servant
David's sake.*

Then it was Isaiah, the old white-bearded man himself, who spoke to a
physician outside the chamber door. "Make a poultice of figs," he said, "and
lay it on the king's boils."

■|

In the twenty-fifth year of Hezekiah's reign the king of Assyria marched his
mighty armies into the west as far as the Great Sea.

He utterly destroyed the kingdom of Tyre and its sea-ports and its
lucrative trade. From that day forward, Tyre was nothing on earth.

Then the king of Assyria turned his attention to all the kingdoms that
had joined into a great alliance, that mighty wall built up between Egypt
and himself. He fought them one by one, and stone by stone they fell before
his bloody, ineluctable assault: Byblos and Arvad and Ashdod and Moab and
Edom and Ammon.

Three nations were left: Ashkelon and Ekron and Judah.

As Assyria marched south along the Great Sea, an Egyptian army appeared and drew up battle lines in order to defend the city of Ekron, but they were beaten back in a morning, and Ekron was defeated in an afternoon, its leaders executed, its people deported.

Now the king of Assyria began to move through a great, sweeping arc into Judah, like a sickle mowing toward Jerusalem. He captured the city of Timnah, cutting off supply lines to the capital. In the Elah Valley he took Azekah and Gath, then marched farther south against Hezekiah's fortress at Lachish. He burned that city to the ground. His soldiers dug a pit for the corpses. One thousand five hundred bodies were covered by the bones of swine and by a casual dirt.

The king of Assyria attacked and defeated forty-six fortified cities of Judah. His brutal advance drove Hezekiah and his small army into the walls of Jerusalem.

Finally, while the Assyrian king himself remained encamped at Libnah, he sent the supreme commander of the empire's armies to Jerusalem, demanding surrender.

The commander took a stand outside the city gates and cried in the language of Judah: "Has any god of any nation ever delivered his land from the hand of Assyria? Where are the gods of Hamath and Arpad? Where are the gods of Tyre and Ashkelon and Ekron? Hezekiah! King Hezekiah! Did the God of Israel save that kingdom? Where are those whom Assyria destroyed a generation ago?"

Hezekiah heard the words. He heard the threat and the scorn both. It was as if Asshur like a bull were stamping the ground outside the city and blasting the sky with his nostrils.

But the king had chosen his course, and now he did not depart from it: he covered himself in the sackcloth of repentance and went into the temple of the Lord, where he spoke softly with the old prophet, Isaiah — these two men together in the low light of ten lamps. There was no other counsel that the king sought except Isaiah's.

"Ah, prophet, Assyria's words have mocked the living God," said the tall king, stooped by age and his heavy meditations. "But you yourself said long ago that God would destroy the pride of that people. Old friend, lift up your prayer for us now."

Then the king himself turned toward the *Debir*, the thick darkness within the Holiest Place, and raised his arms and prayed: "O Lord God of Israel, enthroned above the cherubim, you alone are God of all the kingdoms of the earth: Hear the words which Assyria has uttered, mocking you. Truly, the king of Assyria has laid waste the nations and cast their gods into the fire. But those were no gods at all. They were the work of human hands, wood and stone. Therefore, O Lord our God, come and save us now, so that all the kingdoms of the earth may know that you, O Lord, are God alone!"

Isaiah, standing bolt upright beside the king, but shorter than he, now spoke. He did not touch the king. Neither man moved. Both continued to face the seat of God, and both kept their voices low, whispering.

"The Lord has heard your prayer," Isaiah said. "And the Lord has a word for Assyria:

Against whom have you raised your haughty voice? Against the Holy One of Israel! Have you not heard that it was I who planned your triumphs long ago? But I know your sitting down and your going out and your coming in. And because you have raged against me, I will put my hook in your nose and my bit in your mouth, and I will turn you back the way you came."

That same night, while Hezekiah and the old prophet were praying in the temple of God, the king of Assyria suddenly struck camp at Lachish and began to ride at breakneck speeds away. Rumors had come to him of rebellion in his court, and a violent spirit of anxiety had entered his soul. He didn't even wait to tell his supreme commander of the departure.

Early the following morning Hezekiah's servants found him in the temple and immediately began to shout and chatter. They were amazed by what they had seen.

"My Lord, a hundred and eighty-five thousand troops!" they yelled, their poor eyes gaping.

"The armies around Jerusalem," they said, "the armies made no noises all night long! At sunlight they still lay sleeping. Not a soldier had awakened.

"Then a little child slipped out of the gates and touched a man on his face and ran back to tell us that he was cold. They weren't sleeping! They were dead!

"My lord, there are a hundred and eighty-five thousand Assyrians lying dead at our door!"

22

JEREMIAH

i

After the death of Hezekiah, his son Manasseh rose to the throne and ruled Judah for a long time, forty-five years, during which the kingdom experienced peace.

But this king was not like his father.

A politic, expedient man, Manasseh never withheld tribute from Assyria. All his life he remained an obedient vassal, sending materials for construction in the capital city, Nineveh — even assisting the armies of Assyria against Egypt. Under his reign, Judah enjoyed the protection of the Assyrian bull. Jerusalem sat peacefully upon her hills.

But Manasseh's obedience gave more than money away, and though the swords of Assyria never invaded Jerusalem, the spirit did — and the worship, and the gods, and the altars of that pagan nation.

Manasseh paid homage to the astral deities of his overlord. He erected their altars in the temple itself. He repudiated the reforms of his father, allowing pagan cults to flourish throughout the land. The sacred prostitutes of Ba'al reappeared. Farmers again sought to guarantee good crops by means of fertility rituals — even within the precincts of the temple which Solomon dedicated to the Lord nearly three hundred years ago. Diviners and magicians like those in Assyria now practiced in Jerusalem — beloved of the nobles there.

And as the voice of the Lord was ignored in the land, so was his covenant. So were his laws.

Woe, said the Lord, but no one heard:

> *Woe to her that is rebellious and defiled:*
> *   her officials are roaring lions;*
> *her judges are evening wolves*
> *   who leave nothing till morning.*
> *Her prophets are wanton,*
> *   her priests profane the sacred —*

No one heard the word of the Lord because prophecy was gagged in Judah, and those who protested were punished. Their blood enriched the soil. A rumor in Judah said that the king had sawed Isaiah to death with a wooden saw.

But Manasseh had marched with Ashurbanipal, king of Assyria. He had seen the wild bull, headstrong and vehement, shatter the defenses of Egypt and drive his armies south to Memphis, which he conquered. Ashurbanipal imposed upon the northern reaches of Egypt, the rich delta of the Nile, an absolute Assyrian authority. Even so, it was not enough. The king of little Judah next watched the king of the cruel empire sweep yet farther south to Thebes. The splendid city of ancient Egypt, that white monument on the upper Nile, more than two thousand years old: Ashurbanipal burned it. He took her princes captive. He carried them back to Nineveh, and he executed them.

King Manasseh was a realistic, politic man. He saved the stones of his kingdom from destruction. But not the souls.

ii

Ashurbanipal expanded the Assyrian empire to its greatest limits east and north and west. He was also its last strong king. There was no strength in Assyria after him.

In the year that Ashurbanipal died, a young Judean heard the voice of the Lord speaking directly to him:

> *Before I formed you in the womb,*
> *I knew you.*
> *Even before your mother bore you,*
> *I consecrated you*
> *and appointed you a prophet*
> *to the nations!*

The young man was barely twenty years old. He lived in the small town of Anathoth, about two miles north of Jerusalem. His father, Hilkiah, was a priest. His family had been priests in Anathoth for more than two hundred years.

At dusk one day Hilkiah called his son into his private room and handed him the white linen he'd been wearing that day while performing duties at the temple in Jerusalem.

"Take it to your mother," Hilkiah said.

The garment was soaked with blood. A group of shepherds from Hebron had offered forty beasts upon the high altar. Hilkiah had officiated. Now he was hot and tired.

"Tell your mother I'll need the robe again tomorrow. She has to wash it tonight."

The young man turned and went out into the tiny courtyard of their house. The sun had set. The patch of sky above him glowed deep violet, as translucent as an amethyst.

Hilkiah called behind him, "Wait a minute! I forgot to show you a tear in the hem — "

The young man froze, his eyes wide with listening. "Jeremiah, come here! A bull kicked free and ripped the hem of my tunic. I want your mother to mend — "

But his son didn't move. Whatever he was hearing — it was no human voice. The linen had slipped from his fingers. He was raising his right hand, palm outward, to the open air.

"Jeremiah!" Down the center of the young man's forehead a thick vein stood out, swollen to bursting. All at once he looked to heaven and shouted, "Ah, Lord God! I'm only a child! I don't know how to speak!"

"What?" Hilkiah called. "What did you say?"

Though he was young, Jeremiah had a lean, wasted body, shoulders so bony they made his skull seem huge and his eyes enormous. Now he covered those eyes with the heels of his hands, and sank to his knees on the bloody linen. His thin chest heaved in silent spasms. He was fighting for air. His eyes rolled toward heaven with a wild appeal. He could not breathe —

"What's the matter?" Hilkiah was standing in the doorway. "Jeremiah, what's wrong with you?"

The older man took a step forward — when suddenly his son expelled a great rush of air and slumped to his back on the linen garment, breathing heavily. Hilkiah knelt beside him.

In a little while Jeremiah turned his face to Hilkiah and smiled, bewildered and apologetic. "Father," he whispered, "the Lord put his hand upon my mouth. He closed it and he opened it again."

Hilkiah frowned. He began to brush back strands of hair from his son's wet forehead. "You're as tired as I am," he said, "with less strength to stand it."

Jeremiah blinked his enormous eyes and whispered, "The Lord spoke to me. He said that he has consecrated me a prophet, and that I must speak whatever he commands me."

Hilkiah dropped his eyes, frowning. He saw the linen garment on the ground and reached for it and pulled, but Jeremiah was lying on it. "I'll tell you his words," said Jeremiah, seeking his father's glance.

But Hilkiah said, "Get up. You're rubbing my vestment in the dirt."

"Father, these are his words." Jeremiah sat up. "The Lord said,

> *Lo, I have put my words in your mouth,*
> *words like fire for people of wood:*
> *This day I place you over the nations,*
> *to tear up, to tear down,*
> *to destroy, to destroy,*
> *in order to build and to plant —* "

"Stop it! Stop it! Get up!" Hilkiah the priest was pulling at the linen under his son's body. "Don't you know what you're doing? Stop it!" He took the hem in both hands and gave such a tremendous yank that the little rip opened and the robe tore in two.

"Look at this! Look at this!" Hilkiah cried. He threw the bloody cloth down at Jeremiah, then stomped back into his room. It was very dark now. But no one had yet begun to light the lanterns of the household.

▌▌

Once when Jeremiah was still a boy, five years old, his father took him to Jerusalem. At noon they happened to be standing in the Potsherd Gate on the southeast side of the city when an old man came and said that King Manasseh had just died.

Jeremiah never forgot the moment. The old man spat and pointed through the gate to a deep valley outside the city wall. "There," he croaked. He was shaking with anger. "Right down there, in the valley of the Son of Hinnom, the king burned his children on wooden pyres. He sacrificed them. He said it was a sacrifice. It made a sick sweet odor, like the smoke of rotting fruit."

Suddenly the old man grabbed Hilkiah by the shoulders. "Priest," he begged, "must I mourn him? Manasseh is dead! But how can we mourn the death of such a king?"

▌▌

The day after the Lord had called to him, Jeremiah stepped into the courtyard where his mother was boiling water in a clay cooking pot. "Jeremiah?" she said.

"What, mother?"

She said, "Would you take the pot from the coals and set it over by the oven?" Then she rose up and went out into the street. The clay pot had two handles with which it might be carried, even heavy and hot. Just as Jeremiah reached for them, the word of the Lord came, saying, *Jeremiah, what do you see?*

He said, "I see a boiling pot, facing away from the north."

The Lord said, *Out of the north evil shall break forth against this land. I am calling the kingdoms of the north to set their thrones against Jerusalem and all the cities of Judah. I will utter judgments for all their wickedness in forsaking me.*

But you, Jeremiah, gird up your loins and tell them what I command you. Do not be dismayed by them. Behold, I make you an iron pillar against the whole land. They will fight against you, but they shall not prevail, for I am with you to deliver you!

"Jeremiah!" his mother was crying. "Jeremiah! I have always kept that pot purified! Why are you defiling it?"

The young man looked down and saw that he had tipped the big pot over, spilling the water, dousing the coals, making a mud of the ground between the flagstones.

∎

After Manasseh died, his son Amon was elevated to the throne; but the new king changed nothing of his father's policies, whether inside the kingdom or outside of it. He continued to pay tribute to Assyria and to honor its gods. Indeed, all the gods of Canaan and those beyond the river were welcomed and worshiped in Judah.

Then, at the end of a bare two years, King Amon was assassinated. An old man appeared in the windows of the king's palace, crying, "He is dead! The wicked son of a wicked king is dead! Wash out the temple now!"

But even while the old man was croaking victory from the upper window, three landowners rushed into the palace and came upon him from behind. They slashed his throat and threw his body down to the pavement between the palace and the temple gate. In less than a week these landowners and others like them crowned Amon's eight-year-old son the king of Judah. The boy's name was Josiah. And while he was yet a boy, he was docile and watchful. Others made decisions for him.

But during the twelfth year of his reign, Josiah no longer thought of himself as a boy. He had seen enough of the nations to make decisions for himself, and he began to act like a king. In that year Josiah marched an army north to Samaria and then to Megiddo, cities that once had belonged to old Israel. He entered them, declared them to be under his control, and marched south along the coast of the Great Sea, annexing territory and building a fortress south of Joppa, west of Jerusalem.

Then in the thirteenth year of his reign, when Josiah was twenty-one years old, two signal events occurred: Ashurbanipal died in Nineveh; and, after sixty years of divine silence, there appeared in Jerusalem a prophet of the Lord.

He was a young man, though his body was cadaverous and his skull so domed that he looked ravaged. He had a coarse thicket of hair, and his voice was a whining reed which no one could shut out. Suddenly this man was standing in the Potsherd Gate, facing into Jerusalem, delivering an oracle of the Lord in a nasal wail:

> *What wrong did your fathers find in me*
> *that they went so far from me?*
> *I brought you to a plentiful land,*
> *to enjoy its fruits,*
> *but when you came you defiled my land,*
> *and made my heritage an abomination!*

The people of Jerusalem said, "Who is this? What does he know about heritage and survival and history and reality?"

Yet even while they murmured against him they gathered in the gate and listened. He was passionate. He was dramatic and somewhat frightening. He leaped about while he spoke, sometimes strutting, sometimes bending double with pain.

Now he whirled away from the city and pointed down to the valley below, crying:

For the sons of Judah have done evil in my sight. They have set their abominations in my holy house. They have built a high place in the valley of the Son of Hinnom, there! There! In that place they have burned their sons and their daughters with fire. Therefore, the days are coming, when it will no longer be called the valley of the Son of Hinnom, but the valley of Slaughter! For they will bury bodies in that valley because there shall be no room elsewhere! The dead bodies of this people will be food for the birds and the beasts. In the cities of Judah I will silence the voice of mirth and the voice of the bridegroom and the voice of the bride; for the land shall become a waste.

The prophet paused. He turned and looked at the audience in the gate. Some had covered their ears against his voice; others seemed genuinely shaken; others merely shrugged.

"Who is this ranter?" said an official in the king's service. This was Shaphan, the royal secretary. "Who are his people?"

Certain men from Anathoth heard him and answered. "His name is Jeremiah the son of Hilkiah the priest."

"I know Hilkiah," Shaphan said. "A dependable man. It never occurred to me that he would lose control in his own house!"

"No, sir! It's not his fault."

"But you said this is his son."

"Yes, his youngest. A strange boy. No one has ever been able to teach him obedience."

"Jeremiah. Then he has always been like this?"

"Ever since he was a boy, he brooded. He wouldn't talk for days, then he'd get up in the courtyard and scream that the almond tree had told him secrets. Until this year he was just an embarrassment. Now he's angry. Now he screams in the streets of Jerusalem."

"And that bothers you."

"Yes, it bothers us! He says he's a prophet! Who made him a prophet?"

Shaphan the royal secretary studied the men from Anathoth. "Why are you so passionate about this Jeremiah?" he said.

"If he keeps prophesying like this," they said, "we will kill him with our own hands."

"I believe you mean it," said Shaphan. "But who are you? How do you know this fellow so well?"

"Hilkiah is our father too," the men said miserably. "This fellow, this Jeremiah, this seer — he is our brother."

iii

By the time he was twenty-one, Jeremiah had left Anathoth and found lodging in Jerusalem. In the fourteenth year of Josiah's reign, he began to prophesy the violent advent of a foe from the north. Jeremiah took his stand in various gates of the city, distressing the population wherever he went.

"At that time it will be said to this people and to Jerusalem, 'A hot wind comes!'" Jeremiah tore the air with his high voice. He stood in the Damascus Gate as do messengers from far cities, or heralds of the king. He fixed the merchants with his eyes and cried:

> "Behold, he comes up like clouds,
>   his chariot like the whirlwind;
> his horses swifter than eagles —
>   'Woe! Woe, for we are ruined!'

> *O Jerusalem, wash your heart from wickedness,*
>   *that you may be saved!*
> *How long shall evil ideas*
>   *worm within you?"*

The prophet staggered backward against the stone wall, crying, "My heart! My heart! The walls of my heart! It beats so hard, I can't control it! I hear the sound of the trumpet of war! Disaster follows disaster! The whole land is laid waste! How long, O Lord? How long must I see the horrors and hear the trumpet?"

There was no congregation around the prophet now. He had begun to frighten the people. His feelings shot between extremes. Who could follow his wild transitions? Who could tell that this last collapse was for love of Jerusalem? Jeremiah loved desperately the daughter of his people, Judah. Something in him hated to prophesy her suffering.

But soon the cadaverous man was standing straight again, a solitary figure speaking softly, with terrible articulation. "I looked on the earth," he said, "and it was altogether void, and the heavens gave no light. I looked on the mountains and they were quaking. I looked, and lo — there was neither man nor woman anywhere, and all the birds had fled. The fruitful land was a desert, every city in ruins before the Lord."

Jeremiah walked away. He walked out of the gate, out of the city, down to the Kidron, where he lay down on the dry ground and fell asleep. No one disturbed him.

iv

For three years Jeremiah prophesied in the cities of Judah and the streets of Jerusalem. For five years he troubled the ears of the people. But then he fell silent. In the eighteenth year of Josiah's reign, Jeremiah withdrew from public places. If he was in the city, he was not seen. Certainly, he was not speaking, for the people who had been lashed by his language were experiencing ease again and a sort of peace.

In that year the Book of the Law was found in the temple. King Josiah had already begun to purge the idolatries of Judah. He had heard of the prophecy of Jeremiah and had paid attention to it. At the same time the king's cousin also began to prophesy — and the word of the Lord in his mouth was the same as the word in Jeremiah's. Through the prophet Zephaniah, in the very palace of the king, the Lord God announced:

I will sweep everything from the face of the earth!
On that day I will punish the officials and the king's sons and all who dress

in foreign raiment. I will punish everyone who fills his master's house with violence and fraud.

Like Hezekiah before him, Josiah destroyed the images of Assyrian gods. He tore down the Asherah and the high places of Ba'al. He drove out pagan practices, their priests and their prostitutes. He forbade sorcery and divination and magic in the land. Not only in Judah, but even as far north as Galilee he shut down the local shrines and caused all worship to look toward Jerusalem. And in the midst of this activity, he commanded that the temple be cleansed again of the desecrations of his grandfather, Manasseh. In the eighteenth year of Josiah's reign, while priests were repairing and purging the temple, they found the Book of the Law written upon a long scroll. They gave it to Shaphan, Josiah's secretary, who read it in part, then took it to the king in his private chambers. "Look," he said, "the priests have uncovered an old book!"

Josiah said, "Read it to me."

So Shaphan sat down and read it aloud, from the beginning to the end. The Book of the Law, the ancient statutes of the covenant of God, the holy code first spoken to Moses, older than David and Jerusalem, older than kings in Israel, as old as the exodus and Sinai. When Josiah heard its words, he tore his clothes and wept.

"Great is the wrath of the Lord," he said, "because our fathers have not obeyed the words of this book!"

So the king sent for all the elders of Judah and Jerusalem, the priests and all the people. He gathered them together in the courts of the temple, and then he himself took a stand by the pillar and read the book to them. Next, in their sight and in their hearing, King Josiah made a covenant before the Lord, to walk after the Lord and to keep his commandments and his statutes — with all his heart and soul to perform the words of the covenant which were written in this book.

Then Josiah called for a heifer three years old. When it was brought forward, he commanded that it be cut into two pieces, one half laid on the north side, one on the south with a path between. It was done: blood laced the pavement where the heifer had been dragged apart. Likewise, a she-goat three years old was cut in two and laid beside the heifer, and a ram three years old, a turtledove, and a young pigeon. Then King Josiah commanded the people to join the covenant with him by walking between the halves of the beasts. In that day the people of Judah, both young and old, passed through the blood of the sacrifice and bound themselves one to the other before the Lord, to keep the statutes of the Lord.

Among those who walked in the way of old obedience was a man of twenty-five, whose body was wasted, whose head was huge, whose hair was a wild defiance — but whose countenance was suffused with joy as bright as sunlight.

He smiled and kept silent. There was no need now for the harsh word. The king had returned his people to mercy again.

V

In the twenty-seventh year of Josiah's reign, the Medes and the Babylonians joined in a mighty alliance. In his twenty-eighth year they laid siege to Nineveh, and in three months the capital of Assyria fell. The Medes proceeded to eat up the mountains of Urartu and all the land north and east of the old Assyrian empire.

The Babylonian king pursued the miserable remnant of Assyria's great army eastward to Haran, which he attacked that year and again the next year — until the wreckage of old Assyria fled across the Euphrates River to Carchemish and sent desperate messages to Pharaoh Neco in Egypt: "Help us! We are perishing!"

Their message defined the cry of the whole world in those days. *God, help us!* People everywhere lived anxious and uncertain lives. Farmers and merchants and priests and kings: no one was not threatened. Nations were raging and dying, and the collapse of those ancient empires that once had been fixed stars in the universe made the earth itself a loose and doomful place. Nothing was sure.

Twenty years ago Assyria had invaded Egypt and destroyed its eternal cities forever. But now a new Egypt was emerging, whose Pharaoh Neco was not beholden to the old ways. When the same Assyria, now dying, begged for his help, Neco granted it. Pharaoh Neco mustered an enormous force and marched northeast, out of Egypt and up the coast road of the Great Sea.

King Josiah, now in the thirty-first year of his reign, himself not forty years old, read the Egyptian advance as a threat to Judah. Therefore, he rushed his own armies to Megiddo and drew up battle lines to block Neco's passage.

Neco sent messengers to Josiah, saying: "King of Judah, I am not marching against you, but against Babylon. Let me pass."

But Josiah did not withdraw. Instead, when Neco appeared on the plains of Megiddo, Josiah himself joined the troops in battle, riding among the first chariots, swinging his two-edged sword with power. But an archer shot the king through his neck. He slumped in his chariot. Immediately his driver wheeled around and fled the fighting. He whipped the horses into a furious gallop and drove to Jerusalem as fast as he could go. Sixty miles. When he came full cry through the Sheep Gate, the driver glanced down, then reined his tired horses to a walk. There was no need for haste. King Josiah was dead.

Jehoiakim was crowned king of Judah — but not in liberty, not with autonomy. So soon after Josiah had seized freedom and purged a nation and expanded his northern borders, his son became the king of Judah as a vassal of Egypt. He was forced to pay tribute in the amount of a hundred shekels of silver and ten talents of gold, annually. Jehoiakim laid a heavy tax on the people Judah. No free man escaped it. And the king himself took the benefit.

vi

S uddenly the word of the Lord returned to Jeremiah, saying, *Stand in the gate of the Lord's house and say, "Hear the word of the Lord, all you people of Judah who enter these gates to worship the Lord — "*

∎

Jehoiakim loved strong scents and a luxurious life. On the day of his coronation he opened a large wooden box that had come by caravan from Alexandria. In it were small bags and sachets, jars of alabaster and bottles of glass. From these Jehoiakim selected an oil of calamus, smooth and sweet, and worked it into his beard until that beard stood out like a shining wet sculpture.

Then the king elect rose up and left his private quarters, gathered his servants around himself, and in grandeur went out of the palace door.

It was early in the morning when he stepped into the outer court of the temple. Both courts were filled with people from everywhere in Judah. They broke into roaring as the royal figure passed.

Inside the temple the priests were waiting. It was New Year's Day: already they had thrown open the doors to the bright rise of the eastern sun. Smiles met smiles as Jehoiakim entered the temple — and every priest remarked upon the magnificence of his apparel and his smell.

In solemn ceremony, the priests invested Jehoiakim with the symbols of his office, the royal crown and a royal name which ever thereafter testified to his new identity. Priests poured olive oil on the king's head, allowing it to run down his long hair, his cheeks and beard. It dripped to his shoulders and chest. Then the chief priest stepped out on the porch and shouted:

"Long live King Jehoiakim!"

Immediately the people thundered their acclamation, clapping their hands, blowing on trumpets of metal and horn.

Just as the king himself emerged on the porch, preparing to process to the palace and for the last acts of his coronation, a high, whining voice cut the air like a weapon, destroying the music, destroying the joy of the day.

"Hear the word of the Lord," the voice was wailing. "All you who enter these gates to worship the Lord, thus says the Lord of hosts:
Amend your ways, and I will let you dwell in this place. Do not trust
in these deceptive words: THIS IS THE TEMPLE OF THE LORD, THE
TEMPLE OF THE LORD, THE TEMPLE OF THE LORD!"

The priests rushed out on the porch. They stood between the king and the people, seeking the source of this sacrilege. There! There he was, in the New Gate between the inner and the outer courts! A man as skinny as a stick, wild hair, a huge head. A vein was swollen in the middle of his forehead.

For if you truly amend your ways and execute justice one with another,
if you do not oppress the alien, the fatherless or the widow, or shed
innocent blood in this place, and if you do not go after other gods, then
I will let you dwell in this place, in the land I gave to your ancestors
forever. But you! You trust deceptive words —

"Seize him!" the priests screamed. "Grab that man and silence him! This is the day of the king!"

But those who were nearest the New Gate were stricken by the man's language, by its force and boldness and holy aggression. They said, "He is a prophet," and they could not move. The priests screamed, "He is reviling the temple!"

The prophet, standing on a stone of the gate post, pointed at the priests:
Will you steal, murder, commit adultery, swear falsely, burn incense
to Ba'al and then come before me in this house and say, "We are
delivered!" — only to go on doing the same abominations? Has my
house become a den of robbers in your eyes? My anger will be poured
out on this place, on people and beasts, the trees of the field and the
fruit of the ground. It will burn, and it will not be quenched! I will make
this city a curse for all the nations of the earth!

Suddenly a strange transformation came over the prophet. He ceased speaking, and in the peculiar silence he began to gaze into the eyes of the people nearest him. Then tears were streaming down his wasted cheeks.

"Ah, my heart is sick within me," he whispered. He stepped down from the foundation rock. "Because of the wound of the daughter of my people, my own heart is wounded. Is there no balm in Gilead? Is there no physician there?"

Whereas his cursing fixed the people in fear, the tenderness of this appeal broke the trance. Several men moved forward and seized the prophet, and suddenly he was only thin and weak. The courtyard erupted in confusion and distress. Angry priests came running with the temple guard.

"You!" they snarled with loathing. "Jeremiah son of Hilkiah, we thought we were done with you!"

They commanded the guard to hold him here while the king's coronation proceeded according to law.

So King Jehoiakim passed through the New Gate, staring coldly at the prophet named Jeremiah. The priests and a large element of the people disappeared into the palace — officials, the rich, men who sought important positions in the new king's court. But many people remained in the temple yards, fascinated by the prisoner who could curse them and love them at once.

Before evening the priests returned and accosted Jeremiah. "Who do you think you are?" they said. "Are you above Josiah? King Josiah made this temple the only place of worship throughout all of Judah — *all of Judah!* How can you blaspheme it?"

Then to the leaders of Judah who had followed them from the palace, the priests declared: "Because this man has prophesied that Jerusalem would be a curse for all the nations of the earth, he deserves to die!"

"No, not me! It was the Lord!"

"What?"

Jeremiah had spoken, and the priests were indignant.

"What did you say?"

"It was the Lord who sent me to prophesy against this house," he said. His voice was steady. He turned to the leaders of the people and put his case before them.

"Yes, Josiah brought the worship of the Lord to this house only," Jeremiah said. "But the priests of the temple have forgotten that it is not the house who protects us, but the Lord himself. O people, nor is it your sacrifice which the Lord God loves. It is your obedience!"

A man named Ahikam quietly moved to a place where he could observe the prophet. A reed of a man, his head a bony dome, his eyes big and unbearably sad, Jeremiah looked sixty years old. Yet Ahikam's father had known him since he first began to prophesy, and Ahikam knew that he could not be older than forty.

"Amend your ways," the prophet was saying, looking straight at Ahikam. "Obey the Lord, and the Lord your God will repent of the evil which he has pronounced. As for me, I am in your hands. Only, know that though you put me to death, the word of the Lord will endure."

Jeremiah closed his mouth and waited.

Some of the leaders said to the priests, "If a man has truly spoken in the name of the Lord, how can anyone say that he deserves the death sentence?"

Then the man named Ahikam spoke. "My father is Shaphan," he said, "Josiah's royal secretary before the king died — a scribe, a learned man. He told me of a prophet Micah who prophesied in the days of Hezekiah, saying, *Jerusalem shall become a heap of ruins and the mountain of the holy house a wooded hill.* Did Hezekiah put the prophet to death for that? No, because he feared the Lord! Instead, he begged for mercy, and the Lord repented of the evil he had pronounced. Priests, if you kill this prophet, you will bring that evil upon us now!"

Ahikam's argument prevailed. The leaders believed him, and Jeremiah was not put to death.

vii

In the fourth year of Jehoiakim's reign, Nebuchadnezzar the son of the king of Babylon attacked Neco the king of Egypt at Carchemish on the Euphrates. He struck with power, putting Egypt to flight. He followed Neco south as far as Hamath, where he delivered a second more crushing blow, destroying Egypt's control of territory east of Sinai. Neco went home.

So did Nebuchadnezzar. His father had just died. He went to bury the old king and to establish himself as the king of the Babylonians.

Jehoiakim of Judah smiled. Suddenly he was receiving taxes without having to pay tribute to an overlord.

So the king announced a building program. He spent the tax money for materials, but labor he got for free. He commanded the citizens of his kingdom to work for him. They began to rebuild the old palace of Solomon. They refurbished the chambers of the king.

At the same time the prophet Jeremiah also worked outside the palace, heaping new stones into a pile, stones powder-white from the workman's chisel. Then he climbed his little hill and cried from the top of it:

> Woe to him who builds his house by sinfulness,
>   his upper rooms by a cruel injustice,
> who makes his neighbor serve
>   and does not pay a wage!
>
> Your father ate and drank and practiced justice!
>   He judged the cause of the poor and the needy,
>   and it was well with him!
> But you have eyes for greed
>   and teeth for gain,
>   a fist of violence,
>   and a hand of heavy oppression!

Jehoiakim in his palace commanded his servants to close the windows, but they couldn't. The windows had only just been cut into the new walls.

And the prophet cried: "Thus says the Lord concerning Jehoiakim:

They shall not lament for him,
but with the burial of an ass shall he be buried!
Dragged and cast out of the gates of Jerusalem!''

From that time forward Jeremiah was forbidden to enter the courts of the temple or ever to approach the royal house again.

viii

In the fifth year of Jehoiakim, Nebuchadnezzar returned to the coast of the Great Sea with a massive force. He destroyed the Philistine city of Ashkelon and, like the Assyrians before him, deported its citizens.

In the winter of that year, the people of Jerusalem and Judah proclaimed a fast, and on the coldest day they gathered at the temple of the Lord.

While they were preparing for prayer, a small man climbed to the roof of a storeroom in the inner court, a man bent and studious. He lifted an open scroll before his eyes and began to read. As he read, one of the king's officials recognized the words. He had heard them before, and he knew who had spoken them. He rushed to the house of the king, to the rooms of the royal secretary, and said, "Baruch the son of Neriah is reading to the people from a scroll. The words are the words of the prophet Jeremiah!"

Immediately the royal secretary ordered the small man to come to his chambers. So Baruch came in both shy and afraid.

"Who wrote these words?" the secretary asked.

Baruch said, "I did."

"How did you come to write them?"

"Jeremiah told me to."

"Why?"

"Because Jeremiah cannot come to the house of the Lord, but the Lord still wants his prophet's words to be heard in that place. So he sent me."

"Tell us," said the secretary, "how did you write all these words?"

"Jeremiah spoke, and I wrote his words with ink on the scroll."

The secretary gazed kindly on the small shy man, then he said, "Leave the scroll with me. The king will have to hear it. But you and Jeremiah, go and hide and let no one know where you are."

Baruch vanished.

The secretary then gave the scroll to a man named Jehudi and sent him to a room in the palace where the king sat warming himself. Incense filled the air. A fire burned in the brazier before Jehoiakim. Jehudi said, "I have been sent to read to you from this scroll."

The king frowned, but he said, "Go ahead. Read."

Jehudi read: The Lord says,

> *Warn the nations,*
> *they are coming!*
> *Besiegers from the north ride against Judah,*
> *because she has rebelled against me.*

> *Your ways and your doings,*
> *have brought this upon you!*
> *This is your doom! It is bitter!*
> *It pierces your very heart —* "

Jehudi had not read more than three or four columns when King Jehoiakim leaped from his seat, seized the scroll and a knife, cut off the part that had just been read, and threw it into the fire.

He handed the scroll back to Jehudi, who was stunned and silent. "Go on! Go on!" said the king. "What else does the braying fool have to say?"

Shaking, now, Jehudi read:

Amend your ways, and I will let you dwell in this place. Do not trust in these deceptive words: THIS IS THE TEMPLE OF THE LORD, THE TEMPLE OF THE LORD, THE TEMPLE OF THE LORD!

Again Jehoiakim leaped forward, cut off the words that had been read, threw them into the fire, and commanded Jehudi to read on.

So one read and the other burned the words of Jeremiah, until they had all been burned to ash.

"There," said the king. "The prophet's words have warmed me. Now they are consumed. What harm can they do anymore?"

But the word of the Lord came to Jeremiah where he and Baruch were hiding.

Take another scroll. Write on it all the former words. And concerning the king who burned them, add this: His dead body shall be cast out to the heat by day and the frost by night. And I shall bring upon his offspring all the evil that I have pronounced against them, but they would not hear.

ix

For four years Jehoiakim paid tribute to Babylon. But in the fourth year of his subservience, Pharaoh Neco of Egypt had regained enough military might to meet an advance of the Babylonian armies in the deserts south of Judah. A tremendous battle between the empires was engaged. It made the grey desert a field of bloody mud and flesh. There were heavy losses on both sides, but Neco stopped Nebuchadnezzar — and Jehoiakim, when he heard that Babylon had revealed some vulnerability, chose then to rebel. He withheld his tribute from Nebuchadnezzar and wrote Neco letters of smiling alliance.

▮‖

Jeremiah felt as old as he looked. His stomach hurt continually. It refused most foods tougher or sharper than a porridge of boiled barley grain. For that reason he took no pleasure in eating and he never could put flesh on his bones. He was skeletal and nervous and sleepless — and he hated his condition.

More than that, Jeremiah hated his office. He would rather have been a priest like his father, or a shopkeeper like the brothers who had disowned him long ago.

But God had set prophecy within him like an interior fire. Its furnace was his stomach, its flue his eyes and all his senses. He couldn't strip himself of the office as if it were a clothing. Prophecy was in him night and day. Prophecy caused him to despise unrighteousness and to cry aloud his despising. But he loved the people whom he blamed, so prophecy caused him agonies on their behalf. Prophecy tore him in two, and he hated it.

At forty-seven Jeremiah was as exhausted as a man of sixty-seven. Yet all the cords within him were drawn so tight that when Nebuchadnezzar laughed in Babylon, the prophet was bruised in Jerusalem.

The Lord said to Jeremiah, *Go out and buy a potter's flask, an expensive vessel with a neck so slender it could never be mended if it breaks.*

Jeremiah said, "I am tired. I am so tired, O Lord, of knowing and not knowing — knowing so much of the dangers of my people, yet never knowing enough. Why should I buy a potter's flask?"

Buy it, said the Lord, *then gather some elders and some priests and take them out to the Potsherd Gate above the valley of the Son of Hinnom.*

When Jeremiah moved, his joints ached. Now, walking with an erratic rhythm, he went to the potter's house and interrupted the artisan at his wheel. He purchased a delicate decanter, then went out to find Ahikam the son of Shaphan, a man who had shown him kindness ever since he had been arrested in the temple gate.

Kindness: Ahikam steadfastly gave Jeremiah kindness, reverence, honor — but not love. Not comfort. The prophet was denied such gentle human consolations, for the Lord had commanded him never to marry, never to have sons or daughters.

With Ahikam, now, Jeremiah gathered priests and elders and led them to the Potsherd Gate at the southeast corner of the city.

There the Lord spoke, increasing the fire in Jeremiah's bowels and causing him to sigh.

But no one heard the sighing. God spoke in Jeremiah's voice:

I am bringing such evil on this place that the ears of those who hear it will tingle. Because the people have forsaken me, this place shall be called the valley of Slaughter, for they will fall here by the sword of their enemies. I will make the city a horror, a thing to be hissed at —

Jeremiah drew back his hand and hurled the potter's flask down into the valley, where it shattered.

And the Lord said:

Exactly so will I break this people and this city, that it may never be mended again!

One of the priests, a man named Pashur, spat on the ground at Jeremiah's feet. "This is why we left our sacred duties," he sneered, "to hear you curse Jerusalem? Cursings work, Jeremiah. Cursings work, you foul-tempered destroyer of every good thing. Why don't you throw yourself down into the valley of Hinnom and die?"

Pashur, the chief officer of the temple, scowled and stalked away. The other priests went with him.

Even Ahikam was troubled by the prophecy. "I love the city," he said.

Jeremiah said, "I do, too. Ahikam, I love Jerusalem with all my heart. That's the horror of the prophecy."

But Ahikam could only shake his head in sad confusion and leave Jeremiah alone in the Potsherd Gate.

The Lord said, *Follow those priests. Follow them right up to the temple.*

Jeremiah said, "O Lord, let it be. I have never lent nor borrowed nor defaulted nor begged, yet everyone in the land curses me. Let it be, O Lord."

Stand in the court of my house, the Lord said, *and prophesy!*

Slowly Jeremiah limped up the temple Mount. He entered the inner court where pilgrims were slaughtering beasts for sacrifice and priests were carrying the offering to the altar and smoke was ascending from the broiling meat to heaven.

And through the prophet's piping voice, the Lord, the God of Israel, declared:

Behold, I am bringing upon this city the evil I have pronounced against it, because you've stiffened your neck, refusing to hear my words —

"Enough of cursings!" someone bellowed. "Enough of your wretched cursings, you vulture!"

Jeremiah looked and saw Pashur the priest running at him, with purple rage. He himself, he didn't run. He stood still in the courtyard, mute and sad, until Pashur closed the distance and delivered an astounding blow to Jeremiah's chest — a hit so hard his heart stopped and his vision went red and buzzing filled his ears. Through a pink haze he saw Pashur's fist draw back and then drive forward, into his forehead. His head snapped back. He opened his mouth hugely, trying to suck air into his lungs, but he was falling now. His knees had surrendered. As he went down he noted distinctly each punch he received: his throat, his shoulder, his back, his back — but then he had passed into unconsciousness.

Jeremiah awoke at dusk, unable to move his body. He was in a sitting position, yet hanging backward as if he had been trying to lie down. His arms were drawn out before him, his legs widely separated. Wind blew through his hair. The voices of many people surrounded him. And laughter.

Slowly he realized that he was locked in public stocks. He sat forward in order to ease his wrists, then pressed his forehead against the rough wood between them.

Dusk. The night descended. The people left for their houses. Jeremiah was in the north gate of the temple, bowed and alone. Stars dusted the entire sky, and he hated them. Someone passed behind him singing a cheerful song, and he hated it.

His body was a mass of bruises. His bones felt broken.

"Cursed be the day on which I was born," Jeremiah said, rocking and bumping his skull against the wooden frame of the stocks. "Cursed be the man who announced my birth. Curse him because he did not kill me in the womb."

Frail Jeremiah, his stomach eaten by his angers and his passions, now raised his face to heaven and cried out: "O Lord, you have deceived me and I was deceived!" His voice echoed in the empty courts of the temple. "You are stronger than I am!" he shouted. "You have prevailed. I never did sit with merrymakers. I always sit alone because your hand is upon me — but now my pain is unceasing, O Lord God! Why was I born? For toil and sorrow and mortal shame?"

Jeremiah was shaking his stocks so violently that his wrists were torn and began to bleed. "You, Lord," he screamed. He was beside himself. "You are to me like a deceitful stream in the desert, all dried up when I am dying for water!"

But the Lord said, *If you return, I will restore you and you will stand before me — if you utter what is precious and not what is worthless.*

The next day when Pashur came to release Jeremiah from the stocks, the prophet said to him, "The Lord no longer calls you Pashur, but Terror On Every Side, because he plans to make you a terror to yourself and to all your friends. And this, sir, is what the Lord says:

I will give all Judah into the hand of the king of Babylon. He shall carry them captive to Babylon and slay them with the sword. And you, Pashur, will go into captivity, and there you shall die, and there you shall be buried, you and all to whom you have prophesied falsely."

So said the Lord. So said Jeremiah, whose stomach was not relieved by that saying nor by any other — an aging, dyspeptic man at forty-seven.

∎

In the second year after Jehoiakim withheld tribute from Babylon, Nebuchadnezzar appeared in the north with troops and chariots as countless as the locusts.

He swarmed south toward Jerusalem, consuming cities as he came. It was the winter of the year. It snowed in Jerusalem. One morning the people awoke to a dazzling whiteness, cold air, a perfect calm, and a king as still as a monument. Someone had killed him and left his body lying outside the gate, face up, frozen, pale, and dusted with snow. The oil in his beautiful beard also had frozen.

Egypt did not leave its borders or try to help the kingdom of Judah. Where Nebuchadnezzar marched he caused a black route in white snow. Soon the armies of Babylon drew the black route around Jerusalem like a noose, and then they sat down and ate and waited.

Desperately the people anointed Jehoiachin, son of Jehoiakim, king of Judah — though no one could go out to tell the nation that it had a new king, because the city was surrounded and under siege.

And Jeremiah the prophet sang a song for the sake of the people.

His voice was neither harsh nor whining. He stood in the cold, in the Sheep Gate, singing as if it were a lullaby.

> *Hear and give ear.*
> *Be not proud.*
> *For the Lord has spoken.*

> *Give glory to the Lord,*
> *before he brings the darkness,*
> *and your two feet stumble*
> *on the twilight mountains.*

> *But if you will not listen*
> *my soul will weep in secret for your pride;*
> *my eyes will weep bitterly,*
> *running with tears*
> *because the Lord's flock*
> *has been taken captive.*

Three months later the spring arrived and the rains came down and the earth was prepared for planting. But there was no planting that year.

Jerusalem surrendered to Nebuchadnezzar.

The young king Jehoiachin was carried away to Babylon. So, too, were many high officials and the leading citizens of the kingdom. Ahikam the son of Shaphan found Jeremiah sitting on the ground in the Fish Gate. All bone: the prophet was but bone and gristle. Ahikam knelt down before him and said, "I have come to say good-bye."

"Good-bye."

"Perhaps we will see each other soon?"

"No," said Jeremiah. "We will never see each other again."

Ahikam looked sad. "Never?"

"Never. It is the Lord's desire that I stay in the dying city. But I will write to you."

Nebuchadnezzar's troops took all the treasures of the temple and the wealth of the king's house. They cut in pieces the golden vessels. They led ten thousand people captive, craftsmen, smiths, soldiers, priests, high officers.

Only those who worked the land were left. They stood by the roadside and watched the long departure.

Nebuchadnezzar appointed a governor to oversee this new province of his empire: Zedekiah, twenty-one years old, an uncle to Jehoiachin, the last son of good King Josiah. The City of David was empty now. But its walls were still standing. Jerusalem had that much: walls and streets and roofs and buildings — and the temple of the Lord. The temple was left.

X

Four years passed, during which Nebuchadnezzar did not come west. In four years the little kingdoms persuaded themselves that they were large again, and they gathered in Jerusalem to talk with Zedekiah about rebellion.

Envoys from the kings of Edom and Moab and Ammon and Tyre and Sidon met in the great room of House of the Forest of Lebanon, now echoing with emptiness. Suddenly the door flew open. Sunlight cut into the room, and in the midst of the light stood the prophet Jeremiah, encumbered by a heavy apparatus. Where the prophet went, there was the Lord. And now, to the nations the Lord said:

It is I who made the earth with its people and beasts, and I give it to whomever I please. I have given these lands to Nebuchadnezzar, my servant —

What was this thing hanging from the neck and shoulders of the prophet?

Why, it was a wooden yoke! The yoke-bar of an ox! And leather thongs slung low in front of him, as if Jeremiah had the great throat of a mighty ox. But the man was bone and loose flesh, a shining neck and a great round skull. He could scarcely carry the bar across his shoulders.

But the Lord said:

All the nations must serve Nebuchadnezzar! If any nation will not put its neck under the yoke of the king of Babylon, I will punish that nation with the sword, with famine, and with pestilence!

Just as he came, so the prophet departed. He shut the door behind himself, and the envoys of the nations sat staring at Zedekiah.

"Is he a prophet?" they said.

Zedekiah said, "Yes, but there are other prophets who say other things. Hananiah says that the Lord will never forget his covenant with David, that the Lord will save the City of David."

"Which prophet speaks the truth?"

"I don't know," said King Zedekiah. "I don't know."

xi

Jeremiah wrote a letter to Ahikam and to all the exiles with him.

"Build a house in Babylon," he wrote. "Plant gardens. Take wives, have sons and daughters, and let them marry, too. Seek the welfare of the city where you are. Pray to the Lord on its behalf, for in its welfare is your own.

"For thus says the God of Israel:

Do not let your prophets and your diviners deceive you.

When seventy years are completed for Babylon, I will visit you again and fulfill my promise and bring you back to this place.

For I know the plans I have for you, plans for welfare and not for evil, to give you a future and a hope."

xii

In the ninth year of Zedekiah's governance, Ammon and Judah joined together and withheld tribute from Babylon. As had so many of their predecessors, they hoped for help from Egypt. Nebuchadnezzar marched his armies to Judah. They came and laid siege to Jerusalem.

The siege began in the tenth month of the year, on the tenth day of the month. It was winter and very cold.

Jeremiah was fifty-eight. All his ribs stood out. They could be counted.

Then the Babylonians heard that the Egyptians were, indeed, advancing.

So they lifted the siege and marched to meet them.

In those days Jeremiah attempted to travel to his hometown, Anathoth. But as he walked through the Benjamin Gate, a guard stopped him, struck him, and brought him to the officials of Judah, saying, "Here is a deserter."

"No!" Jeremiah said, "I was only going to Anathoth."

"Why?" the officials asked.

"To buy a piece of property."

"Property in the time of disaster? Your own words condemn you, prophet. You are no patriot, and you do not love Jerusalem."

Jeremiah was beaten and then thrown into prison.

The Egyptians were no enemy. As soon as Babylon massed with force before them, they broke and ran. In two weeks, then, the Babylonian armies were back at Jerusalem, and the city was again surrounded. Secretly Zedekiah sent for Jeremiah.

The prophet was brought into his private chambers, shivering from cold and scabrous from his beating.

Zedekiah said, "Is there any word from the Lord?"

Jeremiah said, "There is."

Zedekiah bowed his head. "I didn't want this," he said. "This was not my choice. I was overruled." Then softly he whispered, "What does the Lord say?"

"That you shall be delivered into the hand of the king of Babylon. That is what the Lord says."

"No, I never wanted this."

"Sir," said Jeremiah, "if you send me back to prison, I will die."

Zedekiah gazed at the prophet a moment, and then said, "Stay in the court of the guard. I will send you a loaf of bread a day."

xiii

In the eleventh year of Zedekiah, in the fourth month, the ninth day of the month, the walls of Jerusalem broke and fell, and the armies of Babylon entered the city in triumph. That night Zedekiah escaped, and with a handful of soldiers rode at breakneck speeds northeast to the Jordan. Early the following morning the princes of the king of Babylon dispatched their swiftest chariots after him, while they themselves sat in the middle gate of the city with their officers and servants, waiting. In the afternoon Zedekiah was brought back to the city, bound, guarded, and walking. He was barefoot.

The princes of Babylon scarcely acknowledged the presence of Judah's last ruler. He was a criminal and a duty. They rose up, stepped into their magnificent chariots, and in a long procession led the defeated Judean away.

Again, Zedekiah was walking. All officials of Judah were walking. So were Zedekiah's children, every one barefoot, walking behind the grandeur of Babylon.

> *My eyes are spent with weeping;*
> *my soul trembles;*
> *my heart is poured out in grief*
> *because of the destruction*
> *of the daughter of my people.*

This miserable cortège was led to Riblah in Syria, to Nebuchadnezzar's western headquarters. There they ate a substantial meal. They slept in beds made of cedar. In the morning they were bathed by Babylonian servants, oiled and combed and scented, dressed in linen from Damascus, then led before the king of Babylon himself. Without passion, Nebuchadnezzar pronounced sentence upon Zedekiah of Judah. Then he tapped a table with the tip of his sword, indicating that the punishment should be carried out immediately.

Zedekiah's hands were bound behind his back. He was placed on stone steps five feet high and forced to look down into a small yard. Soldiers brought his eldest son into the yard, handsome, groomed, appareled in purple as befits a prince. They commanded the lad to kneel and to bow his forehead to the earth. Then, with a tremendous ax, they cut off his head.

Zedekiah moaned. But guards on either side of him forced him still to watch while his second son was beheaded, his third, all his sons. It took two hours.

When the last child lay dead, Zedekiah's guards grabbed his hair, yanked back his head, and pierced his weeping eyes with daggers. This, too, was part of the sentence, that the dying of his children should be the last sight Zedekiah ever saw.

When Jehoiachin had gone into exile ten years earlier, Babylon received him as the king of a defeated nation. He was given a royal attention as long as he lived. But now there was no nation left. Judah had ceased to exist. And on this very day, Jerusalem was in flames. Blind Zedekiah went to Babylon, then, as a criminal. He was not executed. He lived out his natural life in the small, sad communities of Jewish exiles. But for the rest of his days he wished that he had been killed with his children.

xiv

Nebuzaradan is in Jerusalem. The commander of Nebuchadnezzar's guard has come from Riblah with a horde of soldiers and with orders to put the city to the torch.

Another lesser order of the Babylonian king was that Jeremiah the son of Hilkiah should be shown special consideration. Therefore, before the destruction begins, Jeremiah is released from confinement. He is set free. But now the prophet of God is suffering a torment worse than imprisonment.

The city that he loves with all his heart, the city is in flames. Solomon's palace is a high black fire, a bitter smoke. The ancient wooden pillars in the House of the Forest of Lebanon, hard and dry, are burning like candles. The ceiling sags; the beams crack and break; in the roaring of a thousand winds, the roof comes down. Sparks and a foul air rush over Jeremiah. He lowers his head and walks the streets of Jerusalem, weeping. The throne hall is laid naked to the sky. Babylon is cutting the great throne of Solomon into pieces, dumping the gold and the ivory into sacks. The lions that once mounted six steps to the king's seat are carried out and stacked on carts.

Jeremiah wanders to the north side of the city and climbs the ancient stone steps in the Tower of the Hundred. He looks down on Jerusalem without surprise. This is what he said would be.

The temple of the Lord is burning. Its cedars are in flames. Panels and beams and the beautiful roof are all on fire. The sacred furniture has been heaped together in front of the porch. It is burning with a holy fury. Enormous flames go up like sheets in the wind, higher than the prophet in his tower, twisting and reaching like hands into heaven. Jeremiah can feel the heat on his face.

> My eyes are spent with weeping;
>   my soul trembles;
> my heart is poured out in grief
>   because of the destruction
> of the daughter of my people.

Everywhere in Jerusalem Babylonian troops accomplish their business without expression. There is no vengeance here, neither anger nor pleasure. It is only duties. What is valuable, take. What cannot be taken, burn. What cannot be burned, destroy: tear it up or tear it down.

Jeremiah looks at the road that leads north from the Sheep Gate. As far as he can see, it is lined with carts filled and waiting to go. He knows what they carry: Jachin and Boaz, the bronze pillars that stood for three hundred and sixty-five years on either side of the temple door. This morning he watched the soldiers cut them to pieces — together with the candle stands and the great bronze laver of the courtyard. Metal of the highest quality is the cargo in Babylonian carts. Also pots and shovels and snuffers and dishes for incense, the firepans and the bowls, every treasure of the temple, every holy thing, every dear and godly thing, it is all packed in the long caravan bound for Babylon. And the temple itself is pouring forth a vomit of smoke and flame, the temple of the Lord, the temple of the Lord.

"Hey, you! You want to die? Get down from there!"

Look: the rich houses on Zion are burning. A lazy wind is taking the cloud of the city's destruction eastward. Hot stones explode. Listen: here and there, with a dull cracking and the horrible thump of grounded thunder, a building collapses.

"You! Climb down now, or you'll fall with the stones!"

Jeremiah slowly becomes conscious of himself, a sudden pain on his skullbone, heat in his face, his arms wrapped under his stomach. Old man, old man, he should be dying with the city.

There's a soldier in the road below, throwing pebbles at the prophet. One has struck his skull. Jeremiah looks down, now, and the soldier points west toward the Fish Gate. "Can't you see what's coming?" he yells.

Both posts of the Fish Gate have snapped like sticks. They have pitched forward into a dusty rubble. With battering rams and ropes the Babylonians are tearing down the walls of Jerusalem. Yes. Jeremiah feels the concussions in the Tower of the Hundred, yes. He nods to the soldier below. Yes, he's coming down now. Yes.

So the prophet descends and wanders out of Jerusalem. He walks to the Mount of Olives, east of the city. He sits down in a midday darkness, for a billowing smoke blackens the sky above him. There is no sun. There is no City of David.

Is it nothing to you, all you who pass by?
Behold and see
if there be any sorrow like unto my sorrow,
wherewith the Lord has afflicted me
in the day of his fierce anger.

XV

Although every significant citizen of Judah had been deported to villages south of Babylon, Jeremiah wanted to stay in Judah, even in the dead land of his people. He was sixty years old. He was sick unto death. But it seemed to him that his word would serve the poor farmers left behind.

Nevertheless, a group of willful Judeans demanded the prophet's prayers for themselves. They forced Jeremiah to go with them into Egypt. His scribe, Baruch, was also carried away. The prophet's hair was as white as snow. His eyes still were huge, haunted by all they had seen. Under the skin his body seemed all tendon, bone, and gristle. The Egyptians did not understand how one so desiccated could still keep life within his breast.

But yet once more the word of the Lord came to Jeremiah, and he called Baruch to his side.

"I have heard a new thing," he whispered. "Mix your ink. Find a clean scroll. Cut a strong reed pen, Baruch, and write this — for the Lord has commanded that it should be written."

Baruch prepared his instruments and sat once more at his master's side.

Then, in Egypt, Jeremiah dictated words for the sake of the remnant in Babylon:

The days are coming when I will restore the fortunes of my people, Israel and Judah. I will bring them back to the land which I gave their fathers.

Behold, the days are coming when I will make a new covenant with my people, not like the covenant which I made with their fathers when I took them from Egypt — my covenant which they broke, though I was their husband.

This covenant I will put within them. I will write its law upon their hearts, and I will be their God, and they shall be my people. No longer shall each one teach another, saying, "Know the Lord," for they shall all know me, from the least to the greatest. For I will forgive their iniquity, and I will remember their sin no more.

So said the Lord to Jeremiah. Jeremiah dictated it to Baruch, who wrote it on a scroll, and the scroll was preserved.

Jeremiah died in Egypt.

But the promise of the Lord survived.

PART SIX

Letters
from Exile

23

AHIKAM UTTERS
A CURSE

From Ahikam son of Shaphan to the prophet of God, Jeremiah son of Hilkiah: All peace!

My father, it is said that you are in Egypt. Tomorrow a trade caravan will set out for that country; tonight, therefore, I write with the great hope that my letter will find you, and that you are well. Jeremiah, after so many years of misery, be well!

I am directing my letter to Tahpanhes. I have heard that a small colony of Judeans lives there. Perhaps you are among them.

▌

Let me tell you how angry and how sad I am.

Every day I walk from tiny Tel-abib into the flat green countryside. It is ten years since I have been home, yet every day my eyes rise up to see the hills of Judah! I cannot convince them that they will not see the hills at all. They look for the hard brown high and rocky land. My ears listen for the roaring gorges of the rainy season — but all I see are the airy blue spaces and too much green on flat ground.

Yesterday as I walked out alone, I heard a sad sound in the distance: men's deep voices singing slowly, *Ahh! Ahhhhh!* Oh, what a weary melody! They were Jews. They were my brothers. I walked toward the sound until I saw them gathered in a grove of willow trees, and then I was singing too — and by the time I drew near to them, I was weeping.

So then were ten men standing on the bank of the little Chebar canal, all with our heads down, singing a low song, *Ahh! Ahhh.* One man played lightly on a lyre. We were all weeping.

O God, remember Zion! Remember the mountain that has been your dwelling place —

370 | THE BOOK OF GOD

But there is only ruin in Jerusalem! I thought of the temple and I wept. I thought of my great distance from the holy hill of the Lord, and I wept.

Then through the trees behind us came a group of Babylonian guards, all armed.

"Sing a happy song!" they shouted in their own tongue.

Immediately, the man who had been playing his lyre stopped and, without once looking at the foreign soldiers, hung it on a branch of a willow tree. Silently, he sat down. We all sat down.

"Get up!" cried our captors, boisterous, enjoying themselves. "Get up and sing a cheerful song, something your mother sang when she was happy!"

One fellow put his hand on my shoulder and said, "You, Ahikam — you have a good voice. Sing to your God."

In his language I said, "How can I sing the Lord's song in a foreign land?"

Without removing his hand from my shoulder, he produced a small dagger, as narrow as an adder, and laid it across my nose.

So I sang. I sang in the priest's Hebrew so that only my brothers understood. I chose a tender melody, letting the Babylonians think that mindless slaves need only sing a little song to be happy again.

I sang:

> *Daughter of Babylon, you destroyer!*
> *Blessed be the man*
> *who takes your children one by one,*
> *smiling infants, lads and lasses,*
> *and dashes their skulls against the stones!*

When I sang that song I didn't weep anymore.

■

O my father, Jeremiah, if you receive this letter, please send me a word regarding your health. I long to hear from you. Send your letter where you sent the last one: Tel-abib near the Chebar.

Surely God is with you, prophet!

24

AHIKAM MUST MAKE A DECISION

From Ahikam son of Shaphan to Jeremiah son of Hilkiah:

Man of God, forgive me: I need your wisdom now. I am unable to choose between two ways of life — and who else can I write to, if not to you?

You are old, eighty-five, by my calculation, and likely you are very tired. Your voice has been silent ever since Baruch sent many of us your prophecy from Egypt, the little book of comfort, the promise of a new covenant. That was fifteen years ago.

But no one has told us that you are dead yet.

And one reason for my bewilderment is that a new prophet has arisen here, in this country, whose word is very hopeful. He says that our warfare is ended, that we are pardoned. "Comfort!" he cries. "Comfort my people, says your God!"

This prophet declares that God is coming to save us and to take us home again: "Prepare the way of the Lord," he says. "Make a straight highway in the desert for our God."

What do you think of such prophecy? Should I trust it? Should I give over my way of life here, and prepare to go home again? But right now my son has been offered an excellent position, a livelihood infinitely better than our past poverty. Either we commit our lives to this place completely, or we believe the prophet and turn our faces west. It can't be both. But if the prophet is wrong, it will destroy my family.

Let me explain.

When we first arrived in Tel-abib, I farmed a small plot next to that of a man named Murashu. For fifteen years our families shared the labor, tilling, planting, harvesting.

Then Murashu moved to a city named Nippur on the Euphrates River — about fifty miles south of Babylon. There a Babylonian officer happened to notice his daughter while she was standing alone in a field. Murashu's daughter is very beautiful. The officer longed to have her.

So he went to Murashu and said, "Sell me your daughter as a slave for me."

Murashu himself is a shrewd man. I would have shown wrath at such a request, but he rubbed his chin and said, "She is a delicate child, sir. Slavery would kill her."

The officer, sick with love, said, "Then let me take her as my wife!"

Murashu began to weep. "I wish I could honor your desire, but I love my daughter too much to part with her."

The officer rushed away and came back leading a camel. "Will you take this as a dowry?" he asked.

Murashu only wept louder and louder.

The Babylonian officer rushed away and brought three camels, four camels.

Murashu let out a wail of anguish. "Sir," he cried, "my daughter means more than life to me."

But when the Babylonian led a full caravan of twenty-five camels to Murashu's little house, the father dried his eyes and became a father-in-law. He also went into business for himself, and now my old friend is very rich.

He owns seven caravans, five storehouses, three barns, and a house of twelve rooms, with two open courtyards and a fountain in each court.

Murashu no longer prays to the Lord, the God of Israel. He worships Marduk. He says that the Lord seemed glorious on earth only because we had never seen the whole earth — but one day while he was in the city of Babylon, a priest offered to show him the temple where Marduk dwells: Esagila. They passed through court after court, each one grander than the last, until they came to the most interior room.

"This," said the priest, "is Ekua."

My friend stood dumbstruck.

On a dais sat a massive image of Marduk. Above, the roof beams were covered with gold and silver. The walls were sheathed in shining gold. And the great statue of Marduk, the throne on which he sat, the dais itself and the offering table in front of it were all cast in the purest gold. Murashu estimates that there were more than eight hundred talents of precious metal in the room called Ekua.

My family remains miserable in poverty. My wife has begun to cough blood.

Yesterday Murashu came to Tel-abib and asked whether I would permit my eldest son to supervise one of his caravans. It is, he says, a transaction between old friends. My son, at ease in four languages, wants me to accept. His wife, my daughter-in-law, begs me to accept. We would all move to Nippur and live in big houses.

What shall I do? You yourself once wrote that we should make peace with the place where we are. You said that we should seek the welfare of the city where God has exiled us, since in its welfare we would find our own.

Does that advice apply still today?

Well, you must have heard in Egypt that the Babylonian Empire is growing weak. Nebuchadnezzar died ten years ago. The present king is despised by his subjects.

Should we commit our ways to this place, where my son will surely live in luxury and where he may be persuaded by his benefactor to worship Marduk?

Or should we believe the new prophet?

But the prophet's word is hard to accept. He says that in order to redeem his people, the Lord is anointing a Persian, Cyrus the king of Anshan — a pagan!

I have always believed that the anointed one of God must be a son of David. Is the Lord God changing? Can this prophet speak the truth? Will Babylon fall to Cyrus?

O my father, in whom should I put my faith?

I am confused. This misery is worse than poverty. My wife spits blood when she coughs. I — I bleed in my soul.

Are you living, Jeremiah? Will you answer?

Murashu's caravan leaves for Egypt in a week. I am sending with that caravan both this letter and my son. Perhaps he will see you face-to-face in Tahpanhes. Perhaps you will disclose to him the will of the Lord as once you did to me.

Perhaps you will send back with him a word also for me?

All peace, prophet of God!

25

AHIKAM IN JERUSALEM

There is nearly no joy in homecoming.

As soon as we arrived, dry and weary, a priest named Jeshua son of Jozadak built an altar according to the law of Moses, and we sacrificed in thanksgiving. We initiated all over again the burnt offerings morning and evening. We began to keep the appointed feasts of the Lord.

But Jerusalem is desolate and unpopulated. Weeds have cracked the beautiful pavement. And where the temple used to be, wind travels unobstructed. People dragged its old stone away for their own purposes.

So we began to quarry more stone to build a foundation for a new temple. Stonemasons dressed the great blocks and carved them on the temple site itself, fitting them into place.

We have not been able to pay our workers anything besides food and drink and oil. Two years have passed with little rainfall. Our crops failed.

And then the foundation was complete. Priests in vestments led us there, in order to dedicate it. They blew trumpets as they processed. Levites followed with cymbals, praising the Lord: "For he is good, for his steadfast love," they sang, "endures forever toward Israel."

And then when we approached the new foundation, a great shout went up — all the young men crying out in gratitude and joy. My own son raised his hands among the others of his generation: a forest of arms.

But I wept. We wept. The people of my generation wept when we saw this foundation; for we remembered the glory of the old temple. This is a plaything next to that.

So loud was our sorrow, that people at a distance could not distinguish the sound of the joyful shout from that of grieving.

∎

My father, Jeremiah, prophet of God: you will not receive this letter. I will not send it. But the bare writing comforts me. I see you when I write to you.

But you see nothing.

You have neither seen nor received my letters for a long time. When my son traveled by caravan to Egypt, he found your servant Baruch in Tahpanhes, but not you. Your bones already lay beneath Egyptian sand, where our father Joseph lay for hundreds of years before the Lord called us out of slavery.

And now the Lord has called us home again.

The prophet was right. King Cyrus of Persia defeated every kingdom east and west, producing an empire greater than any before him. Then he decreed that the Jews were free to return to Judah. When that decree was announced in Tel-abib, my son came into my small room and knelt beside me and wept. We trembled with joy that we had lived long enough to see Jerusalem again.

My son did not accept the offer of my old friend Murashu. His mother, my wife, died suddenly of a bloody hemorrhage, and the sadness drew us close together. In fact, sadness and suffering have drawn us closer to the Lord as well, because the prophet who spoke of comfort also understood sorrow.

The Lord said, *Fear not, for I have redeemed you. I have called you by name. You are mine. When you pass through the waters, I will be with you. When you walk through fire, you shall not be burned. For I am the Lord your God, the Holy One of Israel, your Savior. Because you are precious in my eyes and honored, and I love you.*

We believed the prophet. We trusted in the Lord.

Now we are home.

I have shown my son the grave where his grandfather Shaphan is buried. It is there that I wish also to be buried.

Very soon, Jeremiah, prophet of God: two or three days at the most. In three days I will follow you down to darkness.

God be gracious to the handful of Jews who must now re-build a temple, a city, a life.

PART SEVEN

The
Yearning

26

MY MESSENGER

i

I have loved you, says the Lord.

The people answer, "How have you loved us?"

Is not Esau Jacob's brother? says the Lord. And I have chosen Jacob. I have loved Jacob. Yet you, priests! You despise my name!

The priests who serve in Jerusalem say, "How have we despised your name?"

By offering polluted food on my altar!

"How have we polluted it?"

By your hearts! You offer blind animals. You sacrifice the sick and the lame to me. Oh, that there were one among you who would shut the door of the temple to keep the rest from kindling fire upon my altar in vain!

ii

There is a temple in Jerusalem again. There's also a priesthood and some measure of sacrifice — but very little holiness.

After the foundation had been laid with shouts both of joy and of sorrow, famine and poverty depleted the people of strength. They were miserable and few, and life was so difficult that no work could proceed on the temple itself. For twenty years the Jews merely existed.

David's ancient kingdom was carved into a small province within the greater Persian realm. Jerusalem was but a minor city in that province, governed from Samaria by a Samaritan. Jews suffered at the hands of those who did not love them.

Then the Persian king Darius granted permission for building the temple again. It took five long years, and when it was finished the sacred building was small and unbeautiful, but functional.

Years passed. Only in small groups did Jews return from exile to their homeland. Some cleared rubble from the old stone buildings in Tekoa and began to live there again. A few built small houses in Jericho, as well as in the land around Bethel. Jerusalem did not flourish. Its population was poor. The city had no walls nor any new building except the temple. For seventy years Jerusalem remained squalid and discouraged.

But then its citizens took hold and began to rebuild its walls. The Samaritan governor commanded them to stop. They didn't. They redoubled their efforts. So the governor complained to the nobles of the Persian Empire, who sent soldiers into the city with swords and an order from the king himself to desist. They did. The wall remains crumbled and useless, a sign of the spirit of the Jews.

Ten years ago the Edomites were driven from their ancestral land by the Arabs. Now they occupy the good ground around Hebron, just south of Jerusalem. The children of Esau, the brother of Jacob, now are a constant harassment to the children of Jacob. And there is no wall for protection.

The people pray: "Destroy the wise men of Edom!"

But this is almost all they pray. To them it seems that God is gone.

iii

I do not change, children of Jacob, says the Lord. I have loved your father. I love you still. Return to me and I will return to you.

The people say, "How shall we return?"

The Lord answers, *Stop robbing me.*

"How do we rob you?"

In the failure of your tithes to me.

"No, O Lord! It is the rain of heaven that fails us! Enemies trouble us, north and south. We are tired. Times are hard. And in seventy years the promises of the prophets have come to nothing."

Children of Judah, you wonder when I shall fulfill my promises?

"We have seen how evildoers prosper. Where is justice in the land? And where is the God of justice?

If justice is absent, the Lord says, *it is absent from your own hands and hearts.*

Behold, says the Lord of hosts, *I send my messenger to prepare the way before me. But who can endure the day of his coming? For he is like a refiner's fire. He will purify the sons of Levi and refine them like gold and silver until they present right offerings unto me. Then the offering of Judah and Jerusalem will be pleasing to me as in the days of old.*

iv

This morning a man left his house and walked down the crooked streets of Jerusalem to the house of a woman. There, solemnly, he made a covenant with her. Before her father and the Creator, the Father of All, this man promised to be her husband all the days of their lives.

Now they are processing back through the city, his groomsmen, her bridesmaids. There are timbrels and dancing. With joy and a little hope they are returning to the young man's house.

This evening they will celebrate. People will put away their poverty for a while: a little wine. Much food. Dancing and public joking about private matters — and tonight husband and wife will lie down together in their own dark room.

But who can say what will happen tomorrow?

Perhaps she will spoil his dinner. What will the young man do then? In these times he may very well rise up and divorce her. It is not uncommon to break the marriage covenant that easily.

And then he may marry another. Perhaps he will choose a heathen woman. Perhaps a Samaritan, since Samaritans are richer and more powerful in the scheme of things. A single Samaritan dowry can overcome a generation of poverty — and a Samaritan father-in-law is as good as God for mercy.

v

But I am the Lord, says the Lord. I change not. Therefore, children of Jacob, you are not consumed.

The temple in Jerusalem is small, not nearly as glorious as the house that Solomon built five hundred years ago. But the Lord remembers the plain temple, and still he utters his word there. Not through the priests, but to them.

For there is also a messenger in the city. A prophet.

But this age neither honors nor recognizes prophets, and there are almost none left in the world.

Therefore, God's present prophet is anonymous. No one shall recall his name hereafter. He shall be known by his office alone, by the service for which the Lord loves him. By calling him, the Lord God has also named him: My Messenger, which in Hebrew is pronounced, *Malachi*.

vi

The day comes burning like an oven, when all the arrogant, all evildoers will be stubble. The day shall burn them so that neither root nor branch is left.

But for you who fear my name, the sun of righteousness shall rise with healing in its wings. You shall go forth leaping like calves. And you shall tread down the wicked. They shall be ashes under the soles of your feet, on the day when I act, says the Lord of hosts.

27

NEHEMIAH

i

The name of the cupbearer of Artaxerxes I, king of Persia, is Nehemiah the son of Hacaliah. Nehemiah serves the king at his palace in Susa, two hundred miles east of Babylon. He is the king's intimate, both guarding and administering the royal apartments. He rose to such high office not by false arrogance and flattery, but by a talent for pragmatism and a faith in his own convictions.

Nehemiah is a eunuch. As cupbearer, he is completely committed to the king and reliable.

He is also a Jew, a worshiper of the great and terrible God. Nehemiah may have lived his whole life in the capital city of Persia. He may serve the Persian government as righteously as any citizen. Certainly, he is respected by the king of Persia himself. But Nehemiah is not Persian.

This is becoming more and more apparent to the king, because his cupbearer is growing disheveled.

It's spring. The rainy season is over. Artaxerxes has just returned from his winter palace in Babylon, specifically to enjoy the luxuriant flowering of Susa, soft in the mornings, pleasant in green evenings. And now the king has finished a satisfying meal. "Wine," he calls. Artaxerxes is sitting on a private terrace with the queen, Damaspia. When he looks up to greet his cupbearer bringing the wine, he sees a man unkempt and distracted. But Nehemiah has always been fastidious in his personal grooming.

"Nehemiah, what's the matter with you?" the king says. "Are you sick?"

Damaspia also looks up.

"No."

"You didn't wash! Damaspia, our good friend is filthy! Have you ever known him to fail his person or his office before?"

But the queen touches the king's wrist. "Softly," she says, gazing at Nehemiah. "This isn't a trespass. This is sadness of the heart."

Artaxerxes frowns at the cupbearer. "Are you sad, Nehemiah?"

"Yes."

"Why? Damaspia, do you know why he's sad?"

The queen holds her peace. Nehemiah stands still for a moment, then he speaks.

"Let the king live for ever!" he says. "Why shouldn't my face be sad when the city, the place of my fathers' graves, lies waste, its walls broken and its gates burned with fire?"

"You mean Jerusalem?"

"Jerusalem. The City of David. Yes."

"But this isn't news. Jerusalem was destroyed a hundred and thirty years ago. Why does that depress you now?"

All at once the words pour from Nehemiah. He keeps his body erect, neither shaking nor spilling wine. But passion turns his tongue into a sword.

"Three months ago my brother Hanani came from Judah to Susa, and I asked him concerning the Jews still surviving in Jerusalem. He shook his head. My brother seemed almost to collapse. 'Trouble,' he said, 'great trouble and shame.' I questioned him all night long until I heard the whole of it, and I learned that my kin had tried to rebuild the walls of Jerusalem. They are harassed by Edomites and Samaritans and nomads and Arabians. They tried to protect themselves with a wall. A wall, my lord! What city of the least value can exist without a wall? But the governor of Samaria applied to the satrap above him, and that man received orders from your servants here in Susa commanding in your name that the Jews must stop building their wall. So the nobles of Samaria came and broke down the work my brother and my people had done. Broke the dressed stones. Broke the hope of the Jews who live in Jerusalem. Broke them."

Nehemiah closes his mouth and remains rigid for a moment, then steps forward and begins to pour the wine.

Softly, King Artaxerxes says, "Cupbearer, make a request of me."

Nehemiah straightens, glances toward the queen, who nods, then turns his face away and starts to whisper. He is whispering aloud, but in Hebrew. He is rocking slightly back and forth. He is praying.

Then, hawklike, he turns back to the king and says, "If it pleases the king, and if your servant has found favor in your sight, send me to Judah, to the city of my fathers' graves, that I might rebuild it."

"Send you to Judah?" Artaxerxes says. "Where would I get another cupbearer like — " But Queen Damaspia touches the king's wrist again, and he falls silent. Finally, he says, "How long will you be gone? When will you return?"

Nehemiah now speaks with pragmatic calculation. "It will take me four years to gather materials and to get there. Would you, my lord, let letters of safe passage be given me for the governors of the satrap beyond the River? — and a letter to Asaph, the keeper of the king's forest, permitting me to take timber for the beams of the gates and the fortress of the temple, for the wall of the city, and for the house I will occupy?"

The king nods, but tips his head toward the queen. "Evidently, Damaspia, our good friend has given the matter a great deal of thought. Did he know my answer before I did?"

Neither the queen nor the cupbearer speaks.

"And he is aware, of course," says the king, narrowing his eyes, "that he's asking the king of Persia to reverse a regal decree."

Nehemiah's face pales. Artaxerxes sees real fear there, but honors the decorum and the courage of the Jew who does not tremble, but continues stout and straight.

Suddenly the king smiles and leans back in his seat. "Four years to get there, Nehemiah? So how long will you be gone? When will you return?"

Though his face is still fixed in fear, Nehemiah swallows and presses forward. "There is one other request," he says, "that the king designate Judah a province of its own, separate from Samaria, and that he appoint me its first governor. In that case, my lord, I would be gone another twelve years. Sixteen years altogether."

Artaxerxes, king of Persia, almost laughs. "Jew, you are a wonder!" He reaches for his cup of wine, raises it to his lips, closes his eyes, and drinks the entire draught.

"It is a delicious spring, don't you think so, Damaspia?" He takes the queen's hand and lays it against his cheek, then to his cupbearer he says, "Wash your face, Nehemiah. Go. Save your city and govern your province with my blessing."

ii

Nehemiah has been in Jerusalem for three days. On the first day he visited his brother Hanani. On the second he honored the sepulchers of the ancestors. Though he arrived with a Persian retinue over whom he has clear authority, he's told no one what he plans to do for Jerusalem. There is good reason for secrecy and for haste.

Now it is the night of the third day. The moon is full, the air chilly. Nehemiah, wrapped in a woolen robe, has ridden a mule to the ruins of the Valley Gate on the southwestern corner of Jerusalem. There he sits outside the gate above the valley of the Son of Hinnom, gazing at broken stone and old char, murmuring softly to himself. He's calculating the job before him.

Two men walk through the fallen gate and join him. "I looked at the north side when I arrived," Nehemiah says. "We'll begin construction there, with the Sheep Gate westward to the Tower of the Hundred and the Tower of Hananel. Then we'll work in a circle against the sun. But this," Nehemiah sighs into the cold night wind. "This."

He urges the mule eastward on the rough ground outside the city — stones cracked and shaggy with weed, sudden falls of loose rock down into the valley on his right — until the columns of another old gate appear in the moonlight.

Nehemiah stops. "The Potsherd Gate," he whispers. "One hundred and seventy-five years ago the prophet stood here and said, *O kings of Judah, I am bringing such evil upon this place that the ears of every one who hears of it will tingle*. Ah, Jeremiah!"

Nehemiah dismounts and whispers again calculations of weight and materials, workers and times, then moves slowly onward.

It is midnight. Nehemiah has inspected the broken wall from the Potsherd Gate to the Fountain Gate, both burned by fire, and now he sees Gihon. Down below in the Kidron Valley is the spring and the long well-tunnel by which David sent his general Joab up into the city to storm it from within, terrifying the inhabitants, destroying their will in a single maneuver. Nehemiah heaves a deep sigh. So much happened between the young, joyful days of David and the lamentations of the prophet Jeremiah.

But Nehemiah can't continue reminiscing. He has a job to do. Besides, they've come to a point where the Kidron Valley drops straight down. The path disappears. Nehemiah whispers to the men behind him, "Enough," then backs his mule to a broader place and returns the way he came.

iii

Sanballat, governor of the province of Samaria, is furious. He strides through the rooms of his administration, throwing his arms up and shouting.

"It's bad enough that Judah should be snatched from me. I can't dispute the laws of the Medes and the Persians. But I *should* be able to control this lisping fool, this upstart in Jerusalem. What did you say he's gotten the Jews to do?"

Tobiah the Ammonite, a rich man from an old and prominent family, is following the governor from room to room, puffing because of his weight. "They're trying to build the walls of the city."

"How long have they been at it?"

"Three weeks."

"With success?"

"Well, the family of Eliashib the high priest has reconstructed the Sheep Gate. It's already been consecrated — "

"Ohhh!" Sanballat cries.

" — and the sons of Hassenaah have laid the beams of the Fish Gate and set its doors, its bolts, its bars — "

"This is too much!"

"Between the gates, the fortress protecting the north side of the temple is right now being — "

"What's the man's name?"

"Nehemiah."

Sanballat strides down the hall and out of his house, to an open yard where the captains of his troops are waiting. There, too, certain allies have gathered from territories surrounding Judah.

"What are these feeble Jews doing!" Sanballat bellows. "Can anyone estimate? — *will* they be able to restore things? Do they plan only to sacrifice? Will they finish this dream in a day? Will they revive the stones from heaps of rubbish? Can they make a wall of burned materials?"

Tobiah follows Sanballat into the yard, chuckling to himself. "Don't worry, my lord!" he calls. "What they are building — if a fox bumps the new wall, he'll break it down."

The captains laugh.

Sanballat, not laughing, turns to Tobiah. "Did you actually talk with this man Nehemiah?"

"I did," Tobiah says. "Geshem the Arab and I went together to Jerusalem. We met Nehemiah in a dirty marketplace. A beardless fellow. Scented and coiffed like a courtier. We said, 'What is this thing you're doing? Are you rebelling against the king?' He answered with religious haughtiness: 'God will make us prosper, but you have no portion in Jerusalem.' I started to laugh. I couldn't help it. The stinking marketplace, this Persian Jewish foppish eunuch surrounded by grim citizens of no country. Oh, I was tickled by the irony. But the fellow turned white and raised his voice and cursed me. *O God*, he cried, *turn their taunt back on their own heads.*"

"That's it!" Sanballat shouts. "Let's send the eunuch home!" All at once the governor of Samaria is raining commands upon his allies: "Geshem and the Arabians, attack from the south. Tobiah, go up with your forces from the northeast. Men of Ashdod, cut straight in from the west. I'm going to hit the city at the north. I swear to burn the Sheep Gate and the Fish Gate and make a smoke of new timber. Move! Move, while there's no wall to stop us!"

‖

In Jerusalem the burden-bearers have begun to fail. For fifty-two days they've carried dressed stone to workers on the wall, and now they stagger beneath their loads. The wall is only half built — a low girdling of stone around the city. They can't stop now, not even for a rest.

But all in one day alone seven reports have come from villages near the cities of Samaria that the enemies of Jerusalem are preparing for a military action. It is evening. Jews are watching the hills for the least movement. "They're coming to kill us," the weary people whisper, "and we have nothing to stop them. Nothing."

Suddenly a trumpet cuts the air above the city, and there stands the little governor from Susa at the top of the Tower of the Hundred, a torch in his right hand, his face bright with flame.

"Do not be afraid of them," Nehemiah cries to Jerusalem. "Remember the Lord, who is great and terrible, and fight for your brothers, your sons and daughters, your wives, and your homes!"

The citizens are not persuaded. "We have never fought before!" they yell. "And you are no captain!"

"But the Lord is! And I am his servant. Listen," cries Nehemiah, having measured the enemy and calculated the potential of his own people: "Here are our stratagems. First, let all the Jews of villages nearby stay in the city night and day. We'll fill Jerusalem. Second, dig a ditch behind the wall, then station yourselves according to families in that trench with swords and spears and bows. Third, since you will be spread out from one another, listen for the trumpet, then rally to the place where the trumpet is. That's where the enemy will be attacking. Fourth, know this and believe it and let your hearts be fortified by it: *Our God will fight for us!*"

Whether the people trust Nehemiah or not, at least they have jobs for the evening and plans for tomorrow. This is new. In Judah there is purpose and encouragement. Yes, and hope. All night long the Jews dig a fine trench. In the morning, Nehemiah divides the working crew into two shifts, one to work and one to watch as long as work on the wall continues. Both day and night, then, there is always a show of force, spears moving back and forth within the city, men crying commands and salutations one to another.

▮

Sanballat the governor of Samaria is writing a letter. This is his fifth to Nehemiah in Jerusalem. His first letter said, "Come, let us meet together in one of the villages in the plain of Ono."

There is good reason why he humbled himself to write that first invitation. Neither he nor his allies had been able to assault Jerusalem because their troops — unused to any real conflict in the peace of Persia — perceived better troops inside the city, troops perpetually alert, hosts of weapons bristling above a growing wall. They refused to attack.

So Sanballat and Tobiah sought to draw this groomed little governor out of the city in order to kill him.

But Nehemiah answered the first letter with a letter of his own:

"I am doing a great work and cannot interrupt it in order to visit you."

Sanballat wrote a second letter, a third, and a fourth. But the eunuch answered each one exactly as he had the first. So Sanballat is writing a fifth letter. He knows what "great work" Nehemiah is referring to. Sanballat knows that all the old breaches in the walls of Jerusalem have been healed. He also knows (by spies in the hills east of the city) that the gates themselves have not yet been built or set in their sockets.

So his fifth letter he dispenses with civility.

"It is reported among the nations," writes Sanballat, "that you and the Jews are building a wall for the sake of rebellion. You wish to be king in Judah. Either you come and speak with me or I will report you to Artaxerxes, the king of Persia." Sanballat rolls the scroll tight and seals it with his seal. He hands it to another man waiting in the room. A Jew. He winks at the Jew and nods vigorously.

"Shemaiah, do this first. And the second thing second. You understand? You know what you are to do?"

Shemaiah says, "Yes."

Sanballat smiles and spills into Shemaiah's hand a pouch of Persian coins, gold, each with the figure of Artaxerxes kneeling, holding a spear in his right hand, a bow in his left.

"You, Shemaiah, prophet of God, are wise to broaden your loyalties. Now you carry a king in your pocket!"

▮

Shemaiah lives in Jerusalem. Now, at his insistence, Nehemiah enters with him a small back room of his house.

Once in darkness and in private, Shemaiah grabs the governor's arm and says, "We've got to meet at the temple, you and I."

"Why?" says Nehemiah.

"To take refuge there."

"Refuge? For me or for you?"

"For you, my lord. For you. Even in Jerusalem there are people who do not love you. They are coming to kill you."

Nehemiah strikes a light in the dark room and peers at Shemaiah. "How do you know this?" he says.

"Am I not a prophet of God?" says Shemaiah.

"God spoke to you, then?"

"To me, my lord. Look, here's a letter the governor of Samaria gave me to give you. Read it and see whether we shouldn't rush for protection in the temple."

Nehemiah takes the scroll, breaks the seal and reads the letter slowly.

"Lies," he sneers.

"Even so, you see how much he hates you."

Nehemiah douses the light and leaves Shemaiah's house. The prophet hurries to keep up with him. They are ascending the hill to the temple.

"Yes," Shemaiah says, growing moist with perspiration, "yes, we'd better go right into the temple, and close the doors behind us. They are coming this very night to kill you — "

Nehemiah stops. Shemaiah takes three more steps before he realizes that he walks alone. When he turns it is a cold eye he finds, glittering and serpentine, gazing dead level into his own.

In a low articulate fury, Nehemiah says, "This is a flat deception, Shemaiah! God did not send you to me. You were paid to make this prophecy."

"No, my lord!" Shemaiah cries. "Oh, no, but I have only the greatest respect — "

Nehemiah slaps him. "Don't your own words *terrify* you, man?" He slaps Shemaiah a second time, and a third. "Prophet, prophet, don't you fear your God? Tobiah and Sanballat hired you! I know — because the Lord would never ask a man such as I am to enter the temple. It is for priests alone. I am a eunuch, Shemaiah! I would profane the place of God!"

Hearing Nehemiah's anger and his language, people are gathering in the street. Shemaiah wishes there were some way for escape, but the people hem him in.

"Sanballat tries to make me sin!" cries Nehemiah. "Tobiah the Ammonite wants me to flee in fear. They plan to give me an evil name, to destroy my authority and to taunt me."

Suddenly Nehemiah grabs the prophet by the beard and yanks his face down until he is on his knees. "Shemaiah, prophet of God, carry this curse to your benefactors. Hiss it in their ears. Say, 'This is what Nehemiah the builder of walls, the governor of Judah, says: *Remember Tobiah and Sanballat, O my God, according to all the evil things they have done. Do not cover their guilt nor let their sin be blotted from thy sight!*' "

iv

And now a new day dawns, cloudless, blue, and beautiful. There has not been such a day in Judah for more than two hundred years.

Jerusalem is filled with people from the countryside, even from as far as the plains of the Jordan. They have all dressed with care, but some stand out like white lilies in a field of darker colors. These are wearing clean linen and carrying the instruments of gladness and thanksgiving and singing.

The Levites are here, mingling among Jews, the children of Judah. They've brought their cymbals, their harps, and their lyres.

And the sons of the singers are here.

The city is alive with motion and laughter. Those still arriving pause to touch the new gates, each one of shining wood, a sure protection for Zion against her enemies, calm glory, jewels in the crown around Jerusalem. Who can express what consolation the completion of the wall has caused in Jewish hearts?

A trumpet unfurls its bright sound across the sky. People turn this way and that to find its source, and then they begin to stream toward the southwest, to the Valley Gate where priests await them in the yard before the gate, and the governor stands on the ramparts above it.

As the crowd swells all in that one place, the priests shake over them a mist of blood. The blood of sacrifice settles like a red breath on the heads of the people. The priests themselves and the Levites have spent the last three days fasting for their personal purification. At the same time they offered sacrifices for the purification of the wall and the gates and the people. Now they are about to dedicate this new thing to the Lord.

"Sing!" cries Nehemiah — whose garments glitter with an orient glory. Dapper Nehemiah, cupbearer to a king — he has built a wall with faith and ferocity!

"Sing!" he cries. "Here at this gate we will divide into two great companies, each to walk the city wall in opposite directions. You praise-singing choirs, split and go first, half to the right, toward the Potsherd Gate, and half with me to the left. Let each half be followed by the leaders of Judah, then seven priests, then eight Levites. And sing! Let there be music from two sides as we walk the wall around, begging the protection of the Lord, giving thanks unto our God!"

And so the people of Judah rise up and walk on the fresh walls of Jerusalem. It is as if a fire has been ignited at the Valley Gate. From there the burning goes in two directions — each with the clashing of cymbals and the sharp strumming of taut string, with full-throated human song and individual shouts of praise: the people process on the top of the wall like bright flame, until the city is surrounded and all the women and the children are clapping and laughing along.

In this way the dedication is accomplished.

Then the two companies descend the wall, one at the Horse Gate south of the temple, one at the Sheep Gate north of it. So they meet again in the courts of the Lord, and there they offer sacrifices, Judah celebrating with a meal of union — for the Lord God has granted them a very great joy. Even at night the celebrations continue in Jerusalem with such gladness that their voices are heard north and south, in Samaria and in Edom. God is with the children of Judah. God is with Jacob again.

28

EZRA

i

Nehemiah has no illusions concerning his accomplishments in Jerusalem — what he can and what he cannot do.

A wall is good and necessary, a weapon protecting the city against enemies from without. A wall lends courage to its citizens, strength to its warriors, peace to its merchants and priests and scholars. But it does not make a people righteous. It cannot protect against the enemy from within.

Nehemiah knows: faithlessness and disobedience destroy a nation at its root. And though a governor may build walls and organize administrations and punish misbehavior, he cannot control the heart. He cannot persuade a people to repent. The Law of God must do that.

But in Jerusalem there are no scribes who love the Law enough. And the priests lack moral force. They are as corrupt as the people. Both neglect the Sabbath with impunity.

In people such as this, a wall breeds pride and a false contentment.

So Nehemiah has written to his benefactor, Artaxerxes of Persia, with one more urgent request: "For the sake of Judah and Jerusalem, send from Babylon Ezra the priest, scribe of the Law of God. The temple here is impoverished. The Jews scarcely know their heritage or their God."

ii

Eight months after he begged for Ezra's presence; five months after the king agreed and the priest organized a grand caravan of the most respected Jews in Babylon; three days after their journey's end, when the caravan disbanded in the countryside outside Jerusalem, on the morning of that day, Nehemiah stands in a fresh city gate and watches as Ezra himself approaches.

A slow, lank man with pouches under his eyes, deliberate in all his movement, Ezra walks in front of a procession of camels, all of them burdened. The priest is very tall, gazing forward like one of his camels. The nearer he comes, the more Nehemiah must tilt his head up in order to look in Ezra's face.

"You are Ezra the son of Seraiah?"

"I am," the tall priest says, pausing.

"Ezra, skilled in the law of Moses which the Lord God of Israel gave to him?"

When Ezra stops, so does the line of camels behind. "And who are you?" he says.

"Nehemiah, governor of Judah, the servant of Artaxerxes." Nehemiah puts forward his hand. "I'm the one who prayed that you would come. Welcome."

Slowly Ezra takes the smaller man's hand, his eyes resting on Nehemiah's splendid robes.

"I have a duty to discharge," the priest says. "Where is the temple?"

So Nehemiah leads the unhurried priest and twelve camels through Jerusalem up the temple Mount. There Ezra delivers all the treasure he has brought from Babylon by order of Artaxerxes. He weighs it and records the weights: Six hundred and fifty talents of silver, silver vessels worth a hundred talents, a hundred talents of gold, twenty bowls of gold worth a thousand darics, and two vessels of fine bright bronze as precious as gold.

As the days pass, Ezra oversees a sacrifice. It takes a month. Nehemiah could have done it in a week, but he is not a priest. Ezra attends to every particular with equanimity, then reviews what he has done: he keeps an accounting. So the Jews who came with him from exile offer to God twelve bulls, ninety-six rams, seventy-seven lambs — and as a sin offering, twelve he-goats.

But if Nehemiah cannot offer sacrifices, yet he can command people.

When Ezra's sacrificing has been completed, the governor of Judah sends out a decree that all the citizens of his province must gather in Jerusalem on the first day of the seventh month of the year: men and women, all who are old enough to hear with understanding.

At the same time he orders workmen to construct a platform of new timber in the square before the Water Gate, a pulpit high enough for thousands to see a single individual standing there. And then Nehemiah meets Ezra in a private room and speaks with passion: "You must read the Book of the Law to this people," he says. He can't control the urgency in his voice. He glares into the pouchy eyes of the priest. "Read it word for word. Read it clearly — and explain it, so that the people understand it. They have forgotten Egypt and the wilderness and Mount Sinai and the words of God which Moses wrote in the law. Ezra, priest, scribe: they have forgotten covenant!"

iii

It is dawn, the first day of the seventh month — a heavy, quiet dawn, though crowds of people have gathered in Jerusalem. No one is speaking. In the square before the Water Gate, a great congregation sits on the ground facing a high, spare platform built of newly hewn wood.

Nehemiah is on the platform. He has commanded the sitting and the silence. He will wait and not grow impatient. He will present the people with a calm aspect.

But soon enough he sees Ezra the priest coming down from the old palace mount, carrying scrolls in his two arms.

While Ezra moves forward through the multitude, Nehemiah descends and goes to meet him. Hands rise around the tall priest. A woman reaches and touches one of the scrolls, then snatches her hand back and covers her mouth. An old man rises, lightly kisses the book, then sits again. And Nehemiah, when he comes face-to-face with Ezra, cannot help himself. He drops to his knees. He, too, kisses the Book of the Law, and he begins to weep. He withdraws. He will watch and listen from a distance, hiding his face and his emotion.

Ezra is followed by twelve important people of Judah. When he ascends the platform, six stand to his right and six to his left, but he is much the tallest, a gaunt chalky figure in the center slowly sweeping his gaze over all the people.

Now he unrolls the book to its beginning. Suddenly, the people rustle and begin to rise. Ezra pauses until the entire square is standing, then he lifts his arms and chants, "Deliver us, O God of our salvation! Save us from among the nations, that we may give thanks to your holy name, and glory in your praise." To the people directly, now, the priest calls in slow measured tones: "Blessed be the Lord, the God of Israel, from everlasting to everlasting!"

The people answer, "Amen!" To Nehemiah it is like the sighing of wind in cedar trees: the people lift their hands and murmur, "Amen." Then they bow their heads and worship the Lord. Ezra watches and waits.

When the whole congregation is seated on the ground again and the square is quiet, Ezra turns his eyes to the words in front of him and begins to read.

"In the beginning," he intones the holy words. "In the beginning God created the heavens and the earth."

"Ahhh," Nehemiah sighs to himself: the words.

Ezra reads with slow articulation. He finds a rhythm in the language and slowly, slowly rocks his body to the reading:

In the beginning God created the heavens and the earth.

The earth was without form. Everywhere was emptiness; everything was darkness. But the Lord sent forth his spirit as a storm on the terrible deep.

And God said, "Let there be light."

And light shined in the emptiness, and God saw that the light was good. He divided the light from the darkness. The light he called "Day." The darkness he called "Night." And when the evening and the morning had passed, that was the first day.

And God said, "Let there be a firmament in the midst of the waters to divide the wild water above from the waters below."

And it was so. God called the firmament "Heaven," and that was the end of the second day.

God said, "Let the waters under heaven flow down to the places I appoint for them that the dry ground might appear." So the waters ran in streams and rivers to the ocean. The waters obeyed their boundaries, and God called the dry land "Earth" and the greatest gathering of waters "the sea," and he said, "It is good."

Then he said, "Let the earth put forth green growing things, plants with seed and trees with fruit so that each kind can reproduce in the time to come." And it was so, and it was good — and that was the third day of the world.

God said, "Now let there be two lamps in the firmament to distinguish day from night. They shall measure the times by their shining, the years, the seasons, and the days." So God set two lamps in heaven — the greater to rule the day, the lesser to rule the night — and some stars. And he saw that it was good.

Evening and morning were the fourth day.

God said, "Let the waters swarm with living things!" God also said, "Let birds fly as high as the heavens!" — and in this manner he created the great sea monsters and the fish and every winged bird according to its kind. And God blessed them, saying, "Be fruitful and multiply: fill the waters in the seas, and the lands and the branches and the bright air of the heavens!"

That was the fifth day.

And God said, "Let the earth bring forth living creatures, cattle and crawling things and the untamed beasts." And it was so, each creature fashioned according to its kind, and God saw that it was good.

"But now," said the Lord God, "now let me make a race in my own image, after my likeness — "

So the Lord God made of red clay a human form, and into its nostrils he breathed the breath of life — and the clay came alive. It rose up on two legs and walked.

That same day the Lord planted a garden in the east, in Eden. He filled it with trees both pleasant to look at and good to eat. In the middle of the garden he placed the Tree of Life and the Tree of the Knowledge of Good and Evil. Then he brought the human to the garden and said, "Behold, I give you plants and animals, fish and fowl, green things, breathing things — everything. Govern it all. In my name, take care of it all.

"*And you may eat of every tree in Eden except the one in the middle. You must never eat of the Tree of the Knowledge of Good and Evil — for in the day that you do, you shall surely die.*"

But when he had placed this single figure in the wide, fruitful garden, God did not say, "It is good." He considered the solitary man and said, "It is not good for anyone to be alone. I will make a helper fit for him."

So God brought him animals, to see what he would call them; and whatever the man called each creature, that was its name. But among these there was not found a helper perfectly fit for him.

So God laid the man down on a green hillock and caused a deep sleep to fall upon him; and while he slept the Lord took one of his ribs and closed up its place with flesh, and of that rib God formed a woman.

Then he woke the man and showed him the woman he had made.

The man laughed in delight and cried: "At last! Bone of my bone, flesh of my flesh!" Then, gently, he approached this second person and said, "Were you taken from man? Then you shall be called woman."

So the man and the woman lived in Eden, naked but not ashamed. And God saw everything that he had made, and behold: it was very good.

This was the end of the sixth day.

And when he had finished all his work, the heavens and the earth and the host of them, the Lord God rested. He rested on the seventh day, and he blessed that day thereby forever. Every seventh day is holy and devoted unto God.

▌▌

Ezra the priest stops reading. He lifts his heavy eyes and looks to the side, seeing nothing. So elegant the words he has just read — so elemental, embracing the whole world — yet to Nehemiah it seems that the priest is bearing a burden greater than any his camels have ever borne.

How cavernous are the minds of the scribes of God! How much they carry in memory!

Suddenly Nehemiah realizes that Ezra need not read the words in order to know them. The Book of Moses lives whole within him. He sees all the words and all the laws in a single glance, as from a high mountain. And though the congregation is receiving the story sentence by sentence, for Ezra the priest every sentence contains the entire story from beginning to end.

Yet, he reads. He reads because he loves the words themselves, and to read each is to honor it.

Ezra turns to the scroll again, draws a slow breath, and continues:

Now, the serpent was more cunning than any other creature that the Lord God had made.

He said to the woman, "Did God say, 'You shall not eat of any tree in the garden'?"

The woman said, "We may eat of the fruit of the trees of the garden; but God said, 'You shall not eat of the fruit of the tree in the middle of the garden, neither shall you touch it, lest you die.' "

But the serpent said, "You will not die. For God knows that when you eat of it your eyes will be opened. You will be like God, knowing good and evil."

When, therefore, the woman considered the tree and saw that it was lovely to look at and good for food and able to make one wise, she plucked its fruit and ate. Next, she gave some to her husband, and he ate.

Immediately their eyes were opened: they saw that they were naked, and they rushed to cover themselves with aprons of fig leaves.

At dusk the man and his wife heard the sound of the Lord God walking in the garden, and they hid themselves. The Lord God called to the man, "Where are you?"

The man said, "I heard the sound of your coming, and I was afraid because I am naked, so I hid myself."

The Lord said, "Who told you that you were naked? Have you eaten of the tree from which I commanded you not to eat?"

The man said, "The woman whom you gave to me — she offered me the fruit and I ate."

Then the Lord God said to the woman, "What have you done?"

The woman said, "No, but the serpent charmed me, and I ate."

So then, in the darkness of the night arriving, the Lord God announced to his creatures the consequences of their sins. To the serpent he said: "Hereafter you shall crawl on your belly and eat dust all the days of your life. Your seed shall be at war with the seed of the woman — and though you may strike his heel, he shall crush his head."

To the woman the Lord said: "The bearing of children shall cause you difficulty and a heavy pain. Yet you shall hunger after a husband, and he shall rule over you."

To the man he said: "Because you disobeyed my word, the very earth is cursed. It shall trouble your labor with thorns and thistles. All the days of your life you shall eat bread in toil and sweat — and in the end you shall return to the clay from which you came. Dust you are: to dust you shall return."

Then the Lord drove the man and the woman out of Eden. At the east side of the garden he set cherubim with flaming swords turned every way, flashing like lightning to guard the gate.

∎

The man was named Adam, after the earth. The woman was called Eve, because she was the mother of all living.

Outside Eden, Adam lay with Eve, and she conceived and bore a son. She named the child Cain. Soon she bore another son and named him Abel.

When Cain grew up, he became a farmer.

Abel became a shepherd.

In time the brothers brought sacrifices to the Lord, each according to his labor. Cain burned a smoky grain; Abel offered a sheep. And though the Lord had regard for Abel's sacrifice, for Cain's he did not.

Seeing that, Cain grew angry. His face fell into the lines of rage.

The Lord said, "Cain, why are you angry? Do well now, and it will be accepted; but if you do not, sin will be lying in wait at your door. Cain, you must master the sin!"

Nevertheless, in the months that followed, Cain kept eying his brother — and finally he said to him, "Let's go out to the fields together."

They went, and while they were there, Cain rose up and killed his brother Abel.

Then the Lord said to Cain, "Where is Abel your brother?"

He said, "How should I know? Am I my brother's keeper?"

And the Lord said, "What have you done? The voice of your brother's blood is crying to me from the ground. Therefore, Cain, the ground shall be shut against you forever. It shall no longer yield its fruit for you; but you shall be a fugitive wherever you wander on the earth."

Cain cried out, "O God, the punishment is too much for me! Because you've driven me from the soil and from your face, anyone might slay me now!"

But the Lord said, "Not so! If anyone slays Cain, vengeance shall be taken on him sevenfold."

And the Lord put a mark on Cain lest any who came upon him should kill him. And then Cain went away from the presence of the Lord and dwelt in the land of Nod, east of Eden.

█

Ezra the priest pauses and looks down on the people who fill the square. The longer he looks at them, the more they cannot return his gaze. They drop their eyes.

"If," says Ezra slowly, "if by resting on the seventh day the Creator blessed that day and hallowed it as a Sabbath forever, then how can you profane the day?"

No one answers him. "I have seen you treading wine presses on the Sabbath," Ezra says. "I have seen you bringing in heaps of grain and loading them on asses on the Sabbath — you sell wine, grapes, and figs on the Sabbath. Why do you do this evil thing?"

Silence. Judah is silent. Jerusalem is borne down by the priest's words — no longer a story, but a very personal sermon.

"I have just read to you the first covenant which God made with the parents of every people of the earth — the covenant which they broke by disobeying his one command. What happened at the breaking of the covenant? Life became difficult. Work became hard. The people who sinned against God also learned to sin against each other.

"The hand of a man shed the blood of his brother.

"In the ages that followed, the descendants of Adam and Eve developed new ways of living." Ezra is not reading now. He is teaching. His pouchy eyes are not judging; they are pursuing an important point. "Some people built cities. Some farmed. Some lived in tents and wandered through the wilderness with flocks and herds. People learned the arts and music. They forged instruments in copper and bronze.

"A few individuals still called on the name of the Lord. Enoch walked so closely with God that when he had lived his full number of years, God took him and he was not.

"But Enoch was unusual. Wickedness entered the world when that covenant was broken. The ground itself was cursed. People grew cunning in killing. A man named Lamech was so proud of his murders that he sang songs about them, and others learned his songs and sang them too.

"Pride prevailed in the world.

"People stole from the heavenly places powers that did not belong to them.

"In those ancient days the meditation of every human heart was evil only, evil continually, so evil that the Lord God was grieved that ever he had made the race, and he said, 'I will blot out those whom I have created from the face of the ground, people and beasts and creeping things and birds of the air, for I am sorry that I have made them.'

Again, the silence in the square before the Water Gate is a heavy one. Nehemiah had prayed for this. He was not sorry that the priest was troubling the hearts of the people — but he was sorry for his flesh, sorry to be a person at all. But then Ezra says in a softer voice, "Yet the Lord God determined to make a second covenant — to start again. Listen, Judah. Jerusalem, listen."

Now the priest bends his eyes down to the book before him and reads:

In those days one man found favor with the Lord. Noah had walked blamelessly with God for six hundred years. To Noah the Lord said: "I am going to destroy all flesh because the earth is sick with violence.

"But you, Noah: Build an ark. Make it of gopher wood four hundred and fifty feet long, seventy-five feet wide and forty-five feet high. Set a door in its side, and cover it with pitch. For I will establish my covenant with you."

Noah did what the Lord commanded. On dry land he built an ark with three levels and a roof and a door.

Then the Lord said, "Noah, go into the ark, you and your wife and your sons with their wives, too. Take with you seven pairs of every kind of clean animal and a pair of every unclean kind, the male and its mate. Take food so that they all might live and continue on the earth in spite of what I shall do.

"*For in one week I shall send a rain by which to blot out every living thing that I have made.*"

Again, Noah obeyed. Two and two, male and female, the footed, the crawling, and the winged creatures Noah drove into the ark. Next went his sons Shem, Ham, and Japheth, their wives, his wife, and finally Noah himself. Then the Lord God shut the door.

On the seventeenth day of the second month of the six hundredth year of Noah's life, the fountains of the terrible deep burst open and spouted water. The wild waters above the firmament also broke through heaven and poured down upon the earth. For forty days and nights water roared over the land, cataracts and waves upon the seas. The ark rose higher and higher until the mountains themselves were covered by the flood and there was water only, water everywhere.

All flesh perished in those days, birds and cattle, the beasts of the field and swarming things. And people. Everyone in whom there had been breath was drowned. Only Noah and those who were with him survived.

After forty days the rain ceased falling. Water continued to cover the earth. But God remembered Noah.

He sent a strong wind across the world and the waters began to abate.

In the seventh month the ark touched the tops of the mountains of Ararat. Noah opened a window and felt the breezes.

He sent forth a dove, but the dove returned to the ark and alighted in its window. She had found no place to perch.

Noah waited seven days and released the dove again. Again she came back, but this time with an olive leaf in her beak. The ark had come to rest in a cradle between two peaks of Ararat. One week later Noah released the dove a third time. She flew toward the southern sun and never came back again.

Then the Lord God said to Noah, "Open the ark. Send forth the living things that they might breed and fill the world again. And you, Noah: go forth as well. Be fruitful and multiply."

So Noah arose. He and his family went out and built an altar and offered burnt offerings to the Lord.

When the Lord smelled the pleasant odor of the sacrifice, he said, "Never again will I curse the ground. Never again will I destroy all living things. While the earth remains, seedtime and harvest, cold and heat, summer and winter, day and night shall never cease."

And God blessed Noah and his children, saying, "Every moving thing that lives shall be food for you. Only you shall not eat flesh with its life, that is, its blood. Life belongs to me. Therefore, whoever sheds human blood, by humans shall his blood be shed. For I made humankind in my own image!"

Then God said to Noah, "Behold, I establish my covenant with you and your descendants after you — that never again shall all flesh be cut off by the waters of a flood. And this is the sign of the covenant which I make between

*me and you for all future generations: I set my bow in the cloud. When I
bring clouds over the earth and the bow is seen in them, I will remember my
covenant, an everlasting covenant between God and every living creature."*

*In the generations after Noah, people began again to multiply. They spoke
one language. Family after family, they spread eastward until they found a
pleasant plain in Shinar, where they settled.*

"Come," they said, "let us make bricks."

*They made bricks by baking and they mortared them with bitumen. Then
they said, "Let us make a city, and in its center build a tower so high it
touches heaven. We will make a name for ourselves, and we will never be
scattered like dust across the earth."*

*So the people went to work, building a monument from the plain up into
the sky.*

Then the Lord God came down to see what the people were doing.

*"Behold," said the Lord, "they are one people speaking all one tongue,
and this is only the beginning of what they will do. Soon nothing will seem
impossible to them!*

*"Come," said the Lord, "let us confuse their language so they can't
understand each other."*

*Therefore, the name of that city was Babel, because there the Lord confused
the tongues of the people. They ceased working together, ceased building or
living together. Like dust the people were scattered across the face of the
whole earth.*

▌▌

Ezra reads, *The face of the whole earth,* and immediately calls out to the
Jews in the square before him: "Twice!"

He draws a deep breath. "Twice," he says, "the Creator tried to establish
his covenant with the people of the world. His second covenant was with
Noah and all his descendants forever — but, as at the first, the people broke
this covenant, too.

"What then?

"What was next?

"What next could the Lord God do for the people he had created, who
now were divided into tribes and tongues and peoples and nations?

"O Judah, don't you know? Don't you remember what the Lord has done?
Israel, are you ignorant of who you are?

"Next God chose one man with whom to make his covenant — and in that
man, one people!"

Nehemiah is breathless because of the sudden passion in the tall priest.
Ezra has come to the goal of his sermon. He is neither weary nor indifferent
now. He drops his eyes and continues reading:

When Abram was ninety-nine years old the Lord appeared to him and said, "I am God Almighty! Walk before me and be blameless. And I will make my covenant between me and you, and will multiply you exceedingly."

Then Abram fell on his face, and God said to him: "Behold, my covenant is with you. No longer shall your name be Abram, but your name shall be Abraham; for I have made you the father of a multitude of nations. I will make you exceedingly fruitful; and I will make nations of you, and kings shall come forth from you. And I will establish my covenant between me and you and your descendants after you throughout their generations for an everlasting covenant, to be God to you and to your descendants after you. And I will give to you and to your descendants after you the land of your sojournings, all the land of Canaan, for an everlasting possession; and I will be their God."

Ezra looks up.

"And who," he calls, "are the nations to come from Abraham? Can you tell me? And then can you say which nation still has that everlasting covenant? The Moabites are the children of Abraham's nephew, Lot. So are the Ammonites. Do they remember the covenant of Abraham? No.

"The Ishmaelites are children of Abraham. Do they remember the covenant? Does anyone on earth remember *them*?

"And Esau was one grandson of Abraham. His children are the Edomites who even today live south of us in Hebron where Abraham pitched his tent. Yet do they remember the covenant?

"Judah! With whom is the covenant?

"Abraham's other grandson was Jacob, whom God named Israel. Israel! It was with Israel that God renewed the covenant. It was Israel whom God took to himself now not as one man, but as a people, as a nation, when he delivered them from the hands of the Egyptians, where they were in bondage.

"You, Israel! Judah, you!"

For ask now of the days that are past, since the day that God created humankind upon the earth — this time Ezra is quoting the Book of Moses from memory.

His voice is rich with the rhetoric:

Ask from one end of heaven to the other, whether such a great thing as this was ever heard of. Has any god ever taken a nation for himself from the midst of another nation, by trials, by signs, by wonders, and by war, by a mighty hand and an outstretched arm, and by great terrors according to all that the Lord your God did for you in Egypt before your eyes? To you it was shown, that you might know that the Lord is God; there is no other besides him. Therefore, you must keep his statutes and his commandments, that it may go well with you, and with your children after you, and that you may prolong your days in the land which the Lord your God gives you forever.

"So, Judah," Ezra says. He whispers it. He leans forward and lowers his voice to a whisper. "So then, is it well with you, Judah? Do you possess the land your God gave unto you? No? Why not?"

Ezra continues quoting:

The Lord our God made a covenant with us at Sinai. He spoke with us face-to-face out of the midst of the fire.

He said, "I am the Lord your God, who brought you out of the land of Egypt, out of the house of bondage. You shall have no other gods before me."

The Lord said, "You shall be holy; for I the Lord your God am holy! You shall reverence your mother and your father. You shall keep my sabbaths: I am the Lord your God.

"Do not turn to idols or make for yourselves molten gods: I am the Lord your God.

"When you reap the harvest of your land, you shall not reap the field to its border. Do not strip your vineyard bare or gather the fallen grapes. These things you shall leave for the poor and the sojourner: I am the Lord your God.

"You shall not steal nor deal falsely nor lie to one another. And you shall not swear by my name falsely, profaning the name of God: I am the Lord.

"You shall not oppress your neighbors or rob them. You shall not curse the deaf or put a stumbling block before the blind, but you shall fear your God: I am the Lord.

"You shall not go up and down as a slanderer among your people: I am the Lord.

"You shall not hate a single brother or sister in your heart, but you shall reason with your neighbors, lest you bear sins because of them. You shall not take vengeance or carry grudges against the sons and daughters of your people, but you shall love your neighbors as yourself: I am the Lord."

Suddenly Ezra pauses. There is a sound in the square, very soft, like running water, and for a moment the priest is mystified. But Nehemiah, nearer the people, knows that sound. It is weeping.

The people of Judah are weeping.

No one wails. No one is crying out. The passage of sorrow through the congregation is as quiet as rainfall.

"Yes, yes," murmurs Ezra. "Now you know. The covenant is with you this day as at the first. As it was with Abraham and Isaac and Jacob; as it was with Moses at Sinai; as it was when David truly possessed the land, so it is this day still. The covenant is with you, that you might keep it again in righteousness and in purity."

But all the people continue weeping, releasing ancient griefs, centuries of sorrow:

You shall be holy, you shall be holy, you shall be holy — for I the Lord your God am holy.

Now Ezra descends from his platform. He begins to walk among the people. He touches the backs of their necks. "Hush," he says. "Don't mourn, don't weep. This day is holy to the Lord your God."

The priest moves slowly. Soon others of his entourage — the Jews, the Levites, and Nehemiah himself — are kneeling here and there among the people, comforting them.

"Go your way," says Ezra. "Eat the fat and drink sweet wine and send portions to the poor. This day is holy to our Lord. Do not be grieved, for the joy of the Lord is your strength."

It is early in the afternoon. The people rise and do as Ezra says. They eat, they drink they send portions to those who have nothing — and soon in Jerusalem there is the beginning of consolation, because the people have understood the words that were declared to them.

So ends the day of the reading.

iv

How long does repentance last? If certain sins have continued a hundred years, and if a people were blind to their condition that long, will sinning suddenly cease? Will there follow a hundred years of righteousness? Or does sorrow die in the dawning of the very next day?

Nehemiah is encouraged by the tears of the people. But he is a pragmatic man, a realist, and in the next months he strives by governmental authority to turn the repentance of Judah into actual obedience.

Are Levites neglecting their duties in the temple? Yes, because the treasury is empty. They are not receiving sufficient funds for a living, so they're finding employment elsewhere, and the temple has fallen into suffering disrepair.

Nehemiah fixes the problem by decree: he requires tithes to be collected throughout his province. He appoints honest treasurers to administer them. He commands the Levites to return to their sacred duties.

Did Ezra blame the people for breaking the Sabbath laws? Good: Nehemiah waits exactly one month, four Sabbaths, to see whether the moral word will have a visible effect. When it does not, he orders the gates of Jerusalem to be shut and locked all Sabbath long, blocking commerce and enforcing a religious rest.

But on the next Sabbath day merchants simply set up market outside the city. Nehemiah explodes. He opens a gate, rides through in a golden chariot surrounded by armed soldiers, threatens every seller with arrest, and drives them away in disgrace.

And then Nehemiah discovers that the grandson of the high priest has divorced his wife in order to marry another. The first marriage lasted a bare two years. The second marriage has just been celebrated, less than three months since the reading of the Law of God. And the second bride is not a Jew. She is a Samaritan with a magnificent dowry. She is none other than the daughter of Sanballat, governor of Samaria.

What decree should Nehemiah make in the face of this outrage?

He goes to Ezra the priest.

They talk in private for a very long time.

■

It is evening, the winter of the year. A cold sleet has begun to cut the air. Nevertheless, a man is sitting on the wet pavement outside the temple, groaning. His clothing is torn, his hair disheveled and dripping, his face aggrieved. There are great pouches under his eyes.

People have gathered around the man, people filled with pity and worry because they love him. They honor him. And they had truly thought it was well with him because they had repented when he taught them the Law. They repented, and he had comforted them.

Yet here is Ezra in a wretched state, and no one can persuade him to get up and go indoors. He has eaten nothing. He has drunk nothing. His groans are deep and wordless — and the longer he abases himself like this, the worse the people feel, helpless and confused and sad.

It is a child who says to the priest, "What are you doing?" And he answers, "I am mourning over the faithlessness of Judah."

This is electric in the people.

"What? *Our* faithlessness?"

"Yours. Didn't you hear who carries the covenant of God? Didn't you understand? Yet you have not separated yourselves from those who practice abominations. You marry Ammonites, Moabites, Egyptians, Samaritans."

Ezra bows his head. The wind blows harder through the temple courtyard. People pull their mantles over their heads, feeling worse than helpless: frightened.

Finally Shecaniah the son of Jehiel speaks. "We have broken faith with God," he says, "but can't there even now be hope for Israel? Ezra, priest, help us make a covenant with God to put away our foreign wives. Please, take the task. We will be with you. Arise, be strong, let all be done according to the Law."

Nehemiah, standing at the back of the crowd, hears Shecaniah's plea and immediately transforms it into a mandate.

That night an order goes forth through Judah that in three days all people must present themselves in Jerusalem, or else forfeit their property and suffer banishment from the congregation of the Jews.

■

From morning to evening, the twentieth day of the ninth month of the year, an icy rainstorm pounds Jerusalem, blinding the beasts and chilling human flesh to the bone. Yet the courtyard of the temple is packed with people. The streets of the city are so crowded that no one can move. Judah, shivering with cold and fear, has gathered to hear Ezra speak a second time:

"You have trespassed and married foreign women and so increased the guilt of Israel," says the priest. "Now then, make confession to the Lord and do his will: separate yourselves from the peoples of the land and from your foreign wives."

The sky darkens. The rain grows heavier. Water soaks the clothing of the people. No one is dry. Everyone is cold. Each can see his breath, grey clouds floating in front of his face: clouds of utterance, because the people are speaking.

"It is so," they say. All their voices sound as if Jerusalem itself were groaning. "We must do as you have said. Let everyone who has taken a foreign wife come before the elders and the judges and put them away, until the fierce wrath of our God is averted from us."

Seldom does a cold rain trigger lightning.

Yet Nehemiah raises his face and blinks at the heavy clouds. He thinks he hears thunder, a muttering in heaven, and he takes it as a sign of divine approval.

29

THE YEARNING

i

AN ORACLE

Rejoice, O daughter of Zion!
Shout aloud, O daughter of Jerusalem!
Lo, your king comes to you,
triumphant and victorious,
humble and riding on an ass,
    on a colt, the foal of an ass.

He shall command peace to the nations,
his dominion from sea to sea
    and from the River to the ends of the earth.

As for you, because of my covenant with you
    I will set your captives free;
For I have bent Judah as my bow,
    Ephraim as my arrow;
I will brandish your sons, O Zion,
    and wield you like a warrior's sword.

Then the Lord will appear over them,
    his arrow going forth like lightning;
the Lord God will sound the trumpet,
    marching forth in the whirlwinds of the south.

On that day the Lord their God will save his people,
*   for they are his flock,*
and like the jewels of a crown
*   they shine on his land.*

Yea, how good and how fair it shall be!
*   Grain shall make the young men flourish,*
*   and new wine gladden the maidens.*

ii

AN ORACLE

Thus says the Lord, who stretched out the heavens and founded the earth, who breathed the spirit into human creatures, Lo, I am about to make Jerusalem a cup of reeling to all the peoples round about!

On that day I will make Jerusalem a heavy stone for all the peoples: all who lift it shall grievously hurt themselves. And all the nations of the earth will come together against it.

On that day, says the Lord, I will strike every horse with panic, and its rider with madness. But upon the house of Judah I will open my eyes. Then the clans of Judah shall say to themselves, "The inhabitants of Jerusalem have strength through the Lord of hosts, their God."

On that day I will make the clans of Judah like a blazing pot in the midst of wood, like a flaming torch among sheaves; and they shall devour to the right and to the left all the peoples round about, while Jerusalem shall still be inhabited in its place.

On that day the Lord will put a shield about the inhabitants of Jerusalem so that the feeblest among them shall be like David, and the house of David shall be like God, like the angel of the Lord, at their head.

And I will pour out on the house of David and the inhabitants of Jerusalem a spirit of compassion and supplication, so that, when they look on him whom they have pierced, they shall mourn for him, as one mourns for an only child, and weep bitterly over him, as one weeps over a firstborn.

On that day there shall be a fountain opened for the house of David and the inhabitants of Jerusalem to cleanse them from sin and uncleanness.

On that day there shall be neither cold nor frost. And there shall be continuous day.

On that day living waters shall flow out from Jerusalem, half to the eastern sea, half to the western sea, and it shall continue in summer as in winter.

And the Lord will become king over all the earth. On that day the Lord will be one and his name one.

iii

AND THE PSALMIST SINGS FOR ALL THE PEOPLE

> *I wait for the Lord, my soul doth wait,*
> *   and in his word do I hope.*
> *My soul waiteth for the Lord*
> *more than they that watch for the morning —*
> *   I say, more than they that watch for the morning.*

PART EIGHT

The Messiah

PART
EIGHT

30

ZECHARIAH

i

An old man with powerful forearms walked five steps from his little house to the workshop behind it, a low stone shed soot-darkened on the inside. It was built of three walls, the fourth open to the south. Interior shelves held hammers, tongs, dies, small smelting pots, ladles, and clay jars containing nails. The workshop was filled with nails of every kind.

Fixed to a stone foundation, in the center of the shop, sat a solid block of metal etched along one edge with grooves of various sizes, but shining and flat on the face of it. Here was an anvil that had served three generations of nailsmiths. More than fifty years ago, it had been bequeathed to this old man by the master who had taught him his craft.

Against the back wall was a brick forge already burning. The old man began to pedal a leather bellows, bringing the fire to white heat. With tongs he introduced a narrow bar of metal into the fire. The bar was squared down its shank. From end to end it was the length of a span. When one end glowed red even to the heart of the metal, the man brought it forth and laid it on the anvil. He raised a hammer and struck so hard that the shed and his body and his face were sprayed with sparks.

This is how he kept burning his beard away. Zechariah the nailsmith had a rough, toughened complexion. His cheeks were mostly scarred. He had no eyebrows nor hair on his forearms; his fingers were perpetually curled and thick, but his upper body was as powerful as it had been fifty years ago when he was nineteen — when his master died and he established his own shop.

With regular, mighty strikes of his hammer, Zechariah tapered the entire length of the metal bar, then shaped its end to a point. He himself had cast six such bars. Today he was beating them into spikes.

Lately there had been a rebellious spirit in Jerusalem. The children and the grandchildren of King Herod were fomenting riots in order to strengthen their own positions against the day when the old king died. Caesar Augustus, therefore, had commanded that several of Herod's sons should be tried in an imperial court — and since Rome executed her

criminals by crucifixion, Herod himself had ordered six new spikes from
Zechariah the nailsmith. Each spike he required to be the length of a span,
which is the distance from the tip of a grown man's thumb to the tip of his
fifth finger when he has spread his hand as wide as he can.

ii

Herod was an Idumean, a descendant of the Edomites who had
moved into Judah centuries ago and had taken up dwelling around
Hebron. In the last hundred years the Idumeans had converted to
Jewish traditions, but the Jews could not completely accept them as kin
and members of the same congregation. They were never persuaded that
these conversions — or that of this king in particular — were anything but
expedient.

In fact, Herod had taken control of Jerusalem by laying siege to the city.
This scarcely inspired love or loyalty. Worse, he came with the favor and
the power of Rome: Marc Antony, master of Roman holdings in Asia, and
Octavian, soon to be Caesar Augustus, had persuaded the Roman Senate
to crown Herod king of Judea, Samaria, and Idumea. He came not kindly,
but conquering.

While the siege of Jerusalem was in progress, Herod sought to mollify his
new subjects by a wedding. He married a Hasmonean, a woman whose family
had produced priests and rulers in Judea for the past one hundred years.
Her name was Mariamne. She was of pure Jewish blood. Her father was the
high priest.

In an extravagant flourish Herod purchased for his bride a necklace of
elegant pearls; they came by elephant all the way from India. He placed
them in a shining ebony box which came from upper Egypt. But the box
lacked hinges and nails. Because of the siege, he was encamped in the hill
country of Judea, and he was forced to use the artisans of that region. Thus
King Herod found an obscure nailsmith, a poor man thirty-six years old,
who fashioned twelve tiny nails of bronze for him. Moreover, he covered the
delicate nails in a golden foil so smooth and beautiful that Mariamne was
charmed and the king did not forget Zechariah.

In the years after the siege, Herod used force and manipulation to
consolidate his rule in the kingdom. When he had established a grim peace
in the region, he began to rebuild Jerusalem on a grand scale. Much of this
work was offensive to the Jews. He built a pagan theater in the city and an
amphitheater nearby. He inaugurated athletic games in honor of Caesar
Augustus, at which the young men competed naked. He began to build for
himself a magnificent palace — and he sent two sons of Mariamne to Rome,

"To enjoy the company of Caesar," he said. There his boys were raised in a manner befitting his own importance, more Roman than Jew.

But King Herod also did one glorious thing for which no Jew blamed him. He tore down the small, functional temple that had stood for five hundred and ten years — ever since the end of the exile — and he doubled the size of the platform on the temple Mount. He surrounded the huge new space with great colonnades on four sides. On the east was the porch of Solomon. Along the entire south side the royal porch was built of four rows of columns, creating three aisles beneath a ceiling a hundred feet high.

Herod began to rebuild the temple of the Lord. The brilliant white edifice that now arose outshone anything Solomon had imagined. The Jewish teachers who followed the progress of this marvel said, "He is atoning for his sins."

And on the day when the new temple was dedicated — though the project would not be completed for many years yet — Jerusalem was filled with teachers and pilgrims and priests, rejoicing!

Herod himself offered three hundred oxen as a sacrifice. He stood high on a royal pavilion and watched the rich, religious commotion with satisfaction. The Levites blew on their ram's horn trumpets and sang; musical instruments clashed and thumped and cut the air; the great altar spat grease, consuming the fat portions of the sacrifice, sending up a white smoke and the sweet smell of roasting meat. And all day long priests were slaughtering beasts on the pavement in front of the altar.

One priest in particular caught the king's attention, an older man, but a powerful one nonetheless: with his left hand he took hold of the ox's horn and pulled back the great head, exposing throat; with the knife in his right hand he deftly sliced one artery; and with perfect accuracy, then, he sent the first spurts of blood into bowls. The rest of the blood ran over the pavement in grooves to a system of drains which carried the blood down to the Kidron Valley.

Herod noticed that this priest was crying. Beast after beast he slaughtered for the sacrifice, never seeming to grow tired while tears kept streaming down his face. It was a ravaged face, thick with scars and wounds; a scraggly beard; mighty forearms — and this most tender weeping!

"Who is that?" Herod asked the priests who stood beside him.

They looked and said, "Zechariah, a priest of the division of Abijah."

The king looked more closely at the weeping priest, who seemed vaguely familiar. "Zechariah?" he said. "Isn't he a nailsmith in the hills of Judea?"

"Yes, the same man."

∎

King Herod murdered Mariamne, his wife.

Her younger brother had been appointed high priest in Jerusalem without his approval. The boy was a Hasmonean barely sixteen years old: clearly, his elevation had been a political move, undermining Herod's personal authority. And when the young fellow presided at his first Pentecost there was such a roar of admiration from the people that Herod decided to end both his popularity and his life.

He invited his brother-in-law to accompany him to the pools of Jericho. The summer was hot. The water was cool. And the king knew how to entertain his friends in a noble style. The boy accepted.

One afternoon a swimming party was organized. Many people filled the pools with games and laughter. King Herod swam toward the young high priest and playfully ducked him under the water. The lad never emerged alive.

In the months that followed, Mariamne's mother refused to accept the death of her son. She accused Herod of murder. She sent her accusation to Cleopatra and to Marc Antony in Egypt. Herod was summoned to make an accounting of himself; and though he succeeded by eloquence and bribery in keeping the friendship of Rome, he bitterly resented the Hasmoneans. He despised his mother-in-law, and he was much inclined to believe every rumor brought to him concerning his wife.

On the slightest provocation he had his mother-in-law murdered. But then jealousy grew violent within him. Mariamne was a beautiful woman. Jews and Romans alike were drawn to her. One day Herod's sister Salome whispered to him of his wife's adultery, and on the next day he had her murdered.

But the death of his wife never lay easily upon his heart.

It was not the crime that troubled him, but her absence, because he never could stop loving her.

∎

The sons of Mariamne were named Alexander and Aristobulus. They were not, in fact, the oldest sons of King Herod; but they were his only offspring with Hasmonean blood — and that, they believed, granted them the real right of succession to their father's throne. They returned from Rome to see to their own interests.

During the same year when Herod's new temple was dedicated, Alexander and Aristobulus strove openly for power in Jerusalem. They plotted among the other children of Herod; they lied and acted treacherously; they intrigued with people of power, and all the while their ambitions seemed to grow more and more immediate. Herod feared that they wanted more than succession, that they were planning rebellions by which to tear the crown from his living head.

Therefore, with instructions from Caesar Augustus, he arrested both his sons, the children of Mariamne. He imprisoned them and had them tried in a Roman court.

The trial lasted more than a year, at the end of which King Herod ordered spikes.

Perhaps he was recalling times more innocent between their mother and himself, when he gave her gifts from India and Egypt. Perhaps his heart was dark with irony. Or maybe it was a mere accident of memory. Whatever the motive, Herod sent an order to Zechariah the nailsmith for six new spikes, each a span in length, by which to crucify his sons.

iii

In the middle of the morning, in the district of Galilee, in the village of Nazareth some three days' journey north of Jerusalem, a middle-aged man crouched at the door of a small stone house. He was running his hand up and down the right jamb, grunting to himself, "Uhmmm."

The jamb was old. The wood was ravaged where past hinges had been torn from it. The door itself was a poor fit, having warped long ago, having suffered the chewings and the kickings of animals and the expansion and contraction of various weathers. All its gaps were blackened. Clearly, household smoke blew out around the door as well as through the windows when the lattice had been thrown open.

Poor little house. It had but the one door and three rooms: the central room immediately within the door, where the family gathered and cooked on a low hearth and kept warm, a room to the left where the sheep and the goats were bedded, a room in the back for sleeping. Here outside, where the man crouched at its door, there was a small walled yard and a garden for vegetables.

"Uhmmm," he murmured, stretching himself to touch the wooden lintel above the door.

His thumbnail was gnarled and black. The palms of his hands were as hard as the handles of old tools.

Suddenly the door was snatched inward and another man stepped out, equal in age to the first man, but smaller, balder, and blinking with a tiny eye.

"Joseph, explain yourself!" he said.

The man named Joseph stood back and lowered his head. Now his hands hung hugely at his thighs. A wild explosion of beard concealed his face beneath the eyes.

The smaller man said, "Last week you were at my lattice. The week before I heard you creeping on the roof. And I waited, didn't I? I waited for the knock. Like any respectable householder, I waited for the greeting and the explanation, but none came to me, no." The little man, finding no response in the hair before him, now addressed the air with vigorous gesticulation: "Joseph comes and Joseph goes and Nazareth says the fellow is odd," he roared. "I myself am a just man. I am willing to listen to explanations, but none do ever come. Joseph! Why are you so interested in my house?"

Joseph mumbled, "Uhmmm," a slow grin dividing his mouth at the teeth.

Suddenly there was the whisper of quick feet inside the house. Joseph's eyes flicked up. The bridge of his nose grew red.

The householder saw the blush, turned, peered into his house, then looked back at Joseph with a shrewd squint of the eye. "Soooo," he said.

Joseph nodded and nodded. Within his beard he whispered a single word: "*Mohar.*"

"Ah, the *mohar*. Am I now discovering that you have come to negotiate something with me, Joseph?"

Joseph nodded.

"To pay me something for the hand of my daughter?"

Joseph nodded.

"My breath is taken away. I can't breathe," said the small man, still fixing the large one with a tight stare. "Yes, yes, this is very sudden. The *mohar*. So you have been talking with Mary, and I didn't know about it?"

Joseph shook his head.

"You have *not* been talking together?"

Joseph didn't even shake his head this time. Having spoken once, he could not speak again. He had raised his eyes. He was staring over the head of the householder. His gaze seemed absolutely fastened to the lintel over the door, as though no other lintel in the world was as charming as this one.

Ah, but the lintel, the door, the whole house, and the sparkling daylight of Nazareth itself were all but a frame for the face within. Pale in the interior darkness, scarcely visible, as though her smile were winter's breath upon the air, was Mary, the daughter of this householder. She had strong brows, a high and even forehead, dark eyes, and a mouth of strong convictions.

"No, father," she declared, "we have not been talking together and you didn't know it."

Her father did not turn around but continued to look at Joseph, who continued to gaze straight past him to Mary.

"We meet," she said. "But there never has been much need for talk between us."

"Is that why you have been creeping around my house, Joseph son of Jacob? To meet with my daughter? To peek in at her? Man, you are as old as I am!"

"Father! Joseph is upright and you know it. He would do nothing rash or unrighteous. He has never been unkind to me — as you yourself know right well! Creeping and peeking? Every time we meet, Father, *you* are lurking nearby."

"Yes!" said Mary's father with energy. "And there has been a great deal of ear-whisperings lately, murmurings I could not interpret. What about *that*? Don't I have the paternal right to ask about that?"

"Father."

"What?"

"Joseph the son of Jacob has been asking me about the *mohar*."

"Oh. Yes. The *mohar*."

"Yes. He wants to marry me."

The bald-headed man frowned. He cleared his throat with such sudden and explosive fury that he seemed to damage himself. Then he drew his lips into a thin purse and announced: "A *mohar*, Joseph, is by ancient and honored custom usually calculated at fifty shekels of silver. Are you prepared to offer me, as compensation for the loss of my daughter, a full fifty shekels of silver?"

There was a long moment of silence. Joseph lowered his eyes. He was a large and powerful man; his great beard alone should have intimidated others — but his meekness gave them a sense of advantage, and his habitual muteness could provoke them to sudden wraths and rages.

Finally, Mary stepped into the doorway and spoke, her voice husky with feeling, her dark brows lifted high: "Everyone in Nazareth knows," she said, "that when his wife died, Joseph spent all he had upon her honor. This is no secret, Father. He sold his tools to buy space in a common cave, a narrow ledge for her tomb. He soaked her linen shroud in aloes and myrrh, very expensive — "

While she spoke Joseph gazed at his advocate with open admiration. What need had he to talk? Mary was so young, her hair soft and long and innocent, divided down the middle. But her chin was stubborn and her mind utterly sure of itself. In fact, it was Mary who conceived a good plan for the *mohar*.

"Joseph," she was saying to her father, "paid for the meals of the mourners — which, as you know, was most of Nazareth, the same good people that now are pleased to call him odd — though he himself fasted through seven days. For the sake of others he made himself a poor man."

"So, Joseph," Mary's father said, thrusting forth a pink lower lip, "so, then, is it your hope to bind my daughter to a poor man?"

"*Father!*"

But Joseph raised his hand.

"It is true, Joachim, that I am poor," he said, nodding and nodding. "But there is a *mohar* I can give." He turned and lumbered out of the yard, leaving Mary and her father alone for the moment.

"Where is he going?" Joachim said, blinking against the natural leakage of his tiny eyes. Mary, on the other hand, crept a little ways after Joseph, her own eyes filled with eagerness.

Soon Joseph returned with a very long, very heavy box hanging by a rope from his right shoulder. He set the box down at Joachim's feet, knelt, drew forth a shining adze, and glanced up. "See?" he said.

Joachim's blinking grew more rapid, his frown the darker.

Joseph pulled out several metal saws so new that Mary could no longer contain herself. She started to giggle. "See, Father?" she said. "Do you see?"

Next came chisels and awls and files, mallets of various sizes, a compass, a fine piece of chalk, a straight edge for measuring, and finally, marvelously constructed of wood and a well-ground blade, a plane. Joseph stroked this last tool with tenderness, then stood up and faced the householder, Joachim, Mary's father, directly.

"I will make for you two doorjambs," he said, "and the lintel and the door — installed. That is my *mohar*. I will weave two wooden lattices. And if your house needs new beams I will hew them too, though it will take me longer to get good wood."

Mary was grinning so hard her cheeks were as bright as pomegranates. "Joseph is a proud man, Father," she said, seizing Joachim's hand and kissing it. "He has always had a craft. You know that. But yesterday he finished making himself a whole new set of tools, and now he is ready for marriage again."

"Well," said Joachim, staring at the instruments scattered in his yard. "Well, this is all so sudden, you know. A father is dizzy. He is gasping with surprise, suffocating — "

"Yes, yes, Father — suffocate. But choke out an answer before you faint. Do you accept Joseph's offer?"

"Mary!" Joachim was wounded. He took his hand back and tucked it under his arm. "Isn't a man permitted a little time to consider the entire future life of his daughter and his son-in-law and the grandchildren to come?"

Mary cried, "Son-in-law? Did you say son-in-law?"

Her father continued, a woeful look on his round face: "Shouldn't a father be allowed to mourn the loss of his only daughter? Joseph, surely you know the goodness of patience and circumspection."

Joseph nodded, sympathy trembling on the rims of his eyelids.

But Mary clapped her hands and cried, "Finish it, Father! Oh, finish it! Set the date for betrothal, that my darling might begin to build you a beautiful house. And when the beams are up," she whispered, moving like breath on a winter's air, floating toward Joseph and touching the backs of his hands, "on the very day the beams are up," she whispered, "we will be married."

iv

S hortly after the autumn harvest, when the mornings were cool and the evenings dry — on Friday, the day before the Sabbath — some three hundred priests began to arrive in Jerusalem. They were coming to assume their sacred duties for the week, while three hundred others were leaving for home again because their duties were done.

Every week this exchange was made with grace and a strict formality. There were twenty-four courses of priests, divided according to family, each division serving at the temple for one week twice a year. When the service of one division was complete, they gave to the next division the keys of the temple and ninety-three sacred vessels, all in solemn ceremony.

On this Friday the division of Abijah, eighth in order of service, was gathering from villages and towns around Jerusalem. Tomorrow their sacred labors began.

Old Zechariah belonged to the clan of Abijah. He came on slow feet, his clothing in one large bag, six new spikes in another.

Normally he entered by the Sheep Gate, the nearest north side entrance to the city. Its road led straight up to the temple. But today he walked west along the northern wall, then south around a corner in the wall. Still outside the city, he passed the broken stone of old quarries. On his right side were tombs the Jews carved in the limestone hills; on his left, near the wall, were gardens ordered, cool, and green. Zechariah paused. He loved the genial peace of it all: olive trees, poplars, myrtle, juniper, hyssop, fig, mulberry, willow. Wealthy people owned these plots; a young man from Arimathea was rumored to have purchased a freshly turned corner; but they seldom sat here to enjoy their holdings. Zechariah did. He was old, somewhat melancholy about the passage of his life. He tended to sit in green places, thinking.

He and his wife were approaching their graves alone. They had borne no children. No generation existed to care for them when they could not care for themselves. No grandchildren. It was the sorrow of both their lives.

Zechariah continued walking. The city wall took a sharp turn westward, but his road went to a gate where the two walls met. He entered Jerusalem through the Garden Gate and was immediately surrounded by the rush and pressure of many people.

On either side of this street, all the way into the city, were shops and merchants, traders and craftsmen both making and selling their wares: woolen goods, carpets, and blankets. Jewelers sat under whitewashed roofs. Flax traders hung their products on smooth wood railings; bakers sold bread as fast as it came from the back of the shop; sandal makers on their stools called to tailors on theirs. This was one of two market streets in Jerusalem, and Jerusalem was thriving: wines, oils, fruits, flour milled from barley, cheeses, eggs, the chicken itself. People were sweeping the great stones of the pavement. Butchers had a street all to themselves. Weavers worked in the southeast portion of the city. Tanners and curriers were required to set their workshops where the smell could not offend either the pilgrim or the priest.

Jerusalem was supported by the rich, vigorous business of the temple. Offerings and tithes fed its treasury, from which the temple servants were paid: stonemasons, sculptors, tapestry makers, those who designed fountains, doctors, barbers, experts in drainage and wells and cisterns. The temple was built of alabaster, stibium, and marble. The courts were paved with wide slabs of smooth stone. Delicate stone lattices three cubits high separated the inner court from the outer courts of the Gentiles. All this required the care of skilled personnel. And all these workers, when they were paid, spent it in the markets of Jerusalem.

The keeping of the temple curtains alone could support a small village. Skilled weavers and knitters had to produce annually two new curtains, twenty cubits wide and forty long. There were twenty-six such curtains hanging in the temple, each woven of six colors on seventy-two strands, each strand with twenty-four threads. It took the steady labor of eighty-two maidens to make two curtains a year.

Zechariah toiled through the crowds until he came to a cross-street. He turned right and lifted his eyes to the final grandeur of King Herod, and he sighed. Here on the western heights of Zion was a palace containing two magnificent banquet halls at opposite ends and rooms enough for two hundred guests — besides the apartments of his ten wives and all his children and all their servants. Soldiers were garrisoned under three mighty towers at the northern end of the building, and all around it were courtyards and gardens and promenades, bordered by canals and lovely pools, fountains and ingenious water spouts.

Zechariah was sixty-nine years old. His wife Elizabeth was sixty-five. They had been married for fifty years. King Herod had been blessed with fifteen children in his old age. Did he know how to give thanks to the Lord? Did he know that each child was more precious than a palace and that the honor each child might render was more enduring than gold?

The old priest sighed again and then diminished himself by approaching the palace. He had to deliver his spikes.

∎

But the king was not in his palace. He had long been sick with an interior affliction whose pain could sometimes grow intolerable. He could not move his fingers, his arms or legs because of the anguish in them. At such times he traveled to the town of Callirrhoe on the eastern shores of the Dead Sea, where there were natural hot springs to ease the aggravation in his extremities.

This time Herod had to be carried the entire distance in a palanquin on the shoulders of six servants. The journey had taken a week.

And now he spent his days stripped to a loin cloth, lying in the steaming water, attended by a secretary and two close counselors.

King Herod genuinely expected to survive this present affliction. Nevertheless, physical pain always caused in him a restless anxiety regarding the identity of his successor. While he lay in the pools of Callirrhoe, therefore, he was revising an old will. He was dictating a new one with sudden barks and fierce decisions naming various sons of his to the throne once he should leave it.

Herod churned the waters with his obsessions.

He had already written and sealed one will naming Alexander, the son of Mariamne, to be his successor — and then another, naming her other son Aristobulus. But these two were about to perish. Two princes and two wills were destroyed, driving Herod to his third will.

"Antipater!" cried the king, dashing water in the yellow baths of Callirrhoe. "Antipater! The son of my first wife, my dear Doris. Inscribe his name on your tablet, sir. Antipater: to him I give my throne, and he will reign over Judea!"

∎

On Friday morning, when lots were cast to determine which priests received which duties for the day, it fell to Zechariah to offer incense in the Holy Place during the *Tamid*, the evening sacrifice.

The old man was speechless with joy. Elizabeth, too, would be glad. This was the first time in all his years as priest that he had ever been selected to offer incense. At his age it would also be the last time.

That afternoon Zechariah entered one of the chambers on the south side of the temple, a small cubicle lighted by thin sunlight through a lattice. There he washed his rough face and body according to the rituals of purification, and then he dressed: clean linen breeches on his old loins; a pure white tunic pulled down from his shoulder to his ankle. With his bent hands he wrapped around his waist a handsome belt also of white linen but embroidered with a single scarlet thread. Finally Zechariah bound his head in a turban as white as his tunic, then went out into the court of the priests and walked to the front of the temple, to the Altar of Burnt Offering.

The *Tamid* began when two priests came and arranged new wood on the coals of the high altar. It sent up a sweet smoke, and a choir of Levites raised their voices in song. At the foot of the altar, a Levite bent down and with one stroke killed a lamb. A priest caught its blood in a bowl, bore the bowl up the altar steps, raised it to heaven, then dashed the blood against the stones of the altar. The Levites struck their musical instruments and sang and sang. Zechariah stood at one side, waiting his turn. Beside him stood another priest, holding a silver firepan.

Now the officiating priest returned to the lamb and cut it into pieces. He washed it, then carried the entire carcass up to the Altar of Burnt Offering and laid it on the fire. While the meat hissed and sent to heaven a linen-white smoke, the priest began to chant the evening prayer. Another priest carried a meal offering up to the fires of the altar, fine flour soaked in oil. The smell of baking filled the air, and the Levites sang and sang.

Now the man who stood by Zechariah touched his shoulder and moved forward. It was their turn.

Zechariah was transported. He seemed to sail up the steps of the temple porch. When he paused at the door and turned, he discovered that his kneecaps were trembling beneath the tunic.

The assisting priest had gone to the Altar of Burnt Offering. With tongs he took good glowing coals from the fire and placed them in his silver firepan; then he, too, climbed the steps of the porch. At the same time another assistant came up with a dish of incense and a silver spoon.

One priest on his left, and one on his right, Zechariah turned and walked through the doors into the Holy Place, his heart hammering. Then it happened again as it had at the dedication of the temple fourteen years ago: Zechariah started to cry. There was no sobbing. Simply, the tears began to stream down his cheeks of their own accord, and he considered it a gift of God, that he could both enter the temple and weep on entering.

Evening light struck at the high windows. A single, magnificent, seven-branched lampstand stood to one side shedding a yellow light. Zechariah and his assistants moved directly toward the small Altar of Incense. The priest with the firepan tipped all its coals into the altar grating. A quick ghost of sparks flew up before them. The other priest set his dish of incense on the side of the altar, then both of them withdrew.

Zechariah was alone.

Water dropped on the coals, spitting and searing him, till he realized that it was his tears.

Oh, then the old priest beamed. He loved dearly the heat of his forge. It was the comfort of a stable life. But *this* heat, this smaller sacred fire touching the same hands and flesh and face — this heat shot his spirit straight to heaven.

Zechariah reached for the little silver spoon, weightless in his thick fist, and scooped it full of powdery incense. He lifted the spoon above the burning coals, then scattered the powder down. It twinkled on the coals like red stars in heaven. He spooned more and more incense into the altar, until great clouds of smoke billowed through the temple, catching streaks of sunlight near the ceiling and pouring out the doors. The crowds outside saw the smoke. They raised their voices in prayer. Zechariah heard them in the distance, saying: *Make haste! Make haste to hear us, O Lord —*

But suddenly the air at the right side of the altar tore apart as if it were a curtain, and fire broke into the room, a pure white flame with its foot on the floor and its crown at the high beams of the ceiling. The heat should have consumed Zechariah's clothing and seared his flesh!

He opened his mouth but could not scream.

The white flame said, "Do not be afraid, Zechariah, for your prayer is heard, and your wife Elizabeth will bear you a son, and you shall call his name John."

It seemed to Zechariah that there now appeared within the standing light a human form; but this was the shading of light in light he saw, a sparkling in the region of the eyes, darkness at the mouth, a spilling of brilliance all down two arms, a torso, and two eternal legs.

Zechariah whispered, "Prayer? What prayer?" The question was a reflex. The man was terrified.

The flame said, "You will know both joy and gladness, for he will be great before the Lord. Your son will turn many in Israel to the Lord their God."

"A son?" the priest breathed.

The bright flame said, "He must drink no wine nor any strong drink. He will be filled with the Holy Spirit even from his mother's womb. He will go before the Lord in the power of Elijah, turning the hearts of parents to their children and the disobedient to justice again, preparing for the Lord a people!"

Zechariah covered his face with his thick hands. "Sir," he said in anguish, "don't ridicule me. I am an old man. My wife is an old woman. It cannot happen as you say."

The flame said, "Look at me."

Zechariah hunched farther down.

The light cried, "I am Gabriel. Look at me!"

The old man uncovered his eyes. *Gabriel?*

"I, who stand in the presence of God, was sent to bring you this good news."

Gabriel, angel of the Deity, appearing here in cosmic fire!

The old man gaped. *Yes!* Yes, there was a human form in light before him.

The angel said, "Old man, because you doubted me, you shall be both deaf and mute until the day these things have come to pass."

■

Outside the temple the choir of Levites had sung themselves into silence. They had finished the cycle of their music. There was no more to sing. Yet the priest appointed to offer incense still lingered within. Finally, two priests in the Nikanor Gate raised long silver trumpets to their lips and released a long, declarative blast. Where was Zechariah? It was time for the drink offering with which the evening sacrifice came to its ending.

There! There was the foolish old man on the temple porch. He was raising his arms. He was opening his mouth and thrusting out his tongue. Everyone knew the word that should come forth: *The Lord bless you and keep you* —

But the priest could utter nothing at all. No blessing, no explanation.

Helplessly he stumbled down the porch steps, his rugged face wet with tears, his eyes gaping. He rushed round to the chamber where he had left his clothing, and he disappeared. Sometime during the night the senile priest must have emerged unseen. Sometime in private he took himself home again.

V

Joseph the son of Jacob presented himself at Joachim's house precisely at noon on the day of his betrothal. He was wearing a clean tunic of coarse woolen weave — sleeveless, roped at the waist, a blue stripe running down its right side from the shoulder to the hem. Over the tunic he had cast a cloak with loose blue fringes at each corner. His hair was oiled. His beard remained a thicket as high as his eyes, but the ends had been trimmed.

Joseph's parents had died seven years ago. Therefore, he came alone. But in his huge hands he carried a rolled parchment with such precious care that one might have regarded this article as his companion and friend. It was soft with age. A cramped writing showed on the visible side. The letters were not Aramaic, but Hebrew. This was news. Joachim had not known that Joseph could read Hebrew.

For his own part, Joachim had invited a goodly number of guests both to witness the betrothal and to enjoy a feast afterward. Mary was his only daughter. Mary, in fact, was his only child. He had no sons. The man Joseph, then, almost as old as Joachim himself, was about to become his son. There was merit in the day. There was reason for celebration.

So people arranged themselves in the little yard before the house of Joachim and his wife Anne. The guests stood on either side, their backs to the walls, forming a pretty colonnade. The dark-haired Mary took a position just inside the doorway, smiling like a white rose. Her mother stood beside her, dropping her eyes and drawing a linen scarf up to the bridge of her nose. Anne strove for the proper expressions of modesty. Not Mary. She had looked forward to this day. Eagerness burned in her eyes, and her white teeth flashed gladness like the sunlight.

Joachim and Joseph faced one another, the father before the door of his house, the suitor just inside the gate.

Joachim now, in a gesture of rigid formality, threw back his bald head, thrust out his bottom lip, and spoke in Hebrew, saying, "For the *mohar* agreed upon, you shall now be my son-in-law." Again he said, "Joseph son of Jacob, you shall now be my son-in-law."

Then Joseph spoke. Actually, Joseph bellowed. He opened his mouth and, oblivious of the energy with which he pronounced the formula, roared: "I came to thy house... for thee to give me thy daughter... Mary... to wife! She is my wife and I am her husband from this day and forever!"

Suddenly Mary lent music to the day. She burst into laughter. Anne turned and tugged her daughter's robe, but there was no stopping the girl now. A hundred emotions played in Mary's face, her eyes shining bright, all filled with loving, her laugh announcing that her husband was an ox, her deep grin adding: *But what a handsome ox, don't you think?*

This was infectious. Guests began to giggle and hide their mouths behind their hands. But they couldn't contain the joy that Mary caused. Soon the yard of Joachim the father-in-law was a rolling, bubbling stew of jubilation. People wept with laughter. Every time someone would slow down and stop, he had only to glance at Mary's blooming countenance and off he went again, laughing till his poor sides ached.

Joseph, however, had not yet completed the steps of his betrothal. With great solemnity he walked through the commotion toward Joachim, holding out before him the precious parchment. Joachim lifted his hands to receive it. Then, when Joseph was relieved of this last thing — the parchment and the duty, both — he heaved a sigh and went into the house to stand by Mary, gazing outward at the guests. His hands hung like dead weights at his thighs; his shoulders stooped because of their great size in a small room; his beard absolutely concealed the mouth and any expression. Joseph might have been suffering some distress at the hilarity that had overtaken the day of his betrothal — except for this, that when Mary turned and touched his shoulder and drew a gauzy public veil across her face, the man's ears flamed a furious red and he was reduced to blowing his nose over and over again.

▮

When Joachim had read all that was written on the document which Joseph had given to him on the day of Mary's betrothal, he returned it to his son-in-law with pride and with gratitude. He never saw it again. Neither did he ever forget the names he found in sequence there, for they defined the sort of grandchild he would one day have:

A BOOK OF BEGETTINGS

Abraham was the father of Isaac.

Isaac was the father of Jacob.

Jacob was the father of Judah and of his eleven brothers.

Judah was the father of Perez and Zerah by Tamar, whose courage preserved herself and her sons when she had been rejected by arrogant men.

Perez went with his father Judah and all the sons of Jacob into Egypt, where Joseph was vizier to Pharaoh. There he became the father of Hezron.

In Egypt Hezron was the father of Aram.

Aram was the father of Amminadab.

Amminadab was the father of Nahshon.

Nahshon lived when Moses led the children of Israel out of Egypt through the sea to the Mountain of God, Sinai. In the wilderness he became the father of Salmon.

Salmon was the father of Boaz by Rahab, who had been a prostitute; but she trusted God and she saved the lives of the men who had come to spy in her city, Jericho. Her own life, then, was spared when Joshua fought that city and Israel entered the Promised Land.

Boaz was the father of Obed by Ruth, a Moabite who loved her mother-in-law so much that she left the land of her birth in order to dwell with Naomi in Israel.

Obed was the father of Jesse.

Jesse was the father of David, king of Israel.

Thus the generations from Abraham to David are fourteen generations.

David was the father of Solomon by Bathsheba, with whom the king had lain in sin but whom the Lord elevated to become herself the mother of a king.

Solomon was the father of Rehoboam the king of Judah when the rest of Israel had torn itself away from him.

Rehoboam was the father of Abijah.

Abijah was the father of Asa.

Asa, who reigned long and well, was the father of Jehoshaphat.

Jehoshaphat was the father of Joram.

Joram was the father of Uzziah.

Uzziah was the father of Jotham.

Jotham was the father of Ahaz.

Ahaz reigned when Isaiah was a prophet. He did not heed the prophet's word. He was the father of Hezekiah.

Hezekiah, whom Isaiah loved and to whom the Lord showed mercy, was the father of Manasseh.

Manasseh was the father of Amon.

Amon was the father of Josiah.

Josiah was a good and faithful king. He discovered the Book of the Law and commanded the whole kingdom of Judah to obey it. He was the father of Jehoiakim and his brothers at the time of the Babylonian Exile.

Thus the generations from David to the Babylonian Exile were also fourteen — all of them named by the names of kings in Israel and Judah. This second list of begettings is royal.

After the Babylonian Exile, Jehoiakim was the father of Shealtiel.
Shealtiel was the father of Zerubbabel, under whom the second temple in Jerusalem was built.
Zerubbabel was the father of Abiud.
Abiud, who lived in Jerusalem when the walls were built again under Nehemiah, was the father of Eliakim.
Eliakim was the father of Azor.
Azor lived when Alexander the Greek marched past Jerusalem, making the whole world his empire. Azor was the father of Zadok.
Zadok was the father of Achim.
Achim was the father of Eliud.
Eliud lived when Judas Maccabeus and his brothers revolted against the foreign rulers of Judea. Eliud rejoiced in their victories, for Judea became an independent land again and the temple was cleansed and dedicated unto the Lord, the God of Israel. Eliud was the father of Eleazar.
Eleazar was the father of Matthan.
Matthan moved from the regions of Jerusalem north to Galilee after it had been added to the territories ruled by the kings of Judea, the high priests of Jerusalem. He settled in the village of Nazareth and there became the father of Jacob.
Jacob was my father.
He told me of the Roman general who fought and killed twelve thousand Jews in order to seize the Holy temple in Jerusalem. He told me, too, of Julius Caesar, who defeated Pompey and raised to power Antipater, the father of King Herod.
I am Joseph.

Upon the evidence herewith recorded,
let it be recognized by those who honor lineage
that my son shall be
a son of David,
a son of Abraham,
a good and godly heritage.

vi

After fifty years of marriage, she comes to believe that she knows her old husband fairly well. She thinks of him often but unconsciously, exactly as she thinks of her familiar little sitting stool where, on long afternoons, she sits her body down and dozes off. (When she naps she holds a bronze spoon in her hand, allowing her arm to hang at her side. Her head droops and droops, and when that spoon slips from her fingers and strikes the floor-stones, she wakes with a start. Enough of sleeping! Back to work.) The husband of fifty years, undemonstrative but trustworthy, obedient to the laws of God and kind to his wrinkled old wife — he has become the blessed furniture of her existence, as much her home as any house might be.

After fifty years even the smallest variations in his habits are immediately apparent.

▌

Zechariah returned too early from Jerusalem and from the duties of his weekly course at the temple. He was too early by a day and a half. He never traveled on the Sabbath. He always walked home on Monday. He walked home in daylight.

But long before the sun rose on the Sabbath, in the chilly autumn dark, Elizabeth was awakened by hammering, the ringing sound of metal upon a harder metal. She lit a candle and went out to Zechariah's shop. There he was, his solemn face glowing orange in the light of the forge, bent to his anvil, his forearms furrowed with muscles tense to the labor, a hammer and a tongs. He struck the red-hot tip of a spike, sending out a shower of sparks.

He was working. On the Sabbath! To her knowledge, her husband had never walked long nor worked on the Sabbath before.

Suddenly he looked up and saw her standing in the night. He gazed at her. His eyes were black pools, hidden in shadow — but she felt his wakeful attention upon herself, upon her bodily self. This, too, was new in the old man. Elizabeth became conscious of the lightness of her robe, of her great flat feet on the cool earth, the long braid in her hair, and the tender flesh at her throat. It was a curious thing: while they were standing thus, Elizabeth blushed.

Zechariah didn't say a word.

He laid his tools down, closed the forge upon its coals and its orange light, stepped out of the darkness, took her hand, and gently led her back to their tiny courtyard. There he put his finger to his lips and nodded, asking silence, perhaps, or patience or understanding.

But she had no understanding. Elizabeth didn't know what was happening to them. She found that she could not draw a steady breath. She was panting.

Her old husband crouched at the cistern and brought up a jar filled with water. Again, without a word of explanation, he beckoned his wife to follow and carried the water into the house, to their sleeping room where the blankets on her pallet were disarranged from sleeping. She felt an urge to straighten them. She set her candle in a sconce, knelt down and spread out her hands to grab the hem — but in the same instant Zechariah lightly knelt beside her.

"Shhh," he said, gazing into her eyes. "Shhh."

The old man's rough face was so filled with wonder that he seemed suddenly a shining being, and shivers ran all down her body. Elizabeth had not been so conscious of his *presence* before, the dear man's nearness.

He poured water into a basin. He moistened a good clean cloth and then, kneeling before her, he began to wash her face.

Slowly, with no haste, he washed himself as well.

He slipped her robe from her shoulders and washed her neck, her arms, and then her bosom.

Ah, she was old! Her ribs were like slats in her sides. She was wrinkled, and her breasts lay as flat as empty sleeves. But Zechariah stroked her old body with such slow wonder, with such sweet, elastic generosity, that the woman could not help but gaze back into his eyes and smile as though she were lovely after all and willing to make a gift of it.

So then the old man blew out the candle. He gathered Elizabeth's braid to one side, lowered her shoulders and her beautiful head down to the pallet. He kissed her, and, marvelously, he came into her.

Elizabeth wept.

Zechariah said nothing at all, neither in the dark of the early morning nor in the light of the following day.

31

MARY

i

The houses of Nazareth were built on the steep sides of a hill that faced east and southeast. They received a morning sunlight. The soil, too, was good for growing vines and vegetables. The weather was kind because of the hill's protection, and the rainfall was generous. But there was only one spring of water for the entire village, so Nazareth always remained small. Those who lived there knew one another very well.

Six months after her betrothal to Joseph, in the spring of the year when the rains had passed and the ground was green, Mary sought a little privacy by climbing the slopes above the village. On the crown of the hill she found a chalky-white path and took it, wandering first westward, then south. She removed the veil which she as a woman betrothed was required to wear in public. She released her hair from its hood. She allowed the wind of high places to bathe her face, to raise her hair like a long black wing, to blow through her loosened clothing. Suddenly she came to a sheer rocky drop on the southern ridge. She stopped and stared into the great green plain of Esdraelon, then she burst into tears.

Mary sat down and gave herself over to sobbing, taking huge whooping breaths and shaking her shoulders. It felt very good to cry, though she hadn't a notion why she should be crying — except, perhaps, that she was alone. She had not been truly alone since the betrothal, when every citizen in Nazareth declared her a woman and began to watch her as if she were a girl again.

The valley beneath her feet was lovely, patchy green and yellow, divided into the plots of the farmers, the wheat and barley just springing up.

Oh, she felt so sad. Yes, and at the same time happy. Excited. Not content, really. Scared.

Mary bowed her head, buried her face in her arms, and wept.

Suddenly a hand seized her shoulder in a very strong grip. In the same instant thunder crashed at her ear. She jumped and would have tumbled from the cliff, but for the hand that held her.

The thunder said, "Hail!"

Mary opened her eyes, terrified. There was no one there. No *one* there, no person, no hand at all — but a dazzling pillar of light, its base upon the rocky hill, its pinnacle endless in the heavens.

The light said, "Hail, O favored one, the Lord is with you."

Mary gaped, withdrawing from the radiance by pushing backward on the earth.

The light said, "Don't be afraid, Mary."

The light said *Mary*. It called her by name! She paused. She leaned forward and peered into the illumination as though it were glass and had depth, and then it seemed to her that she saw a human figure, magnificent in size, smooth in proportion, a face attentive and looking back at her. The face said, *Mary*.

Oh, my Lord! It is your angel!

The angel said, "Mary, you have found favor with God. Behold, you will conceive in your womb and bear a son, and you shall call his name Jesus.

> *He will be great;*
> *he will be called the Son of the Most High;*
> *to him will the Lord God give*
> *the throne of his father David,*
> *and he will reign over the house of Jacob forever!"*

Mary, altogether unconscious of herself, Mary on her hands and knees, gazing upward into the primal light, her body casting no shadow whatever though her face was warmed by the light — Mary said, "Ah, sir, no, sir. I think this cannot be, because I am a virgin. I have never known a man."

But the angel said,

> *The Holy Spirit will come upon you,*
> *and the power of the Most High will overshadow you;*
> *therefore the child to be born will be called holy,*
> *the Son of God!*

There seemed, then, a dimming of light, as though the heavenly pillar were resolving itself into white cloud.

Yet the angel was still speaking: "Mary, go see for yourself that nothing will be impossible with God. Visit your kinswoman Elizabeth, who is very old. She, too, has conceived a son. This is the sixth month with her who was called barren."

Mary whispered, "I am the handmaid of the Lord. Let it happen to me according to your word."

So then there was no angel at all, but a cloud blowing out over the plain of Esdraelon, spreading, changing shape, seeming an eagle with two wings flying, casting a shadow wide enough to cover the fields of yellow and green.

ii

Joachim's house was very old. Five generations old, at least. In order to change the beams, Joseph had to remove the entire roof. He cleared its topsoil first, upon which a spring grass had been allowed to grow, for the root-mat gave strength and the grass a protection. Then he broke the rolled, sunbaked clay that covered a very old lathing, thin slats supported by the beams themselves. The beams had suffered two fires over the generations. The damage had been hidden by a ceiling of clay plaster; but it was now his father-in-law's notion to build a little room on the roof, and Joseph had recognized that the present structure would not sustain the continual combined walking and weight of Joachim and Anne, two bodies beloved of God, to be sure, but very round.

During the winter rainy season — just after the ceremonies of betrothal — Joseph had paid attention to the door-work, the window lattices, and the interior preparations. He scored the ceiling plaster and scraped it down. Now that the rains had ended, he began on the roof.

Daily he saw Mary. Always upon arrival, he grinned and pulled his beard and flapped a hand in her direction. It used to be that he felt like a fool in her presence, lumbering and wordless, while she could so quickly utter light laughter and sentences of brave, whip-cracking intelligence. But now she wore a veil and seemed demure! That eased him, though it was only a seeming. Mary giggled often under the veil, her dark brows rising with sweet expression, like the wings of sparrows.

No, the real difference between Joseph's bashfulness and his comfort was that he had settled into the trust of the betrothal and found it consoling. Joseph was forty years old, given rather more to stabilities than to passions. And he was working again. His days had purpose and a schedule. And he himself had grown confident of Mary's love. The woman, so young and smart and beautiful, would be constant.

They planned to marry in summer, when Joachim's house was altogether finished.

But in the spring — exactly three weeks after Joseph had begun his work on the roof itself — Mary suddenly wasn't there.

For three days Joseph came and waited to wave his greeting, but she didn't appear and he felt her absence terribly. He lost concentration for the job. Yet he said nothing to Joachim or Anne. He hid his growing anxiety.

This was his nature. It was the hardest thing in the world for the big man to do, to speak his feelings or his fears — especially when they involved confusion and guilt. Ignorance snatched speech right out of his mouth.

Was Mary avoiding him? Had he offended her somehow?

Neither was her father saying anything to Joseph these days, but he, at least, was visible. From time to time he would stick his head out of the house and scowl at his son-in-law with a black, speechless anger.

What had Joseph done? At home alone, the poor man began to sink into despair.

And then in the evening of the fourth day, Ann came unannounced to Joseph's house. He went out to greet her and saw that she had brought lentils and onions and rice in a pot. She entered his little courtyard, and he watched her as she kindled a fire of dried brush and dung. Dung burns slowly, with much smoke. Apparently she intended to linger a while.

When the fire was hot, she poured olive oil over the vegetables and the grain in her pot and began slowly to stir. Joseph liked lentil stew.

While she was stirring, Anne said, "Joachim does not know that I have come. You needn't tell him nor fear that I will tell him. This is our business."

She fell silent, staring into the stew. Like her husband, Anne was nearly as wide as she was high. When she meditated, her mouth compulsively pursed over and over again. A network of wrinkles laced her lips.

Suddenly she said, "Won't you allow us even to talk?"

The stew had begun to send forth a pleasant aroma. Joseph had found himself grateful for Anne's presence. But this question immediately caused anguish in his breast. He didn't know what she was talking about.

"What?" he said.

Anne said, "Are you going to keep her from me? Even from me?"

Joseph peered at his mother-in-law, seeking understanding.

"Who — ? Keep who from you?"

Anne turned to the door. "Mary!" she called. "Mary, can we talk together?"

Joseph widened his eyes with horrible comprehension and spoke: "You don't know where Mary is?"

Anne stopped stirring the stew. "No," she whispered. "Don't you?"

Joseph rose to his feet and grabbed his beard. There was no guilt in him now. Only fear. He had a fierce urge to run out into the countryside looking for Mary.

Anne's eyes, too, were filled with panic.

"But she took her clothes!" Anne said. "Last Sabbath Joachim and I went to the synagogue in Japhia. Mary said she wanted to be alone. It was late when we got home. The house was dark and she was gone. She took her clothes. Joseph, if she isn't here, where is she? Didn't she tell you anything?"

By the sixth month of her pregnancy, Elizabeth the wife of Zechariah, sixty-five years old, was blooming.

"God has smoothed my wrinkles," she said. "He has filled my breasts with life again and given my bony body weight for a while."

She called herself a gourd. She said she was like a cucumber, so quickly had she swelled up. Her womb was full. A baby! In three months, when Elizabeth turned sixty-six, she would also bend forward and bear a baby into the world. Oh, she spent her days attending to the domestic work as if she were young again, and except in the afternoons when she took dozy little naps on her sitting stool, Elizabeth spent the daytime humming and whistling and singing songs.

Then early one evening she heard a rapping on her door. She wiped her hands and went to see who was there.

Zechariah didn't hear the knock. Zechariah wouldn't have heard a hammer on his anvil or thunder in the heavens. Ever since the night of his "vision of angels," as he described it in writing for her — the old nailsmith had been completely deaf and dumb.

So Elizabeth opened her door herself — and there stood her nephew's child, Joachim's little girl, whom she had not seen in years. "Mary!" Elizabeth cried. "Pretty Mary, it's you! But you're alone!"

But this was no common visit.

And Mary was not a child anymore.

Her dark brows were lifted in an intense appeal, and her eyes were filled with beseeching. Clearly, she had come with a question.

Then several things happened so swiftly that they were all one thing, and that thing was the revelation of God.

Mary's eyes dropped to Elizabeth's breasts and then to her belly. In the softest of whispers, she said, "Hail, Elizabeth."

Immediately the baby in Elizabeth's womb leaped up to her heart, and old Elizabeth shrieked.

Because Elizabeth suddenly understood everything: the child inside of her, the reason for Mary's appearing, the glory of the days in which they were living, the great thing that God was starting to do!

"Oh, Mary!" Elizabeth cried. She grabbed her young niece by both her arms and pulled her into the house. "Mary, blessed are you among women, and blessed is the fruit of your womb!"

Mary mouthed the words, *My womb?*

Elizabeth gathered the woman in a crushing embrace and howled, "What a gift has been given me, that the mother of my Lord should come to me!"

Mary said, "You know about me?"

Elizabeth released her, covered her face, and began to cry.

"Mary, I know!" she said. "I know what child is in you right now. As soon as you spoke to me, the babe in my own womb jumped for joy, and that was a prophecy. Oh, sweetheart, blessed are you to have believed that the Lord would fulfill the word he spoke to you!"

"He told me that I would conceive a child," Mary said to Elizabeth. "He said that the child would be holy, the Son of God! He said my baby would be called the Son of God."

Elizabeth stepped past Mary and shut the door of the room. She returned, took her niece by the hand, and led her to a small, three-legged stool. Gently Elizabeth urged her to sit, then she knelt down before Mary, and the two women gazed at each other, one whose hair, all white, was gathered in a braid, the other whose hair hung all around her shoulders like a black cape.

Mary whispered, "Things are changing, Elizabeth! I think God is turning the whole world upside down. What do you think?"

The older woman started to nod, but the words were pouring from Mary now: "God is lifting up the little people, a lowly maid like me, Elizabeth. He is blessing me! Next he will knock the mighty from their thrones! And hungry people will eat, and rich people will go hungry! Things are changing! I know it. The world will not be the same tomorrow. Does anyone else know this, too?"

Elizabeth reached for Mary's hands and put them on the tough roundness of her own womb. "This baby knows it," she said. "And maybe my old husband knows something, too."

"God is rising up, just as he did for Israel in Egypt." Mary's eyes were filled with a hectic brightness. The times themselves were converging in her mind. Elizabeth watched the young woman fairly explode with understanding. Mary said, "God is remembering his people! He is remembering the promises which he made to our ancestors, to Abraham and to Abraham's children forever. Oh, Elizabeth, my soul magnifies the Lord! I can't help it anymore. My spirit is rejoicing in God my Savior!"

▌▍

Mary stayed with Elizabeth and Zechariah for three months after that. Often the women murmured and chattered together as if they were the same age, not a half one hundred years apart. And when the commotion caught his eye, Zechariah would look up and smile as well; but his participation was limited.

On the other hand, he was forever tender with his wife now. He touched her cheek with the backs of his fingers. His eyes were voluble with expression, and Elizabeth's eyes were ears of an excellent listening: she understood.

It was Elizabeth who remembered Joachim and Anne and Joseph. She sent word that Mary was visiting, acting now as her companion and soon as her midwife.

Then, when the old woman went into labor, she took immense satisfaction in screaming. She paid attention to the strapping pain, the astonishing strength in her old body, and she gave voice to every new degree of hurting. She screamed like a sixteen-year-old. Everyone in the village knew that the day had arrived, that a baby was coming to a woman who had been barren longer than most of them had lived.

It was a boy.

Elizabeth had known that it would be a boy. Zechariah had written it down on tablets: *A son, filled with the Holy Spirit already in your womb. A son, and we shall call his name John.*

When her jubilant screaming was done and the thin thread of infant squalling had begun, then the neighbors knew, and soon they came to visit. They praised the newborn baby; they rejoiced with his mother; they grinned at his old father, bobbing their heads up and down as if he had lost his brains as well as his hearing.

On the eighth day of the child's life, friends and relatives of Zechariah and Elizabeth gathered for his circumcision. In the midst of the ceremony, a rabbi began to refer to him as "Zechariah." They were naming the boy after his father: Zechariah.

But when she understood their intent, Elizabeth stood up and cried, "No!" She moved toward her son saying, "He shall be called John."

"John?" said the rabbi. "There's no one named John in your families." He turned to Zechariah, who was sitting on a three-legged stool, oblivious of the interruption.

The rabbi stood directly in front of the nailsmith to get his attention, then he pointed at Zechariah and made huge mouth gestures: ZECH - AHHH - RYE - AHHH! Next he pointed at the baby and repeated the same four enormous syllables, bobbing his head up and down, seeking agreement.

Old Zechariah watched but showed no new expression. Neither did he acknowledge the rabbi's massive interrogative. Instead, he rose up and went into the other room, then came back with a writing tablet. Standing where the rabbi and others could see what he was doing, he wrote on the tablet in Aramaic: *His name is John.*

Everyone who saw the inscription marveled.

And immediately Zechariah's tongue was loosed, and he began to speak — softly, softly praising God.

Elizabeth covered her mouth, overcome with emotion. He had not spoken since the night of their making love.

Except for the soft singing of Zechariah's new voice, silence fell upon the room. The rabbi himself had been struck dumb. Who could doubt that this was the work of the Lord?

In the land where the people had not heard a prophet for hundreds
of years, Zechariah, a nailsmith and a priest, an old man with a savage
countenance was filled with the Holy Spirit and singing the prophecy of God:

"Blessed be the Lord God of Israel," Zechariah sang, "for he is visiting
his people! He has raised up a horn of salvation for us in the house of his
servant David, exactly as he promised — that we should be saved from the
hands of those who hate us.

"God is remembering his holy covenant! God is remembering the oath
he swore to our father Abraham, to grant that we, being delivered from our
enemies, might serve him without fear, in holiness and righteousness all the
days of our life!"

Now the old man moved toward his baby boy. "You, my son," he
whispered. "You, John," he sang in greater voice, gathering the child into
his powerful arms,

"Ah, you will be called the prophet of the Most High,
because you will go before the Lord to prepare his way,
to give his people knowledge of salvation
in the forgiveness of their sins,
through the tender mercy of our God,
when the day shall dawn,
giving light to those who sit in the shadow of death,
light to guide our feet into the way of peace."

iii

Spring turned into summer. The sky remained bright blue and cloudless
all day long. The lack of a roof in the dry season was not a problem.
Therefore, Joseph could work at a careful pace, making sure that
no one would ever be able to find fault with his *mohar*, keeping his mind
completely on his work, refusing to think of anything except the precision
and quality of his work.

Then, suddenly, the beautiful Mary was home, smiling at him, kissing the
few naked places on his person, his ear, his forehead, his neck — and poor
Joseph lost concentration all over again.

He felt anger and fear together, because Mary had put herself in harm's
way, traveling alone without a word to anyone. Yet he could not scold the
woman.

He felt hurt that she hadn't trusted him enough to tell him of her
journey. Even now she offered no explanations. Part of the man guessed
that this was her own affair. Part felt sad that she would conceal some

important thing from him. But the very sadness prevented him from asking. It wasn't in his nature to demand. Moreover, if he had attempted to open the topic at all, between his first word and his second Mary would have produced a whole speech, very eloquent, and he would have forgotten all his thought in hers.

Joseph, therefore, kept his questions to himself.

But soon he saw that Mary was not the same as she had been at their betrothal, and the confusion increased.

She spoke less. Her eyes had become strange, as if gazing away from the world — gazing inward, perhaps. Her face had taken a high flushed color. It was growing rounder. She herself seemed to him radiantly lovely. Changed. Not girlish, but gathering on her frame a woman's softer loveliness. Nevertheless, she often climbed to the roof and watched him work. Then she would rush to him and hug him very, very hard — ignoring the mud and his sweat.

Soon his anger passed away in such hugging. His hurt was healed. Fear remained, perhaps because the woman was not talking, not chattering as she used to do — though she smiled as perpetually as the moon.

And then, during one particularly long hug when Mary began to sob, Joseph felt several physical changes that had been hidden from his eyes before: Her breasts had grown large and proud. Her body was generally rounder. And between the wings of Mary's hips, a tough lump had formed, pressing back upon the man who hugged her. Joseph stepped back and searched her face. Her tears were rain under sunshine: she was beaming, her dark brows raised so high, her teeth blinding white, her eyes peering out of mystery.

But the face was fuller. Her lips were thicker.

With an uncharacteristic boldness, Joseph reached and placed his hand upon her abdomen. Mary stopped smiling. She watched him, now, with thin lines of fright.

Yes. There was a baby in Mary's womb!

Joseph took his hand back. Silently he went to the edge of the roof, descended the ladder, and walked away through the village to his home. He went inside and lay down upon his floor and hid his face in the crook of his arm and began to cry.

Joseph had not cried since the death of his first wife.

In the evening there came a knock at his door. He rose up to open it, expecting Mary. But it was Anne, short and round and grey and sad. She went to his hearth and kindled a fire of dry sticks and dung. Joseph stood back in darkness and watched. Anne hung a small stew pot over the flames and stirred it until it bubbled, then she poured some into a dish and handed the dish to him, together with a brass spoon. She went up on tiptoe and kissed his beard, then turned and left.

Joseph's mind was filled now with one thought only.

That night before he went to bed, he brought out his writing instruments and a precious page of parchment.

Carefully, stroking every letter with painful precision, for his hands were very large and his nails gnarled, he wrote formal words on the parchment. They granted Mary release from the contracts of betrothal. They mentioned reasons of ritual impurities, mild causes but legal ones nonetheless. They did not mention adultery. Joseph could not write adultery. He could not lay upon Mary — whom he loved, whom he could not stop loving — public accusations of adultery.

His mind was very clear that night.

Tomorrow he would find two witnesses and in their presence give this document to Mary personally.

Now he unrolled his sleeping pallet and lay down and, mercifully, fell asleep.

∎

In those days King Herod discovered that Antipater, his oldest son, successor to his throne, had been responsible for the assassination of his own uncle Pheroras.

Pheroras was Herod's brother. He had been an able commander of Herod's armies. Thirty years ago Pheroras had brought the siege of Jerusalem to a triumphant conclusion, allowing Herod to enter and to rule there.

This same Pheroras had just been poisoned. He died shouting and whimpering in Herod's rooms — and he terrified the old king with thoughts of his own mortality.

Therefore, King Herod destroyed his third will and testament. He ordered his son Antipater brought to trial, and he began to consider which other son was trustworthy and true.

∎

While Joseph was sleeping on his decision to divorce Mary, the voice of an angel called to him in a dream.

"Joseph, son of David," the angel said, "you should not fear to take Mary home as your wife, because the infant conceived in her is of the Holy Spirit. She will bear a son, and when she does you must call his name Jesus, since he will save his people from their sins.

"God is fulfilling prophecies, Joseph!

> Behold, a virgin shall conceive and bear a son,
> and his name shall be called Emmanuel.

Emmanuel," the angel said. "Emmanuel, God with us."

When the son of Jacob woke up on the following morning, he moved more quickly and more lightly than he ever had in his life.

He lit a fire of dry sticks, then burned the parchment in its flames.

He washed himself. He brushed and brushed his beard. He oiled his hair. He donned his one clean tunic and his Sabbath robe, then fairly ran to the home of Joachim and knocked on the door.

But there was wailing inside the house, a voice filled with outrage and pain. No one heard Joseph's knocking. The voice was howling, "How could you bring such disgrace on — "

Hearing that, Joseph made a fist and pounded the door with all his might. "Joachim!" he bellowed. "Joachim, open your door and let me in!"

The house became very still. No one spoke. No one moved.

"Joachim," Joseph roared, "open this door."

"Go away." It was Joachim's voice, whining piteously: "You don't have to finish the room. Just go away and leave us alone."

But Joseph only roared the louder: "No, I will not leave until we've set the day for my wedding to your daughter. And you're right. I don't have to finish the roof. But I will. After we are married."

The little house seemed altogether deserted after that, so long did silence last inside. Then Joachim called softly, "Joseph, do you know that Mary is with child?"

Joseph said, "Yes, I know."

"And Mary my daughter says that you are not the father."

"She's right. I'm not the father."

The new wooden door on Joachim's house opened a crack. A tiny eye peered out. "And you wish to marry her anyway?"

"Yes. I do."

Joachim threw open the door and burst into tears. "I am overcome with happiness!" he cried. "I am suffocating in gladness!" He spread his arms and moved toward his son-in-law, but Joseph saw one figure only.

Pale in the interior dark — scarcely visible, as if she were winter's breath on the air — Mary was gazing out at Joseph, hesitating, chewing her bottom lip. Oh, the worry in her features broke his heart!

Joseph couldn't help himself: he ran past Joachim and gathered Mary into his arms and held her tightly to his body.

"I love you," he whispered in her tender ear. "Don't cry, don't cry. I love you, Mary, and I know who is sleeping in you, and I will love him, too. It is well. All is well. I know what God is doing, and I love you."

iv

In the year before he was assassinated, Julius Caesar had drawn up a will in which he named his nephew Octavian as his son. When the old dictator died, then, young Octavian stepped into his father's glory by changing his name to Gaius Julius Caesar Octavianus.

There followed seventeen years of struggle for power in Rome. Its empire reached from Britain to Asia Minor and Syria, from Egypt through Africa to Spain. This was a bloody period for Rome, but it was also the slow, intelligent, methodical rise to power of Octavian: to supreme power, finally, in all the Roman world.

He never took upon himself the trappings of royalty. Faithfully he observed all the formalities of traditional republican rule. He never characterized his position with a greater title than *princeps*: "the first citizen." Nevertheless, the Roman Senate and the people conferred upon him the title *Augustus*: Reverend, a person commended to deities and to people alike, one bearing within himself the qualities of divinity.

At the same time, he dropped his birth name in public and assumed the name of his adoptive father, Caesar.

Thus, by his thirty-sixth year Gaius Octavianus became Caesar Augustus, in power and in practical fact the first emperor in Rome, a phenomenon whom the inhabitants of certain provinces began to worship as a son beloved of the gods: *Soter*, they called him, Savior, for he now inaugurated a period of peace so deep and sweeping that throughout the known world old wars ceased, merchants traveled everywhere without fear, commerce developed in safety, prosperity appeared, prosperity descended to tired lands and sat down and smiled.

In the fourteenth year of his reign, Caesar Augustus made a grand sacrifice to Roman gods for the peace of the world. At the same time he ordered that a marble altar be built to honor this remarkable state of human affairs. In the eighteenth year of his reign he dedicated the altar, a marvel of sculpture around which stood a wall carved with the stories of Rome: Romulus and Remus suckled by the she-wolf, Mother Earth with children on her knees, figures depicting air and water. The monument was called the Ara *Pacis Augustae*, Augustus' Altar of Peace.

In the twentieth year of his reign, the fifty-sixth year of his life, these words were inscribed in stone to celebrate the birthday of the Emperor:

The birthday of the god was the beginning of the good news to the world on his account.

In the twenty-third year of his reign, Caesar Augustus decreed that the people of the provinces throughout his empire should be enrolled. This enrollment would constitute a general census; the information gathered would facilitate the levy of taxes upon every household in every territory in the whole Roman world. In order to cross-check families and to produce a lasting and effective record, heads of households were ordered first to return to their ancestral cities or villages — the places of their parents — and then to await documentation there.

So Joseph the son of Jacob left Nazareth in Galilee and, obeying imperial decree, set out for Judea. Mary, his wife, went with him. They were bound for Bethlehem, the city where King David had been born one thousand years before, because Joseph was descended from the house of David.

Mary rode the donkey. Joseph had fashioned a small, rolled saddle to support her back. She had nearly reached the term of her pregnancy. The infant inside her was huge. She was breathless and tired, swollen in her hands, wrists, and ankles. Her long hair had lost traces of its beauty. But the angel had said of her son:

> To him will the Lord God give
> the throne of his father David —

"Of his father... David." Therefore, Mary had insisted, and no one could deny her, neither her mother nor her husband: Mary was determined to go with Joseph to bear her boy in the city of his father David.

It was Mary's conviction that the great and distant Caesar Augustus was nothing more than a tool in the hands of the Most High God. For she could conceive of no reason more valid for this decree of the Emperor, than that her holy child would now be born in Bethlehem.

■

A shepherd led his smallish flock down the side of a hill to a grassy valley. It was dusk, so he descended into shadows; but he knew the valley by heart. Low stone walls created several protected areas, folds for his animals. He stood between two gates in the wall, each leading into separate enclosures, and he called the flocks toward himself. As they approached, he turned the fat-tailed sheep through the gate on his right. The goats he nudged to the left. He was counting them, watching carefully for signs of disease or of any injury a beast might have received during the day's pasturage.

He was a young man, studious in his countenance, given to the thoughtful, internal frown. Thin lips. His lips were compressed with thinking. He wore leather sandals and a camel's hair cloak. There were two leather bags attached to his belt, one bulky, one stoppered for water.

When he had finished his count, he closed the rough wooden gates and sat down with his back against the right one, then drew from the larger bag bread and cheese and began to eat.

He allowed his eyes to rise to the stars, bright glittering sands on the shores of heaven. Absently, he lifted his right hand and blotted out ten thousand stars.

"Simon!"

He brought the hand down again and turned.

Two other shepherds with two more flocks came over the ridge of the western hill. These flocks were much larger, pale in the starlight, a hundred white shadows floating down the dark slope toward him.

"Simon, are you there? Have you gathered brush yet? Where is the fire? Why haven't you made a fire for us? It's going to be cold tonight."

∎

Mary rode slowly toward Bethlehem. Joseph led the donkey, but Mary's condition controlled its speed: the beast walked with a long bobbing of its head.

The enrollment had already begun before the tiny family arrived. Bethlehem's regular activities had been drowned in the great flood of Jews. Children of David filled the village and the hillsides around about. Roman officials had established their booths on the ridge road which went north from Hebron to Jerusalem and passed directly through Bethlehem. Citizens waiting to register stood in long lines from morning till late afternoon. Then they ate and they rested. Most would return to the census takers again tomorrow. It was a monumentally slow process. The inns were crowded. Strangers slept side by side on the earthen floor, or in lofts. The owners of the inns withdrew to the smaller, private rooms built on roofs of their buildings.

It was dusk when Joseph led his donkey and his wife through the gate and into the village. Though there were few people wandering the streets, he knew immediately how burdened Bethlehem was with humanity: the very air vibrated with the breathings, the low murmurings, and the talk of ten thousand people — like hornets humming inside a hive.

But Mary had begun to glisten in the moonlight. More and more she was leaning back against the ridge of her wooden saddle, grimacing. Her teeth shone white.

Just once as they approached the gate she had whispered, "It's time, Joseph. It's time now." She did not have to repeat it. The word had triggered soft explosions in his brain: *It's time, Joseph.*

The glistening on her brow was sweat.

For a moment the carpenter felt completely helpless. Mary must not bear her baby in the open, in some dark corner; yet he could think of no *place* which could accommodate them. Every human den or nest was inhabited. The dark village was a crush of population.

Then the donkey shook its head and began moving of its own accord. It shuffled into an easy trot. Joseph called sharply, twice, for a halt. But because the beast continued trotting, he was forced to run alongside, gripping Mary's wrists in one hand and bracing her back with the other.

Joseph, it's time!

The donkey took a narrow street downhill. It wound around a large inn to the back, where a cave had been dug as a sort of basement in limestone. Here Joseph smelled the warm consoling odor of many beasts, the russet sting of a clean dry hay. The cave was enclosed by a rude wooden fence. The donkey stopped at a gate and waited.

Mary gasped. Joseph could hear the grinding of her teeth and a deep internal moaning: *It's time, it's time!*

He lifted the wooden bar of the gate. Immediately the donkey entered and walked to the back of the cave where several feed troughs had been carved in the virgin stone. Other beasts lying about on straw swung their heavy heads to watch this new intrusion.

Mary cried out and fell from the donkey.

Joseph caught her. Her body astonished him. It was like iron ingots, heavy and very hard, all her muscles doubled down and flexing: "Ahhh!"

With his feet Joseph kicked together a huge pile of clean straw. He laid Mary there. He laid her down in such a way that her robe became her bedding, covering all the straw beneath her.

Suddenly Mary threw back her head, bent her torso up at the belly, then crouched forward, howling: "Oh, Joseph!"

For the second time that night Joseph felt completely helpless. His face was on fire with fear and foolishness.

He was not a midwife!

But Mary reached and grabbed his big hands and pressed the palms of them to her vulva, crying, "Not yet! Not yet! Hold it in, Joseph. Hold it back till I'm ready — Ahhh!"

He felt the baby! Joseph felt the round crown of the baby's head, slick and warm — and pulsing! Pushing out of Mary! It seemed to the carpenter that he had just fallen off the top of a high cliff and that he would soon hit stones below — but the drop between was breathless and exhilarating!

Gently he pushed back, denying the child entrance into this world.

Mary was twisting her body around, first to her left side, then over on her hands and knees. Joseph kept his hand in place, overcome by his wife's extraordinary strength and wisdom.

"Steady me!" she cried. "Get behind me, Joseph — please don't let me fall!"

She rocked up on her heels. She rocked back against the huge chest of her husband. He released the infant's head between her legs and caught the woman at the hips.

Now Mary, squatting, her knees straining apart, hunched her body down. She started to scream — but the sound was cut to solid silence by the monstrous effort she was making. Joseph trembled. His throat was raw. He smelled the mossy scent of Mary's sweating. Her hair was a thick tangle under his face, all filled with dust and straw. Now a squeal, thin as a harp string, endlessly long, began to sing in the cave-stable: *Eeeee* — Joseph felt the sound between his arms. It was Mary's tiny cry, growing stronger, growing louder, never breaking for a breath, a surge of power gathering within her and driving downward, driving her baby out into the world: *Now!*

There was a quick slurping sound, and suddenly a baby lay on his back in straw under his mother, his face confronting Mary's face directly. She burst into tears. She fell backward against Joseph, howling in delight and relief and in pain and in great sorrow. The baby kicked and wrinkled his face and began to cry. Mary reached up and pawed the beard of her husband. Then she was pulling him down by it: "Wash him, wash him, wash my baby, wash the blood away, wash him perfectly clean, wash him and salt him, then bring me my knife."

Joseph stood up. His muscles did not want to stretch. He walked like a drunk man to their knapsacks and found there the linen cloth that Mary had packed for the baby. Also, salt and a lantern and a knife.

When he knelt down and lit the lantern, he saw Mary in the grip of another task, bent forward, pushing against something else inside of her, as if there were another baby coming.

He also saw what a quantity of blood and water had soaked into the straw between her legs, and he pitied his wife.

And the infant, streaked with mucus and blood: as he washed it, he watched the tiny body turn from blue to a light pink and then to a rose color as if small fires had begun to burn within him. He wiped the baby clean. The baby sighed. Joseph could not stand the glory of the moment: the baby sighed.

Mary uttered a final shout, and the afterbirth flushed out, and now she looked as wet and exhausted as gravestones after rain.

"Joseph," she whispered, "please bring him here."

Joseph laid the baby upon Mary's breast.

Mary bit linen and tore off a thin strip. With this she tied a knot in the cord that had connected the holy child to her body. Then she took the knife and cut that connection forever. Both the mother and the baby cried.

"Jesus," she whispered. She gathered him to her bosom and rocked him. "Jesus, Jesus. Little Yeshi. Here you are. And I love you, baby."

Mary opened the linen cloth. Slowly she began to wrap it round her baby, tight enough to assure him he was still embraced as in a womb, tight enough to be her love upon him even after separation, loose enough to allow the child to live and breathe on his own.

In the lantern light Joseph saw the great beasts surrounding them. They had raised their heads, sniffing the air. Perhaps a birthing scent spoke even to them of primal matters.

"Joseph?"

"Yes?" he said.

"Do you want to hold our baby?"

The huge man was a plain ox, thick in all his parts, a heavy ruinous creature. And the child in his arms was so light, composed of such crushable sticks. But Jesus opened his eyes and looked at the huge head and the beard above him. Little Jesus gazed at the hairy ox, and he was not afraid. Therefore Joseph, filled with the sense of his undeserving, began to weep and quickly laid the tiny boy in a feed trough for safekeeping and for sleeping.

Mary whispered, "You see? You bore the baby, too."

Ah, Mary was generous! And beautiful. She put her swollen fingers to her brow and wiped the sticking strands of black hair back.

"Joseph," she said softly, "would you come here with your clean cloths? Husband, would you darken the lantern and come and wash me, too? Would you wash all my parts clean again?"

∎

By midnight the fires of the three shepherds had collapsed into sparks and red embers. Simon and the two others who joined flocks and shared the long night watch had also subsided into silence.

One sent soft, moist snorings up toward heaven — a tough old man, content. One sat wakeful upon the stone wall, slapping it sometimes with the flat of his rod in order to warn wild animals away.

Simon had gone to lie among the sheep for warmth, but he wasn't sleeping. He was gazing thoughtfully upward and enjoying the periodic huffings and sighs of the larger ewes.

All at once the stars began to explode.

Simon leaped to his feet.

The sheep stumbled up, bleating and running back to the stone walls.

The stars — in tens, and then in tens of thousands — were flashing like white fires in the black sky! They began to move.

Like burning bees, like a great whirling swarm of bees, the stars were crossing heaven from the east to the west.

Simon stood immobilized. Even the sheep were fixed in attitudes of awful fear.

Between the glorious motion of heaven and the dark earth below, there now appeared a single, endless pillar of a pure white fire.

And the fire spoke, and Simon understood what it said.

The fire cried, "Don't be afraid!"

No, *not* the fire — but a figure within the fire! The brilliant form of a human, smooth and huge and very beautiful, his feet upon the mountains.

An angel of the Lord!

The angel said, "I bring good news of great joy which shall come to all the people. For to you is born this night in the city of David a Savior who is Christ the Lord! And this will be a sign for you: you will find a baby wrapped in swaddling cloths and lying in a manger — "

Suddenly that swarm of the fiery heavenly host swooped down and filled the lower skies, praising God and singing:

> *Glory to God in the highest!*
> *And on earth peace to the people with whom he is pleased!*

How long the enormous chorus lasted, Simon did not know. The air itself was the music of these angels. When they withdrew again to heaven, and the night was dark, Simon thought he could hear nothing but what he had heard, *Gloria*, still ringing in his ears; and he thought he was blinded to the common things around him, stone and sheep, his companions and his own hand.

But the older man that had been snoring whispered, "Simon?" — and Simon heard that very well.

"Simon," said the shepherd, "did you see that, too?"

Simon gazed solemnly at his friend and under common starlight nodded.

The third shepherd joined them.

The old man gaped at them both and whispered, "And did you hear what the angel said to us?"

Simon nodded.

"It was the Lord," the old man said. "It was the Lord who made these things known to us."

Simon stepped out of the sheepfold and carefully closed the gate. He pushed the gate of the goats, testing its latch, then he began to walk up the northwest slope of the valley. The other men joined him. At the crest of the hill Simon broke into a run. Faster and faster he ran, until he was flying. His heart was very light. His legs were tireless. His eye saw the fires of Bethlehem immediately, and he kept his sight there while they grew to meet his nearness.

Simon did not even pause at the edge of town. He sailed the narrow streets knowing nothing, yet trusting his foot to find the right place. And it did.

Here, cut in limestone under a large inn, was a cave. Inside the cave was the soft glow of an oil lantern. Simon crept forward, the first of the three to arrive. He bent down and, emboldened by the angel's word, entered.

In the shadows of a single flame, Simon saw a man sitting down, a large man with a great, fierce beard all round his face. The man nodded and did not challenge Simon. So the young shepherd lingered and looked and saw a woman resting upon the man's knees. She seemed exhausted, but she was awake. Beside her was a stone manger. Within the manger, clean yellow straw. Upon the straw, wrapped in strips of linen cloth, was a baby also awake and watchful.

Simon sighed. The air went forth from him in a long and inarticulate sound: *A Savior! The Messiah!*

As the other two shepherds crept in and knelt by Simon, the woman glanced up and smiled.

"Mother," Simon said, "your baby is the most beautiful baby I have ever seen. As soft as the nose of a lamb."

The older shepherd gave Simon a rude poke.

"As soft," said Simon, "as the pillar of cloud by day."

The baby closed his eyes and slept.

The shepherds all covered their faces with their hands. After a while, they turned and left.

V

By the eighth day of the child's life, Joseph had found lodgings for his little family. There was a room, therefore, shelter and water, quietness and privacy for the circumcision of the boy.

Mary laid him naked upon her knees. Joseph knelt before them — then, pulling the flesh with one hand and cutting around it with a knife in the other, he removed the infant foreskin.

The baby's eyes popped open. For a moment he seemed to be considering some vile offense in the world. Then his mouth opened, he drew breath, and he released a long, loud, lusty yell. Mary laughed at his infant shock. Her laughter bounced the baby left and right on her knees. Joseph, who was trying to wash the little wound, could scarcely catch it.

"Mary," he said. But he was a soft-spoken man. Who could hear him?

He called again, "Mary!"

But her voice was a *gloria* of angels. The tears had moistened her black lashes. They caused a radiance around her eyes. The baby's tears were merely angry.

"Mary!"

"Yes," she gasped. "Yes, I know, I know: his name will be Jesus."

As soon as she said *Jesus*, the laughter died within her. She gathered the little boy to her bosom, and his fussing, too, was stilled, and the room was quiet now.

Joseph murmured, "Yes. His name is Yehoshuah — Jeshua. His name is Jesus."

∎

When the time came for them to be purified according to the law of Moses, Joseph and Mary carried the baby to the temple in Jerusalem and then back to Bethlehem again, all in a single day.

At noon they approached the temple Mount from the south, amazed at the long white elegance of the Royal porches facing them. Hushed with humility, the carpenter and his wife entered the crowded colonnade and moved among four endless rows of columns which supported lofty ceilings, all covered with carvings, like the very heaven for richness! They crept from table to table where merchants were doing business.

Finally, they purchased two turtledoves to offer as a sacrifice, then went into the great open Court of the Gentiles.

They walked to the east side of the stone balustrade which surrounded the inner courts and the temple itself — the wall beyond which Gentiles could not pass, under penalty of death. They went through the Gate called "Beautiful" into the Court of Women.

Once there, Joseph took the baby Jesus into the crook of his left arm; he held the turtledoves in his right hand and prepared to go alone into the innermost Court of the Priests and Israelites, where the Altar of Burnt Offering was —

But a man cried, "Wait!"

He was an old man. His motion was crippled by his great age. But his manner was categorical: instinctively, Joseph obeyed and waited while the man approached.

"This is the one!" he cried. "This is the one whom the Holy Spirit promised I would see!"

His shouting was high and whining. He drew a great deal of attention. "Oh, Simeon!" people muttered. They were used to his presence here. He returned every day, saying that he would see the Messiah before he died.

"Oh, Simeon!" they said. But the old man seemed shameless, so filled with one thought that no other thought had meaning for him.

"Give us the child," he panted as he came to Joseph. "Let these poor bony arms touch and cradle the Lord's Christ. Yes! Yes — "

Again, Joseph obeyed.

The baby was awake and unafraid. He gazed up into the fierce and ancient face of the man named Simeon, and Simeon whispered, "Yes, yes. O Lord, yes! I'm ready. I can die in peace, now, as you promised. These poor dim eyes are seeing the salvation which you have prepared for the whole world, a revelation for the Gentiles and glory for your people, Israel!"

Neither Joseph nor Mary said a word. They stared at the stranger who held their baby, gaunt old man, bent down and bony.

Suddenly he raised his face and peered into Mary's eyes.

"Your baby is set like a building stone in the scheme of things," he said. "Many in Israel will fall because of him. Many will rise. But he is a sign, woman, whom most will deny." Simeon narrowed his eye and lowered his voice to a private whisper: "Indeed, a sword will pierce through your own soul, too! All the secret thoughts of the people are going to be revealed."

Simeon handed her the baby. Mary took him and held him, and still she made no answer. But neither did she forget. Everything that was said and done in the early days of Jesus' life his mother kept in her heart — everything, pondering continually and seeking understanding.

∎

King Herod was familiar with the eastern custom of paying homage to potentates upon significant occasions.

Six years ago, when he had finished building Caesarea on the sea and was dedicating it by a magnificent series of athletic contests, certain envoys arrived from nations abroad with gifts of rare value. They came to pay homage to Herod. They came in caravans, camels and donkeys and carts full of goods, and they were received as grandly as they came. It was a tradition the king appreciated.

Herod himself had sent gifts westward to Gaius Julius Caesar Octavianus when that man became "Augustus." At other times he met Caesar face-to-face to offer his personal homage. When he sent his sons to Rome, they had carried heaps of eastern treasures. And in return Caesar called him a "friend and confederate."

It was not strange, then, that in these latter days a caravan arrived from the east. Magi had come to pay homage in Jerusalem. And though there had been no communication to prepare him for the envoy, King Herod waited to receive their request for an audience. He waited to be gracious unto them.

The request never came.

Instead, it was told to Herod that the Magi were asking questions about someone else — one who had just been born king of the Jews.

"We have seen his star in the East," they said, "and we've come to worship him."

Him? *Who?*

Herod was very sick in those days. He couldn't walk; he could not bend his joints without pain. His legs and feet lacked blood and were perpetually cold; an aching as hard as stone in his shinbones; his toes were turning black.

Of his own accord, however, he sent word to the Magi that good rulers grant their guests a visitation. If they had needs, he said, he would be pleased to satisfy them. Would they wish to present themselves at the door of his palace? Though he could not come out to them, they would surely be welcome within.

In the meantime Herod began to think in extremes. What bloodline would foreigners know about? Who held any greater right to the throne than he? Jews, surely; but *Davidic* Jews! A son of David had always sat on the throne until the exile — and even then it was prophesied that such a son would be anointed again. "Anointed" in Hebrew is *Messiah*.

Suddenly Herod was shooting down the halls of his palace, commanding his scribes to seek out certain information: was there a prophecy regarding the anointed one of God? The Messiah? Saying where he would be born?

Yes! Dreadfully, there was such a prophecy. Scribes brought to Herod the scroll of the prophet Micah, and they read it aloud in his hearing:

> *And you, O Bethlehem in the land of Judah,*
> *are by no means least among the rulers of Judah;*
> *for from you will come forth a ruler*
> *who will shepherd my people Israel.*

"Ahhh!" A foul sound escaped the old king's mouth: "Bethlehem!"

The men from the east were grateful for Herod's invitation. They accepted, and with great ceremony they entered his palace and then his apartments.

Herod contrived to smile. He looked at the Magi, these readers of stars, men of no royalty nor any apparent distinction, and he smiled.

"How long since the birthing star appeared?" he asked.

Bowing and scraping — obsequious fools! — they told him.

"Ahhh. Yes," said Herod. "Well, the little king whom you are seeking is likely to have been born in Bethlehem. It's a short journey south of here. Go to Bethlehem. Search diligently for the child. And when you have found him, bring me word, that I may go and worship him, too."

The Magi left him.

By nighttime they had left Jerusalem, too — somewhat sooner than Herod had expected.

███

Early in the morning Mary woke to hear soft noises outside the house where they were lodging, the sudden blast of camels blowing air through their narrow nostrils.

Camels?

She moved the lattice and looked out. Camels — yes, indeed. Camels were resting on their bellies in the road, their haughty heads held high as if they belonged right here in Bethlehem.

Some people were gathered on the far side of the beasts, servants, it seemed. On the near side, standing and talking with Joseph, were three men of great dignity and subtle mystery. Her poor husband was uncomfortable.

He stood with his huge hands helpless by his thighs, his whiskers twitching around invisible fits of anguish; yet the civility of the three foreign men seemed in no way disturbed by the carpenter's bluff inhospitality.

One of them touched Joseph's shoulder and pointed toward the house. Joseph began, then, to nod and nod. He turned and walked toward the door of the house. The three men bent down and picked up boxes of various sizes and followed Joseph.

Swiftly Mary withdrew from the window. She pulled on a loose blue robe, rushed to her baby and gathered him up in her arms, then stood in the middle of the room facing the door.

It opened.

Joseph came in, speechless — shrugging his shoulders, whirling his eyebrows, trying desperately to communicate something to Mary, but speechless.

Behind him, one by one, the men of foreign raiment and foreign aspect entered the room. They glanced at Mary and nodded. But they gazed long and long at Jesus.

Suddenly the three men bowed all the way down to the ground. They leaned forward and pressed their foreheads to the floor. Delighted by the motion, the swirling sound of robes, and the rush of new odors in the room, the baby raised his two hands and waved them furiously in the air, grinning with his whole mouth, jumping in his mother's arms, and cackling.

The three men sat back upon their heels, and each placed his box at Mary's feet.

The first man opened his box and lifted out a dull yellow medallion. Gold.

The second man took out small cakes of an incense for burning.

The third man showed to the child a small white alabaster flask which, when he pulled the stopper from it, filled the room with mysterious smells. "Oil of myrrh," he whispered, "a gift for the king of the Jews."

Little Jesus grew solemn. His eyes became still and grave — a golden color. Apparently myrrh had a strong effect on the child.

The camels outside blew heavy steams of breath into the air.

And Mary took the alabaster flask and closed it with its stopper. She, too, had grown sober and uncomfortable. Graciously she bent her head and acknowledged the veneration of the Magi. But privately to Joseph she said, "Put these things away. Hide them. I think they are dangerous for our son."

▌▌

Herod never saw nor heard from the Magi again.

In three days he sent servants to Bethlehem to see why they were lingering so long. The servants returned to say that they were not lingering at all. They had vanished.

There was no hint of a smile in the king's face now. His eyelids grew heavy with insult and fear and an ancient, unrequited rage. His countenance turned white. He did not sleep. By the morning of the fourth day he had made three decisions.

Before the noonday sun was high, each decision had become a public decree; by the afternoon each was in process; by night all would be done.

First: King Herod sent a command to the prison officials responsible for guarding his son Antipater. "Since the man has been found guilty of conspiring in the death of my brother Pheroras, and since I, Herod, can discover no reason whatever for clemency, crucify him."

Second: King Herod sent an entire regiment of his army to Bethlehem with the absolute, irrevocable order to break into the houses of its citizens; to find and identify every male child two years old and younger, to gather these babies in an open place — and to kill them, every one.

Third: King Herod required his personal servants again to prepare a caravan — as well as his personal palanquin — for an extended journey. The pain in his legs was intolerable. His fingers had grown cold as night and had fixed themselves in a clench. He desperately needed relief. All he could think of now was to lower his troubled body into the hot baths of Callirrhoe.

Two days later, the old king was laid upon mountains of soft blankets, wrapped inside his palanquin, and hoisted to the shoulders of his servants, young and strong.

But the slightest motion was to him such torment that they stopped often and made very slow progress down the hard road from Jerusalem to Jericho. Indeed, that little trip, not halfway to Callirrhoe, consumed three days of the king's life.

And so it was that five days after his final murders, a son and hundreds of sons, King Herod himself ceased breathing. He died lying on pillows in Jericho, his eyes wide open, seeing nothing.

vi

By the time the soldiers had arrived in Bethlehem to kill the children, Joseph was gone. The Lord had warned him in a dream, and he had fled with his family south to Egypt. Later, when they heard of Herod's expiration, they returned by a round route to Nazareth, avoiding Judea altogether. Archelaus, Herod's son, ruled that province now, and he was a man more brutal than his father.

Gladly Mary and Joseph came back to their own small house again, and this child entered his life with a common baby joy.

Jesus was by nature healthy, alert to the world around him, quick to learn, quicker to touch and to test. He had his mother's spacious forehead and, like her, the smooth intensity of balanced eyebrows — though she was always likelier to laugh than he was.

All through these years, Mary maintained her delight in life, and Jesus was the apple of her eye. Daily he gave her reasons for laughing. "Yeshi!" she would cry, lifting her hands helplessly to heaven, "Oh, Yeshi, a little salt makes a very big hunger. A lot makes a very bad face!"

So Mary would laugh and Jesus would wrinkle his small face in quizzical smiles.

He climbed the hill behind Nazareth. He prowled the highland, exploring even to the brow of the hill that overlooked the Esdraelon Valley. His mother found him there, and she did not laugh. Neither did she cry out, though he could have fallen to his death. Quietly she came and sat beside him and surrounded him with a strong arm, and pressed him to her side, where her heart still hammered in fear.

She pointed to the puzzle-patches of farmland that covered the valley floor.

She whispered, "Right there, Yeshi. Hundreds and hundreds of years ago. There was a prophetess named Deborah who destroyed Jabin the king of Canaan — right there — because Jabin's army was riding in chariots and God sent a rainstorm and the rain turned the whole valley to mud and the chariot wheels got stuck."

Mary began to rock her body. She hummed three notes, and then she sang:

> *The kings, they came and fought;*
> *by the waters that flowed past Megiddo*
> *great Canaan arrived to fight,*
> *but they got no spoils of silver.*
> *March on! March on!*

> *For the stars of heaven joined the war;*
> *they dropped from their courses fighting,*
> *and Kishon exploded her banks in torrents,*
> *sweeping the kings away:*
> *March on, my soul with might!*

So sang Mary, while Jesus, gazing at farmland, watched an ancient war. No, Mary did not laugh that day.

But she taught Jesus other songs. And she taught him the lilies, the flowers, the grasses and all growing things, seed and soils, and how to pray. She taught him prayer by praying herself, and he watched with a swift understanding. She taught him thrift — not grimly, nor bitterly, but with ingenuity and a glad self-sufficiency. She taught him to sew. And to cook.

Joseph, stolid and laborious, taught Jesus to read and to write, both in Aramaic and in Hebrew.

Joseph took Jesus to the synagogue.

Joseph never laughed.

When Jesus asked about that, he told his boy he was too old to laugh. He had lost the knack a while ago. But Mary's laughter, he said, was like his own.

"It is enough," he said.

In those days Joseph's huge bush of a beard was shot through with white. His eyebrows had started to grow. There was almost no face left to look at. A nose.

In the spring of the year when Jesus turned twelve, his parents decided to take him with them to Jerusalem, to celebrate there the feast of the Passover.

It was a four-days' trek in company with many families from Nazareth. Almost everyone walked, though a few rode donkeys. The distance from Galilee to Judea was not easy, since the hills between Samaria and Jerusalem were cut across by sudden, precipitous gorges; and there were innumerable caves along the way where thieves lurked.

In Jerusalem the people of Nazareth dispersed, each family to find its own lodgings.

It was at this point — just upon arrival, approaching a two-story house in the valley between the high hill of Zion and the temple Mount — that Mary and Joseph always looked for Zechariah. Since all the priests of all the divisions were on duty for the Passover, Zechariah would come early and prepare for his relatives and cheerfully greet them as they arrived.

But today no Zechariah came out of the house, neither the priest nor the nailsmith. Instead, Elizabeth appeared in the doorway and waved. She tried to smile. But as Mary drew closer, the smile broke. The tiny old woman lowered her head and lifted her arms, and Mary knew. Mary knew. She walked into her great-aunt's embrace. Each woman fell on the neck of the other, and they wept together for the sake of Zechariah.

"He died in his sleep," Elizabeth said. "John and I have come to Passover alone this year. Oh, Mary, I am so glad to see you."

On the day of the sacrifice of the lambs, Joseph took Jesus outside the city to the east, to the Mount of Olives, where there were two great cedar trees. Under one tree a man was selling nothing but young doves. Under the other tree there were four shops offering everything necessary for sacrifices: lambs, sheep, oil, and meal.

Joseph purchased a sheep, one year old without spot or blemish.

As they led the sheep down into the Kidron Valley and back to the city, he said, "Every year at Passover, Rabbi Baba ben Buta brings three thousand head of livestock to the temple, right into the Court of the Gentiles. There he sells the sacrifice to pilgrims. I would rather buy ours here."

Joseph showed Jesus how to wash in preparation for the sacrifice.

Together they entered the white, multitudinous, noisy courtyards of the temple. Smoke rose to the beautiful sky. Levites were singing on the steps of the temple. Periodically, trumpets blew from the pinnacle at the southwest corner of the royal porch. Hundreds of people were streaming in one gate with walking sheep, while hundreds more streamed out another, carrying bloody cuts of meat and the hide of the carcass, neat and whole.

Within the inner Court of the Priests and the Israelites, Joseph knelt down and held his sheep with an arm around its chest, awaiting his turn. Jesus stood by, watching.

Soon a priest approached, and a Levite beside him. The priest inspected the animal closely, mouth and ears, stomach, and the roots of its wool; then he handed Joseph a small clay bowl and stepped back. Joseph, still kneeling, placed a hand on the head of the sheep. Suddenly the Levite seized its whole snout in his left hand, shut off the wind, and with a single sweep of a silent blade, cut the animal's throat, causing a sigh and a bloody yawning there. Two fountains of blood began to spurt.

The Levite lowered the front portion of the beast, aiming the blood into Joseph's bowl which, when it was full, the priest took, together with the loose, woolly body. The blood he threw against the altar. The sheep he skinned and butchered with amazing speed. He washed the pieces of meat, lifted them up to the Lord, then returned them to Joseph, and Joseph gave some to Jesus, who had seen it all with a steadfast and unblinking eye.

This is the food that Joseph and Mary and Jesus consumed that night with a ritual care — and not them only, but Elizabeth and John as well. Zechariah's family reclined with Joseph's family that night, singing hymns and remembering.

For this was the Passover, the ancient story all over again, the Exodus by signs and wonders and the salvation of Israel, whom the Lord bore out on eagles' wings and brought unto himself. And this was the same Lord who had loved an ancient nailsmith, allowing him to see a new thing before he died. Zechariah had stood on the mountain with Moses and seen the promised land.

On the following day Elizabeth and John went home.

Mary and Joseph lingered through the last day of the feast. Early in the morning they gathered with their friends from Nazareth, and the whole group set out northward.

They traveled till evening, when people began to put up tents, preparing for the night. Mary set some stew over a fire, then went to tell Jesus that it was time to eat.

But Jesus was nowhere to be found.

She began to run from tent to tent. People shrugged and shook their heads. Relatives were sympathetic, but they couldn't help her. No one had seen Jesus anywhere the whole day through.

"He's a boy," she said over and over. "He's only twelve years old!"

And now it was dark on earth. The distant hills were pure black silhouettes. The only light was the fires of families who had sat down to eat.

Mary rushed back to Joseph, crying, "Let's go! We've got to go back! Either he's lost on the wayside, or else Jesus is in Jerusalem alone!"

So they walked all night long, alone, ascending the difficult roads to Jerusalem as quietly as they could, for fear of robbers and thieves.

In the city itself and in the light of day they began a long search, questioning strangers, knocking on the doors of many houses. Mary couldn't eat. She had begun to suffer such torments of guilt that she grew dirty and unkempt. Her dark hair knotted and grew ratty. Her face was pale, her dark eyes staring.

"My fault, my fault," she kept muttering. "He isn't even thirteen. I should have been watching. It's my duty to watch out for him."

They had been to the temple. It was the first place they had looked, both the outer and the inner courts. Nothing — though more than once Mary thought she saw the wide forehead of her son among the people. Nothing. Now, therefore, she returned to the temple no longer to look, but to pray. It had been three days.

Mary went away from the crowds. She thought she would seclude herself behind a column in the porch of Solomon. As she entered the place she heard soft voices to the left, so she turned to the right. But suddenly one high, piping voice began to speak, and she recognized it. Jesus! It was her son's voice!

Mary flew around the pillars and found some ten men sitting in a circle, old men, young men — and a boy! Rabbis, they were. Teachers and students and —

"Yeshi!" she shrieked. All talking came to a halt. "Yeshi, what are you *doing* here?"

Everyone turned and looked at her. Jesus turned, too, but with level eyes and a maddening calm.

A rabbi said, "The lad is studying the Law. He has a marvelous understanding — "

Mary hardly heard him. She ran to Jesus and took his face between her hands. "What have you done to us?" she hissed. She was going to cry. She could feel it coming. She did not want to cry. Therefore, she shouted at the top of her lungs: "Your father and I have been searching the city for days! I would never have treated my parents like this! Yeshi, I've been dying with worry!"

"Mama," the boy said, "why did you have to search?"

"What? What are you saying?"

"But didn't you know where I would be? Didn't you know that I must be in my Father's house?"

Mary stopped shouting. She released her son's face, seeing pink marks where her hands had squeezed him. No, she did not understand this thing which he said. Neither did she understand him.

This she knew now as never before, that she did not understand her son. And this too: that she had to cry. No matter the place or the company, she lowered her head and covered her face and began to cry.

Then it was Jesus who rose up and took her by the arm and led her to a more private part of the porch and there consoled her by patting her on the shoulder. He patted her and held her hand and sat with her as long as she needed.

32

JOHN THE SON OF ZECHARIAH

i

In those days there lived on the wilderness shores of the Dead Sea a community called the Essenes, people who were waiting for the absolute reign of God: *Thy kingdom come*, they begged in many ways. They separated their daily lives from the entanglements of world economies and the taint of governments, declaring themselves to be the New Covenant. The Essenes felt that their community was a visible sign of that kingdom where the temple of the Lord would be built not of stones but of people completely obedient to him.

They avoided luxury and every impurity. They studied the laws of Moses and strove to keep them in every particular. They were especially observant in matters of cleanliness since it was their purpose to be a present witness of the future and eternal kingdom. This present age was coming to an end! And since its faithful populations must learn how to prepare, the Essenes wrote their teachings on scrolls.

Regarding the signs of the end of the age, they wrote that there would arise two messiahs, *the priestly and the lay*. When the duly anointed high priest and duly anointed king appeared — *messiahs anointed of Aaron and of Israel* — then all the scattered hosts of Israel would be gathered together, and *the earth would be filled with the knowledge of God like the waters which cover the sea*.

In language most formal, they wrote that the lay messiah, the king, would be a *Scion of David who shall in the Last Days reign in Zion, an offering of the booth of David now fallen down*. By "fallen booth" they meant the Law. They felt that the laws of Moses had been long neglected, justice and ritual purities, both. He, they wrote, as the anointed king, *will arise to bring salvation to Israel*.

Of the anointed priest they wrote that he would be *the Expounder of the Law*.

These were the signs of an end and a beginning — the end of an unrighteous age, the beginning of the direct reign of God, as once he ruled Israel when they wandered in the wilderness.

Therefore, when a man named John began to cry in the Judean wilderness, "Repent, for the kingdom of heaven is at hand!" the whole community of Essenes began to tremble with excitement. For John was the son of the priest Zechariah, and his mother had been of the house of Aaron!

Surely, he was that priest!

His preaching was a fierce and fearless exposition of the Law. Surely the end which the prophets had foreseen was finally at hand! Hadn't Isaiah prophesied: *The voice of one crying in the wilderness, "Prepare the way of the Lord! Make his paths straight!"* Yes, and this John was no respecter of persons. He told the truth. He lived dependent on no one's welcome nor anyone's wealth. And he was as concerned for the laws of cleanliness as the Essenes themselves. He offered Jews a ritual washing. He preached a baptism of repentance for the forgiveness of sins.

Coming from the wilderness near the Dead Sea and from houses on Zion, the Essenes trooped to the places where John the son of Zechariah preached.

Many other people went out to hear him. Multitudes came from Jerusalem and all the regions of Judea to the shores of the Jordan to be baptized by John, confessing their sins.

ii

John the son of Zechariah had hands as huge as his father's, shovels at the ends of his wrists. Like his father's, they were hard and dark, though he was not a nailsmith. In fact, he had no craft for earning money. He survived on the poor fare of the wilderness; he ate insects, locusts, and the wild honey he found in rocks and trees; he drank water, and sometimes as gifts from those he baptized he drank the milk of goats. He gathered wood and slept on the hard ground. It was simple survival that had made his hands hard. He lived as his ancestors had lived two thousand years before him, Abraham and Isaac and Jacob: a wilderness existence.

And he dressed like the nomad, wearing a rough mantle of camel's hair. He dressed (so noted the Essenes) like the prophet Elijah, wearing a leather girdle around his waist.

None of these details was lost on the citizens of Judea.

Many yearned to see signs of the kingdom and the restoration of their holy covenant. They hated subservience. They hated Rome. The Roman presence was a perpetual abomination. If a Gentile spat on the ground, a Jew had to cross the street to avoid the discharge or risk his own impurity.

Gentiles exhaled filth. They ate their food defiled; they stripped naked for public games; they used coin that offended the laws of God; they profaned the land, taxed poor Jews beyond their means, and murdered them upon a whim. Pontius Pilate, the new Roman Procurator of Judea, was brutal in his governance and cold in execution. Nor were the sons of Herod any better. No kings, they! They ruled at Rome's behest. Not a genuine Jew between them, since neither one so much as pretended a righteous worship. They built palaces of luxury by the labor of citizens more faithful than they. Ah, there was such a yearning in the land, a deep, weeping desire for the return of the kingdom of the Lord God of Israel. Therefore, while some people separated themselves and struggled to obey the laws of Moses, others formed fierce military units and planned by might and rebellion to restore the freedoms of Israel. In the name of the jealous Lord God they made a public denunciation of iniquitous foreign influence, idolatries, Jewish apostasies. These were by nature and by political definition Zealots.

So great was the yearning that when the rumors flew through Jerusalem — "He wears leather like Elijah! He bows to none but God! He refuses to eat with sinners, and he preaches the Law without compromise!" — multitudes went out to hear this John the son of Zechariah and to be baptized under his huge hands.

Nor did they turn away from his harder words of judgment. The times required iron expositions.

"I have seen wildfire race through dry fields," John cried. He was standing on a flat stone, head and shoulders above the people. His hair fell in wild tangles down his back. His voice was a battering — and the people felt consoled.

"I have seen," John cried, "small beasts rush from the flames, squeaking and bleating in terror. And then, as the bright burning consumed even the edges of the fields, I saw the silent ones stream out, the hidden ones, slick snakes whom we do not see until they've bitten us shin and heel."

John threw out his arms to indicate the entire crowd before him. "You brood of snakes!" he bellowed. "Who warned you to flee the fiery wrath to come? What are you doing here? Do you think a little splash will wash you clean? Or do you trust your heritage to protect you when this age ends and the judgment of God precipitates the eternal covenant? You children of Abraham! You children of that older covenant, there comes now a covenant so new that each must enter one by one. Every heart must prove the truth of its own purity, its own *new* purity."

John paused. He snapped his body straight and stood fixed for a moment, a narrow column above the people. He had the capacity to be with them and absent, both at the same time — indifferent. It was a troubling habit, since it broke focus. The circle had no center.

More quietly, now, John said, "People, people, prove your purity. Reveal your heart by the work of your hand. Let seeming and being be the same in you. Bear fruits befitting repentance. I tell you, even now the axe is laid to the root of the trees; every tree that does not bear good fruit shall be cut down and cast back to the dry fields where the fires shall consume them."

John stepped down from his stony platform and began to walk through the crowds downhill toward the Jordan.

He was a man of a large frame and lean muscle, a gaunt jaw, deep-set eyes. Perhaps his hands seemed the larger because his forearms were shrunken around their two bones. He walked with the long loose stride of a bedouin.

Five men fell in step behind him, clearly familiars of his, disciples.

The rest of the people hesitated. There was no protocol here. Should they follow? Should they wait for a smile and a nod? But John was not given to smiling. How should civility treat one who makes even the wilderness his private portion?

One of the Zealots ran down the path after him, crying, "Sir! Sir! What are we to do, then?"

John stopped, turned, and looked at him. The Zealot shrugged and tried to smile. He was a soldier rudely weaponed, a member of those insurgent groups that hid in Judean caves and fed on the produce of farmers. "What," he said, "is the right thing for us to do?"

"Stop robbing the common folk," John said. "Rob no one, not by violence, not by false accusation." Suddenly he lifted his voice. "To every soldier here," he called, "those in the temple guard, those under Herod Antipas, be content with your wages!

"And let every person here be generous: if you have two coats, give one to the man who has none. If you have food enough, share it!"

John turned back and continued descending to the river. Apparently, this exchange had broken any hesitation. The multitude flowed down behind him.

Two tax collectors crept near him and whispered, "Teacher, what about us?"

In a full voice, without breaking stride, John said, "Collect no more than is appointed for the people of your region. Will you become poor for the loss of income? Yes. Will your families suffer the reduction? Yes. Will you wish, therefore, to quit your unpopular position? Yes, and that will be a decision you must make within your own heart. But to tax people above the legal designation is not a choice for citizens of the kingdom of God."

"Please, sir?" an elderly woman stood on the bank of the Jordan and spoke as John descended. "Teacher, please?" She was dressed in widow's weeds. "I'm a Jew," she said. "But before the coming judgment I am nothing more than a convert. Wash me like a convert. Please, sir, baptize me."

John the son of Zechariah approached the woman and peered into her eyes.

"You know the need of your repentance?"

She nodded.

"And you trust the forgiveness signed by this washing?"

She nodded — trembling now. John took her elbow in his large hand, then, and led her out into the water. They waded ten paces together, fifteen long paces. He held her elbow to steady her. They sank to their waists.

John spoke a word into the woman's ear. Suddenly she crouched and rolled forward and vanished under the bubbling surface.

John waited while the river flowed to smoothness, then he slapped the water with the flat of his hand and called, "Woman, in repentance you are clean! Child of the light, citizen of the kingdom to come, *arise*!"

He reached into the river, then brought the woman up by her shoulders. She made an explosive exhalation, threw back her head, whipping the air with her hair and sending a circle of water up to the sunlight. She began to laugh. Her widow's clothes clung closely to her body. Her eyelashes sparkled with water drops.

John's mantle was splashed dark. The long ends of his hair and beard dripped water. He turned toward shore, and that gesture seemed to release all the people lined up along the water. Like a herd of thirsty animals, they all began to wade toward John: tax collectors, soldiers, Pharisees, Sadducees, shepherds, shopkeepers, potters, butchers, scribes, the reverential Essenes — people filled with a terrible yearning. Jews. They rushed out into the Jordan, repenting, confessing their sins in a grand cacophony, seeking each to be baptized by John and so to enter the kingdom.

John cried, "Yes, I baptize you. But there comes after me one so much mightier than I that I am not worthy to stoop and unloose the thong of his sandal! I baptize you with water. He will baptize you with the Holy Spirit and with fire."

iii

In the midst of the multitudes that came daily to the Jordan for baptism, there appeared one figure separated from the rest. John turned and saw the man standing upriver among some reeds, waiting. Reflected sunlight played upward from the water on his face, trilling the flesh below his eyebrows and cheekbones, below his nose and his chin.

He had amber eyes, gazing directly at John.

He was clean-shaven, like a Roman — or, it occurred to John, like one of the prophets mournful for the future, for they would shave their beards.

Amber eyes! John recognized those golden corneas, polished, laconic, and nearly translucent. No one else had such a fathomless gaze. This must be the cousin John had not seen since the Passover when his father had died.

Eighteen years ago! Eighteen years, and still those eyes had that lidded rich regard. This was the one of whom his mother had said once, "He is my Lord."

The man among the reeds lifted his hand in greeting.

John nodded. Jesus, then! This was Jesus!

Jesus began to wade downriver, to the deeper water where John was standing.

When they stood face-to-face, John saw copper flecks in the iris of his cousin's eye.

Jesus said, "John, baptize me."

For a moment John hesitated.

"John," said Jesus, "baptize me." Without waiting for an assent, he closed his eyes, sank down and slipped under the water. His long hair lingered on the surface for a short while, then it, too, was pulled down into darkness and disappeared.

These were swift, breathless events for John. So much raced through his mind: his family, his past, his fierce convictions, the future of his people, Israel.

The day and the weather and all events now tightened down to one small focus: this air, this round patch of river, flat and calm in the sunlight, and this sudden, preternatural silence.

Time seemed to collapse — and when John came to himself he could not remember how long Jesus had been lying on the riverbed.

In a quick panic he slapped the water with the flat of his hand and cried: "Child of the light and the kingdom to come, rise up!"

There was a continued, shining silence — then Jesus, like a great fish, heaved from the water, and immediately the heavens above them split asunder and there flew down a dove, a white dove, a blinding white dove which alighted on the shoulder of Jesus — white fire beside his face — and in that same instant a voice broke from heaven, saying: *This is my beloved Son, in whom I am well pleased.*

Immediately Jesus began to move from John toward the eastern shore of the river. His expression was intense but unreadable. His manner seemed so nearly wolfish — like a predator following an invisible scent — that the people on land backed away and made a path for him.

Jesus was withdrawing from the public with some fierce purpose.

And then John saw that the white dove was flying in spirals ahead of Jesus, leading the way.

Oh, that was no common dove! That was none other than the Holy Spirit who had brooded over the wild waters of creation and then again the waters of the flood!

John folded his huge hands at his throat and whispered: "You, Jesus, greater than me — your life shall be more terrible than mine. Wherever the Holy Spirit is driving you now, God help you there! God help you, cousin."

iv

J esus is in the wide, dry spaces of the wilderness. Except for the savage beasts that paw the spoor where he has wandered, he is solitary.

The Spirit that seized him at his baptism has sent him deep into the desert, far from civilization, far from people and comfort and shelter and food. In forty days Jesus has eaten nothing. The scoop of his abdomen makes skeletal all his bones. At night he shivers in the cold. In the morning his lips are cracked. His tongue is swelling. He cannot swallow. By midday the heat of the sun grows intolerable, like a brass weight on his shoulders.

Jesus sits with his back against one stone of a dolmen. The flat capstone — a table on boulders higher than a man when he is standing — casts the shadow in which he sits. His head has sunk between his knees. He is pressing his forearms against his stomach.

Suddenly he feels the presence of coolness. Not a wind. An element, rather: something like ice nearby.

Jesus raises his head and sees light above him on the dolmen, a column of white light rising from this ancient rock into the sky, the radiance of a cold, ineluctable power.

Within the polish of this light there is the image of a beautiful man. Indeed, the light *is* this splendid figure near to Jesus, who is crouching in the dull ache of starvation.

With unctuous sympathy, the light speaks.

"Yeshi," it says, "if you are the Son in whom God takes such pleasure, why shouldn't you comfort yourself and eat?"

Jesus neither stands nor answers. He regards the icy light as though it were a savage beast sniffing too close to him.

The light smiles. "Command these stones to become bread," it says. "You have that power. You can do that."

Jesus bows his head and closes his eyes and in a hoarse voice whispers: "It is written, *No one lives by bread alone, but by every word that issues from the mouth of God.*"

"Ah, yes, we can both quote Scripture," says the light, "you to hide within it, I to call you forth and grant you knowledge, fame, and a universal name!"

All at once the cold becomes an engulfing, binding pressure on Jesus from his ankles to his face. A wind arises and begins to scream. When Jesus opens his eyes he finds that the light has completely surrounded him, canceling the desert in a pale fog. Then he feels a footing beneath him. He stands, and the light releases him, lightly moving to one side, smiling — and so Jesus is able to see that he has been transported to the highest corner of the temple wall, below which all Jerusalem is scattered like pebbles. Here the priests blow trumpets to cry in the New Year. Here is thin air and a giddy height.

The cool light speaks. "Jesus," it says, "if you are the Son whom God loves, cast yourself down. For it is promised in the Psalms, *He shall charge his angels to guard you. They will bear you in their hands to keep you from dashing even your foot against a stone.* In such a public place, who could not recognize that you are the darling of the Almighty God?"

But Jesus stands dead still in the lofty air and whispers, "It is written, *You shall not tempt the Lord your God.*"

In a flash Jerusalem vanishes, and Jesus is not on the temple wall. He is infinitely higher than anything made by hands — and the frozen light is now a snow where he is standing, the white rind of a cosmic mountain. This is the peak that rose first above the waters when God's diluvian wrath drowned all earthly things except for Noah and his kin. This is the eminence from which all the world is visible, from sea to sea to sea.

Now it is the great glacial ice that speaks, the crawling capstone of dolmen earth.

"Jesus of Nazareth, look!" it booms. "See the kingdoms one by one, the jewels of creation. Mark their power and their glory. Review their histories from the beginning till now, from now until forever. All this, all these wonders will I give into your hands — to rule them all — if you but bow down and worship me."

But Jesus does not look at the kingdoms of the world. He sits down on the terrible mountain and closes his eyes and whispers, "But I know you. I know what sort of angel you are. Satan, tempter, betrayer — begone! For it is written, *You shall worship the Lord your God, and him only shall you serve.*"

In that same instant, Jesus is sitting with his back against one boulder of a dolmen in the desert under a severe sunlight. For the sun has circled the sky and has taken his shade away.

He draws lines with his finger in the dust. In Hebrew he writes the words: *The devil departs. For a season.*

V

W ho are you?"

"Why do you ask? Is this a secret? I am John the son of Zechariah."

"Yes, yes, everyone knows your name. What we don't know is your authority. What status do you claim under God? Why do you baptize?"

It was the cool of the evening. The sky had a winy beauty which, as his disciples knew, always comforted John at this turning between day and day. Tonight he was obviously tired. None of the disciples would have spoken to him now. But strangers didn't know any better.

After the crowds had gone home for supper, John had stretched himself
on a grassy hill outside the tiny transjordan village named Bethany. He had
folded a goatskin as his pillow beneath his head. Four of the disciples were
sitting in conversation at a distance. Nearer, close to his side, a fifth disciple
was squatting by a heap of hot coals, broiling fish.

And then came this delegation from Jerusalem, priests and Levites
representing the temple and the Sanhedrin. The hems of their wonderful
garments were dry and clean because they forded the Jordan on donkeys.

They dismounted, approached John on the grassy hill, and greeted him
loudly enough to rouse him.

John squinted up at them, leaned on one elbow, and nodded his own
greeting in return.

Under these odd conditions, then, the delegation began its inquiry:

"John the son of Zechariah, who do you claim to be? No one can deny the
power of your preaching. It burns like a fire throughout Judea. But neither
does anyone know by what right you do these things. Are you," they said,
"the Messiah?"

No one was laughing, neither John nor his interrogators nor the quiet
disciple broiling fish nearby. So great was the desire for the coming of
God's Anointed One, that the question was repeated often among the Jews,
touching every charismatic individual who appeared: *Is this the one? Has
Messiah finally come?*

On the other hand, the same desire in so many people could empower
false Messiahs to do harm in the land.

"Are you the Messiah?" the delegation asked.

John shook his head. "No," he said. Tough and lean in his mantle of
camel's hair, he said, "I am not the Messiah."

"Who then?" said the priests. "Are you Elijah whom God promised to
send before the great and terrible day of the Lord?"

John said, "I am not."

"Then what of that prophet?" The delegation was standing in a
semicircle at John's feet. He had continued to recline before them.
"Moses wrote that God would raise up for us a prophet just like him.
He said that the Lord would put his words in that prophet's mouth, and
of those who didn't heed those words, the Lord himself would require a
recompense — "

"*But the prophet,*" said John, quoting Moses, "*who presumes to speak in
the Lord's name what the Lord had not commanded —* " John paused and
sighed. " *— that same prophet shall die.*"

"Yes. Moses wrote that, too. So are you that prophet?" the priests asked.

"No."

"Then who are you? Sir, we must have an answer for those who sent us.
What do you say about yourself?"

John gazed at the delegation a while, then said, "A voice." He lay back on the ground again, his head resting on the goatskin pillow. He closed his eyes. "Tell your superiors," he said, "that you went out into the wilderness and there you met a voice, nothing more, nothing less. And wherever you traveled, over mountains, valleys, rough land, and water, that voice was crying, 'Make straight the way of the Lord!' "

John folded his huge hands upon his chest. Soon he was breathing with a deep regularity.

The priests and the Levites glanced at one another, amazed. Then they called to the disciple who was broiling fish. "You, man. You, there, what's your name?"

The disciple said, "Andrew."

"Andrew," they said, "do you see what your master is doing?"

"Yes," Andrew said. "He's sleeping."

"Well, wake him up! Who does he think he is? Not only does he insult us, he's insulting the whole priesthood in Jerusalem who sent us to him. Wake him up, or we will."

Andrew stood up smiling. "The man is tired," he said. "I'm sorry, sirs, I won't wake him — and I won't let you try. But here is some fish. You may share a meal with us, if you wish."

Evidently they did not wish. Without another word the officials mounted their donkeys and rode through darkness in the direction of Bethany.

▮

Early the following morning Andrew himself woke up to the sound of John's voice, a joyful, energetic cry.

John was standing on the grassy hill, peering eastward into the sunrise. He had shaded his eyes with his left hand. "There," he called, waking Andrew.

John raised his right hand and pointed straight into the light. "There," he said. "There he comes!"

Andrew and another disciple climbed the hill to John's side, trying to see what he was pointing at.

"There!" John cried. "Don't you see him? That is the Lamb of God who takes away the sin of the world!"

Andrew saw someone walking in their direction. Tangled hair. He looked emaciated, gaunt in the cheek. His step was slow and cautious, as if all his bones were brittle.

John said: "Forty days ago I baptized that man, and I saw the Spirit descend from heaven as a dove, and remain on him. Then the Lord God, who sent me to baptize with water, said to me, *He on whom you see the Spirit descend and remain, this is he who will baptize with the Holy Spirit!* Yes, and I heard the voice from heaven declare that he is the Son of God. His name is

Jesus. He comes from Nazareth."

The solitary figure had drawn near enough now that Andrew could see his features. Light brown eyes, calm and lidded. They regarded John with friendly recognition. Then they looked directly at Andrew himself and at the other disciple.

The Lamb of God: this Jesus had a thin growth of beard, perhaps a month's growth, neither oiled nor brushed, unkempt.

He said to John, "It is well."

John nodded and answered, "Yes, cousin, it is well. And it shall be well. Are you hungry?"

"Plain bread," Jesus said. Then, to Andrew he said, "Do you have any fish? Have you been fishing yet this morning?"

Andrew swallowed. He couldn't immediately answer. In fact, he was by occupation a fisherman, but —

Jesus said, "I'd like some fish to break my fast."

Andrew immediately took to his heels and ran toward the village in order to find some fish.

By the time he returned, the new man was washed, combed, clean-shaven and waiting. He had a wavy, raven-black hair — and eyes of a peculiar hue: a dazzling brown, like disks of polished gold. His glance was steadfast, his complexion ruddy, his whole aspect comely.

"There's no need to hurry," he said to Andrew. "Where did you find my breakfast?"

"My brother," Andrew answered breathlessly. "Simon. He doesn't sleep much. He had already netted some small fish in the river."

All morning Andrew could not tear his attention from this visitor. He watched how Jesus blessed the food, how he ate, how he spoke with John, gazing directly at him, maintaining a soft, insistent tone, how he shaped individual words with a careful rounding of the mouth, how he stood, how he moved, with what grace he prepared to depart — and then, in that moment of departure, Andrew suffered an exquisite physical longing to follow him. It felt like the rending of silk inside his breast.

Jesus began to walk down to the river alone, toward the ford that led to Jericho. Andrew watched him go, pursing his lips and sighing.

Suddenly a great hand fell on his shoulder. John was beside him, the master unto whom he had given commitment. Young Andrew! — his heart cracked between two desires.

But John said, "Go, my son. Go. That's the man whom I told you about, whose sandal I'm not worthy to unloose because he is so much greater than I am. I baptize with water for this very reason, that he might be revealed to Israel. Why shouldn't that begin with my own disciples?"

John kissed the anxious young man and whispered, "Andrew, it is right: he must increase, while I must decrease. Go."

vi

W hen Herod the Great had died a generation ago, his dreams of a proper succession died with him.

The final codicil of his final will had named his son Archelaus as king. It had also granted limited territories to two other sons who thus became "tetrarchs." Philip received lands north and east of the Sea of Galilee. Antipas controlled two provinces: Galilee in regions west of that Sea, and Perea east of Jordan and the Dead Sea as far south as the fortress Machaerus, as far north as the city of Pella.

But because of immediate infighting with his brothers and a spontaneous revolt in his own lands, Rome stripped Archelaus of his title as king, demanding first that he prove he deserved to rule. In the next ten years he proved, rather, that he merited no power at all. He treated both the Jews and the Samaritans with such cruel brutality that Caesar Augustus banished him to Gaul and reduced both Judea and Samaria to a common province under a governor.

Thereafter Rome allowed no "king" at all in the lands that Herod the Great once had ruled.

Tetrarch Philip governed in quiet obscurity for thirty-eight years. He died without children to receive his territories.

Antipas, on the other hand, mimicked his father. He founded a city on the western shores of the Sea of Galilee and built it according to Greek designs. He named it after the Roman Emperor Tiberius. And since, like his father, he cared little for Jewish laws and sensibilities, he blandly chose as the site of this new city a very old burial ground. Jews absolutely shunned the handsome and unclean place. Antipas responded by importing Gentiles in order to bring a population into his city. In Jewry, then, this ruler's arrogance created a Roman invasion, a community which was oblivious to all that was holy.

But who could make a public condemnation of these actions? Antipas maintained a standing army, weaponed, suspicious, and violent; and like his father, Antipas would easily murder the mouths that threatened his strength. He called himself by his father's name: Herod Antipas.

When Herod Antipas was forty years old, he fell in love with the wife of his brother. Her name was Herodias. She had a daughter named Salome. But Herod Antipas was already married. Therefore he divorced his wife — bringing down upon himself the rage of her father, king of the desert kingdom, Nabataea — and then married Herodias.

Such was the power of a tetrarch. His will was law, whether or not it alienated his subjects, offended his neighbors, or broke the holy commands of God.

∎

The more John preached, the less people connected his name to the name of his father, Zechariah. Throughout Judea and Samaria and Galilee and Perea, up and down both sides of the Jordan, he became known as "John the Baptizer."

And that ceaseless cry, *Repent, for the kingdom of heaven is at hand*, rang like a tocsin wherever he went. John caused distress in cities and in the countryside: some suffered spiritual distress, truly striving to prepare for the kingdom, while others feared that a heavenly kingdom must displace earthly kingdoms and economies. Moreover, certain authorities worried that the desire for heaven's approach would drive zealots mad enough to sabotage the more worldly powers.

A tocsin wherever he went — and John seemed to appear wherever the water was. He baptized multitudes everywhere on the Jordan, from the lowland near the Dead Sea even as far north as Salim where springs produced abundant water.

And all his baptizing was given the sawtooth of the law. He announced the need of each person's purity before God. He demanded a deep, internal turning of the heart. He declared that an impassable gulf divided worldly governance from governance of the Lord, and as a caustic example he referred to the flagrant disregard of covenant displayed by the tetrarch of the very province in which he, John, and this great congregation presently were standing.

"Herod Antipas, do you hear me?" John the Baptizer cried. Ears burned at the royal name; faces went down; but a hundred minds remembered what John said.

"I stand in a low valley," he crowed. "You sit on mountains of power. Yet my voice will reach you." John raised that voice to the pitch of an eagle's shriek and cried: "Listen, Antipas! It is not lawful for any man to take his brother's wife! Why do you think you are different? However you whitewash the union, you and Herodias have bound yourselves with cords of sinning! But the Lord has sent his anointed here, *here*! — and he comes like a farmer at harvest coming to his threshing floor. Even now the winnowing fork is in his hand. He is ready to clear it, Antipas! Wheat he will gather into his bins, but the chaff he will burn with unquenchable fire!"

∎

Three months after he had baptized Jesus of Nazareth, while John and his disciples were strolling over dry hills east of the Dead Sea — just at eventide — a band of soldiers came riding up the slopes on strong Egyptian mares. Twenty horsemen. They made such a headlong thunder of their coming that the ground trembled. John stopped and looked. The bloody light of the sunset bathed their helmets. To a man they were dressed in battle gear.

But they were following no road nor discernible path. They came like a low cloud, gathering density as they ascended the hills. Soon enough it became apparent that the Baptizer was the target of this swift contingent.

John told his disciples to leave him immediately. They took several steps backward, but they could not leave. They became a silent, helpless audience.

Among the galloping horses was a cart, bouncing on light wheels. Suddenly, in dust and sound, the soldiers surrounded John. Two of them leaped to the ground. One grabbed the Baptizer by his hair; the other looped rope around his legs and his torso and, finally, his neck. As huge as John's hands were, the outline of his body under such a binding revealed him to be miserably lean.

So this lean man was lifted up and heaved into the cart, and without a word the soldiers mounted, reined their horses around, and galloped back down the slopes the way they had come.

John's disciples stood a while in silence. Then the entire company began as one body to walk.

They walked all night long in the dark, in a southerly direction, for they had recognized the insignia of the troops that had taken their master away. They were walking toward the fortress at Machaerus, a massive, unbreachable stronghold, one residence of the tetrarch.

They had no doubt: Herod Antipas had imprisoned John the Baptizer in his dungeons there.

33

ANDREW

i

Perhaps the brothers Andrew and Simon were alike at the core. Perhaps they shared a sort of tympanic sensitivity, highly alert to the people and the events around them. But the effects of that awareness were different in each, and they managed their feelings differently, and they could not have had bodies more dissimilar.

Andrew's mood was ever blowing left and right in the winds of the people around him. In glad company he, too, was glad and gladder than most, beaming blessings on everyone. If there arose contention, he grew gloomy and withdrew. If there was some unreadable silence, Andrew felt isolated and suffered anxieties for the future. He was long-fingered, quick, twitchy, and watchful. But he was so trammeled by shyness that he suppressed whatever might call attention to himself: his heart and his mind went tripping forward at furious speeds. But in public his tongue grew thick and his thoughts too small to mention.

Simon, on the other hand, was a blunt fellow. Physically blunt: short-fingered, broad-chested, powerfully knit and crowned with a skullbone as round as a Roman's. He wore a beard so thick and dark, the whole head looked like a war club. He could explode in talk. No ties to his tongue. He gave every impression of self-confidence. Simon was the wind that blew his brother about, in almost any company the source of a boisterous gladness, or of contention. But one sign of a vulnerable heart within him may have been the bluff cynicism with which Simon met matters of consequence and human emotion. *Ho, ho! You can't dupe me. I won't be anybody's fool.* Or perhaps he wore the suspicious exterior for protection, since he could be a man of sudden, deep, and dangerous loyalties — dangerous because they were so absolute.

Simon was full of young bluster, girding himself and going wherever he wanted to go!

Andrew went one way only — following Jesus.

"He stopped. He turned and he saw me, but I hadn't made a sound. I'd been creeping, you know — hiding, sort of. He said, 'What are you looking for?' And I said the first thing that came to my mind. I said, 'Where are you staying?' No, Simon, actually I said, '*Rabbi*, where are you staying?' I called him Rabbi, and then I blushed and almost ran back to John, because who gave me permission to call him my teacher? But he said, 'Come and see.' No blame. No question. No hesitation. He told me to go with him, and I did. We forded the Jordan together. What do you think about that? We went to a small house near Jericho, and he invited me in, and I went in, and I spent the night with him. What do you think about that?"

"What should I think?" Simon said.

"Well, but it's Jesus," said Andrew.

"You said that. I know six men named Jesus, and five of them are madmen."

"But John said he was the Lamb of God."

"The what?"

"The Lamb of God — who takes away the sin of the world."

"What does that mean?"

"I don't know. Sacrifice, maybe?"

"You sacrifice a *goat* for sins. I never heard of a lamb that bore the sins of the people."

"There's the Passover lamb. Ask John."

"Andrew, I like John. I traveled with him, didn't I? A whole year through, the same as you. But I didn't always take his meaning, even when I went and asked him four times over. Besides, he's in jail."

Andrew paused, stood up straight, and fixed his brother with an anxious look. His voice grew soft with intensity. "But I'm not in jail," he said. "And I know what I've seen with my own eyes and touched with my own hands, and I know what he has done to me. Jesus, Simon. This one is not a madman. Jesus, deep as a root in the ground. And in my breast. Even now, while I'm away from him, my heart yearns to be back again."

Andrew's eyes were shiny with emotion. Simon had also stood up by now, though his gaze was turned to the mist that sailed the still waters of the lake. The brothers were mending breaks in their fishnets with new flaxen cord. Dusk was descending. There was only a little light left in the day.

Simon said, "I'm sorry, little brother. I didn't mean to fight with you. Tell me what you've seen."

Andrew said, "I didn't always understand John either. But I was too nervous to ask."

"He was always talking about fire," said Simon. "The man seemed so fierce, I kept waiting for him to burst into flame."

Andrew and Simon now shook out two hand-casting nets and laid them open on the grass. The nets were made of a hemp meshing, cone-shaped, with weights around the wide mouth to pull it below the surface. Simon began to string a new cord through the loops of the smaller mouth.

Andrew said, "They tried to kill him."

"Kill John?"

"No, Jesus. They tried to throw him off a cliff. It was his own hometown. The people he grew up with. His own synagogue.

"When Herod Antipas arrested John, Jesus decided to return to Galilee. We took a route straight through Samaria. Simon, everything the man does has a strange, calm power. He met a woman at the well outside of Sychar, and just by talking to her — by his words alone — he caused such awe in her that she ran back to town saying, 'Could this be the Messiah?'

"We stayed two days in that place, so we didn't get to Nazareth until the day before the Sabbath.

"But as soon as we arrived, Jesus' mother went to tell an elder of the synagogue that he was there, and the elder invited her son to read from the prophets and to preach the next day.

"I like her. I like Mary. She and Jesus look alike. They have the same wide forehead and the same widow's peak. But she's so proud of him and so sure she knows what's best for him, that sometimes she pushes him into embarrassing positions.

"When we entered the synagogue that Sabbath, old men patted his head, saying, 'Yeshi, Yeshi, do well today.'

"Little children ran to him screaming, 'Do me! Do me!' Jesus didn't seem offended. 'See how sick I am?' the children cried, running in circles around him. 'Two broken legs. I'm dying. Heal me, Miracle Man.' The news precedes us wherever we go. Everyone knows what Jesus can do.

"He knelt down and snatched two children to himself, one in each arm. He gave them kisses on their necks until they squealed at the whisker-tickling and laughed with delight. No, he was not offended by their games.

"Worship began. Prayers, a reading from the Law, then the attendant handed Jesus the scroll of the prophet Isaiah. He unrolled it and he read it. He sat down and began to preach — and that was the beginning of our trouble."

By now the brothers had folded their nets and stowed them fore and aft in a wide-bodied rowboat. The boat had a short mast center-forward, wooden bins for sorting fish, some barbed fishing spears lodged along the gunwales, and a rough flooring since the fishermen stood up to cast the nets, then knelt to pull them in again.

Together they pushed the prow into the lake. Andrew jumped in and moved forward. Simon bowed behind the stern, shoved the boat free of the grassy bank, then stepped inside and took an oar. It was dark on the waters. The last light was dying in the west, the direction which the brothers faced as they rowed away from the land.

Andrew kept talking:

"Jesus read the passage in Isaiah where it says, *The Spirit of the Lord is upon me, because he has anointed me*. Anointed 'me' — anointed someone to preach good news, to give sight to the blind, to proclaim the year of the Lord's favor. So far, so good. But when he preached, Jesus turned himself into that 'someone.'

"He said, 'Today this scripture is fulfilled in your hearing.'

"Right away I heard somebody grumble, 'Who does he think he is?'

"Jesus said, 'The time foreseen by the prophets has come. The kingdom of God is at hand. Repent,' he said — just like John. But then the next thing John would never dare to say: 'Repent and believe what you hear and see in me.'

"Well, that did it. The whole synagogue took offense. They shouted that he was only a carpenter's boy and had no right to such proud language.

"But Jesus did not back down. He said, 'No prophet is acceptable in his own country.'

"People hollered even louder. 'Prophet? So, Yeshi, you're a prophet now? You are *both* the anointed one of God *and* a prophet?'

"They couldn't stand it. Simon, I don't know how their anger changed from shouting to action — but soon the men had carried Jesus out of the synagogue and were driving him up the hill behind Nazareth. I ran to be with him. This was a mob. These people were enraged. They were forcing Jesus toward the edge of the hill. Simon, they planned to throw him over the cliff!

"But then Jesus grabbed my arm and pulled me sideways, and suddenly we were hidden in the bushes. He grinned and winked at me. 'All my childhood I played in these hills,' he said, and he led me away by another path.

"Even then he was calm. That's what I'm telling you, Simon — how confident the man is. He knows something. He has something that no one else has. What is that thing? Well, I'm starting to believe him. When he says, *The Spirit of the Lord is upon me*, I think he is telling the truth."

Andrew moved to the prow of the boat where he lit an oil lamp. It made an island of yellow light, while all around them the sea was black.

"So we left Nazareth," he said. "Six days later we came here to Capernaum."

Andrew opened his net and laid it loosely on the floor. Simon, in the stern, did the same. Each brother in his own time took hold of the weighted rim of his net, then lifted it, whirled it, spun it out into the darkness where it made a flat slapping on the water and sank.

They stood a while in contemplative silence, holding the drawstrings of their nets and staring up into the night sky busy with a million stars. Then they knelt and dragged their nets back in. No need to kneel: both nets were empty.

For the rest of the night they cast their nets but caught nothing at all.

ii

On the morning after they had arrived in Capernaum, Jesus and Andrew separated for the day. Andrew was anxious to find his brother. He'd heard that Simon was staying with his wife's family in Capernaum.

Jesus went to the synagogue. It was a remarkably balanced and beautiful building — built, in fact, by a Gentile, a centurion, a righteous man who honored the Jews by means of this expensive gift.

But this was the Sabbath, and Jesus had come to observe the day, to worship, and then to teach whomever he found willing to listen.

By mid-afternoon he was sitting among a group of pious Jews who were curious to hear the Scriptural exposition of this new rabbi.

But the more they listened, the more curious they became, because this man offered no exposition at all. All the scribes and rabbis grounded their teaching on passages from the Scripture — except Jesus of Nazareth! This fellow didn't support his word by reference to Moses or the prophets. Instead, he spoke as if he were his own authority. He seemed to assume that his word was true for this reason alone, that he had spoken it!

It was an astonishing display — for some Jews a disturbing one, but for others, bold and admirable. Something new was happening in Galilee!

Then suddenly the Sabbath decorum was shattered. A wailing arose in a corner of the room.

"*Aieee*! Get away from me!"

It was a ghastly howling, altogether unrestrained. Then a man emerged from darkness clutching his robe at the throat, his eyes rolling in horror. His hair was greasy and wild. "What, what, what," he wailed, stumbling toward Jesus: "What do you have to do with us?"

The pious people backed away from the man, troubled and embarrassed. "Oh, Shobal," they said. "Oh, Shobal." They knew him. They pitied him. He had lurked for years in the backstreets of Capernaum, mumbling and fretting in cryptic language. And they feared him. More properly, they feared the demon within him. For Shobal was a meek man of limited sense; but his demon was cold, deadly, and unclean.

Now Shobal, stumbling forward, his mouth slurred open, the flat of his left hand raised against the new rabbi, howled, "Jeeeeesus of Nazareth, have you come to destroy us? I know you! I know you! *Aieee* — I know who you are, *You Holy One of God!*"

Jesus had not arisen from his seat. With half-lidded eyes he regarded the coming apparition, a man eaten by the demon within, and he shook his head. "They call you Shobal?" he murmured. "Yes, they call you 'basket.' What you carry in you — it is not of you."

Then Jesus cracked the air with a cry as with a hammer: "*Silence!*" The entire synagogue echoed the command. No one moved. In a quieter voice Jesus said, "Come out of the man."

Shobal fell like timber. His limbs shuddered, drumming the floor. The wailing that came from his mouth grew louder and louder until it seemed to break loose from the man and fly out of the beautiful building and into the earth.

Now there was in the room a silence nearly palpable, like white wool settling upon every living soul. Jesus reached down to Shobal and stroked his wild hair smooth again; then he helped the exhausted man to his feet and together they went out into the sunlight.

"What is this?" the people said. "A new teaching? An amazing authority! Why, he commands even the unclean spirits, and they obey him."

They ran out of the synagogue and followed Jesus.

By evening the whole city was gathering around him, bringing friends who were sick with diseases, relatives who were possessed by demons. And Jesus healed them. He touched them. With his fingertips he brushed their foreheads, their faces, their lips, and their feet. With his golden gaze he peered into their eyes. And ever in his private voice he whispered, "Here, here, here is the mercy of God. Here. Here."

iii

Very early the following morning, even before the sunrise, Jesus slipped from his sleeping quarters and left to find a lonely place outside the city, a secluded place for praying.

But Shobal had been dozing right outside his door.

And Shobal, now given to ripping fits of wonderful laughter, jumped up and ran after him, south along the lake shore, roaring his delight.

Shobal's liberty was Jesus' capture. Soon a crowd of citizens was pouring from Capernaum after the weak-minded Shobal and his miraculous friend.

Jesus turned and observed this human river for a moment, then made a decision. He cut left and walked down to the Sea of Galilee where two rowboats had been dragged ashore. Beside each was a pair of fishermen, washing their nets. Four men. One of these was Andrew.

"Andrew," Jesus called.

"Master! Good morning!"

"Do you see the people coming?"

"Yes. Oh, my — yes!"

"Would you and your brother row me out a little way and anchor there? I want to teach. But I need a proper distance and a pulpit."

Andrew grinned. "Of course," he said. "Simon?"

Simon said nothing, but put his shoulder to the boat and drove it into the water.

Jesus and Andrew boarded.

"Grab your nets!" Jesus said. And just as the crowd was running down the slopes to the sea, Simon heaved the boat completely into the water, leaped aboard and took an oar.

In the early morning over still waters a man's voice can travel ashore as easily as an eagle glides.

Jesus sat down in the back of the boat, facing the people. Simon did not drop anchor. He placed himself behind Jesus and kept both oars in the water. By his own adjustments he held the stern and the preacher perfectly landward.

Jesus said, "The kingdom of heaven is at hand."

The sun had just arisen like a solid flame at the far side of the sea. The bodies of the listening citizens, therefore, were suddenly in a clear and fierce relief, though the boat, the mast, and the teacher inside were all to them in silhouette.

The brothers Simon and Andrew, on the other hand, saw Jesus' back in a burning light — and though his hair was raven-black, they could see under sunlight a deep red hue. The rabbi's black hair burned scarlet in its depths.

Jesus said, "To what shall we compare the kingdom of heaven? What parable shall we use for it? The kingdom of heaven is like a grain of mustard seed. When sown in the ground it is the smallest of seeds. But when it grows it puts forth branches so long and large that the birds of the air can make nests in its shade — and then of all shrubs it is the greatest!"

Suddenly Jesus turned and whispered to Simon, "Think about this: your meek little brother is my first little seed."

Simon opened his mouth, but Jesus had already turned back toward the beach.

"Listen!" he cried. "Here's a different story altogether! Once upon a time a sower went out to sow his fields. He cast the seed abroad with great sweeps of his hand. Some of it fell on the hard path, and the birds came and ate that seed before nightfall. Some fell on rocky ground and thin soil. Soon young seedlings appeared, but when the sun grew hot they withered and died because they had no root. Other seed fell among thorns. The tough thorns grew up with the tender plants, choking them and overpowering them so that they bore no fruit.

"But much of the seed fell on good soil where it flourished and brought forth an abundant harvest, yielding thirtyfold and sixtyfold and a hundredfold!"

At the top of his lungs, Jesus cried: "Those who have ears to hear, let them hear!" Then he stood up and turned away from land and from the people with a finality.

He looked at Andrew sitting in the bow of the boat. "Good morning, fisherman," he said. He broke into a dazzling smile. "Andrew, I've worked up an appetite. Do we have some fish for breakfast?"

Andrew shook his head. "No," he said. "I'm sorry, we have no fish at all."

"Well, look here," said Jesus, still smiling. "Here are your nets still in the boat. Put out to deep water and let them down for a catch. I can wait to eat."

"Master!" Simon boomed. The thick beard hid his mouth; but his voice roared like a lion in a cave. "What's the point?" he said. "We've been toiling all night long with nothing to show for it."

"All night?" said Jesus with a seeming sympathy.

"Yes."

"And you caught nothing?"

"No, nothing."

"And this is your profession? This is how you make a living? This is the thing you're best at? Ah, poor fellow!" Jesus beamed at Simon, his eyes flashing, his whole face filled with delight. "Do it anyway. Do it because I ask you to."

Simon glowered at Jesus, then said, "At your word I will let down the nets," meaning: *it's your responsibility.*

So they rowed past the shallows, brought their oars in, allowed the boat to drift on its own, unfolded their nets on the floor, then both brothers cast nets from either side at the same time.

The instant the nets hit water, the lake around them began to boil with activity. All at once they were floating in a shoal of fish so dense that the nets bulged and tugged and grew too heavy to haul inside.

"John!" Simon bellowed. He stood erect and roared inland: "John, James, get out here!"

The other boat that had been resting ashore was suddenly afloat and coming with great sweeps of its long oars.

"The nets are tearing!" Simon cried.

When the second boat arrived, all four men worked the two nets, pulling and pouring living fish out on the floorboards until their ankles were hidden in slippery bodies, until the boats themselves were sinking nearly to the gunwales.

Then while three men labored with cheer, the fourth man, Simon, grew visibly agitated. Again and again he shot a nervous glance at Jesus, who sat in the stern. Finally, Simon turned from the nets and waded through fish to the back of the boat where he fell down at Jesus' knees and said, "O Lord, I am a sinful man! More sinful than I ever knew. Depart from me!"

At his confession the fishing ceased. Andrew and John and James stood up and looked at the sight: massive Simon sunk among the wet fish, bowing down to Jesus. They, too, let go of their nets. Immediately the lake relaxed, the water grew calm, the morning returned to a smiling silence — and

Jesus' next words, though spoken softly, were perfectly clear and ever thereafter remembered.

"Simon, don't be afraid," he said. Then he looked from man to man in both boats. "Follow me," he said, "and I will make you fishers of the human soul."

When they had brought their boats to land again, the men began to follow Jesus. Simon son of Jonah, James and John the sons of Zebedee — as Andrew had before them, they left their occupations, their boats, their possessions, their houses, and their families, and they made their homes with Jesus.

By the following morning, Simon had shaved his beard. He showed up with pure white cheeks under the sunburnt thunder of his forehead.

When he saw the change, Jesus burst out laughing.

The blunt, roundheaded man stuck out his bottom lip and frowned.

But that only caused Jesus to laugh the louder.

"O tender soul!" he cried. "You have a mouth for pouting after all!" He reached and pinched Simon's white cheek.

That pinch destroyed the big man's concentration, and he astonished himself by laughing along, barrel-chested and booming. So did Andrew, filled with gladness in glad company. So did James and John.

"Simon bar-Jonah, as smooth as a boy! Why did you shave your face?"

Simon grew serious again. "To be like you," he said. "To be like my master."

iv

That afternoon Jesus and Andrew and the sons of Zebedee went home with Simon. He had insisted. He was full of a rage to humble himself and serve them all — foot-washings and cool drinks and food and rest. But when they arrived at the house, they found that Simon's mother-in-law had gone to bed with chills and a violent fever.

Simon's desire to serve evaporated. Instead, Jesus performed a service of his own.

He entered the woman's room and knelt by the pallet where she lay shivering. He gazed into her moist face, curled back the grey hairs stuck to her brow, then took her by the hand. Lightly he raised her to a sitting position. She opened her eyes and focused her vision upon him. She blinked and swallowed.

Slowly Jesus rose to standing. Gently he took the woman's weight upon himself and raised her also to her feet. By the time the bedclothes had fallen away from her, the fever, too, was gone. She swallowed again and licked her lips and drew a huge breath of air as if she were inhaling some wonderful scent — and then it was she, flushed pink and grinning and strong again, who served the five men in her house.

All through the meal Simon relished the miracle his master had performed. He kept asking his mother-in-law how it felt to be healed, then blowing out great woofs of air, completely bedazzled.

Andrew withdrew into silence. With one or two others he might possibly join a conversation. But five was too many. Five left no gaps for a shy man's word. He was content to listen.

Therefore, when supper was done and everyone else was enjoying their talk, Andrew alone heard a hoarse voice whispering at the window, "Sir?" Softly, patiently: "Sir?"

Andrew got up and went outside. It was already night, but in moonlight he could make out a figure in the alley between two houses. Someone was lurking in shadow, timidly whining at the window, "Sir? Sir — "

Andrew said, "What's the matter here?"

The supplicant whirled around and crouched by the wall. Yet he held his ground. He didn't bolt when Andrew began to approach him. Instead, he crept one tiny step forward and croaked, "Are you — ?"

The motion brought the man into a patch of moonlight, and suddenly Andrew saw the sheen of stone-white skin, the unreal porcelain glaze of leprosy: it shined down the hairless scalp and the neck of the solitary man.

A leper! Andrew froze. Lepers defiled people. The law forbade them human contact. This was itself a flagrant violation, to enter the city at all.

Then the man fell down on his face and whispered, "Master."

"No!" cried Andrew. "No, not me!" In horror he stumbled backward, tripped, and started to fall; but he was caught from behind by two firm hands.

"Master," the man croaked, "if you will you can make me clean."

Andrew was released, and Jesus stepped forward, peering at the leper in moonlight.

"I will," he said. He put both his hands on the silvery scalp as if in blessing, and he said, "Be clean." The leprous flesh seemed to turn into a powder. Jesus stroked the man's head and neck, brushing away the white dust of the disease. New skin appeared and the man was made soft and fresh, clean.

"Now, go your way," Jesus said. "Show yourself to the priest and offer the gift that Moses commanded. But do not breathe a word of this to anyone. Tell no one what I've done for you!"

Andrew was surprised at how sternly Jesus spoke to the man. He sounded almost angry. But by the following morning Andrew decided that Jesus knew what the leper was going to do.

Clearly, the man had not obeyed his healer, for the news had spread everywhere in Capernaum. Greater and greater multitudes besieged Jesus this day and the next, this week and the next.

So swiftly and so far abroad flew the reports about Jesus, that people began to gather from all the cities of that region. They came from Bethsaida on the north shore of the lake, from Chorazin, a city built on the basalt hills, from Magdala, a center of fishing and shipbuilding, a city of wealth and a loose reputation.

People traveled from everywhere in the ancient territories of Zebulun and Naphtali, the western and northern portions of Galilee.

■

One day when Jesus was preaching in the house of Simon's mother-in-law, the multitude was so dense that Andrew had to flee the place. People filled every room. They crowded the doorway as well as the streets around the house, and those at the edges of the congregation stood on tiptoe, straining to hear what Jesus was saying.

Andrew intended to keep his distance until the evening, when people would have to go home. But then he noticed four men coming down the street, carrying a light bed frame among them.

On the frame lay a young man whose spine was doubled back upon itself. It thrust his chest up, bared his throat, and bent his neck back at a hard angle, so that even lying down the poor fellow was forced to stare back the way that he had come.

The four men turned a corner and then stopped, stunned by the great sea of people before them.

"Oh, no!" they said. "We'll never get through."

The young man on the bed frame made a yowling sound. Evidently it was a question.

"No," said his friends. "We have to go home."

The yowling grew guttural and passionate. The crooked man barked and jibbered and seemed close to choking. His friends pleaded with him. "Gimel," they said, "he's surrounded by a thousand people. No one can break through that wall."

Now Gimel started to cry with his mouth wide open. So hopeless were his inarticulate sobs, that Andrew was moved to step forward and to speak.

"You came to see Jesus?" he asked.

The four men shrugged and shook their heads. "Little Gimel has been paralyzed for three years," they said. "If this Jesus of Nazareth cannot help him, maybe he's meant to be paralyzed for the rest of his life."

"Ahhh!" Gimel wept. "Ahhh-ha. Ahhh-ha."

Andrew felt the tears rising in his own eyes. So he acted.

"Do you see that mattock there?" he said. "Bring it and follow me."

He led the four men and their friend down a secluded alley. They came to the house at its back, where there was a staircase up to the roof. Andrew heard the animal murmuring of many people within. He also heard Jesus' voice above all else. He climbed the stairs to the top, then called, "Come up, and bring little Gimel with you."

Carefully the four men ascended to the clay roof.

Andrew pointed to a near section of the roof and said, "Crack it. This area is over the room where Jesus is preaching. Break through right here."

"Through the roof?" one man asked.

Andrew smiled. "You need some sort of door to Jesus, don't you? I'm giving you one."

With strength, then, that man lifted the mattock and dealt the roof a wonderful blow.

Andrew heard chunks of ceiling fall inside. Then there was a perfect silence. He felt giddy to be so rash. Even Jesus had stopped talking.

While one man swung the mattock the others plucked up pieces of sunbaked clay. Next they tore out the branches that had held the clay — and so they opened a long hole in the roof.

Faces gaped up from the interior darkness. People had pressed backward, making a space directly below the roof gap.

Gimel's friends tore his bedding into strips which they tied to the corners of his frame. Together, now, they leaned toward the hole and lowered the thin, bent body of their friend into the room, setting him down right in front of Jesus of Nazareth.

They dropped the cloth strips and lay on their stomachs to watch what might happen. Andrew, too, lay down beside them.

Jesus looked up, directly at Andrew, then turned his attention to the paralyzed lad at his feet.

"Take heart, my son," he said. "Your sins are forgiven you."

Blasphemy! Andrew heard an immediate hissing in the house. The word hissed was a horrible accusation: "Blasphemy." He looked and saw several well-known scribes murmuring among themselves. These men studied and taught the laws of Moses in reverential detail: recondite in knowing, fierce in the preservation of the law, they could not keep still before a profanation. So they were murmuring loudly enough for others to hear, "Who does he think he is? No one can forgive sins except God alone!"

"What?" said Jesus. "What is your question, sirs?"

Andrew heard an iron severity in Jesus' voice. The master was glaring at these scribes as if they were jackals in a corner.

"I'll tell you your question," Jesus declared. "You're wondering which is the easier to say and the harder to prove: whether I say, 'Your sins are forgiven,' or else, 'Rise and walk.' Well, sirs, in order to show you that the

Son of man truly has power to forgive sins, I will do the lesser thing with visible proofs. Watch! Listen!"

Jesus knelt down and in a tempered voice said, "Rise, lad. Gimel, get up and fold your bedding and go home."

The body of the young man relaxed. For a moment he lay flat on his bed, then he rolled over, stretched with a trembling luxury, and stood up.

Immediately his four friends clattered down from the roof.

Andrew was glad for them. But he had seen how bitterly the scribes had received Jesus' rebuke. For them there had been no goodness in the healing of a paralyzed man.

From his vantage on the rooftop, Andrew watched as Gimel now broke through the crowds and ran to his friends, waving his arms in limber joy. He watched, too, the small knot of sullen men who also were moving away from the people, their heads bent in a dark dialogue together.

V

T he next day at noon Jesus was walking down the main thoroughfare of Capernaum. Shops and booths lined both sides of the street, various foods for sale and dry goods, craftsmen offering skills, coppersmiths, barbers, butchers, oil merchants, tailors, potters.

In the midst of the marketplace a tax officer sat behind his table, collecting from the other businesses taxes required by Herod Antipas.

This is where Jesus stopped, at the toll booth.

He gazed at the tax collector, a dour man of grey complexion, a bony nose, and sunken eyes. When the collector noticed the gaze and looked back, Jesus said, "Your name is Matthew?"

"Yes," said the collector.

Jesus said, "Follow me."

Immediately, Matthew the tax collector stood up and left his business and followed Jesus.

Because of their royal patrons, tax officers took generous portions of the revenue for themselves. They were not much loved by the population. In fact, Matthew seemed to have lived a spare existence despite his generous income. But on this particular night he loosened his purse and spread a rich feast in honor of Jesus of Nazareth.

Not only did Jesus come, grateful for the good food; not only did his disciples come, Andrew, Simon, John, and James; but many of Matthew's acquaintances came as well, other tax collectors, people who ignored the laws of Moses, and some who lived in an obvious immorality. They all reclined at the same table. They all joined in noisy conversation.

And news flew through the city that Jesus had been seen entering this place of questionable reputation.

When he and his disciples bade the rest of the company good night and left Matthew's house, they noticed in the shadows a group of scribes who had gathered to confirm what they had heard.

"What rabbi eats with tax collectors and sinners?"

Jesus paused and said, "Those who are healthy need no physician. Those who are sick do. Write this down somewhere, you righteous scribes; memorize it; sing it as a song:

> *I am not come to call the righteous;*
> *But sinners to repentance.*"

Jesus continued walking down the dark street of the city. In a moment he spoke again, this time to his disciples alone.

"Unto you it is given to know the secrets of the kingdom of heaven," he said. "But to those who are outside, I will always speak in parables so that seeing they may not see, and hearing they may not understand."

Andrew gasped and stopped walking. "Ah, Jesus!" he wailed.

"Andrew? What's the matter?"

"Then I am outside the kingdom. You just said that I'm outside the kingdom of heaven!"

Jesus also stopped. "How did I say such a thing?"

"Because I *don't* understand," Andrew wailed. This was a genuine anguish. Andrew was overcome with loneliness and very close to tears. "When we were in the rowboat you told the people a parable about a farmer sowing seeds. I heard it. Jesus, I truly heard it, but I don't understand it."

"Simon," Jesus said, "do you?"

"I remember it," the big man answered. "Hard ground, rocky ground, thorny ground, I remember it."

"But you don't understand it."

"No."

"John? James? Don't any of you know this parable? Ah, how shall you know all the parables?"

Jesus began to walk again. The disciples had no choice but to follow. There was a breeze blowing in the direction of the lake and drawing the cold with it. The men wrapped their robes tightly about themselves.

Jesus said, "The sower sows the word. His seeds are the word of God broadcast over all the people. Those who are like the beaten path receive the word with their hearing only. Soon Satan comes and snatches it away from them. Those who are like the thin soil over rock — they receive the word with joy and quickly shoot up in the sunlight. But they have no root. So when tribulations and temptations come, they are scorched in the heat

of that light. They wither and die. Those who are like soil among thorns —
they hear the word. It roots in their hearts. But as they go on their way they
are choked with the cares of the world, with riches and pleasures and lusts,
so they bear no fruit in the end. But those who are like the good ground —
Andrew, they receive the word in an honest and good heart; they hold it fast;
they live in patience; and they bring forth some thirtyfold, some sixtyfold,
and some a hundredfold." Jesus stopped in the road. "Andrew," he said,
"do you understand the story now?"

"Yes," said Andrew, very softly. "Thank you."

Jesus said to them all, "The kingdom of heaven is like a treasure hidden
in a field. When someone happens to find it, he covers it up again and in
sheer joy goes and sells all his worldly possessions, then he returns and buys
the entire field."

Jesus said, "Or, the kingdom of heaven is like this: a merchant spends
his whole life searching for fine pearls; yet when he finds a pearl of perfect
purity, he sells all that he has and buys that single jewel and counts himself
perfectly content.

"Tell me, Simon," Jesus said, "have you understood all this? James, John,
have you?"

"Yes," they said.

"Good," he said. "Go home. Go home, now, and sleep. You are mine. You
needn't worry. I want to go up into the mountains to pray. Good night."

vi

In the morning Jesus' disciples discovered that he had not returned all
night long. He was not in Simon's house.

They went out and looked for him, but found him nowhere in the city.

As they moved from building to building and street to street, their
numbers began to swell. Gimel went with them.

Gimel bounded ahead of them like a gazelle in a grassy field. When his
four friends saw Andrew, they immediately attached themselves to the
group as well. Shobal was there, grinning with wet lips. Matthew came.
And Philip, who had grown up in the same city as Simon and Andrew.
There were Zealots and Pharisees and Essenes. There were those who
had been followers of John the Baptizer. Men and women, both rich and
poor, citizens of cities large and small. Two women of some rank and
substance walked side by side: Joanna, whose husband was a steward of
Herod Antipas, and Susanna. Their clothing was cool and dyed light purple.
Another woman followed, a pale young woman who had lived in Magdala
until Jesus quietly and privately had cast seven devils out of her. Her name

was Mary. She also walked with the multitude into the countryside to find him whom she called *Rabboni*, My Teacher.

Simon preceded them all with a robust stride. He seemed to have made up his mind.

"Remember what Jesus said last night?" he asked Andrew, who was keeping pace with him, but dolefully. Andrew lacked his brother's vigor. His narrow forehead was written with worry.

Andrew murmured, "He said that we are his."

"No, no! He said he was going up into the mountains. Don't you remember that? I do! Going into the mountains to pray. We'll find him."

So there was a destination. Simon led the great crowd north and west into the hills, five and ten miles throughout the morning, higher and higher as they went.

To Andrew, the hill country seemed mazy and unforthcoming. It did not reveal secrets. People could wander among the caves, cliffs, ravines, the dead-stone heights, and never be seen again.

But Simon had the innocence of sunny bluster. Andrew followed his brother simply because of that grand self-assurance, and in the end he wondered whether Simon had been following the Spirit of God after all, but unaware.

Because it happened that the people following Simon lifted their eyes all at once — exactly as if they were of one mind and one body — and spied a solitary figure standing on rock above them: a man whose long hair blew eastward, snapping like a black flag in the noonday wind, whose white tunic outlined an efficient frame, whose eye even at this distance acknowledged them and seemed to know their names.

Jesus.

He stepped backward and vanished.

Pell-mell the people rushed up to the rocks where he'd been standing and found on the other side a small valley, a high mountain valley. Its floor was grassy, scattered with tiny lilies, gentian, wintergreen, and white limestone; its walls were rounded like a cup and rimmed with choppy rock; its far side formed a concave slope of stone, a natural canopy.

It was under that canopy that the people saw Jesus. He was seated like a candle on a sconce-like shelf of limestone. He said, "Peace be with you." He said it in his natural voice, yet the people were astonished by the nearness of his word. Sound in this valley was an intimacy, a murmuring into personal ears.

"Peace be with you," Jesus said, and the people began to settle themselves on tussocks of grass, on the rising sides of the valley — near to Jesus and far from him: they filled the little amphitheater with color and life.

Jesus allowed his gold-bright eyes to linger here and there among the people, plucking forth individuals, Philip, Matthew, Shobal, Mary from Magdala, Gimel, Andrew, Simon.

An eagle wheeled the blue air above him. Sparrows flitted among the shrubs. Jesus spoke.

"Blessed are the poor in spirit," he said, "for theirs is the kingdom of God."

Andrew bowed his head to listen. Why had he worried? How could Jesus ever have gotten lost in the mountains — he whose confidence knew this world in all its particularity, both its visible form and its invisible spirit. Andrew felt ashamed of himself and also much relieved. It was his blessing, to be humble.

Jesus said, "Blessed are those who mourn, for they shall be comforted.

"Blessed are the meek! They shall inherit the earth.

"Blessed are those who hunger and thirst for righteousness. They shall be filled."

Andrew thought of John the Baptizer, his first master and his friend. Could he be filled in the Machaerus dungeon?

Jesus said, "Blessed are the merciful, for they shall obtain mercy.

"Blessed are the pure in heart. They shall see God.

"Blessed are the peacemakers, for they shall be called the children of God."

Jesus paused a moment, then added an urgency to his tone: "Blessed are those who are persecuted for righteousness' sake, for theirs is the kingdom of heaven — "

Ah, then John can be filled, thought Andrew. For the Machaerus prison *is* his righteousness!

" — and blessed are you," Jesus was saying, "when others abuse you and persecute you and utter every manner of evil against you falsely, on my account! Rejoice then, and be glad, because your reward is great in heaven. Oh, my children, you are joining a sacred company, for it is in exactly this way that people persecuted the prophets before you."

Jesus fell silent and swept his gaze over the great variety of disciples seated everywhere in the valley. Andrew felt a sudden start of recognition: Jesus' eyes! They were the color of a golden wheat field, ready for the harvest. They had the same soft rolling motion as a wheat field bowing beneath the breezes, and the texture was forbearing.

To those gathered before him, Jesus said, "You are the salt of the earth. But if the salt has lost its savor, with what can it be salted again? It's no longer good for anything except to be cast on pathways to kill the soil and be ground underfoot.

"You," he said, "are the light of the world. But who would light a lamp and put it under a bushel? It must be set on a stand, giving light to the whole house. Let your light so shine that everyone may see your good works and give glory to your Father in heaven.

"Now, you must never think that I have come to abolish the law or the prophets. Children, I have come to fulfill them!

"You have heard that it was said to our ancestors, *You shall not kill; whoever kills shall be liable to judgment.* But I say to you that everyone who is angry with his brother shall be liable to judgment. Yes, and whoever insults his sister shall be liable to the council. And whoever says, 'you fool!' shall be liable to the pits of fire.

"You have heard that it was said, *You shall not commit adultery.* But I say to you that everyone who looks at a woman lustfully has already committed adultery with her in his heart.

"Again, you have heard that it was said, *An eye for an eye and a tooth for a tooth.* But I say to you, do not resist one who is evil. If anyone strikes you on the right cheek, turn to him the other also. If anyone sues you for your coat, let him have your robe as well. If anyone forces you to go one mile, go with him two. Give to him who begs from you, and do not refuse him who would borrow.

"You have heard it said, *You shall love your neighbor and hate your enemy.* But I say to you, love your enemies. Pray for those who persecute you, and you will be children of your heavenly Father — because God makes his sun rise on the evil and on the good; he sends rain upon the just and the unjust alike. You must be perfect, as your heavenly Father is perfect."

Jesus lowered his face and looked down into his hands. Yet his voice was audible from the lowest to the highest rocks of the valley. "When you pray," he said, "do not heap up empty phrases as the Gentiles do. They think they will be heard for their many words. Your Father knows what you need even before you ask.

"When you pray," he said, "pray like this:

> *Our Father in heaven,*
> *Hallowed be your name.*
> *Your kingdom come,*
> *Your will be done*
> > *on earth as it is in heaven.*
> *Give us today our daily bread,*
> *And forgive us our sins*
> > *as we forgive those who sin against us.*
> *Save us from the time of trial,*
> > *And deliver us from evil."*

Jesus raised his face again. "People," he called, "do not lay up for yourselves treasures on earth, where moth and rust can consume it, where thieves break in and steal. But lay up for yourselves treasures in heaven! Neither moths nor rust nor thieves are there — and where your treasure is, there will your heart be also.

"I beg you, do not be anxious about your life, what you will eat or drink, or what you will wear. Look there! Look at the birds of the air. They don't sow or reap, yet your heavenly Father feeds them. Aren't you of more value than a thousand birds? Which of you by taking thought can add one day to your span of life? And why do you worry about your clothing? Consider the lilies around you now, how they grow. They don't toil or spin, yet I tell you, even Solomon in all his glory was not arrayed like one of these. If God so clothes the grass of the field which today is and tomorrow is cast in the oven, won't he clothe you so much more, O people of little faith?

"Therefore, don't be anxious anymore. But seek first the kingdom of God and his righteousness, and all these things shall be yours as well."

Jesus stood up.

A stiffer wind had begun to blow. Small clouds scudded the sky.

Jesus' black hair rose and fell like loose soil.

"Judge not," he called, "that you be not judged!

"Why do you notice the speck in your brother's eye and miss the log in your own? That's hypocrisy. First take out your log, and then you can see clearly to pluck the speck from your brother!

"Ask, and it will be given you! Seek, and you will find! Knock, and it will be opened unto you! Or which of you, when your children ask for a loaf, would give them a stone instead? If you who are by nature evil give good gifts to your children, how much more will your Father in heaven give good things to those who ask?

"Whatever you wish that others would do to you, do the same to them!

"O my children, enter by the narrow gate. For the gate which leads to destruction is wide and easy. But the one which leads to life is narrow and hard.

"Everyone who hears these words of mine and does them will be like a wise man who built his house on the rock. The rains fell, the floods came, the winds blew and beat upon the house, but it did not fall because it was founded on rock!

"Everyone who hears these words and does not do them will be like a foolish man who built his house on sand. The rains fell, the floods came, the winds blew and beat upon that house, and it fell, and great was the fall of it!"

Abruptly, Jesus turned and stepped through a cleft in the valley wall and was gone. No one tried to follow him — not even Simon. Jesus' departure had a certain finality about it: he had separated himself. Simon quietly began to return the way that he had come. So did the rest of the people.

Andrew no longer worried about Jesus. Perhaps because his own shy spirit suffered in the blunt, boisterous, self-confident public, he seemed to understand his master's withdrawals. The most significant decisions must be made in private. The hardest knots must be loosed in solitary prayer.

Andrew descended the mountain thinking, *Jesus is praying. He has found a lonely cove, and he is praying.*

∎

In the afternoon of the following day, Jesus appeared on the shore of the Sea of Galilee, south of Capernaum. Most of the disciples who had heard him preach yesterday on the mountain gathered around him again.

It was clear from his manner that Jesus did not intend to preach today. He didn't sit or else find an elevated position for himself. Instead, he began to walk among the crowds, sometimes laying his hand on a shoulder, sometimes gazing into an individual's eyes.

Neither was he offering the people pleasant greetings. He was not smiling. Jesus was thoughtful and solemn.

He stopped before Simon and stood there so long that the big man's cheeks blushed crimson.

Jesus said, "Simon, you" — then he walked to James and John, the sons of Zebedee who were standing side by side. "You," he said, "and you."

Andrew knew what Jesus was doing. His poor heart hammered because of the enormity of the event: Jesus was choosing those who would be bound to him hereafter, whose lives would be altogether defined by the life of this man, Jesus of Nazareth. Salt; light; the poor in spirit; the meek, the peacemakers — the persecuted! No chosen one could ever be the same again. Nor could that one choose his own way any more.

Andrew trembled. He knew what he was watching: death.

Jesus chose Philip and Bartholomew and Matthew and Thomas and James the son of Alphaeus and Thaddaeus and Simon the Zealot and Judas Iscariot.

And the last one whom Jesus chose had also been the first: Andrew, who then ran away from the crowds and the seashore and hid himself in a small room in Capernaum and burst into tears.

34

MARY MAGDALENE

i

In those days Jesus began to travel to the cities in Galilee and all the surrounding territory, preaching the good news of the kingdom of God. With him went the twelve disciples and certain women whom he had healed, women who had devoted their lives to Jesus no less than Simon or Andrew. Among these was Mary from Magdala. The disciples called her "Magdalene." Wealthier women like Joanna the wife of Chuza supported the traveling group with their money and their means. Mary, poor and pale and bruised about the eyes, ministered unto Jesus otherwise, quietly serving his more personal needs, food and cleanliness, clothes and rest and music.

She never drew attention to herself. She had no family left in Magdala. This was her family. If she couldn't be a daughter, she could be a servant. If she couldn't be a mother, she could be a maid. It was enough. But it was also very precious, and precious things, she had discovered, trouble the soul because they might be lost or taken away. Mary Magdalene remained small and thin and hushed. No, she would not draw attention to herself. She would not jeopardize the delicate gift that had been given her.

After two months' travel through the northern and middle regions of Galilee, Jesus began to move south. He bypassed Nazareth and walked five miles southeast, along the valley of Esdraelon to a town called Nain.

Just as he and his disciples approached the city gate, they heard a public lamentation, and they saw a funeral procession emerging in slow measure. Six young men came carrying a bier, flat boards wrapped in white linen, upon which lay the body of a lad no older than they. Immediately behind them walked a woman, sobbing and stroking the body of the dead.

Among those who stood by watching was a wide-eyed girl. Jesus knelt down beside her and whispered, "Who is that woman?"

The child whispered back, "His mama. It's her boy that died. It's her only boy. And she's a widow woman."

"Are you sad for her?" Jesus asked.

The child nodded. "He was a nice boy. He loved his mama." Her lip began to thrust out. "I am so very, very sad."

Jesus said, "Me, too."

The woman's hair draped her face and cheeks. Her robe was torn open. Her weeping was so desolated that there was no force to it, only moaning.

Jesus patted the little girl's shoulder, then stood up and walked to the grieving widow.

"Don't cry," he said. He reached and touched the bier in order to stop the pallbearers.

"Please," he said, "hold it firm and steady."

This interruption confused people in the procession. They leaned left and right to see what was happening, but no one complained. The man at the bier acted with an evident authority. They watched.

Jesus leaned over the face of the corpse. He studied it a moment, then said, "Young man, I say to you, arise."

There came the sound of a tight sneeze. The dead lad sucked a huge chestful of air and sneezed again, rolling up into a sitting position. The bier bounced and swayed in the grip of the six bearers. Once more the lad put his hands to his nose and sneezed heartily.

People gaped. The pallbearers trembled, nearly dropping their charge. But the dead youth was looking around with a common question in his eyes. "Mother?" he said. "Mother, where are you?"

Jesus took the lad's hand and pointed. "There she is" — almost unrecognizable in the dishevelment of grief and wonder. He took her hand, too, and said, "Woman, here is your son."

For a moment no one approached this tiny reunion. The citizens muttered to one another: "God has visited his people!"

And Mary Magdalene, hidden among the disciples of Jesus, thought to herself, *She has had her baby twice.* Mary's face flamed with gladness and admiration. *Once she bore him herself, and once my rabbi bore him back to her. Ah, twice a mother!* Every fiber in Mary's being was maternal.

◼

Jesus stayed for several days in Nain, then he continued on his way to Jerusalem where he wanted to celebrate the feast of the Passover. But rumor flies faster than people walk.

The report of his miracle in Nain raced south through Judea and Perea and even to the fortress of Machaerus, where John the Baptizer was imprisoned.

When he heard it, John called two of his disciples to himself and said, "But he was to baptize with fire! I *know* he was to keep the wheat and burn the chaff in an unquenchable fire. Yet I hear of healings and ease and what? — that he eats with sinners!"

John the Baptizer was wasted to bone. He had but a narrow cell, a
little water, and no sunlight at all. His food and his light, rather, were his
visions of the kingdom of God. He survived upon his fierce anticipation of a
kingdom of absolute righteousness.

"Go to Jesus," he said to the two disciples. "Ask him if he truly is the one
to come, or should we look for another."

As quickly as they could, John's men ran north on the transjordan route
from Abila toward Amathus.

The very next day they saw a huge crowd of people on the east bank
of the Jordan near the mouth of the Jabbok. Such a multitude in an
uninhabited place persuaded them that Jesus was there. So they turned
from the road and descended into the Jordan Valley and found him in the
very center of activity — like the hub of a great wheel turning. All faces,
young and old, yearned toward him. And he was never still. He was never
mute.

His long black hair kept falling forward as he laid hands upon people
lower than he, crippled people, children, the sick still lying on their backs
— and they were healed. His smile flashed like sunlight on the sea. Or else
a dark cloud crossed his brow and the crowd was hushed, like fields before a
storm. By sudden barks, by spouts of verbal fire, he cast out evil spirits. He
covered the eyes of the blind, and when he removed his palms he removed,
too, the darkness. Blank, wandering eyes turned suddenly raw in the
sunlight — seeing.

The disciples of John pushed their way through this huge mass of people
until they were close enough to be heard.

"Jesus!" they shouted. "Jesus of Nazareth! John the Baptizer has sent us
to ask you a question!"

Jesus paused and scanned the crowd till he identified the source of
these voices.

"You've come from John?" he called.

"Yes."

"You've seen my cousin?" Jesus began to wade toward them with a bright,
eager expression: "How is he?"

"Concerned," the two men said. They did not embrace Jesus when he
came near. Instead, bluntly, they said, "Are you the one who is to come, or
should we look for another?"

"John the Baptizer wants to know?"

"Yes."

"But tell me, is he well?"

One of the men said, "Sir, he survives on righteousness. He feeds on his
expectations of the kingdom of God. John is exactly as well as these things
are — and he will not be well if he cannot believe in you. Are you the one
to come?"

The eagerness had drained from Jesus' face. With a quiet, somber authority he said, "Tell John what you yourselves have just seen: the blind receive their sight, the lame walk, the dead are raised, and the poor have the good news preached to them. Surely, John will have read these signs in the prophets. Surely he will understand them."

There was a certain finality in Jesus' tone. This would not be a light visit after all.

John's disciples had no response.

Jesus said, "Go now, and tell my cousin for me: Blessed are those who take no offense in me."

As soon as the two disciples had departed, Jesus cried out to the entire crowd around him, "Be careful! Don't find blame in what I say! Instead, remember what you saw when you went out to the wilderness to be baptized by John. Not a reed shaken by the wind. Not a man in soft raiment. No: you saw a prophet, and more than a prophet! I tell you, this is he of whom it is written, *Behold, I send my messenger before your face, who shall prepare your way before you.*"

Then, in a murmur so soft only those closest to him could hear it, Jesus said, "There is no one born of women greater than John — yet those who are least in the kingdom of God are greater than he."

Mary Magdalene heard that difficult word: *The least are greater than John.* She turned it over many times in her mind.

▌

Four days later, Mary Magdalene was suffering the pains of a pure delight. In spite of herself, the woman would dash ahead of the company of disciples, then rush back and try to suppress her gladness and fail. At every turning in the road, at every new rise and horizon, Mary ran to see if Jerusalem was visible yet. Simon had told her of its walls and towers — and of the temple there. She wanted to see the high stone, stone so white it blinds a pilgrim's eyes!

Until she'd been healed of her rages, the woman had never been farther from Magdala than Tiberias, where the Roman air seemed more congenial. Things religious had galled Mary then. Now they delighted her.

For the first time in her life Mary Magdalene was a child unafraid to feel glee and to show it to those around her. Today she was swift on her feet. Her legs were like wings for speed, like feathers for lightness.

They were going mostly uphill, the beautiful hills! Spring had caused such tender greenness on the rolling landscape. It looked like the folds of a great green robe cast down on the earth. God's robe! Look: early green figs! And look: the common people went about their business as if it meant nothing to be living in the shadow of majesty! O Jerusalem! Jerusalem!

And there it was!

Mary could scarcely breathe.

They were approaching Jerusalem from the northeast. The city wall was massive left and right — not pure white, but mighty! There, in the central portion of the wall and looming over it with battlements, was the tower of the Fortress Antonia. Beyond that, but not yet visible, the temple.

They were moving toward the Sheep Gate. By now Jesus and the disciples had been caught up in a running stream of people, many of them shepherds coming to sell their sheep at a market just inside that gate, flocks of sheep for the pilgrims and their Passover.

But before they entered the gate, Jesus turned aside and walked toward a large stone enclosure, a mystery to Mary. It had four unequal sides of pillars and beautiful balustrades supporting a rail waist high. From the outside it looked like a large, open pavilion with roofed porches at every corner and one in the middle of the longest side. Jesus entered the middle porch. His disciples followed — Mary last of all, creeping slowly and peering around herself.

Why, the porches gave into a reservoir! A pool as huge as a lake! With steps descending to the water. Mary leaned over and saw the steps disappear in a green gloom. Then she stood straight, aware of a universal groaning.

All around the steps lay invalids in the dry pools of their own rags: the blind, the lame, the paralyzed. This beautiful structure contained such misery.

Jesus walked among these people. Some turned to look. Some raised hands of begging. Some called to him. But he stopped beside an elderly man whose shins were whip-thin and twisted backward. The man gave him a glance absent of interest, then turned away.

Jesus said, "Do you want to be healed?"

"Ha!" The man's laugh was sharp and sardonic. "What d'you think we're all doing here?" he sneered.

Jesus said again, "Do you want to be healed?"

"Thirty-eight years I've been lying by this pool," the man spat. His cheeks were sunken and creased. "Thirty-eight years, always alone and no one to help me. So when the angel troubles the water for healing, I start crawling there but someone always steps down before me. Do I want to be healed! Ha!"

Jesus neither knelt nor touched the man nor made the slightest gesture. "Rise," he said. "Take up your pallet, and walk."

All this Mary watched with the maternal benevolence that flooded her whenever she saw Jesus heal another human. She clasped her hands together and beamed as the old man drew his legs beneath himself, then rose to stand. She waited next to hear the shout of joy that always followed such a healing, but it never came. The man looked down and stomped his feet, chewing, chewing his toothless gums, testing his bones, and muttering that the left leg still felt stiff.

Jesus had already begun to walk to the porch door. Mary followed, confused by the man's reaction to his healing.

"Wait! *Wait!*" A cry behind her: "What do you think you're doing?"

An angry cry! Mary shrank with guilt and fear.

"Man, you can't do that! This is the Sabbath!"

Mary crept to a pillar and looked backward and saw five men wearing the broad phylacteries of Pharisees. They had surrounded the cripple whom Jesus had just healed. They were yanking at the rolled pallet in his arms, while he with gristly strength was hanging on to it.

"Sinner!" the Pharisees snapped. "The Mishnah forbids you to carry your bed on the Sabbath."

"Well," said the fierce old man, "tell it to *him*! That's the one who told me to take it up."

Him, of course, was Jesus, just leaving the portico.

Mary's heart twisted within her. So dear to her were the mercies of her master that she simply assumed the whole world likewise honored and praised him. But these Pharisees were retracting their lips in an obvious hatred. "Jesus of Nazareth!" they hissed. "How often has he flouted Sabbath law? Someone should kill that calf before it becomes a bull."

Kill? Did they say *kill* the calf? Mary began to tremble. Perhaps she had misunderstood them. Who could hate Jesus? For all the bad people in the world, why would anyone hate Jesus? And how could they talk of murder? Dangerous! Say it, do it! The word is the door to the deed. Oh, this was dangerous! Mary knew by experience the thrill one feels just to *think* of killing. One could do anything then! Kill? The horrible memory swelled in Mary.

She fled from the pool. She ran to Jesus as fast as she could go. She caught up to him just as he was walking through the Sheep Gate into Jerusalem. She put herself immediately behind his left side. She did not grab him. She had no right to presume. Nevertheless, she soon found that her forehead was pressed against the back of his shoulder, so closely did she follow; and she could smell the scent of his hair; and she was not crying. No, she didn't cry. But neither did she see Jerusalem upon her first entering in, the white stones, the dressed stones, the golden stones of the temple of the Lord.

ii

After the Passover Jesus and his people traveled north again, taking a route through Samaria since he would with equal passion speak to Samaritans as to Jews. They spent a night in Sychar, where the citizens received the entire company with gladness and hospitality and a noisy faith.

They ate meat that night, unusual in the diet of common folk and itinerants because it was so expensive and people did better to shear a sheep than eat it. But the Samaritans of this place had met Jesus nearly a year ago and had placed a sacred trust in him ever since then. His returning gave them the perfect reason for a party.

Moreover, there was a woman here whose affection for Jesus was so grandly dramatic that none could *not* laugh and dance within the sphere of her jubilation.

"You!" she bellowed the moment she noticed him coming toward the city. "It's *you!*" she cried, and she started to run.

She was a human of formidable proportion. She was a globe, an earth, a maker of her own weather.

Jesus stopped, half raising his arms in helplessness. The disciples shrank backward. It looked like the convergence of worlds!

The woman came layered in paints, green at the eyes, rouge on the cheeks, henna in her hair, orange henna on the palms of her hands.

"Yoo-hoo! Teacher! Master!" She waved her great arms over her head, gathering speed. Jesus stood completely alone. His eyes grew large. His jaw sagged.

"Oh, Lord, it's so *long* since I've seen you!"

Just a year ago this same woman was known as an eater of men. Every husband she had married died. Five of them. And none dared to be the sixth. Therefore, the man she lived with wouldn't marry her, and the people of Sychar wouldn't talk to her.

But one day Jesus of Nazareth appeared at the city well, and in spite of everything — her race, her reputation, her outrageous size and dress and behavior — he talked with her as though she, too, were a daughter of the kingdom. Then *she* it was who trumpeted to the city the marvel of this man, *she* who brought believers to him by her own massive transformation and her booming green-and-red-and-henna witness: *Come and see a man who told me all that I ever did! Can this be the Messiah?*

Now, it may be that on the afternoon of her going forth in headlong joy to greet the returning Jesus, one of her small toes hooked a root. Whatever the cause, gladness fled her face. Terror widened her green eyelids. The great woman shrieked, "Master!" and seemed bodily to lift from the earth. "Master! *Catch me!*"

Jesus, directly in her orbit, uttered a single astonished bark: "Ha!"

For years thereafter the disciples debated the elements of his next act, whether it was a miracle or the desperate strength of a man in peril of his life.

He caught her.

Or perhaps it's more accurate to say, he broke her fall.

In the very last instant, as belly-first the flying woman descended, Jesus whirled around, bent, took her wallowing plunge upon his back, staggered forward three steps, and fell on his face.

The city of Sychar, its citizens, and all the followers of Jesus observed a long moment of silence. Clearly, the woman had bruised the master's dignity. Had she also broken some of his bones? No one could tell. He was buried facedown beneath a hill of flesh.

In the voice of a little girl, the woman spoke: "Master? Are you — "

A small puff of dust appeared near the region of Jesus' mouth. Then a snuffling sound. Then more dust blew out with a rapid force. Actually — the sound was more like choking. And the whole mass of human flesh had begun to heave and shake. Jesus was striving to turn, his face in a grimace, all his breath gone out of him. The woman initiated efforts to climb off, but then Jesus sucked in an enormous wind and opened his mouth and burst into laughter. He was laughing! He had been laughing already in the dust! His eyes were closed, his black lashes bright with tears, his mouth stretched wide by the ear of the woman, producing wonderful booms of laughter.

And when he had turned all the way over, he threw his arms around his massive admirer and hugged her, and she blinked and began to giggle, and he cried, "Woman, don't love me so much! You could crush me with all your loving!"

He released a long fountain of laughter. All his disciples and all of Sychar joined him, roaring at the mountainous love before them.

And so it was that the celebration had already begun, laughing and dancing and the eating of meat — though Jesus said that for him the better food was ever to do the will of his Father, to accomplish his work.

Sir, the woman had said at their first encounter, *I perceive that you are a prophet.* Then she put to him the question that most divided Jews and Samaritans: *Our ancestors worshiped on Mount Gerizim. But your people say that Jerusalem is the place where people ought to worship.*

Who had the right religion? People killed and people died because of this question. But now an itinerant teacher gave a gaudy woman its final answer:

Woman, Jesus said, *the hour is coming — indeed, it is already here — when you will worship the Father neither on this mountain nor in Jerusalem. God is spirit. Those who worship him must worship in spirit and truth.*

The woman had fallen silent then. All her cosmetics became ineffectual. Honesty opened her eyes and made them beautiful: a human soul begging life.

I know that Messiah is coming, she said. *When he comes, he will show us all things.*

And Jesus, steadfastly returning her gaze, said, *I who speak to you am he.*

iii

O n the first Sabbath after his return to Capernaum, Jesus entered the synagogue and sat down to teach those who were willing to hear him.

Mary Magdalene took her place among the women, but she often cast her eyes toward the cloak that Jesus was wearing, and the blue fringes on it. She had washed it the day before, using a new mixture: a gentler alkali and liquid dripped through the ashes of another kind of soapwort. The fabric of Jesus' garment was delicate. It had begun to wear thin from too many harsh washings. She meant to preserve it — but not at the expense of true cleanliness.

While her attention was turned into the big room, Mary noticed that a man was moving toward Jesus. At the same time, all the small groups of teachers and students fell silent. They, too, were watching. By the length of their fringes and the width of their phylacteries, Mary recognized many teachers as Pharisees, ferocious for the laws of Moses.

Jesus, too, stopped teaching.

He raised his golden eyes, welcoming the man who approached him.

"I," the man said, "was a stonemason, sir. I made a living with my hands."

The stonemason drew his right hand from under his robe. It was atrophied, as if boiled to the bone and dried a dead-grey. Jesus looked at the withered hand while everyone else looked straight at Jesus.

Something was going on in the synagogue, something Mary could not understand. Her face grew hot. She hated this leering, watchful, critical silence. What were all these people waiting for? Why did they seem so angry?

The man said, "Jesus, I beg you to heal me so that I don't have to beg in shame anymore."

Suddenly Jesus rose to his full height and said, "Come here. Don't be afraid. Come and stand here in the midst of everyone."

The man made apologetic murmurs to people as he went toward Jesus. He bowed his head, self-conscious. But he obeyed. He came.

Jesus put his hand on the man's shoulder, then glared bright golden all around the room and said, "I know exactly what you are thinking: that it is not lawful to heal on the Sabbath. You're waiting to see if I will break the law. Scribes, Pharisees, students of Moses, let me put it to you another way. Is it lawful on the Sabbath to do good — or to do harm? To save a life, or to kill?"

No one answered him.

Jesus clapped his hands once, hard. The synagogue jumped. Mary's heart failed inside of her. "Tell me, then," Jesus shouted. "If your sheep falls into a pit on the Sabbath, which of you will not grab it and pull it out?"

Still, no one answered him.

"And wouldn't you say," he cried, his eyes flashing: "Wouldn't you, even in terms of the law, say that a human is more valuable than a sheep? So! Then it is lawful to do good on the Sabbath!"

Jesus' face changed. The corners of his mouth turned down in sorrow, and he shook his head slowly, slowly. "Such a hardening of the heart," he said. "My Father works on the Sabbath, and I am working on the Sabbath. Truly, truly, the Son does nothing of his own accord, but only what he sees the Father doing. For the Father loves the Son and shows him all he is doing. Even greater works than these will he show him, that you all may marvel."

Then Jesus gripped more tightly the shoulder of the man beside him. "Stonemason," he said, "stretch out your hand."

The man raised his right hand and reached it out as far as he could. It opened. It unfolded like a rose and was whole.

Jesus did not sit down again. He strode out of the synagogue.

But Mary held very still. She was filled with fear. For her master seemed intent upon danger, as if he wanted to make cruel people angry.

The Pharisees: she could hear their whispering even now. She closed her eyes and covered her face, but it didn't matter. She heard their wrathful accusations: *Worse than breaking Sabbath laws, now the man is making himself equal to God!*

And they said, *Not by the Lord does he heal. Jesus of Nazareth belongs to Beelzebul. By the prince of demons he casts out demons!*

And again, they said: *How shall we destroy him?*

■

Yet, on that same afternoon Jesus uttered a word so holy and so consoling that Mary's fears were drowned in a private flood of gratitude.

Many of the disciples were gathered at the house of Simon's mother-in-law. Certain scribes and Pharisees had come demanding to see some sign to prove the authority of his words.

Jesus was saying, "It is an evil and adulterous generation that seeks a sign. No sign shall be given it except the sign of Jonah." At that moment, Andrew came into the room and signaled for Jesus' attention.

Jesus noticed and nodded, but continued speaking. "For as Jonah was three days and three nights in the belly of the whale," he said, "so will the Son of man be three days and three nights in the heart of the earth — "

Now he looked in Andrew's direction and said, "Yes?"

Andrew tried to move through the crowd, but Jesus said, "Say what you have to say from there."

Andrew looked distressed, but he spoke anyway.

"Your mother is outside," he said, "asking you to come out and speak with her. Your brothers are there, too."

Jesus didn't move. Slowly he turned his gaze to everyone who surrounded him, person by person.

As if asking Andrew a question, he said, "Who is my mother?"

This caused Andrew to swallow and frown.

Again Jesus said, "Where are my brothers?"

Andrew shrugged.

Mary, suddenly, was ramrod straight and perfectly alert. And then it seemed to her that Jesus turned his soft, wheat-colored eyes directly toward her.

"Here," he said, "is my mother and my brothers and my family. Here. For the one who desires to do the will of my Father is my sister. And my brother. And my mother."

Oh, sheets of glory fell on Mary now! Radiance and gratitude, and who was queen? She was conscious of none but her master and herself — and she was queen! So high past fears! Lifted higher than loneliness, she had been elevated into the family of Jesus!

Truly, Mary from Magdala had a family, and she would be home wherever the Lord was present, forever.

iv

So heavy were the crowds all Sabbath after Jesus healed the stonemason's hand, so insistent were the arguments and accusations of scribes and Pharisees, that by nightfall he was exhausted. He drew his closest disciples apart and said, "Let's get to the boats." Mary saw that his shoulders sagged forward, making a cave of his chest. "Let's cross to the other side of the lake."

Under cover of the night, then, some twenty disciples took separate routes down to the shore.

Altogether, three rowboats pushed out into the Sea of Galilee. Mary watched which one Jesus entered and managed to climb into the same boat, though she was forced to crouch amidships on the floor.

Jesus, she saw, also went down to the floor in the stern. He lay on a small cushion and fell asleep.

So did she. She curled up. She listened to the rhythmic knocking of the rowlocks and the light flapping of the sail above her — then she dozed, and all the darkness of the night came close around her, like a coverlet.

Suddenly someone stepped on her.

No apology. A great foot crushed her shoulder, and she woke to feel the boat dropping. It hit bottom, rolled, and a screaming wind blew spume like dry salt into the boat. It tore through the sail. Lightning flashed. The man

506 | THE BOOK OF GOD

who'd stepped on her shoulder was trying to drag that sail in, but failing. Thunder cracked beside them. Men at the oars were throwing their bodies backward in tremendous efforts to control the boat. Its bow pointed upward. It stood on its stern. Then the stern was slammed by a great wave, kicked high in the air, and the boat plunged down to the pits of the deep. Water broke over all, and Mary was under it. She could drown in the boat. The seas were mountainous. She grabbed the gunwale in both hands to breathe and was nearly pitched overboard.

Lightning lit the low cloud.

Men were hoarse with bellowing.

Bailing was useless.

Now the sail shredded altogether. It clawed the air like fingers.

A booming voice yelled, "Teacher! Teacher! Don't you care?" It was Simon! Simon was the one who could not get the sail down. Now, hugging the mast, he had swung round to the stern and was shouting with panic and anger, "Don't you care if we perish here?"

Under stuttering flashes of lightning, Mary saw Jesus sit up in the back of the boat. He held the sides in both hands and rode the crests of two waves, one after the other. Then in spite of the wild pitching, he stood up on the back thwart and spread his arms and cried out louder than the winds, louder than the crashing seas: "Peace!" His body seemed small below the lightning and the violent night. Nevertheless, his voice was the thunder itself: "Peace!" he commanded. "Be still!"

And the boat sighed and settled into smooth water. The sleeves of the torn sail dropped straight down on Simon's shoulders. No one spoke. A universal calm covered everything, so that it was the disciples' ears roaring, unaccustomed to quietude. Little waves slapped the hull.

Simon, gaping and blowing sprays of water, whispered, "Who is this? What kind of man is this?"

Jesus said, "Why are you afraid? Have you no faith?"

But Mary wasn't afraid. Mary's heart was firm and brave, and even the seas were home to her, because Jesus was there.

▌▌

The eastern shores of the Sea of Galilee were inhabited by a pagan people called the Gerasenes, though the disciples saw none when they beached their boats there the following morning. They had made landfall in lonely territory, some distance from any city.

In fact, they happened to come ashore near limestone cliffs whose faces were broken and forbidding. All up and down the stone was scored by narrow pathways and riddled with countless tombs.

While the small band of Jews sat below the cliffs to eat their breakfast, a piteous wailing descended to them, a sweet, thin agony like a beautiful flute filled with sorrow.

Mary searched the honeycombed walls above her, but saw nothing. She couldn't place the source of the wordless misery. But she felt very sad, mortally sad, just hearing it. The bread became dry in her throat and she could not swallow it.

Nor did the wailing cease. If the other disciples heard it, they gave no sign. Mary rose up and walked south along the cliffs. Sometimes the wailing tightened a pitch; sometimes it lowered into moaning; but it continued without pause, as if the graves themselves could breathe and sing.

Farther south where there was grass on the slopes, Mary noticed a herd of pigs coming over a low ridge, a large herd, and she saw swineherds following them. She ran toward the swineherds, calling, "Sir! Sir, someone's crying on the cliffs back there."

One swineherd high on the hillside crossed his hands over his staff and stared at her.

"He's hurt!" Mary called. "I think he's hurt. I've cried like that, but only when I was terribly hurt. Can you hear him? Do you know him?"

"Leave him alone," the swineherd said, returning to his pigs.

"What?" cried Mary. "Do nothing?"

The swineherd ignored her.

"You know him, don't you?" Mary shouted.

Abruptly the swineherd lifted his staff and pointed it at her. "Who are you?" he demanded.

"My name is Mary. From Magdala."

"A Galilean."

"Yes."

"A Jew."

"Yes."

"You people! You and your pompous laws, despising us for eating pork, then meddling in our lives. Go home. You don't know what you're talking about. Go on home."

Jeeeeee! Jeeee — High and horrible, the wailing tore the morning air above the tombs. Such a mortal bereavement! — it pierced Mary to the heart. "How can you ignore that?" she yelled.

"Idiot," the swineherd sneered. He slapped pigs with the side of his staff. "The man likes graves. He's bedeviled. Knocks his skull with stones, slashes his flesh. We tie him with fetters, he snaps them. We tie him with chains, he breaks them — "

"Is *that* what you do to those possessed?" Mary was near tears. "Tie them with iron?"

"Go on! Get out of here, you self-righteous, trifling Jew!" the swineherd yelled. Then he released a hoarse laugh. "There!" he yelled, pointing. "There's your demoniac, the object of your affections!"

Mary looked and saw a man completely naked, leaping from rock to rock on the cliff face, screaming, *Jeeeee! Jeeeee* — and throwing stones down at the disciples on the beach below.

"Jeeeeesus!" he was shrieking. "What d'you have to do with me, Jesus? Jesus! Jesus, Son of the Most High God!"

Suddenly the madman vanished — then just as suddenly he appeared farther down. "Jeeeesus, did you come to torture me before the time?" Now he put his head down and started to run top speed down the stones toward Jesus, screaming, "Don't hurt me! Don't hurt me! Don't hurt me!"

Mary, too, was racing back as fast as she could.

Jesus was walking forward, separating himself from the disciples.

The man dropped to flat land, howled, and kicked sand in a manic dash at Jesus.

Jesus called, "What is your name?" At once it looked as if the naked man took a blow to the throat. His legs flew out in front of him and he fell hard on his back.

But he rolled over and, crouching on his hands and knees, answered Jesus. In a multitudinous growl he said, "My name is legion; for we are many!"

"Ah, legion!" Jesus was striding forward. "Warrior devils! Soldier devils! Five thousand craven devils — you know my name!" he cried. "I command you, come out of that man!"

"Wait!" In a beautiful, flutelike sorrow, a choir of voices wailed from the mouth of the naked man, "Jeeesus, we beg you, don't send us into the abyss! Send us into the swine on the hillside."

Mary, creeping close behind her master, heard him mutter, "Go."

Immediately the naked man slumped to the ground.

But suddenly the pigs on the green slope splayed their short legs and they raised an abominable squealing. They began to stampede downhill. The swineherds jumped about, cursing and swearing, but they could do nothing to control their herds. Two thousand swine like a living mudslide were tumbling downhill. They ran squealing over the beach and into the lake, where they thrashed the water and gargled and spluttered and died — until the entire lake was covered with the floating, rolling barrels of pig corpses.

An empty hillside. The swineherds, too, had fled.

But Mary Magdalene had already gone to Simon's boat and cut down the hanging rags of his sail. She found a skin of clean water and gathered up her own robe, then returned to the man who had been wailing. He lay unconscious on the ground.

Carefully, by slow strokes, Mary washed him. She washed his thin hair. She used the narrower strips of sail to bind his new wounds, all the while murmuring, "I know, I know, I know what you've suffered, I know it very well." With her fingertips she probed lightly the muscles of his arms, unable to find the strength that might have snapped chains and fetters: his poor, lean neck was gristle and tendon, and she could hide her whole hand in the hollow of his collarbone.

Finally, Mary wrapped him in her robe. Jesus had made the madman clean within. She had rendered him clean without. She felt glad for the shared ministration.

The disciples, too, seemed to approve her new independence. Andrew whispered, "Thank you."

Then, over the low ridge in the south, people began to appear, natives, Gerasenes moving on the balls of their feet, suspicious, ready to bolt in an instant.

They gaped at the sea-full of drowned pigs. "See?" said the swineherds in front of all. "Do you believe us now?"

The Gerasenes crept down the slope, then stopped in a tight knot on the beach, amazed: the man that had been filled with demons was sitting at the feet of Jesus, clean and clothed and sane.

"Get away!" the swineherds called from their distance. "Jew, depart from here. Go on, go home. Leave us alone, now."

Slowly Jesus arose, preparing to oblige them.

But to the man whom he had freed of demons he said, "Stay here among this people. They need your word and your living example, sir. Return to your own house and declare how much God has done for you."

∎|

The sky was bright blue when Jesus and his disciples returned across the lake. The heavens had been scrubbed clean by the storm that had nearly swamped them the night before.

Again, Jesus took his place in the stern of Simon's boat. He sat on the back thwart facing the prow, his bare feet planted wide on the deck before him, elbows on his knees, his face buried in his hands. The hair hung down like a veil, a tangled black mass covering head and arms and legs to the shin.

Mary sat on the floor near his feet, straining to hear her rabbi's breathing. She wanted to hear a regular exhalation. She hoped that he was sleeping in his dark seclusion.

Without moving, Jesus said, "You are a healer, Magdalene. You know the hurts, and so you are a healer. Shalom."

Mary glanced at the occlusive black curtain, her heart racing on account of his word.

She said, "Lord, do you know that my fingers are always cold? Even when I feel warm, they're chalk white and cold, and I worry that I leave traces of coldness on everyone I touch. You can't wash the cold away."

Jesus, his head slung down between his shoulders, didn't answer.

Then Mary heard a sigh so deep that the man's whole body shuddered. She assumed that he had fallen asleep, and she was glad.

▌

People saw the three boats coming. By the time they touched land, people had already begun to gather along the Capernaum shore.

Jesus bound his hair back in a headband and bent to help Simon and Andrew drag their boat up on shore. They stowed the oars and other equipment. Simon had just cut down the last shreds of sail from the yard of his stout mast; the disciples had just begun to wash the boat's interior when a small, red-faced man threw himself through the crowd and fell at Jesus' heels.

"Master!" he panted.

"Jairus!" said Jesus. "What's the matter?" He knew the man. He had often seen Jairus arrange worship in the Capernaum synagogue.

"Master, my child is dying!"

"Your daughter?"

"Every breath is weaker than the one before! She's dying right now! Please, come and lay your hands on her. Please!"

Jesus said, "Take me to her."

Jairus jumped up and pleaded with people to move — then he and Jesus, the disciples and most of the multitude began to flow through the streets toward high ground near the synagogue.

"Hurry, hurry," Jairus whined, pumping his short arms. "Get out of our way! Hurry!"

Suddenly Jesus stopped. Unaware, Jairus continued to plow forward, but Jesus was looking at the crowds directly behind him.

"Who touched me?" he asked.

Simon released a harsh laugh. "Touched you?" he cried. "*Touched* you! This is a mob. Who *didn't* touch you?"

Jesus ignored the ridicule and shouted: "Who touched my tunic just now? I felt the power go out of me — "

Jairus noticed that the crowd had come to a complete halt. He was struggling helplessly against a human wall. Then he saw that the master was no longer with him, that the multitude was watching Jesus in another exchange altogether.

People had withdrawn from Jesus, making a circle of space before him. A thin, frightened woman was crouching down in that space, a wasted body covered with the sores of ill nourishment.

"Jesus!" Jairus called. "There's no time! My daughter has no time left!"

But Jesus' back was turned. He was listening to the woman whose words rushed out as if she were arguing for her life:

"But I've been bleeding for twelve years, and nothing has stopped the flow, nothing, not even the doctors. I spent everything I had on doctors and they only made me worse than before, but then I saw you coming across the lake this morning and I thought: If I just touch the hem of his garment I will be well — "

Abruptly she paused. She shrank backward in alarm. Jesus had taken a step toward her and dropped to one knee.

" — so I touched your tunic, you see — " she breathed, her eyes terrified. Jesus was stretching his hands toward her face.

" — and I'm well, now. I'm well. I'm not bleeding — "

Jesus drew the woman's grey face to his shoulder and patted her back. "Daughter," he whispered, "your faith has made you well. Go in peace."

When Jesus rose up and walked toward Jairus again, the small man could not look at him. Neither was he trying to fight through the crowds toward his house any more. His face was white, drained of expression, his eyes sightless.

Another man spoke to Jesus with an air of superiority. "No need," he said, nodding as if he and Jesus were level-headed men while Jairus was a child requiring guidance. "You may as well go your way," the man said. "Jairus' daughter is dead."

Blankly Jairus looked here and there, as if he'd lost something.

Jesus seized Jairus by his shoulders and, glaring at the messenger, said, "Jairus, do not be afraid. Do you hear me? Just believe. Now is the time for believing!"

Jesus took Jairus' elbow and led him with great strides toward his house. The master's eyes flashed like weapons in sunlight; nor did he temper their aggression when he approached the house and heard tumultuous grieving inside. Women sat in the courtyard blowing on the wooden pipes of sorrow and wailing as loud as they could.

Jairus blanched and pulled backward.

Jesus still led him into his house. Jesus cried, "Stop this noise! The child is not dead but sleeping!"

These were professional mourners. They were paid to be sad, and they thought they knew their business. They took just an instant to process what Jesus had said, then they broke into sardonic laughter.

But Jesus' eyes burned a more terrible heat. He released Jairus, tore the headband from his hair, opened it into a leather strap, and physically drove the mourners out of the house. He called Simon and John and James to join him, then he shut the door.

At once the aspect of the master changed.

"Where is the child?" he asked.

Her mother answered, "This way."

She led them into a back room where a single candle burned. The girl had been clothed in clean linen. Her large eyes were closed, the eyelids fringed with a rich black lash. Her eyebrows were high, beautifully etched; but her cheek was alabaster, and her fingertips a lily white.

Jesus stepped to her pallet and took her hand in his.

"Talitha," he said, "cumi."

Damsel, I say to you: arise.

As though she were waking from sleep, the child opened her eyes and looked at the faces surrounding her and smiled.

Jairus fell on his knees beside her, weeping.

"Papa," she said, "what's the matter?" She sat up and began to give his back many little pats.

Her mother clasped her hands and whispered. "She's twelve years old! She's very smart."

Simon cleared his voice and said, "Child, do you know who this man is? Do you know who healed you just now?"

Jesus said to her mother, "Yes, I can see how smart she is. She's also hungry. Why don't you find her something good to eat?"

V

In that same season, Jesus took his closest disciples and left Capernaum. For several weeks they traveled from village to village toward the central portions of the province — toward Nazareth.

On the way the master grew quieter. He preached less. There was less quickness or humor in his glance. Often he seemed oblivious of the conversation around him. And every time he bade farewell to the people of a village, he seemed more burdened than before, compressing his lips in thought.

Finally Jesus drew the disciples into a private grove of olive trees and sat and disclosed his soul to them.

"These people make me feel so sad," he said. "They are distressed and scattered — like sheep without a shepherd. They need the presence of shepherds. Their souls are ready to be harvested for the Lord."

Jesus looked specifically at the twelve whom he had chosen — all sitting on the ground and gazing back at him. "I am conferring upon you power and authority," he said, "to cure diseases and to cast out unclean spirits. The Lord of the harvest sends you. I send you. Go forth two by two. Go to the lost sheep of the house of Israel, preaching that the kingdom of heaven is at hand. Heal the sick, cleanse the lepers, cast out devils. Take nothing for the journey except your staff: no bread, no bag, no money in your belt.

Wear one coat only. Go in sandals. Where you enter a house, stay there till you leave the village altogether. But if any village refuses to hear you, leave it — and when you go, shake the dust off your feet as a testimony against it.

"Simon?"

The large disciple stood up. Jesus rose, too, and embraced him. As they stepped apart, swiftly, Jesus reached and pinched his bald cheek and grinned.

"Andrew? James? Judas? Matthew?"

One by one he sealed the disciples' commission with an embrace.

"No need to wait. Nothing to buy. Let those who hear you also feed you. Pray to your Father in heaven. Go."

The order had been swiftly given. It should as swiftly be obeyed. In that same hour, then, the disciples divided themselves into pairs and departed into the world.

They were an apprehensive lot. This switch from disciple to preacher seemed far too soon. How could they trust their own knowledge or skill? Only slowly did they find their voices.

But from the beginning they used the words that Jesus had used, begging people to repent.

Soon they were anointing sick people with a glistening olive oil, and then they became giddy with excitement when the sick were healed.

vi

In Nazareth, in the home of Jesus' mother — the same house where her rabbi had been raised from a baby — Mary Magdalene baked a basketful of raisin cakes with honey, very sweet. She filled a flask with good thick cream and a bag with ripe figs and pomegranates. Then she gathered her goods together and by a winding path climbed to the top of the hill behind the city.

It was mid-afternoon when she went. She appreciated the breeze into which she walked on that high ground. It came from the Great Sea to the east, still carrying a salt smell and causing in her the sense of spaciousness.

Ahead of her — sitting on rock at the edge of the hill, staring out over the green Esdraelon Valley, his back to her — she saw Jesus, and she paused.

Mary had a piece of news for him which would be very difficult to deliver and even more difficult to hear. Bad news. Right now she regretted her born expression, always frowning, always sober. She wished it were in her nature to smile lightly and make cheerful, senseless conversation.

Well, but she had the cream and the pomegranates.

Jesus shifted his gaze. He angled his head to the left. Suddenly, under the sunlight, she saw that her rabbi's black hair reflected a deep red sheen.

That discovery raised a small commotion in Mary's breast, and she blurted: "Raisin cakes, Rabboni! A little lunch, sir, while you are sitting here!"

Jesus turned and smiled. To Mary his eyes were as steadfast as medallions. He was radiant and ruddy, his teeth perfectly white. Foolishly she bustled toward him, her face warm with feeling, then she raised her eyes and saw the drop-off, the depth of the valley before them, and she gasped. She buckled at the knees and began to fall.

But Jesus caught her elbow as well as most of the food. One round pomegranate bounced over the edge of the rock and was swallowed by the blue air.

"Oh, my!" Mary whispered, pressing backward but peering down into the valley.

"Sit," said Jesus.

In a fleeting whisper Mary breathed: "Rabboni, I didn't want to bother you."

"Sit, sit," Jesus said. He had not released her elbow. He was settling her slowly to the ground. "Sit with your back to the stone. You'll feel less like sliding into the abyss. Did you bring enough food for two? Ah, yes. Exactly enough."

He picked through her basket and chose a raisin cake and handed it to her. "Mary from Magdala," he said with a formal tilt to his head, his cheeks bunched like beds of spices: "would you be pleased to dine with me?"

Mary took the cake and nibbled at it, wishing her face were round and easy with common happiness. But she knew she had the countenance of pale longing.

Jesus selected another cake, sighed, bit hugely, and chewed — looking out over the wide valley.

"Ah! You baked it with honey," he said. "What a pleasure. What a pleasure this afternoon has become."

He glanced at Mary. "For years this was my hiding place," he said. "When I was a lad I hid here in plain sight, swinging my feet over the world. Mary, it really is a map of the world of our people. Look there."

Jesus raised his left hand and pointed across the vast patchwork of farmers' fields and orchards and vineyards to the eastern reaches of the valley.

"Twelve centuries ago Deborah the prophetess, the judge of God, fought King Jabin and the Canaanites in that very place. Jabin came riding down this valley with an army of mighty iron chariots. But the earth trembled, and the heavens dropped! The clouds dropped water. The Kishon became a torrent. God mired Jabin's chariots in mud, and Deborah's light-footed armies rushed down to victory." Jesus turned and smiled. "My mother loves that story. She has told it to me again and again — right where you are sitting now."

Mary whispered, "Thank you."

Jesus raised his eyebrows. She couldn't help noticing that he had a forehead as broad and noble as his mother's. Each had the same distinctive widow's peak — though his mother's hair was streaked with grey and pulled severely back.

"Thanks for what?" Jesus said.

"Well, it's your hiding place," Mary whispered. "And I'm sitting in it, too."

"Ah," said Jesus. "So you are. Pale Mary! The alabaster maiden from Magdala is swinging her feet above the whole world." He smiled again, then pointed to the extreme southeast.

"There," he said. "Do you see that ridge of hills at the edge of the valley?"

She nodded that she did, and he continued: "It was called Mount Gilboa. One thousand years ago King Saul and his son Jonathan died in battle on that mountain. And then King David wept for their deaths. For both of their deaths, for his brother and for his enemy."

Jesus plucked a fig from the bag by her knee and held it just in front of his lips. "*Saul and Jonathan*," he murmured, "*beloved and lovely, swifter than eagles, stronger than lions*. That's what David sang in his sorrow."

Jesus bit into the fig and chewed.

Mary said, "Rabboni?"

"Yes?" he said.

"You are a good man."

"Well, so you say," he said. "But there is none so good as God."

"You do good things," said Mary. "You do good things for everyone who comes to you. I have never seen you do a bad thing." She paused, having come to a distressful question. "Then why are so many people angry at you?"

"These are excellent figs," Jesus said. "But I like your raisin cakes better. It's the honey I like."

He chewed with a slow clenching of his jaw muscles. Mary could hear the popping of tiny fig seeds between his teeth.

Jesus said, "God is doing a new thing. It's the change that troubles some people. The old covenant is passing away. A new one is coming. But new wine requires new wine skins. Old skins would burst from a new ferment, and all the wine would be lost. The old traditions cannot contain what the Father is doing through me. Even the rules for the Sabbath have to change."

"Are you sad when people get angry at you?"

"Sad," said Jesus. "Yes."

Mary's heart was moved inside of her.

"But I have to do what I see my Father doing. The Father loves the Son and shows him all that he himself is doing — and greater things than these will he show him, that they may all marvel."

"Greater things, Rabboni?" Mary said. "Oh, I need no greater thing than this, that I can bake you raisin cakes, and you may enjoy a bite or two."

Jesus still stared out over the valley. His eye had a faraway look, and his words a grave formality, like the tolling of a bell. "The hour is coming," he said, "and now already is, when the dead will hear the voice of the Son of God, and those who hear will live. Even those in tombs will come forth."

Mary dropped her gaze and stared into the palms of her hands, so pale that she could see the blue veins there.

"Why," she whispered softly, nervously, "why did you heal me? I didn't ask, but you healed me."

Jesus neither shifted his gaze nor said a thing.

This frightened Mary. Three weeks ago it would also have silenced her, but she was growing more independent. And this moment of unexpected intimacy granted her a certain boldness, so she spoke:

"The Gerasenes told me what they do to people possessed by evil spirits," she said. "They tie them with iron. Rabboni, they tie them with fetters and chains. But I heard that man, that demoniac, wailing among the tombs, and I knew exactly how he felt. He despised himself! On account of the devils living inside him, the man hated everyone and despised himself in the hatred. It's a horrible loneliness! I know. I know! And among all people on earth, this hatred hates you, Jesus, the most. But you healed that man. Why did you heal him?"

Still, Jesus continued to stare into the distances. There was the white worm of a scar on his cheek. The rest of his face was darkened by the sun, but the new skin of that scar had remained white.

Mary said, "Did you heal him because you were sorry for him?"

Then she said, "Did you heal him because it's what you're supposed to do?"

Poor Mary! Bold or not, her heart was hammering to be asking such questions. "Did you cast the evil spirits out of that man because you loved him?" she pleaded. "Did you love him, Rabboni? Can it be that you loved him?"

Softly, Jesus spoke. "All that I do," he said, "all these miracles, healings, and wonders — they are signs pointing to the one glorious deed which the Father has sent me into the world to accomplish. Yes, there is love, Mary. God loves the world."

Mary whispered, "I wanted to kill you."

Jesus neither turned nor looked at her.

Mary was shaking from her shoulders to her knees. Her fingers felt like ice.

"The moment I saw you standing at the end of the street, staring at me, I felt such a strong urge to murder you. And I loved the feeling. And I hated myself because of it. Ah, Rabboni, I was filled with seven faces of hatred and seven voices of sorrow. When my own mother died, I laughed! I despised the laughter, but I laughed! When my father died, I ran out of the city of Magdala shrieking with laughter. I ran all the way to Tiberias. I made the Romans laugh with me. I rollicked and carried on and played the fool until we were spending both night and day in a mindless laughter. And then I saw you at the end of a street, your eyes like level suns, and you were not laughing. You were a cold, unwinking judge, making the devils in me tremble like the strings of a lute. You made me sick to my stomach. I ran at you! I was very fast. My fingers were knives. Beardless face! White throat! I was going to kill you by cutting your throat. I flew at you, my knives flashing — "

Mary had not planned this tirade. It was horrible! She had never told the story before, to herself or to anyone else — never!

"I am the one," she whispered. "I am the one who put that scar on your cheek. No one but me. I feel so sad for it. But in that moment it seemed to me that a fire came out of your mouth and burned the devils in me until they ran away. The hatreds, the laughter and murder and loathings, they all went out of me, and I grew small and I was so weak that I couldn't walk. But you touched my face, and I rose up and followed you, and you did not deny me, and that has been my comfort ever since. It is enough. Truly, it is enough.

"But sometimes I wonder why you did it. Is there a reason why you healed that woman in Tiberias? Did you feel sorry for her? Or is it just what you are supposed to do? Or... did you perhaps love her, Rabboni?"

There passed a long moment of silence while Mary held her breath, purely ignorant of how the master might answer her questions.

Finally Jesus said, "Would you hand me the flask of cream? I'd like to wash the raisin cakes down with a swallow of cream."

But Mary was immobile. She could not move. He had asked for the cream. But such shame was running through her limbs that they were paralyzed. *Oh, Mary, why can't you hold your tongue?*

Jesus reached for the flask himself. Mary's head was bowed down, her shoulders rounded; she was circling into herself.

Jesus said, "Why did you make these cakes with honey? Are you celebrating something?"

But I am a part of his family, Mary thought. *He said I was among his sisters and brothers. He said it, then he looked at me.*

Jesus touched her elbow. "Do you want some cream?" he said.

She shook her head.

"The honey is expensive," he said. "And I know you, Mary from Magdala: you are a frugal soul. Why did you bring honey all the way up to the top of the hill for me?"

O Lord! O my God — the bad news! Mary had forgotten the real cause of her coming here. *Forgive me! Forgive me!*

But she could not raise her face to look at him. How unworthy she was to be the messenger of such news as she had now to offer.

"John," she said softly, nearly broken by humility and the weight of her words. "His disciples came to Nazareth this morning and told us: John the Baptizer is dead."

That was the news. It had been spoken. But Jesus said nothing.

Mary filled the void with more talk.

"Herod Antipas gave a banquet," she said. "His wife's daughter danced. She danced so well, he vowed a vow. He vowed to give her whatever she wanted. She went to her mother. Her mother said, 'Ask for the head of John on a plate.' Her mother hated John for blaming their marriage as sinful."

All of Mary's strong emotions now rose up and flowed from her eyes. She couldn't help it. She began to weep.

"The girl," she said, "did what her mother told her. She asked for the head of John on a plate. Herod Antipas was sorry. But he had made his vow in public. He couldn't deny it. So he sent a soldier of the guard into the prisons, and the soldier beheaded him — "

"Ahhh!" Jesus released so sharp a cry that Mary looked up. He had wrapped his arms around his stomach and was rocking slowly backward and forward.

Mary's tears poured down like a rain. "The soldier of the guard came back to the banquet with John's head on a plate," she whispered. "He gave it to Herod. Herod gave it to the girl. The girl gave it to her mother."

"*O my cousin! My cousin!*" Jesus wailed. His chest was heaving. He had thrown back his head. Mary could see the white rim of his bottom teeth. "O John! O my dear Baptizer!"

Jesus crouched down and rolled sideways until his head lay on Mary's lap. "Woman," he murmured, "would you hold me a while?"

Mary raised her hands above the face of her master, not touching him but spreading her palms as if in blessing. Then she whispered, "Yes, I will."

She lowered her hands and began to stroke his black hair from the temple to the shoulder.

"Rabboni, Rabboni," she whispered over and over until the day had descended into night and it seemed to her that her master was sleeping.

And still she whispered, "Rabboni."

35

SIMON PETER

i

I didn't know. How could I know? The days were bright and free and full of promise, and we were a glad company — and successful besides. Jesus sent the twelve of us in pairs through villages preaching and healing, and we grew so excited, because of his trust in us and because of the authority he gave us. We returned with joy crying, *Lord!* clapping our hands: *Lord, in your name even the demons obey us!*

We called him "Lord."

And then he, the Lord, blew off the top of my head with an observation ten times mightier than ours. We had said "demons." But he said "Satan." He said, *I saw Satan fall like lightning from heaven.*

What power! What a man! Strong, firm, smart, and — strong. In those days I was giddy with goodness and happiness. I had no idea what was going to happen.

He told us. He said it. He repeated it several times over, filling in the details. *This*, he said, *is what they will do to me.* And *there*, he said, locating it. And *for three days.* He said it would last three days. Even so, I didn't comprehend it. Like stone I stayed ignorant. Maybe it was willfulness.

Maybe I didn't want to know.

ii

Overnight, it seemed, Jesus changed. He used to laugh and relax. He had an easy, ambling stride, you know. Interested in nearly anything. Would listen as much as talk. More so. After supper we could make a great cackling of our talk, and he'd lean back and listen, flicking his eyes here and there. Interested.

But when the twelve of us returned from our missionary journeys, we saw how tight his face had become. He had a restless urge to move. He wanted to get away.

There were so many people coming and going that we couldn't even find time to eat. Jesus said that we looked tired after our tour of preaching. That was the reason he gave.

"Let's sail to some private place apart," he said. "You need the rest."

But there was an urgency in him that hadn't been there before. He didn't lean back and listen any more. He was thinking things. He began to draw his lips into a whistle, thinking of things.

So we boarded our boats, and I sailed mine into the lead, and we began to travel east along the north shore of the Sea of Galilee. Jesus didn't sleep. For the first hour he sat with his head bowed. Then I looked shoreward and saw a great herd of people pacing us on land, and other people running from the villages to join them. I yanked a halyard and made some comment, and he looked up, and then that was all he looked at: those locusts, those vultures who would devour him with never a thought for his well-being.

In another hour Jesus pointed to an inlet that opened backward to a green field. "Put in there," he said.

In fact, that's where the herds were gathering. They were pouring down into that field and pressing close to the water.

"There?" I said. "You think *that's* a private place?" People lined the beach like locusts crowding an oak tree so thick they'll break it.

"There," he said, and I didn't argue. I shut my mouth and made for land. I heard him mutter, "God have mercy," and I knew his mood. "God have mercy on them," he said. "They are like sheep without a shepherd."

All this was different, you see. Jesus wasn't cheerful anymore. Even when he started to teach all those people he had the knot of frowning in his brow. Intense.

I remember that he begged them always to pray and never to lose heart. He told them stories: *There was a judge who neither feared God nor cared for people. And there was a widow who kept coming to that judge, saying, "Vindicate me against my enemy." He refused. The judge refused until he grew so irritated by her constant coming that he said, "I will vindicate her, or the woman will wear me out!"* And then the Lord made sure the people understood his stories: *Even so will God vindicate those who cry to him day and night!*

He told them a story about people who trust in themselves and despise others: *Two men went into the Temple to pray, one a Pharisee and the other a tax collector. The Pharisee stood and prayed thus with himself: "God, I thank thee that I am not like other people, extortioners, unjust, adulterers — or even like this tax collector. I fast twice a week. I give tithes of all that I* get." But the tax collector, standing in the back, would not even lift his eyes to heaven, but beat his breast, saying, "God, be merciful to me a sinner."

And all those sheep-people were watching him and nodding, but the Lord frowned and made sure of the meaning: I tell you, this man went down to his house justified rather than the other. For those who exalt themselves will be humbled, but those who humble themselves will be exalted.

On and on all afternoon the Lord taught like that. Sober. Pleading — almost as if his eyes were arms reaching into the crowds and grabbing people one by one.

And then it was growing late, but Jesus didn't look like he was going to quit. You see? — he was forgetting the plain, daily things. So I had to go and remind him.

I crouched down with my back to the crowds and whispered, "Master, do you know how late it is? The people are hungry. Soon they'll be cold and tired, too. Send them off to the villages round about for food and lodging."

Common sense. Basic needs at the end of the day.

But the Lord turned that intense stare at me and said, "No, they don't have to leave."

Suppertime, eventide, and he said that they didn't have to leave. And then he said to me, "You feed them."

Me? I should feed them?

Jesus didn't blink. Neither was he laughing. I made a joke of it. I said, "I guess you want me to break into my great treasury and buy two hundred days' worth of food — "

"Simon," he said. He interrupted me without the ghost of a smile. "How much food do we have?"

How was I to know? And what difference could it make?

But my dutiful brother pushed his face between us and said, "There's a boy here with five barley loaves and two fishes."

Jesus, still staring at me as if I were the one responsible, said, "Ask the people to sit on the grass, and bring the food to me."

So I told them to sit, and they sat. Sheep. A great, bleating flock of sheep all up and down the green field. Five thousand men, plus the women, plus the children!

But Jesus stood alone at the edge of the lake. He took the loaves and the fishes in his hands, and looking up to heaven he blessed them and broke the loaves and gave them to us, his disciples, to distribute among the multitudes. We did. And I'll tell you what: we came back to the Lord for more, and he gave it to us, and we handed out bread and fish until every man and every woman and every child was satisfied. By nightfall I was grinning. I had a terrible tickling in my stomach, and I would have laughed out loud if everyone else had not been so solemn.

He had been right! I had been wrong. Against all common sense and reason and facts and reality, the man could fill whole populations with food and still have enough left over for his nearest and dearest friends.

Bursting with pride I went among the people again and began to gather the *uneaten* fragments. We disciples took up twelve whole baskets!

So I walked where Jesus stood on the shore, ready to admit my huge stupidity and pound him on the back for this miracle too. But I didn't. Even in the twilight I could see that there was no triumph in his face, no gladness or calmness either. His lips pursed: he was thinking, thinking. But he saw me coming.

"Simon," he said, "tell all the disciples to board their boats and start back the way we came. I will dismiss these people myself." For just a moment his expression softened and he put his hand against my cheek. "I want to go up in the mountain to pray," he said. "I want to go alone."

When the Lord touches my cheek like that — pinches it, really — he befuddles me. I huff and blush and cannot talk.

So we left him ashore and pulled out toward dark water.

Mary Magdalene always sits dead center in my boat, underfoot when I raise or reef the sail. And she sits in the bottom, not on a thwart. I've asked her a thousand times to stow herself where she belongs, but she doesn't answer me and she doesn't move. Sickly child! No meat on her bones. How do you argue with silence and pitiful eyes? I give up. But I step on her sometimes and I wonder whether it doesn't hurt her. She doesn't say.

That night I had to gather the sail in altogether. The wind was contrary, and the waves were swelling so that we couldn't tack. We had to row, and the rowing itself was a backbreaker — the more so since Mary was crouched at our ankles, as miserable as a mouse, uncomplaining.

What took two hours during the day now ate up most of the night. Our muscles were cracking. The boat heaved high, causing the oar blades to skip from the water: useless! It'll snap the spine, that sudden flip of the oar.

Then Andrew cried out above the wind, "Look!"

And I looked off starboard and let out a yell. There was something on the black water, something coming — a human form, an apparition. The roots of my hair tightened.

But it spoke.

The ghostly figure said, "No, don't be afraid! It's me!"

It was Jesus! Walking toward us on the rolling seas!

Now I *did* burst out laughing. Great whoops of laughter — not only that the Lord had come after all, but that he had come in so grand a manner.

"O Lord, is that you?" I cried. "Can I do that, too? Jesus, let me come to you on the water!"

He said, "Come."

So I stood up big as a tree. I stepped my left foot on the gunwale and swung my right foot over and put it on the water, and the water took my weight. It was a long, slick surface — yes! But steady enough for both my feet.

I was doing it! Everything in me wanted to throw back my head and bellow with laughter. But then Jesus rose ten feet on a huge swell, and I — the sea, the water and my body — sank into a deep trough, and my heart flew out of my mouth, and I felt my feet pop below the surface, and I shrieked, "Lord, save me!"

Jesus was right there. He put out his hand and grabbed my arm and said, "O Simon, such little faith! Why do you doubt?"

After he helped me into the boat and got in himself and moved to the stern, the wind ceased completely, and I sat shivering all over my flesh, trembling in my bones. I was cold to the marrow. I could not keep still. Then I became aware of a small hand patting my knee, and I looked down.

It was Mary's hand. The mouse who crouched beneath my thwart was peering up at me from her wet, white, anxious face and patting my knee.

iii

When we landed south of Capernaum, Jesus sent Judas and Matthew directly to the city market for two weeks' provisions.

We're not going to stop in the villages this time.

I'm not going to preach.

We will not be begging bread, neither as itinerants nor as guests.

We're going out of Galilee. We're going alone. I want to talk to you.

And we left.

Jesus didn't join the general chatter. He strode in front of us all. Disciples straggled behind. Women and men, there were about twenty of us. I hung near his shoulder as best I could, but when the road was level, he moved at a brisk pace, his black hair streaming back from his brow, his light eyes lidded against the wind. I confess, I puffed a little.

Jesus looked neither left nor right. His lips were white, fixed in a soundless whistle, thinking, thinking. Whatever he had to say to us, he was saving it up. I figured it must be mighty important to need its own place for the telling — and that place outside of our own country. We took the road from Capernaum southwest toward Mt. Tabor, winding up into the hills. Then, still five miles north of the mountain, Jesus cut straight west, ten miles to Sepphoris. But he didn't enter that city either. We passed north of it and continued west. West! I had never before in my life seen the Great Sea! After Sepphoris we descended to a very rich plain, the grainfields just starting to dry for harvest, orchards and palms and fruits growing everywhere. When we came near the sea and the salt air, I saw that the land to our left was swampy. To the right it broke into rocks. On both sides there were only patchy gardens.

And then we saw the sand dunes. Ha! My bare face grinned to feel the stinging wind, all washed with salt. My nostrils opened wide, and my skull felt light. The Great Sea! I could hear the breakers off to the south, crashing on the long beaches. And then we climbed to the breast of a dune, and there was the sea itself, everywhere north and south and west, endless as the heavens, a blue-green water so clear you'd think it was a heavier air. Ha ha! And here was the city of Ptolemais, blinding white in the sunlight! A port city. I could board the big ships there! I could be a voyager off to Egypt or to Rome!

But the Lord did not go down into Ptolemais.

We turned north on the road that follows the coast. Twenty-five miles to Tyre. Out of country, and going farther all the time. The people that passed us were Gentiles. We tightened our ranks in these regions. Rushed in a small clump forward. Jesus was not tempering his speed.

Nor had he spoken more than the fifty plain words to us since we left. We were five days out by now. I worried about this pondering of his. What happened while we were gone preaching? Jesus was still young, you know. Thirty-two. Rabbis live long. They grow thin and wrinkled and grey, and I fully expected to care for my Master when his eyes dimmed and his teeth fell out. I wanted to carry his old bones on my own back. But Jesus seemed to be spending all his wisdom and all his strength right now on this fierce thinking. Like a furnace in his brain.

John the Baptizer, my brother's first master, had been beheaded. That happened. But I asked Jesus if he was thinking about John, and he said there was no need for that anymore.

Then a woman began to follow us. Not a Jew. A Gentile. A screechy sort. First she ran along the side of the road, staring at Jesus; then all at once she raised a piercing cry in thick accents: "Sir! Sir! Son of David, have mercy on me."

I cut near her and told her to go away. Even in foreign territories people demanded his attention! He wanted to be alone. He wanted to be thinking.

But she cried louder, "My daughter is vexed with a demon!"

Jesus kept walking.

I blocked her way and said, "You're a Syrian. Your daughter's a Syrian. We're Jews! Accept the facts and leave us alone!"

But the woman clawed past me and chased after Jesus, howling, making a scene. Begging!

"Master, I'm sorry!" I called. "I can't make the goy listen. You tell her to go home."

For once he listened to me. Jesus stopped and frowned at the woman. That alone should have chilled her. His words were even worse.

"I was sent to no one but the lost sheep of the house of Israel," he said. Jews, just like I said.

But this Syrian did not fall back in shame. She came *to* Jesus, sank to her knees and said, "Lord, help me."

Jesus said, "It isn't right to take bread from the children and cast it down to the dogs."

Now those were harsh words! He frightened *me*. I don't think I'd have been that tough on the woman.

Yet, Jesus' scolding didn't break her. She said, "Yes, Lord, but even the dogs get to eat the crumbs that fall from their masters' tables."

For the first time that season I saw the expression of the Lord go soft. He smiled. He smiled: the cheeks bunched under his eyes, and he said, "Woman, great is your faith!" Then he reached and took her elbow and raised her to his level again. "Go home," he said. "The devil has left your daughter. She is healthy and hungry and waiting for you to come home."

The woman was transfigured. She took to her heels and ran back the way we had come, and I was feeling happy that Jesus had smiled, but when I glanced at him, his eyes were hard again and blaring at *me*.

"So, Simon," he said. "Did I do right or wrong by the goy and her small sick Syrian whelp? What do *you* say the facts are now?"

"Lord," I said, "you always do the exactly right and perfect thing."

But then came this young man with a look of dopey appeal, and I wondered if we would ever get away. I had seen it often enough in the last twenty months: heal one, heal a multitude.

This particular fellow was deaf. And he had a speech impediment. So his friends had come to speak for him. They asked Jesus to lay hands on the boy in order to heal him.

In fact, Jesus did more than merely touch him. He led the fellow apart and put his fingers into the ear holes. He spat and touched the tongue. Then, looking up to heaven, Jesus sighed. It's the hugeness of that sigh which I can't forget. Jesus was not smiling. I'd say he was praying without words. I'd say he was begging heaven.

Then he said to the deaf man, "Ephphatha."

Be opened.

Well, the young man's ears were opened and his tongue was loosed and right away he was prattling as plainly as a rabbi.

Jesus said, "Listen to me! You must not tell anyone what I have done for you — "

But the fellow only laughed a loud, rude laugh and ran toward his friends all full of new words and a wagging tongue.

"Did you see that?" he cried.

And his friends shouted back, "That Jew does everything well! He makes deaf people hear and dumb people speak!"

Suddenly Jesus seemed to be flying. His face was entirely shut. His stride was so swift and so long that I myself had to run to keep up, and I could maintain that only for short bursts at a time.

∎

We did not enter the city of Tyre either. In the next several days Jesus veered east again and we traveled into the region of Caesarea Philippi. So we'd gone a great half-circle through several lands and soils and geographies.

Then one morning, suddenly, the Lord was talking again.

We were sitting in sight of the cave where some of the source-water of the Jordan comes from. In that cave there's a shrine where pagan people have worshiped their gods forever. But the water, you know: that's the water that flows into the northern end of the Jordan valley, and then into the Sea of Galilee, and on and on through all our tribes and our families, past Pella and Samaria and Jericho, even into the Salt Sea forever.

Behind us rose Mount Hermon whose snow and whose dew feeds the Jordan, too. There is where the river really begins. The mountain makes the headwater.

We had eaten our breakfast. We were relaxing on grassy patches among some low black boulders. Basalt, you know. Jesus was sitting in the scoop of a single rock as though it were a throne.

I truly believe that I would have forgotten this setting — or at least that I would not recall the detail — except for what Jesus did to me that day.

Softly he said, "What do you hear about me when I am not present?"

Instantly we all shut up, watching him. His voice had come like rain from a blue sky. He was looking at the backs of his hands, his fingers spread apart, and he was wearing a headband, his hair held back behind his ears. You see how all this is fixed in my memory? Every detail.

He said, "Who do people say that the Son of man is?"

Amazingly, my brother answered first. He never talks in a group. But the words jumped out and he gasped and then he shut up again for the rest of the day. He said, "John the Baptizer! Some say you are . . . John."

Jesus looked up at Andrew and nodded.

Then here came the second shocker. Mary Magdalene spoke. The shy white woman agreed with my brother. "That's what Herod Antipas thinks," she said. "He's afraid that you are John come back to blame him."

Well, then ideas and answers came pouring from all of us:

Philip said, "Some say you're Elijah, returning because the terrible day of the Lord is about to strike fire and burn like an oven."

Judas hollered, "Or Jeremiah!"

James: "Yes! Yes! One of the old prophets raised to life again!"

Jesus raised his hands, his eyes as bright as new coins flashing sunlight.

"But who," he said, cutting through the chatter, "who do *you* say that I am?"

I answered then. I said the most natural thing there was to say. But if Andrew and Mary Magdalene had surprised me, well, I must have dumbfounded the whole company of disciples.

I said, "You are the Christ, the Son of the living God."

Everyone shut up. Everyone spun around and looked at Jesus. To get his reaction, I suppose.

And this is what the Lord did: he broke into a proud smile. He beamed on me, shaking his head in wonder, and I blushed so hard my vision went red.

"Blessed are you, Simon son of Jonah," he said. "Flesh and blood did not reveal this to you; but my Father who is in heaven, he revealed it to you! From now on your name shall be Peter. On this rock I am going to build my church — and the powers of death shall not prevail against it."

All the disciples shifted their staring from Jesus to me. Maybe to see what *my* reaction would be. He called me "Peter." Stone. The Lord gave me a new name. The more I thought about it, the more my chest swelled, big as Mount Hermon.

And here's the next thing Jesus said to me: "I will give you the keys of the kingdom of heaven, and whatever you bind on earth will be bound in heaven, and whatever you loose on earth will be loosed in heaven."

I know about the giving of keys. Sometimes a landowner will give his chief servant the keys to his holdings. It means he trusts this servant with his own authority!

And Jesus said to me: *I will give you the keys of the kingdom of heaven!*

Oh, my! That day is fixed in my mind forever, caves and shrines and water and black boulders and Mount Hermon. I hardly knew what Jesus meant. I was as ignorant as a child — but I was a *chosen* child, you see! A favorite.

Now Jesus rose from his stony throne and began to walk down to the ancient pagan cave. He said he was thirsty. As he went, that thoughty look returned to his face, as if he felt some terrific pressure on his temples. After such a sunny smile, to see the gloom again — oh, that bothered me.

He said, "Things are going to change now." He heaved a sigh. We all were moving with him now toward the little spring of water. He said, "I have to go to Jerusalem. When I get there, I will suffer many things from the elders and the chief priests and the scribes. I'm telling you now so that you need not be surprised when it happens. It will happen."

Jesus knelt down by the spring, cold from the earth. He made a cup of his hands and scooped water. Just before he started to drink, he said, "I will be killed in Jerusalem, and on the third day be raised — "

I spoke again. I said the most natural thing there was to say.

Well, my feelings were so hurt by Jesus' words. Be *killed*? Was this the gloomy thing he'd been thinking about all the time?

I grabbed his wrist and shouted, "No!" The water splashed from his hands. "No, God won't allow it!" I cried.

On account of my feelings, I was gripping him with all my strength. But he started to pry my fingers from his wrist. He had terrible power in his hands.

I blustered on. Surely he knew that I was arguing out of love for him! "O Lord," I said, "this can never happen to you!"

He was standing, holding me at the forearm, his eyes like white hammers. No smile, no pride any more: anger!

He said to me, "Get behind me, Satan."

Ah, my heart failed. Another name! A vile and hateful name!

He did to me what he said to me: he began to drag me bodily away from his face, pushing me back behind him.

He said, "You are a hindrance to me. You care for the things of this world more than the things of God!"

He let me go. I was suddenly so weak that I slumped down to the ground.

No, but I do care for the things of God! And I love you, Lord Jesus! This is so confusing. One minute I'm Peter, the next minute I'm Satan, but I didn't change! How can plain love cause such outrage in the Lord?

I huddled on the ground. I couldn't say another word. I was afraid of Jesus then.

He ripped off the headband and shook out his hair and said to the rest of the disciples, "If you want to come after me, you've got to deny yourself and take up your cross and follow me. Those who wish to save their lives will lose them. Those who lose their lives for my sake will find them."

Jesus spoke with force. He said, "If someone is ashamed of me and of my words, the Son of man will also be ashamed of him when he comes in the glory of the Father and of the holy angels."

I felt worse and worse. I rolled on my side and covered my face because the tears were coming. *Does Jesus think I am ashamed of him?*

Then he cried in a loud voice, "The Son of man will be delivered into the hands of human authority, and they shall kill him, and the third day he shall be raised."

The second time he said it!

Oh, Lord Jesus, do you think I'm ashamed of your words? Are these the words you think I'm ashamed of?

"I tell you truly," Jesus said, "some of you here shall not taste death till you see the Son of man in power and in his kingdom."

He knelt down again and cupped his hands and drank. A long, long drink. He must have been very dry.

Just watching that common gesture made me feel guilty and alone.

iv

For five days Jesus didn't talk to me. Neither did I talk to the others. I kept my distance.

But on the morning of the sixth day he found me eating my breakfast alone. James and John were hovering behind him — as if they were afraid of me. What an odd thought! It can't have been true.

"Come with me," Jesus said. "I have something to show the three of you."

I got up and followed.

We walked to Mount Hermon. By midday we were climbing the mountain itself.

Finally Jesus showed us a cleft in some rock and asked us to wait there while he went on alone.

"To pray," he said.

We waited. We settled down between the halves of stone and watched as Jesus climbed farther up the side of Hermon. He'd found a narrow ledge, a steep one. His left side was against the sheer rock, his right side naked to the spaces and the plains below.

John whispered in my ear, "Simon, why are you mad at us? Did we insult you?"

This was a shocker. "I'm not mad at you," I said.

"Every day you go off by yourself, glowering."

"I don't glower!"

John shrugged. "When I greet you, you start working your fists like you're going to hit me."

"No, no," I said. "It's me. It's my mood that's the problem."

"You're not thinking of leaving Jesus? Like you left John the Baptizer?"

"Oh, John, no!" I was horrified. Had I seemed such an enemy these last days? But I thought everyone was mad at *me*! "Where else could I go?" I said. "No one has the words of eternal life except Jesus."

Jesus: he had ascended to a shelf of rock that jutted over the emptiness. *O Lord, did you, too, think that I would leave you?*

He had raised his eyes and his hands to the sky. He was praying. He looked like a wax candle set in a niche. He looked like a white statue standing in an alcove cut in the wall of the mountain. Far above us!

Jesus, believe me! No matter what happens, I will never, never leave you!

All at once it seemed to me that his head caught fire! No, not fire: glory! A pure white radiance blazed all around the Lord's head, and his face shined like the sun, and his clothes grew brighter and brighter — whiter than any fuller on earth could make them!

I jumped up, my whole body exploding with gladness!

Oh, what a sight the Lord was granting us. I knew it as soon as I saw it: this was his true majesty!

John cried, "Who is that? Who's that with him?"

James bellowed, "Moses! Oh, John, that's Moses of old! Can't you see the flaming veil over his face?"

But there were two men with Jesus, one on either side, talking and nodding as if the three had known each other all their lives.

Jesus! Jesus, who else has come to honor you?

And I heard it said: *Elijah.*

So I shouted to James and John, "That other man is the prophet Elijah!"

And I ran out from our cleft in stone, and I started roaring as loud as I could: "Master! Master! It's good to be here! Let us make three booths, one for you and one for Moses and one for Elijah — "

Immediately a thunderclap knocked me backward. I hit the ground with my shoulders. I saw a dazzling cloud come and cover the whole mountain, and from that cloud like thunder there fell a mighty voice, saying, *This is my beloved Son in whom I am well pleased. Listen to him!*

I was stunned. Everything went dark. The thunder rolled itself up and went quiet. I felt as if I were in the silence under the sea, hardly able to breathe.

But then I felt something like feathers on my cheek. I opened my eyes and saw Jesus standing over me, Jesus alone.

"Come," he said. He was smiling. His eyes were both common and kind. "Don't be afraid," he said, lifting me by my hand. "It's time to go down the mountain again."

And when James and John were also with us, he said, "Tell no one this vision until the Son of man is raised from the dead."

V

Some time after we had returned to Capernaum, the collectors of the Temple tax set up their tables in the marketplace. Every male among us has to support the worship of the Temple by annual dues of a half-shekel.

So when Judas and I were buying cucumbers at a booth nearby, one of these petty officials hollered to me: "Simon, doesn't your teacher pay the tax?"

I said, "Of course he does."

"Well, show me his money," he said.

Judas was with me. He had the purse. We had the payment. But the toad provoked me by rapping the table grandly with his knuckle. "Put it here," he said. "Put it here and all is clear!"

Faster than thought I whacked his board with the flat of my hand so hard his eyeballs spun. "Keep what you see!" I said.

Judas let out a cackle of laughter, and we left.

Back at my mother-in-law's house we told Jesus about the tax-collecting lizard.

Jesus said, "What do you think, Simon? From whom do the kings of the earth take tribute, from their own children or from others?"

"From others," I said.

"Then the children are free," said Jesus. "And the children of the king shall forever be free —

"However," he said, draping his arms over our shoulders, mine and Judas', "so that we do not offend the officials of this world, go down to the sea, cast out a good hook, and look in the mouth of the first fish you catch."

We did. That same afternoon I pulled in a good-sized carp. When I pinched its mouth open I found a clean piece of money. A shekel.

One shekel, of course, is two half-shekels. That's two payments of the Temple tax.

With the fish-coin, then, we went to the collector's booth and paid the snake two taxes. I gave him the carp as interest. I told him that his eye and its eye had much in common.

Judas liked my joke. He hated the authorities worse than I did. As we walked back to the house, he giggled and giggled about fish-eyed officials — until it occurred to him that I had paid dues for Jesus and for myself, but not for him.

Immediately his mood changed.

"Go back!" he said. He planted his feet in the middle of the street and said, "Tell the man to write my name down instead of yours."

Judas has always been a moody little fellow. But lately he seems ready to pick fights all the time.

"No," I said. "It's done. The deal is done."

Judas pushed it: "Tell him the tax is for me."

"Why?" I said.

"Because my tax isn't paid yet."

"So pay it yourself."

"You won't miss two drachmas," he said. "Besides, you didn't earn the half-shekel. You found it."

"I worked for it. I fished it!"

"Jesus told us *both* how to get that coin."

"Judas, just pay the tax," I said. "You have the money. I've seen you divide yours from the rest of the treasury."

He glared at me. He's got these huge bushes of eyebrow and a tiny head. Judas stood in the center of the street, glaring at me.

I shrugged and turned to go.

He screamed, "Simon son of Jonah, you owe it to me."

"I don't owe you anything," I said, still walking away.

"Oh, yes, you do! You owe *everyone*! Peter, favored by the Master. High and mighty, proud of his brand-new name!"

Now Judas was racing after me: "Everything comes your way, doesn't it?" he yelled. "And you think you deserve it, don't you? Do you know how you strut and swagger? You look down on us! You puff up that hollow chest of yours and clap us on our backs because you think everyone is tickled just to be near you. You think you're the greatest in the kingdom of heaven, don't you?"

"All right, let's talk about that," I said. I was at my mother-in-law's courtyard. I turned around and blocked the door and put my finger in Judas' face.

"Who really thinks he's greatest?" I shouted. "I'll tell you who. It's the fellow who gets to walk with the Lord, who already has more than anyone needs, and who still isn't satisfied! That fellow thinks he deserves more. Pride, Judas! That's real pride. And when you add self-pity, it's plain *ugly*!

"Judas! You snivel about a half-shekel when you yourself have been chosen by Jesus!"

I turned into the courtyard, and there stood both James and John.

James said, "Judas has a point, you know."

What? A *point*? "So is this a gang against me now?" I said.

James said, "You *do* act as if we're not equals anymore. You spend most of your time with Jesus."

"I didn't choose me!" I shouted. "Jesus chose me. I didn't name me! Jesus named me. So who are you going to blame?"

Give it to John: he never shouts. Always soft-spoken, always pretending to be the one reasonable voice in any argument. Self-control. The snot! The superior, sanctimonious snot!

"It never was the gift," he mused, "nor the giver we questioned, but the attitude of the receiver. Humility!" he said with a crinkle-eyed smile. "Learn humility, Simon Peter."

James, a great wit, began to talk about polishing rock, cutting boulders to pebbles. Judas began to giggle and flap his oversized eyebrows. That drove James to childish absurdities. He started listing the basic properties of stones: millstones, whetstones, tombstones —

I was shaking, ready to slap the joke down his throat.

But John said, "Come, come, Simon has a point, too. If we mock his name we mock Jesus' own decision."

"But he lords it over us!" Judas said.

James said, "And he thinks he's the greatest in the kingdom of heaven — "

The very words that Judas had said earlier! Yes, they *had* been discussing me behind my back.

John said: "Well, isn't that precisely the point, James? The kingdom of heaven? Let Simon enjoy his reward now. Truly, let him. We will receive ours when the kingdom finally comes."

James got a huge smile on his face.

Judas, however, dropped his bristly bushes into a black frown.

James said, "Yes, yes, yes, Simon. Oh, yes! We have asked Jesus to grant us a favor when he comes in his glory — "

Ah, listen to the sons of thunder. A new voice! James whirled around and saw Jesus standing in the doorway.

"Listen to the booming," Jesus said.

He called the brothers *Boanerges*, "sons of thunder."

Suddenly everyone's behavior changed. We all grew quiet. I felt my old guilt burning in my cheeks. I hate that blush! I hate to show my feelings so clearly so often.

Jesus came into the courtyard and sat down facing James and John.

"What favor do you want me to do for you?" he said. "This is as good a time as any to ask it."

The brothers glanced at one another. They glanced at me and Judas, too, but nervously. James said, "Grant us to sit one at your right hand and one at your left, in your glory." He swallowed and grinned.

Now I was truly struck dumb. Were we arguing about greatness? Had we been blaming pride? Well, this "favor" was the entire Tower of Babel!

But Jesus nodded, as if thinking seriously about it. Then he said, "You don't know what you're asking." In a solemn tone he asked: "Are you able to drink the cup that I drink?"

James and John said, "Yes!"

Jesus frowned and asked again, "Are you able to be baptized with the baptism with which I will be baptized?"

Like idiots the brothers grinned and babbled. "Yes, yes, we are able!"

Jesus heaved an enormous sigh. I heard that sigh. I stared at the sons of thunder.

Jesus said, "Well, the cup and the baptism shall be yours, too. You will drink, and you will suffer. Yes. But to sit beside me is not mine to grant. Simon Peter," Jesus said to me, "go get the rest of the disciples and bring them here."

I nodded solemnly. I bowed deeply in obedience. And I went.

When we had all gathered in the courtyard, Jesus said, "You know that those who rule the Gentiles lord it over them. It shall not be so among you. Listen to me: whoever would be great among you must be your servant, and whoever would be first must be slave of all. For the Son of man came not to be served but to serve — and to give his life as a ransom for many."

Suddenly he raised his voice and called, "Bernice!"

A tiny child peeped into the courtyard from the street.

"Come here," Jesus said to her, and she crept in. Jesus gathered his long hair back over his shoulders, then spread his arms — and with a burst of energy the little girl flew to him and landed in his lap.

The face of the Lord lost its heaviness. I saw his white teeth. He smiled at the tiny rag of life in his lap — the girl now peering peacefully at us from the cave of her protection, the arms and the breast and the garments of Jesus — and his golden eyes glittered in kindness.

Then he said, "With regard to greatness in the kingdom of heaven, I tell you that unless you turn and become like children you will never enter there. Those who humble themselves like this child, they are the greatest in the kingdom of heaven.

"With regard to greatness on earth," he said, "I tell you that those who receive one such child in my name receive me. But those who cause one of these small souls who believe in me to sin — it were better for them to have millstones tied around their necks and to be drowned in the depths of the sea! Do not despise even one of these little ones. For in heaven their angels always behold the face of my Father."

Jesus bent his head down and whispered in the ear of tiny Bernice. She rolled her wide eyes round and round, listening. She covered her mouth and asked a question. Jesus pointed at Judas, sitting on the ground with his back to the wall. Bernice giggled. She slid from Jesus' lap, tiptoed over to Judas, whose eyebrows started jumping all over his head, and then she kissed him on the tip of his nose. He turned crimson and frowned like a clap of thunder. Bernice skipped out to the street, laughing with glee.

And Jesus said, "If your brother sins against you, go and tell him his fault between you and him alone. If he listens, you've gained your brother again."

I said, "Yes, but how often shall my brother sin against me and I forgive him? Seven times?" There was a gang of disciples I had to deal with.

Jesus shook his head. "Not seven times," he said, "but seventy *times* seven.

"Listen," he said, "the kingdom of heaven can be compared to a king who wanted to settle accounts with his servants. When he began the reckoning, one was brought who owed him ten thousand talents. The servant couldn't pay, of course; so his lord commanded that he should be sold, together with his wife and children, in order to cover the debt. The poor fellow fell on his knees and implored the king to have patience. 'Give me time,' he begged, 'and I will pay you everything.'

"The king took pity on that servant. He forgave him the debt and released him into freedom again.

"But just as the man went out, he met another servant who owed *him* a hundred denarii. He seized his fellow servant by the throat and said, 'Pay what you owe.' The poor man fell on his knees and implored the first servant to have patience with him. He promised that he would with time pay everything he owed. But the first servant refused to listen. He had the poor man thrown into prison till he should pay the hundred denarii.

"When the king heard what had taken place, he summoned the first servant to himself. 'You wicked man!' he said. 'I forgave you your whole debt! Shouldn't you have had mercy on your fellow servant as I had mercy on you?'

"In wrath the king delivered him to the jailers till he should pay the ten thousand talents.

"So also will my heavenly Father do," said Jesus, his eyes cast down to the flagstones under his feet, "to those who do not forgive their brothers from their hearts."

And then, so softly I could hardly hear it, Jesus murmured, "Simon? Judas? James? John? How much do you suppose I have forgiven you?"

vi

Then we left.

Jesus departed both the city of Capernaum and the province of Galilee for good. He set his face toward Jerusalem. We weren't wandering anymore. We had some-where to go. And I guess we had a certain time to be there.

When we were about a day's journey from Capernaum, a scribe rushed up to Jesus!

"Teacher!" he cried. "Teacher, I want to follow you wherever you go!" I understand that desire perfectly. I remembered when I first felt it over two years ago in my rowboat.

But Jesus said to him, "Foxes have holes, and birds of the air have nests. The Son of man has nowhere to lay his head."

We kept walking. We: those who had become his most loyal followers, men and women, a small and separate group, though multitudes still poured from the villages we passed. Always the multitudes. Always.

Then one of the disciples figured out that we were never going back to Galilee together. He went to Jesus and said, "Lord, let me first go home and bury my father."

Jesus said to him, "Follow me and leave the dead to bury their own dead." You see? His manner was firm. His changing was done. His mind was made up.

A woman from one of the villages watched us for several days from a distance. Then she came near and said, "Jesus, I will follow you. But I have to say good-bye to those who are at my house."

He said to her: "No one who puts her hand to the plow and then looks back is fit for the kingdom of God."

There was a heaviness to his sayings now. His motion seemed heavy, too. Actually, he had grown leaner in the last year, but he moved as if his bones were dense, as heavy as lead.

Just after we entered the province of Samaria, Jesus sent James and John ahead to a village to prepare them for his coming.

Within an hour the brothers came back. James was furious.

"They are refusing to let you in," he said. "They say it's because you're traveling to Jerusalem. You're a risk and a danger to them, they say. Lord, do you want us to call fire down from heaven and consume them, as Elijah did?"

Here is an example of the heaviness in Jesus. He looked so long at James that the man grew nervous and couldn't return the gaze.

Finally he sighed and said, "The Son of man came not to destroy lives, but to save them. If one village does not receive us, another will. Come. Let's find that other one."

One night while we were sleeping in the fields, I saw a white form gliding like a ghost to the place where Jesus lay. It settled upon him, and there it stayed. The roots of my hair tightened. I felt something like dread.

So I rose up and crept closer to see what night spirit sat by my Master.

But it was no spirit at all. It was Mary Magdalene. She was lying behind him, stroking his hair.

"What are you doing here?" I hissed. "Things are bad enough already. You want to give his enemies bigger sticks to beat him with?"

She didn't answer. She looked up at me from her white face, her dark eye sockets, and her chin began to tremble.

Without moving so much as a finger, Jesus spoke.

"Simon, see what you've done? You made her cry," he said. "Is there a good reason for that? But no one else has come to comfort me. No one else has considered that I might be grateful for the comfort. Go away, Simon Peter. Go away. I am so tired now. Go."

So I went back to my own pallet and lay down and cried.

I'm a simple man. I try to do what is right. That's all. Simple rightness, with all my might. But sometimes the Lord was such a mystery to me that I seemed unable to do anything but wrong. I didn't understand. I could not understand him. And when he withdrew into his absolute darkness, it always made me feel sad and lonely, as though the whole universe were lit by one lantern on the prow of a boat and above is the night and below are the black seas, and the lantern gutters and goes out.

Mary, I'm sorry. You know things I cannot know — stupid man that I am! I'm sorry, I'm sorry, I'm sorry I made you cry.

36

SON OF FATHER

i

In those days the Jews taught that there were ten degrees of holiness on earth, ten concentric circles, those of lesser holiness surrounding those of greater, more concentrated holiness until all surrounded that perfect cube of darkness, the Holy of Holies in the Temple.

Circles in circles like wheels in wheels: the land of Israel itself was the first circle and the first degree of holiness.

The city of Jerusalem was the second.

Into these two spheres anyone on earth might travel, whether by freedom or by force, whether Jew or Samaritan or Gentile; their presence did not diminish the holiness of the greater rounds, and if they came devoutly they could themselves participate in the holy.

The third circle was the Temple mount, into which traffic entered daily, from which it daily departed. Buying and selling took place in here, particularly as it supported the rituals of sacrifice and the Temple.

But the fourth degree was an absolute wall against those who were not Jews. Immediately within the porticoes around the Temple was the Court of the Gentiles, a great paved yard where proselytes were admitted, where a pilgrim might buy an animal to sacrifice, where even a Roman could wander without polluting the sacred places or bringing the wrath of God down upon himself.

But within that vaster court was a balustrade, a terrace walled with a stone lattice, and one gate only through which Jews could pass and no one else. None but Jews. Visible to everyone along this wall were stone inscriptions in Latin and Greek prohibiting the entrance of Gentiles under the penalty of death. This wall, in Hebrew called hel, was the fourth degree of holiness.

The fifth, inside the Court of the Gentiles through that single gate called Beautiful, was the Court of the Women.

The sixth was the Court of the Israelites, where priests and the male Jew might enter, but not the female. Here laymen slaughtered their own sacrificial offerings and butchered the carcass. The priests caught the blood and carried the cut parts up to the Altar of Burnt Sacrifices, there to burn them before the Lord.

Now, the area closely surrounding the altar and the Temple proper was reserved for priests and Levites alone. This was the seventh circle, the seventh degree of holiness on earth.

The strip of pavement between the altar and the porch of the Temple itself was the eighth.

The ninth was the sanctuary inside the Temple, furnished with the altar of incense, the table of showbread, the golden candlestick.

And the tenth — that Most Holy Place, occluded from the rest of the Temple by a double veil of fine twined linen, blue and purple and scarlet — the tenth was a room in which God's ineffable holiness dwelt among the people, the *Debir*, a room dreadfully and completely dark, thirty feet wide and thirty feet high and thirty feet deep.

Here one man only ever entered, the high priest — and he but once a year.

ii

Ten days before the Feast of Tabernacles — in those cooling weeks of September after the farmers have finished harvesting their date orchards and their vineyards, in that brief respite before they have to sow their fields in barley and wheat — seven men of the tiny village of Japhia in Galilee gathered their families together and began to travel to Jerusalem for the feast.

That they were going was not unusual. Jews from every province — Jews, indeed, from all the nations of the world — streamed to the holy city for the joyful celebration at the end of the autumn harvest. But this particular band of Galileans took an odd route south. Moreover, they made several peculiar stops on the way. Therefore, they drew the attention of the Roman authorities, and they were followed.

Instead of striking southeast toward the Jordan and then down, as did most Galilean pilgrims, they went due south into the royal estates of Herod Antipas, where they spent two days lingering in tents, then they traveled west by southwest through Samaria straight to Caesarea on the sea. They camped outside the city two more days. It was here that the Roman governor of Samaria and Judea maintained his residence. In fact, he wasn't present at the time. He was in Jerusalem, holding court in the palace of Herod the Great, as was his custom during the high festival days of the Jews. Nevertheless, three men from the Galilean band walked back and forth in front of his residence morning and evening for two days, seeming to study it.

Then it was that Roman suspicions were aroused.

After the Galileans had broken camp and departed along the coast road south, an imperial servant left Caesarea for Jerusalem carrying ten crystal goblets to the governor there. He was a corpulent, smiling man, a courtier full of goodwill for everyone, Roman or fanatical, it didn't matter. He rode with one driver in his chariot and two armed soldiers in attendance.

It was observed that the Galileans, having traveled south from Caesarea on the coast highway, took the road inland from the city of Joppa. A reasonable itinerary, the same one which the imperial servant himself soon took.

Reasonable, too, was the brief detour which the Galileans made in Sharon, the coastal plain between Joppa and Lydda. They purchased seven calves from a herdsman there. The Roman courtier was knowledgeable enough of Jewish ritual to recognize the beasts they sacrificed.

More curious, however, was the stop they made just twelve miles east of Lydda. The place was Beth-horon, one of two towns situated on a ridge which guarded the road's ascent from the coastal plain into the rough hill country west of Jerusalem. In the middle of the morning the band of Galileans simply stopped. The women began a great babbling. Gossip, most likely. They saw to the children, the goods, and the animals, while their husbands left them alone.

The seven men climbed the Beth Horon ridge, itself not a difficult climb — but then they hiked back through sharp rock and thorn bushes so thick that a Roman of some girth made sacrifice to follow. But if he hadn't followed, he would never have discovered the place where the Galileans were going: a narrow defile in which was a natural limestone terrace and a cave, both completely concealed to an outside eye.

The imperial servant did not try to descend the rugged wall of the defile. He had left one of his soldiers with the driver at the chariot. The other now lay down with him at the edge of the wall and watched as fourteen more Jews emerged from the cave and greeted the Galileans and sat down to talk.

Brigands, perhaps. Robbers who made the cave their hiding place. Or revolutionaries.

The visitation lasted an hour. It might have gone on into the afternoon, but it was interrupted.

One of the brigands dominated the conversation, a man both lank and graceful. Agile. He moved much when he spoke, a passionate fellow, immensely articulate even to Roman ears — and, yes, an insurrectionist! As his voice rose, one could hear a vilification of everything Gentile.

"Jealous!" he was saying. "Jealous for the laws of the Lord, abominating the coin of the goy and his taxes — "

Suddenly the imperial servant had a great desire to sneeze. At the same time he commenced to perspire, moistening all the creases of his flesh and drizzling sweat into his eyes. He had just realized who the orator was — and the luck of his discovery made him very excited.

This was the son of a prominent rabbi in Jerusalem, the son of a man whose hatred for Rome was so massive and so magisterial that even among a race of haters the only one to equal his despisings was his son, the orator before them now! The father was a ranter. Ah, but the son was feral and dangerous, a murderer capable of attacking even Jews whose zeal was less than his. So notorious was he that the public knew him by a nameless name: "Son of Rabbi," they called him, and "Son of Father."

Oh, what a nest of serpents! Seven Galileans, fourteen Zealots — and a leader! *The* leader!

The heavy Roman courtier turned to his companion and whispered, "Do you know who that is? It's Barabbas!"

Then he sneezed. Once, twice, three times. He went into a fit of sneezing. When finally it had run its course, he looked up and saw the revolutionary called Barabbas standing above him in sunlight, his short sword drawn.

The Roman tried to smile with peaceable goodwill and genuine beneficence upon the cold Jew staring down at him, but his nose and eyes were wet from the sneezing. The smiling did not succeed. He felt the edge of the sword bite through his flesh, even to the neckbone.

iii

In those days the ruler of the Roman Empire was Tiberius Claudius. Caesar Augustus had adopted the man before he died in order to control the choice of his own successor.

Tiberius was already fifty-six years old when he ascended into power. He determined not to add to the size of the empire Augustus had created, but rather to preserve it. From the beginning of his reign he sought to unify all Roman provinces not only under one governance but also under one mind and in one spirit. To that end he encouraged every race within his realm to worship the dead Augustus as the son of gods, an associate with whatever gods the people acknowledged. In the figure of Augustus, Tiberius hoped to establish a symbol, a force, a focal point for the loyalty of all the tribes and tongues in the empire.

Let people invoke Augustus, and the state itself would hold their souls.

Therefore, the present emperor rejected foreign cults. This Jews knew only too well: his policies threatened disaster to those whose laws could know no God but one God. The leaders in Jerusalem scrutinized with keen attention every new decree that issued from Rome. And the legions who

came, the centurions, the legates, and the governors — every arriving
Roman caused greater anxiety among the chief priests and the Sanhedrin,
those who in narrow limits ruled the Jews.

Already Tiberius had banned Druidical rites and practices throughout
the empire.

What else? Ten years ago, upon a pretext of scandal in that place,
he destroyed the temple of the Egyptian mother-goddess, Isis. Then he
crucified her priests in public, inviting the entire population to observe the
slow exposure and the death of such religious leaders.

What else unnerved the Jewish leaders? In the city of Rome itself, when
he heard the rumor that four Jewish men had conspired to steal a woman's
treasure, Emperor Tiberius commanded that the entire Jewish community
should be driven from the city into exile.

From such practices there was no safety. Against them there was neither
intervention nor appeal. Moreover, they were coming closer and closer to
the center of the center of holiness.

For in these last years the courts of the Roman emperor had appointed
a new governor over Samaria and Judea, Pontius Pilate, an insulting,
irreligious man. Immediately he began to mint for his provinces coin
bearing pagan images. Jews had no choice but to use it, touch it, receive it,
spend it. So there was no secret about this governor's intent: he meant even
by his sarcasms to diminish what few privileges Jews had preserved from the
days of Herod the Great.

Indeed, this governor wanted to abolish the laws that separated and
distinguished them.

Pontius Pilate maintained the seat of his government in Caesarea by the
sea. But it was Jerusalem which required his greater attentions. Soon after
he had arrived, he ordered his troops to encamp within the walls of the city
of Jerusalem — in the second circle of holiness.

"Raise your ensigns high," he commanded his captains, "so that every
Jew can see the images of the emperor affixed to them!"

The Jews saw. And fiercely the Jews protested.

Pharisees, Zealots, scribes, men jealous for the laws of God went to the
place where the governor resided and cried out against him in the streets.

Pilate threatened to cut them down where they stood.

They didn't weaken. They only cried the louder. One old rabbi stepped
face-to-face with a young soldier, who tentatively drew his knife. In a single
motion the rabbi ripped open his tunic, grabbed the soldier's wrist, and
forced the edge of the knife across his own bony breast faster than the
Roman, horrified, could yank it back again.

The rabbi stood bleeding and unblinking, a devout ferocity in his eyes. It
was the same wild look that all these Jewish protesters had. When the new
governor recognized in them a genuine readiness to be slaughtered and to

die, then he himself backed down. He commanded the offending symbols to be removed from their holy city.

Pontius Pilate trod more lightly among the provincials after that. But he did not keep his foot indoors. With somewhat more circumspection, but with cruelty after all, he stepped on the toes of some Jews, and on the skulls of others.

iv

In the seventeenth year of Tiberius Caesar, during the Jewish celebration of the Feast of Tabernacles, Pontius Pilate, who was holding court in the palace of Herod the Great issued an order for the execution of seven Galilean men.

"Reprisals," he said. "The murder of an imperial servant, a Roman citizen, cannot pass without punishment."

A contingent of ten soldiers armed with knives and spears and swords, shields, helmets, greaves, and armor, marched in close order out of the palace. Faces forward, themselves an iron military unity, they marched through the center of the city, down into the Tyropoeon valley and up the other side to the Huldah Gates on the south side of the Temple complex. They did not hesitate, but marched through the Royal Portico into the Court of the Gentiles. It was crowded with pilgrims. People fell backward. People dashed out of the way of the soldiers' grim progress. Some yelled for the Temple guard. Others hurled epithets and curses at the Romans. But the armed soldiers looked neither to the left nor to the right. Swifter than any could warn of their coming, they marched through the gate called Beautiful, past the balustrade, *hel*, the fourth degree of holiness, into the fifth and then the sixth: the Court of the Israelites.

In that place, seven Galileans were slaughtering seven calves for sacrifice. All but one of the calves lay dead, and that one had the knife already at its throat. Three of the beasts were being butchered, the new meat draining its blood down channels in the Temple pavement. Rivers of dark blood ran in these channels from the altar eastward, through a drainage system underground into the Kidron valley, which was made extraordinarily fertile thereby.

The captain of Pilate's soldiers barked a single command.

The presence of Gentiles in this place was so unthinkable that it caused a space of perfect silence, as though the universe had paused to consider some wonder. But this was the paralysis of horror. Absolutely no one, neither priest nor Israelite, could utter a word. No one moved.

And in that space of strange serenity, the soldiers obeyed their captain's command. They stepped quickly and efficiently among the Galileans and slashed six throats, mingling their blood with the blood of the calves, their sacrifice.

The captain approached the seventh man, whose face was linen-white and gaping. He noticed the fellow's youth, a naïvete unusual among Jewish revolutionaries.

Without emotion the captain said, "Whom did you go to meet at Beth-horon?"

"I don't know." A breaking voice. A boy.

The captain struck him across the face. "Who murdered the governor's servant?" he said. "Who stole ten crystal goblets?"

The Galilean raised his open hands. "Truly, I don't know the man."

The captain struck him again.

"I don't know his name!" cried the youth. "I never heard his name! I hardly knew what we were doing there!"

"Then you saw him?"

"Yes! Yes!"

"So you can tell me of this murderer?"

The Galilean's feet were huge, but his legs were meatless, thin. They would break like dry sticks. "They called that man something you could say of any man," he whimpered. "The son of a father."

"They said it in Hebrew?"

"Yes."

"They said Bar-abba?"

"Yes."

"Thank you." The captain wound the fingers of his left hand into the hair of the frightened revolutionary. "And what do they call you?" he said.

"Gimel," the young man whispered, "because I was crooked once — like the Hebrew letter gimel."

"Well, Gimel, it should come as no surprise to you that the murders of Barabbas also cause the death of Jews."

With his right hand the Roman drew his dagger across this throat, too, and the blood of the seventh Galilean ran with the blood of his brothers down to the soil of the Kidron valley.

V

Three times in two weeks the high priest convened the Jewish governing council in order to discuss the deterioration of relations between Rome and Jerusalem. They met in the Chamber of Hewn

Stone below the pavement of the Temple courtyard. This room of mighty pillars was forever in shadow, lit by lamps and always chilly.

The first meeting of the council occurred immediately after the execution of seven Galileans. It was a hasty midday gathering. Scarcely forty men arrived. As many as thirty members were traveling out in the province or else were unaware that Gentiles had intruded in the holy places of the Jews.

High priest Caiaphas allowed an hour of passionate shouting while he sat and said nothing. Priests and Pharisees strode about the stony room weeping, condemning the sacrilege, begging God to preserve the holiness of his name. Even more than the murders of Galileans, it was the profaning of the Temple that most enraged these men.

Finally, Caiaphas spoke. In a single speech, by calm oratory and a resistless sequence of reasons, he first acknowledged the issue that consumed the council, then turned their attentions from one enemy to another.

"In the Court of the Israelites," he said, "ten Roman soldiers have killed seven Galileans. For that you are angry at the Romans. And well you should be. But what can you do about it?

"Members of the Sanhedrin, we have no choice but to be realistic. Under whose dispensation do we rule? Surely in matters most religious, under the Lord's. And this is a matter of religion, yes. On the other hand, the practice of our religion and all the rites of the Temple remain free only insofar as we are granted that freedom by Rome. In matters of civil law and the governing of Jewish people as *people*, we rule under the dispensation of the Emperor and his prefect in this province: Pontius Pilate — who ordered the soldiers to enter our sanctuary.

"Now, by your leave," said Caiaphas, "I will ask you several questions. First: What happens to our authority if Rome decides to withdraw the dispensation which no other race possesses in the empire? Second: What raises Rome's displeasure more than revolutionary rhetoric? And more than acts of revolt, what provokes its fury? Third: Who is more heedless and loud for insurrection than the Zealots? — than *all* those who seek a messiah of military designs? Oh, members of the Sanhedrin, *they* are the dangerous ones! If these people — over whom we still exert some control — are not held in check, then our rule, our authority, the Temple and all its holy ritual will be lost. We have lost them before.

"Fourth question: And from whence do the most intense of Zealots come to threaten the seat of our power here? Why, from Galilee! Always from Galilee.

"My brothers, the seven Galileans are not without some culpability of their own. The Romans may not be friends of ours. They surely are not of our blood. But they are the ones we must appease, even while we quench the fires of the radicals who *are* our kin and our children.

"This, sirs, is expedience," the high priest said.

Then he stood up and said: "Go out. Go immediately to the priests and the people in the Temple courts. Ease their minds. Then go to all the people in Jerusalem, both the citizens and the pilgrims here, and calm them, too. By your own composure and by gentle ministrations settle the people. I'll go find some valid reason for Pilate's execution of these Galileans, something we can offer the pilgrims to satisfy their questions. But you must turn their hearts to the keeping of the feast. Remind them that it is the most joyful of all our festivals. Go."

During the next several hours the council members scattered throughout the city, presented faces of beneficent kindness, words of comfort, pledges of stability.

No, no, all was in order, they said. The Temple had been purged. Sacrifice continued. None need hang back. There was neither threat nor danger to anyone. It had been, the council protested, a single affair. In fact, these Galileans had brought the judgment upon themselves.

What had they done?

Well, they had committed heinous crimes. What crimes? Well, the priests and the elders gave their earnest word to the people that when they were able to reveal the nature of the Galileans' crime, they would. They surely would.

∎

Early the following day, the high priest convened the council again. This time all seventy members were present.

Caiaphas said, "Pontius Pilate tells me he has evidence that the Galileans murdered an imperial official, an innocent courtier, a Roman citizen who served in the governor's residence in Caesarea."

"What evidence? How does he know this thing?"

"A charioteer and a foot soldier found the official's body. He had followed the Galileans into the hills above Beth-horon, but when it grew late and he hadn't returned, they went looking for him. His throat had been slashed. He was, they said, a heavy corpse in difficult terrain. It took a while to drag him out again."

Caiaphas spoke with slow circumspection, calm and grey and saturnine. He sat on a stone seat, dressed in the white linen of his office, making a cage of his fingers before his face. He was not given to personal passions. Rather, he was concerned for the efficiency of public machines.

"But," certain Pharisees objected, "did this chariot driver see the murders? And if not, how can he know who committed them?"

Caiaphas said, "Excellent question. Nevertheless, Pilate has it by confession from a dying Galilean that they had gone into the hills to meet the man whom people call 'Son of Father.' "

"Barabbas? That smoking firebrand?"

"The same."

"Bold robber! Cunning thief! Scourge of the merchants and the Romans. The people adore him."

"They do. But they shouldn't."

"Well, but he gives a poor Jew hope. He makes the old man young again by driving a hot blood through his veins."

"He turns Jews into Zealots," Caiaphas declared. "He makes the Romans nervous, which makes me very nervous indeed."

"But the people adore him!"

"Right. And the more they do, the greater the danger he is to us."

"Then how do you plan to handle Barabbas without a riot?"

"Brothers, I propose that we set one of our foes against the other, keeping our hands hidden and our hearts clean."

Quietness spread through the Chamber of Hewn Stone. The entire Sanhedrin, as conscious of the tension in present events as the high priest was himself, gave tacit approval to his intentions, if not yet to his proposal.

"Indirectly, without promise or commitment," Caiaphas said, "I indicated to the governor that we might be able to name the Zealot's hiding places, and that we might — again, through a whole Babel of indirections — communicate those places to him."

"You would serve the Romans!"

"I would save the Temple, sir! I will use any expedient to keep the Temple holy!"

"So! And I suppose that you in your fine linen know how to locate the cave rat, Barabbas?"

"This," said Caiaphas, "is what I say: Ask the rabbi. And if the rabbi, his father, will not divulge his son's hiding place to us, then we will censure the rabbi. We'll make the *father* known to Rome, that Rome may do as it pleases with him."

■

Two weeks later the council gathered again in the Chamber of Hewn Stones.

By then the Feast of Tabernacles had concluded without insurrection or incident. The pilgrims — more than one hundred thousand of them — had left for home, uplifted. Jerusalem was reduced to its more peaceful population of fifty thousand. It had scrubbed its white stone streets clean of the worshipers' dirt and had returned to common commerce and an easier routine. Pontius Pilate, too, had gone back to Caesarea by way of the Beth Horon road, taking a good many troops with him.

The Sanhedrin was meeting in regular session to discuss both a death and a capture.

The man whom the common people called "Son of Father" had been found and imprisoned in a cell underneath the palace of Herod the Great. That was the capture.

But the father himself, the old rabbi long notable in Jerusalem, had died with the fierce serenity of an undiminished hatred. He had kept completely silent regarding the haunts of his son. The Romans were forced to execute him and then, in their usual brutish manner, to find Barabbas on their own.

vi

A centurion stood before a small house of sunbaked clay. It was scorched black around the windows, the lintel, and the doorway. The door itself had fallen outward into the road, cracked with char. Ribbons of smoke still rose from the interior straight up into blue sky. There was no roof. The beams and the weave of branches had burned, and all its mud had collapsed into the house. It smelled rank. A bitter ash.

"Whether you see them or not, sir," the centurion called, "my troops completely surround you now. Arise and come out, or we will come in, and then you will never rise again."

The centurion waited. He lowered his head and sighed. His name was Longinus. He had been an officer in the legions for nineteen years, transferred from cohort to cohort, promoted by small degrees. Now he was less than a year from retirement and very tired. His men were from Gaul. Longinus was himself a Roman citizen. The Gallic soldiers knew each other well. Of him they knew discipline, the crack of his vine-staff on their backs, absolute command and obedience, but they did not know the man. Nor should they, of course. Yet he was tired of the loneliness, too.

Suddenly the door that lay by the road shifted. It slid sideways, and dust blew out as from an exhalation.

"What's that?" Longinus said. "Soldier, the door moved. Lift it up. Watch out — the wood's still smoldering."

In ranks around the burned-out house the hundred Gauls stood armed, cuirass and helmet flashing in the sunlight, some slouched, some alert, all of them looking like a broken wooden fence.

The soldier closest to Longinus walked to the door, gingerly touched its edges, then began to lift the near end slowly from the road. It was made of three heavy planks joined by crosspieces, top, middle, and bottom.

"*Di meliora!*" the centurion breathed. Then: "Don't drop it!" he shouted. He rushed forward and knelt down in the shadow of the door.

There was a child underneath it. A girl. Blood soaked her hair. Blood and a black dirt smeared her lower quarters, her legs, and the soles of her feet. Blood filled the whorls of her ears. Her small shoulder, white as alabaster, was perfectly clean — but both her hands were split and seared with burning. Her palms were sloughing a wet flesh. She was breathing, but unconscious.

Strangely, when he lifted the child in his arms, it was the pure white and naked shoulder that most broke the centurion's heart.

He glared at the house and roared in a hoarse voice: "Do you keep a count of the people who suffer for you? Does it matter? Here is a child dying because you hid in her house! Come out, you *scelus*! Come out and see whether she is your sister or just another Jewish sacrifice!"

Longinus felt the sting of tears in his eyes. Ah, he was too old for this anymore.

A voice came out of the house: "Who kills children?"

The words were huge, echoing: "Who has slaughtered all the villages around Beth-horon? Was it a Jew or a Gentile?"

The voice was magnified by round, hollow plaster walls. So, then: Longinus had a fix on the fugitive.

"It was no one but a Jew," he cried back, "that triggered our just and necessary response!"

"Oh, Roman! A cohort comes for one man! Ten centurions, one thousand soldiers crawling the countryside, bludgeoning people in the streets and burning their houses! Roman! Roman! Is that a just response?"

With one hand, Longinus clutched the child to his bosom; with the other he signaled his men into the tiny courtyard of the house, mouthing the word: *Cistern.* They began to creep toward the gap that had been a door, four with spears, four with swords.

Longinus shouted, "But one sole Jew had only to surrender in order to stop the cohort. You, Barabbas, hero of the people — you chose your neck over their safety. And now what? Now I shall clap my hands and crack that neck, and you will have gained nothing at all."

He meant it. He was sick of these Zealots who considered their cause more holy than human life. Destructive, fanatical people. Religious! Blind to the benefits of Roman order and Roman roads and the peace that Augustus bequeathed the world!

The eighth soldier had just crept through the stinking brick. The centurion shifted the child in his arms, preparing to clap this insurrectionist to death.

But she coughed. The little girl opened her eyes and looked up. She saw the martial aspect of the man who held her, and she began to shriek — powerful, piercing, terrified cries: "*Mama! Mama! Mama —* "

Immediately, louder than the child's terror there came from the house a wild bellow: "Roman jackal! What are you doing?"

And the Zealot Barabbas vaulted the black wall, lean, athletic, and enraged. He landed face-to-face with the centurion. But before he could draw breath, ten Gauls seized him, buckled his knees, and bound his arms behind him.

The child was stunned to silence by the brutality. She gaped. She began to shiver in the centurion's arms.

"Nothing," Longinus said. "I am doing nothing but cradling a baby who is afraid of me. Nothing, sir, so meaningful as you are doing."

Barabbas spoke with a voice like a whistling whip, spitting hatred: "She was trying to open the door, Roman," he said. "She was trying to save me from the fires your people set. But the door was ablaze on the inside. I could not get near it. And then it dropped outward."

"Do you know her?"

"She is a Jew."

"Yes, but do you know her?"

"All Jews are precious to me."

"Yes, sir. Yes: you are a very great man, and this is but one Jew. A baby Jew. A girl. Are Jews also precious to you one by one?"

Barabbas paused and looked directly at the child. "She is my sister's daughter," he said.

"Thank you," said Longinus. "I will take her to your sister. Where does your sister live?"

"My sister is dead," said Barabbas. "My brothers are dead. Our father died two days ago. Only our mother is left alive. In Jerusalem. Perhaps you will spare her life if she has a child to feed. Or perhaps you will kill them both."

"Barabbas," said Longinus, too weary to argue, too old and too lonely to bear the dry hatred of these rebellious provincials anymore: "for the record, what is your legal name? I'll write my report, and we can be done with each other forever."

Barabbas spat in the dust.

The centurion sighed. "For your niece, then, so that I lodge her with the right family after all, what is your name?"

Barabbas — on his knees, bound, and bowed to the ground — twisted his face into a grimace of genuine pain. "Yehoshuah," he said, speaking it fully in Hebrew: Yahweh Is Salvation.

The little girl reached out a hand from which hung damp ribbons of skin. "Yeshi, Yeshi," she whispered. "Jeshua."

Longinus turned to the soldier who was recording information on a tablet. He dictated an official time, date, and place for the arrest. Then he repeated the name of his captive in his own tongue: "Jesus Barabbas," Longinus said. "The prisoner's name is Jesus."

37

TO JERUSALEM

i

JUDAS

The instant he heard of the capture of Barabbas, Judas Iscariot gasped and cried out: "The people! The people!"

Suddenly, he saw! Judas was able to see! Understanding struck him with the force of lightning. He nearly wept at the inspiration. Why had he never seen it so clearly before?

A friend from Judea, a Zealot, found him in Perea.

In the middle of October Jesus had crossed the Jordan with his disciples north of Pella. They were traveling slowly through the northern portions of Perea, when the young Zealot arrived from Jerusalem and drew Judas aside to tell him the horrible news: first, Pontius Pilate had surprised certain Galileans in the Temple precincts and mingled their blood with the blood of their sacrifices. Next, the governor went looking for Barabbas in the towns around Beth-horon, punishing the people, actually killing their children in order to secure that man's surrender. Barabbas himself was captured ignominiously in a tiny place.

"A tiny place," the Zealot said, "a lonely house, burned down to the ground — "

And Judas cried: "The people!"

All at once an entire strategy was vouchsafed to him exactly as oracles are given by God to the prophets.

"It should have been Jerusalem," he said, dazzled by the insight. "There should have been a hundred thousand Jews around. Watching! Ready to riot! But *ready*," he said. "The Galileans — they were not ready. And Barabbas — he missed the pregnant hour by a week. It should have happened at the Feast of Tabernacles. Holy time, holy place, holy people, all the people, crowds of people from everywhere on earth, outraged at the revelations of Rome and ready to fight! Yes!"

So Judas had a plan to think about.

Perhaps it would have remained merely a dream, another scheme for the saving of Israel, except for the events of the very next day.

Some Pharisees from the southern part of the Perean province saw Jesus on the road with his disciples. They recognized him and paused to talk. For once it seemed that they genuinely wished to be helpful.

There were three of them. In fact, Judas recognized one as having been a supporter of John the Baptizer, even after his imprisonment. Judas himself had considered following John. He liked the boldness of the man and the whiplash of his rhetoric. But John was a cold man, truth be told. He seemed unable to acknowledge the contributions of others, the personal qualities that someone like Judas brought to the group.

When Jesus had greeted the Pharisees, they said to him, "Teacher, get out of here." They spoke with intensity. "Go north to the Decapolis or west into Samaria," they said, "but don't stay in territory Herod Antipas controls. He wants to kill you. He said it himself. More than ever these days, kings are nervous and rulers are taking counsel together. The times are dangerous for people of a public praise."

Jesus smiled. Judas thought how his Master's eyes had the yellowish steadfast stare of a cat: how cool his response! How nearly sarcastic in the face of danger!

Jesus said, "So, you have occasion to speak to Herod?"

The Pharisees nodded. "Now and again."

Jesus, still smiling, also nodded and said: "You go tell that fox these words exactly: *Behold, I cast out demons and perform cures today and tomorrow, and the third day I finish my course. Nevertheless, I must go on my way today and tomorrow and the day following. For it cannot be that a prophet should perish away from Jerusalem.* Those words exactly."

The Pharisees did not smile. Nor did they wish to keep talking. They promised to carry that message to Herod, then they uttered words of a heavy farewell and left, continuing north.

Judas, on the other hand, could scarcely contain the tumult of feelings in his breast.

Jerusalem — of course! Jesus was going to Jerusalem, slowly to be sure, but boldly and openly. No one could *not* know his going or his destination. And so wonderfully notorious was he that the rulers themselves were afraid of him. Ha! There might indeed be substance to his plan.

Judas Iscariot gazed at Jesus, blinking furiously against tears of pride. None of the other disciples seemed to recognize the true nature of the man they were following, the explosive potential in his subtle face.

What potential? Why, a power no less than Messianic!

Now that the Pharisees had departed, Jesus was speaking again. A large group had formed around him — yet perhaps it was Judas alone who understood the deepest meaning of the Master's words. He memorized them. His proud, passionate attention could not help but keep them in his mind as a manifesto for the future.

These are the words that caused his tears and turned his dream into a firm commitment:

Jesus said, "I came to cast fire upon the earth, and Oh! how I wish it were already kindled!"

Jesus' face was transported with the vision — the same vision, surely, as Judas was seeing.

The Lord said, "Do you think I've come to give peace on earth? No, I tell you, but division! Hereafter in one house there will be five divided, three against two and two against three, father against son and son against father, mother against daughter and daughter against her mother."

Judas whispered to himself certain more ancient words which these words recalled: *The day comes, burning like an oven, when all the evildoers will be stubble. The day that comes shall burn them up, says the Lord of hosts.*

Judas' heart was hammering. He tested the word. He whispered, *Messiah*.

Now Jesus raised his voice so that no one should miss the saying: "When you see a cloud rising in the west," he cried, "you say, 'A shower is coming.' And so it happens. When you see the south wind blowing, you say, 'There will be scorching heat.' And it happens. You hypocrites!"

Someone giggled. It was Judas who giggled. He couldn't help it. Jesus had uttered the sharp word *hypocrites*.

"You hypocrites!" Jesus cried. "You know how to interpret the appearance of earth and sky. Why, then, do you not know how to interpret the present time?"

Judas was overcome with gratitude. He bowed his head and covered his face. For he it was who had the gift! He could interpret. And it seemed to him that Jesus recognized that mystery between them alone.

Yes, yes, more certainly than roundheaded Simon Peter — since he knew more deeply than Simon what such a title truly meant — he spoke in his heart his personal confession: *You are the Christ! And we shall tread down the wicked! On the day when you act they shall be ashes under the soles of our feet, O Lord, O Messiah, Jesus, Son of David, the One who was to come — you!*

ii

MARY OF BETHANY

Jesus will sometimes find lodging with us. He arrives unannounced, often in the middle of the night. We rise up in the morning and find him sitting in our courtyard under the grape arbor, resting. He says he rests best sitting up.

My sister is immediately delighted to see him. "Well!" she says, clapping her hands and causing every soft part of her body to wobble: "Well, then! We must make cakes!"

During these last three years he has usually come in the company of his disciples. He first makes sure that they all have food and places to sleep in Bethany, then he slips silently into our courtyard.

But in the years before there were disciples — and several times since, truly — he has arrived completely alone.

I am convinced that Jesus spends the odd night under our arbor then steals away before the sunrise while we're still sleeping. Martha denies it. She says a man as civil as Jesus would never neglect the proprieties of a guest, greetings and eatings and compliments, permitting a host, she says, to be a host. But I think he prays here. And he leaves something of his spirit behind when he has gone. I seem to smell it. It is like a scent on the morning air.

Our little village lies about a mile and a half from Jerusalem, on the far side of the Mount of Olives. It's a convenient distance from the city — and Jesus must come to Jerusalem. He cannot keep away. Passover draws him. Passover has always drawn him here. And Pentecost, at the end of the barley harvest. And the Feast of Tabernacles. Last year, on the last day of that feast, Martha and I were there when Jesus suddenly stood up in the porches of Solomon and cried out, *If you are thirsty, come to me! All who believe in me, come and drink! For it is as the Scripture has said: "Out of his heart shall flow rivers of living water!"*

That saying caused a furious division among the people. Some of them questioned whether the Christ could possibly do any more signs than Jesus was doing. This was such a wonderful word that it caused the soles of my feet to tingle. At the same time there were rumors that the chief priests had sent officers into the Temple precincts to arrest Jesus. They didn't. The feast ended peaceably. But he was busy every day until the end — and that's the point. Jesus is always busy in Jerusalem, exhausted by the evening, in need of a quiet place apart. A sleepy village, an enclosed courtyard, a grape arbor.

He did not come to the Feast of Tabernacles this year. Maybe he knew there would be violence. I should ask him.

But he came to the Feast of Dedication. Hanukkah. Winter. Dreary, cold, wet December. But these were good days, after all. Even in my sleep I knew he had come.

"Martha," I said before either one of us had gotten up. "Martha, Jesus is here."

She was immediately awake. "How do you know?" she said.

"I can smell him," I said.

"You what?"

"It doesn't matter how I know," I said. "What matters is how we meet him. Martha?"

"What?"

"Please allow the man to rest. Let him arrange his day the way it pleases him best. Martha?"

She didn't answer. She gave her blankets a rough tug, got up, and went to the stove to kindle a fire.

Jesus was there, of course, hunched beneath the arbor. His arms were folded across his chest, his head leaning to the side, his wide brow frowning, his eyes closed. Sleeping, I think. And shivering for cold. I had just gone into the back room for a blanket, when I heard my sister start clucking like a hen:

"Jesus, Jesus, you'll catch your death out here. Come inside. It's going to rain. I've a good fire going — and we must make cakes."

So then I saw them both enter the house, Jesus first, bowing his head slightly at the low lintel and then smiling to see me. Martha second, a small storm of helpfulness.

I have always liked the fact that the Master shaves his face. When he smiles I can see all the lines. His cheeks wreathe from the high bone to the chin. It's a generous smile, even when his eyes — as lately they do — remain solemn.

So Jesus entered, smiling at me. I smiled back and shrugged, and we both measured our love for my sister Martha, who was oblivious of such communications, who was already bustling toward the clay stove to feel the sides of it for heat. No one is better than Martha for the consistency of a barley dough and the perfect temperature of a stove.

Olives were ripe. They were pressing them even then at Gethsemane. Martha went out to get fresh oil.

While she was gone, Jesus sat on a low stool. I sank down on the floor before him, and we began to talk.

I asked him about praying, how he does it when he is alone. I was thinking of the grape arbor.

"Lord," I said, "teach me to pray."

He has the eyes of evening suns in autumn. There is something of the far horizon underneath his looking.

He said, "When you pray, say 'Father.' "

"Father?" I said. And I thought, *Call the Lord God Father?*

Jesus put his wrist to his chin and continued, "Father, hallowed be your name. Your kingdom come. Give us each day our daily bread — " He smiled suddenly, wreathing his cheeks, and his eyes came very near. I think he was thinking of Martha and her daily cakes. Then he said, "Forgive us our sins, for we also forgive every one who is indebted to us. And lead us not into temptation.

"I tell you, Mary," Jesus said, leaning slightly forward, "if you ask, it will be given you. Seek, and you will find. Knock, and it will be opened to you. What father gives a serpent to children who ask for a fish? Well, if human parents know how to give good gifts to their children, how much more will the heavenly Father give the Holy Spirit to those who ask?"

I nodded and nodded all the while that Jesus was speaking. When something moves me deeply, I forget my face and my flesh. I seem to rise and inhabit the words as if they were huge rooms, warm mansions. Ah, Lord Jesus, immensely generous!

Martha bustled into the house, her arms full, her cheeks jiggling with haste and work and pleasure.

"I told Lazarus that the Master was here," she announced. "He'll be coming over for cakes," she said. "So much, so much to do!"

And do she did. The very air changes when my sister gets busy. It snaps as if cluttered by tiny lightning. It takes my breath away.

Soon the fresh oil was crackling and we began to smell fish. Where had she found fish so early in the morning?

"My sister," I called out loud. "The miracle worker!"

There came a sudden thump, dough thrown on a wooden board. When I turned, I saw Martha standing behind me, her fists on her hips, her expression hard and dark.

"Lord," she said, "don't you care that my sister has left me to serve alone? This morning she ordered me not to intrude upon your life. She said you needed rest. But here she sits, talking and listening, the perfect private pupil, keeping you to herself. So which of us is intruding after all!"

In that moment I realized that I had been wrong: Martha is *not* oblivious to the subtle communications that pass between the Master and me. She loves him, too. I know that. But I always thought it a more robust love, tougher and less tender. Ah, now I think that I have sinned against her.

Martha said, "Tell Mary to let you alone. Tell her to get up and help me."

But Jesus did not remove his gaze from her.

"Martha, Martha," he said, "you are anxious and troubled about many things. Only one thing is needful. Mary has chosen the good portion which shall never be taken away from her."

We ate her meal in a heavy silence after that.

When our brother Lazarus came into the house, he knew immediately not to ask questions. Martha's jowls were shaking; the flesh of her neck was blotchy red. We learned long ago to heed the signs of our sister's moods.

But shortly after breakfast Jesus went to her and touched her shoulder and said, "Martha, come with me."

He invited Lazarus and me in the same manner, calling us by name and saying, "It's the Feast of Dedication. Put on warm robes and walk with me into Jerusalem."

We did. We walked up over the ridge of the Mount of Olives, and I felt very good then. The sight of the Temple there — the porches, the high walls of massive stone, the pinnacles above them, and the great doors of the sanctuary itself — always fills me with comfort and assurances.

By now it was apparent to me that this was one of Jesus' private visits, a personal withdrawal. He must have left his disciples across the Jordan in Perea. Whether he had planned to sacrifice his privacy by taking the three of us with him to the Temple — well, that's another matter. I think it was the morning's mood that persuaded him.

But the generous Lord was talking also as we walked.

"Martha," he said, "how often have you repeated the Psalm, *The Lord is my shepherd*? Well, think of me as your good shepherd. The good shepherd lays down his life for the sheep. A hired hand, who does not own the sheep, sees the wolf coming and runs away. He leaves the sheep to be snatched and scattered by the wolf. He flees because he cares nothing for the sheep. I will never do that to you."

Jesus walked with a long, slow stride. I know that he was moderating his speed for Martha's sake. Her legs are short and, though she is a strong woman, after all, the hills cause her to puff.

Jesus' black hair had a fine dusting of mist on it.

Now he spoke in a lower tone, terribly intimate, and it seemed to me that his words were very heavy.

"I am the good shepherd. I know my own and my own know me, as the Father knows me and I know the Father. Martha, I will lay down my life for my sheep. This is the reason why the Father loves me, because I lay down my life that I may take it again. No one will take it from me, but I will lay it down of my own accord. I have power to lay it down, and I have power to take it again. This is the charge I have received from my Father."

Jesus fell silent, then, and we, too, were very quiet after that, all three of us, each thinking our own thoughts.

I felt afraid.

He led us into the Temple by way of the northeast corner, the gate through which the priests lead out the red heifer for sacrificing on the Mount of Olives.

A cold wind was blowing from the east. It had been to our backs while we walked; now it cut through our clothing, and I saw that Lazarus looked ashen. Martha's teeth had begun to chatter. Her eyes were swollen — because of what Jesus had said, I think. He led us into Solomon's portico, which was walled on its eastern side, a good protection against the weather.

As we walked among the great colonnades, people began to follow us. Many recognized Jesus. Soon a crowd had gathered, and we could hardly walk anymore.

Then a man called out, "How long will you keep us in suspense? If you are the Messiah, tell us so in plain words!"

I felt Martha grow tense beside me. Her breath whistled in her nose.

Jesus looked at the man who had challenged him and called out over the heads of the multitude, "I told you, sir, and you do not believe!"

His tone was absolute. He was not arguing. This was not a debate. Jesus was making a declaration as elemental as a mountain.

"The works I do in my Father's name," he called, "bear witness to me. But you do not believe because you do not belong to my sheep."

Jesus reached and took Martha's hand in his. I doubt anyone saw the gesture but me. Her face flamed.

Now Jesus shook back his long hair and called out for the whole multitude to hear: "My sheep hear my voice, and I know them, and they follow me, and I give them eternal life, and they shall never perish, and no one shall snatch them out of my hand! My Father, who has given them to me, is greater than all, and no one is able to snatch them out of the Father's hand. I and the Father are one!"

Some of the people broke into howling when they heard that, as if they were in pain. Others bared their teeth and picked up stones and drew back to throw them at Jesus.

His eyes flashed. "I've shown you many good works," he cried. "For which of them do you stone me now?"

"Not for good works," they yelled back, "but for blasphemy. You're a man, but you're making yourself out to be God!"

"If I am not doing the works of my Father," Jesus cried, "then don't believe me. But if I am doing them, even though you don't believe me, believe the works, that you may know that the Father is in me and I am in the Father."

Just then three officers of the Temple came plowing through the crowds, their left arms wrapped in ropes with which to bind a prisoner — Jesus, by the look in their eyes. Many people roared approval and made a way for them. Others tried to block their progress.

One of the officers outpaced the other two. He broke through alone and lunged at Jesus — but then ran straight into the folded fists of my dear sister Martha, who brought them up beneath his jaw with such wonderful force that his teeth snapped together on the tip of his tongue. For a moment he stood drooling and bleeding and bewildered. Martha was so short he couldn't tell where the hit had come from.

In that moment, Jesus vanished. No one saw him leave. No one saw him anymore.

So we went home alone, bending our heads against the dreary wind and holding close to one another, all of us thoughtful, though Martha seemed to have overcome her shivering.

All this took place two months ago. We haven't seen Jesus since then. But we've heard that he and his disciples are just over Jordan, in the same place where John first baptized at the beginning of his ministry.

And yesterday our brother Lazarus lay down on his bed and could not get up again. He's very sick. Martha thinks we should tell Jesus right now.

I myself, I think we ought to let him alone a while — let him arrange his days as he sees best.

iii

THOMAS

Thomas was trying to put his finger on the changes around him. It wasn't just the places where Jesus chose to go. It was the *times*. And the winds, the very taste of the air.

Surely the disciples themselves were changing. As long as he'd known Andrew, the man had been a quiet, withdrawing sort. But in recent months Thomas noticed that Andrew's silences were different. Not so much shyness, but a mute, wall-eyed anxiety.

Thomas said to him, "What's the matter?"

Andrew looked away and swallowed. "I don't know," he said.

Once Matthew had called Thomas the Esau of disciples. A scholar's joke. "What does that mean?" Thomas had said. Matthew nodded, grey as the grave, and said that he was a blunt hunter with questions. Thomas decided to take it as a compliment.

"Don't know?" the blunt hunter said to Andrew. "You haven't slept once in seven nights. You jump when somebody sneezes. What's the matter?"

Slowly Andrew revealed his thought: "This place. These stones. That bank of the river — this is where we first saw Jesus. John was preaching here." Andrew spoke in a hushed voice. "Right there," he said, pointing toward the Jordan. "That's the very spot where he baptized the Lord."

Thomas said, "So? What's the matter with that?"

Andrew looked at him, his eyes moist and pink — some sort of fear —
then he shuddered and he walked away.

Changing.

Judas, on the other hand, was perfectly gleeful. Especially when Jesus
harangued the crowds that were coming out to him, Judas would vibrate
like a harp string, and his bushes of black eyebrow would jump up and down
with delight.

Well, but that was in fact the most troubling change: what Thomas called
"The New Harangue." Jesus. The Teacher himself.

Ever since he had returned from the Feast of the Dedication, Jesus
seemed touchier than necessary. Or what? What? Hard to say. Critical?
Angry? Some fever was in him. Some painful or sacred zeal had been ignited
behind his eyes.

Thomas agreed that sins and sinners needed a public judging. Every age
must have its prophet. And prophets must be bold. But sometimes Jesus
seemed to lose plain sense and caution. Already the powerful people in
Jerusalem hated him. Now, with things like this "New Harangue," Jesus was
enraging his enemies, and these men, when they are enraged — they will
kill you.

So the disciples were on the east side of the Jordan, and Jesus was
standing on a flat stone, head and shoulders above the ever-present crowds,
preaching the same as he had preached from the beginning: "No servant
can serve two masters," he was saying, "for either he will hate the one
and love the other, or else be devoted to one and despise the other. You
cannot," Jesus preached, "serve God and mammon."

Well, then the Pharisees who were also always in these crowds muttered
to each other, "Two masters? What about the one who serves both God and
the devil — the *prince* of devils?"

Abruptly Jesus turned on them. "You! You justify yourselves before
men!" he cried, his voice like a battering ram. "But God knows whom you
serve, you hypocrites! What you exalt in the halls of human power is an
abomination in the sight of God!"

A Pharisee shouted, "You have a demon! You're a madman!"

Jesus' hair hung down his shoulders like a cape. To the entire crowd he
cried, "Beware the leaven of the Pharisees, which is hypocrisy!"

"What are you saying, Jesus of Nazareth?" shouted the Pharisees. "What
is this 'leaven' supposed to mean?"

Jesus cried, "Leaven means evil!"

Thomas climbed a stone to see who was challenging Jesus. It was the
biggest Pharisee among them, his throat engorged with anger.

"You blame *us*?" the Pharisee bellowed. "We know Moses and the
prophets! We know the law better than you, Jesus! Or if you know it, so
much the worse for you, since you do not keep it!"

"Keepers of the law," Jesus said with silky scorn.

Thomas looked and saw a smile on Jesus' face. Mirthless, kindless, cold as iron.

"Keepers of the law, are you?" He repeated the phrase like a refrain. "Excellent keepers of every visible law, yes. Washing the outside of the cup and the dish, washing your bodies so perfectly clean, both finger and chin."

Suddenly Jesus threw up his right arm. His eyes flashed, and he shouted, "You fools! Inside you are full of filth! He who made the outside, didn't he make the inside, too?"

Here it came. Thomas knew the signs and he feared the consequences, but nothing would stop Jesus now.

"Religious legalists! Hypocrites — woe to you!" he shouted. "For you tithe mint and dill and cumin, but you neglect the weightier matters of the law, justice and mercy and faith. Blind guides, straining out a gnat and swallowing a camel!

"Woe to you, hypocrites! You make your phylacteries broad and their fringes long. You love the place of honor at feasts, the best seats in the synagogues, honor in the marketplaces, being called rabbi. You are like whitewashed tombs, outwardly beautiful but full of dead men's bones within, full of hypocrisy and iniquity!

"Woe to you! You load the people with burdens hard to bear, but do not touch the burdens with one of your own fingers.

"Woe to you! You build tombs for the prophets whom your fathers killed. Yet you do again what your fathers did before. You serpents! You brood of vipers! How are you going to escape the devouring fires of Gehenna? Therefore the Wisdom of God says, *I will send them prophets and apostles, some of whom they will kill and persecute* — so that the blood of all the prophets, shed from the foundations of the world, may be required of this generation! I tell you, all the blood, from the blood of Abel to the blood of Zechariah, shall be required of this generation!"

Suddenly Jesus fell silent. The entire multitude seemed to be holding its breath. The day itself was still and windless.

Thomas looked at the face of the Master and was also moved to an aweful silence. The fires were out. Suddenly Jesus was pale and sad and very tired.

Slowly the Lord descended from his stony platform. Slowly he began to walk downhill toward the Jordan, staring again into the distance, due west.

People pressed backward, making a path for him.

Jesus began to speak again — scarcely above a murmur; but yet by a mystery everyone heard him. From the front of that congregation to the very back, every heart heard his words and every mind remembered them:

"Jerusalem, Jerusalem," he mourned, "killing the prophets and stoning those who are sent to you! How often would I have gathered your children together as a hen gathers her chicks beneath her wings, and you would not!

O my people, your holy house is now forsaken. I tell you, you will not see me again until you say, *Blessed is he who comes in the name of the Lord.*"

Jesus walked down to the Jordan and out into its waters. There he stood with his back to the crowds, waist-deep in the river, neither speaking nor turning around.

It was as if the sun had blackened. The people dispersed. They withdrew to their cities in Perea and Judea and Samaria: Bethabara, Qumran, Jericho, Jerusalem, Bethlehem, Emmaus, Lydda, Joppa, Sychar. They went home and did not come back.

By evening, only the disciples remained.

Mary Magdalene cut a pomegranate into halves and walked out into the water and stood next to Jesus a while.

Andrew said to Thomas, "That is the exact spot where John baptized him. And they killed John. What do you think they'll do to Jesus?"

Judas was beside himself, actually relishing the situation. At one point he said to Thomas, "Do you have any idea how many people go up to Jerusalem for the Feast of the Passover?"

Thomas said, "What's the point? Why do you want to know?"

Judas said, "I know! I already know how many."

"Then," snapped Thomas, "why did you ask me?"

But Judas could not contain himself. "One hundred and twenty-five *thousand!*" he cried. "Add to that the population of the city, and what do you get? One hundred and *eighty* thousand!"

"What's the point, Judas?"

"The point, Thomas, is that even a hundred Roman legions can't survive such a force."

From the river Thomas heard singing. He turned from Judas and strolled down to the banks of the Jordan. Mary, in a thin uncertain voice, was singing ancient verses meant for dancing, a common thing, very familiar:

> *Catch us the foxes,*
> *the little foxes*
> *that plunder the vineyards:*
> *Our vines are in blossom — come!*

She fell silent, and after a while she returned to the other women in the small camp of the disciples.

The closer one gets to the Dead Sea, the fewer fish there are in the Jordan. Simon Peter and James and Matthew therefore spent the afternoon snaring small fowl for supper. Joanna and Susanna and Mary Magdalene plucked the birds, dressed them, put them on wooden spits, and began to roast them. The meat sizzled and sent a pleasant odor into the air. The moods of the disciples softened.

Though he did not understand the changing times any better than before, Thomas saw the fires and smelled the roasting meat and felt consoled. The homely business of supper comforted him.

Near dusk Philip and Andrew came back from a trip into Machaerus. They had purchased several newly forged swords, each about two feet long with sheaths concealable under a tunic. Judas had given them money from the common treasury.

After night had fallen Jesus joined the band again, and everyone was together.

They arranged themselves on the ground. Jesus looked up to the dark heaven and gave thanks, and then the food was passed around.

While they were eating Jesus began to speak. "I know how you feel," he said. "You're right. Nothing will ever be the same again. But listen to me, my friends: Never fear those who can kill the body only. Rather, fear him who, after he has killed, has power to cast into the fires of Gehenna, too.

"But aren't five sparrows sold for two pennies? And not one of them is forgotten by God. Why, even the hairs of your head are all numbered. Therefore, fear nothing at all, for you are of more value than many sparrows.

"When they bring you before the synagogues and the rulers and the authorities, do not be anxious how you are to answer or what you are to say. For the Holy Spirit will teach you in that very hour what you ought to say.

"Fear not, little flock. It is your Father's good pleasure to give you the kingdom."

After that Jesus became quiet again. Then, when they were done eating, he went off by himself alone.

Thomas saw that Jesus' words had caused Mary Magdalene to cry.

He went to her and said, "What's the matter?"

She looked at him from her bruised eyes. "What's happening, Thomas?" she said. "Jesus is like a man in a thunderstorm — but no one else can see the wind or the rain. Thomas, where is he? What's happening to us?"

Thomas said, "He has gotten too angry these days. It'll get us into trouble."

Mary said, "No, I don't think Jesus is angry."

"Didn't he just rage at the Pharisees?"

"I think he's worried, Thomas. I don't think he hates the Pharisees. Maybe he's so sad it sounds like anger."

"Maybe," said Thomas. "But I get very nervous when he tells us not to be afraid."

∎

On the next day a man came to the disciples and asked where Jesus was. He said he had a message for him.

Simon Peter said, "Give me the message. I'll take it to him."

The man said, "I'm a friend of Martha and Mary in Bethany. They say: *Lord, he whom you love is ill.*"

After that the two men engaged in conversation for about an hour. Thomas listened. Judas, too, stole close and listened.

Simon questioned Martha's friend about tensions in Jerusalem, movements of troops, the mood of those in authority, rumors regarding the provinces. Though the man was but a plain citizen of the city, gossip ran strong, and he could tell Simon what the people were saying. He said that everyone knew the name of Jesus there, and that most people had some sort of opinion.

Judas said, "They like him, right?" He clapped his hands and answered the question himself: "Yes, yes, Jesus is the darling of the common folk. They adore him!"

When Jesus returned that afternoon, Simon gave him the message: *He whom you love is ill.* Jesus sighed. His face grew the more sorrowful, but he said nothing. He went and sat by the river and said nothing at all.

That day passed and the next day, too. Jesus was a ghost among the disciples. Once while he was sitting and staring westward, he allowed Mary to comb his long hair with slow strokes: *Catch us the foxes, the little foxes —* Suddenly she began to wash his clothes for him. It caused all the disciples to wash their garments, so that by the morning of the third day the bushes along the Jordan were covered in a festival of white robes, drying.

At noon Jesus said to the disciples, "Let's go into Judea again."

Simon's eyes darted among all the disciples as if looking for someone to say something. No one did — so he blurted the thought in his head: "Rabbi, they want to *kill* you there! Don't you know that? We'd be walking straight toward disaster."

Jesus said, "Aren't there twelve hours in the day? Those who walk in the day don't stumble because they have light. But those who walk in the nighttime stumble, because the light is not with them."

Simon Peter just blinked.

Thomas, too, did not know how that saying applied to Judea.

Then Jesus said, "Our friend Lazarus has fallen asleep. I am going to awaken him out of sleep."

Simon nearly exploded. "If he's sleeping, let him sleep! The man's on the way to recovery."

Jesus said, "Peter, he's dead. And for your sake I'm glad I wasn't there, so that you may believe. Please, let's go to him."

Dead! Lazarus was dead. Of course that required some honorable response. But Jesus was talking about Judea, where hatred and danger waited for them. Torn between friendship and fear, no one had a thing to say.

Finally, it was Thomas who spoke, that blunt hunter, simple Esau.

"I don't understand it, so I can't explain it," he said to the other disciples. "And I'm afraid of the consequences. But I think we should go with the Master. I think we should be ready to die with him."

iv

MARTHA

It was spring, almost the end of the rainy season. In two weeks the fields near Jericho would be ready for the barley harvest; two weeks after that the lowlands would be ready, and in a month the higher fields and the mountains.

Dreariness was nearly over. The sun was ruler of the day. The land was fat and rich, the crops abundant, the early green figs full on their branches.

Shepherds were preparing to lead huge flocks of yearlings toward Jerusalem. Soon hundreds of thousands of sheep would be bought and sacrificed at the Passover.

And those Jews who lived in foreign countries — Parthia, Mesopotamia, Asia, Crete, Cyrene, Egypt, Arabia — had already set out for Judea and Jerusalem and the feast.

There was an energy in the weather, a heightened excitement in people generally.

But for Martha of Bethany, the sister of Lazarus, there was no goodness in the season nor any kindness left in the world.

She was sitting in the corner of their sleeping room, her bedding rumpled and soiled. She didn't care. Her poor hair was unbrushed. She was herself unwashed. The creases in her heavier flesh were damp from the motionless sweat of long sitting. Periodically, people looked in through the door. She didn't care what they saw. They asked if there was something they might do, bring her food or sit and weep with her. Martha didn't even respond. She didn't care.

Ten or fifteen friends were sitting with her sister Mary in the large room. Sometimes they raised their voices and wailed. It irritated Martha, who kept her arms folded and made no sound at all.

Lazarus had died in this room. On her pallet.

He had lain sick for seven days. In seven days his force wasted away. He grew yellow and gaunt. The flesh of his face retracted from the mouth and nostrils and eye sockets as if someone were tightening it. Then he died. Four days ago he died.

He died late in the evening, when the tiny family was alone. By Martha's desiring, Lazarus lay on her pallet all that night while she and Mary stayed in the same room, anointing him with a sweet-smelling oil, weeping and whispering together, trying to remember things.

At dawn they announced the death, and the mourners gathered. Many, many people began to lament, tearing their garments, sobbing, sometimes uttering screams so shrill that Martha's jaw would snap shut. This is the reason why she had wanted the night with her brother and sister alone: quietness. Plain quietness.

Certain women then wrapped Lazarus in long linen strips. Men brought a new bier. A procession formed at the door of their house — good friends carrying the bier and the white corpse high at their shoulders — then Mary and Martha went forth in front of a sad company, walking out of Bethany to the tombs some distance from the places where people lived.

Three days ago, then, Lazarus was buried.

And the mourners all came back to their house. And Martha took to her room, yesterday and today — tomorrow, too, for all she cared. She had ceased to care about anything.

His face. They had even wrapped her brother's face in the white cloth. He had gone faceless through the town to the crypt, and now he lay behind a stone with neither face nor feature of any sort, a rough-hewn slab of rock, the door forever shut.

An elderly woman looked into Martha's room. She whispered something, then turned and started to go, but Martha became suddenly alert.

"Wait!" she called. "What did you say?"

"I said that Jesus is coming. He's on the road from Jericho."

"Ha!" It was a flat, sarcastic laugh. They had not received so much as one word from him before Lazarus died! Even their messenger, when he returned from his mission to bring the Lord back, had no communication from Jesus.

Martha came up from the floor in a swift, pumping motion, then lowered her head and fairly ran through the large room and out the house.

"The road from Jericho!" she shouted aloud. "Yes, and how long ago didn't we send friends down that road, begging help! Ha!"

Martha had a short stride. Neither was she a light woman. Nevertheless, she was strong. She moved at a steady pace until she saw Jesus ahead of her, then she broke into a lunging run.

Jesus stopped and waited.

When Martha got to him she made two fists and began to beat him on the chest. She hit him and hit him and for the first time since Lazarus died she burst into tears.

"Why weren't you here?" she wailed.

Jesus stood watching Martha with golden eyes.

"If you had been here, my brother would not have died!"

Now Jesus grabbed her fists in his own hands. Martha stopped struggling. She put her forehead against his chest and sobbed.

"Even now I know," she said, "that whatever you ask from God, God will give you."

Jesus said softly, "Your brother will rise again."

"I know," Martha whined. "I know, I know — in the resurrection at the last day."

Jesus said, "I am the resurrection and the life. Those who believe in me, though they die, yet shall they live. And those who live and believe in me shall never die. Martha?" Jesus stepped back so that she had to look at him.

"Martha," he said, "do you believe this?"

She nodded. She looked up and allowed her eyes to enter the halls of his endless gazing, and whispered, "Yes, Lord, I believe that you are the Christ, the Son of God, he who is coming into the world."

Jesus released her wrists and laid his hands on Martha's head. Then, smoothing her fierce hair with many strokes, he said, "Go tell Mary that I would like to see her."

So Martha hurried home again. Jesus was right: her hair was unkempt. Her clothing was dirty. Even her mouth tasted foul. She should cook. She should wash herself and make cakes.

She ran through the courtyard, into the house, still filled with people, and knelt beside Mary and whispered, "The Teacher is here. He's calling for you."

Immediately Mary rose up and the two women went out together. Martha led her to the Jericho road to Jesus, and all the mourners followed. All of them.

As soon as Mary saw Jesus, her face collapsed and she started to cry all over again. She came toward him and fell at his feet. "Lord," she said, "if you had been here my brother would not have died."

Jesus drew a heavy breath. He lifted his eyes to all the grieving people.

"Where have you laid him?" he said.

Mary whispered, "Come and see."

Suddenly the tears began to stream from the Lord's eyes. He was weeping.

"See?" a woman said to Martha. "See how he loved your brother?"

Now the whole procession followed Mary and Martha and Jesus by a winding path to the tombs east of the village. Jesus did not speak. Martha and Mary walked on either side of him.

"There," Martha said, pointing to a small cave with a slab of new stone covering the front of it. "That's where we buried my brother."

Jesus moved ahead of the rest, close to the tomb. He ran his finger along fresh gouge-marks in the stone, then turned to the mourners and pointed to three men. "Please," he said, "come and take the stone away."

Martha was shocked. "Lord, it has been four days since he died!" she said. "There'll be a horrible odor."

Jesus looked directly at her and said, "Didn't I tell you that if you believed you would see the glory of God?"

Martha had no answer.

Jesus turned and watched while the stone was removed from the grave. Then he lifted his eyes and said, "Father, I thank you that you have heard me. I know you hear me always, but I say this for the sake of these people — that they may believe it was you who sent me here."

All at once the Lord Jesus cried out in a ringing voice: "Lazarus! Come forth!"

Martha gasped and began to pant. The sound of his cry had caused her heart to hurt within her.

The black interior of the tomb now filled with a dim white shadow. The shadow grew thick and moved, then the dead man emerged, his hands and his feet still bound in linen strips, his face still hidden by the white cloth.

Jesus walked to Martha and put his hand on her shoulder. "Unbind him," he said, "and let him go."

V

JOSEPH OF ARIMATHEA

As soon as the men in the Chamber of Hewn Stones came to order, the high priest announced his reason for convening the council again under unusual circumstances.

"Jesus of Nazareth," he said. "This Jesus of Nazareth is seizing the imaginations of the people. Tens of thousands say they belong to him. Actually, they say they *believe* in him. They love the signs, they marvel at his wonders, and now it is reported that he has raised a man from the dead. Dead for four days, his soul surely gone from the body, yet — so these enthusiasts say — Jesus of Nazareth gave him life again. He is *here*, sirs. Right now the dead man is walking the streets of Bethany, and people can go and see the proof for themselves."

"So, then," said a member of the council, "what are we going to do?"

Another man, a Pharisee, said, "It isn't these signs only. It's his rhetoric, too. Jesus of Nazareth denounces us wherever he goes. Not the Romans, but *us*, his own people."

"He's a Galilean, isn't he?" said a third. "How many messiahs have come out of Galilee in the last years? It's a cauldron of revolution."

"But *this* one damns us in public and the people love it! His language is fiery. His effect is frightening."

"What are we going to do about him?"

"If we let him go on like this, soon the whole country will be chasing after him."

"And if he appears at Passover this year, he could tear the city apart with riot."

"Yes, and then what? Why, the Romans will come and destroy both our holy place and our nation."

"What are we going to do?"

"I think we should murder the fellow he raised from the dead."

"Where is Jesus now? Is he still in Bethany?"

"No. We checked. Even before rumors of this resurrection hit Jerusalem, he and his followers had vanished."

"So we don't know where he is."

"Maybe we want him at the Passover so we can find him."

"Well, surely we should give orders that anyone who knows where he is must tell us immediately."

"It's done. We've already done that."

"Do you know that Passover pilgrims are even now arriving in Jerusalem? People are coming early because they want to see this Jesus of Nazareth."

"What are we going to do about him?"

Caiaphas the high priest now rose to speak. He had allowed the chatter to go on long enough.

"Listen carefully," he said, "and take the full meaning of my words. It is expedient for us that one man should die for the people, and that the whole nation should not perish."

All the men fell silent. Someone whispered, "Ah — like Barabbas!"

The huge room in which the council met had vaulted hallways thirty feet high, resting on eighty-eight pillars of massive stone, above which were the Temple courtyards.

By one of these pillars sat a man in expensive robes, his dark beard neatly trimmed.

While others delivered themselves of various opinions, this man leaned back and held his peace. He was not given to sudden judgments, nor to changing the judgment once he had expressed it. He was, therefore, much respected by the rest of the council. He had built his own fortune by business acumen, by public honor and private honesty. He was a genuine seeker of the kingdom of God. His name was Joseph of Arimathea, and he felt within himself deep stirrings of admiration for this Jesus of Nazareth.

When Caiaphas pronounced it "expedient" that one man should die for the people, Joseph took the full meaning indeed — and more, perhaps, than Caiaphas himself had meant thereby.

Leaning back by his pillar of huge stone, Joseph believed he had heard a prophecy: *One man shall die for the nation, and not for the nation only, but for the children of God scattered everywhere in the world.*

At the same time, the rest of the council rose up and declared in passionate unanimity, "Then he must die! To save us from riots and the Romans, Jesus of Nazareth must be put to death!"

vi

JUDAS

For several weeks Jesus had secluded himself and his disciples in a small town east of the Jordan at the very edge of the desert.

Then, early one Sabbath, he said, "Let's go."

Simon Peter said, "Go where, Lord?"

Jesus said, "To Jerusalem. For the Feast of the Passover."

Judas Iscariot let out a squawk of joy, and his stomach went into spasms. The time was at hand! Jesus and he: they had a plan together, and now they were about to execute it.

Every disciple suffered a private response to Jesus' announcement. They walked in silence the morning long. The women drew near to other women. They walked in tight company together. No one was happy but Judas. But then, neither did anyone know what Judas knew.

By the time they came near to Jericho, a crowd had attached itself to him again.

There was a blind man sitting by the road, begging.

Suddenly he reached out and grabbed the hem of Andrew's robe. "Who's passing?" he asked. "It sounds like someone important is passing."

Poor Andrew was caught by surprise. He stammered, "Jesus. It's, um, Jesus of Nazareth — "

Immediately the blind man began to wave his arms and shout, "Jesus! Jesus! Son of David! Have mercy on me!"

People everywhere turned to look. "Jesus? *Jesus* is here?"

Simon Peter, clearly tense, bellowed at the beggar, "Shut up!"

But he only shouted the louder, "Jesus! Jesus!"

Simon lunged at the man.

Judas burst out laughing. "No use to threaten him, Simon," he laughed. "The fellow is *blind*!"

Simon glowered. Judas went into a fit of giggling, and the beggar kept shouting, "Son of David!"

"Andrew," Jesus called, "bring the man to me."

Andrew did.

And when the blind man stood before him, Jesus said, "What do you want me to do for you."

"Lord," he said, "let me receive my sight."

Jesus said, "Receive your sight. Your faith has made you well."

Immediately sight illumined the man's eyes, his whole face and posture. He was suffused with joy, and in the same loud voice that had been begging, he began to praise God for the good thing done. Then he, too, joined the multitude following Jesus.

Down Jericho streets the people moved, past pools and parks and gardens and great villas. Jericho had been a city built by Herod the Great. He had wintered here. He had perished here. He left behind a rich municipality — and especially rich for those who gathered taxes here.

Jesus stopped beside a gracious garden. The whole congregation behind him also stopped.

Then he threw back his head and called out: "Zacchaeus! Zacchaeus, come down!"

There was a man in the tree above him. A little man. When he dropped from the branches and stood self-consciously in front of Jesus, everyone was surprised that he was also a *rich* little man! A tax collector! This fellow owned the most lavish villa in all Jericho.

Jesus said, "I must stay in your house tonight."

Little Zacchaeus beamed. He said, "You, O Lord, and your disciples, too!"

Judas nearly burst with admiration for his Master. Lo, there wasn't a level of society which he had not touched and bound to himself.

A beggar and a rich man, both in a single day — and the rich man would be most helpful for the cause!

On the following day they drew near Bethany at the Mount of Olives, no more than a mile and a half from Jerusalem. Jesus called to himself the sons of Zebedee and pointed toward a tiny village opposite, Bethphage.

This, for Judas, was the only disappointment in an otherwise perfect day: that Jesus had not chosen him.

"Go into that village," Jesus said to James and John, "and you will find a colt tied on which no one has ever sat. Untie it and bring it here. If anyone asks why you're taking it, simply say, 'The Lord has need of it.' "

Judas watched them walk into town. Even at that distance, he saw the colt that they untied. Some people stopped them and asked a question, but when the brothers pointed uphill toward Jesus, they let them go again.

Then here they came, leading the colt.

Judas knew exactly what was going to happen. Therefore he was the one who showed the disciples — no, he showed the entire multitude! — what sort of demonstration should now erupt around his Master. He tore off his robe and threw it over the back of the colt. Simon saw that. He grinned and did the same. So did Matthew and Mary Magdalene — they heaped the colt with a humble saddling. Then James and John lifted Jesus himself and set him on the animal, and Jesus began to ride. The King! — he was riding toward Jerusalem.

As he went, more and more people threw their garments down in the road before him. It became a carpet of clothing and praise. People ran back to groves of trees and cut branches, then rushed forward and spread them also in the way. A vast, laughing multitude surrounded him now, some running ahead, some following. Excitement raced from heart to heart like fire in a dry field. They shouted and sang songs.

Then, as they were descending the mount to the gates of Jerusalem, the voices of thousands of people all became one voice, one massive music, singing, *Hosanna to the Son of David! Blessed is the King who comes in the name of the Lord. Hosanna! Hosanna in the highest!*

Judas was delirious. The city gates began to pour forth another mass of people equal to the first. Those who came out converged with those who were coming in, so the singing was doubled and the roar of it cracked the high blue vaults of heaven. It seemed that all Judea was spiraling down to this sole place for the praise of Jesus of Nazareth. Oh, what a mighty army! Now truly, the very legions of Rome must tear off their greaves and beg for mercy.

Certain rulers with bright red faces had also come out of the city. They fought their way to Jesus on the colt.

"Teacher!" they screamed, "control your disciples! Tell them to shut up!"

But Jesus shouted, "I tell you, if these were silent the very stones would cry out!"

Judas laughed with magnificent glee. He couldn't help himself. He was sailing on a sea of victory, surely, surely! And the water was the people, and the ship was his Lord, and the wind was behind them, surely!

Shaking with laughter, seeking quick camaraderie, he glanced up at Jesus — and suddenly there descended to the earth a horrible silence! Or so it seemed. Judas felt as if he and Jesus were alone beneath a green sea where there was no sound but the voice of Jesus only.

Because Jesus was crying!

He was not rejoicing in the public acclaim nor glorying in the advent of his kingdom now. He was crying! He was gazing at the stones of the city and allowing tears to run down his face.

Was Judas the only one who could hear the tragic sobbings of the Master? He wanted to grab Jesus and shake him. *Don't lose heart now!* Judas howled in his heart.

Jerusalem, he heard Jesus saying, *O Jerusalem, would that even today you knew the things that make for peace. But they are hid from your eyes. For the days shall come when your enemies will surround you and dash you to the ground, you and your children within you. They will not leave one stone upon another in you, because you did not recognize the time of your visitation.*

For just a moment Judas suffered a stark panic. The words might be words of a defiant messiah, but the tone was defeat. The tone was melancholy. Judas screamed out loud, "The kingdoms of the world, Master! The jewels of creation! Their power and their glory all are yours, if you will fight for them!"

Immediately it broke the spell: the thunderous song of the people rushed in again, and Judas heard roarings on every side. He and Jesus once more were riding the great surge of royal power through the city itself! They were at the very gates of the Temple.

Jesus dismounted. The Lord went afoot, now, majestic and wrathful, through the Triple Huldah Gate in the southern wall of the Temple, his golden eyes fixed and flaming. The disciples could scarcely keep up with him.

Then Judas saw where Jesus was going. The booths. The hundred shops in the southern portico. The tables, the selling of animals for sacrifice, the money exchange, commerce in the precincts of the Temple.

As he approached the busy marketplace, Jesus twisted three cords into a whip. Then he cried in a piercing voice, "Away! Away!" and began to crack his furious whip over the heads of merchants.

Judas trembled with pleasure. Now it was starting. This was Messiah! Jesus, hurling fire to earth! Jesus, the howl of God, whose voice is a rod of iron: *Judgment has come, O you people!* For look how the Master flings to the pavement the coins of the money changers! How he tips their tables over! And those who sell sheep and oxen and pigeons — them he drives out of the Temple, crying accusations like a Zealot: "Away with these things! Away! It is written, *My house shall be a house of prayer.* But you have made it a den of thieves! Away!"

All these things took place on the first day of the week, the Sunday before the Feast of Passover. On that day Judas said in his soul, *This is he whose coming is a refiner's fire — and who shall endure it now? Who shall be standing when this week is done?*

All the way back to Bethany, Judas wiped tears from his eyes and sighed with excitement.

But that was the last time he felt such joy. That was the last time Judas Iscariot was glad, for the rest of his life.

∎

Even before dawn the following day, when no one else was stirring, Jesus woke John, left Bethany, and slipped into the old part of Jerusalem through the Potsherd Gate. Judas, filled with a high anticipation for the glory of this day, followed.

The Potsherd Gate gives into the Tyropoeon valley, which transects Jerusalem from north to south. Jesus and John walked north a while, their heads bowed down, then they climbed the ancient steps which led up the west slope of the valley to the upper city. Here were the houses of wealthier people and narrow streets between them.

Judas had to draw nearer in order to keep them in view. It nagged him that he was reduced to the role of a spy: but no one else knew the mind of the Messiah as well as he. Judas had to be always available.

Jesus and John walked past the ritual baths of the Essenes on the southwestern side of the city, then turned north and ascended Mount Zion in the direction of Herod's palace. Pontius Pilate was in residence there till the end of Passover, he and his legions. Judas nodded sagely. The Master was about to rise up and lead a mighty rebellion of the people: of course he would first scout the Praetorium, that seat of Roman power.

But Jesus never got that far.

Certain Essenes lived on the southwestern corner of Mount Zion, members of the same community that dwelt in the desert, obeying the laws of Moses and looking for the coming of the kingdom of God. These are the people who thought that John the Baptizer was the Priest at the end of the ages — just as others thought Jesus was that other figure, the King at the end of the ages.

Now Jesus and John stopped before one of the Essene houses, an elaborate structure of white stone and iron lattices. He knocked lightly on a door which faced down the mount to the west. A man stepped out. There was a rich mosaic on the pavement of the vestibule and, behind the first building, a higher house, an upper room well protected by the rest of the compound.

The three men bent their heads together for a brief exchange of words, then separated.

So here was Judas' second irritation: the brief meeting had looked very much like an assignation. Strategizing. Some kind of planning in which he, Judas, had no part!

Swiftly, now, Jesus was striding back the way he had come.

He turned a corner and shocked them both by suddenly appearing face-to-face with Judas.

"What are you doing here?" Jesus said.

For a moment Judas was dumbfounded. He could feel his eyebrows twitching. "Someone," he said, "someone had to watch your back."

"Why?" said Jesus.

Why?

The answer was so obvious to Judas that the question astonished him. Unless Jesus was testing him. Or unless he was speaking cryptically to conceal from John the secrets that existed between them.

Judas smiled and whispered, "Lord, you know."

Jesus did not smile. He frowned. "I know that you have purchased swords," he said. "Judas, *you* should know that I have no need of swords."

Messiah has no need of swords! The saying excited Judas, but that excitement became the measure of his disappointment in the rest of that day, Monday. Every indication of strength and purpose and rebellion stopped right here. Jesus sighed. His face sagged. The melancholy mood fell upon him again, and Judas became confused.

"Master? Master, what are we going to do?"

But Jesus and John were already retracing their route to the Tyropoeon valley.

Just at the bottom of the ancient steps to the lower city, they met Philip and Andrew and the beginnings of a morning crowd.

"Lord," said Philip, "there are several Greeks here, who came to the feast especially to see you."

Jesus heaved another crushing sigh and then, for no reason that Judas could discern, delivered a little lesson on death. "The hour has come for the Son of man to be glorified," he said. "Truly, I say to you: unless a grain of wheat falls to the earth and dies, it remains just a grain of wheat. But if it dies, it will bear much fruit."

Jesus looked directly at Judas and said, "Those who love their lives will lose them. But those who hate their lives in this world will keep them hereafter, eternally — "

All at once the Master groaned and sank to his knees. He folded his arms across his stomach and bent forward. The people became a sepulcher for silence. And Judas felt his face grow hot with distress. He was embarrassed for the Lord, suddenly revealing such pain! Such weakness.

"Oh, my soul!" Jesus cried. "My soul is so troubled! And what should I say now? 'Father, save me from this hour'? No."

Slowly he lifted his head and rose to standing again. "No," he said. "It was for this very reason that I have come to this hour. Therefore I say, 'Father, glorify your name — ' "

As if in answer, the sky exploded.

"Thunder!" the people cried.

But John whispered, "An angel was speaking to him."

"So, so," said Jesus softly. "That was a voice from heaven — for your sake. Now begins the judgment of this world. Now the prince of this world will be driven out. And I, when I am lifted up — I will draw all people to myself."

Judas said, "Lord, what do you mean, *lifted up?*" It sounded like exaltation. Judas wanted to pursue exaltation.

But Jesus looked heavy and sick. "It's the reason I need no swords, Judas," he said. "To those who have ears to hear, it reveals what sort of death I am going to die."

Death and dying. Morbid and disconnected conversation: that's all that happened on Monday. The passions of the people began to dissipate. Surprise was lost. Surely the authorities were contriving ways to contain Jesus, his person, his force, and his effect.

And Judas began to be afraid.

■

On Tuesday Jesus went with his disciples to Jerusalem and into the courts of the Temple.

A light rain was falling, so they gathered under the roof of the Portico of Solomon, and there Jesus continued his talk, but he took no action. Absolutely none.

He told a story about a landowner who had let his vineyard out to tenants. When the harvest had been taken in, the landowner sent a servant to get from the tenants his due, but they beat him up. He sent a second servant and they beat him, too. The third servant they murdered. So the landowner decided to send his son. "His beloved son," Jesus said. "Surely they would respect his son."

But when the tenants saw that it was the son, they thought to make the vineyard their own by killing the landowner's only heir.

"What will the landowner do," Jesus said at the end of his story, "when he finds that the tenants have executed his son? Put his beloved son to death? Don't you think he will come and destroy them, too?"

Judas saw certain members of the ruling council among the people in Solomon's porch. He noticed how stiff and selfconscious they became when Jesus spoke of executions. Quickly they left the area. But Jesus let them go. He hadn't so much as engaged them in dialogue. No action. Only talk.

A scribe said to him, "Which commandment is the first of all?"

This was such a common question, an old rabbinic test; yet Jesus answered it.

"*Love the Lord your God will all your heart and all your soul and all your mind*," he said. "This is the first and great commandment. And the second one is like it, *Love your neighbor as yourself.*"

Judas couldn't believe it. This sounded like conciliation! Even so did the gentlest, most maundering rabbis teach their students. There was neither prophecy nor power in such talk! Where was the messianic cry? Where was the captain of the hosts of heaven and the catalyst of revolution on earth?

The Passover was only days away. Multitudes were filling Jerusalem like a hive with energy and expectation.

And Jesus was muttering rabbinic love.

Later, as they wandered out of the Temple, that thick-minded dullard of a disciple — Thomas — paused to marvel at the walls.

"Look, Teacher," he said. "How huge the stones are, yet how close the masonry!"

Jesus responded in odd, distracted tones: "The time is coming when not one stone will be left on another. They will all be thrown down."

Again, Judas was confused. The Messiah was to restore the Temple and Jerusalem. Twice, now, Jesus had spoken of the city's destruction.

At the Mount of Olives Jesus turned and looked back at Jerusalem. The rain had stopped. The clouds had lifted. A bright sun caused the entire city to shine resplendent on its hills, ten degrees of holiness, the crown of God!

But Jesus drove Judas mad by heaving another, bottomless sigh.

To provoke him, Judas said, "When, Lord? When will the beautiful stones come down? Tell us what signs we can look for that these things are finally going to be accomplished?"

Jesus said, "When you hear of wars and rumors of wars, don't worry. They are not the end. Nations will rise against each other; there will be earthquakes and famines — but these are just the beginning of the birth pains.

"Listen to me: the gospel must first be preached to all the nations. And those who preach it will be hated for my name's sake."

Jesus looked at Judas. "But you asked for signs," he said. "Your dreams, Judas, are both greater and lesser than you know. Here are your signs: when you see the desolating sacrilege set up where it should not be, *then* let everyone in Judea flee to the mountains. For then will occur such tribulation as has never been — no, not from the beginning of creation.

"Signs? After the tribulation the sun will be darkened and the moon made dim, and the stars will fall from heaven!

"And then the Son of man will come in clouds with power and glory, all the angels surrounding him. He will sit on his glorious throne, and all the nations will be gathered before him, and he will separate them one from another as a shepherd separates the sheep from the goats. The sheep he will place at his right hand, and the goats at his left. And which, Judas, do you think will be saved? And why do you suppose they will be saved? Because of war? Because of triumphs and victories and grand defeats?

"Listen to my last parable of all:

"The King will say to those at his right hand, *Come, O blessed of my Father, inherit the kingdom prepared for you from the foundation of the world. For I was hungry and you gave me food. I was thirsty and you gave me drink. I was a stranger and you welcomed me, naked and you clothed me, sick and you visited me, in prison and you came to me.*

"But the righteous will ask, 'When, Lord, did we see you hungry and feed you? Or thirsty and give you drink? When did we welcome you or clothe you or visit you?'

"And the King will answer them, *Truly, when you did it to one of the least of my brothers and my little sisters, you did it unto me.*"

Judas put his head down and started to walk away.

Jesus said, "Wait! There is one more part to the parable. The King will say to those at his left hand, *Depart from me, you cursed, into the eternal fire prepared for the devil and his angels. For I was hungry and you gave me no food. I was thirsty and you gave me no drink, a stranger, naked, sick, in prison and you did nothing at all for me.*

"But they, too, will ask, 'When did we see you hungry or thirsty or a stranger or in any need and did not minister to you?'

"Then the King will answer, *Truly, as you did it not unto the least of these, you did it not unto me.*

"Now, Judas, go your way. Hear with your ears. See with your eyes. Watch for the coming of the true kingdom of God. Watch, I say, for it will surely take you by surprise!"

■

That evening the disciples and Jesus went to eat with Lazarus in Bethany. They reclined around a table while his sister Martha served them.

Then Lazarus' other sister Mary entered the room and walked to Jesus carrying an alabaster flask of ointment, pure nard, extremely expensive. She went behind him, where his feet were stretched out on the floor, and she knelt down. She broke the flask and anointed the feet of her Lord with a slow flow of oil. Then she wiped them in her long hair, and the house was filled with the precious scent.

In a choked voice, Judas Iscariot said, "What about the poor, Lord? What about those who are least in the world? Shouldn't this ointment have been sold for three hundred denarii, and the money given to *them*?" His face was red with emotion.

Jesus, too, reacted with emotion. "What's the matter with you?" he said. "Who are you to blame this woman?"

Judas' eyebrows rose to his hairline. He couldn't utter a word.

"Let her alone," Jesus continued. "She has done for me the good work, sir, that no one else has thought to do. She has anointed my body in advance of my burial. The poor will be with you always. I, on the other hand, will not always be with you. Mary understands that. Do you? *Do* you? Do you, sir, take my meaning now?"

Judas could not so much as nod. He was suffocating in humiliation.

By sunrise on Wednesday, Judas had made up his mind.

He resolved to accept confusion no more. He did not understand Jesus; he could not penetrate the Master's recent talk; but he could take matters into his own hands and *create* the clarity that he and the times required.

Everything that Judas had foreseen was coming to pass: multitudes had gathered in the holy city, intense with anticipation. They were like dry kindling waiting for the flame. That flame must be some precipitating act by his Master.

Jesus was not acting. But perhaps Judas could himself trigger that act.

Clearly, the revolutionary power lay with Jesus of Nazareth. It was Jesus whom the people had extolled as Messiah just three days ago. And then Jesus had exhibited a divine wrath in the Temple. Bold in opposing the authorities, mighty in his miracles, absolutely transporting in his rhetoric, Jesus had to be the Messiah! Perhaps these latter hours he had become a reluctant Messiah, but no one else fulfilled prophecy as he did.

Therefore, Judas had decided not to plumb the reluctance, but rather to force the Lord into action.

He would arrange a confrontation from which Jesus could not withdraw *except* by openly displaying his messianic power.

Judas would bring the enemies of Jesus directly *to* him — yes, and to his disciples, too! When the enemies attempted to attack both him and those whom he loved, the Lord would have no choice but to take up his royal power and reveal himself as the anointed one, the King!

On Wednesday morning, then, Judas presented himself to the chief priests and the captains of the Temple, and said, "You've given orders that anyone who knows where Jesus of Nazareth is must come and tell you."

"We have," said the chief priests.

"And I suppose you wish to arrest him somewhere apart from the multitudes."

"Continue."

"Well, I can lead you to him when he is in a private and an unprotected place."

They said, "But you're not a stranger to us, sir. We know that you are one of his disciples. Why would you betray your own Master to us?"

Judas replied immediately. "For money," he said. "Pay me and I'll do it. Pay me enough, and I'll do it soon."

The chief priests acted exactly as Judas thought they would. This part of the plan worked very well. In order to bind him to themselves, they weighed out thirty pieces of silver then and there, and poured it all into the bag Judas had brought for that purpose.

38

JESUS

i

S imon Peter thrust his head into the room and said, "Where should we go to prepare for the Passover? Do you have a place in mind?"

Jesus looked up from the scroll he'd been reading. "I do," he said. He stood and walked to the lattice and called: "John, would you come in here?" Then he sat down on the floor again, his back cradled by the corner of the room, his wrists on his knees, hands loose.

"What are you reading?" said Simon the Rock.

"Songs of comfort, Peter," Jesus said, "songs of comfort and strength."

John came in and stood by Simon.

Jesus couldn't help it. He smiled at the incongruous pair: tough, smooth-shaven Simon, his head shaped like some weapon the Romans would make, cheeks puffing, breathing hard, his arms ever bent for action — and John, sweet John of the enormous eyes and the ascending eyebrows, pliable John who, though he would with his brother James strut and thunder, could nevertheless smile for Jesus such an ethereal smile that, seeing it, Jesus suffered the warm breath of love in his bosom. Of all the disciples, Simon Peter loved Jesus loudest and strongest. John seemed nearly indifferent to such passions — yet it was John who caused them most.

Smiling, then, Jesus said, "Go to Jerusalem. Listen: go round by the Kidron valley and enter at the southwest through the Gate of the Essenes. When a man carrying a pitcher of water passes you and starts to climb Zion, follow him. John knows the way. John even knows the house where he will stop. But we won't know if the place will be safe today. Therefore, ask the householder to show you the guest room where we can eat the Passover. If all is well, he will take you to a large upper room already furnished. Prepare the meal for us there."

They left. Jesus closed his eyes and imagined their going: Simon in the lead, Simon huffing and bustling a brave obedience, all full of his mission. Though John knew better where they were going, in his serenity it would never occur to him to lead.

Soon Simon and John faded from Jesus' mind. The smile vanished. The little bloom of loving he had felt drooped within him. The air went out of his mouth in endless sighing. His breast collapsed.

Jesus took up his scroll again and read:

> *I love the Lord because he has heard my supplications.*
>   *The snares of death encompassed me;*
>   *I suffered distress and anguish.*
> *Then I called on the name of the Lord —*
>   *"O Lord, I beg you, save my life!"* —

He stopped reading. He bowed his head and allowed his hair to fall like a curtain between his face and the eyes of any who might enter his room in Bethany now.

"Abba," he whispered.

It was Thursday.

This was Thursday of the week of the Passover, the thirty-third year of his life.

"Abba. Abba," he whispered.

Thursday, the fifth day of the week in which he was to die.

ii

At evening Jesus entered the upper room with ten of the disciples. Simon and John met them there. The table was neatly set. Already the prescribed foods had been brought in, filling the room with a rich aroma: lamb, unleavened bread, a sauce of bitter herbs, wine.

The table, low to the ground, was shaped like a C so the servants could enter the middle and approach each place. One would not sit at such a formal meal. The table was furnished with low couches on three sides of it; one reclined on these.

The room was spare. There were few ornaments in the house of the Essenes. Along the wall another narrower table held water and towels. A rug received the sandals of the people as they came in. Already the candles were lit. It was dusk outside. Breezes bent the candle flames. Shadows were gathering at the high ceiling.

Jesus, when he had removed his sandals, went to a central place at the table. The others found places to the left and the right of him. Jesus motioned them to recline. So, in a genial ripple of motion and chatter, the twelve disciples lay down on the couches, crooked their left elbows, and propped their heads on their hands.

Jesus continued to stand, looking down both sides of the table.

"I — " he said, "With all my heart I have earnestly desired to eat this Passover among you before I suffer — "

Conversation ceased. Faces tilted toward him: his people, frowning, questioning, exhibiting surprise and a sudden blinking pity — his foolish people, still ignorant of what was to be, though he had told them; he had told them! He had said it clearly and often. His poor sheep-people, his munching followers, his disciples.

"I tell you, I will not eat it again until it is fulfilled in the kingdom of God."

While they watched him, then, Jesus shed his robe and went to the side table and picked up a clean towel and tied it around his waist in the manner of a servant. He gathered his hair in another towel, which he wound as a turban around his head. He poured water into a pitcher and carried it to the nearest disciple, the last one in sequence around the table. Then, in a room completely hushed, Jesus knelt down and began to wash that disciple's feet.

He moved to the next and washed his feet, too.

And the next.

So still was the room, that each small splash of water could be heard. Andrew began silently to cry.

So did Judas, though his eyes were wide open and blazing with an odd ferocity. Jesus felt that Judas' feet twitched the instant he touched them, and he knew: cosmic elements, light and darkness, were contending in this poor disciple's soul.

He moved on, then, to Philip and Matthew and James and the blunt, frowning Thomas.

Last of all, Jesus came to Simon.

Simon Peter, forever proud of his humilities! — he snatched his thick feet back beneath his robe and said, "What! Are you going to wash my feet?"

Jesus sighed and said, "You may not now understand what I'm doing, but you will in the future."

"No!" Simon said, his bare jowls trembling. "You will never wash my feet."

Something tightened in Jesus' throat. "If I do not wash you," he said, striving for kindness in his voice, "if you do not let me serve you, you will have no part in me."

Simon shot his feet out again, pleading, "My hands, too, Lord! Wash my hands and my head!"

As he rubbed the hard soles of Simon Peter's feet, and then again as he toweled them dry, Jesus said, "Those who have bathed do not need to wash — except for their feet — for they are clean all over."

By now the light outside the lattices had diminished to a deep blue. The room trembled and shifted in yellow candle flame.

Jesus removed the towels and laid them again on the side table. He put his arms through the short sleeves of his own robe, shook his hair free, and took his place, reclining among the disciples.

"Do you understand what I've just done to you?" he said. "You call me Teacher and Lord, and you are right because that's what I am. Now: if I, your Lord and Teacher, have washed your feet, then you, too, must wash one another's feet. This is an example. Blessed are you, my friends, if you do it!"

He paused a moment. "Come," he said. "Let's eat."

They did. The twelve disciples began to eat, but there was nothing common about this meal anymore, nothing merely traditional, however ancient the practice. These men took their food with deliberation, as if every gesture required a conscious deciding.

Jesus did not eat.

He gazed into the faces that surrounded him, in some sense filling himself with his dear friends. But he had to temper his intensity: simply glancing at Andrew caused that man to stop chewing and begin blinking against his tears again.

Each face. Each disciple. Thomas, focused on the food, biting with strong clenches of the jaw muscles. Matthew, grey scholar, cutting his pieces very small. The battling eyes of Judas, that black explosion of eyebrow which snapped and twitched like the wings of a dying insect.

Compulsively, Jesus sighed. Suddenly, sorrow was tearing at his soul as with something like grappling hooks. Heat rushed into his face, and Jesus groaned aloud. The disciples glanced up and immediately stopped eating, looking guilty.

Almost inaudibly, Jesus whispered, "One of you is about to betray me."

The whole company gasped, as if Jesus had cracked the table with an ax.

"What?" said Thomas. "What did he say?"

Andrew, in perfect anguish, choked: "Is it me, Lord?"

Jesus noticed that Simon made some sort of signal to John. John nodded. And then, because he lay in the place of honor, immediately to Jesus' right, John leaned his head against Jesus' bosom, and said, "Who, Lord? Who is it?"

At that same moment Judas was reaching his bread to the sauce of bitter herbs. "Rabbi," he said, "is it me?"

Jesus picked up a piece of bread and dipped it in the dish with Judas. He said, "The one who is sharing the sauce with me, he is the one."

Judas froze. He raised his eyes and stared at Jesus, his whole face writhing, beseeching, defying —

Jesus returned the gaze with a level looking and whispered, "The Son of man shall surely go as it is written of him; but woe to that man by whom he is betrayed! It were better for him if he had not been born."

"What?" Thomas said. "What did he say? I can't hear what he's saying!"

Like tearing roots from the soil, Judas took his eyes from Jesus and covered them. "Master." He whispered as softly as Jesus: "What do you want of me?"

Jesus, fixed upon the face of Judas, whispered, "That you waste no more time, whatever you choose to do, do it quickly."

Judas took three brief and separate breaths, then by the strength of his thin arms he forced his body upward and away from the table. He walked to the door, opened it, and was swallowed by the darkness.

Night air wandered into the room, moist and cold. Simon got up and closed the door and lay down again on his stomach.

There was neither eating nor speaking in the room after that. Soon the candle flames stood as straight as soldiers — and all the shadow along the walls seemed a solid thing.

Jesus felt as if the light itself were dying. Only a little was left in which to live and to love his disciples.

"Children," he said, "yet a little while I am with you — but then you will not see me, because where I am going you cannot come.

"A new commandment I give to you," he said. He formed these words in his mouth as if he were carving them in stone — uncrushable words, the memorial he absolutely must leave behind:

"Love one another," he said. "Even as I have loved you, you must love one another. By this will the whole world know that you are my disciples — if you have love for one another.

"Do you love me now? Then you will keep my commandment when I am not here.

"And I will pray the Father, and he will give you another Counselor to be with you forever, the Comforter, the Holy Spirit, even the Spirit of truth.

"But I will not leave you desolate. I will return to you. Yet a little while, and the world will see me no more, but you will see me. Because I live, you will live also.

"In the meantime, children, you will weep and lament. I am so sorry to tell you so. The world will rejoice, and you will be sad. Worse, already tonight you will fall away from me. All of you, just as it is written: *I will strike the shepherd, and the sheep shall be scattered abroad.*"

"No!" Jesus recognized the shout immediately: Simon Peter. He had found something to say, and he was up on his knees to say it: "No, Lord! Though they might, I will never fall away from you!"

Jesus wondered if this clamorous disciple knew how often his voice sounded like mere whining. "Simon, Simon," he said, "Satan asked to have you. He wanted to sift you like wheat. But I have prayed for you, that your faith may not fail."

Simon thumped the table: "Lord, I'm ready to go to prison with you."

"To prison?" said Jesus. "Oh, Peter, this very night before the first rooster crows twice, you will deny me three times."

But Simon raised his arm and declared, "Even if I have to die with you, I will not deny you."

In fact, Jesus had ceased listening to Simon's bluster.

He gathered himself into a formal position, sitting cross-legged before the table. He took the unleavened bread in two hands and elevated it in a motion so dignified, so noble and holy, that Simon and every other man in the room was reduced to an aweful silence.

Aloud, Jesus blessed the bread. He brought it low and broke it and then handed it to the disciples, saying, "Take and eat."

They obeyed. Jesus watched. And when they all were eating the bread, he declared: "This is my body, which is given for you. Do this in the remembrance of me."

Their chewing became massively slow.

Jesus took the cup of Passover wine and lifted it and gave thanks, then he gave it to the disciples exactly as he had given them the bread. While they were drinking, he said, "This is my blood of the covenant, shed for many for the remission of sins. Do this, as often as you drink it, in the remembrance of me."

And while they passed the cup one to the other, Jesus began to sing. He rocked his body back and forth like the old men who prayed in the synagogue. He closed his eyes and rocked and sang in a strong voice:

> *Praise the Lord, all nations.*
> *Extol him, all you peoples!*
>   *Great is his love,*
>   *his steadfast love*
> *and his faithfulness lasts forever.*

Those who had finished drinking joined the song, but softly.

When the song was done, Jesus bowed his head and closed his eyes and took John by the hand.

"Come," he said. "It's time to go."

So they all stood up and filed out into the dark night and descended the stairs from the upper building to the lower one. They passed through the courtyard and out the west-facing door which gave down the side of Mount Zion. But Jesus led them down the eastern slope of Zion, praying softly as they went: *Abba, Abba, Abba.*

The wind had died. Houses were closed against the vapors of the night. Jesus took his small band down the long steps, the ancient steps into the lower city.

Father, I've given them the words you gave me. They know I came from
you. They believe you sent me —
Through the City of David they walked, through roads a thousand years
old, dim and unlit. The stars gave a dead light. The disciples had neither a
lantern nor a torch. Jesus persisted in his praying:
Holy Father, keep them in your name, that they may be one, even as we are
one —
Out of the city by the Potsherd Gate and down again into the Kidron valley.
The walls of Jerusalem rose high on their left side. On their right, like silent
eyes, were the whitewashed tombs of the wealthy. And Jesus still was praying:
The glory you gave me I've given them, that they may be one as we are
one, I in them and you in me, that they may become perfectly one, so that the
world may know that you have sent me, and that you love them even as you
love me —
And so, as was his custom whenever he stayed in Jerusalem, Jesus came in
the dark shadow of the night to the Mount of Olives, and there he stopped.

∎

"Stay here."
Jesus' words were short and bitten.
To eight of the disciples, he said, "Stay here. While I pray."
Touching Simon and James on their shoulders, then taking John's hand
in his own, Jesus entered a private olive grove called Gethsemane. There
was no light beneath these ancient trees, whose trunks were great twists of
shadow. Jesus moved by memory.
As he walked, breathing became difficult for him. His legs felt numb and
heavy.
"My soul," he groaned. "My soul is sorrowful. Even unto death."
He stopped. His throat was thickening. There was no controlling this
anymore.
"Wait here," he said, releasing John's hand. His voice sounded harsh. He
knew it would get worse. He barked, "Watch with me!" and rushed through
the grove the distance of a stone's throw, then stumbled and fell face down
on the ground. He drew his knees up under himself like a man palsied. He
drove his fingers through the soil and howled, "Abba! Abba!"
Then the storm broke. Jesus wailed aloud from earth even unto heaven:
"ABBA, FATHER, TAKE THIS CUP AWAY FROM ME!
Take this cup away from me.
Remove it, O my God.
I don't want to drink such suffering.
Abba, Abba — I don't."

Silence. Jesus breathed through his nostrils, his cheek in the dirt. No wind. No light. No sound, not the rustling of leaves nor the call of an evening insect. Nothing.

Without lifting his head, by a terrible effort, Jesus uttered words more reasonable: "Father, all things are possible with you. You can abolish the cup. You can make this hour pass away from me — "

Sweat pooled in the bridge of his nose. It drizzled into his eyes, burning, and dropped to the earth as thick as blood. Jesus was suffering powerful oppositions. He wanted his prayer to be both truthful *and* obedient, but these seemed to be adversaries within him, each demanding his soul.

Jesus retracted his lips and ground his teeth and for a long while could utter nothing at all. But then he had brought his mind and his breathing and his horror under greater control, and he spoke the last part of his prayer in meek syllables:

"Nevertheless, not my will, Abba," Jesus said. "Let yours be done."

He lay a while in perfect quietness then, weak, empty, and exhausted.

Finally he rose up. His legs trembled under the natural weight of standing, but he was able to make his way back to James and Simon and John.

When he came to them, his heart sank into deeper and deeper loneliness. Their bodies lay like sacks at the bases of two trees. By the slow draw of easy breathing, Jesus knew that they were sleeping, all three.

"What, Simon?" he said to his oblivious disciple. "Couldn't you watch one hour with me? The spirit is willing, but the flesh is so weak."

Jesus composed himself. By conscious thought he stood erect and dignified. Then he saw small firelight below him, at the foot of the Mount of Olives, so he bent to his disciples and shook them one by one awake.

"Arise and look," he said, "Look down the mountain. See? The hour has come. My betrayer is at hand — "

Simon snorted, then made a great show of being on guard and seeing the torch-fires that wound up the path from the Kidron valley, a long line of winking lights.

Jesus went out of Gethsemane and began to rouse the rest of his disciples. They, too, had been overwhelmed with weariness. They woke foolishly, clearing their throats, complaining like children, not quite comprehending where they were or what was about to happen.

But then the smoking torches began to arrive. There came, too, the soft clashing of armor, scabbards, swords. And suddenly, from three sides at once: soldiers appeared — the troops and officers of Herod Antipas' armies, as well as captains of the Temple police. In front of them all Jesus recognized a nervous little figure, a taut fellow whose torch blazed brighter and blacker than the others: Judas, mirroring a smile, his great eyebrow fairly flying from his head in a manic show of civility.

Judas raised the torch above one disciple and then another, peering into their faces, chattering, "Yes, yes, greetings to you, yes," and moving on.

Jesus, watching the progress of the small zealot, suffered an enormous sadness.

Finally, Judas spied him where he stood. The man's mouth grew tighter in smiling, but his eyes swelled with begging. He began to bob his head as if Jesus and he shared secrets.

He came so close to his Teacher that Jesus could see the pores in his flesh. Loudly Judas exclaimed, "Hail, Master!" Then he went up on his toes, and he kissed him.

A servant of the high priest called, "Is that our man, then?"

Judas backed away, saying nothing, staring at Jesus.

The servant began to stride forward with a knife and a rope.

Suddenly, someone huge hurtled past Jesus, bellowing and slashing the air with a short sword.

Judas screamed, "Simon, Simon! Messiah is here!"

Simon Peter struck the rope and the knife from the servant's hands and in a wild stroke cut off the man's ear.

But Jesus sprang forward and grabbed Simon from behind. He tightened his left arm against the big man's throat, and with his right hand stripped the weapon from Simon's fingers.

"Put it up!" Jesus growled in Simon's ear. "Those who take the sword perish by the sword."

Simon went slack. Jesus released him. "Don't you know," he said, "that I could ask my Father for twelve legions of angels and he would send them to me?"

Jesus reached down and picked up the severed ear of the servant and touched it again to the side of the man's head and healed him. At the same time he found Judas in the throng and glared at him. With a raw, specific condemnation, he declared, "But I would never ask my Father for such a thing, or else the Scriptures would never be fulfilled."

Little Judas dropped his torch. It seemed an involuntary act. Yet he left it on the ground. He hesitated no more than the time it takes to shrug one's shoulders, then vanished.

Jesus, now drawing himself erect before the captains of the Temple, said, "Have you come out with swords and clubs to capture me like a robber? Day after day I sat in the Temple teaching, and you didn't seize me then. But," he said, starting to stride toward them, "this is your hour, and the power of darkness."

As if his word were their command, the soldiers also moved forward. In torchlight they began to bind Jesus' arms.

One of the disciples bleated in fear. This was proving to be a very large contingent of soldiers. The more they filled the area around Jesus, the more the disciples shrank backward.

Jesus watched as terror overtook his children and they fled. Some crept away. Some dodged and raced away. But they all scattered, all of them, till no one was left and Jesus was completely alone.

iii

John!" It was a hoarse, guttural whisper, unrecognizable.

"John! Is that you?"

John had been hurrying through the narrow streets of the lower city. He froze and flattened himself to a wall. The night was impenetrable.

"John son of Zebedee! Where are you?"

The young man almost crouched down in order to hide. Instead, he surprised himself by calling out, "Who's that? Who's there?"

The whispering stopped. Except for a distant clatter of running feet, the city was still as stone. John suffered a moment of panic — then a hand grabbed his shoulder. He whirled and delivered a blow to the side of someone's head. It cracked his knuckles, and he yelped.

The voice said, "Relax. It's me, Simon."

"Simon!" John snapped. "What's the matter with you?"

"Sorry," said Simon. "Sorry. Where are you going?"

John, rubbing his hand, began to walk at a quick pace.

Simon followed.

"I know you've got some sort of a plan," he said.

John bent his elbows and started to trot. Simon, puffing harder, ran, too.

"First you went toward Bethany like the rest," Simon said. "But then you stopped. I saw you. You turned round and came back to the city. I followed you. You knocked on someone's door. Who was that? I saw him rush out ahead of you, throwing on his robes as he went. You're going after him now, right?"

"Yes, Simon — and if I don't get there when he does, I miss my chance. You've already taken more time than I can spare."

John broke into a steady running.

"Get where?" Simon called. "What chance?" The bigger man was having trouble keeping up.

"To be with him!"

"Him? Who?"

"Jesus! To be with Jesus!"

"Jesus? Where?"

"The high priest's palace!"

"Jesus!" Simon exclaimed. "That's exactly what I thought!"

But John said nothing now. He was running swiftly up the ancient steps to Mount Zion. Simon, gasping for air, fell farther and farther back.

On the heights of Zion other people were hurrying through the dark streets, too, all converging northeast of the Essene quarter. John tempered his speed to match theirs. He didn't want to attract attention. These people were members of the Sanhedrin, summoned suddenly by Caiaphas to his palace. John knew of the meeting. It was a trial. Joseph of Arimathea had told him.

He turned a corner and ran along a low wall, then stopped at the gate of the high priest's courtyard. It was shut. But there, just inside, was Joseph himself, peering anxiously into the night.

As soon as he recognized John, he spoke to the maid who was keeping the gate, gestured toward John, then dashed through the courtyard to stairs that led to an upper chamber.

The maid came and opened the gate to John.

There was too much light in here. Officers were standing by a central fire, warming themselves. Lanterns were attached to the walls round about. John felt uncomfortable. He bowed his head and began to walk toward the stairs, when a voice boomed, "John! John — here! Out here!"

Simon, lathered and breathless, was standing at the gate.

Quickly John went to the maid who had admitted him and smiled. "That man is also a friend of the high priest," he said.

The maid glanced back and forth between the two men, suspicious. Finally she went and opened the gate.

If Simon came in, he was on his own.

John was already mounting the steps to the chamber whose windows glowed with an interior light. Voices grew louder the closer he came, the general murmuring of many men. John did not try to enter. He crept along a stone walkway that circled the outside of the room till he was hidden from the courtyard below, then he brought his face close to a window grill and looked inside.

Men's heads blocked his vision. They were standing with their backs to the wall. But they nodded and muttered and craned to see, so John caught glimpses of the proceedings within.

Jesus! A head moved and John saw Jesus! His heart leaped: there stood Jesus, solitary in the center of the room, as calm as a white candle, though his clothes and his flesh were soiled, and the hair that hung down his back was a falling mass of knots.

A voice inside said, "Testimony!"

Heads moved, all looking in one direction and blocking John's view.

"Testimony!" said the voice, dominant, self-confident.

A lesser voice, farther inside the room, called out: "He spat in my son's face."

The heads swiveled to the new speaker, and John could see Jesus again — profile, facing the front of the room, which was cut from view by the window casement.

His arms were still bound behind him! But he seemed motionless by choice, his lips pursed as if forming one letter of the alphabet, one sound forever.

"Spat in your son's face?" said the voice of silken authority, and Jesus was hidden again. "What sort of charge is that?"

"Uncleanness! Bodily discharge. The spit defiled my boy."

Someone else called, "No, it healed your son of blindness!"

"It got him thrown out of the synagogue, too!"

"Not enough!" declared the voice in the front of the room. This must be the high priest, Caiaphas. "I want more damning testimony!" There was menace in the tone.

Then people began to shout out a series of accusations:

"He has broken every Sabbath law, working, walking, cooking on the Sabbath!"

"Noted," said the high priest.

"He eats with sinners."

"Noted!"

"He scorns our father, Abraham!"

"He casts out demons by the power of demons!"

"He says he can forgive sins — "

"Noted. *Noted!*" The high priest raised his voice in procedural scorn. "We've heard it all before, and none of it warrants execution."

The room was stung to silence.

The head directly in front of John bowed down and he saw Jesus framed by the window, still erect, his beautiful forehead filled with thought.

"Who brings against the defendant," Caiaphas said with smooth articulation, "witness concerning a capital crime, an offense deserving death?"

Suddenly the head at the window snapped up and, inches from John's face, called, "I do!" John swallowed hard. The nearness left him trembling.

The man moved from the window into the room and stood by Jesus.

"Give God the praise," the invisible judge intoned. "What have you to say?"

Rubbing his chin, the witness said, "I heard the defendant announce that he was going to destroy the Temple!"

"Good, sir! Sabotage and sacrilege are killing offenses. Very good!"

"Yes," cried another man, rushing to the side of the first. "Yes, he said he'd destroy the Temple made with hands and in three days build another *without* hands!"

"Wait," said Caiaphas.

But already a third man was clapping for attention and shouting: "I heard it, too! Just this week!"

"No, no, no," the first man shouted. "No, the defendant said it three years ago, exactly."

"Shut up!" The voice of the high priest dominated the room. "Trifling witnesses, you're ruining your own testimony."

The three men crept to the farther wall, and Jesus remained alone in the center of the room.

Then Caiaphas himself appeared.

John saw the high priest approaching Jesus, a wizened, insinuating man, hunched at the shoulders, moving on a soundless tread. Over clean white linen he wore a blue woven robe whose hem was edged with bells of gold and pomegranates of cloth. On his head he wore a grand turban.

Caiaphas found a mark immediately before the slender form of the Lord and stepped on it. Then he lifted his face and parted his lips in smiling.

Jesus returned the look but did not smile.

Caiaphas said, "What? Have you nothing to say in answer to these charges? You've never been afraid to speak. Go ahead." Caiaphas made a show of bowing his head to listen. "Defend yourself."

But Jesus held his peace.

John's heart was hammering within him, seeing these two in such proximity. Jesus had a lean, regal posture. But he was filthy, and Caiaphas was arrayed in the glory of Aaron.

"You do not choose to talk?" said Caiaphas. "Then I choose, and you shall have no choice *but* to speak!"

The high priest drew himself up to his full height and said, "I adjure you by the living God to tell us whether you are Messiah, the Christ, the Son of God."

Softly Jesus said, "I am."

John gasped and covered his mouth.

Jesus was still speaking: "And you shall see the Son of man, sitting at the right hand of power, coming with the clouds of heaven."

"The man is dangerous," Caiaphas muttered. Then he said, "Blasphemy." More loudly still, "Blasphemy!" He seized the throat of his robe and tore the cloth apart. "What need do we have of witnesses, when the man blasphemes in the very midst of the council?"

Caiaphas withdrew from Jesus, out of John's sight. But his insinuating voice filled the chamber: "What say you, reverend sirs? What sentence does the Nazarene deserve?"

"Death."

First one and then another said, "Death."

Then the whole company of witnesses and counselors were condemning Jesus in a glad chorus of unity: *Death!*

It was as if some prohibition had snapped in the room. Men surged in toward Jesus. John wound his fingers through the window grill, tormented by the scene. Men were spitting in Jesus' face and hitting him in the head. They covered his eyes and cried, "Prophesy, Christ! Who was it that hit you?"

John backed from the window. Sick with sorrow, he turned away.

Just then he heard footsteps in the narrow road behind the high priest's house. A man was running: John looked and in the spill of window light recognized the small form of Judas Iscariot, dashing away at a wild pace. It was the last time any disciple saw Judas.

∎

SIMON PETER

John left me alone. He disappeared. I had no idea where he went, and I had no friend in that place. He did. I didn't.

And even as the servant was opening the gate, she kept staring into my face. That was unnerving enough. Then she spoke, and I glanced down at her, and that's how I lost sight of John in the courtyard.

What she said was, "Aren't you one of that man's disciples?"

Took my breath away! I had just gotten there.

"What man?" I said.

"You know," she said. "The man they arrested."

"No," I said. "No, I'm not."

I brushed past her and since John was nowhere in sight, I went to the fire in the middle of the courtyard — as if I had business in that place and knew exactly where I was going.

It was a common fire on a cold night. Officers of the Temple guard were warming themselves. Servants, too. I put out my hands and ducked my head down. Jesus was somewhere in the palace. I meant to stay.

But that maid wouldn't leave me alone!

Soon I felt that people were looking at me. Made my flesh crawl. I glanced up, and there she was, talking to the officers. "This is one of them," she said. "He's a disciple of the Nazarene."

"Woman," I said, "I don't know and I do not understand what you're talking about."

But I moved to the forecourt. A colder place, but darker, too.

I love Jesus. I loved Jesus then — desperately. That whole night it was hard for me even to breathe, because I kept seeing him tied up. He was somewhere in the high priest's house, with people who wanted to kill him. How could I leave? I kept wringing my hands. Helpless! I wanted to throw my body at the doors and burst in and beat them all with clubs!

I don't know how long I paced in that dark place.

An hour, maybe.

But then — I'll tell this part as truthfully as I can — then four things happened, one right after the other.

First, the shouting. All at once there came from an upper chamber the slurred shouts of many men. They were laughing as if they were drunk. I went back into the courtyard to see what was happening —

But a soldier blocked my way and said, "You *are* one of them."

I said, "No."

He said, "Don't lie to me. You're a Galilean."

I said, "No," and tried to push past him.

But he struck my chest and said, "Don't you recognize me?" He struck me again. "I was there when you cut off my cousin's ear!"

"Damn you!" I yelled. "Damn you!" People started to look, people in the courtyard, people pouring out of the upper chamber. Two guards reached for their weapons. It drove me crazy. I raised my right hand and screamed, "I swear by the city of Jerusalem that I know nothing of the man! I do not know — "

Then this is the third thing that happened.

Jesus came out of the upper chamber, his arms bound behind him. He turned and looked down at me. He saw my right hand in the air.

And this is the fourth thing.

Somewhere in the night a rooster started to crow.

I lowered my hand and covered my mouth and turned away from Jesus and ran out of the courtyard. I ran out into the city. I ran down a dark alley and fell to the ground with my face in my hands and I burst into tears. I cried and cried and could not stop.

This is the whole truth.

iv

Friday's dawning was uncertain. It was the end of the latter rains. Clouds had crept in from the sea and covered Jerusalem in a sky as undefined as the sea itself, a grey weight under heaven. Dawn, then, was a lessening of shadow, an odor of moisture, and a dirty light.

Now and again a thin, drizzling rain fell.

The palace which Herod the Great had built more than fifty years ago was enclosed by a wall of massive stone forty-five feet high. Within the wall were rich green gardens, covered promenades bordered by canals, lovely pools, curious water fountains. The palace had more than a hundred apartments, two magnificent banquet halls, roofs constructed of long beams carved with brilliant decorations, barracks for several legions of soldiers, stables. But thirty-three years ago King Herod had gone down to death, and now — all his ambition for the glory of his name and the kingship of his son having failed — the place was named for the Roman governor who held court here during the high feast days of the Jews: it was called the Praetorium. Pontius Pilate walked its promenades. His troops occupied its barracks. Rome ruled.

A principal gate in the Praetorium wall opened eastward to the wide public square of the upper city. Guards stood in towers on either side of the gate, though in these days they did not shut its huge doors: Jews who intended to celebrate the Passover would never defile themselves by entering the residence of a Gentile.

But Roman law required prosecutions and sentencing to take place in public. In order to render legal judgments, then, Pilate met with the people of Judea in that square east of the royal palace. A *tribunale*, an elevated speaker's platform, had been erected in that place. When court was in session, a large wooden chair was brought out and set upon this platform, the magistrate's seat. When Pontius Pilate sat therein, he *was* Rome.

In the dirty dawn of Friday, high priest Caiaphas stood at the very edge of the ramp that led to the Praetorium gate and rapped the hard end of his staff on the flagstones.

"An audience and a judgment!" he called.

Behind him a miserable group had gathered in the public square: soldiers of the Temple guard, certain leading members of the Sanhedrin, and in their midst — his wrists bound in front of him, his face soiled and tired but otherwise unremarkable — Jesus of Nazareth.

"Pontius Pilate, Procurator!" the high priest called, clearly but loudly, not obsequiously. "Here is a criminal of such public threat that Rome must hear the indictment and pass sentence and execute her sentence now, today, before sunset and the Sabbath!"

Having made his formal petition, the high priest returned to those who stood under the grey drizzle in the open square. Other members of the Sanhedrin showed more anxiety than he did, murmuring among themselves about the charges they would bring.

Jesus allowed his eye to wander over the spacious pavement. He focused on the far southeastern corner. His lips tightened, and his jaw clenched.

Several women and a man were lurking in that corner, their hoods drawn up against the weather. Their faces were mostly concealed, but he recognized them. Andrew, his first follower. He must have brought the women here. Mary Magdalene, pinched and pale. Joanna and Susanna and Mary of Bethany. And her sister Martha, short and solid.

Jesus closed his eyes with unutterable sadness.

Suddenly two Roman soldiers thrust a wooden shaft between his elbows and his back. They each took an end and drove him forward to the front steps of the platform. Pilate's chair was in position. Pontius Pilate himself was ascending steps at the back of the platform: the judge and the accused arrived at the same time.

A servant raised a shield over Pilate's chair, to protect him from the rain.

"Now, then," said Pilate, sitting down and beckoning the high priest forward. "What's the charge?"

The Roman wore his hair cut short. His knuckles were dimpled, his fingers fat, his upper lip low in the middle and high at the sides, as if it were deformed by too much blowing of trumpets. It gave him an expression of perpetual sneering.

Caiaphas said, "We found this man, Jesus of Nazareth, perverting our nation."

"Yes?" said Pilate. "And?"

"And," said Caiaphas, "sedition. He says that he is Messiah, a king."

Pilate frowned. "Why have you come to me?" he said. "Your 'Messiah' is your religion. Judge him according to your own law." The governor made motions to stand and go.

Caiaphas snapped to attention. "No! We must come to you!" he said. "We don't have the authority to put a man to death."

Pilate did stand up then. "Death?" he said. "You think he's committed a capital offense?" He stepped forward and squinted into Jesus' face, then said, "Bring him in. I'll interrogate him inside."

By the rod at his back, the soldiers dragged Jesus after the governor, through the gate, into the Praetorium itself.

In a broad hallway Pilate again sat down. Jesus was positioned directly in front of him. There was a bowl of fruit at Pilate's left hand.

"I have no time for this," he said. "Make your answers short. Jesus of Nazareth, are you the king of the Jews?"

Jesus, bent forward by the rod through the crooks of his elbows, nevertheless raised his head and looked into Pilate's eyes. "Do you say this on your own?" he said. "Or did others tell you this about me?"

"What! Am I a Jew?" Pilate sneered. "Your own chief priests delivered you to me. What have you done?"

Jesus said, "My kingdom is not of this world. If it were, my subjects would be fighting for me — but my kingdom does not belong here at all."

"So," said Pilate, "then you are a king?"

"*You* say I am a king," said Jesus. "The reason I was born into the world is to testify to the truth. All those who belong to the truth listen to my voice."

"Truth?" said Pilate abruptly, half out of his chair. "What is truth?"

Shaking his head, he walked out into the wet morning, while the accused was driven stumbling behind him. This time Jesus was forced to climb the steps to the *tribunale*.

As he came to the top, he saw Pilate's back and heard his confident announcement: "I find no fault in this man."

Immediately a clamor arose in the public square. Crowds were gathering now. Certain members of the Sanhedrin came forward, lodging further charges against Jesus.

"He stirs the people to insurrection, even from Galilee to this place!"

Pilate glanced toward Jesus: permission to respond.

Jesus said nothing.

"He's a known revolutionary!"

Pilate nodded, but Jesus said nothing.

"He has forbidden his followers to give tribute to Caesar!"

Each time an accusation was presented, Pilate invited some reply from Jesus, but he held his peace. He pursed his lips. He looked every accuser squarely in the face, but he himself said nothing.

Finally Pilate raised his hands for silence. He stepped forward on the platform, prepared to render his ruling.

"I examined this man and found no evidence for any of your charges," he said. "But your outrage is real, and it must be satisfied. Therefore, I will order the accused to be scourged with a whip of knotted cords and weights of metal. The *flagellum*. After that I propose to honor your custom of releasing one prisoner at the Passover. I will release this man, Jesus of Nazareth."

There was a moment of perfect stillness. The high priest looked trapped, unable to respond.

Suddenly a voice cried from the back of the crowd, "Jesus? Jesus *who*?"

It was a woman perhaps fifty years old. She began to push her way forward, crying, "Jesus of Nazareth? Not Jesus of Nazareth!" She was clothed modestly, like a rabbi's wife, though her robes were drenched and her progress was broken by the weight.

Jesus watched her coming. So did Pontius Pilate and Caiaphas the high priest. The woman's features were hectic with fear and a wild hoping.

"No," she was calling, "not Jesus of Nazareth, but Jesus *Barabbas*! My son! My son! Set my son free!"

Jesus recognized the rage of maternal love in this woman, and he admired her.

Caiaphas seemed to catch fire as she came nearer. He reached for her, took her elbow, escorted her to the very lip of the platform and, trembling with compassion, cried to Pilate, "Yes! This woman's son. If you choose to honor the custom, sir, release unto us Jesus Barabbas!"

A handful of Zealots clapped their hands and yelled, "Barabbas! Barabbas!"

The governor was stunned. "The man is a murderer," he said. "You yourself asked for his arrest, and I agreed!"

Caiaphas said, "I know which is more dangerous to both of us!"

Pilate snapped, "Only one of them has killed a Roman."

But Caiaphas and the chief priests were already encouraging the crowds, common folk of common loyalties, who drowned Pilate's words with their chanting: "Barabbas! Son of Father! Release unto us Barabbas!"

This grew to a thunder in the square. People came rushing from everywhere in the city. More and more voices took up the chanting. The crowd was swelling into a mob.

"BARABBAS! BARABBAS!"

Only those on the *tribunale* could hear the governor issue orders to a centurion: "Take him to the barracks. Whip him. And make it bloody, man!"

Four soldiers grabbed Jesus and dragged him back through the Praetorium gate. There was no care in their going. Haste! Brutality. The multitude was achieving that swollen rocking rhythm which every Roman feared, because riot was at the heart of it.

Make it bloody, man!

In the barracks soldiers stripped the clothes from Jesus' body. His hands were tied to a post with thongs. Out of nowhere a lash whistled, stung his shoulders with little pinchings, then ripped backward and set his flesh on fire.

Again, the whistle and the lash and the nettle-stings. Again, an audible tearing of his skin, then he heard someone cry out in sympathy.

The whistle, and Jesus couldn't help it: he flinched. The whistle: he drew one knee up to his stomach. The whistle: and Jesus realized who was crying out. The whistle: it was himself.

The whistle. The whistle. Jesus began to taste blood in his breathing, in his mouth and nose. He stopped making noises. Darkness closed around the edges of his thought. The whistle. He sagged. He hung heavy from his wrists.

The whistle.

As though from far away, Jesus watched several soldiers place on a man's brow a circlet of thorny briars. Next they threw over his back a billowing purple robe, as huge as the sky.

Hail, king of the Jews! Ha ha! Hail, robed in blood, thou bloody king!

But then Jesus himself was on his feet. Walking. Under rough fibers his skin was sticky and wet. A thick liquid was running down his legs. The soles of his feet kept slipping in it. His back was unbendable. Jesus knew that it would hurt soon. This was the Father's will.

Then he was standing on one side of the *tribunale*, confronting the multitude. Pontius Pilate was gesturing toward him and shouting: "Behold, the man!"

On the other side of the *tribunale* now stood another man, athletic, dark-eyed, fiery, and very clean. How neatly combed was he! Jesus strove to stand erect, but failed. His robe was woven of iron and stone.

Pilate shouted, "*Now* what do you say? Which man should I release to you — Jesus Barabbas, or Jesus of Nazareth?"

The multitude had found a single voice. "BARABBAS!" it bellowed.

Pilate looked troubled. "Then what shall I do with this man?" he cried.

"CRUCIFY HIM!" came the thick-throated chorus, priests and people and Zealots and pilgrims, but no distinction among them now. They were the mindless mob: "CRUCIFY HIM!"

Jesus lifted his eyes and looked to the southeast corner of the square, where he had seen some of his followers in the dirty dawning. Suddenly he gasped and nearly collapsed.

"Why should I crucify him?" Pilate was crying. "What evil has he done?"

Caiaphas leaped to the platform and shouted at the top of his lungs, "We have a law, and by that law he ought to die, because he made himself the Son of God!"

Jesus had spied his mother. She was clinging to John. Woman of no means, woman who had borne him, woman whose clothing was dark with the morning rain — she was staring at him with horror, her mouth wide open. *The will of the Father! The will of the Father!*

Pilate was shouting at Jesus, "What's the matter with you, man? Have you nothing at all to say?"

Caiaphas, too, was shouting: "Crucify him, Magistrate, or else you are no friend of Caesar's, because he pretends to be a king like Caesar!"

"CRUCIFY HIM!" The huge crush of people was wheeling toward riot: "CRUCIFY HIM!"

"What, then?" shrieked Pontius Pilate. "Shall I crucify your king?"

The high priest turned purple with fury: "We have no king but Caesar!"

And the voice of the multitude resolved itself in an endless, ponderous roaring: "*CRUCIFY!*"

So Pilate sank down into the judgment chair and gripped the armrests and delivered his verdict. He released the man that had been arrested for insurrection and for murder.

But Jesus of Nazareth he turned over to the will of the people. He ordered a centurion and a small contingent of soldiers to lead him outside the city and to crucify him.

V

Jesus is dragging a heavy wooden beam up the center of the street.

In fact, two soldiers tried to lay it on his shoulders, but the weight of the rough wood startled the lacerations in his back, and the pain became so intense that something like light exploded in Jesus' skull, and he slipped to the ground in a faint.

So now he is cradling one end of the beam under his left arm and bumping its other end over the stones of the street.

Each stone is a Sinai.

There are spike holes near the extremities of the beam. It has been used before.

Jesus is moving north, slowly, toward the Garden Gate.

He is wearing his own robe again, and his tunic, though they have lost their shape, scabrous, befouled by human discharge.

His hair, because he bends so far forward, hangs nearly to the ground.

The sandaled feet of a centurion are walking in front of him, just within his vision. He is following these feet.

There is the sound of wailing behind him. He has heard such lamentation before, sometimes genuine, sometimes conventional. For Lazarus. For Jairus' daughter. For the son of the widow in Nain.

The beam sticks between two stones. Jesus groans and drops to his knees, and the lumber hits ground. He doesn't blame the crossbeam, the *patibulum* to which he will be nailed. He just can't carry it any more.

Motion makes his skin scream. And beneath all, his bones are weak and tired.

Someone is parting his hair and drawing it back from his forehead. He is able to see. An elderly woman, her eyes swimming in tears, wipes his brow with a rich linen cloth, then presses it into his hand.

And the centurion seems kindly enough, middle-aged, gruff. He has spoken to the soldiers — Gauls, by the look of them — who even now are placing the wooden beam on the back of another man. Jesus is overcome with gratitude. His chest heaves with weeping.

He rises and finds his body very light.

He walks forward.

Immediately the procession lifts its voice again in lamentation.

Jesus turns, shaking his head. "Daughters of Jerusalem, don't weep for me," he says. "Weep for yourselves. The days are coming when they will say, 'Blessed are the wombs that never bore and the breasts that never gave suck.' In those days people will beg the mountains to fall on them and the hills to hide them."

Jesus hands the linen cloth back to the woman who had wiped his face with it. "For if they do these things when the tree is green," he whispers, "what will happen when it is dry?"

The cloth is bloody. He is sorry for that. But he turns and walks.

The morning drizzle has turned to rain. Everyone is wet. And the sky is more than merely grey now. Darker clouds are rolling in from the west. There is a breeze. It's nine o'clock in the morning, Friday.

Out through the Garden Gate they go, and yet farther north. The stone city wall runs north and south on his right-hand side. Jewish tombs are cut into the rock on his left. Here is a hillock by the side of the road, a rocky mound in which four stout poles are fixed, forever ready to receive the crossbeams and the bodies of criminals sentenced to crucifixion. The hill allows a public viewing. It is called Golgotha.

The centurion halts here and hands Jesus a jar of liquid. He lifts it to his lips and tastes it, but then refuses to drink. This is wine mixed with myrrh, a narcotic. It is not in the will of the Father.

Four soldiers strip Jesus down to his loincloth.

At the same time another group of soldiers arrives. They bring two more men with crossbeams on their backs. These men do drink. They drain their jars completely dry.

All three now are stretched on the ground, each beside a different pole. Jesus stares at the black clouds lowering. His back is a field of fire. He cannot swallow. He wishes he could swallow, but his tongue is thick and stuck to the roof of his mouth.

Someone lifts his head by the hair, then pillows it on wood.

His arms are yanked left and right as far as they will go, palms up.

A cold point touches his wrist.

Jesus hears the thump of a maul on metal: once, twice. He feels a spike probing the bones in his right arm: once, twice, three times. As the bones separate and the spike bites hard wood, a dull pain pulses up into his armpit and his neck. This is the will of the Father.

His left arm, likewise, is nailed to the crossbeam.

Then, by pikes and human strength, Jesus is lifted bodily from the ground. Soldiers climb ladders behind the stout pole, hauling him up and allowing him to swing from his arms alone until the *patibulum* is lashed to the pole and the cross is formed. The soldiers descend. In front of him they bend his knees and drive a third spike through his ankles. His muscles convulse. He begins to tremble as if he were very cold. His teeth chatter. He bites his tongue but doesn't notice, except that there is the taste of blood in his mouth.

"Father."

Jesus speaks through bloody foam and through shivering, even while one of the Roman soldiers climbs the pole behind him.

"Father, forgive them, for they know not what they do."

That soldier hangs a shingle at the very top of the cross. Printed on it in Hebrew and Greek and Latin, by order of Pilate himself, is the legend: *Jesus of Nazareth, the King of the Jews.*

Now the troops responsible for these crucifixions settle on the ground and begin to divide the criminals' clothes among themselves. They cast lots for the various pieces.

Rain falls steadily now, and the breeze is stiffening. Nevertheless, pilgrims still travel up the road and into the city. They see the inscription above him and grin.

Certain Pharisees are standing by, nudging one another. "He saved others," they laugh. "What do you think? Can he save himself? Ha ha."

Derision is common at crucifixions. It takes a man so long to die. Citizens participate. But Jesus' shoulders are pulling apart. He can scarcely hear human voices over the shrieking of his own pain.

"If you are the Son of God, prove it by setting yourself free!"

"Hey, King! King of the Jews, jump down from that cross and we will believe in you!"

The criminal hanging to his left is laughing. "Messiah! Messiah!" The man is gasping in genuine laughter. "Ha ha, *now* I meet Messiah! Been waiting all my life, ha ha! Been waiting since the days of Daniel, hee hee! And look! He shows up *dying*! Well, Messiah," he hisses at Jesus, "save yourself and save me, too!"

"How can you say that?" The other criminal is not laughing. "Don't you fear God? We are justly condemned, but this man has done nothing wrong. Jesus?" he whispers.

Jesus, roused by the devotion in the utterance, lifts his head and looks. The man's tendons are cracking through his neck and shoulders.

"Jesus of Nazareth, you healed my mother of bleeding," the criminal whispers. "Doctors nearly destroyed her. I hated them. I hated everyone in authority. But you said that her faith had saved her. Now I am touching you, Jesus, as she did. And I'm begging you to remember me when you come into your kingdom."

The poor child! Frightened of dying, casting his life to the one crucified beside him. Jesus struggles for breath and answers: "Truly, today you will be with me in Paradise."

All at once the wind dies. Black clouds close like fists in heaven. Even the beasts are silent, and travelers hurry toward the city now. A storm is coming.

Jesus drops his eyes, sees familiar women at his feet, and involuntarily cries out. This is the sorrow! This is suffering greater than whips and spikes and a universe of derision. His mother is there. Mary, still supporting herself by gripping John's arm, is looking directly at him, pleading with him. Her face is at the level of his waist. She is crying. She is fifty years old, grey and frail, and her eyes are begging him: *Why? Why are you dying?*

Jesus wants to howl his grief to the black skies. He cannot touch his mother any more. He cannot receive her love any more. Oh, God! — in his condition he is not worthy of the love of anyone. And this! Is the will . . . of the Father!

"Woman, woman, woman," he murmurs to his mother. He rolls his head toward John. "He is your son now."

To John Jesus whispers, "And she is your mother. Please take her away. Care for her."

He shuts his eyes. He is occupied by elemental things, life and death. His body hangs heavily from the extended arms and the metal spikes at the ends of them. Whenever he moves, his bones make grinding sounds and the pain descends into his pelvis and he loses control of all his physical functions. He groans in human filthiness.

Jesus opens his eyes again. His mother and John are gone.

The day is dark with a thick darkness.

Thunder rumbles deep in heaven. There is a pause of preternatural calm. Then lightning forks the belly of the clouds. The crash follows immediately, and all at once the wind is shrieking down the Jewish tombs. Trees bow and rise again, the leaves torn forward like women's hair.

The road to Jerusalem clears swiftly of people. The soldiers huddle on the lee side of the hill.

It is noon. And now, when the flashes of lightning themselves are extinguished, the earth is utterly black. Darkness an hour — while the fierce wind makes the rain sting like sand on the skin, and no one, no one exists in all the world but Jesus and his wretched body. If he should call out, who would hear? The wind pulls and snaps his hair like a banner. All his wounds have tongues. They are screaming in pitches higher than hearing.

Darkness another hour — darkness, coiled and thick, itself a power entoiling him, binding his chest and his heart and his mind. Jesus can neither think nor breathe. He is sunk down in *tehom*, the great engulfing flood of the dead, the deeps that boil beneath creation. He has been swallowed by chaos. This is the place: it is here that he is dying.

Darkness the third hour — and now he knows obliteration. Jesus has been blotted out of the Book of Life. Not even God is here.

"Eli?"

No, not even his Father, whose will he is even now obeying, the Father who has loved him from the beginning, whom he has loved, whom he has called Abba.

"Eli? Eli?"

Where is his Father now? Has the Son become so foul that even God cannot look upon him?

It is Jesus of Nazareth who howls out of *Sheol*. None but him. He can hear the words. They are his own words. He howls them up to heaven:

"*My God!*" he shrieks. "*My God, why have you forsaken me?*"

Silence.

The universe is silenced by that cry.

Jesus throws his body outward from the cross. His ribs splay apart in the straining. His shoulders form hollows at the pits of his neck. His mouth is an empty canyon.

Someone says, "Was he calling Elijah?"

"I don't know," says someone else. "Wait and see."

A third person is running through the darkness toward the crosses.

Jesus allows his body to droop. The weight of it draws out his arms, closing the cage around his lungs, constricting his breathing. He can breathe only in faint pants. But he whispers, "I'm thirsty."

"Yes! Yes!" cries the person who has been running toward him. "Yes, drink this."

On a long stalk, this most civil individual raises a sponge to Jesus' lips. He sucks and tastes a common wine. He drinks. Jesus has never drunk so sweet a drink in all his life before.

The rain has ended. The wind has died. A little light sifts down like flour from the clouds.

"It is finished," Jesus gasps. "Father. Into your hands I commend my spirit."

His body falls far forward. His head sinks down between the wings of his rising arms. His heavy black hair, his long wet hair falls over his head like a curtain. An everlasting sigh issues from his open mouth, and that is the end. He dies.

vi

The centurion under whose watch three men were executed outside Jerusalem on the Friday of Passover week retired soon afterward. His twenty years were up. He might have continued in the legions, of course, seeking promotions. But his spirit could no longer be committed to the military.

Nor to Rome, for that matter.

He felt, in fact, released from all the entangled demands by which his life had been lived.

His name was Longinus.

He told the story often, how the man on the middle cross died quickly, almost as if it were an act of volition, a choice he could make.

Jesus of Nazareth, the King of the Jews: there had been a spring storm more terrible than any Longinus had experienced before; and then, as the world was emerging from the darkness, Jesus asked for a drink and he, Longinus, having anticipated the request, was already coming by with some thin wine in a sponge. He lifted the sponge to Jesus, who drank and who then bestowed upon the Roman such a generous and completely personal smile of thanksgiving, that Longinus caught his breath. *So to be known!* he thought to himself. *How can this man possibly know me?*

But the man said something like, "It's all over now," and he put his head down, and he died. Like choosing it. Like the last breath was no more difficult than the first had been. Like making a gift of the remarkable moment to the one who had given him drink. To Longinus: *Here. This is for you.*

Therefore Longinus had said, "Surely, this was the Son of God." And though he said it spontaneously, he never took it back again. He believed it.

Nor was he alone. Some women had watched this man's dying from the beginning. They had stayed through the storm. And the instant he died they knew he was dead and they drew near. They looked at his body with more than affection. They gazed at it with such deep and speechless yearning that they could not cry.

Even in spite of the pain of the yearning, Longinus wished that something in his life might mean that much also to him.

Later that day, he saw again that expression of fathomless yearning. This time in the eyes of a man. A man of some wealth and authority.

About five o'clock in the afternoon, Pilate called Longinus into his presence and asked whether Jesus of Nazareth were truly dead already.

"Yes," the centurion said.

"What, in less than half a day? Everyone else takes days to die."

"It's unusual, but I saw him die. He's dead."

"And I suppose you sought the evidence of it?"

"Well, I wouldn't have, except that the Jews want all three taken down before the evening. Their Sabbath."

"I know, I know," Pilate said. "There's a fellow here who wants the body of Jesus the Nazarene. A member of their Sanhedrin. Joseph. He wants to bury him in his own tomb. You are sure, then — he's dead?"

"My lord, we went to break the legs of the criminals to hasten their dying. But Jesus was already dead. A soldier proved it by piercing his side with a spear. The blood that flowed out was mingled with water."

Pontius Pilate waved a fat hand in front of his face. "I will never understand this people. Never. Go tell that fellow Joseph he has my permission. He's waiting in the shadows of the gate. Go."

It was in the eyes of Joseph of Arimathea that Longinus saw the yearning for the second time. Therefore, he attached himself to the Jew.

They returned together to Golgotha.

Joseph — a man well-groomed and richly dressed — knelt down on the earth and unrolled a linen cloth. It was an expensive piece, close-woven and white. Then he leaned a ladder against the back of Jesus' cross. He took a rope and an iron claw, and climbed up behind the body, which still hung from its arms, away from the pole. Joseph looped the rope around the chest of the dead. Then, pulling the ends back under his armpits and over the crossbeam, he tossed them down to Longinus.

With sudden, violent wrenches of the claw, Joseph yanked the spike from Jesus' left wrist. The body swung out and hung from the right arm.

Longinus tightened the rope, taking Jesus up somewhat. Joseph applied himself to the right spike. It whimpered in the wood, and Jesus slumped altogether forward into the loop of rope. Longinus felt the weight in both ends of the rope.

"Hold him, sir," Joseph whispered. "Hold him."

He scurried down the ladder and stood below the slouching corpse, under the face and the black rain of the dead man's hair. He put the claw to the spike through Jesus' ankles. Longinus heard that he was weeping when he pulled that spike.

Even as Joseph spread his arms to catch the corpse, he glanced to the centurion and whispered, "Now," and Longinus paid the rope out, and Jesus came down into Joseph's arms, one at the bend of the knees and one around his shoulders. The head fell over Joseph's left arm. The mouth opened up under Joseph's close gazing, and then again Longinus saw that holy yearning in his eyes.

Joseph of Arimathea was holding his whole treasure in all the world — this world and the next one, too.

He lay his Lord upon the white shroud. He wound the linen around him.

And here came the women again. They knelt like flowers around Joseph's tender wrapping. They each touched the broad, bloodless forehead of the dead man before it, too, was covered in cloth. Then they watched as Joseph took the shoulders and Longinus took the feet and together they bore the body to Joseph's tomb, carved in rock with others of the Jews.

Joseph knelt down and backed in. Longinus knelt and went forward. They lifted the body to a low ledge cut in stone on the right. They came out again and rolled a wheel-sized stone down a groove that had been etched just outside the sepulcher, until the heavy stone covered the door.

So, then, it was done.

Jesus of Nazareth was buried.

Evening fell. The Sabbath arrived.

But Longinus did not observe it. He was not a Jew. Neither was he the Roman he had been. The events of that day inaugurated for him a time of crippling confusion.

In the next days he did two things:

He left the army completely, seeking no reward at his departure, no villa to which he might retire, no final recognition. As far as his superiors were concerned, Longinus had perished from the face of the earth.

And then he went through Jerusalem seeking a small child whose hands had been disfigured by burning half a year ago, who had nearly died from a blow to her head. This little girl had no parents. Her grandmother was elderly and widowed. She had an uncle — but whether he felt obliged to care for her, Longinus could not know.

Therefore, the Roman decided that if the girl had been abandoned, he would raise her as his own. For he was the man responsible for her troubles and her injuries.

If, on the other hand, her uncle loved her and was caring for her after all, then Longinus would offer his help as a brother to Barabbas, a second uncle to his niece. And if that were not acceptable, then he would be a servant to them both.

39

THE NEW COVENANT

i

There was no gathering of professional mourners that Saturday. No voices at all were raised in a public lamentation.

It was the Sabbath. Religious law forbade engaging in thirty-nine various forms of work on the Sabbath. One could comfort the bereaved as a friend or relative. But not as a professional.

Then again, it was not required of mourners on *any* day to lament the death of a criminal.

Jesus of Nazareth had been executed. His death had been completely legal. This wasn't a loss. It was a restoration of order and the public good. One doesn't lament a healing.

And what of those who loved him?

They were in hiding.

They muted their grief. No one in Jerusalem heard their crying, neither the authorities nor the great milling herd of pilgrims come for the Passover. Someone calculated that the number of sheep sacrificed that week was two hundred and fifty-five thousand, six hundred. Into so vast a blood-red sea the death of one Galilean dropped with scarcely a splash. And when several hundred thousand lambs are bawling before their slaughter, who can hear the voices of two humans weeping?

Just as well.

Those who loved Jesus did not want to be heard. They were terrified.

Simon Peter, John, Matthew, James, Andrew, Thomas, Philip — all of the twelve except Judas — had returned one by one, spontaneously, to the house of the Essene and to the upper room where they had eaten their last meal with the Master. Here they huddled all day Saturday behind locked doors.

The women went to Bethany.

So many Marys, all like blossoms wilting: they sat at home with Martha and Lazarus. Mary their sister rose to serve them. She brought towels moistened in cool water. Martha rocked herself, round as a barrel, and listened to singing.

Mary, the Lord's mother, would be quiet a while, her head bent. But then the storm of her sorrow would strike as if in the forehead: she would fall backward clutching her temples in two hands and deliver herself to wailing. Her hair had been as dark as her son's once. Now even from her widow's peak it was streaked with silver, and the sword was in her soul. Joanna and Susanna, who sat on either side of the grieving mother, fanned her when she wept. They nodded and murmured words of consolation and beat air into her face with relentless force until her sobs subsided. Then they, too, turned and listened to the singing.

Mary Salome, the wife of Zebedee, the mother of John and James, also was there in the house, though she had chosen to sit somewhat out of sight behind Martha's large clay firepot. She'd been at the tombs when they buried Jesus. There, too, she had concealed herself in the darkness. Mary Salome *had* heard the words that Jesus uttered from the cross. *All* of them — including the terrible sentence that joined *his* mother to *her* son. Because he was speaking from his death-engine, the new relationship seemed as solemn as a wedding. It confused her regarding herself. Had she lost a son as well? Therefore, she retreated into darkness a while.

Mary Magdalene, her lips gone bloodless; the flesh around her eyes so blue and wounded; her fingers twitching like the limbs of a spider; her thin bones shivering — this Mary was not crying. She was singing. Her voice was little, like a child's, like a small bubble of water. But it was absolutely accurate. And the melody was lovely.

That's why the women were listening. Because the melody was sweet and the song was happy. There was no sorrow in this song. It was a tune for love and dancing:

"Catch us the foxes," she sang, "the little foxes that plunder the vineyards." Then softly, softly: "Our vines are in blossom — come!"

And again she sang: "My beloved speaks and says to me:

> *Arise, my love, my bright one, come!*
> *For the winter is past and the rain is gone,*
> > *the flowers are voices*
> > *for song and all choices,*
> *and turtledoves laugh in the land —* "

Mary Magdalene paused in the midst of her singing. She spent a moment in reflection. Then she said, "His locks were wavy, as black as a raven. His eyes were like doves by springs of water, bathed in milk and beautiful."

The women listened, and all the women nodded. His eyes were like doves. They knew what Mary meant.

ii

E arly Sunday morning, as soon as the Sabbath restrictions were lifted and they could in good conscience travel distances, three women left Bethany for Jerusalem, Mary Magdalene, Mary Salome, and Joanna.

Midway around the northern rise of the Mount of Olives, Mary Magdalene stopped and looked at the others.

"Did you feel that?" she said. "Did the earth tremble?"

Each woman was carrying cloths and a jar in her arms, myrrh in one, frankincense, nard. They meant to anoint the corpse of the Lord with spices, their final honor to him whom they loved. It was only the third day since he had been buried.

"It seemed that the ground moved under my feet."

"It *did* move," said Joanna.

Mary Salome said, "But there was no sound."

Neither was there light yet, though the stars were dimming in a charcoal sky. Dawn was behind them.

"Let's go."

"Hurry. Please hurry."

They skirted Jerusalem on its northern side, then turned south to the garden in which Joseph's tomb had been newly hewn in rock. Mary Magdalene was peering forward and muttering, "But who will roll the stone?" She couldn't make out which sepulcher was Joseph's. The wall of the city was on their left, blocking any eastern light. All the tombs were in shadow.

Suddenly Joanna shrieked and dropped her jar.

Mary Salome dropped hers, too. It shattered.

A pillar of white light, bright as a blade, had shot down from heaven and stood on the stone of Joseph's tomb. That stone was lying flat on the ground.

Mary Magdalene gasped. The dawn air smelled of myrrh.

A voice said: *Don't be afraid.*

It seemed to Mary that the light contained the figure of a man, glorious in every aspect and so bright that brightness itself was his clothing.

The man said, *You seek Jesus of Nazareth, who was crucified. He is not here. Behold the place where they laid him. Then run to tell his disciples that he goes before you into Galilee. There you shall see him as he said to you.*

The light withdrew into heaven, leaving the women blinded and terrified. That voice had been no consolation.

Mary Salome gathered her robe up and started to run back the way that they had come.

Mary Magdalene, void of all expression, began moving toward the tomb itself.

"Mary, *don't!*" Joanna rushed forward and pulled at her sleeve, but then she shrank back from the open tomb, wailing, "Mary, please! It was an earthquake! It was the Romans or the wrath of God. Whatever happened, it's all over now. Mary, please, let's go!"

Mary did not respond. The small, solemn, pale woman now knelt down directly in front of the black hole in stone.

This was more than Joanna could bear. "We can't tell *anyone*," she cried, and dashed after Mary Salome.

Mary Magdalene bent forward and stretched her hand into the shadow of the sepulcher. Cold air. A dead air, but no odor. On the right side in darkness she touched a flank of hewn stone. With her fingers' tips she measured upward one cubit and came to its surface: this was the ledge upon which they had laid the body of the Lord. She reached deeper in darkness, preparing to touch his rigid corpse — but found nothing. Felt nothing. There was nothing there.

Mary's stomach twisted. He was *gone*! He *was* gone, as the blinding white figure had said!

Mary jumped up.

Daybreak: there were flecks of golden fire over Jerusalem, south between the stone wall and the hill of crosses. She ran through the Garden Gate into the city and up the road that led to Zion. She ran to the house of the Essene and beat on his door. She beat and beat till someone came and opened it. Then she rushed through the vestibule, out the back to a second building built higher than the first, up its stairs to another door, which was locked: "Simon!" she cried. "Simon! Simon, open the door!"

Not since Jesus had driven the demons out of her had Mary moved with such strength and ferocity. If Simon didn't open the door soon, she had a mind to crack it like a cask with her forehead. *Behold, Mary! Mary Magdalene is crazy again!*

But Simon did open the door.

And Mary immediately was chattering:

"They took the Lord out of the tomb, out of the *tomb*, Simon, Joseph's tomb, the tomb itself, and we don't know where they put him — "

Simon grabbed her and demanded, "Are you sure?"

Mary said, "It was dark, but I put my hand in — "

But Simon Peter was already racing down the steps and out into the street.

John cried, "Simon, I'm coming, too." He flew past Mary. He ran so fast that he outdistanced Simon.

Mary followed both men. She caught up to Simon at the Garden Gate, and when they both came to the tomb they found John kneeling at the entrance peering into it.

Simon pushed John aside and went in.

The morning light had strengthened. Mary could see what Simon Peter was looking at inside: the shroud — still in its windings on the ledge, but flat. And there was the cloth that had covered Jesus' head, rolled up in a place by itself.

Now John, too, crawled into the tomb. The two men crowded the small space, so Mary pulled back and stood aside, shifting her weight from foot to foot.

When the men came out they were shaking their heads and saying nothing.

"Simon?" Mary begged. "John?"

But they began to walk away, each consumed by his own thought.

Mary ran ahead and stood directly in front of Simon Peter. "What are you going to do about it?" she said. "How will we find his body?"

Simon put his big face close to hers. She saw his jowls trembling. "Leave it alone!" he said. "Don't you think we're in enough danger already?" Then he walked away. John followed.

Mary watched until they disappeared into the city and then, finally, she began to cry.

No, Mary Magdalene was not strong again. She was weak and helpless and sad and desolate. And now that the tears had begun, she could not control herself at all. She went to the place where Mary Salome had broken her jar of myrrh. She knelt down and gathered the pieces and tried to fit them together again. But she couldn't. She could hardly *see*. Weeping filled her vision with such a rain of sorrow, that all the world was blurred.

She dropped the clay shards and howled like a small child lost. *Yes, Mary is crazy again, and she doesn't care. She doesn't care.*

"Woman?"

Someone was calling to her.

"Woman?" It was a clear voice, breaking through the morning and the roaring in her head.

"Woman," it said, "why are you weeping?"

Huffing with her sobs, Mary looked up and thought she saw the gardener coming.

"Because they took my Lord away," she sobbed, "and I don't know where they put him."

The man said, "Who are you looking for?"

"Oh, sir!" Mary said, rising up, "if you are the one who carried him off, tell me where he is and I'll get him myself."

Now the man stopped directly in front of her — long, dark hair through her swim of tears. A white tunic. Clean-shaven.

In a soft, familiar voice, the man said, "Oh, Mary."

She gasped.

She looked and saw the beautiful forehead, the raven black hair of her dear Lord Jesus and his steadfast, golden gaze!

"*Rabboni!*" she cried.

"Hush, hush, child — hush." Jesus placed a finger to his lips. "You cannot cling to me now," he said. "I haven't yet ascended to my Father. But go to my friends and tell them that I am ascending to my Father and your Father, to my God and your God."

Oh, yes, Mary Magdalene was very strong indeed, and swifter than the north wind blowing toward Jerusalem. She was fair and she was lovely now, her lips like a scarlet thread, her cheeks like halves of a pomegranate.

The morning was still young when she arrived for the second time at the upper room and stood in the doorway laughing into the dark den of gloomy disciples.

Mary couldn't help herself. It was his great grim mouth that drove her to it. She threw out her arms and ran to Simon Peter crying: "Simon, dance with me! Hug me and spin me around, because I have just seen the Lord. *He is alive!* Simon, Simon, he has risen from the dead!"

iii

On that same morning, the third day of their desolation, one of the disciples decided to go home and perhaps to stay there permanently. Cleopas told the others that he wanted to take his daughter out of harm's way — which meant out of Jerusalem, away from the authorities that had arranged for the death of their Master. Besides, he argued: what should keep him here anymore? The wheel was off the wagon, the axle broken; it would not move again. Jesus was dead. Life itself was ashes now. Cleopas said that he was tasting the dry soot of futility in his mouth.

What he didn't say was that he was angry.

If he stayed with the other disciples, he knew that sooner or later he would attack them. Words for sure, words of a monumental scorn for these blithering fools. But he'd hit them, too, and if he had a club in his hand he might very well break skulls.

So he took his daughter and left.

Their house was in Emmaus, about seven miles west of the city. It was one of the villages Pilate had ravaged in order to capture Barabbas. Oh, yes, Cleopas had a sort of singing fury in his heart. As they went, he found himself reviewing all the things that had happened since they had come to Jerusalem.

Each detail was new tinder to the fire.

His daughter, eighteen years old, walked quietly beside him, sometimes asking the question that kept him talking. She, too, had been a disciple of Jesus. By her own deciding. But part of that decision, Cleopas knew, was her desire to take care of him, her father. She was good at listening.

"Abba," she said, "you're more than sad, aren't you? You're something else."

He stuck out his bottom lip. "I'm so angry I can hardly breathe," he said.

She said, "Why? Who are you angry at?"

And he would have answered the question by naming a thousand names — but just then he realized that there was a stranger pacing them, walking the same road in the same direction.

As soon as Cleopas glanced at him, the stranger said, "Friends, what are you talking about?"

All at once Cleopas' daughter stopped and put her head down and began to cry. Until that moment it had not occurred to him that she would be as sorrowful as he. Cleopas made a fist and growled, "What do you *think* we're talking about?"

The stranger shrugged. "I don't know," he said.

"What's the matter with you?" Cleopas said. "Are you the only visitor who doesn't know the things that have happened in Jerusalem these days?"

"What things?" said the stranger.

But his daughter answered before he could. "Concerning Jesus of Nazareth," she said gently. "He was a prophet mighty in deed and word before God and all the people. But the chief priests and the rulers condemned him to death. They crucified him," she whispered. "He died," she said. "But we had hoped that he was the one to redeem Israel."

Cleopas, hearing such despair in his young daughter, suddenly realized who he was angry at.

"This morning an idiot woman told us that the grave was empty and that Jesus was alive," he said. "Simon went and looked. They were right. The grave was empty. But that means absolutely nothing. And he who caused us to hope has now become the death of hope! Jesus, Teacher, Messiah — pah! This is what that dead man taught me: to hate life because everything is vanity and nothing is more than a striving after wind!"

Cleopas was furious with Jesus.

"Ah, you foolish fellow," the stranger said, "slow to believe what the prophets have spoken!"

If his daughter hadn't put her arms around him and held him so tightly, Cleopas would have hit the man.

Softly, earnestly, she asked, "What *did* the prophets say?"

"That it was necessary for the Christ to suffer these things in order to enter his glory."

"Abba?" she whispered. "Abba, let's walk."

Cleopas obeyed.

Then while they walked toward Emmaus, the strange man spoke, holding their attention, fascinating them both with the depth of his knowledge, and causing in them a rebirth of wonder. For, beginning with Moses and the

prophets, he interpreted in all the scriptures the things concerning Messiah
— how everything that had been prophesied was fulfilled in Jesus.

Except the absence, Cleopas thought. *Messiah would never have left us
alone.*

It was near evening when they came to Emmaus.

As they approached their own home, Cleopas' remarkable daughter took
the strange man's hand and said, "The day is nearly over. Sir, stay with us.
Let us prepare a meal for you."

The man had steadfast eyes, utterly unthreatening and unafraid. He
smiled his agreement. Cleopas surprised himself by feeling some pleasure at
the stranger's acceptance.

But when they all sat down to eat, their visitor smiled and began to act as
if this were *his* house and *he* were the host. He took the bread and blessed it
and broke it and gave it to them.

In the instant they touched the bread, their eyes were opened. As if just
waking up, Cleopas recognized the features of the Lord, his eyes like polished
amber. The stranger had been Jesus all along! But in that same instant, Jesus
vanished. Cleopas and his daughter were sitting at the table alone.

"Now I know," the woman breathed, luminous with awe, so devout that it
caused her father almost to weep. "Now I know why my heart was burning
while he talked to us on the road!"

They rose up — both of them, father and daughter, fresh with joy — and
hurried back to Jerusalem to tell the disciples what had happened on the
road, and how the Lord was known to them in the breaking of the bread.

▌

That same evening ten disciples were huddled in the upper room. The door
had been locked more than three days now, the windows shut against spying
eyes. The air was fetid.

Thomas, irritated with the indolence of the others, had gone out to find
food.

Some of the men dozed on their backs on the floor. Some sat as if in
conversation, though no one was speaking.

The table where they'd eaten the Passover last Thursday had been
removed. The side table remained. Two candles burned fitfully on either end
of it. The room shuddered in shadow.

Simon Peter was pacing back and forth like a lion behind bars. It was his
restlessness that caused the candle flames to bow and gutter.

Matthew said, "I've lost count."

James said, "Of what?"

"How many times the rock-man has thrown himself east and west in our
small country."

"The man's a menace," James said. "If he lands on someone, he'll crush him — then there'll be ten of us."

"Grim talk, James."

"Grim times, Matthew. We're hiding here because the leaders want to blot us out. You know Simon has never been a tranquil man. But look at him now. He's out of control. Who knows what he'll do? Yes, he could get someone killed."

Andrew said, "Something's troubling my brother."

"Oh, poor Peter!" James exclaimed. "As if there's no trouble for anyone else! Jesus is dead. Does your tender brother mourn him more than the rest of us?"

Andrew put his head down, near tears.

Matthew, as dry as chalk, murmured, "No need for ridicule, James."

John said, "Maybe Jesus isn't dead."

James turned on him. "Women talk!" he sneered. "The talk of hysterical women!"

"I was at the tomb, James," John said. "His body was not there."

Matthew spoke moderating words. "Absence is no proof," he said.

"A stolen corpse!" James declared.

John said, "But his windings were still there. And the cloth that had covered his face was rolled up in a place by itself. What, then, brother? Neat thieves? Tidy thieves?"

James fairly shouted: "No need for ridicule, John! I'm just asking for proof. I haven't seen any proof."

Andrew raised his eyes and whispered, "The curtain that hides the Most Holy Place in the Temple — when Jesus died it tore in two, from the top to the bottom."

"How did you know that?" James sneered. "Were you there?"

"No," Andrew murmured, withdrawing again into himself. "Simon told me. Simon was there."

James the son of Zebedee jumped up shouting, "What is the *matter* with you, stone-head? Don't you have any sense?"

Simon stopped pacing and looked at James. "What?"

"Do you deliberately endanger us, or are you just stupid?"

"What are you talking about?"

"Ahhh!" James growled, turning away, "he's another Judas."

Andrew gasped.

Simon's body snapped into a fighting posture. "James," he bellowed, "explain yourself!"

James whirled about and matched the bellow: "No, you explain yourself, you public spectacle! What were you doing in the Temple when Jesus was dying?"

"Praying!" Simon shouted. He began to move toward James with his knees bent, his elbows crooked, his fingers like grappling hooks. "I was begging forgiveness."

James, too, lowered himself for the attack and spread his arms.

Matthew began to stand, saying, "Brothers, there are other enemies — "

At the same moment Andrew flew toward Simon and John rose up in front of James.

But James, glaring at Simon, whispered with calculated spite: "Get behind me, Satan!"

Simon howled like a wild beast, his face distorted by violent emotions. He stumbled backward a moment, then he gathered his body into a low projectile and prepared to launch himself at James. There was such a haunting in his eyes that the disciples instinctively fell away from him.

Suddenly a beam of blinding white light split the room at its center.

And then it was no light at all, but the bright figure of a human, standing among them, standing directly between Simon Peter and James.

And then the figure was Jesus.

He said, "Peace be with you."

Simon dropped to the floor, sitting with his legs straight out in front of him. James gaped. No one spoke. Andrew knelt down and covered his face.

Jesus allowed his eyes to travel over each man in the room. He was so clean! — his clothing radiant, his arms like rounded gold, his body an alabaster column. He opened his white robe so that they could see the scar in his side. He showed them, too, the spike scars at the ends of his arms.

John breathed, "It is you, Lord."

The eyes of the disciples began to shed fear and to glitter at the sight before them: "O Lord, it's *you!*"

Again Jesus said, "Peace be with you," and nodded to make the word personal unto each one of them. Then he said, "Friends, you know that the Father sent me into the world. In the same way I now send you. Not just disciples anymore — I make you my apostles."

Jesus stood over Andrew and placed his hands on the shy man's head. The breath that descended from the Lord's nostrils seemed scented of myrrh. Andrew smelled myrrh as Jesus touched him and said, "Receive the Holy Spirit."

Likewise, Jesus placed his hands on John's head and breathed on him: *Receive the Holy Spirit.* And on James, on Matthew and Philip and Nathanael and all the disciples. Last, he came to Simon Peter.

Throughout this gentle ceremony Jesus was saying: "If you forgive the sins of the people, their sins will be forgiven. If you hold their sins, they will be held fast."

Then, with such civility that it seemed the right and proper thing to do, Jesus departed, and no one tried to stop him.

All ten men remained motionless, enshrouded each in his own wonder.

James whispered: "Mary Magdalene was right."

Andrew said to himself: "Judas should have waited."

Simon, in a corner alone, muttered, "What am I to do? O God, what am I to do?"

Suddenly the door banged open and all the disciples jumped up, ready to protect themselves. Who had left the door unlocked? But in came Cleopas, pounding his right fist into his left hand and crying, "We have seen the Lord!"

His daughter behind him nodded with shining eyes, "Yes, it's true. We've seen the Lord."

∎

A week passed. Stories about the Lord's appearances began to spread privately among his people. Lazarus and Mary and Martha heard them. So did Joseph of Arimathea. Well, it was his tomb. Someone had to tell him that it had not been robbed in the manner he thought.

A man named Nicodemus searched out the disciples. He was a member of the Sanhedrin. James met him, then, in secret and with much caution. But the fellow confessed an ever-growing fascination with Jesus; and now that there were stories of his resurrection, Nicodemus could not stay silent any more.

"Is it true?" he begged of James.

James said, "Why do you want to know?"

Nicodemus said, "Three years ago he told me I had to be born again to enter the kingdom. *Born again*, he said, *of water and the Spirit*. If he's alive after dying, you see, then his word is true. And he said, *Whoever believes in the Son of man may have eternal life*."

James the son of Zebedee said to Nicodemus, "Yes. It's true. Jesus was raised from the dead."

"Ah!" The member of the Jewish Council couldn't contain himself. He plucked at his robes, he rubbed his chin, he smiled and frowned, he looked glad and bewildered and transported. "See?" he said. "Oh, sir, do you see? This is what I know. This is what I was told, that God loved the world so much, he gave it his only Son, and those who believe in him will never perish. They will have eternal life."

As the stories of the Lord's appearing spread, so did remembrance of his teaching — and so did joy.

Shobal, whose name means Basket, the odd fellow out of whom Jesus had cast an evil spirit, suddenly walked into the upper room and started to laugh. A drooling, lank sort of laughter. He tried to stop, but he couldn't. He laughed and laughed, and the first one to laugh with him was Mary the mother of Jesus, who had not laughed in many a year. Mary and Shobal laughed like children together, holding hands and turning circles. And most of the disciples became infected with this dithering joy. They barked and bellowed and giggled and roared.

"Shobal," cried Philip, "however did you get here from Capernaum?"

But Shobal only winked and nodded and laughed.

Simon Peter stood to the side and smiled, but he didn't laugh. He couldn't. It wasn't in him to laugh these days.

Thomas was downright peevish in the midst of such groundless gladness. "You're living in some illusion!" he growled.

Simon answered him: "No, we really have seen the Lord."

"Just like Mary Magdalene saw him, right?"

"She did," said Simon.

"People *want* to believe he's alive," Thomas said. "I don't blame that. It's natural. But it is not natural to turn your wants into your reality. That's dangerous."

Simon Peter had no heart for the debate. But James did. Vigorously he proclaimed: "He was here, Thomas, in this very room, while you were gone looking for food. Jesus appeared, even though the doors were locked, and showed us his scars and blessed us, each one of us!"

Thomas, the "blunt hunter," got very specific then. "If I can't see it, I can't believe it. Tell you what, James, let me touch the scars from the spike; let me put my hand in his side, and *then* I'll believe it."

On Sunday night the disciples were again gathered in the upper room. Again, candles were burning at either end of the table. There was a general quietness among the people there, repose before sleep. Softly Simon Peter was murmuring prayers — psalms, by the sound of it. He looked dark and forbidding. He hadn't shaved for ten days now.

But Thomas felt himself to be alien here. Everyone else seemed bound together by some ethereal experience which excluded him. His mood was sour. He was planning to leave these people and this place but he hadn't yet decided where to go. Certainly, he didn't feel like sleeping now.

Then someone directly behind him said, "Peace be with you."

The voice was murmurous and personal. Thomas began to turn around — then leaped to his feet, all his nerves singing.

It was Jesus! Between two candles on the table, there stood Jesus, solemn and erect! Candlelight brushed the sides of his face with an orange warmth and shade. He was looking at Thomas, though the other disciples, too, were rising now and forming a semicircle.

"Come here," Jesus said.

No one moved. Thomas sent furtive glances left and right, but all the men were waiting on him. Jesus was speaking to none but him: "Thomas, come here."

Slowly Thomas approached.

As he did, Jesus opened the palms of his hands and said, "Reach out your finger. Examine my wounds."

Thomas wanted to say, *No need, no need, Lord.* But he was crushed and couldn't speak.

Jesus opened his robe so that his flesh was visible from the ribs to his hip. "Reach out your hand and put it into my side," he said.

But Thomas wrapped his arms around his own chest and began to sink down to his knees. *No need, Lord.*

"Thomas, once and for all I tell you: Do not be faithless but believing!"

The poor disciple, now completely bowed down before Jesus, whispered, "My Lord and my God!"

Jesus put his hands on Thomas' head. The scent of myrrh spilled through the room, and Jesus said, "Have you believed because you've seen me? Hear my final beatitude: Blessed are those who have not seen and who nevertheless believe."

iv

SIMON PETER

I let my beard grow back. The first days I was too sad to shave. Didn't think about it. But then the Lord Jesus rose from the dead exactly as he said he would — exactly, you see, as he *said*, which is part of the problem, because I never really paid attention to that saying, because I didn't believe he would *die*, so how should I even *consider* that he could come back to life again? — but he did, exactly as he said he would, rise up from the dead and he appeared in person before us, and I was astonished, I was speechless, I was so *glad* for him and so overjoyed for the whole world, but yet at the same time I was sick inside myself. I can't describe this. It's impossible. Nothing is greater than this. God is here. God is in Jesus. The kingdom of God begins in Jesus! And as much as I *know* that, as much as I love and *believe* it, that's how much I loathe myself. That's how horrible I feel. Because I'll never enter that kingdom. I don't deserve to. I gave up my right. I denied my Lord. I rejected him to save myself. Do you understand this? It's at the time of crisis that the truth comes out, and I . . . I'm the one who swore he didn't know Jesus. So after the first days I let my beard grow on purpose. It would be hypocrisy to think that I could be like my Lord anymore.

Mary Magdalene said we should go to Galilee. Mary Salome and Joanna agreed. They said that an angel told them that Jesus would meet us there. So we went. Everyone. All the disciples. A very happy band. Much chatter and singing. The weather was beautiful, clear and dry. The barley fields were white for harvest. I saw it all in gratitude — and in sorrow.

Jesus' mother walked by John. She looked so lovely that I felt like crying. Thomas and Matthew were becoming good friends. My brother spent most of his time with Mary Magdalene. Shobal came with us, grinning like a puppy.

By the time we got to Capernaum, I couldn't stand it anymore. I had to do something, something I could throw my body into but something familiar so I wouldn't have to *think*!

I said, "I'm going fishing," and ran away from the lot of them.

I had given my boat to my brother-in-law. He's a careful fisherman. Nets, lines, spears, mast, sail, oars — it was all in good condition. But he wasn't there, and I didn't ask. I inspected the equipment and prepared the boat. Then at dusk, just as I was shoving off, here came a group of disciples, not a thought in their heads except to follow my lead.

My brother came with me. Mary Magdalene, too, tucked herself down in the middle of the boat.

James and John and Nathanael began to get their boat ready while we pulled away. They knew where we would drop nets. They would find us.

That night the stars were like sand on the seashore. The black sky was swollen with stars. Mary dozed. Andrew and I did not talk. We worked. I was grateful for the darkness and the work. It didn't bother me that we caught nothing.

In the grey light of the morning I heard James calling, "Simon? Simon?"

I spied the Zebedee boat some distance through the mist. It was riding high in the water. They hadn't caught anything either.

"Simon, let's go in."

So we shifted positions. Mary moved into the prow. My brother and I took oars and began to pull for shore. He and I faced the red bubble of the sun as it broke horizon and set the lake on fire.

Suddenly Mary said, "Who's that?"

We looked over our shoulders. There was a man standing on the beach, his tunic like a flame in the sunrise light.

"Ho! Children!" he called to us. "Have you caught anything?"

James yelled, "No!" Their boat was just off our stern.

The man on shore called: "Cast your nets on the right side and see what you catch!"

Immediately, John stood up in his boat and swept his net open and cast it to the right. It sank for a moment, then it came to life, the water boiling and churning with fish.

James went crazy. He almost lost the lead lines when he cast his net. It, too, foamed up with fish. And Andrew cast in the same direction, and I did, too, before we realized that each net was so heavy it needed two men to haul it in.

"Simon!" John was calling. All four of us were straining just to bring the nets near the gunwales. "Simon, it's Jesus! That is the Lord on shore!"

The word went through me like a sword, a sweet, terrible pain. I looked through the burning distance and in a mystery saw every feature of his face. So I couldn't hold still. I lashed my net to the gunwale. I tied my work clothes close to my waist and threw myself into the sea and swam for shore as fast as I could.

Stupid! Stupid! When I came up out of the water I couldn't think of anything to say. I stood there feeling wretched.

Jesus had kindled a charcoal fire. Bread and fish were already laid on it, breakfast for one. He didn't look at me. He looked to the boats still struggling shoreward. So there were those who belonged to him, working and worthy — and here was I, idle and unworthy.

Andrew had also lashed his net to the gunwale. He was rowing the boat alone. Nathanael and John rowed while James kept their huge catch close to the side of the boat. As they came close, I waded back into the water and helped drag the nets onto dry land. We spread out a wide carpet of glittering fish.

Jesus said, "Bring some of the fish. Come and have breakfast with me."

We sat. Jesus sat among us. He served us one after the other. He served me last. I couldn't eat.

Neither was he eating. He kept looking at me.

Oh, those eyes, dead level and lidded! He would not stop looking at me. I wanted to crawl away. And I *would* have, but he opened his mouth and spoke to me.

"Simon son of Jonah," he said, "do you love me more than these?"

"Yes, Lord!" I think I shouted the answer. It came *immediately*, all on its own: "Yes, Lord, you know that I love you."

He neither smiled nor blinked. Solemnly he said, "Feed my lambs."

Did he mean it? Was he granting me a place with him? I held that notion very tenderly, very uncertainly.

But still, he did not stop staring at me.

And he spoke again.

"Simon son of Jonah, do you love me?"

The same words. The second time.

Carefully — because I *meant* it and I wanted him to believe that I meant it — I said, "Yes, Lord. You know that I love you."

He said, "Tend my sheep."

Even then this wasn't over. He kept looking at me. And now I knew what was coming, and it did come.

For the third time he said, "Simon son of Jonah, do you love me?"

I bowed my head and started to cry like a child. He was asking and he was telling, both. He knew. He knew. He knew how many times I said I did not even know him. He knew.

I couldn't raise my face to him. I said, "Lord, you know everything. You know that I love you."

There was a great silence after that. Someone was moving, but no one said anything.

And then I felt his hand on my shoulder. Jesus was kneeling in front of me. He crooked a finger beneath my chin and lifted my head, and I looked through my tears and saw his eyes filled with such kindness that I only bawled the harder.

He said, "Feed my sheep."

Yes! Jesus was offering me a place in the kingdom.

Be a shepherd of my flock.

Yes, Lord! Yes!

"Peter, when you were a young man," he said, "you used to fasten your own belt and go wherever you wanted to go. But when you grow old you will stretch out your hands and someone else will fasten a belt around you and take you where you don't want to go. Do you understand?" His expression was ancient and earnest, filled with meaning: *Peter, do you understand? I am telling you the sort of death you will die, by which you will glorify God.*

I nodded. I understood.

So then he stood up, and he said to me all over again what he had said at the very beginning.

He said, "Follow me."

V

In those days the priests in Jerusalem purchased a potter's field south of the city at the confluence of its three valleys, the Tyropoeon, the Hinnom, and the Kidron valleys.

They paid thirty pieces of silver for the land and designated it as a burial place for strangers who died in Jerusalem.

They had determined that this money was good for no other use. Certainly, it could never have been returned to the Temple treasury. It was, they said, blood money.

It had the taint of two deaths on it.

∎

Judas Iscariot had kissed Jesus, saying, *Hail, Master.*

Jesus did not praise his disciple. Neither did he seize the moment or the power. He said, *Betray.* He called the act a betrayal.

Simon had tried to fight on the Master's behalf. Judas had cried out his title, *Messiah!* But Jesus disarmed the one and rebuked the other, and every dream died, and all the world was darkness then: *There shall be no legions of angels here. You have mistaken me, Judas! Of all my disciples, you have disappointed me the most.*

Judas dropped his torch.

He fell back into the night.

When the procession of soldiers led Jesus through Jerusalem to the high priest's house, Judas followed. Then he stood outside the back wall, waiting.

He had never desired anything for his Master but power and glory and dominion. Not the arrest. Not captivity. Not death, not ever death.

Jesus is an eloquent man. He will persuade them of his innocence.

But then the word came down from the windows above: *Blasphemy!*

And the question: *What sentence does he deserve?*

When the council began to cry, *Death, death,* Judas bolted from the high priest's house. He ran down into the Tyropoeon valley then up the Temple hill. He dashed through seven degrees of holiness and even breached the eighth: through the Court of the Women, through the Court of the Israelites, into the Court of the Priests where he thrust himself between the High Altar and the porch.

Priests rushed to block him there. His presence was a profanation.

I have sinned! wailed Judas Iscariot. *I sinned against innocent blood!*

That's your affair, not ours, the priests snarled. *Get out of here!*

Judas tore a pouch from over his shoulder. He took hold of its long leather strap and whirled it round his head like a sling. The priests scattered. The pouch was as heavy as a weapon. But then it burst open, and silver coins flew ringing over the stone floor of the porch and into the sanctuary of the Temple, the ninth degree of holiness.

Then he walked away.

Jesus Iscariot crossed the Temple courts to the extreme southeastern corner. This was the largest section of Herod's wall, brutal in size and conception. Its dressed stones were more than thirty-six feet long. They weighed one hundred tons. Within the spaces of this heavy masonry, Judas climbed stone stairs to an old storeroom. It had a high small window facing east. Outside, the wall dropped straight down from a pinnacle of the Temple into the Kidron valley. Inside, the window admitted a little dawn light.

Judas looked around the dim room. One lamp, cold and dead, hung from the ceiling by a tough hempen cord. Judas stood on stools to untie the cord, first from the ceiling and then from the lamp.

He tied one end tightly around the leg of a stool, then he set that stool under the eastern window and stood on it.

He looked out at the Mount of Olives, black in front of the grey dawning. The heavens were thick with cloud. It would storm today.

Judas tied the other end of the cord around his neck and crawled out on the window's stone ledge. He turned so that he was facing into the room, kneeling, waiting. Slowly he rocked backward past the balance point, then he relaxed. The cord yanked the stool up from the floor. It caught in the window casements and stuck there.

∎

Regarding the thirty pieces of silver which Judas Iscariot had flung into the Temple, the priests said, "It isn't lawful to put this in the treasury again. It is blood money."

So the field which they purchased by means of that silver they called Akeldama: The Field of Blood.

∎

One morning Mary of Bethany awoke with the familiar sensation that the Lord was outside, sitting in their courtyard under the grapevine, praying. For a moment she lay still, content that he should have come. But then the events of the last month rushed into her consciousness, and she cried, "Martha, Martha," and she dressed, and she bounded outside to see if he were really there, but he wasn't.

Yet she could not go back into the house. She was restless. She walked through Bethany looking left and right, as if she might find something important. Martha must have roused Lazarus. The two caught up with her at the edge of the village.

"Where are you going?" Martha demanded, out of breath.

"I don't know," Mary said. "I don't know."

But her intensity drew others from the houses round about, and they followed.

"Where is she going?" they asked.

Martha said, "My sister knows what she's doing."

Mary went a little ways on the Jericho road, then turned aside and found herself walking a thin stony path toward the tombs.

That's where she was going. To the tombs!

And others were doing the same thing!

From towns all over that area people came, one by one, two by two, in groups; they were streaming toward that honeycomb in white rock, the places where their kin were buried.

What was this universal yearning?

They told one another that they had awoken that morning thinking of their dead. They were coming, they said, to honor the memories.

At first Mary saw about a hundred people crossing the fields from several directions. But the closer they came to the tombs, the more she saw. Like spokes on a wheel the crowd was converging, becoming more dense, numbering four and five hundred!

There was a general air of excitement.

Mary felt such a tugging in her breast that she broke into a hard run ahead of the rest.

So she was the first to see the Lord standing in front of Lazarus' empty grave, facing her, gazing at her with his golden eyes and smiling.

Behind her the noises subsided as those arriving also saw the Lord.

And when the whole multitude had fallen mute with awe — as if they were living stones in the countryside — Jesus spoke.

"I tell you truly," he said, "the hour is coming when your relatives lying dead in this place, and all the dead everywhere, will hear the voice of the Son of God — and those who hear will live."

Jesus, dressed in white, stood erect as a cedar tree, his black hair cascading to his shoulders, his manner quiet and dignified.

"All those that the Father gives me will come to me," he said. "And those who come I will never cast out. For I have descended from heaven to do the Father's will. This is his will: that I should lose none of those whom he has given me. And this is his will: that all who see the Son and believe in him should have eternal life, and I will raise them up at the last day!

"I am the bread of life," Jesus said. "Those who come to me will never hunger.

"I am the light of the world. Those who follow me will not walk in darkness but will have the light of life."

He said many things that morning. And by some mystery Mary remembered everything: *I am the way and the truth and the life.*

His beautiful voice never grew loud. Instead, it entered her mind as a music, a low, personal murmuring, like a lullaby: *Do you remember the shepherd, Mary?* She bowed her head to listen. *The shepherd who dies for the sheep? The shepherd called Good? And do you remember that once I said I was he? I am.*

Soon his voice alone consumed her attention, as though it were a soft stream flowing over pebbles, endlessly various, ever the same. After a while she lifted her eyes and saw that he wasn't there any more.

Yet the Lord's voice still murmured in her mind: *I am. I am. I am —*

∎

It was on a Tuesday, thirty-eight days after Jesus had risen from the dead, that the disciples received a short, urgent message from Mary and Martha and Lazarus: *We have seen the Lord in Bethany*!

Simon Peter didn't hesitate. He set out immediately for Judea. The others followed.

Andrew made the journey mostly in silence, glad to hear the jubilant chatter of the rest — glad, too, to find Mary Magdalene often at his side. Their quietness was both mutual and pleasant.

On the first night of their trip south, the disciples stayed in Sychar, telling the Samaritans what they had seen and heard: that Jesus was alive, that he had appeared to them in Jerusalem and then in Galilee, that recently he had shown himself to more than five hundred people in one place, and that they were on their way to see him again. Such palpable excitement! A huge woman with henna in her hair and bracelets on both arms hit the table with her fist and cried, "I knew it!"

The second night they spent in Jericho with Zacchaeus, eating well and sleeping in his fine, large house.

From Jericho to Jerusalem the road was fifteen miles, uphill, and rocky. If they hurried, the disciples could cover the distance in about six hours. But the day was bright and cloudless, and the hearts of the disciples were expansive, so they set out midmorning at a leisurely pace.

As they walked, Andrew drew near to his brother and spoke quietly, so that no one else might hear the question.

"Simon, forgive me if I'm doubting you," he said, "but did the curtain in the Temple really tear in two?"

His brother's cheeks were clean-shaven again, scrubbed to a blush. His hair had been cut and washed and brushed until it puffed up like lamb's wool. Simon strode chest-forward as if he were a wondrous thing to behold. This was the old Simon. That's why Andrew could hazard the question.

"Yes," said Simon. "I didn't *see* it, you understand. But I *believe* that it tore from the top to the bottom."

Simon walked a while thinking, then said, "See, the priests rushed out of the Temple scared to death. And they *said* it tore. And I saw a fear in them — I mean a stark *terror* in them — which proved it. They *looked* like men who had got caught staring into the *Debir*, you know. The Most Holy Place. They had seen the darkness of God, and they thought they were going to die."

Now Simon glanced at Andrew and seemed to consider whether he ought to say more than this.

He did.

"There's another reason why I believe it," he said in a sober tone. He stared down at the road before him.

"I have seen that darkness, too. I know that terror. The priests and me —
we've experienced the same thing.

"Andrew, do you remember that Jesus said I would deny him?"

Andrew remembered. He whispered, "Yes."

"He was right. I denied him three times in order to save my life. And while
I was denying him the third time, he suddenly came out and looked at me,
looked straight at me! Such a painful, painful expression! Oh, Andrew, I
thought I had lost him. I was in darkness then, and that was the darkness
of God! I expected to die. No, I wanted to die. The priests were killed by the
tear in the Temple. I was killed by my sin."

The disciples had just begun to climb the eastern slope of the Mount of
Olives, but Andrew was unaware of the landscape. He was feeling such pity
for his brother that the tears began to stand in his eyes.

Simon saw it. "No! Wait!" he exclaimed. "Everything is all right! Andrew,
don't you know what Jesus was doing on the shore the morning we caught
so many fish? He was forgiving me."

Simon punched Andrew on the shoulder. "Smile, brother! I understand
the curtain now. It ripped and God broke out. I mean, nothing divides
us from him anymore. I mean, that's what Jesus has done. That's what
forgiveness is." Simon began to strike his breast: "The mercy of God —
right here, right now!"

Suddenly Thomas cried, "Look!" He clapped his hands and pointed and
shouted, "There he is!"

The disciples raised their arms and their voices and started to race uphill.

Andrew's heart leaped within him. Jesus was standing on a stony rise at
the highest elevation of the Mount of Olives, waiting.

But then Andrew went more slowly than the rest. The wind was pulling
at the Lord's white robe. He was like a marble column under the blue
firmament. And this is why Andrew did not run to be near him: he feared
what was to come. So splendid in sunlight was the Lord's appearance that
Andrew was disquieted. A royal Lord Jesus! He might have been holding a
scepter in his right hand, or a sword, or seven burning stars.

Thomas, too, was impressed by the grandeur of Jesus' person. "Lord," he
cried as he approached the top of the mountain, "will you *now* restore the
kingdom to Israel?"

Jesus said, "It isn't your place to know the times or seasons which the
Father chooses." His voice had a brazen quality, like a trumpet.

The disciples ranged themselves below him. None climbed to his level.
Andrew stood behind them all.

Jesus said, "You are my witnesses now. Preach repentance. In my name
preach the forgiveness of sins. Open the scriptures to people. Show them
that the Christ had to suffer and die and on the third day be raised from
the dead."

Andrew began to cry. The Lord's words were a valediction, rhythmic, heavy, and divine. All the disciples were quiet. No one moved. Motion might destroy the moment. A small cloud came sailing over Jerusalem from the west.

Jesus said, "You are my witnesses. Go into the city and wait there until you are clothed with power from on high. But when the Holy Spirit has come upon you, preach! Preach first in Jerusalem, then through all Judea and Samaria, and then to the ends of the earth."

While he was saying these things, Jesus was lifted up from the ground. He rose higher and higher, his black hair streaming in a distant wind, until the small cloud passed beneath him and he was taken from the sight of the disciples.

Andrew watched the cloud. When it continued eastward, there was only the blue sky, yet Andrew and all the disciples gazed into that as if something more should happen.

As softly as feathers, two men in white robes appeared beside them.

"Ah, men of Galilee," they said — and the world rushed in on Andrew again, loud and raucous and harsh and fiercely lit.

All the disciples moved. Holiness broke. The sky was shut like a lid.

But the two men said, "Why are you looking up into heaven? Don't you know that this Jesus, who was taken up from you, will come again in the same way you saw him go?"

Andrew, the last to climb the mount, was the first to leave. He didn't wait for the others. He went alone down the western slope of the Mount of Olives into the Kidron valley and into the city. As far as he knew, all the disciples separated, each taking his own way into Jerusalem.

But he was empty, body and soul. There wasn't a single word within him that he might speak it to another, or a thought that he might think it. His heart had been drained. His face was stunned and blank. He had stopped crying when he stopped seeing Jesus.

vi

Some days later — certainly more than a week later — Andrew was sitting in the upper room of the house of the Essene on Mount Zion. He assumed he was alone. He had no idea how long he'd been in this place or why he had chosen it, but he began now to be aware of the times because of the general commotion outside.

The city was filled with pilgrims again. It was the Feast of Weeks, when people brought their firstfruits to the Lord, the source of rain and growth and goodness. In Greek the day was called the *Pentecost* — the fiftieth day after Passover. During these seven weeks since the Passover, all the barley had been harvested and after that all the wheat.

It was Sunday. That's the noise that Andrew heard. The tromping of tens of thousands of people toward the Temple. Today two loaves of bread would be offered to God by the priest on behalf of the people. The loaves had been made from the flour of the new wheat crop and baked with leaven. Devout Jews had arrived from every nation under heaven, because this was a feast of solemn joy. A feast! Before the day was done, everyone would eat, the impoverished and the strangers and the Levites.

Andrew knew the feast. Andrew knew the times. Andrew had been righteous since his youth, keeping all the rites and all the ceremonies of Moses. Such obedience had endeared him to John the Baptizer.

Perhaps this was the day when he would begin to neglect righteousness. Andrew was very, very tired.

But then he heard a soughing sound, a low moan just outside.

"What's that?" he whispered to himself.

To his surprise, somebody answered, "The wind." Philip was with him in the room. "The wind in the lattice," he said.

But the sound didn't cease. Nor did it vary its blowing with gusts. It grew steadily stronger, first whistling like breath in a flute, then raising a continual howl.

Andrew's body began to tingle. His fingers twitched at his chin.

Several people stood up and moved to the window. Why, there were six and seven disciples here!

"It sounds like a gale," Matthew said, "but not a leaf is trembling! Not a pilgrim's hair is out of place."

"And people are looking here," Thomas said, peering into the street. "They're looking in this direction, as if *we* were the wind!"

Suddenly Simon Peter burst into the room, daylight exploding behind him. "Do you feel it?" he shouted. "It's coming! It's coming!"

Immediately he ran out again.

Mary Magdalene came in.

Andrew jumped to his feet, itching to do something. "What's he talking about?" he asked.

Simon Peter was bellowing down to the street below, "Up here! We're up here!"

James said, "Who's he calling to?"

John was at the window, his face brightening with delight. "The crowds, I think," he said. "They've turned back from the Temple. They're starting to come up here."

Mary Salome, John's mother, came in, blinking with confusion. John saw her and ran to her and embraced her. "Mother," he said, "Simon is right. It's coming right now."

Then Peter was back in the room and people were pouring in behind him, and Andrew saw on his brother's head something like a tongue of fire, and Simon was talking, talking with energy, but talking in a language Andrew had never heard before.

The roar of the wind was not a sound anymore. It was a storm within his own soul now. Andrew was filled to bursting. So he opened his mouth and began to speak as enthusiastically as Simon, but in a different language altogether. Ten people turned toward him with understanding.

All the disciples had tongues of flame resting upon them. And all were speaking in various languages. And foreigners understood them. And this was the Holy Spirit! Yes, this was power from on high, the promise of Jesus, and *that's* what Simon had been bellowing about.

Andrew was a trumpet. His whole being sang with the breathing of God. Oh, he was a healthy man! Oh, he had such wisdom to impart. And he lost nothing in the pouring forth. He only gained. He would never be drained again.

People standing on the steps outside said, "They're drunk! They didn't save their wine for the feast! They drank it at dawn."

"*No!*" Simon Peter rushed to the door of the room and boomed, "No, we are *not* drunk!"

This disciple had come into his strength. His speaking silenced the room and the crowds outside and the city over several streets.

"You are witnessing what Joel prophesied long ago," Peter said. "God is pouring out his Spirit. As Joel said, *In the last days your sons and your daughters will prophesy, and I, says the Lord, will show wonders in heaven and on earth: blood and fire and vapor of smoke; the sun shall be turned into darkness and the moon into blood — but those who call on the name of the Lord will be saved.*"

Peter turned left and right, embracing everyone with his voice, those in the room and those all down the streets.

"Listen to me," he called. "You crucified Jesus of Nazareth. He did mighty works and wonders. He did everything in righteousness, yet you killed him by the hands of outlaws. But this was the plan of God! And God raised him from the dead again. We are witnesses of this fact.

"Not only has he been raised here on earth, but he has also been lifted up to the right hand of God in power and authority. What you see and hear today — this is the work of Jesus!

"Oh, let the whole house of Israel know that God has given Jesus to us as our Lord and our Christ!

"Repent! People, repent and be baptized in the name of Jesus Christ for the forgiveness of your sins — and you, too, will receive the Holy Spirit. The promise is for you. It is for your children. It is for everyone!"

Andrew held his peace as long as Peter was preaching. So did the rest of the disciples. But now the Spirit that had blown through him blew over the crowds of people, and those who had understood Andrew's language before, now came near and took hold of his robe.

Please, they said in their foreign tongue. *Baptize us.*

Andrew lost shyness that day. And the anxiety that had made the world seem so dangerous and uncertain — that, too, passed away. He never was a loud man after that. And he would always rather answer than ask. But the words came easily to his lips. And the proper gesture waited ever within his reach. And over and over again he said what the Lord had taught him to say:

"Damsel," Andrew said, tilting the child into the water, "I baptize you in the name of the Father and of the Son and of the Holy Spirit."

And this was good and true and right and holy, because before he left the Lord had said: *Lo, I am with you always, even unto the end of the world.*

EPILOGUE

T his, then, is the story that was told through the years and the
centuries and the millennia to come.

The disciples preached it in Jerusalem, adding more and more
people to their company until the number of those baptized swelled into
the thousands.

At the same time the council and the leaders in Jerusalem strove to
silence them. They were as threatened by the disciples as they had been by
Jesus because the assembly growing around them was large and well-knit
and committed to this Jesus as to one alive and mighty. It was an assembly
distinct from the Synagogue — an *Ecclesia*, a Church. Peter and James and
John formed the core leadership in Jerusalem. Therefore, the priests and
the Temple guard imprisoned them and commanded them not to preach.
When the disciples disobeyed, stirring the people up further, the high priest
arrested them again and beat them and charged them upon their lives to keep
silence. But always upon their release they continued to tell the story anyway.

After twelve years of increasing conflict, King Herod Agrippa took bloody
measures against this growing Church. He ordered the execution of James
the son of Zebedee. James, the first disciple to die for telling this story,
was beheaded.

Nevertheless, the story still was told.

Simon Peter traveled out into Judea and up the coast of the Great
Sea. With some hesitation he preached to Gentiles as well as to Jews
— especially in Caesarea, the seat of the Roman governor and an active
seaport. When a Roman centurion named Cornelius heard the story, he
received the Holy Spirit no less than the disciples had on Pentecost. Peter
marveled: "Even the Gentiles who believe in Jesus are forgiven their sins!"
And he baptized the household of Cornelius in the name of Jesus Christ.

From there the story spread north along the seacoast.

Among those who persecuted the followers of Jesus was a Pharisee born in
Tarsus at the northeastern sweep of the sea, a Jew of wild intelligence and

passionate legalism. He hated those who scorned the laws of God. He saw
the Church as subversive and dangerous. But then the story that he strove
to abolish rose up and overwhelmed him, becoming his only reality. The
man's name was Saul.

While riding to Damascus with an order from the high priest to arrest
believers there, Saul was blinded by a flash of heavenly light and a voice of
accusation: *Saul, Saul, why do you persecute me?*

He was thrown to the ground by the light.

"Who are you, Lord?" he cried.

The voice said, *I am Jesus, whom you are persecuting. But rise and enter
the city, and you will be told what you are to do.*

For the rest of his life he never doubted that the Lord Jesus had made
his last resurrection appearance to him, to Saul, "as to one born out of due
time." So the story was true. The man repented of his persecutions. Three
days later he was baptized. To indicate the radical change within himself, he
changed his name to Paul, and after a period of preparation and prayer, he,
too, began to tell the story — in Greek, to the Greeks.

It was twenty-five years after the crucifixion of Jesus when Paul began to
travel through the Roman Empire. He preached in Cyprus and in the lower
cities of Asia Minor. He preached in the northern cities, too, then crossed
over into Macedonia and traveled south into Greece: Philippi, Thessalonica,
Berea, Athens, Corinth.

Paul maintained a written correspondence with the churches he
established in these places, repeating the story again and again. To the
church in Corinth he wrote:

> *For I delivered to you as of first importance what I also received, that*
> *Christ died for our sins in accordance with the scriptures, that he was*
> *buried, that he was raised on the third day in accordance with the*
> *scriptures —*

For twelve years Paul told the story with passion and intelligence. He
could transfix multitudes by his words. Therefore he became as threatful
to the authorities as had any disciple. Once while he was at the Temple
in Jerusalem, certain people cried out, "This is the man who is teaching
people everywhere against the law and against this place! He has defiled
the Temple!" The accusations aroused a mob that dragged Paul from the
Temple into the street and began to beat him to death. A riot began.

The Roman Tribune sent centurions and soldiers to enforce peace. They
arrested Paul. They bound him in two chains and carried him to prison while
the violent mob followed, screaming: "Away with him! Kill him! He has no
right to live!"

While Paul was in prison it was discovered that his opponents were plotting to murder him; so the Tribune in Jerusalem transferred him to Caesarea, where he was to be tried under the Roman governor.

Paul had an advantage over the other disciples: his parents had acquired Roman citizenship. He was born a Roman. When his imprisonment in Caesarea lasted more than two years without a final ruling on his case, he exercised his right as a Roman and appealed directly to Caesar for justice.

This required his appearance in Rome. Therefore the prisoner was taken by ship through storms and treacherous seas to the capital of the empire.

Paul lived there under house arrest another two years.

From his confinement in Rome he wrote a letter to the church in Philippi, saying:

> *Rejoice in the Lord always; again I say, Rejoice! Let everyone know your forbearance. The Lord is at hand. Have no anxiety about anything, but in everything by prayer and supplication with thanksgiving let your requests be made known to God. And the peace of God, which passes all understanding, will keep your hearts and your minds in Christ Jesus.*

There the Bible falls silent.

But the Church has continued. And the story has been told for two thousand years.

It is said that Paul was executed outside the walls of Rome along the road to Ostia.

It is said that Simon Peter also traveled to Rome, where he became the first bishop, chief guardian of the Church, and that his life was brought to a violent end, that his hands were stretched out on a cross at the foot of Vatican Hill.

It is said that Andrew, Simon's brother and Jesus' first disciple, told the story of his Lord in Scythia and in Greece, and that he was crucified on an X-shaped cross.

It is said that John the son of Zebedee and Salome was the only disciple not to suffer martyrdom. Even today people declare that John was with Mary the mother of Jesus when finally she lay down and died.

And this is sure: that every continent on earth has heard the story to various effects. Countless are the languages in which it still is told. Innumerable the hearts that have been shaped by it.

Walter Wangerin, Jr.
October 24, 1995

Hara

SYRIA

Tyre ●

●Damascus

C A N A A N

ISRAEL

C A N A A N ●Jerusalem

EGYPT

● Rome

MACEDONIA

Corinth● ●Ath

Mediterranean   Sea

Cr

ASIA

GALATIA

SYRIA

● Ephesus

● Antioch

CYPRUS

Caesarea ●
● Jerusalem
JUDEA

Alexandria
●

EGYPT